lonely planet

Panama

DISCARDED

Comarca de
Kuna Yala
p221

Colón
Province
p206

Bocas del Toro
Province
p178

Panamá
Province
p72

Panama City
p40

Chiriquí
Province
p152

Coclé
Province
p92

Darién
Province
p235

Veraguas
Province
p134

Península
de Azuero
p110

THIS EDITION WRITTEN AND RESEARCHED BY
Carolyn McCarthy

Contents

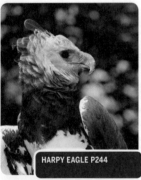

ALFREDO MAIQUEZ/GETTY IMAGES ©

HARPY EAGLE P244

ALFREDO MAIQUEZ/GETTY IMAGES ©

TRADITIONAL *POLLERA* P269

Contents

UNDERSTAND

SURVIVAL
GUIDE

SPECIAL FEATURES

Welcome to Panama

From clear turquoise seas to the coffee farms and cloud forests of Chiriquí, Panama can be as chilled out or as thrilling as you wish.

Endless Summer

With a spate of deserted islands, chill Caribbean vibes on one side and monster Pacific swells on the other, Panama sits poised to deliver the best of all beach worlds. And a whole other world begins at the water's edge. Seize it by scuba diving with whale sharks in the Pacific, snorkeling the rainbow reefs of Bocas del Toro or setting sail in the indigenous territory of Kuna Yala, where virgin isles wear nary a footprint. Meanwhile surfers will be psyched to have world-class breaks all to themselves. Hello, paradise.

Cosmopolitan Panama

The dazzling blue coastline and shimmering skyscrapers say Miami, though many joke that you hear more English spoken in Panama. Panama City is nothing if not culturally diverse and driven, rough-edged yet sophisticated. Always a work in progress, construction is underway to add a subway and complete the massive canal expansion. But it's the particulars that make it special. Pedal the coastal green space, explore the historic Casco or attend an avant-garde performance and you will realize this tropical capital isn't just about salsa, that's just the backbeat.

The Great Outdoors

In Panama, nature is all about discovery. Explore the ruins of Spanish forts on the Caribbean coast or boat deep into indigenous territories in a dugout canoe. Wildlife is incidental: a resplendent quetzal on the highland trail, the unruly troupe of screeching howler monkeys outside your cabin or the breaching whale that turns your ferry ride into an adrenaline-filled event. Adventure tourism means zipping through rainforest canopies, swimming alongside sea turtles or trekking to sublime cloud forest vistas. One small tropical country with two long coasts makes for a pretty big playground.

Lost World Adventure

You don't have to make it all the way to the Darién to get off the beaten path – though if you do, you'll hit one of the most biodiverse spots on the planet. Go where the wild things are. Soak in the spray of towering waterfalls near highland Santa Fé. Visit one of Panama's seven indigenous groups through community tourism. Live out your castaway fantasies in the Kuna Yala or idle on a wilderness beach in Península de Azuero. Howl back at the creatures sharing the canopy. Panama is as wild as you want it to be.

ALEX BRAMWELL/GETTY IMAGES ©

Why I Love Panama
By Carolyn McCarthy, Author

In a world where the wilderness and native cultures are disappearing, Panama – against all odds – continues with its essence intact. Trekking through exuberant rainforests, seeing indigenous culture and sailing between pristine tropical islands opened up my sense of wonder. The wildlife viewing is astounding – from expected places, like the waters of Isla de Coiba to patches of preserved forest just outside the capital. For me Panama is a confluence – an explosion of nature, cultures and beliefs in that messy, musical arrangement that's everyday life in Latin America. All that energy feeds you, and you see the world in new ways.

For more about our authors, see page 320

Panama

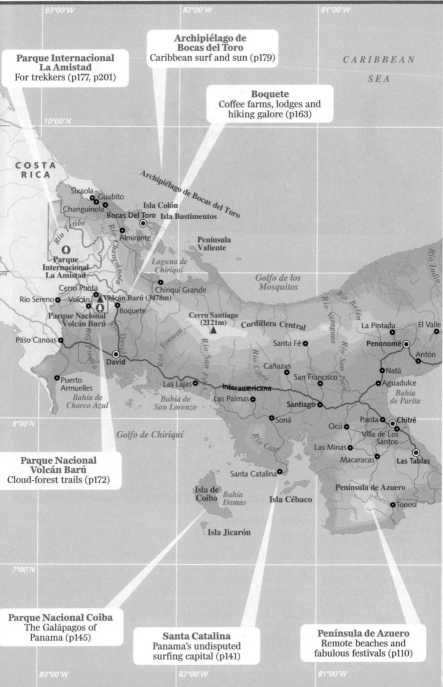

Parque Internacional La Amistad
For trekkers (p177, p201)

Archipiélago de Bocas del Toro
Caribbean surf and sun (p179)

Boquete
Coffee farms, lodges and hiking galore (p163)

CARIBBEAN SEA

COSTA RICA

Sixaola
Guabito
Changuinola
Isla Colón
Bocas Del Toro
Isla Bastimentos
Almirante

Península Valiente

Parque Internacional La Amistad

Río Teribe
Río Changuinola
Laguna de Chiriquí

Golfo de los Mosquitos

Chiriquí Grande

Río Indio
Río Belén
Río Veraguas

Cerro Punta
Volcán
Volcán Barú (3478m)
Boquete

Cerro Santiago (2121m)
Cordillera Central

La Pintada
El Valle

Río Sereno
Parque Nacional Volcán Barú

Santa Fé
Penonomé
Antón

Paso Canoas
David

Río Fonseca
Río Cobre
Río San Pablo

Cañazas
San Francisco
Natá
Aguadulce

Puerto Armuelles
Bahía de Charco Azul

Las Lajas
Interamericana
Las Palmas

Santiago
Bahía de Parita

Bahía de San Lorenzo

Soná

Ocú
Parita
Chitré

Golfo de Chiriquí

Las Minas
Villa de Los Santos

Río Caté

Macaracas
Las Tablas

Santa Catalina

Península de Azuero

Isla de Coiba
Bahía Damas

Isla Cébaco

Tonosí

Isla Jicarón

Parque Nacional Volcán Barú
Cloud-forest trails (p172)

Parque Nacional Coiba
The Galápagos of Panama (p145)

Santa Catalina
Panama's undisputed surfing capital (p141)

Península de Azuero
Remote beaches and fabulous festivals (p110)

83°00′W   82°00′W   81°00′W

10°00′N

8°00′N

7°00′N

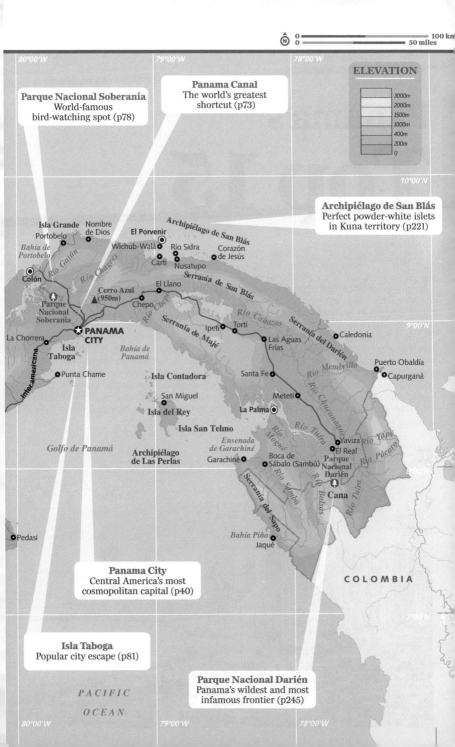

N 0 ━━━━━━━━━━ 100 km
  0 ━━━━━━━━━━ 50 miles

Parque Nacional Soberanía
World-famous
bird-watching spot (p78)

Panama Canal
The world's greatest
shortcut (p73)

ELEVATION

3000m
2000m
1500m
1000m
400m
200m
0

10°00'N

Archipiélago de San Blás
Perfect powder-white islets
in Kuna territory (p221)

Isla Grande   Nombre
Portobelo   de Dios   El Porvenir
Bahía de   Wichub-Walá   Río Sidra   Corazón
Portobelo   Carti   de Jesús
                                    Nusatupo
Colón   *Río Gatún*   *Río Chagres*   Serranía de San Blás
        Cerro Azul   El Llano
Parque   ▲(950m)   *Río Cabazas*
Nacional   Chepo   Serranía del Darién
Soberanía   *Río Chepo*   Ipeti   Tortí   Caledonia
                Serranía de Majé   Las Aguas   9°00'N
La Chorrera   ★ PANAMA   Frías
        Isla   CITY   *Bahía de*   Puerto Obaldía
        Taboga   *Panamá*   *Río Membrillo*   Capurganá
Punta Chame   Isla Contadora   Santa Fe
                                        Meteti   *Río Chucunaque*
                    San Miguel   La Palma
                    Isla del Rey   *Río Tuira*   8°00'N
                                        Río Yapé
                Isla San Telmo   Yaviza
Golfo de Panamá   *Ensenada*   El Real *Río Púcuro*
            Archipiélago   *de Garachiné* Boca de   Parque
            de Las Perlas   Garachiné   Sábalo (Sambú) Nacional
                                        Darién
                                    Río Sambú   Cana
                        Serranía del Sapo *Río Balsas* *Río Tuira*
Pedasí

Panama City
Central America's most
cosmopolitan capital (p40)

COLOMBIA

7°00'N

Bahía Piña
Jaqué

Isla Taboga
Popular city escape (p81)

PACIFIC

OCEAN

Parque Nacional Darién
Panama's wildest and most
infamous frontier (p245)

80°00'W   79°00'W   78°00'W

Panama's
Top 15

Panama City

1 Panama City (p40) is high-octane Latin America: think *ceviche* (marinated seafood), casinos and stacked skylines. For this city of nearly one million, transformation is in the air: a new coastal green space, an anticipated biodiversity museum soon to open and a subway system under construction. Sure, the traffic resembles a boa constrictor digesting one megalithic meal, but its appeal persists. People are real here and nature is never very far away. Beauty lives in the skewed rhythms, incongruous visions and fiery sunsets.

Panama Canal

2 One of the world's greatest shortcuts, the canal (p73) cuts right through the continental divide, linking the Atlantic and Pacific Oceans. And it's worth marveling. Just as stunning as the hulking steel container ships passing through the locks are the legions of creatures watching from the jungle fringes. Two visitors centers offer viewing platforms and museums that showcase the construction and its expansion. There's also worthwhile boat and kayak trips on the waterway. Or you can book a partial transit and squeeze through the locks yourself.

1

ZOYA STATENKO/GETTY IMAGES ©

Casco Viejo

3 Don't miss Panama City's historical neighborhood of Casco Viejo (p45), full of crumbling convents and cobblestones. The colonial architecture may hark back to Havana, but this is not a spot where time stands still. It's as much about today's urban mix as the eclectic, easygoing vibe. The Cinta Costera, a new green space, takes walkers and bikers from downtown to the tip of the peninsula. On sticky evenings artist's booths line the promenade, couples dine under parasols and skinny boys cannonball into the bay.

Santa Catalina

4 This surf village (p141) is all small town, with just one paved road. Here, nature is a delight and 'resort' is still a foreign word. The biggest draws are the world-class waves that roll in year-round (but peak in February and March). The town is also the launching pad for excursions and diving trips into the wildlife-rich Parque Nacional Coiba (p145), an island journey that may be heavy in logistics but worth every dogged effort. Right: Fishers, Santa Catalina

Wildlife-Watching

5 Bring your binoculars. With more than 300 mammals and 900 bird species, Panama is crack for naturalists. Scarlet macaws, toucans, sloths and squirrel monkeys are just a few local stars. As a spectator sport, wildlife-watching is nothing short of thrilling, but it's the calls, cries and rumbles of the rainforest that will stamp your memory forever. Serious birders might head to the highlands to spot a resplendent quetzal (p169) or brave the Darién for a glimpse of the legendary harpy eagle (p244). Top right: Brown-throated three-toed sloth

Parque Nacional Coiba

6 Often compared to the Galápagos, this remote marine park (p145) is a veritable lost world of pristine ecosystems and unique fauna. Spy flocks of scarlet macaws, enormous schools of fish, migrating humpback whales with calves, and manta rays scuffing the ocean floor. Scuba divers might even glimpse a hammerhead or a whale shark. Most importantly, it's still wild, with few visitors and little infrastructure. Not long ago an infamous prison operated on the main island, but now everyone comes here by choice. Right: Hawkfish

The Highlands

7 In the tropics, the highlands are the equivalent of a breath of fresh air. Panama's highlands range from lush forests with tiny golden frogs to mist-covered coffee plantations. From Panama City, weekenders take to El Valle (p94) and El Copé (p107). Boquete (p163) is the classic mountain town, but if you are looking to get off the beaten path, the tiny hamlet of Santa Fé (p137) has true mountain tranquility, with local-led horse rides and hikes to waterfalls with swimming holes. Paradise is not lost.

Archipiélago de San Blás

8 With little to do but negotiate the price of a coconut, sway in a hammock or snorkel in turquoise waters, many find it to be paradise here. Locally known as Kuna Yala, this 400-plus island archipelago (p221) in the Caribbean is an independent indigenous territory steeped in tradition. Most guest lodges are remote palm-fringed islets surrounded by clear waters, while Kuna residents live on community islands teeming with livestock, commerce, and thatched and cement homes. Below: Traditionally dressed Kuna woman

ALFREDO MAIQUEZ/GETTY IMAGES ©

ADAM CROWLEY/GETTY IMAGES ©

Península de Azuero

9 Sweet landscapes of sculpted hills, lonely beaches and crashing surf feed the growing buzz that this rural peninsula (p110) has become today's hot getaway. Yet the strongest impression is one of tradition. Spanish culture has deep roots here, evident in the charm of tiled colonials, country hospitality, religious festivals and elaborate *polleras*. Playa Venao (p131) has emerged as a major surf destination, while the more remote Playa Cambutal (p132) is still the wild beach of your dreams. Top: Colonial-style cottage, Villa de Los Santos (p119)

Archipiélago de Bocas del Toro

10 No wonder this Caribbean island chain (p178) is Panama's number one vacation spot. *It's all good*, say the locals. Pedal to the beach on a cruiser bike, hum to improvised calypso on Isla Bastimentos, and laze over dinner in a thatched hut on the waterfront. Lodgings range from cheap digs to stunning jungle lodges and luxury resorts. Surfers hit the breaks, but there's also snorkeling with dazzling corals and oversized starfish or volunteering to help nesting sea turtles. Bottom: Cayos Zapatillas (p193)

Water Sports

11 Soaking up the best of Panama means getting wet – dive with whale sharks, kayak around uninhabited islands or raft in the highlands. For many, it's fantasy enough to dive waters teeming with tropical fish. The Pacific is the best place to spot marine mammals, including whales, especially in spots like Parque Nacional Coiba (p145) and the Golfo de Chiriquí (p159). The Caribbean is known for its colorful coral and giant starfish around Bocas del Toro (p178) and the powdery white-sand beaches of the Archipiélago de San Blás (p221).

Parque Nacional Volcán Barú

12 Panama's only volcano (p172) dominates the misty Chiriquí highlands. At 3478m it's also the highest point in the country. Enthusiasts can make the steep and usually muddy predawn climb for the reward of viewing both the Atlantic and Pacific Oceans at the same time. Another, perhaps saner, option is the Sendero Los Quetzales (p173), a stunning trail that traverses the park, crosses over the Río Caldera and provides the chance to see exotic orchids, tapir and resplendent quetzals. Bottom: Golden-headed gecko

Festivals

13 A window into the country's wilder side, Panama's many festivals also reveal the breadth of cultures in this small country. From Caribbean Congo (p216) celebrations in Portobelo to the vibrant folkloric traditions of the Península de Azuero, the three-day Kuna stomp that is Nogagope (p224) or Panama City's open-air jazz festival (p53), all of Panama loves a good rum-soaked time. When it's all over, a replenishing bowl of 'Get Up Lazarus' soup (a potent seafood soup) at Mercado de Mariscos (p59) is in order. Top left: Congo dancer

Boquete

14 Equal parts adventure hub and mountain retreat, Boquete (p163) is a magnet for expats, retirees and travelers of all stripes. Bird-watchers come for a glimpse of the resplendent quetzal, while adventurers come to climb a mountain, ride a zip line or raft the white water. But what really moves this small town is the principal crop of the world: coffee. Coffee farms dot the countryside, with tours showing the process from leaf to cup. Fuel up, and you're ready for the next adventure. Top right: Coffee berries

Parque Nacional Soberanía

15 A quick day trip from the glass towers of Panama City and you're in one of the world's premier bird-watching sites. Parque Nacional Soberanía (p78) has one of the most accessible tropical rainforests in Panama. While out on the trail, look for sloths, howler monkeys or white-face capuchins. On Pipeline Rd more than 500 bird species – from toucans to motmots – have been sighted. For an alternate view of the canopy, climb the towers at Rainforest Discovery Center (p79) or visit the neighboring Emberá and Wounaan communities. Bottom right: Keel-billed toucan

Need to Know

For more information, see Survival Guide (p282)

Currency
US dollar ($)

Language
Spanish

Visas
Generally not required for stays of 90 days.

Money
ATMs widely available. Credit cards accepted in some areas.

Cell Phones
Local SIM cards can be used in unlocked phones.

Time
Eastern Standard Time (GMT/UTC minus five hours)..

When to Go

Bocas del Toro
GO Sep–Oct & Feb–Mar

Panama City
GO Sep & Dec–Mar

Boquete
GO Dec–Apr

Santa Catalina
GO Dec–Apr

Jaqué
GO Jan–Apr

Tropical climate, wet & dry seasons
Tropical climate, rain year-round
Dry climate
Warm to hot summers, cold winters

High Season
(mid-Dec–mid-April)

➡ Corresponds with the Pacific-side dry season.

➡ Little rain in Panama City and elsewhere south of the continental divide.

High Season Peak (holidays)

➡ Includes November festivals, Christmas and New Years plus Easter holidays.

➡ Hotel rates may be up to double that of normal rates.

➡ Resorts, festival towns and beaches are crowded with Panamanian vacationers.

Low Season
(mid-April–early Dec)

➡ Corresponds with rainy season in most of the country.

➡ Rain is sporadic: check regional climate guides, many destinations can still be enjoyed.

➡ Lodging rates and resorts are better priced.

Useful Websites

ATP (www.atp.gob.pa) Official national tourism website.

Visit Panama (www.visitpanama. com) The more-limited English-language version of the ATP site.

The Panama News (www. thepanamanews.com) English newspaper useful for culture and local politics.

Lonely Planet (www.lonelyplan et.com/panama) The popular Thorn Tree forum, travel news and links to other useful sites.

Panama Info (www.panamainfo. com) Good travel resource.

Casco Viejo (www.cascoviejo. org) Panama City information.

Lanic (http://lanic.utexas.edu/ la/ca/panama) Academic links from the University of Texas Latin American Information Center.

Important Numbers

Panama has no regional dialing codes.

Panama country code	☎ 507
International access code	☎ 106
Directory assistance	☎ 102
National tourist information	☎ 526-7000
Police	☎ 104

Exchange Rates

Australia	A$1	US$1.03
Canada	C$1	US$0.98
Euro	€1	US$1.29
Japan	¥100	US$1.01
New Zealand	NZ$1	US$0.84
UK	UK£1	US$1.53

For current exchange rates see www.xe.com

Daily Costs

**Budget:
Less than US$65**

➡ Dorm bed: from US$7

➡ Dine on *comida corriente* (set meals), visit markets and street stalls

➡ Plan sightseeing via bus, DIY visits to beaches and waterfall hikes

**Midrange:
US$65–US$180**

➡ Double room at a midrange hotel: US$45–US$120

➡ Some fine dining, activities (snorkel rental or surf lessons) and regional flights

**Top End:
More than US$180**

➡ Double room at a high-end hotel, resort or lodge: from US$120

➡ Guided trips with bilingual naturalist guides

➡ Internal flights and car rental

Opening Hours

Opening hours vary throughout the year. Throughout the book we list high-season hours, which are usually reduced in low-season.

Banks 8:30am–1pm or 3pm

Restaurants 7am–10am, noon–3pm and 6–10pm; closed Sunday

Offices 8am–noon, 1:30–5pm weekdays

Government offices 8am–4pm

Bars & clubs 9pm or 11pm–3am

Malls & shops 10am–9pm or 10pm

Supermarkets 8am–9pm

Arriving in Panama

Tocumen International Airport (Panama City) Most international flights arrive here. Hire taxis at the transport desk in the airport (from US$27). It's a 40-minute ride to downtown. In daylight hours local buses (US$1.25) depart every 15 minutes for Albrook Bus Terminal, near the regional airport (one hour), and other destinations.

Aeropuerto Enrique Malek (David) Located 5km southeast of the Costa Rican border, David's airport frequently handles flights to and from San José. It's about 5km from town. Take a taxi (US$5) or a shared taxi (US$2).

Getting Around

As most Panamanians use public transportation, it's reasonably priced and connections are frequent.

Bus Most cities have a bus terminal with frequent regional departures and connections to Panama City and Costa Rica.

Car Rentals are not cheap but roads are generally in good condition. Some areas, including Panama City and many rural areas, are very poorly signposted.

Train Mostly a novelty, goes between Panama City and Colón.

Air Domestic flights depart Panama City from Aeropuerto Albrook and arrive in destinations throughout the country.

For much more on **getting around**, see p293

First Time Panama

For more information, see Survival Guide (p281)

Checklist

➡ Check the validity of your passport.

➡ Check the visa situation and government travel advisories.

➡ Organize travel insurance.

➡ Check flight restrictions on luggage and camping or outdoors equipment.

➡ Check your immunization history.

➡ Contact your credit card provider to see if it includes car rental insurance.

What to Pack

➡ Passport

➡ Phrasebook

➡ Swimsuit

➡ Digital camera and charger

➡ Flip-flops

➡ Sun protection

➡ Poncho or rain jacket

➡ Binoculars

➡ Strong insect repellent (30%–50% DEET)

➡ Refillable water bottle

➡ Drivers license, if you plan to rent a car

➡ Field guide

Top Tips for Your Trip

➡ Don't flag a taxi in front of a high-end hotel if you don't want to be charged tourist rates off the bat; taxis aren't metered so walk a block – it pays!

➡ Outside the cities, many perfectly good lodgings don't have a handle on email and websites. Don't get frustrated if no one sees your reservation – the hotel email might have been created by a precocious nephew who never checks it. If you have even basic Spanish, call ahead.

➡ Panamanians are used to foreigners dissing local idiosyncrasies – such as drivers not using signals or crowds that can't form lines. Instead, ask *why* it is the way it is and you'll have a lively conversation.

What to Wear

Locals rarely wear shorts if not at the beach. Bring light-weight pants or skirts and short sleeves. Dining and night-life can be formal in the capital. Bring proper dress shoes or sandals, a skirt or dress for women, and pants and a dress shirt for men. Pack a light sweater for over air-conditioned restaurants and bus rides. A fleece and lightweight shell are necessary for highlands. For hiking, long sleeves and quick-drying pants help keep the bugs away.

Sleeping

Book lodgings two to six months ahead during high peak times such as the week preceding Easter, the November festivals and the weeks surrounding Christmas and New Year. See p282 for more accommodation information.

➡ **Hotels** Abound in midrange and high-end categories; for a cheap option check out private doubles in hostels.

➡ **B&Bs** A recent midrange phenomenon; most common in the capital, Boquete and Bocas.

➡ **Hostels** Cheap and spreading in Panama; range from quiet digs to party central.

➡ **Lodges** Running the gamut from rustic to high-end; good places to commune with nature, mostly in the highlands.

Money

Prices in Panama tend to be slightly higher than in other parts of Central America, such as Guatemala and Nicaragua, though they are about on par with Costa Rica.

ATMs are widespread except for in the Darién, on Isla Contadora and the Archipiélago de San Blás.

Some midrange and high-end hotels will take credit cards, as will most adventure tour outfitters. Nicer restaurants will also take credit. The cards most commonly accepted are Visa and Mastercard. If you are planning on charging a big-ticket item, it's best to check in advance. Most cards charge a fee (between 3% and 10%) for international use.

For more information, see p287.

Bargaining

It's OK to bargain at markets and street stalls, but educate yourself first by asking around to get an idea of the pricing of different items and the specific factors that contribute to the quality.

Tipping

→ **Restaurants** Tipping should be 10%; check to see if it's included in the bill.

→ **Taxis** Tipping is optional, but you can round up a dollar or two, especially at night.

→ **Guides** It is customary to tip US$1 to US$2 per person for day tours, with more substantial tips (from US$10 per day) for naturalist guides.

Panama hats (p104)

Etiquette

→ **Asking for help** Say *disculpe* to get someone's attention; *perdón* to say excuse me.

→ **Personal space** Don't be surprised if locals have fewer boundaries about personal space than what's customary in North America and Europe.

→ **Visiting indigenous communities** Ask permission to take photos, particularly of children, and dress more modestly than beachwear. Bargaining may be appropriate for buying crafts but not for lodging and food. The best gifts for children are those that are useful (pens, paper, creative games or books).

→ **Surfing** Novice surfers should be aware of 'dropping in'.

→ **Hitchhiking** Picking up hitchhikers in rural areas is common. If you get a ride from a local, offer a small tip.

Language

Spanish is the national language of Panama, and knowing some very basic phrases (p299) is not only courteous but also essential. That said, English speakers are easier to find here than in other parts of Latin America. Some restaurants feature English-speaking menus and it's certainly the standard for guides. If you visit Kuna Yala, learning a few words of Kuna beforehand (p227) is a great way to warm relations.

If You Like...

Beaches

Kuna Yala Known for perfect and plentiful postage-stamp-sized islets with turquoise waters. (p221)

Isla Contadora Vacation like a high-roller on this island of mansions and gorgeous beaches with a good dose of privacy. (p83)

Golfo de Chiriquí The national marine park boasts islands of monkeys, nesting turtles and plenty of patches of sand just for you. (p159)

Farallón Within reach of the capital, this wide, brilliantly white resort beach is a natural beauty perfect for long strolls. (p101)

Nightlife

Casco Viejo Dart across the cobblestones between underground bars, brew pubs, wine bars and live music venues. (p64)

Bocas del Toro With Aqua Lounge's aquatic trampoline and the strange shots at Mondo, it's the scene of the young and the brave. (p189)

Tántalo Bar The best exotic cocktails and rooftop bar rolled into one – you could only do better by booking its dominatrix-themed suite. (p64)

Boquete Focusing on expats, places like Mike's Global Grill, with its games and Cheers-style counter, offer comfort and *cerveza* for the homesick. (p171)

Romantic Getaways

Los Quetzales Cabins Cabins tucked into the rainforest canopy, with fireplaces and the mountain air buzzing with hummingbirds. (p176)

Casco B&Bs A hefty dose of pampering with this vibrant old-world neighborhood right out the door. (p53)

Archipiélago de Bocas del Toro From secluded ecolodges to thatched beach huts, these resorts can erase the world beyond. (p179)

Playa Los Destiladeros This tiny cove seduces with achingly blue skies, a secluded beach of pounding surf and candlelit dinners for two. (p129)

Outdoor Adventures

Nivida Bat Cave Trek to this massive Caribbean cavern rife with nectar bats; perfect for a subterranean swim. (p196)

Parque Internacional La Amistad True wilderness hiking without the drama of the Darién; access via the highlands or Caribbean coast. (p201)

Sportfishing Azuero While Chiriquí and Bahía Piña hog the glory, organize guided fishing trips here for quite reasonable rates. (p110)

Volcán Barú Terribly steep, hard and invariably foggy and muddy, but how else can you view both oceans at once? (p172)

Surfing

Santa Catalina It's all about world-class waves here, and hostels boast front-row seats. (p141)

Eco Venao This lush ecoresort fits all budgets and serves as the best base camp for Azuero surfers. (p131)

IF YOU LIKE... WATER SPORTS

Azure, turquoise or crystal clear: the waters of Panama beckon you to join in the fun. Whether it's snorkeling coral reefs or rafting through verdant canyons, options abound.

Playa Bluff Powerful barrels rush this wilderness beach; avoid May to September when turtles nest. (p192)

Playa El Palmar A Panama City weekend break with two surf schools and a white-sand beach as your playground. (p90)

Off-the-Beaten-Track Destinations

Soposo Rainforest Adventures Step off the gringo trail to sleep in stilted huts and explore remote Naso villages. (p202)

Santa Fé Dancing butterflies, swimming holes and giant waterfalls grace this humble mountain town. (p137)

The Darién Steeped in indigenous culture and exotic wildlife; with permits required, checkpoints and delays, the real trouble is arriving. (p235)

Wildlife

Isla Barro Colorado Nature geeks shouldn't miss this rainforest, the most intensely studied area in the Neotropics. (p79)

Parque Nacional Coiba Dive with a whale shark, spy scarlet macaws or search for endemic howlers. Wildlife is epic here. (p145)

San-San Pond Sak Sloths, river otters and the occasional manatee inhabit this little-known Caribbean wetland near Changuinola. (p201)

Isla Bastimentos From July to August, loggerheads, hawksbills, greens and leatherbacks hatch on the north shore. (p195)

Parque Natural Metropolitano A patch of rainforest amid Panama City. Don't mind the titi monkeys on the trail! (p48)

Top: Snorkeling, Archipiélago de Las Perlas (p83)
Bottom: Strawberry poison-dart frog (p196)

Month by Month

TOP EVENTS

Festival de Diablos y Congos, February–March

Carnaval, February–March

Feria de Azuero, April or May

Panama Jazz Festival, January

Festival of Nogagope, October

January

With dry season and tourist season at their peaks, this is a big month for travel in Panama. It's prime time for kitesurfing and swimming, since Pacific Ocean temperatures are at their warmest and the wind is up.

Panama Jazz Festival

The weeklong jazz festival (www.panamajazzfestival.com) is one of the biggest musical events in Panama, drawing top-caliber international musicians from jazz, blues, salsa and other genres. Held all over the city, the open-air events are usually free. (p53)

Fiesta del Mar

Held at the end of the month on tiny Isla Taboga, a boat ride away from Panama City, this new tradition seeks to revive island culture with a weekend festival (www.fiestadelmarpanama.com) of Calypso music, dancing and food events. (p81)

March

It's prime time for surfing on both Pacific and Caribbean swells. High season is winding down. Events related to the religious calendar may take place in February or March.

Carnaval

On the four days preceding Ash Wednesday, general merriment prevails in Panama City and on the Península de Azuero. This anything-goes, multi-event period features street parades, water fights, costumes and live music til the wee hours. (p53)

Festival de Diablos y Congos

Held every other year, this Congo festival celebrates rebellious slave ancestors with spirited public dancing featuring beautiful masks and costumes. Participants assume the role of escaped slaves and take captives on the street. (p216)

Semana Santa

During Holy Week (the week before Easter), the country hosts many special events, including a re-enactment of the crucifixion and resurrection of Christ. On Good Friday, religious processions are held across the country.

May

With sporadic, refreshing rain showers, the weather is generally pleasant throughout the country. May begins a five- to six-month nesting season for both loggerhead and green sea turtles on the Caribbean coast.

Feria de Azuero

Held late April or early May, this rural festival in the historic colonial town of Villa de los Santos features singing competitions, folk dancing and the quaint attractions of a rural agricultural fair.

🎎 Fiesta de Corpus Christi

Forty days after Easter, this religious holiday features colorful celebrations in Villa de Los Santos. Masked and costumed dancers representing angels, devils, imps and other mythological figures perform dances, acrobatics and dramas. (p120)

July

Though it's the middle of the rainy season, the weather is relatively dry on the Caribbean side. It's also off-peak for visitors and hotels offer better rates.

🎎 Nuestra Señora del Carmen

Celebrating the patron saint of Isla Taboga, this event held on July 16 starts with a procession parading the virgin statue, followed by fire breathing, games and dance.

🎎 Festival de Santa Librada

Celebrating the patron saint of Las Tablas, this July 21 event has huge street celebrations, music and dance, in addition to solemn religious services and processions. Held in the festival-happy Península de Azuero.

🎎 Festival de la Pollera

Hundreds of young beauties parade through Las Tablas wearing traditional *polleras*, handmade lace dresses that can be worth tens of thousands of dollars. Beyond that, it's a raucous street festival with music, food and dance. Held July 21.

August

Breeding humpback whales can be observed in the Archipiélago de Las Perlas. Mid-month Panama City celebrates its founding in 1519 with a stream of events. Rainy season continues.

🎎 Festival del Manito Ocueño

Among the country's best folkloric events, this three-day bash features traditional music and dancing, and culminates in a country wedding. Held the third week of August in the rural village of Ocú.

September

The rain usually lets up a little, particularly around Panama City. Still low season, it's a good time to travel around the country with no need of reservations.

🎎 Feria de la Mejorana

In late September, Panama's largest folkloric festival draws musicians and traditional dancers from all over the country to tiny Guararé on the Península de Azuero. With oxcart parades and *seco* cocktails, it's a fun time to soak up tradition. (p122)

October

October 12 is Día de la Raza (Colombus Day), a dubious legacy nonetheless celebrated by every high school

brass band letting loose. Throughout Panama, some very different yet excellent festivals are well worth attending.

🎎 Festival of Nogagope

Kunas converge on Isla Tigre for three days of tireless traditional dancing. It's visually engaging and fully authentic. Held from October 10 to 12, it's followed by a three-day fair with art shows and canoe races. (p224)

🎎 Festival of the Black Christ

On October 21, thousands honor the black Christ in Portobelo. Many make the pilgrimage on foot from the capital. Miracles aplenty have been attributed to the black Christ. After a night-time procession there's dancing and drinking til the wee hours.

November

Don't come to Panama for business between November and December as the whole country takes off to celebrate multiple independence-related holidays in November, followed by the Christmas holiday. Panama City empties out and beaches are full.

🎎 Día de Independencia

On November 28 Panama celebrates its independence from Spain with parties and revelry throughout the country. Most locals head to the beach and enjoy a drink or 10. Book any travel well ahead.

Plan Your Trip
Itineraries

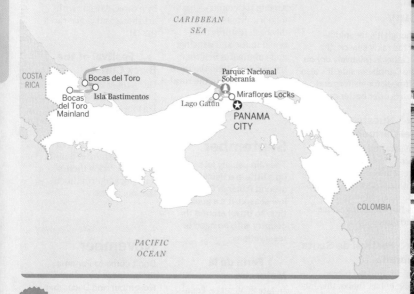

CARIBBEAN
SEA

COSTA
RICA

Bocas del Toro

Parque Nacional
Soberanía

Bocas
del Toro
Mainland

Isla Bastimentos

Miraflores Locks

Lago Gatún

✪ PANAMA
CITY

COLOMBIA

PACIFIC
OCEAN

1 WEEK Essential Panama

For a taste of tropical Panama, this trip takes you to the hyper-charged capital. Explore the city and see colonial ruins and landmarks like the famous Panama Canal while getting a dose of rainforest adventure. Take the grand finale of a chill Caribbean getaway.

Start by imbibing the rush of **Panama City**, the country's vibrant capital. Make a visit to Panamá Viejo to admire the grandiose ruins of Spain's first Pacific settlement, destroyed in a massive pirate raid. Walk or pedal along Cinta Costera, downtown's

coastal green space, to the *ceviche* (seafood) stands at the Mercado de Mariscos. Continue to the historic neighborhood of Casco Viejo, with hip plaza restaurants and rooftop bars amid crumbling ruins, galleries and 18th-century churches. Take in the scene strolling the romantic Paseo las Bóvedas.

Take a day trip to nearby **Miraflores Locks**, where observation decks put you front and center with mammoth ships as they shimmy through the canal. Follow with a rainforest visit nearby. Options include checking out the wildlife-rich **Parque Nacional Soberanía**, a favorite

Casco Viejo (p45), Panama City

of avid birders. Climb a canopy tower to search for toucans, capuchin monkeys and sloths or paddle a kayak on Lago Gatún alongside howler monkeys and sunbathing crocodiles.

From Panama City, fly to **Bocas del Toro** for four days of chill Caribbean vibes. Hire a water taxi to snorkel the clear waters filled with tropical fish and colorful coral reefs. Explore Isla Colón riding a cruiser bike out to Playa Bluff or Starfish Beach. Work up an appetite riding the waves and spend your evening wining and dining on the waterfront in quirky Bocas Town.

Split your time between this laid-back hub and a more remote setting such as **Isla Bastimentos**, with thatched resorts and jungle lodges, for a true island getaway. If you want to really get under the skin of the culture, take a chocolate tour on the Bocas del Toro **mainland** or visit indigenous groups on other islands with a community tourism initiative.

Fly back to the capital for another shot of urban decadence in the city's many open-air restaurants, sleek bars and salsa clubs.

CARIBBEAN
SEA

COSTA
RICA

Parque Internacional
La Amistad

Cerro
Punta

Volcán

Sendero Los Quetzales

Boquete

David

Orange
Blossom Road

Santa Fé

El Valle

PANAMA
CITY

Santa Catalina

Parque
Nacional
Coiba

COLOMBIA

PACIFIC
OCEAN

GREG NEWINGTON/GETTY IMAGES ©

Pacific Coast & Highlands

2 WEEKS

Whether you're traveling on buses or with your own wheels, hit the Interamericana for a route that alternates between scenic beaches and highland cloud forests.

Spend your first few days exploring **Panama City**, taking tips from the previous itinerary. Then head west along the Interamericana, where you can stop for a leisurely seafood lunch and pass the hours playing in the waves at one of the string of beaches along the Pacific coast. The next stop is **El Valle**, a mountain retreat surrounded by lush cloud forests and green peaks. Return to the Interamericana, taking a quick stop at one of Coclé's roadside attractions, then take the turnoff for **Santa Fé**, a tiny highland town amid sparkling rivers and gorgeous waterfalls.

For surf time, backtrack to the Interamericana and detour to the surf village of **Santa Catalina**. Soak up the laid-back vibe at thatched restaurants and join the local surfing kids nailing the waves on the town beach. Another very good reason to stop here is to connect to **Parque Nacional Coiba**, a far-flung yet pristine island in a vast marine park. Snorkeling, diving and hiking are all top-notch; although there's minimal infrastructure, it's worth staying a few days.

Head via David to the popular highland retreat of **Boquete** in Chiriquí. Enjoy the great hiking, go rafting, take a canopy tour and fill up on mountain-grown coffee. Birders can stalk the resplendent quetzal. Choose from among fine dining options and sleep sound in clean mountain air.

If you have your own wheels, take the new **Orange Blossom Road** to Volcán, a very scenic shortcut. Otherwise grab a bus via David to **Cerro Punta**. Retreat to a charming rainforest cabin before hitting the trail to hike the **Sendero Los Quetzales**, a stunning trail through wildlife-rich cloud forest. If traveling by bus, you can loop back to Boquete on this hike. If adventure *still* calls, from Cerro Punta you can access the trails of **Parque Internacional La Amistad**. Take a guide – the Panamanian side of this international park is virtually undeveloped and largely unexplored.

If you need to save time, you can fly back to Panama City from David.

ALFREDO MAQUIEZ/GETTY IMAGES ©

Top: Highlands, Coclé Province (p92)
Bottom: David (p153), Chiriquí Province

Bicoastal Explorer

If you're itching to get off the beaten path, this seafarer route will bring you to the less touristed Península de Azuero on the Pacific coast, the Afro-Caribbean heartland and the furthest reaches of Kuna Yala (and possibly even Colombia).

Start in the capital of **Panama City**. From there, take a ride in the luxury train along the historic Panama Railroad through the Canal Zone to **Colón** to admire the Unesco World Heritage Site of **Fuerte San Lorenzo**. While in the area, check out the Panama Canal expansion at the nearby **Gatun Locks**. Using **Portobelo** as your base, explore 16th-century Spanish forts, boat out to deserted island beaches, scuba dive or attend a festival.

Return to Panama City to travel to the **Península de Azuero** by bus. From time to time traditional festivals take over the streets of these tiny colonial towns. If your visit coincides, join the revelers! Otherwise, check out workshops where regional artisans craft Panama hats, lace dresses and colorful *diablo* (devil) masks. Make your base **Pedasí** for leisurely trips to the beach and a friendly village atmosphere. Move on to the more remote **Playa Venao** to enjoy a pretty half-moon bay, meet other travelers and ride some waves without the crowds. If turtles are hatching, it's worth making the pilgrimage to **Isla de Cañas**.

When you're ready, return to the capital and take a 4WD or flight to **Kuna Yala**, a string of hundreds of pristine islands ruled by the Kuna. Thatched huts on dozens of islands run the gamut from bare-bones to creature comfort, with meals and excursions always included. Snorkel and swim to your heart's content, or charter a sailboat for the grand tour. Highlights include snorkeling the reefs and wrecks of **Cayos Holandeses** and meeting the locals on the tiny community island of **Isla Tigre**.

At the end of your trip, return to Panama City via **Burbayar Lodge**, in a stunning mountain setting on the edge of the Kuna mainland, with great hiking and wildlife-watching. If you are heading on to South America – and bent on adventure – consider a three- to four-day sailing or boat trip to Colombia.

Top: Kuna Yala (p221)
Bottom: Scarlet macaw

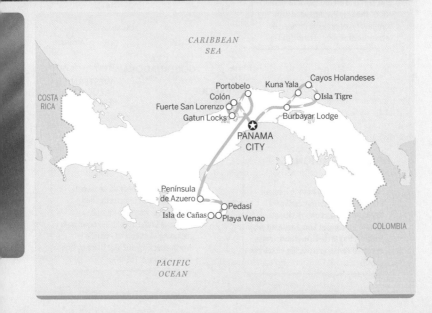

Off the Beaten Track: Panama

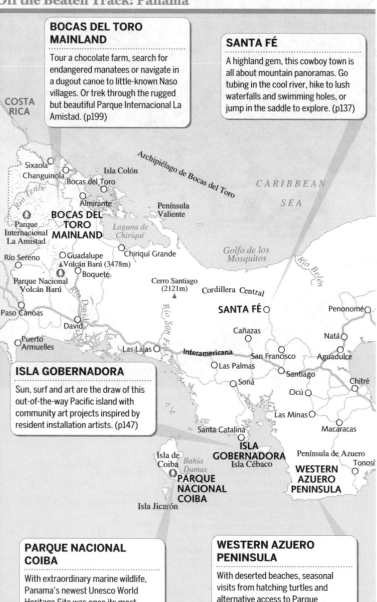

BOCAS DEL TORO MAINLAND

Tour a chocolate farm, search for endangered manatees or navigate in a dugout canoe to little-known Naso villages. Or trek through the rugged but beautiful Parque Internacional La Amistad. (p199)

SANTA FÉ

A highland gem, this cowboy town is all about mountain panoramas. Go tubing in the cool river, hike to lush waterfalls and swimming holes, or jump in the saddle to explore. (p137)

ISLA GOBERNADORA

Sun, surf and art are the draw of this out-of-the-way Pacific island with community art projects inspired by resident installation artists. (p147)

PARQUE NACIONAL COIBA

With extraordinary marine wildlife, Panama's newest Unesco World Heritage Site was once its most infamous island prison. Far-flung yet pristine, this little-visited park offers excellent diving and wildlife-watching. (p145)

WESTERN AZUERO PENINSULA

With deserted beaches, seasonal visits from hatching turtles and alternative access to Parque Nacional Coiba, this little-known area including Mariato and Palmilla is worth checking out. Get there by bus from Santiago. (p148)

Map labels: COSTA RICA; CARIBBEAN SEA; Sixaola; Changuinola; Isla Colón; Archipiélago de Bocas del Toro; Bocas del Toro; Almirante; Península Valiente; Parque Internacional La Amistad; BOCAS DEL TORO MAINLAND; Laguna de Chiriquí; Golfo de los Mosquitos; Río Teribe; Río Sereno; Guadalupe; Volcán Barú (3478m); Chiriquí Grande; Boquete; Cerro Santiago (2121m); Cordillera Central; Río Belén; Parque Nacional Volcán Barú; Paso Canoas; David; Río Chiriquí; Río San Félix; SANTA FÉ; Penonomé; Cañazas; Natá; Puerto Armuelles; Las Lajas; Interamericana; San Francisco; Aguadulce; Las Palmas; Santiago; Chitré; Soná; Ocú; Las Minas; Santa Catalina; ISLA GOBERNADORA; Isla Cébaco; Península de Azuero; Tonosí; WESTERN AZUERO PENINSULA; Macaracas; Isla de Coiba; Bahía Damas; PARQUE NACIONAL COIBA; Isla Jicarón

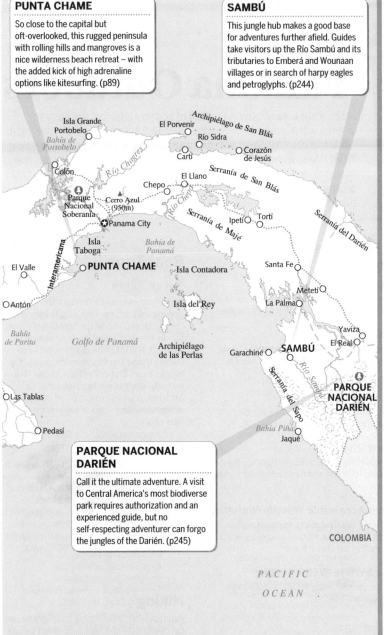

PUNTA CHAME

So close to the capital but oft-overlooked, this rugged peninsula with rolling hills and mangroves is a nice wilderness beach retreat – with the added kick of high adrenaline options like kitesurfing. (p89)

SAMBÚ

This jungle hub makes a good base for adventures further afield. Guides take visitors up the Río Sambú and its tributaries to Emberá and Wounaan villages or in search of harpy eagles and petroglyphs. (p244)

PARQUE NACIONAL DARIÉN

Call it the ultimate adventure. A visit to Central America's most biodiverse park requires authorization and an experienced guide, but no self-respecting adventurer can forgo the jungles of the Darién. (p245)

Isla Grande
Portobelo
Bahía de Portobelo
El Porvenir
Archipiélago de San Blás
Río Sidra
Corazón de Jesús
Cartí
Colón
Río Chagres
Serranía de San Blás
El Llano
Chepo
Parque Nacional Soberanía
Cerro Azul (950m)
Río Chepo
Serranía del Darién
Panama City
Serranía de Majé
Ipetí
Tortí
Interamericana
Isla Taboga
Bahía de Panamá
El Valle
PUNTA CHAME
Isla Contadora
Santa Fe
Antón
Metetí
Bahía de Parita
Golfo de Panamá
Isla del Rey
La Palma
Yaviza
El Real
Las Tablas
Archipiélago de las Perlas
Garachiné
SAMBÚ
Río Sambú
Serranía del Sapo
PARQUE NACIONAL DARIÉN
Pedasí
Bahía Piña
Jaqué
COLOMBIA
PACIFIC OCEAN

0   100 km
0   50 miles

Plan Your Trip

Panama Outdoors

With a cosmopolitan capital full of sparkly casinos, it's easy to overlook the appeal of Panama's outdoors. But it's worth making it your top priority. Start with the astounding wildlife: primates swing from trees, whales breach offshore and butterflies dart across the forest floor. Ride a dugout canoe through jungle waterways, snorkel around jewel-toned reefs, trek to misty heights or surf huge Pacific tubes. Refuel with fresh coffee from the highlands, and then repeat.

Best of Panama Outdoors

Best Surf Beach

Laid-back vibes, access to Parque Nacional Coiba and world-class waves: it's all at Santa Catalina.

Best Hike

Sendero Los Quetzales is a beautiful 8km route, running between Cerro Punta and Boquete in Chiriquí Province.

Best Sportfishing

If you want to break a sportfishing world record, your chances are high at Bahía Piña.

Best Dive Site

Parque Nacional Coiba has extraordinary marine wildlife; you might spot hammerheads or a whale shark.

Best Accessible Wildlife-Watching

More than 500 bird spices have been sighted along Pipeline Rd in Parque Nacional Soberanía – hit the trail and start counting!

Best White-Water Rafting

Tackle the white water of Río Chiriquí from May through to December.

Boat Trips

River Trips

Partial canal transits through the Miraflores Locks are the best way to appreciate the canal, and one of the highlights of any trip to Panama. Another great option is to watch wildlife from a kayak on Lago Gatún. In the Darién, tours cruise up Río Mogué to an Emberá village. In the Wekso sector of the Parque Internacional La Amistad, travelers can explore indigenous villages heading upriver on motorized dugouts.

Ocean Trips

The 226km-long Archipiélago de San Blás is a thrill for ocean explorers. Run as an autonomous region by the Kuna, it has hundreds of coconut-fringed islands and islets surrounded by turquoise waters. Independent travelers can travel by small boat between the islands, or charter sailboats through the area and even continue on to Colombia.

Hiking

Panama offers everything from dry tropical rainforests and highland cloud forests to humid jungles and blistery mountain peaks.

Starting near the capital on the shores of the canal, Parque Nacional Soberanía contains a section of the historic Sendero Las Cruces. Closer to Panama City, Parque Natural Metropolitano boasts a number of short but rewarding hikes in plush rainforest that literally skirts the edge of the capital.

Popular highland retreats include Boquete, El Valle (nestled into the extinct volcano now known as Valle de Antón), and Santa Fé, surrounded by rivers, waterfalls and cloud forests. All feature hikes in a pristine mountain setting.

Chiriquí is home to two of Panama's most famous hikes, namely Volcán Barú and Sendero Los Quetzales in Parque Nacional Volcán Barú. While Los Quetzales is more scenic in poor weather, ascents up Barú, which is Panama's highest peak, can offer views of both oceans on a clear day.

Recommended remote destinations include the Las Nubes sector of the Parque Internacional La Amistad. With trails only accessible with a guide, it is as rugged and unchartered as Central America gets.

Diving & Snorkeling

Panama's underwater world spans two great oceans, and abounds with colorful coral gardens, towering rock shelves, sunken wrecks and a rich diversity of marine life. Fans of multicolored reef fish and bathtub-warm water should head for the Caribbean, while more advanced divers in search of enormous pelagic animals and remote dive sites should head to the Pacific. Three major spots in Panama that have a deserved reputation for fine scuba diving are the Archipiélago de Bocas del Toro, the Caribbean town of Portobelo and the Pacific coast Isla de Coiba.

The Caribbean islands of Bocas del Toro have a thriving dive community. During the rainy season (mid-April to mid-December) underwater visibility is extremely poor – nearly 40 rivers deposit silt into the seas around the islands, which turns the water a murky green.

Near historic Portobelo, 16 major dive sites feature underwater attractions including a 110ft cargo ship, a C-45 twin-engine plane, soft-coral-laden walls, offshore reefs and rock gardens.

The best diving in Panama is around Isla de Coiba, the centerpiece of a national marine park accessed via Santa Catalina. Divers here scout for enormous sharks, including schools of hammerheads, blacktips and white-tips as well as the occasional tiger or whale shark.

The Kuna prohibit dive operators from working in the Comarca de Kuna Yala, but the snorkeling is some of the best in Panama.

Surfing

Although the joy of Panama is riding some of the lesser known surf breaks – or even discovering your own – the country has two world-class spots in Santa Catalina and the Archipiélago de Bocas del Toro. Even these are significantly less crowded than similar spots in neighboring Costa Rica.

The face of a typical wave at Santa Catalina is 2m, though during February and March 4m waves are fairly common. Waves are at their best during medium to high tide when rides approaching 150m are possible. On the Caribbean side, the islands of Bocas del Toro offer some of the best and most varied surfing in Panama, especially from December to March.

Surfing spots are also found in the provinces of Panamá, Los Santos, Colón and Chiriquí.

Fishing

Panamá means 'abundance of fish,' and with 2988km of coastline, there's no problem finding a fishing spot. Freshwater

DIVING RESPONSIBLY

➡ Never anchor on the reef and take care not to ground boats on coral.

➡ Avoid touching or standing on living marine organisms. Polyps can be damaged by even the most gentle contact. If you must hold on, only touch exposed rock or dead coral.

➡ Watch your fins. The surge from fin strokes can damage delicate reef organisms and clouds of sand can smother organisms.

➡ Make visits quick to underwater caves, as trapped air bubbles damage organisms.

➡ Resist the temptation to collect or buy corals or shells or to loot marine archaeological sites.

➡ Do not feed fish and never ride on the backs of turtles.

anglers usually set their sights on trout and bass, while serious sportfishers ply the seas for trophy fish including tarpon, sailfish and marlin. Freshwater angling can be pursued independently, especially in the highland rivers of Chiriquí and Veraguas. In the Canal Zone you can fish for peacock bass in Lago Gatún and the Río Chagres.

For deep-sea fishing, Panama offers three world-class areas – Bahía Piña, the Pearl Islands and Isla de Coiba – all served by extremely professional fishing outfits. In the Darién's Bahía Piña, more International Game Fish Association world records have been broken than anywhere else on the planet. This top spot is served exclusively by Tropic Star Lodge. The seas around Isla de Coiba are home to several species of sport fish including yellow-fin tuna, wahoo, dolphin, Spanish mackerel, jacks and rooster fish.

Cycling

Owing to its compact size and modern infrastructure, Panama is the perfect country to unleash a little pedal power. As with all long-distance cycling, you need to prepare yourself both physically and mentally for the rigors of the road. The major factor when considering a lengthy bike ride is the weather. With heat a serious factor, riding in the early morning and resting in the heat of the day is a good strategy. Also, it's not entirely safe to ride in the rain. Throughout much of the country, the rains come from mid-April to mid-December, though the Caribbean has rain

virtually year-round. Beyond the capital, you're essentially on your own, but never underestimate the prowess of the village mechanic.

Wildlife-Watching

Unlike the savannahs of Africa, wildlife-watching in the Neotropical rainforest is an exercise in patience and stealth – a little luck doesn't hurt either. Although it's unlikely you'll come across top predators such as jaguars and pumas, primates and lesser mammals are commonly sighted. Top national parks for watching-wildlife include La Amistad, Volcán Barú and the Darién. Closer to the capital, Parque Natural Metropolitano and Parque Nacional Soberanía are easily accessible and quite good.

Highlights

Nowhere else in the world are rainforests as easily accessible as they are in this tiny sliver of a country. To make the most of your wildlife-watching experience, pick up a good field guide. Some highlights include:

➡ **Two- and three-toed sloths** Found only in Neotropical rainforests, these ancient mammals came into being when South America was isolated. Curled up high on a branch, they are hard to spot. They spend 16 hours a day asleep or inactive but are busy with digestion.

➡ **Mantled howlers** Greeting sunrise and sunset with booming calls that resonate for kilometers, howlers are incredibly vocal. Their antics are also good storm indicators.

⇒ **Jaguars** The largest cat in the Americas, jaguars are incredibly rare and elusive, though their evidence is all around, from dried spoors to fresh tracks.

⇒ **Parrots and macaws** Panama has more than 20 species, including five macaws. Big macaws can be identified by their huge bills, bare facial patch and long, tapered tails.

⇒ **Toucans** The spectacular multicolored bill is a giveaway. This powerful tool is full of air cavities and quite lightweight. A serrated upper mandible helps grip slippery fruits and intimidate other birds.

Bird-Watching

With more than 900 bird species in Panama, all you need to do to spot feathered friends is to get a good pair of binoculars and hit the trails. Two popular spots include Pipeline Rd in Parque Nacional Soberanía and Burbayar Lodge in Panamá Province. Panama Audubon Society (p52), located in Panama City, organizes the annual Christmas bird count on Pipeline Rd, and runs bird-watching expeditions throughout the country.

White-Water Rafting & Kayaking

Whether you take to the water by raft or kayak, Panama boasts some excellent opportunities for river running. The most famous white-water runs are the Ríos Chiriquí and Chiriquí Viejo. The unofficial river-running capital of Panama is the highland town of Boquete. Sea kayaking centers are Bocas del Toro and Chiriquí Provinces.

Regions at a Glance

Located at the heart of the Americas, Panama is the crucial link. The Panama Canal joins the Atlantic to the Pacific, wedding east to west in global commerce. In the last century, the canal defined Panama, but it's what lies just beyond which may define the next. Pristine beaches, lush rainforest and big city nightlife are major assets. English is widely spoken, yet the lost world of rainforests and dugout canoes is never too far off. The canal expansion will mean further growth and glitz. But for now, you can still pick an empty islet and play survivor for a day.

Panama City

History
Cuisine
Nightlife

Colonial Echoes

Wander the cobblestone streets of the Casco Viejo, admire the 16th century ruins of Panamá Viejo or peddle the brand new Cinta Costera for the long view. History's most notorious explorers, pirates and marauders have preceded you.

Tastes go Tropical

Panama chefs are reinventing traditional ingredients and refining tropical tastes, and the capital's lively dining scene is finally reflecting its cultural plurality, with more options than ever.

La Rumba

From rooftop cocktails with city views to live salsa bands and open-air graffiti bars, Panama City nightlife is dynamic, daring and ever hip.

p40

Panama Province

Man-Made Marvels
Rainforests
Island Getaways

Panama Canal

The expansion of this 80km cross-continental shortcut is even more reason to see the Panama Canal. Few know there's also fishing, kayaking and wildlife-watching off the shipping lanes.

Jungle Love

Rainforest adventure and some of the best wildlife-watching is just outside of Panama City. For nature on steroids, reserve ahead for the exclusive Smithsonian Tropical Research Institute tour.

Island Escapes

Isla Contadora makes a great city escape, with pristine beaches and deserted isles – for a price. On a budget? Flee to Isla Taboga for the day. Both now have frequent ferry service.

p72

Coclé Province

Highlands
Latin Tradition
Beaches

Mountain Time

Coclé's highland retreats are prime weekend getaways. El Valle is an established resort town with boutique hotels and charming waterfall walks. For something wilder, replenish yourself in the deep forests of Reserva Privada Távida or Parque Nacional Omar Torrijos.

Latin Tradition

Pick up a panama hat, the signature product of Coclé, at a street-side stand, or take an up-close look at the production of fine cigars and cane sugar on a factory tour.

Sun & Sand

Wide pearly beaches are signature Coclé. With an airport coming up and resorts popping up, it's poised to boom. Stop in Farallón or Santa Clara to kick back for a couple days.

p92

Península de Azuero

Festivals
Deserted Beaches
Turtle Nesting

Take it to the Streets

If the peninsula is the heart and soul of Panama, then festivals are its pulse. Villa de Los Santos, Las Tablas and Guararé are the best places to get your groove on.

Deserted Beaches

With access improving, the rugged Azuero coast may not remain solitary for long. Its essence is still wild, especially the further you go down the coast.

The Moonlight Hatch

From late August through November, thousands of endangered olive ridley sea turtles reach remote Isla de Cañas in the wee hours to hatch their eggs.

p110

Veraguas Province

Surfing
Diving
Country Roads

Ride a Wave

With some of the biggest breaks in Central America, Santa Catalina surfing is deliriously good. Big tubes and long rides attract the experts (especially December through April); beginners have their own sandy-bottom spot.

Underwater Wonders

Pure delight for divers and snorkelers, Parque Nacional Coiba hosts amazing biodiversity. It's out of the way, but well worth a visit.

Country Roads

Brave the winding lanes to the rugged and relatively undiscovered landscapes of the highlands. The village of Santa Fé makes an ideal base for waterfall hikes with swimming holes, river tubing and horseback riding.

p134

Chiriquí Province

White Water
Hiking
Highland Lodges

Make a Splash

Adrenaline addicts head to Boquete, the highland town that's a major hub for rafting and kayaking. You can paddle year-round on the Río Chiriquí or Chiriquí Viejo.

Hit the Trail

The iconic Quetzal Trail weaves through gorgeous highland forest in search of its namesake. Brave Volcán Barú or set out expedition-style to Parque Internacional La Amistad.

Highland Lodges

A delicious treat in high country, cabin lodges in the coffee farms of Boquete and cloud forests of Cerro Punta and Buena Vista take the chill off with fireplaces, bottles of wine and hot tubs.

p152

Bocas del Toro Province

Beaches
Surfing
Community
Tourism

The Stunning Sandbox

Many an idyllic palm-fringed crescent is a bicycle ride or boat taxi away from Bocas town. Take care of the many starfish on its namesake beach as well as on Red Frog Beach.

Surf's Up

While second to Santa Catalina, Bocas offers the most varied waves in Panama, with plenty of options to get beginners on board. Then a cool Caribbean vibe reels you in to stay.

Go Local

Connect with local and indigenous cultures through the popular Oreba chocolate farm tour, visit a Ngöbe-Buglé community on Isla San Cristóbal, or have a real adventure in little-known Naso country.

p178

Colón Province

History
Diving
Caribbean
Culture

Steeped in History

Old Spanish fortresses, the Panama Railroad and the canal expansion: the tumultuous history of Colón is Panama's most compelling. Take a day tour from Panama City or spend a few days around Portobelo.

Underwater Treasures

While it does not rival the clear waters of the Pacific, there's enjoyable diving to soft coral walls, offshore reefs and wrecks. Keep an eye out for eagle rays, nurse sharks and reef sharks.

Caribbean Culture

Colón drums to its own beat. To get a sense of this vibrant Congo culture, it's worth checking out the artist workshop in Portobelo or attending a festival.

p206

Comarca de Kuna Yala

Islands
Indigenous
Culture
Arts

Islands

With hundreds of idyllic islands and waters of Technicolor turquoise, you could indeed do much worse. Resort islands comprise little more than thatched huts with sandy floors and a few hammocks, but what more do you need?

Kuna Culture

With the world of the strong, self-governing Kuna very different from mainland Panama, it's well worth engaging a local guide or host. Community islands will further your cultural understanding.

Molas

Beautiful and often exquisitely crafted, these colorful panels of intricate embroidery are the signature of Kuna culture and Panama's most beloved craft.

p221

Darién Province

Nature
Indigenous
Culture
Sportfishing

Nature

The lush rainforest of Parque Nacional Darién belies the most ecologically diverse park in Central America. Getting there's another story...

Indigenous Culture

Remote pockets of Emberá and Wounaan peoples have inhabited these forests for centuries. With a guided expedition up the Río Sambu, the most intrepid of travelers can learn about real jungle survival.

Reeling in the Big One

Bahía Piña is the granddaddy of sportfishing destinations; more world records have been made here than anywhere. An exclusive fishing lodge has all the trimmings.

p235

On the Road

Panama City

POP 699,500 / ELEV SEA LEVEL / AREA 2561 SQ KM

Best Places to Eat

➡ Maito (p63)

➡ Mercado de Mariscos (p59)

➡ Country Store (p63)

➡ La Rosa Mexicano (p62)

➡ Granclement (p59)

Best Places to Stay

➡ Las Clementinas (p54)

➡ Saba Hotel (p55)

➡ Magnolia Inn (p54)

➡ Luna's Castle (p53)

➡ Dos Palmitos (p58)

Why Go?

The most cosmopolitan capital in Central America, Panama City is both vibrant metropolis and gateway to tropical escapes. Many worlds coexist here. Welcoming both east and west, Panama is a regional hub of trade and immigration. The resulting cultural cocktail forges a refreshing 'anything goes' attitude, more dynamic and fluid than its neighbors.

Unflinchingly urban, the capital rides the rails of chaos, with traffic jams, wayward taxis and casinos stacked between chic clubs and construction sites. A center of international banking and trade, the sultry skyline of shimmering glass and steel towers is reminiscent of Miami. In contrast, the peninsula of Casco Viejo has become a thriving colonial neighborhood where cobblestones link boutique hotels with underground bars and crumbled ruins with pirate lore.

Escape is never far. Day trip to sandy beaches (Pacific or Caribbean), admire the canal, or explore lush rainforests of howler monkeys, toucans and sloths.

When to Go

➡ **Jan** In the peak of high season, the weeklong Panama Jazz Festival features open-air concerts and events held mostly in the historic neighborhood of Casco Viejo.

➡ **Dec-mid–Mar** High season is dry season, with sunnier weather for outdoor cafe dining and day trips to the beach; hotel rates are up and travelers should book ahead.

➡ **Apr–Nov** Low season prices and occasional rain showers, though a rain reprieve usually comes in October. A slew of public holidays in November mean ubiquitous parades, party events and closures.

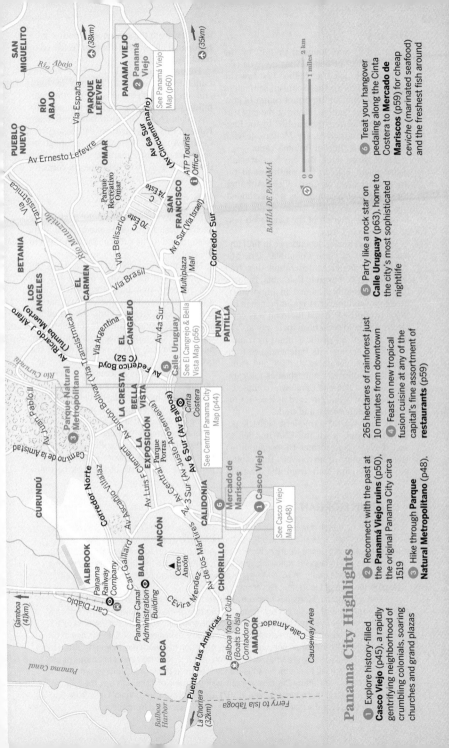

Panama City Highlights

1 Explore history-filled **Casco Viejo** (p45), a rapidly gentrifying neighborhood of crumbling colonials, soaring churches and grand plazas

2 Reconnect with the past at the **Panamá Viejo ruins** (p50), the original Panama City circa 1519

3 Hike through **Parque Natural Metropolitano** (p48),

265 hectares of rainforest just 10 minutes from downtown

4 Feast on new tropical fusion cuisine at any of the capital's fine assortment of **restaurants** (p59)

5 Party like a rock star on **Calle Uruguay** (p63), home to the city's most sophisticated nightlife

6 Treat your hangover pedaling along the Cinta Costera to **Mercado de Mariscos** (p59) for cheap *ceviche* (marinated seafood) and the freshest fish around

History

Panama City was founded in 1519 by the Spanish governor Pedro Arias de Ávila (Pedrarias), not long after Balboa first saw the Pacific. Although the Spanish settlement quickly became an important center of government and church authority, the city was ransacked and destroyed in 1671 by the English pirate Captian Henry Morgan, leaving only the stone ruins of Panamá Viejo.

Three years later, the city was reestablished about 8km to the southwest in the area now known as Casco Viejo. Although the peninsular location was well defended, the Spanish overland trade route faded upon the destruction of the Caribbean port at Portobelo in 1746.

Panama gained independence in 1821 and became part of Gran Colombia; a decade later the regional confederation dissolved and Panama belonged to Colombia. Panama City subsequently declined in importance, though it would return to prominence in the 1850s when the Panama Railroad was completed, and gold seekers on their way to California flooded across the isthmus by train.

Panama declared its independence from Colombia on November 3, 1903, and Panama City was firmly established as the capital. Since the Panama Canal was completed in 1914, the city has emerged as a center for international business and trade.

The city's greatest modern setback occurred in 1989, when the USA invaded to oust dictator (and former US collaborator) Manuel Noriega from power. The capital suffered damage both from the invasion itself and from the subsequent looting, with residential blocks of El Chorrillo destroyed by combat-ignited fire.

Following the handover of the Panama Canal from the US to Panama in 1999, and the subsequent closure of American military bases in the country, Panama City has taken charge of its own destiny. Today, Panama City is by far the wealthiest city in Central America. With a spate of foreign investment and the Panama Canal expansion, the city is poised to continue its constant transformation.

◉ Sights

Panama City stretches about 20km along the Pacific coast, from the Panama Canal at its western end to the ruins of Panamá Viejo to the east.

Near the canal are Albrook airport, the Causeway and the wealthy Balboa and Ancón suburbs, first built for the US canal and military workers. The colonial part of the city, Casco Viejo juts into the sea on the southwestern side of town. In the south, the Causeway has numerous restaurants, bars and fine vantage points on the edge of the ocean.

The main drag is Av Central, which runs through Casco Viejo to Parque Santa Ana and Plaza Cinco de Mayo; between these two plazas, the avenue is a pedestrian-only shopping street. At a fork further east, the avenue becomes Av Central España; the section that traverses the El Cangrejo business and financial district is called Vía España. The other part of the fork becomes

---

CAPTAIN MORGAN

After sacking Panama in 1671, Captain Henry Morgan burnt the city to the ground, massacred its inhabitants and made off with the richest booty in the Americas. Because his actions violated a peace treaty between England and Spain, Morgan was arrested and conducted to England the following year, but acquitted since he supposedly had no prior knowledge of the treaty. In 1674 Morgan was knighted before departing for Jamaica to take up the post of Lieutenant Governor.

Although Captain Morgan is best remembered for his nefarious exploits at sea, the last several years of his life in Port Royal (the 'Sodom of the New World') is the stuff of legends. Here, he lived out the last years of his life spending the riches of Panama.

The events surrounding his death remain a mystery. He died in 1688, at the age of 53, leaving behind an immense personal fortune. Although his death has been attributed to tuberculosis and dropsy (edema), the local lore has it that world's most infamous pirate simply drank himself to death. Now his legacy lives on in the form of spiced rum.

To see the legacy left by Captain Morgan, visit the ruins of Panamá Viejo, the original settlement that he thoroughly sacked in 1671. Or check out Casco Viejo's Iglesia de San José, which houses the golden altar – the only item – salvaged from the raid.

PANAMA CITY FOR CHILDREN

Panama City has a variety of attractions to enthrall and entertain kids. The city's new Cinta Costera has waterfront paths and a playground. The setting also hosts sporting events and occasional fairs. Another park option is Parque Recreativo Omar (p43), the local answer to New York City's Central Park, with greens that were once a golf course.

A perfect reward for a day well spent is ice cream, and Casco Viejo's Granclement (p59) is a parlor that even mom and dad would beg to visit.

Great rainforest excursions abound. At the Rainforest Discovery Center (p79), kids can walk short paths and check out the wildlife from the top of a 32m tower. Other good options include visiting Summit Botanical Gardens & Zoo (p78), which has kid-focused programs, a small zoo and trails. Alongside huge canal boats, jungle boats cruise along Lago Gatún, fishing for peacock bass or just spotting troupes of monkeys, birds and other animals.

Isla Taboga is another interesting day trip, with plenty of sand to play in and a cool ferry ride that's a blast for small travelers.

For more adventure, families can visit an Emberá village in the Parque Nacional Soberanía, tour the old cannon-lined forts in Portobelo, or take a moderate hike through Parque Nacional Soberanía (p78), or even just in town at Parque Natural Metropolitano (p48), where the chances of spotting a monkey or toucan are pretty good.

The Panama Canal Railway, which links the two oceans, provides a lovely journey along the canal and through rainforest. Kids might also enjoy a visit to the Miraflores Locks, especially since the new museum there has lots of eye-catching multimedia exhibitions and is hands-on in parts.

If you need a respite from the heat (or the rain), head to Centro de Exhibiciones Marinas (p52) to get close to Panama's amazing underwater world. Or if all else fails, stroll down to Multicentro Mall (p67) – a mall with dozens of shops and restaurants, a movie theater and an internet cafe.

Av Simón Bolívar and, finally, Vía Transístmica as it heads out of town and across the isthmus toward Colón.

★ **Museo de Arte Contemporáneo** MUSEUM
(☎262-3380; www.macpanama.org; Av de los Mártires, Ancón; admission US$3; ⊙9am-4pm Mon-Fri, to noon Sat, to 3pm Sun) This wonderful privately owned museum features the best collection of Panamanian art anywhere, an excellent collection of works on paper by Latin American artists, and the occasional temporary exhibition by a foreign or national artist.

Museo de la Biodiversidad MUSEUM
(Museum of Biodiversity; www.biomuseopanama.org; Causeway) Pending inauguration in 2013, the Museo de la Biodiversidad is set to be a landmark museum with extensive botanical gardens. Biodiversity is celebrated with vivid visuals, and outdoor and ocean exhibits. World-renowned architect Frank Gehry, who designed the Guggenheim Museum in Bilbao, Spain, designed this controversial structure of crumpled multicolor forms. It's located near the tip of the Causeway.

Parque Recreativo Omar PARK
The biggest park in the city is filled with children, joggers and the occasional salsa class. Located in Omar, behind the San Francisco neighborhood. Access from Vía Belisario.

Panama Canal Murals HISTORIC BUILDING
(Balboa; ⊙7:30am-4:15pm Mon-Fri) FREE The story of the monumental effort to build the Panama Canal is powerfully depicted in murals by notable artist William B Van Ingen of New York. The murals are mounted in the rotunda of the Panama Canal Administration Building. The paintings have the distinction of being the largest group of murals by a Northe American artist on display outside the USA.

The murals tell the story of the canal's construction through four main scenes: the digging of Gaillard Cut at Gold Hill, where the canal passes through the Continental Divide; the building of the spillway of the Gatún Dam, which dammed the Río Chagres and created Lago Gatún; the construction of one of the giant lock gates (the canal uses some 80 of these gates); and the construction of the Miraflores Locks near the

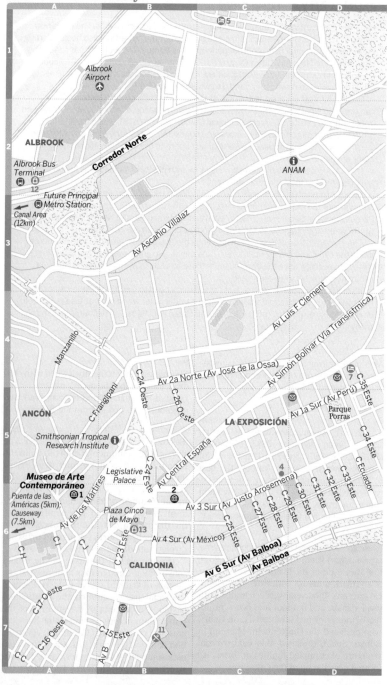

Pacific entrance to the canal. A frieze located immediately below the murals presents a panorama of the excavation of Gaillard Cut.

Van Ingen is also known for his murals in the Library of Congress and the US Mint. These he produced for US$25 per sq ft; the finished murals cover about 1000 sq ft.

It's closed on weekends, but guards may allow visits between 10am and 2:30pm if you ask politely.

Museo Afro-Antilleano   MUSEUM
(☑ 262-5348; cnr Av Justo Arosemena & Calle 24 Este; admission US$1; ⊙ 8:30am-4:30pm Tue-Sat) The small Afro-Antillean museum has exhibits on the history of Panama's West Indian community, particularly their work building the railroad and later the canal.

Baha'i House of Worship   TEMPLE
(☑ 231-1137; ⊙ 10am-6pm) On the outskirts of Panama City, the white-domed Baha'i House of Worship is the mother temple for all of Latin America. It looms like a giant egg atop the crest of a hill, with a beautiful, breezy interior.

Readings from the Baha'i writings (in English and Spanish) are held Sunday mornings at 10am. Any bus to Colón can let you off on the highway, but it's a long walk up the hill. It's 11km northeast of the city center on the Vía Transístmica.

◉ Casco Viejo

Following the destruction of the old city by Captain Henry Morgan in 1671, the Spanish moved their city 8km southwest to a rocky peninsula on the foot of Cerro Ancón. The new location was easier to defend, as the reefs prevented ships from approaching the city except at high tide. The new city was also easy to defend as a massive wall surrounded it, which is how Casco Viejo (Old Compound) got its name.

In 1904, when construction began on the Panama Canal, all of Panama City existed where Casco Viejo stands today. However, as population growth and urban expansion pushed the boundaries of Panama City further east, the city's elite abandoned Casco Viejo and the neighborhood rapidly deteriorated into an urban slum.

Today, Casco Viejo is half crumbling, half high-end. The restoration of Casco Viejo is a work in progress, so be aware of your surroundings and exercise caution while exploring this fascinating neighborhood.

Central Panama City

The newly restored architecture gives a sense of how magnificent the area must have looked in past years. Declared a Unesco World Heritage Site in 2003, the area is getting international recognition. The construction of a controversial coastal highway around the peninsula has preservationists fuming.

Plaza de la Independencia   PLAZA
In this plaza, in the heart of Casco Viejo, Panama declared its independence from Colombia on November 3, 1903.

Iglesia de San José   CHURCH
(Av A) This church protects the famous Altar de Oro (Golden Altar), the sole relic salvaged after Henry Morgan sacked Panamá Viejo.

According to local legend, when word came of the pirate's impending attack, a priest attempted to disguise the altar by painting it black. The priest told Morgan that the famous altar had been stolen by another pirate, and even convinced Morgan to donate handsomely for its replacement. Morgan is said to have told the priest, 'I don't know why, but I think you are more of a pirate than I am.' Whatever the truth, the baroque altar was later moved from the old city to the present site.

Teatro Nacional   THEATER
(☑262-3525; Av B) Built in 1907, the interior of this ornate theater has been completely restored. It boasts red and gold decorations, a once-magnificent ceiling mural by Roberto Lewis (one of Panama's finest painters) and an impressive crystal chandelier. Performances are still held here. For information visit the office at the side of the building.

Plaza de Francia   PLAZA
At the tip of the southern point of Casco Viejo, this beautiful plaza pays homage to the French role in the construction of the canal. Its large stone tablets and statues are dedicated to the memory of the 22,000 workers who died trying to create the canal.

Most of the workers died from yellow fever and malaria. Among the busts is a monument to the Cuban doctor Carlos J Finlay, whose discovery of how mosquitoes transmit yellow fever led to the eradication of the disease.

On one side of the plaza are nine restored dungeons that were used by the Spaniards and later by the Colombians. Although they're now home to some rather upscale art galleries and shops, you can still see the original stonework. Also on the plaza are the Teatro Anita Villalaz and the Instituto Nacional de Cultura.

Instituto Nacional de Cultura   GALLERY
(INAC; ☑211-4034; Plaza de Francia; ⊙8:30am-4pm Mon-Fri) INAC is responsible for maintaining the country's museums and other cultural institutions. There is a small gallery on the 1st floor that displays works by Panamanian artists.

Paseo las Bóvedas   LANDMARK
This esplanade runs along the top of the sea wall built by the Spanish to protect the city. From here, you can see the Puente de las Américas arching over the waterway and the ships lining up to enter the canal.

Palacio de las Garzas   HISTORIC BUILDING
(Presidential Palace; Av Alfaro) The Palacio de las Garzas is named after the great white herons that reside here. The president of Panama lives on the upper floor.

Club de Clases y Tropas RUIN
(Antiguo Club Union; Calle 1a Oeste) This abandoned ruin was once the favorite hangout of General Noriega, though it was virtually destroyed during the 1989 US invasion. Some fresh paint was selectively applied in early 2000, when scenes from the movie *The Tailor of Panama* were filmed here. Now it occassionally hosts raves and club events.

Parque Bolívar PLAZA
In 1826, in a schoolroom opposite this park, Simón Bolívar held a meeting urging the union of the Latin American countries. Bolívar eventually succeeded in liberating Bolivia, Colombia, Ecuador, Peru and Venezuela, united as Gran Colombia. Although unable to keep Gran Colombia together, he is nonetheless venerated as a hero throughout Latin America.

Museo de Arte Religioso Colonial MUSEUM
(Museum of Colonial Religious Art; ☑ 228-2897; cnr Av A & Calle 3; admission US$1; ⊙ 8am-4pm Tue-Sat) Housed beside the ruins of the Iglesia y Convento de Santo Domingo, the Museo de Arte Religioso Colonial has a collection of colonial-era religious artifacts, some dating from the 16th century.

Just inside the ruins' doorway, the Arco Chato is a long arch that had stood here unsupported for centuries. It even played a part in the selection of Panama over Nicaragua as the site for the canal since its survival was taken as proof that the area was not subject to earthquakes. It collapsed in 2003 but has since been rebuilt.

CONTROVERSY RINGS THE CASCO

A Unesco World Heritage Site, the Casco Viejo neighborhood in Panama City is the city's oldest, with a rich architectural and cultural heritage. After a long decline during the 20th century, when wealthy families abandoned the area in favor of the modern downtown area, restoration has come full swing.

Panama City, now a metropolitan area of more than one million residents, experiences ever-increasing traffic congestion. As a partial response, the government completed the Cinta Costera I project (Coastal Belt) in 2007. This involved filling 4km of Panama Bay along Avenida Balboa from Paitilla to the Mercado de Mariscos. In 2009 the fill and road were extended some 500m to the access road to Casco Viejo (Cinta Costera II).

In 2011 the government announced plans to continue the coastal highway toward the Bridge of the Americas. A contract was signed with Brazilian construction company Odebrecht for US$780 million to construct a tunnel under Casco Viejo connecting the Cinta Costera II with a link to the bridge. However, after the signing the government altered its plans for the tunnel, citing high costs, and suggested road construction on an ocean fill around the Casco.

This announcement incited a great deal of public debate about the project and its impact on the cultural patrimony of the Casco Viejo. The tranquil area, located on a peninsula with 270° ocean views, would now be ringed by a highway on the sea. Citizens groups led by Casco residents have suggested other alternatives that would not impact the neighborhood.

After preparing an Environmental Impact Study in 2011, which many considered deficient because it did not consider alternatives, the Ministry of Public Works and Odebrecht began the construction of an ocean bridge in front of Casco that would not involve filling the beach and shore. Instead, the road would be elevated on 177 pilings some 8m above the sea and 200m offshore.

Unesco's World Heritage Committee has consistently recommended that the government select the tunnel alternative and perform a thorough analysis of alternatives, along with their cultural, environmental and social impacts. The government maintains it has complied with Unesco's World Heritage Committee requests.

However, civil groups opposed to the project assert that authorities have failed to meet Panama's international obligations. The project is slated to finish by June 2014. As a result, the World Heritage Committee could potentially place the Casco Viejo on its List of World Heritage in Danger, one step before delisting the site.

Daniel Suman is a professor of environmental and coastal law at the University of Miami.

Casco Viejo

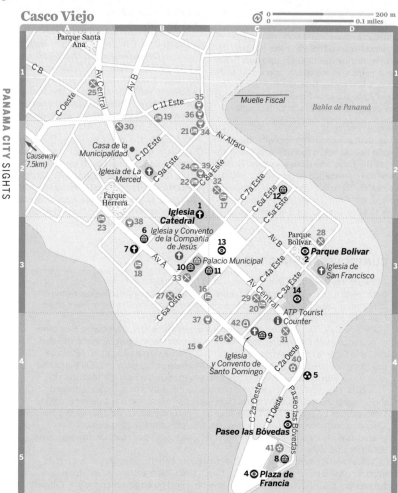

Museo del Canal Interoceánico   MUSEUM
(Canal Museum; ☎211-1649; www.museodelcanal.
com; Calle 6a Oeste; admission US$5; ◔9am-5pm
Tue-Sun) This impressive museum is housed
in a beautifully restored building that once
served as the headquarters for the original
French canal company. The Panama Canal
Museum (as it's more commonly known)
presents excellent exhibits on the famous
waterway, framed in their historical and
political context. Signs are in Spanish, but
English-speaking guides and audiotours
(US$5) are available.

Museo de Historia de Panamá   MUSEUM
(☎501-4128; Calle 6a Oeste, Palacio Municipal;
◔8am-4pm Mon-Fri) **FREE** The modest Museo de Historia de Panamá has a small
selection of exhibits covering Panamanian
history from the colonial period to the
modern era.

◉ **Parque Natural Metropolitano**

Up on a hill to the north of downtown, this
265-hectare **national park** (☎info 232-5516;
www.parquemetropolitano.org; Av Juan Pablo II;

Casco Viejo

admission US$1; ⊙8am-5pm Mon-Fri, to 1pm Sat) protects vast expanses of tropical semi-deciduous forest within the city limits. It serves as an incredible wilderness escape from the trappings of the capital. Two main walking trails, the **Nature Trail** and the **Tití Monkey Trail**, join to form one long loop with a 150m-high *mirador* (lookout) offering panoramic views of Panama City, the bay and the canal, all the way to the Miraflores Locks.

Mammals in the park include tití monkeys, anteaters, sloths and white-tailed deer, while reptiles include iguanas, turtles and tortoises. More than 250 known bird species have been spotted here. Fish and shrimp inhabit the Río Curundú along the eastern side of the park.

The park was the site of an important battle during the US invasion to oust Noriega. Also of historical significance, concrete structures just past the park entrance were used during WWII as a testing and assembly plant for aircraft engines.

The park is bordered on the west and north sides by Camino de la Amistad and to the south and east by Corredor Norte; Av Juan Pablo II runs right through the park.

Pick up a pamphlet for a self-guided tour in Spanish and English at the **visitors center** (☑232-5516; admission US$1; ⊙8am-5pm Mon-Fri, to 1pm Sat), 40m north of the park entrance.

Canopy Tower   TOWER
(☑269-9415; www.anconexpeditions.com) Scientists set up this research crane to study the forest canopy, a complete ecosystem 30m to 50m up from the ground. Previously off-limits to the public, Ancon Expeditions has exclusive access to take tourists up to the treetops. It provides an entirely different view of the rainforest. Book ahead.

⊙ Panamá Viejo

Founded on August 15, 1519, by Spanish conquistador Pedro Arias de Ávila, the city of Panama was the first European settlement along the Pacific. For the next 150 years it profited mainly from Spain's famed bullion pipeline, which ran from Peru's gold and silver mines to Europe via Panamá. Because of the amount of wealth that passed through the city, the Spaniards kept many soldiers here, and their presence kept the buccaneers away.

In 1671, 1200 pirates led by Captain Henry Morgan ascended the Río Chagres and proceeded overland to Panama. Although the city was not fortified, it was protected on three sides by the sea and marshes, and on the land side was a causeway with a bridge to allow tidal water to pass underneath. But to the bewilderment of historians, when Morgan and his men neared the city, the Spanish soldiers left this natural stronghold and confronted the buccaneers in a hilly area outside town.

It was the first of many mistakes in battle. After the Spanish force fell to pieces nearly everything of value was either plundered and divided up or destroyed by fire.

For the next three centuries the abandoned city served as a convenient source of building materials. By the time the government declared the ruins a protected site in 1976 (Unesco followed suit in 1997), most of the old city had already been dismantled and overrun.

So little of the original city remains that its size, layout and appearance are the subject of much conjecture. Today, much of Panamá Viejo lies buried under a poor residential neighborhood, though the ruins are a must-see, even if only to stand on the hallowed grounds of one of Central America's greatest cities.

For safety reasons it's best to explore the area during the daylight hours.

Mercado Nacional de Artesanías   MARKET
(National Artisans Market; Av 6 Sur; ◷9am-6pm) Panamá Viejo buses will drop you off at the Mercado Nacional de Artesanías behind the first remnant of ruins as you approach from Panama City.

Museo de Sitio Panamá Viejo   MUSEUM
(☑226-8915; www.panamaviejo.org; Av 6 Sur; admission US$3; ◷9am-5pm Tue-Sun) The highlights are an impressive scale model of Panamá Viejo prior to 1671 as well as a few surviving colonial artifacts. Signs are in Spanish, though a brochure and tape recording recount the site's history in English. An optional extra is climbing Mirador de la Torre, the lookout tower.

The cost of entry depends on what you wish to see, with the higher price including both Museo de Sitio Panamá Viejo and a trip up to the *mirador* (admission US$3 to US$6, children US$0.50). Children under eight are not allowed to go up the tower.

🏃 City Walk
Panamá Viejo

START PUENTE DEL MATADERO
FINISH PUENTE DEL REY
LENGTH 3.5KM; 1.5 TO 2 HOURS

Panamá Viejo was founded on a coastal bar alongside a shallow cove. The primary government buildings were at the mouth of the cove, also a port. All of the major Catholic religious orders – the Franciscans, Dominicans, Jesuits and Augustines – were present. The best houses and most of the convents were built on the narrow strip of land along the beachfront.

Visitors enter the sector over a modern bridge parallel to **1 Puente del Matadero**, an awkwardly over-restored stone bridge that took its name from a nearby slaughterhouse. It marked the beginning of the Camino Real to Portobelo.

Continuing two blocks east along Av Cincuentenario are the ruins of **2 Iglesia y Convento de La Merced**. Erected by the Mercedarian friars in the early 17th century, the buildings actually survived the fire that swept the city following Morgan's assault. However, the church's facade was dismantled by friars and moved to Casco Viejo, where it can be seen today.

Also bordering the avenue are the remains of **3 Iglesia y Convento de San Francisco**, erected by the Franciscans. The church faced the sea and stood on a massive base. The churches were Panamá Viejo's most outstanding buildings. All were rectangular, with stone outer walls, timber roofs, internal wooden supports and a lack of towers. The adjoining convents had inner courts surrounded by wooden galleries, and the larger ones had enclosed gardens and orchards.

The colonial city followed a grid plan with a main square. The lots tended to be narrow, and the houses often consisted of two or three stories. There's not much left of the city's sole hospital, **4 Hospital de San Juan de Dios**. Much of the remains were scattered when Av Cincuentenario and a side road were put in not long ago.

Just north are the spacious ruins of a church and convent, **5 Iglesia y Convento de la Concepción**, erected by the nuns of Nuestra Señora de la Concepción. Most of the ruins, which cover the better part

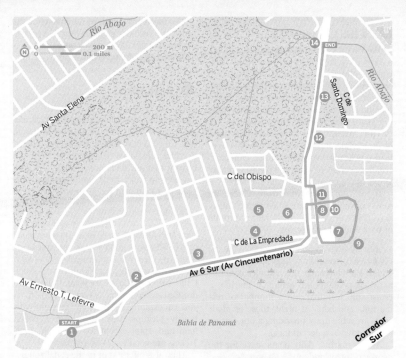

of two blocks, were part of the church – little remains of the convent.

The Jesuits arrived a decade or so after Dominican friars and built **6 Iglesia y Convento de la Compañía de Jesús**, whose stone ruins are visible today.

Also facing the Plaza Mayor were the **7 Cabildo de la Ciudad** (City Hall) and the **8 Casas de Terrín**, houses built by one of the city's wealthiest citizens, Francisco Terrín. Most of the better houses were built from timber and placed wall to wall, with small inner courts, open-air kitchens and separate wings for the servants. Some had ground-floor galleries and balconies, and most had plain exterior walls. A few of the fancier homes were built from stone and their ruins remain. The poor had far simpler dwellings, usually thatched huts built with cheap materials such as reeds.

The center of power resided at **9 Casas Reales** (Royal Houses), a complex ringed by timber ramparts and separated from the city proper by a moat. Within the complex were the customs house, the royal treasury, a prison and the governor's house. Despite the obvious historical importance of the site, past governments have allowed sections of the property to be used as a landfill and for horse stables. Only scattered walls remain of the once impressive structures.

10 Catedral de Nuestra Señora de la Asunción, built between 1619 and 1626, is the best-preserved building. In traditional fashion, it was designed so its two side chapels gave the cathedral a crosslike shape when viewed from the heavens. The bell tower was at the back of the church and may have served double duty as a watchtower for the Casas Reales. The main facade, which faced the Plaza Mayor, is gone – only the walls remain.

Immediately north of the cathedral are the massive ruins of **11 Casa Alarcón**, the town's best-preserved and largest known private residence, which dates from the 1640s. Just north, **12 Iglesia y Convento de Santo Domingo** is the best-preserved church. The convent dates from the 1570s, though the church was built 20 or more years later.

13 Iglesia de San José belonged to the Augustine order. Of special interest here are the building's vaulted side chapels, an architectural feature seldom seen in Panama.

14 Puente del Rey is visible from Av Cincuentenario near the northern edge of town. Built in 1617, it may be the oldest standing bridge in the Americas.

☉ The Causeway

At the Pacific entrance to the Panama Canal, a 2km palm-tree-lined *calzada* (causeway) connects the four small islands of Naos, Culebra, Perico and Flamenco to the mainland. The Causeway is popular in the early morning and late afternoon, when residents walk, jog, skate and cycle its narrow length.

The Causeway also offers sweeping views of the skyline and the old city with flocks of brown pelicans diving into the sea. Others arrive here simply to savor the pleasant breeze at one of the many restaurants and bars.

If you don't have your own vehicle, it's most convenient to take a taxi to the Causeway (US$4 to US$8). Any of the restaurants or bars can call one for you.

Fuerte Amador Resort & Marina　　　MARINA
(☑ 314-1980; www.fuerteamador.com) At the end of Isla Flamenco, this complex contains a two-story shopping center, a marina, a cruise-ship terminal and a number of restaurants and bars. At night, these open-air spots are a big draw, providing a fine setting for cocktails or a decent meal.

At the marina, daily boats leave for the nearby resort island of Isla Taboga.

Centro de Exhibiciones Marinas　　　MUSEUM
(Centro Natural Punta Culebra, CEM; ☑ 212-8000; adult/child US$5/1; ☉ 1-5pm Tue-Fri, 10am-6pm Sat & Sun) Ideal for families, the CEM is operated by the Smithsonian Tropical Research Institute (STRI). This informative marine museum features two small aquariums and a nature trail through a patch of dry forest containing sloths and iguanas. Signs in English and Spanish.

Separate aquariums contain fish from the Pacific and the Caribbean, allowing you to compare the two sets. Staff on hand can explain to you the reasons for the differences. Exhibits examine the role that Panama's marine resources play in the country's economy, and the destructive effects of harvesting fish and shrimp by net.

Exhibits include a small six-sided building with sweeping views of the Bahía de Panamá, built by Noriega for intimate gatherings. Today, it has exhibits on the history of Panama's indigenous cultures.

Outside, large, intelligent illustrations of vessels allow visitors to glance out at the ocean and identify the types of ships waiting to transit the canal, aided by a telescope.

The forest just south of the Puente de las Américas (visible from the center) is a surviving patch of dry forest, which once lined Central America's Pacific coast. Keep your eyes open for three-toed sloths and other wildlife.

🏃 Activities

Barefoot Panama　　　TOUR
(☑ 6780-3010; www.barefootpanama.com; city tour per person US$79) Prompt and professional, this tiny agency does a great city tour of Panama that takes in everything from the history to flora and fauna. There are also day trips to San Lorenzo and Gamboa, with visits to a Wounaan indigenous village.

City Sightseeing Panama　　　BUS TOUR
(☑ 392-6000; www.citysightseeingpty.com; Av Justo Arosemena & Calle 29 Este; 24hr ticket adult/child US$29/24) A good way to get your bearings is by these red double-deckers that loop the city. Stops include Multicentro Mall, Calle Uruguay, Casco Viejo and the Amador Causeway. Service is hop-on, hop-off, so you can explore the sights all you want with hourly pickups. Departures run between 9am and 4pm, except for the night tour. Tickets are good for 24 or 48 hours.

They also offer a tour of the canal zone.

Panama Audubon Society　　　OUTDOORS
(☑ 232-5977; www.audubonpanama.org) Holds bird walks and monthly meetings with interesting speakers at Parque Natural Metropolitano visitors center. It's a good opportunity to get to know some Panamanian bird-watchers and to learn more about tropical bird species. Both English and Spanish are spoken.

Bikes n More　　　BICYCLE RENTAL
(per hour from US$4; ☉ 8am-6pm Sat & Sun) At the Causeway entrance, Bikes n More operates a booth where you can rent a bicycle.

🎓 Courses

Casco Antiguo Spanish School　　　LANGUAGE COURSE
(☑ 228-3258; www.cascospanish.com; Calle 4a Oeste, Casco Viejo; 20hr intensive per week from US$195) This new reader-recommended Spanish school sits in the heart of the Casco. In addition to private and group lessons, they also offer accommodations and activities.

Institute for Spanish Language Studies　　　LANGUAGE COURSE
(ILERI; ☑ 260-4424; www.isls.com/panama; Camino de la Amistad, El Dorado) Located in the suburban El Dorado neighborhood, this

language school offers four hours of one-on-one instruction per day, five days a week. Costs start at US$275 for the first week, with optional extra homestays (US$175 per week).

✨ Festivals & Events

Panama Jazz Festival   JAZZ
(www.panamajazzfestival.com) A blast, the Panama Jazz Festival is gaining momentum as one of the biggest musical events in Panama, drawing hundreds of thousands of spectators for a weeklong festival mid-January. It's held all over the city. Open-air events are usually free, while big-draw theater spectacles require tickets.

Carnaval   FESTIVAL
Carnaval in Panama City is celebrated with merriment and wild abandon in the days preceding Ash Wednesday, between February and March. From Saturday until the following Tuesday, work is put away and masks, costumes and confetti come out, and for 96 hours almost anything goes.

Festivities begin with a coronation of Carnaval queen on Friday, followed by a small Saturday parade with the queen and her court. Vía España fills with people, music pours from all directions and spontaneous dancing breaks out. Masked characters cavort among the crowd. Colorful street vendors wander through the throngs of people, and improvised entertainment abounds. The party moves indoors at night – into cantinas, private clubs and hotels – where combos play Afro-Cuban and typical Panamanian music, and the dancing and drinking continue till dawn.

On Sunday folk-dance groups decked out in Panama's national costumes join the queen and her attendants in the afternoon parade down Vía España, traveling from near Vía Brasil to near Av Federico Boyd (the exact beginning and ending points vary from year to year). To cool the sunbaked masses, fire and garden hoses are turned on the crowd. The amount of water sprayed on party-goers during Carnaval in Panama City during these four festive days equals the amount the city uses during the previous four months.

The madness peaks on Shrove Tuesday with the biggest parade of all. Floats of all sizes rule the avenue, not the least conspicuous of which is the traditional entourage of transvestites. Most of them carry a razor in each hand as a warning to macho types that a punch thrown at them will not go unanswered.

Carnaval officially closes with the first rays of sunlight on Wednesday morning, when the hardiest celebrants appear on the beach of the Bahía de Panamá to bury a sardine in the sand – a symbolic gesture intended to convey the end of worldly pleasures for the Lenten season.

🛏 Sleeping

Panama City offers every kind of accommodations, though its midrange lodgings tend toward overpriced.

Boutique lodgings are on the rise. After extensive renovations, old-world charmer Casco Viejo is an excellent option, with many restaurants and cafes in walking distance.

Fast-paced, modern Panama is best experienced in the overlapping neighborhoods of Bella Vista, Marbella and El Cangrejo. However, a highrise fire in October 2012 revealed that Panama City firefighters lack adequate equipment to fight blazes above the 8th floor; something to think about in this sea of soaring steel and glass.

For those who prefer the quiet life, outlying neighborhoods have excellent B&B options. These include the former US-occupied neighborhoods of Clayton, Albrook, Ancón and Amador, which are located in the Canal Zone.

Casco Viejo

★ Luna's Castle   HOSTEL $
(☑ 262-1540; www.lunascastlehostel.com; Calle 9a Este; dm/d/tr incl breakfast US$13/30/39; @🛜) Housed in a creaky colonial mansion, Luna's masterfully blends Spanish colonial architecture with funky, laid-back backpacker vibes and great service. A bit loony and very friendly, it's the kind of hostel people keep talking about long after their trip. Its latest feature is a helpful activites concierge, whose expertise ranges from planning a sailboat trip to finding the best mojito.

Ample dorms (US$2 extra for air-con) are stacked with bunks and the shared bathrooms get a frequent scrub. Perks include free bikes, laundry service and a basement movie house showing popular flicks.

Panamericana Hostel   HOSTEL $
(☑ 202-0851; www.panamericanahostel.com; Calle 10 & Av A, Plaza Herrera; dm/d incl breakfast without bathroom US$13/28, d incl breakfast US$38; @🛜) Billed as a 'design hostel', this four-story newcomer offers equal doses of pop art and playfulness. It seems big, with 29

rooms, many stenciled with Panamanian slang, some with huge views. Wall murals, cutouts and black lights offset a whole lot of white space. The soon-to-open rooftop bar offers an amazing panorama, but might be detrimental to R & R.

Hospedaje Casco Viejo HOSTEL $

(☎ 211-2027; www.hospedajecascoviejo.com; Calle 8a Oeste; dm/d incl breakfast without bathroom US$11/22, d US$25; P @ 🛜) Every inch of this old hostel – pending renovation – has seen heavy use, but it's hard to get picky at these prices. The best room is the dormitory, with well-spaced single beds. Perks include a communal kitchen and an open-air courtyard. It's on a quiet side street near the Iglesia de San José.

★ Magnolia Inn INN $$

(☎ 202-0827, 6551-9217; www.magnoliapanama.com; Calle Boquete cnr Calle 8; dm US$15; r US$80-135; ❄ 🛜) Every little detail speaks to the thoughtfulness of this cool inn, a restored three-story colonial run by American expats. Air-conditioned dorms are grown-up friendly, with orthopedic mattresses, quality bedding, individual lamps and numerous power plug-ins. Shared bathrooms and kitchen are immaculate and service is top-notch. Ample doubles with city views come stocked with minifridges, flat-screen TVs and coffee makers.

Tango lessons (US$8) are offered in the ballroom on Monday nights. There's also a personal taxi service with English-speaking driver.

Las Clementinas BOUTIQUE HOTEL $$$

(☎ 228-7613; www.lasclementinas.com; Calle 11 & Av B; d incl breakfast from US$275; ❄ @ 🛜) 🍃 All happy families may be the same, but great hotels have their particularities. This one, with its antique regional maps, recycled hardwood floors from the canal, and unusual relics from the original house, feels like authentic Panama. The restored colonial has six airy suites, a leafy courtyard and wonderful restaurant.

Guests get the opportunity to locally engage with free cruising bikes and housemade pocket guides including listings of the best neighborhood dives. Original tours visit marginal areas where tradespeople such as traditional tailors work, to show the many complex issues of the city.

Casa del Horno BOUTIQUE HOTEL $$$

(☎ 212-0052; www.casadelhorno.net; cnr Calle 8a & Av B; d incl breakfast from US$250; ❄ @ 🛜) A great addition to the neighborhood, this modern understated haven manages to be boutique yet still feel very Panamanian. Decor includes exposed original stone walls, polished cement and large art prints of Congos by photographer Sandra Eleta. There are two penthouses with Jacuzzi and eight rooms, which feature soft lighting, wine cellar, mini HD entertainment center and private balconies.

Concierge service and in-room massages are a plus. There's a great cafe and upscale restaurant onsite.

Canal House B&B $$$

(☎ 228-1907; www.canalhousepanama.com; cnr Calle 5A Oeste & Av A; ste incl breakfast from US$210; P ❄ @ 🛜) 🍃 Exclusive and elegant, this grande dame B&B is where Agent 007 slept when in town. Fine details in the three luxury bedrooms include iPads, blown-glass lamps and embroidered pillows. Shared spaces are lovely and service rates impeccable. Though located in the Casco, it feels removed, with climate-controlled rooms and double-glass windows sealing out street noise (and yes, part of the ambiance).

Green-gold certified, the hotel recycles and separates waste, in addition to using energy-saving lights and biodegradable detergents. It also works with the Cal y Canto Foundation to train and employ Casco residents.

Tántalo BOUTIQUE HOTEL $$$

(☎ 262-4030; www.tantalohotel.com; cnr Calle 8a Este & Av B; d incl breakfast from US$159) Industrial chic has hit Casco hard. Various artists were commissioned to make the rooms of this 12-room boutique hotel. Do oversized spikes on the ceilings humor your fantasies? With oversized murals, stenciled Bukowski quotes and stripped-down decor, none of the rooms are shy – or too serious. A brick lobby with living vegetation wall at the bar says, 'Welcome, what's your story?'

Los Cuatro Tulipanes APARTMENT $$$

(☎ 211-0877; www.loscuatrotulipanes.com; office Av Central btwn Calles 3 & 4; apt from US$140; P ❄ 🛜) Ideal for travelers yearning for a little independence and privacy, the 'four tulips' are in fact a set of luxury apartments in distinct Casco Viejo locations. While each is unique, all are elegant restored spaces with features like handpainted tiles, hardwood details, high ceilings and private terraces. Some have a concierge.

Kitchens come fully equipped, and maid service, wi-fi, cable TV and coffee and tea are included.

Caledonia

Caledonia is central to city highlights, but itself is a very working-class area not frequented by outsiders. Given that foot traffic dwindles in the evening, it's best to take taxis at night.

Mamallena HOSTEL $

(☎6676-6163, 393-6611; www.mamallena.com; Calle Primera Perejil; dm/d incl breakfast US$13/33; ❄@📶) On a residential street that's somehow survived the wrecking ball, this small, homey hostel nails the mark on service. Amenities include 24-hour desk service, pancake breakfasts and DVD library. High-ceiling dorms have air-con at night and the cute motel-style doubles offer considerable privacy. The onsite travel agency offers sailing to San Blas and popular day trips.

Renovations with more doubles and a swimming pool are coming.

Hotel Andino HOTEL $$

(☎225-1162; www.hotelandino.net; Calle 35 Este; s/d US$49/55/65; P❄📶) Rooms at the Andino come up short on charm, but they're big, clean and equipped like a start-up apartment. Request a king-size and you can also get a two-burner stove for some self-catering adventures. If you don't feel like leaving the hotel, there's a bar and restaurant, making it a convenient choice to crash overnight between bus departures.

Hotel Costa Inn HOTEL $$

(☎227-1522; www.hotelcostainn.com; Av Perú near Calle 39 Este; d incl breakfast US$76; P❄@📶🏊) In a part of town famous for surprises, these no-nonsense rooms are good, but probably overpriced unless you are very keen on the pool and gym. Try for a room on the 4th floor; they're notably better than those on the lower levels. Euros are accepted. Guests get a free airport transfer and there's a travel agency on the premises.

El Cangrejo, Marbella & Bella Vista

As central as it gets, these neighborhoods have no lack of restaurants or bars within walking distance. However, it is also one of the noisier spots in town, with snaking traffic and honking horns dominating the daytime hours.

Panama House B&B $

(☎263-4366; www.panamahousebb.com; Calle 1a de Carmen 32, El Carmen; dm/s/d without bathroom incl breakfast US$15/35/45, s/d incl breakfast US$55/65; P❄@📶) In a cozy colonial near Vía Brasil, this congenial home is lovely and sought-after. Fresh rooms have safe boxes, high ceilings, warm light and tiled bathrooms with scalloped sinks. Mattresses are a bit slim. Guests of all ages congregate in the communal kitchen, lounge area or on the lush hammock patio.

Hostel Villa Vento Surf HOSTEL $

(☎6101-4841, 397-6001; hostelvillaventosurf.com; Calle 47 No 7, Marbella; dm/s/d/tr incl breakfast US$15/35/40/45; ❄@📶🏊) This relaxed newcomer sits in a suburban-style home around the corner from the nightlife hot spot of Calle Uruguay. Young internationals come for the swimming pool or the easy-access partying, though it's a relatively calm spot (all laptops engaged) and staff is nice. It's a bit unkept, though. Bunks crowd larger dorms, but air-con keeps them cool. Breakfast is pancakes and coffee.

Hostal Balboa Bay GUESTHOUSE $

(☎227-6182; Calle 39 Este No 21, Bella Vista; dm incl breakfast US$13, s/d US$35/50; ❄@) Though quiet and clean, rooms are of widely varying quality and service can be spotty as well. It's currently undergoing renovations – check for changes in rates. It's central but gets less traffic than the competition. The neighborhood gets deserted at night so take taxis.

Saba Hotel HOTEL $$

(☎201-6100; www.thesabahotel.com; Vía Argentina s/n, Bella Vista; d US$120; ❄@📶) Modern and cheerful, the Saba is a great value addition to Bella Vista. With lots of glass and bamboo, there's a sustainable theme that's probably more stylish than substantive. Still, you can practice yoga, get a carrot juice at the detox bar or order room service watching your flat-screen TV. Service is great and there's a restaurant onsite.

Baru Lodge B&B $$

(☎393-2340; www.barulodge.com; Calle 2nda Norte H-7, El Carmen; s/d incl breakfast US$60/70; ❄📶) Tasteful and cordial, this inn sits on a residential street central to the action. Rooms are sleek and modern, with subdued colors and soft lighting. The English-speaking owner makes guests right at home. Cable TV, fast wi-fi and air purifiers are among the

El Cangrejo & Bella Vista

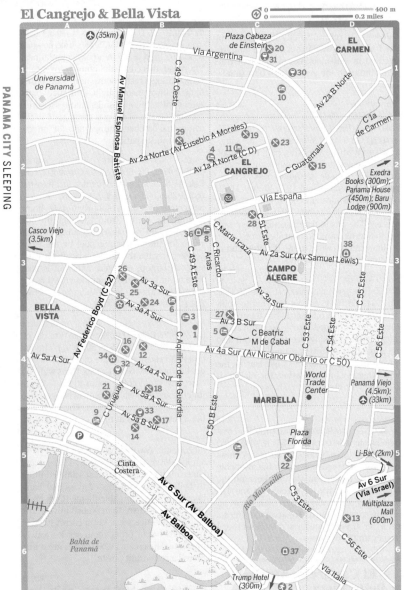

perks. The garden patio has wicker seating, where continental breakfasts are served.

Getting here is a challenge, as streets are unmarked, but you can tell the taxi it's located behind Exedra Books.

Executive Hotel   HOTEL **$$**
(☎ 265-8011; www.executivehotel-panama.com; cnr Calles 52 & Aquilino de la Guardia, El Cangrejo; s/d incl breakfast US$95/105; P ❄ @) Bustling and efficient, this business hotel is centrally located in El Cangrejo with an endless array of

El Cangrejo & Bella Vista

prim white rooms. While rooms are definitely too skinny, we like it because the service is friendly and caring. It's also the secret spot in the city for outstanding North American breakfasts at the 24-hour cafe.

Coral Suites Aparthotel　　APARTMENT **$$**
(☎269-3898; www.coralsuites.net; Calle D; s/d US$99/110; P❋@≋) This all-suites hotel is serviceable for traveling executives who require their amenities, or long-term visitors in need of more than a hotel room. Suites are unremarkable yet functional, with spacious bathrooms, bouncy mattresses and fully equipped kitchens. Staff is pleasant and guests have use of a full gym, business center and 24-hour rooftop pool.

DeVille Hotel　　BOUTIQUE HOTEL **$$$**
(☎206-3100; www.devillehotel.com.pa; Calle Beatriz M de Cabal near Calle 50 A Este, Bella Vista; ste incl breakfast from US$270; P❋@) A sweetheart of a hotel, DeVille has won a devoted clientele for its classy, tasteful digs and sterling service. Beautifully appointed rooms feature antique Thai dressers glistening with inlaid mother of pearl, marble-topped antique tables set with Louis XV chairs, and the finest-quality US-made mattresses with custom bed linen made of Egyptian cotton and goose-feather pillow.

All of the 33 rooms are suites and offer luxury par excellence. While it's comfortable and functional enough for the most distinguished executive travelers, it's also undeniably romantic – a hard balance to strike.

Toscana Inn　　HOTEL **$$$**
(☎265-0018; www.toscanainnhotel.com; Calle 1a A Norte, El Cangrejo; s/d/tr incl breakfast US$108/121/138; P❋@❖≋) The best of the bunch on this hotel-lined street, with wonderful service and a modern look and feel. Beds have firm mattresses and brocade covers in ample rooms with flat-screen TVs and leather sofas. Showers feature shaving mirrors. You can get away on the 6th-floor terrace, and facilities include an onsite business center and a nice adjoining cafe.

Hotel Continental　　HOTEL **$$$**
(☎265-5114; www.continentalhotel.com; Calle Ricardo Arias & Vía España; d incl breakfast from US$125; P❋@❖≋) This well-located casino hotel has that swinging, tropical style more common to Havana than Panama, thanks to the open architecture, cool breezes and abundance of fresh-cut flowers. Service is oft-praised and recently remodeled rooms are tasteful and spacious. At current rates it's a steal.

Suites feature eye-popping skyline views from the sitting area, the bed and even the walk-in closet. Of course, the real action happens poolside – grab a cocktail and watch it all swirl by.

Bristol Panama
LUXURY HOTEL $$$

(☑265-7844; www.thebristol.com; Calle Aquilino de la Guardia, Bella Vista; d incl breakfast from US$219; P❄@🛜🏊) The elegant Bristol features oriental carpets, flamboyant orchids and precious woods, and that's just the lobby. Rooms are refined and lovely. No more do-not-disturb tags here – heat sensors determine if rooms are occupied. Other five-star amenities include a spa, 24-hour butler service and free cell-phone loan. The restaurant, run by an award-winning Panamanian chef, is currently getting an update.

Le Meridien
LUXURY HOTEL $$$

(☑297-3200; www.starwoodhotels.com; cnr Calle Uruguay & Av Balboa; d US$380, ste from US$550; P❄@🛜🏊) Created by 100 artists, there's cool digital art and even birdsong in the elevator. Yet, while daring and innovative, some details are simply off. Internet is US$15 extra, rooms have laminated wood walls and furniture seems a bit cheap given the all-out setting. A little Le Mediocre. But the rooftop pool offers a delicious city skyline view.

There's also a Clarins spa onsite and a swish fusion restaurant.

San Francisco & Punta Paitilla

Similar to Bella Vista, San Francisco is a central, busy location with the added perk of having the biggest green space in this part of the city – Parque Recreativo Omar. Punta Paitilla is a peninsula of modern high rises that juts into Panama Bay.

Hostal Casa Margarita
B&B $$

(☑394-5557; www.hostalcasamargarita.com; Casa 97, Calle Los Claveles; s/d/tr incl breakfast US$75/88/115; P❄@) Irresistibly cozy and chic, this stucco house features seven smart, impeccable but simple rooms with colorful touches, flat-screen TVs and minifridges. A huge garden and breakfast patio has ample space to lounge or dally over a complete breakfast with fresh fruit. Guests also get kitchen use, but the real treasures here are the warm hosts.

Trump Hotel
LUXURY HOTEL $$$

(☑215-8800; www.trumphotelcollection.com/panama; Calle Punta Colón; d from US$176; ❄@🛜🏊) A logical step if you already have the Burberry coat or Chanel bag, this long-anticipated hotel resembles a mirrored sail on swank Punta Paitilla. Staff filter out gawkers. The 369 rooms feature neutral palettes, pillow menus and ubiquitous ocean views, though some housekeeping was found lax. The infinity pool oozes ambiance, but it's so on display that few dare go.

Canal Zone

Hostal de Clayton
HOSTEL $

(☑317-1634; www.hostaldeclayton.com; Edificio 605B, Calle Guanabana; dm US$15, d with/without private bathroom US$45/38; P❄@🛜) Reminiscent of an army barracks, this friendly hostel is located on the site of the former US army base of Clayton, a well-heeled residential area. The rooms and amenities here are perfectly suited to the budget traveler, but for those without bus savvy or the budget for taxis, the location leaves you adrift in suburbia.

Hostal Amador Familiar
INN $

(☑314-1251; www.hostalamadorfamiliar.com; Casa 1519, Calle Akee, Balboa; dm incl breakfast US$15, d with fan/air-con US$30/35; P❄@🛜) If you like quiet, this big red canal house offers bargain private rooms with old-home charm. Tiled high-ceiling rooms with rod iron beds and sashed windows are worn out but clean; dorms are dark and less appealing. A highlight is the dining patio and open-air kitchen where breakfast is served. Service is sadly lax.

The location is just off the causeway, a US$5 taxi ride from the center.

★Dos Palmitos
B&B $$

(☑391-0994; www.dospalmitos.com; 0532B Guayacan Terrace, Ancon Hill; s/d incl breakfast US$75/88; ❄@🛜) If your attraction to Panama is more about wildlife than wild life, check out this tucked-away Canal house B&B. There are just four rooms decorated with *molas* (colorful hand-stitched appliqué textiles made by Kuna indigenous people) and vintage newsclips and featuring immaculate wooden floors, king beds and wicker furniture. The backyard terrace offers bird-watching and abundant breakfasts featuring homemade bread and fresh juice. Angeline the host also offers transportation and tours.

It's on the quiet Ancon hill – a good place to take a walk, but for dining variety you will need a taxi.

La Estancia B&B **$$**
(2314-1417; www.bedandbreakfastpanama.com; Casa 35, Quarry Heights, Ancon Hill; d incl breakfast US$95; P✱@✇) Perched atop Cerro Ancón and surrounded by tropical flora and fauna, La Estancia is a small cement apartment building converted into a tranquil and friendly B&B. Rooms are plain, uncluttered and clean. Breakfasts are excellent, best enjoyed on the patio while gazing upon the Puente de las Américas.

Albrook Inn INN **$$**
(2315-1789; www.albrookinn.com; Calle Hazelhurst 14, Albrook; d/ste incl breakfast US$99/143; P✱✲) Set amid lush greenery and removed from city chaos, this lodging near Albrook airport aspires toward country inn but feels a bit lackluster and impersonal. Motel-style rooms have modern decor and flat-screen TVs but could be roomier. A small kidney-shaped pool spruces up the garden. Ideal for an early morning domestic flight.

Country Inn & Suites HOTEL **$$$**
(2211-4500; www.countryinns.com/panamacanalpan; cnr Avs Amador & Pelicano; d/ste US$135/149; P✱✲) They say there are only two lodgings overlooking the canal: one is the prison holding Noriega, the other is this chain hotel. Though reminiscent of a retirement community in Panama City, Florida, it's well run and a good value, with causeway access and a huge swimming pool. Rooms boast private balconies overlooking the Puente de las Américas.

✗ Eating

Boasting the most innovative contemporary cuisine of Central America, Panama City is a fun place to dine out. There are literally hundreds of places to eat and, thanks to a big immigrant population, cuisine from every corner of the globe.

Casco Viejo is home to a number of boutique eateries and European-inspired cafes. Bella Vista, the self-proclaimed restaurant district, is the best spot in the city for lightening the wallet and satisfying the taste buds.

With so many salaried earners on their lunch break, the banking district of El Cangrejo is home to a number of pricey eateries. They also tend to be slightly more conservative and less trendy.

Owing to the wealth of city denizens and the popularity of dining out, reservations are a good idea. Although you can probably get a table most days of the week, don't even think about just showing up on Friday or Saturday night without phoning ahead.

For groceries and self-catering, stop by the 24-hour Supermercado Rey, which has several locations throughout the city, including one in El Cangrejo, and another inside the El Dorado Mall.

Street vendors sell everything from shaved ice to grilled chicken or *empanadas*. In the evening, sausage, *papas rellenas* (stuffed potatoes) and arepa (savory corn cake) stands on Vía España do a brisk business and the food is cheap and good.

✗ Casco Viejo

★Mercado de Mariscos MARKET **$**
(Av Balboa; mains US$2.50-14; ☺lunch Mon-Sat) Above a bristling fish market, an unassuming restaurant is *the* place to get your seafood fix. Come early as service at peak time is painfully slow. Gems include whole fried fish and cavernous bowls of 'Get Up Lazarus' soup (a sure hangover cure).

Outside, stands ladle out delicious US$2.50 plastic cups of *ceviche* (seafood marinated in lemon or lime juice, garlic and seasonings), including classic concoctions, Mediterranean-style (with olives) and curry.

La Petite Bretagne CREPERIE **$**
(Av Central; mains US$8; ☺10am-5pm Tue-Fri, to 10pm Sat, to 3pm Sun) Revitalizing a formerly sketchy corner of the Casco, this adorable cafe ladles up authentic buckwheat crêpes from Brittany. Preparations are light and fresh eg fresh salads come with tart passionfruit dressing. The caramelized onion tart manages an airy crust – it's melt-in-your-mouth good. But don't skip dessert, namely an endorphin-enducing velvety chocolate fondant.

Granclement ICE CREAM **$**
(Av Central; gelato US$2.80-4.20; ☺1-3pm & 4-7pm) Pure pleasure defines these intense tropical fruit gelati and intense, creamy flavors such as basil, orange and chocolate, and ginger. A few scoops of these fussy Italian creations will sweeten a leisurely stroll through the Casco.

Café Per Due ITALIAN **$**
(26512-9311; Av A; pizza US$5-12; ☺9am-10pm Tue-Sun; ✍) Our pick for a quick bite, this

Panamá Viejo

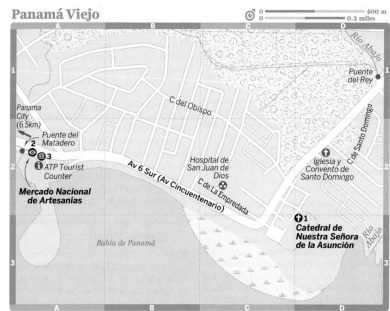

Panamá Viejo

◎ Top Sights

1 Catedral de Nuestra Señora de
la Asunción D3

2 Mercado Nacional de
Artesanías..A2

◎ Sights

3 Museo de Sitio Panamá Viejo.............A2

🛍 Shopping

Mercado Nacional de Artesanías (see 2)

casual Italian-run eatery serves scrumptious
thin-crust pizzas. Check out the bacon and
blue cheese or the fresh tomato, basil and
garlic. Mozzarella is not skimped on. For
privacy, try the tiny brick courtyard with a
couple of tables.

Super Gourmet   DELI **$**

(Av A; mains US$5-9; ⊘7am-7pm Mon-Sat, 10am-
3pm Sun) Stocking gourmet goods that range
from wine to wasabi peas, this is the perfect
pre-picnic stop. You can also grab soup or a
baguette deli sandwich with roasted chicken
and peppers, pastrami or three cheeses; the
half-portion is probably enough. For breakfast, eggs on English muffins or arepas hit
the spot.

Café Coca Cola   PANAMANIAN **$**

(Av Central; plates US$3-6; ⊘7:30am-11pm; ✸)
A neighborhood institution, this old-school
diner comes complete with chess-playing
señoras and no-nonsense waitresses. TVs
broadcasting soccer matches seal its status
as a den of the working class. Of course,
the real reason you're here is to eat out on
hearty platefuls of rice, beans and the fea-
tured meat of the day without breaking the
bank.

Diablo Rosso   CAFE **$**

(📞262-1957; www.diablorosso.com; 6th St & A Ave;
mains US$4-10; ⊘11am-7pm Tue-Sat; 🛜) This
art cafe with biting social commentary and
quirky folk art would be perfectly at home in
Buenos Aires' Palermo neighborhood. You can
also enjoy a frothy cup of cappuccino, cheesy
arepas piled high with eggs, hearty vegetarian soup or spinach quesadillas. Check for art
openings or Tuesday night art cinema.

Restaurante L'Osteria   ITALIAN **$$**

(📞212-0809; Av B; mains US$13-18) A current
hot spot in a new boutique hotel, this Italian-
run brick bistro is all that – if you order
smartly. Crusted cheese rice balls and leafy
green salads make a nice starter. Gnocchi
with fresh ricotta and percorino cheese, unu-
sual pastas and well-priced arugula pizzas

are highlights. The downside is hiccups in service (especially if you send the wine back).

Ego y Narciso FUSION $$
(☑ 262-2045; Calle 3, Plaza Bolívar; mains US$8-20; ⊙ noon-3pm Mon-Fri, 6-11pm Mon-Sun) With cosmopolitan flash, this tiny restaurant is perfect for appetizers and drinks. Outdoor tables on Plaza Bolívar offer extra ambiance. Graze on quality *ceviche,* octopus toasts with balsamic reduction and tender kebabs.

Manolo Caracol PANAMANIAN $$$
(☑ 228-4640; Av Central near Calle 3 Oeste; tasting menu US$36; ⊙ noon-3pm & 7-10:30pm Mon-Fri, 7-11pm Sat) Manolo's immerses you in tropical tastes, rescuing what's native, toying with flavors, paring them down and surprising you. Tiny courses pair opposite flavors and textures, such as beef tongue sprinkled with sea salt, fire-roasted lobster drizzled in olive oil and tart mango salad with crunchy greens. Not every dish sings, but the fun is adventuring through them.

Drinks are extra, but there is a fine selection of wine to splurge on. An open kitchen allows you to watch the cooks dodging flames, a lively backdrop to the warm, colonial style with bold art and heaped bowls of fruit.

✗ El Cangrejo & Bella Vista

New York Bagel Café CAFE $
(Plaza Cabeza de Einstein near Vía Argentina; mains US$3-9; ⊙ 7am-8pm Mon-Fri, 8am-8pm Sat, 8am-3pm Sun; ✿ 🛜) More San Francisco than Brooklyn, this fully American creation nonetheless packs in expats with freshly baked bagels, lox and oversized breakfasts. They also serve handsome burgers. The setting offers jazz, soft sofas and your assortment of laptop geeks.

Sabores de la India INDIAN $
(Calle 51; mains US$3-10; ☑) With Bollywood on the telly and staff and cooks from the continent, this unassuming spot is a fast track to your spicy food fix. Vegetarian options are plenty (with tofu), there's also a succulent chicken tikka, garlic naan and spicy daal with requisite fixings. Big appetites should check out the US$10 lunch buffet.

Shalom Bakery KOREAN, BAKERY $
(Av 3a Sur, Bella Vista; mains US$3-8; ⊙ 7am-9pm Mon-Sat) Breakfasts are pretty conventional

BEST TAKE-OUT

Panama City is not big on take-out, but any of these goodies could satisfy an urge to brown bag a picnic to the Cinta Costera, Parque Recreativo Omar or Casco Antiguo, for US$10 or less:

Petit Paris (Marbella; ⊙ 6:30am-8:30pm) Baguettes and croissants at this bakery and cafe.

Lung Fung (Av Periodista & Vía Transístmica) Shrimp chow mein at this place in Chinatown.

Caminito de la Empanada (p63) Argentine-style snacks like spinach or spicy beef empanadas.

Super Gourmet (p60) Wine, cheese and deli goods.

(ie bagels and eggs), but it's worth delving into Korean staples such as *bulgolgi* (rice with the tenderest beef) or seaweed rolls. The small cafe is strewn with lovely travel photos on clothespins. There's live jazz twice a month on Saturday evenings.

Athens GREEK $
(Calle 50, Bella Vista; mains US$5; ⊙ 11am-11:30pm Thu-Tue) Fresh and casual, this Greek eatery serves warm pitas with hummus, satisfying Greek salads, gyros and pizzas. It's ideal for families and large groups, with long hours and plenty of indoor and outdoor seating.

Crêpes & Waffles CREPERIE $
(☑ 269-1574; Av 5a B Sur, Bella Vista; mains US$5-10; ⊙ noon-10pm Mon-Sat, 9am-10pm Sun; ☑) Ideal for an afternoon pick-me-up or a quick bite before clubbing, this salad bar and crêpe factory has something for everyone. Spinach, ricotta and tomato are a good standby, but the sweet crêpes, with fillings such as cheese, apples, chocolate and caramel, are delectable. There's also a salad bar.

Niko's Café CAFETERIA $
(Calle 51 Este near Vía España; mains US$3-8; ⊙ 24hr) Spawned from a Greek immigrant who once sold food from a cart, Niko's has become one of Panama City's most successful chains, with locations throughout the city. These sprawling 24-hour cafeterias serve hearty portions of inexpensive food ranging from made-to-order breakfasts, Panamanian dishes and desserts.

La Mar
PERUVIAN $$

(☏209-3323; www.lamarcebicheria.com; Calle Guatemala s/n, El Cangrejo; mains US$9-18; ⏰11am-3pm & 6-11pm) Serving Peruvian classics in high style, La Mar is part of superchef Gastón Acurio's empire. Start with a tart pisco sour – they pack a punch (in a good way). The *degustación* plate lets you try four varieties of *causas* (like burgers) or *ceviche*. Potato *causas* come delicate and creamy. For timider palates, *arroz chaufa* (fried rice) is fluffy and flavorful.

The setting is sleek. Dress well and reserve ahead – it gets busy.

Sukhi
THAI $$

(☏395-6081; Calle Beatriz M de Cabal; mains US$8-13; ⏰11:30am-10pm Mon-Sat) In a cheerful cafe, this casual newcomer offers lovely, though not the most authentic, Southeast Asian food. Start with the fried calamari with ginger-cilantro dipping sauce. Flavors pop in the green bean green curry while Ladna comes in fragrant beef broth with broccoli rabbe. Service is good and the price is right.

Market
INTERNATIONAL $$

(www.marketpanama.com; Av 5A A Sur near Calle Uruguay, Bella Vista; mains US$8-28; ⏰noon-11pm Mon-Sat, 11:30am-9pm Sun) With blackboard specials, brick and bustle, this bistro is US-style. There's an emphasis on style and quality, though the menu is riddled with comfort foods. Salads come in oversized bowls and you can top off your order of Angus beef with interesting sides such as creamed spinach or green beans with bacon. It is wildly popular for weekend brunch.

Smoke Shack
AMERICAN $$

(Av Federico Boyd s/n; mains US$9-23; ⏰noon-11pm) Southern BBQ has nestled into an unlikely home on this busy downtown corner. High-stacked burgers, pulled pork sliders, real smoked beans and waffle fries are done right. That and indoor-outdoor seating, football on the tube and clockwork service bring in the crowds.

Masala Indian Cuisine
INDIAN $$

(☏225-0105; Av Justo Arosemena, Bella Vista; mains US$8-18; ⏰noon-11pm) Nothing complements hot and humid tropical climes quite like a fiery plate of Indian curry and an ice-cold Kingfisher lager. Cozied up with floor pillows and colorful textiles, Masala offers a full complement of traditional dishes from the subcontinent ranging from tikka masala to lamb vindaloo, with a good selection of vegetarian dishes.

Ozone
INTERNATIONAL $$

(Calle Uruguay, Bella Vista; mains US$7-16; ⏰noon-3pm & 6-10pm) Packed with worker bees at midday, Ozone is a local fixture serving enormous portions of good food. Too bad the ambiance is wanting – the dark location was once a garage. But if you're hungry, a huge salad, wrap or hummus is bound to satisfy, and the chocolate cake is a winner.

Wine Bar
ITALIAN $$

(Av Eusebio A Morales; US$7-17; ⏰5pm-1am) Some say this Italian bistro with an encyclopedic wine list is the best dinner value in town. Certainly, it is popular among the local cognoscenti. The pasta is satisfying, or you can order appetizers such as a plate of soft and hard cheeses and enjoy the patio.

Martín Fierro
STEAKHOUSE $$

(☏264-1927; Av Eusebio A Morales, El Cangrejo; steak US$12-20; ⏰noon-3pm & 6-11pm Mon-Sat, noon-9:30pm Sun) For serious steaks, there is only one name in Panama City, and it's Martín Fierro. Top selections include the best in US-imported New York rib steaks, grass-fed Argentinean fillets and locally raised Panamanian cuts. The salad bar and selection of Chilean wines round out your meal.

★ La Rosa Mexicano
MEXICAN $$$

(☏301-0488; Av 5a B Sur near Calle Aquilino de la Guardia; mains US$10-28) No soggy burritos here. This chic eatery offers modern Mexican in a Cirque du Soleil setting. Start with guacamole handmade at your table. The cocktails are stunners, try the watermelon margarita topped with a sprig of rosemary. Menu highlights include red snapper, salad with jicama and roast pumpkin seeds and, for dessert, a dizzy-good *cajeta* (caramel) with sea salt. Service is sterling.

Restaurante Matsuei
JAPANESE $$$

(☏264-9562; Av Eusebio A Morales, Bella Vista; mains US$18-39; ⏰noon-11pm Mon-Sat, 5:30-11pm Sun) With a proud quarter-century tradition, Matsuei is one of Panama's finest raw fish experiences. Imported fish means varied offerings from *unagi* (eel) to *maguro* (tuna) on offer. Non-sushi eaters could try the piping hot sukiyaki, cloud-light tempura or countless other Japanese standards. Bargain hunters should try the fixed lunch (US$12).

La Posta
ITALIAN $$$

(☏269-1076; www.lapostapanama.com; Calle Uruguay, Bella Vista; mains US$12-42; ⏰noon-2:30pm & 6:30-10pm Mon-Sat) A staple on the Panamanian food scene, with seasonal menus and lovely presentation. The tropical setting says hacienda, with a breezy dining room decked with white linens and big wicker chairs. Start with octopus three ways or a beet salad with crisp bacon vinaigrette. Organic chicken and fresh pastas stay in the comfort zone but ultimately satisfy.

✖ San Francisco & Punta Paitilla

Caminito de la Empanada ARGENTINE $
(Punta Paitilla; mains US$2; ☺7:30am-7:30pm Mon-Sat) Cheap and tasty, with a selection of tiny savory Argentine empanadas, filled with meat, cheese or veggie mixes, or *medialunas* (crescent rolls).

Parillada Jimmy PARRILLA $$
(☑226-1096; Av Cincuentenario, San Francisco; mains US$9-15; ☺11:30am-11:30pm) The long, open porch with high ceilings and wrought-iron chandeliers lends a farmhouse feel to this Panama City institution. An open grill sears some serious cuts of beef, chicken and country-style sausage. Located in the San Francisco district just east of the Multiplaza Mall, Parillada Jimmy packs in lunchtime diners and an after-work crowd.

★**Maito** PANAMANIAN $$$
(☑391-4657; www.maitopanama.com; Av 3M Sur, San Francisco; mains US$8-27; ☺noon-3pm Mon-Fri, 7-11pm Mon-Sat) With style and pedigree, Maito toys with the classics, tinkering in everyday Caribbean, Latin and Chinese influences. While results are mixed, it's still worthwhile. Start with a watermelon Waldorf salad. Ribs glazed in passion fruit prove tender but lack the crispness of the duck chow mein. Seafood risotto in squid ink proves divine. There's garden seating and impeccable service.

✖ Canal Zone

Country Store CAFE $
(☑232-7204; Calle Tomas Guardia 583, Ancón; US$4-10; ☺8am-6:30pm Mon-Sat) Serving country breakfasts and baguette sandwiches, this adorable outdoor garden cafe is a great addition to Ancon Hill. Tití monkeys watch over as you enjoy fresh salads, split a pizza or dip into baked goods with a cup of organic coffee roasted in-house. They also sell goods from a nearby farm.

♥ Drinking & Nightlife

Bars and clubs open and close with alarming frequency in Panama City, though generally speaking, nightlife is stylish, sophisticated

---

THE SECRET LIFE OF THE CAUSEWAY

All four of the Causeway islands once comprised Fort Grant, which was established in 1913 to guard the southern entrance to the canal. Between 1913 and WWII, the USA made Fort Grant into the most powerful defense complex in the world.

In 1928 two 14in guns with ranges up to 44km were brought to Panama. Mounted on railway carriages, they could be moved across the isthmus via the Panama Railroad to defend either entrance to the canal (the Pacific-side emplacement for the railroad guns was on Culebra). You can still see the tracks today on the driveway leading up to the Centro de Exhibiciones Marinas. The concrete rooms nearby, now used by marine-center staff, once housed the guns' ammunition.

In 1941 the Japanese assault on Pearl Harbor showed that carrier-based aircraft could attack successfully far beyond the range of artillery. Suddenly obsolete, many of the big guns were retired from service even before the end of WWII. However, in 1942 the US military was still determined to bulk up their defenses, and paid the enormous cost of US$400,000 to build a command post on Isla Flamenco.

The Causeway, its four islands and a chunk of the peninsula leading to the Causeway, were turned over to Panama in October 1979 in compliance with the Torrijos-Carter Treaty of 1977. Today, part of the Fuerte Amador shopping center is built on a massively protected bombproof structure that was needed 'for use in case of emergency and vital to the security of important data,' according to the US general who ordered its construction. Even today, the US military will not disclose what data was so important that it needed to be stored at the center of a rock island.

and fairly pricey. The well-to-do denizens of the capital love a good scene, so it's worth scrubbing up, donning some nice threads and parting with a bit of dough. You might regret blowing your budget the next morning, but that's the price you pay to party with the beautiful people.

Big areas for nightlife include Casco Viejo, Bella Vista and the Causeway.

For the latest on what's happening, *La Prensa* (www.prensa.com) has weekend listings in the Thursday and Friday editions or on its website; look for the 'De Noche' section.

Doors usually open at 11pm. Under new law, all bars and clubs close between 2am and 3am, except for casinos, which now can't serve alcohol. Remember to bring ID. Most clubs have a cover charge of US$10 to US$25; this varies greatly depending on the place, the date and the time.

Casco Viejo

★ Havana Panamá   LIVE MUSIC
(Av Alfaro; cover US$10; ⊙ Thu-Sat) Old school rules this vintage salsa bar replete with bandstand and leather booths. You'll have to don your finest threads (there's a dress code) and enter behind a swooshy velvet curtain. A complete salsa band rocks the house.

Mojito sin Mojito   BAR
(cnr Av A & Calle 9a Este) With a stripped down, warehouse atmosphere, this very local bar welcomes guys in flip-flops and chicks in stilletos with equal openness. Best for beer on tap and a burger (either veggie or regular). If you're feeling smart, chat up the trivia-giving bartender.

Bar Relic   BAR
(Calle 9a Este; ⊙ 9pm-2am Tue-Sat) Wildly popular with travelers and hip young Panamanians, this cavernous hostel bar is a hit. Service is friendly and patrons easily mingle in the ample courtyard with shared picnic tables. Hungry? Try the pulled-pork sandwich. Not only are you partying outside (a rarity in Panama City) but you're next to the historical wall of the city.

Tántalo Bar   COCKTAIL BAR
(cnr Calle 8a Este & Av B; cover US$5-10; ⊙ roof deck 5pm-2am) Though they serve reasonably priced lunches (think wraps with patacones), this ultra-hip cafe-bar is best known for sunset happy hours on its rooftop deck. Pair your cocktail with tapas. Cover is

charged after 10pm, but to get a spot on the tiny roof deck, show up around 7pm.

La Vecinidad   BAR
(Av A; ⊙ 8pm-3am Thu-Sat) 'One place that hasn't lost the essence of the neighborhood,' describes manager Super Nick, a former gang leader turned rapper and businessman. Open-air and tagged with graffiti, this hangout is a worthy stop for a cold one tasting of the true diversity of the Casco.

La Rana Dorada   BREWERY
(Av Alfaro s/n) Replete with shiny brass fixings and wooden stools, this wonderful pub is Panama City's first brewpub of small craft beers and a worthy start. After-work happy hour is just catching on, but it goes gangbusters here. Along with a draft, pizzas are popular. A second location is on **Vía Argentina**.

Platea   JAZZ
(⬛ 228-4010; Calle 1 Oeste) With exposed brick walls and a small, intimate stage, this jazz club wouldn't feel out of place in Greenwich Village. As the night wears on, both bohemians and society folk hit this swinging spot, making for some excellent people-watching over expertly crafted mojitos.

Around the City

The district of Bella Vista is home to Calle Uruguay, a strip of trendy bars and clubs reminiscent of Miami's South Beach. DJs usually pull from a broad repertoire, from salsa and merengue to UK and US '80s classics, with electronic music (house, drum 'n' bass) liberally added to the mix. The scene is young and you can expect to pay to play here. Moreover, clubs change hands quick in this neighborhood, so its best to ask locals about the latest and greatest additions.

S6is   CLUB
(Calle Uruguay, Bella Vista; ⊙ from 9pm Tue & Thu-Sat) Pronounced 'seis' (as in the number 'six'), this club caters to *miembros del club,* aka the beautiful people. There's a fine selection of electronic music worthy of the megaclub scene but with a more intimate and loungy vibe.

Cayucos   CAFE
(Causeway) Located on the Causeway, this open-air resto-bar sits on the water with excellent views of the city. While not exactly a bar, it's the perfect ambiance for the first

cold beer of the evening or a leisurely drink on the weekend.

El Pavo Real
PUB

(Vía Argentina, Bella Vista; ☺ noon-midnight Mon-Sat) A mix of Panamanians and expats gather over games of darts or pool at this British pub-restaurant. The old location was made famous by John le Carré's thriller *The Tailor of Panama* but pub grub continues to satisfy and there's occasional live music.

Wine Bar
JAZZ

(Av Eusebio A Morales) With more than 200 wine selections from around the globe on offer, this is the spot to leisurely share a bottle, with a selection of soft, blue and hard cheeses. Live jazz starts at 9pm most nights of the week.

Li-Bar
LOUNGE

(Calle 76 Este, San Francisco) Cold as a meat locker, this upscale lounge is popular with 30-something Panamanians. It is more chill than other spots, but clubbers still come dolled up to the nines.

Lum's
PUB

(☑ 317-6303; Bldg 340, Corozal Oeste off Carretera Diablo, Ancón; mains US$6-12; ☺ from 11am Mon-Sat) Occupying an old cavernous hangar that once housed machinery for the Panama Canal, Lum's is an expat hangout of choice. Satellite TV, pool table, foosball and a handful of tap beers pack in the crowds on weekends. The menu is heavy on ribs, steak and other grilled mains. It's located in Ancón on the edge of the canal.

Starlight
LOUNGE

(☑ 269-4626; Av 5a B Sur, Bella Vista) The lion's den of karaoke, this older club has no cover, you just have to consume a drink and muster the courage to croon under the disco rays.

Zona Viva
CLUB

(Causeway) On the Causeway, this closed compound hosts nightlife spots ranging from dance clubs to low-key watering holes. Pick your theme, be it pirate bar or Egyptian club. For some it's *pura racataca* (without class), for others it's a fishbowl of fun. Since ID is checked at the complex gate it's considered more secure than most.

Gay & Lesbian Venues

Maybe it's an egalitarian move, but the best gay scene in Panama City is actually found at the city's hippest bars and clubs, not in gay-specific establishments. For some, the gay and lesbian bars give so many 'all you can drink' promotions that they turn out to be sloppy spots not all that conducive to meeting and mingling.

BLG
CLUB

(Av 4a A Sur; ☺ from 10pm Wed-Sun) Located in the heart of Panama City's nightlife scene, this out-and-proud club serves an incredibly diverse clientele. BLG sees its share of top-notch DJs, and it's hard not to have a good time when there's a free open bar included in the cover charge (from US$3).

LOCAL KNOWLEDGE

PANAMA CITY AFTER DARK

Panama City's nightlife scene is arguably the most diverse in Central America. It is a mishmash of martini bars, historic lounges, casinos, strip joints and secret underground haunts, all of which generally start thumping around midnight and shut down when people are ready to leave.

Three main districts represent the city's most popular entertainment options. For glamour, hit the diva-dense **Calle Uruguay** district, stopping in the street late at night for the obligatory spicy Colombian arepa. Cover charges here are ubiquitous as are dress codes and thumping electronic music. Across town, **Zona Viva**, located at the neck of the Amador Causeway, offers a slightly cheesier alternative that's pedestrian-friendly and based mostly outdoors: expect cheap drinks, security pat-downs and a primarily Panamanian crowd.

Panama City's most alternative (and perhaps fastest growing) nightlife district is **Casco Viejo**. Set within roughly 10 blocks of cobblestone, the Casco's nightlife is about as far from sterile as it gets: offbeat bars, Brazilian lounges and hidden salsa clubs draw visitors eager for some neighborhood authenticity.

Matt Landau is the author of www.thepanamareport.com

☆ Entertainment

If you're not looking to get blotto, there are numerous ways to spend a moonlit (or rainy) evening in the city. A good place to start is the arts section in the Sunday edition of *La Prensa* or the back pages of the *Panama News*.

Cinemas

Panamanians have a love affair with Hollywood and there are many air-conditioned cinemas in and around the city. Panamanians also love to gamble, and there are a few flashy casinos where you can get in on the action. There are also opportunities in the capital to see traditional folk dancing and live performances of music and theater.

Panama City's modern movie houses show mostly Hollywood films (with Spanish subtitles) for US$4.50. VIP showings serving alcoholic drinks, with comfortable leather seats, cost US$10. Most theaters offer half-price regular tickets on Wednesday. For listings and show times, pick up a copy of *La Prensa* or go to www.prensa.com and click on 'cine.'

Albrook Cinemark   CINEMA
(Albrook Mall) Next to the Albrook bus terminal. There's also one in the Multiplaza Mall.

Multicentro Cinemark   CINEMA
(Multicentro Mall) Mainstream cinema, with some dubbed titles and some with subtitles. Near Punta Paitilla.

Casinos

None of the casinos in Panama City are on the verge of stealing business away from the megacasinos of Las Vegas, but there are three attractive and popular houses of chance in the capital city. Most are inside top hotels such as the Sheraton, Miramar Inter-Continental and Hotel Continental. With the passing of a recent law, casinos no longer serve alcohol.

Traditional Dance

Restaurante-Bar Tinajas   TRADITIONAL DANCE
(✆ 263-7890; www.tinajaspanama.com; Av 3a A Sur near Av Frederico Boyd, Bella Vista; entry US$5; ◷ Mon-Sat) A good place to see traditional Panamanian folk dancing, this dinner show is a classic. Sure, it's touristy, but nicely done just the same. Shows are held Wednesday to Saturday at 9pm with a US$12 minimum per person for drinks and food. Reservations recommended.

Theater

For current listings of plays and shows, check out www.teatrodepanama.com.

Teatro Anita Villalaz   THEATER
(✆ 501-4020; Paseo las Bóvedas, Plaza de Francia, Casco Viejo) A historical spot in Casco Viejo to see live performances.

THE JAZZ SOLUTION

Once a down-and-out section of the city with crumbling architecture and serious poverty, Casco Viejo is coming into a new chapter. Making a strong push towards revitalization, the neighborhood is home to dozens of new restaurants, cafes, shops and renovated historical buildings. In the midst of this architectural revival, another less tangible one struggles to take place: that of the Panamanian music community.

Jazz great and native Panamanian Danilo Perez returned here to the musical conservatory where he learned his first notes to establish **Fundación Danilo Perez** (✆ 211-0272; www.fundaciondaniloperez.com; Av A 1069), a musical foundation which has generated over US$1 million in youth scholarships. It also sponsors the Panama Jazz Festival, a wildly popular citywide event featuring artists from all over the world.

In an interview with *El Casqueño*, Perez says, 'Through the discipline of music we can create relevant leaders and good citizens. We can solve many of society's problems.' Youth are chosen from inner-city Panama and all parts of the country, including Colón and the Comarca de Kuna Yala. Some grants take students as far as the Berklee School of Music and the New England Conservatory. Many come back to the music conservatory to teach others and complete the cycle of community participation.

The Panama Jazz Festival is held every January, with a week of events in theaters around the city, culminating in a free Saturday concert in the Casco's Plaza de la Independencia. The foundation in Casco Viejo also houses a library and music museum and is open to the public (admission free).

Teatro En Círculo THEATER
(☑ 261-5375; www.teatroencirculo.com; Av 6 C
Norte near Vía Transístmica) Plays and musicals
are scheduled regularly.

Teatro Nacional THEATER
(☑ 262-3525; Av B, Casco Viejo) Casco Viejo's
lovely 19th-century playhouse stages ballets,
concerts and plays.

🛍 Shopping

The city has a number of markets where you
can purchase handicrafts native to regions
throughout the country. Here, you'll find
a range of handmade goods from baskets
made in Emberá villages to *molas* from
Kuna Yala.

A number of shopping malls, some quite
high end, highlight the increasing love of
Americana in Panama. Consumerism aside,
these air-conditioned spots can be a good
place to escape the heat.

⭐**Karavan** ART
(☑ 228-7177; www.karavan-gallery.com; Calle 3a
Oeste, Casco Viejo; ☉ 9:30am-5pm Mon-Fri, 10am-
5pm Sat, noon-5pm Sun) An excellent place to
find original Kuna embroidery with modern
designs and Congo art from Portobelo, with
artisans working onsite. Karavan commissions local artists and works closely to develop new talent.

Mercado Nacional de Artesanías MARKET
(National Artisans Market; Panamá Viejo; ☉ 9am-
4pm Mon-Sat, to 1pm Sun) A good choice for
memorable souvenirs.

**Mercado de Buhonerías y
Artesanías** MARKET
(Av Central España; ☉ 9am-5pm Mon-Sat) This
bustling outdoor spot is a great place to
shop for Panama's crafts.

Reprosa JEWELRY
(☑ 269-0457; www.reprosa.com; cnr Av 2 Sur &
Calle 54 Este; ☉ 9am-7pm Mon-Sat) Sells quality *huacas* (replicas of pre-Columbian gold
pendants) and necklaces made of black onyx
and other gemstones.

Joyería La Huaca JEWELRY
(☑ 269-7254; www.joyerialahuaca.com; cnr Calle
Ricardo Arias & Vía España) A reputable jewelry
store in front of Hotel Continental.

Exedra Books BOOKS
(☑ 264-4252; Vía España at Vía Brasil; ☉ 9:30am-
9:30pm Mon-Sat, 11am-8:30pm Sun) Easily one
of Central America's best bookstores.

Albrook Mall MALL
(Albrook; ☉ 10am-9pm Mon-Sat, 11am-8pm Sun)
Next to the bus terminal, this mall has a
cinema, supermarket and dozens of stores,
including American and European chains.

El Dorado Mall MALL
(Av Ricardo J Alfaro; ☉ 10am-9pm Mon-Sat, 11am-
8pm Sun) Near one of Panama City's newer
Chinatowns, El Dorado also has restaurants,
shops and a cinema.

Located near Corredor Norte and Parque
Metropolitano in El Dorado area.

Isla Flamenco Shopping Center MALL
(Amador Causeway, Isla Flamenco; ☉ 10am-10pm)
This place is small but nearby you'll find the
best selection of open-air restaurants in the
city.

Multicentro Mall MALL
(www.multicentropanama.com.pa; Av Balboa,
Paitilla; ☉ 10am-9pm) Has a cinema and shops,
along with many outdoor restaurants.

Multiplaza Mall MALL
(Vía Israel & Vía Brasil, Punta Pacifica; ☉ 10am-9pm)
The biggest downtown mall, with designer
shops, restaurant and cinema. It's east of
downtown, on the way to Panamá Viejo.

ℹ Information

DANGERS & ANNOYANCES
Casco Viejo is the focus of an ambitious urban
renewal program, but it's still a work in progress.
Generally speaking, the tip of the peninsula
southeast of the Iglesia de la Merced is safe for
tourists and heavily patrolled by police officers
on bicycles. Always exercise caution, and stay
where it's well lit and where there are plenty of
people around.

Casco Viejo gets an undeserved bad rep,
though you should not underestimate how
quickly the neighborhood can change. As you
move away from the tip of the peninsula (north
of Parque Herrera), you will be entering high-
density slums. Other high-crime areas include
Curundú, El Chorrillo, Santa Ana, San Miguelito
and Río Abajo.

Calle Uruguay, the clubbing hub of the city,
also attracts opportunists. Don't take your full
wallet out at night. We have heard reports of
women going up to male travelers to hug them
and taking their wallets.

Taxis generally allow unrelated passengers to
share the cab but robberies do occasionally occur. It's best not to get into a taxi with a passenger. If you speak Spanish, you can offer a slightly
higher fare to keep your taxi to yourself. Evaluate
any taxi you hail before getting in (check for door

DAY TRIPS FROM PANAMA CITY

Looking to get out of the city for the day? Here are some author-tested suggestions.

➡ Laying eyes on the awe-inspiring **Panama Canal**, which cuts a channel across Panama from Colón (Atlantic) to Balboa (near Pacific); boat from Balboa in Panama City for a five-hour tour through locks to Miraflores Lake

➡ Spotting feathered friends along Pipeline Rd in Parque Nacional Soberanía (p78)

➡ Visiting the world-famous tropical biology center on **Isla Barro Colorado**

➡ Escaping to the flower-dotted island of **Isla Taboga**

➡ Surfing gnarly breaks along the **Pacific Coast**

handles and taxi licensing numbers). It's very common for taxis to refuse fares to destinations simply for their own convenience.

There are occasional reports of robbery near the ruins of Panamá Viejo – don't go after sunset, and always keep an eye out.

Panama has become stringent on drug control, which sometimes means roadblock checks of drivers and their passengers. Always have your passport with you.

When walking the streets of Panama City, be aware that drivers do not yield to pedestrians. Sometimes it's best to approach intersections as Panamanians do – look both ways then run like hell.

EMERGENCY

Police (☑104)

INTERNET ACCESS

Most lodgings have wi-fi, and internet cafes are plentiful in Panama City, especially in the El Cangrejo banking district.

MAPS

Instituto Geográfico Nacional (Tommy Guardia; ☑236-2444; near Av Arturo del Valle at Transistmica; ◷8am-4pm Mon-Fri) Just off Av Simón Bolívar opposite the Universidad de Panamá. Has an excellent collection of maps for sale.

MEDICAL SERVICES

Medicine in Panama, especially in Panama City, is of a high standard.

Centro Médico Paitilla (☑265-8883, 265-8800; cnr Calle 53 & Av Balboa) This medical center has well-trained physicians who speak both Spanish and English.

Centro Metropolitano de Salud (☑512-6600; Corosel Los Ríos; ◷7:30am-noon & 1-3pm Mon-Fri) Offers yellow-fever vaccinations with international certificate (required for travel to Colombia if returning) for a minimal charge.

MONEY

ATMs are abundant throughout the city. The Banco Nacional de Panamá counter at Tocumen International Airport is one of the few places in Panama City that exchanges foreign currency.

HSBC (Vía España) Changes Amex traveler's checks with no fee; US$5 per transaction for other types of checks.

Panacambios (☑223-1800; Vía España, Ground fl, Plaza Regency Bldg; ◷8am-5pm Mon-Fri) Buys and sells international currencies.

POST

Many hotels sell stamps and some will mail guests' letters.

Main Post Office (Av Balboa btwn Calles 23 & 24; ◷7am-5:45pm Mon-Fri, to 4:45pm Sat) Holds poste restante items for 30 days.

Post Office (Plaza las Americas; ◷7am-5:45pm Mon-Fri, to 4:45pm Sat) Only post office for mailing packages. There's a second branch nearby.

TELEPHONE

Tarjetas (phonecards) valued at US$3, US$5 and US$10 can be purchased at pharmacies for local and regional calls from any card phone.

TOURIST INFORMATION

ATP (Autoridad de Turismo Panamá) offices give out free maps. The usefulness of a given office depends on the individual employees; few speak English.

Autoridad de Turismo Panamá (ATP, Panama Tourism Authority; ☑226-7000; www.atp.gob. pa; Vía Israel, Centro Atlapa, San Francisco; ◷8:30am-4:30pm Mon-Fri) Panama's tourist bureau is headquartered at the Atlapa Convention Center in the San Francisco neighborhood. Enter at the rear of the large building. ATP gives out free maps and information on things to see and do. There are also ATP information counters in Casco Viejo and Panamá Viejo.

ANAM (Autoridad Nacional del Ambiente; ☑500-0855, 315-0855; www.anam.gob.pa; Building 804, Albrook; ◷8am-4pm) ANAM can occasionally provide maps and information on national parks. However, they are not organized to provide much assistance to tourists.

ℹ️ Getting There & Away

AIR

International flights arrive at and depart from **Tocumen International Airport** (📞 238-4160, 238-4322; www.tocumenpanama.aero), 35km northeast of the city center.

Domestic flights depart from **Albrook airport** (Aeropuerto Marcos A Gelabert; 📞 315-0403), aka Aeropuerto Marcos A Gelabert, in the former Albrook Air Force Station near the canal.

Air Panama (📞 316-9000; www.flyairpanama. com) covers domestic routes. At the time of writing, the online system was out of order and it was best to go to Albrook airport in person to buy tickets. Since this requires extra planning and logistics, it's best to check with your lodging on the current situation.

Flights within Panama are inexpensive and short – few are longer than one hour. However, if traveling to the Darién, Isla Contadora or Comarca de Kuna Yala, it's quite possible that the plane may make multiple stops. You'll find that prices vary according to season and availability.

BOAT

There are regular ferries to Isla Taboga and Contadora, leaving from Panama City's Balboa Yacht Club.

BUS

Albrook Bus Terminal (📞 303-3030; www. grantnt.com) Albrook Bus Terminal, near the Albrook airport, is a convenient and modern one-stop location for most buses leaving Panama City. The terminal includes a food court, banks, shops, a sports bar, storage room, bathrooms and showers. A mall lies next door, complete with a supermarket and cinema.

Passengers must buy a multiuse card or *tarjeta* to pay the US$0.10 terminal tax before entering the bus area by turnstile (it also serves to use bus terminal bathrooms). You can avoid this inconvenience by offering another person in line cash to swipe their card for you.

For assistance, go to the Information booth.

Metrobus (www.tarjetametrobus.com; fare US$0.25-1.25) All local buses are on the new Metrobus system with designated bus stops and clean, new buses. Cash is not accepted. Passengers must buy *tarjetas*, rechargable orange cards, at a special kiosk in Albrook terminal or at designated locations (such as supermarkets or main bus stops, all listed on the website). If you don't have one, try offering another passenger reimbursement for swiping their card.

Both **Panaline** (📞 227-8648; www.viajeros. com/panaline) and **Tica Bus** (📞 262-2084; www.ticabus.com) serve San José, Costa Rica; see their websites for hours.

Canal Zone buses depart from the Albrook terminal to Balboa and Clayton, Miraflores Locks, and Gamboa, leaving every 45 minutes. In transition, these buses will soon be run by Metrobus with the same card system.

CAR

Daily rates start from US$35 per day for the most economical cars, including unlimited kilometers and insurance. The following agencies have branches at both the Albrook and Tocumen airports.

Avis (📞 238-4056; www.avis.com.pa)

Budget (📞 Tocumen 238-4069; www.budget panama.com)

Hertz (📞 238-3751; www.hertz.com.pa)

National (📞 238-4144; www.nationalpanama. com)

TRAIN

Panama Railway Company (PCRC; 📞 317-6070; www.panarail.com; Carretera Gaillard; one-way adult/child US$25/$15) This glass-domed luxury passenger train takes a lovely

---

FLIGHTS FROM PANAMA CITY

The flights listed in the table show the approximate cost for one-way fares.

DESTINATION	COST (US$)	FREQUENCY
Achutupu (San Blás)	80	daily
Bocas del Toro	116	multiple daily
Changuinola	117	multiple daily
Corazon de Jesus (San Blás)	74	daily
David	117	multiple daily
Isla Contadora	69	daily
Ogobuscum (San Blás)	80	4 weekly
Playón Chico	78	daily
Sambu (Darién)	82	3 weekly

ride from Panama City to Colón daily, leaving at 7:15am and returning at 5:15pm. The train follows the canal, at times surrounded by nothing but thick vine-strewn jungle. If you want to relive the heyday of luxury train travel for an hour or two, this is definitely the way to do it.

Note that the Panama City terminus is actually located in the town of Corazal, a 15-minute cab ride from the capital.

ℹ Getting Around

GETTING INTO TOWN
From the Airports

Tocumen International Airport is 35km northeast of the city center. The cheapest way to get into the city is to exit the terminal, cross the street (to the bus shelter) and catch a bus to the city. Taxis can be hired at the Transportes Turísticos desk at the airport exit; they're a much faster means of getting into town, though somewhat costlier. Beside the desk is a taxi stand, with posted prices (from US$27). Don't be distracted by touts offering rides at ridiculously high prices; they take their cut from the taxis.

From the Albrook Terminal, airport buses (US$1.25, one to 1½ hours) marked 'Tocumen Corredor' depart every 15 minutes. You can also take a taxi from downtown (from US$27).

The Albrook airport north of Cerro Ancón handles domestic flights. The easiest way to get to/from the airport is by taxi; the ride should cost between US$3 and US$5.

From the Bus Terminal

All long-distance buses arrive at the Albrook bus terminal; from here there are connections throughout the city. Routes (such as Vía España, Panamá Viejo) are displayed in the front window and cost US$0.25. If you arrive after dark, it is recommended that you take a taxi (US$3 to US$5) to your destination.

BICYCLE

The only spot to rent bicycles in Panama City is at the Causeway entrance. Both **Moses** (☎ 221-3671; ☉ 9am-7pm Sat & Sun) and Bikes n More (p52) operate booths with rentals starting at US$4 per hour for mountain bikes. You can also rent tandems and rickshaw bikes.

BUS

Panama City is almost done phasing out its *diablos rojos* ('red devils') for modern, safe, air-conditioned buses by Metrobus (p69). Rides cost US$0.25 to $1.25, with the higher cost for corredor routes.

Buses run along the three major west-to-east routes: Av Central–Vía España, Av Balboa–Vía

BUSES FROM PANAMA CITY

DESTINATION	COST (US$)	DURATION (HR)	FREQUENCY
Aguadulce	6.35	3	33 daily
Antón	4.70	2	every 20min
Cañita	3	2½	11 daily
Chame	2.60	1¼	37 daily
Changuinola	28	10	8pm daily
Chitré	9	4	hourly
Colón	3.50	2	every 20min
David	15-19	7-8	15 daily
El Copé	6.50	4	9 daily
El Valle	4.25	2½	hourly
Las Tablas	10	4½	hourly
Macaracas	10	5	5 daily
Paso Canoa	17	8	5 daily
Penonomé	5.25	2½	48 daily
Pesé	9.65	4½	6 daily
San Carlos	3.25	1½	25 daily
San José, Costa Rica	40	16	2 daily
Santiago	9	4	20 daily
Soná	10	6	6 daily
Villa de Los Santos	9	4	18 daily
Yaviza	14	6-8	8 daily

Israel, and Av Simón Bolívar–Vía Transístmica. The Av Central–Vía España streets are one-way going west for much of the route; eastbound buses use Av Perú and Av 4 Sur; these buses will take you into the banking district of El Cangrejo. Buses also run along Av Ricardo J Alfaro (known as Tumba Muerto).

Metrobuses stop at official bus stops and the Albrook bus terminal near the Albrook airport.

TAXI

Taxis are plentiful but problematic. Some do not travel (or even know) the whole city, so don't be surprised if they leave you standing on the sidewalk upon hearing your destination.

Taxis are not metered, but there is a list of standard fares that drivers are supposed to charge, measured by zones. One zone runs a minimum of US$2; canal zone destinations run up to US$6. An average ride, crossing a couple of zones, would cost US$3 to US$4, more for additional passengers or if it's late. Always agree on a fare before you get into the cab or, better, ask your hotel to estimate the fare to your destination and then simply hand the driver the money upon arriving. Taxis can also be rented by the hour.

Watch out for unmarked large-model US cars serving hotels as cabs. Their prices are up to four times that of regular street taxis.

America (☎ 223-7694)
America Libre (☎ 223-7342)
Latino (☎ 224-0677)
Metro (☎ 264-6788)
Taxi Unico Cooperativa (☎ 221-3191)

Panamá Province

POP 1,713,070 / ELEV SEA LEVEL TO 100M / AREA 11,887 SQ KM

Best Spots to Explore

➡ Parque Nacional Soberanía (p78)

➡ Panama Canal locks (p73)

➡ Lago Bayano (p91)

Best Places to Stay

➡ Canopy B&B (p80)

➡ Burbayar Lodge (p91)

➡ Canopy Tower Ecolodge (p79)

➡ Nitro City (p89)

Why Go?

Panamá Province has a rich history of pirates, plunder and pearls. Although the most populated province in the country, Panamá can be as big or as small as you want it to be. Tranquil rainforests and sizzling beach scenes are yours to explore and the comforts of the capital are never more than an hour away.

The principal attraction remains the world's most daring engineering marvel. Explore the Panama Canal and its expansion by visiting its locks, boating through its watery recesses or hiking along its jungle-clad shore. It is also the unlikely host of one of the most accessible and best-studied tropical rainforests on the planet.

Day trips from the city abound, ranging from beaches and surf breaks to ferry trips to the island village of Taboga. Further flung are the Archipiélago de Las Perlas, attracting everyone from the moneyed elite to the occasional *Survivor* TV series.

When to Go

➡ **Dec–Apr** Trade winds and dry weather translate to a perfect time to windsurf or kitesurf; beaches are usually full and hotels charge high-season rates.

➡ **May–Nov** Low-season rates in resorts and hotels translate to huge savings; calmer conditions mean wakeboarders can have their fun.

➡ **Aug–Oct** Migrating humpback whales put on spectacular displays, best viewed around Isla Taboga and Archipiélago de Las Perlas.

History

Throughout the 16th and 17th centuries, the Spanish used the isthmus as a transit point for shipping plundered gold between Peru and Spain. The main route was the famous cobblestoned Camino Real (King's Hwy), which linked Panamá to Portobelo, and served as the only road across the isthmus for hundreds of years. In the 1700s, however, the route was abandoned in favor of shipping gold around Cape Horn owing to repeated pirate attacks, the most famous of which was Captain Henry Morgan's sacking of Panamá Viejo in 1671.

As early as 1524, King Charles V of Spain had ordered a survey to determine the feasibility of constructing a trans-isthmian water route. But it wasn't until the 1880s that any country dared to undertake the momentous project of carving a trench through these dense jungles and mountains. The first canal attempt came from a French team led by Ferdinand-Marie de Lesseps, bolstered by his prior success building the Suez Canal.

Sadly, the French team grossly underestimated the difficulties and some 22,000 workers died during the construction attempt. Most lives were lost to yellow fever and malaria, which led to the establishment of an enormous quarantine on Isla Taboga. It was not yet known that mosquitoes were the disease vector.

Several decades later, the Americans learned from the mistakes of the French and succeeded in completing the canal in 1914. Today, the waterway rests firmly in the hands of the Panamanian government, and the face of the canal is rapidly changing as an ambitious expansion is made.

AROUND PANAMA CITY

No visit to Panama City would be complete without taking a day trip to its famous waterway – though just remember that the Canal Zone is much, much more than just the canal. The rainforest surrounding the canal is easily accessed and one of the best places to view a variety of Central American wildlife.

Panama Canal

One of the world's greatest artificial marvels, the canal stretches 80km from Panama City on the Pacific side to Colón on the Atlantic side, cutting right through the continental divide. Around 13,000 vessels pass through the canal each year and ships worldwide are built with the dimensions of the Panama Canal's locks (305m long and 33.5m wide) in mind. In 2010 the canal brought in US$2 billion in revenue.

Ships pay according to their weight, with the average fee around US$30,000. The highest fee was around US$376,000, paid in 2010 by the cruise ship *Norwegian Pearl;* the lowest was US$0.36, paid in 1928 by Richard Halliburton, who swam through.

The pre-expansion canal has three sets of double locks: Miraflores and Pedro Miguel Locks on the Pacific side and Gatún Locks on the Atlantic side. Between the locks, ships pass through a huge artificial lake, Lago Gatún, created by the Gatún Dam across the Río Chagres, and the Gaillard Cut, a 14km cut through the rock and shale. The passage of each ship releases a staggering 52 million gallons of fresh water into the ocean.

Panamanians voted to expand the canal in 2006. The US$5.25 billion plan will widen and deepen existing navigation channels as well as enable the construction of two new locks. Originally planned for inauguration at the canal's 100-year anniversary, it now seems that the expansion will not open until 2015.

⊙ Sights

◉ Miraflores Locks

Miraflores Visitors Center   MUSEUM
(☑276-8325; www.pancanal.com; viewing deck/full-access US$5/8; ⊙9am-5pm) The easiest and best way to visit the canal is to go to the Miraflores Visitors Center, located just outside Panama City. The recently inaugurated visitors center features a large, four-floor interactive museum, several viewing platforms and an excellent restaurant serving sumptuous buffet spreads within panorama view of teh canal transit. Tip: the best time to view big liners passing through is from 9am to 11am and from 3pm to 5pm, when they are more frequent.

To get there, take any Paraíso or Gamboa bus from the Albrook Bus Terminal in Panama City. These buses, passing along the canal-side highway to Gamboa, will let you off at the 'Miraflores Locks' sign (US$0.35) on the highway, 12km from the city center. It's about a 15-minute walk to the locks from the sign. Otherwise, you can take a taxi; there's a 30-minute wait at the locks and from there you get driven back to the capital. Expect to pay no more than US$20 for the round-trip – agree on the price beforehand.

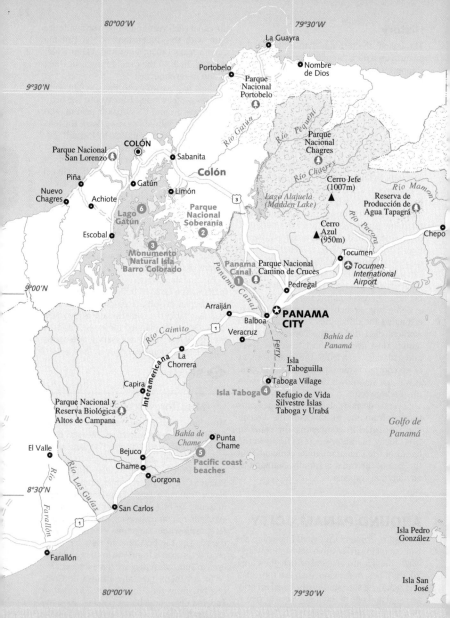

Panamá Province Highlights

1 Lay eyes on the awe-inspiring **Panama Canal** (p73), an engineering marvel in the midst of an expansion

2 Spot feathered friends along Pipeline Rd in **Parque Nacional Soberanía** (p78), one of the world's premier bird-watching sites

3 Visit the world-famous tropical biology center at **Monumento Natural Isla Barro Colorado** (p79), the most studied patch of rainforest in the world

4 Escape the urban grind of the capital on a day trip to the flower-dotted island of **Isla Taboga** (p81)

5 Soak up the sun, surf gnarly breaks and make the most of romantic hideaways along the **Pacific coast beaches** (p89)

6 Paddle a kayak or fish for peacock bass on **Lago Gatún** (p76), and spot some howler monkeys in the canopy

Panama Canal

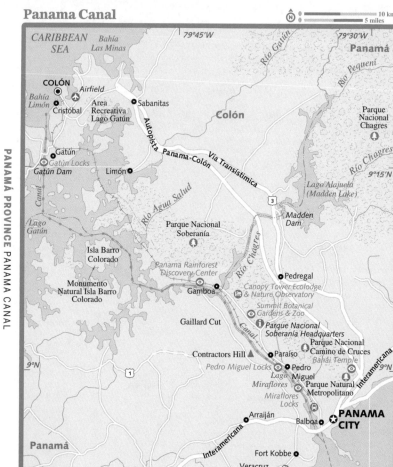

Other Locks

On the Caribbean side, the Gatún Locks have viewing platforms that also show the canal expansion.

Pedro Miguel Locks   CANAL

FREE North past the Miraflores Locks, the Pedro Miguel Locks are seen from the highway to Gamboa. One hundred meters beyond the locks there's a parking strip where onlookers can watch ships transit the canal.

Activities

Yala Tours   ADVENTURE TOUR

(☎6641-6676, 232-0215; www.yalatourspanama.com) This small Swiss-run operation provides specialized trips throughout Panama, but also day trips to Gamboa and the canal area. A highlight is kayaking in Chagres River and Lago Gatún (while watching canal ships mow through!). There's also a canal boat tour in Lago Gatún, wildlife-watching and hiking in Parque Nacional Soberanía, as well as cultural visits to an Embera village.

Jungle Land Panama
TOUR

(☑ 213-1172; www.junglelandpanama.com; all-inclusive package adult/child overnight US$175/130) Offers the novelty of a jungle retreat with canal ships passing by. Captain Carl hosts guests on a charming wooden, three-story houseboat. It's in Lago Gatún, from where fishing, kayaking and nocturnal safaris are at your fingertips. Day trips also available. Leaves from the Gamboa public boat ramp.

Canal Bay & Tours
BOAT TOUR

(☑ 314-1339; www.canalandbaytours.com; partial/full transit US$115/165) Offers partial canal transits every Saturday morning. Boats depart from Muelle (Pier) 19 in Balboa, a western suburb of Panama City. They travel through the Miraflores Locks to Lago Miraflores and back, and then cruise out into the bay for scenic views of the city. These tours last 4½ hours (make reservations in advance). One Saturday every month, it also offers full transits, from Balboa to Cristóbal on the Caribbean coast, passing all three sets of locks. The transit takes all day (from 7:30am to 5:30pm). Check the website for dates of upcoming transits.

Ancon Expeditions
BOAT TOUR

(☑ 269-9415; www.anconexpeditions.com) The highly recommended Ancon Expeditions offers regularly scheduled canal transits. It's a good idea to book in advance as this is one of the company's most popular offerings.

Panama Canal Fishing
FISHING

(☑ 6678-2653, 315-1905; www.panamacanalfishing.com; all inclusive day trips from US$445) If you have dreamed of reeling in the big one in the Canal Zone, the signature tour is fishing for peacock bass in Lago Gatún and the Río Chagres. Introduced by an American looking to boost his pastime, this species is now considered a plague. By fishing, you do a great favor to the lake.

Canal Zone

The Canal Zone is home to a number of impressive attractions, especially if you're into wildlife-watching, hiking and bird-watching. On a day trip from Panama City, you could visit the Miraflores Locks and finish at the Parque Nacional Soberanía and the Panama Rainforest Discovery Center. With prior

PANAMÁ PROVINCE CANAL ZONE

EXPANDING THE CANAL

Betting on growing international shipping needs, the Panama Canal is expanding. One of the biggest transportation projects in the world, this US$5.25 billion mega-project is slated to finish by 2015. New locks will be 60% wider and 40% longer. Container traffic is expected to triple. But will it be able to meet increased world shipping needs?

As container ships get bigger and bigger, the need to accommodate them is plain. Proponents of the expansion expect the increased traffic and volume through the canal to inject a huge boost into the Panamanian economy. The country will maintain its current role as the maritime logistics center in the Americas, and everything from the Free Trade Zone of Colón to the international financial hub of Panama City is likely to boom. It may even increase tourism, since the new locks will be able to accommodate large cruise ships.

The rationale for the expansion is that the demands of the international maritime shipping community have changed. Although as much as 5% of the world's total sea commerce traverses the Panama Canal, the Suez Canal in Egypt, which is capable of handling larger vessels, serves more than 6%. Furthermore, the Panama Canal is already operating at more than 90% of its maximum capacity and will reach its saturation point in less than five years.

The biggest challenge the Panama Canal faces is luring the enormous post-Panamax vessels, which currently depend on either the US Transcontinental Railroad or the Suez Canal. But those in favor of the canal expansion are hoping that this lucrative market will adopt the Panama route, especially as trade volumes between Asia and the continental east coast increase. There is concern that the expansion will not offset its construction costs. Furthermore, critics from all sectors of society are pessimistic that the government can actually pull off the project at its stated price tag.

Financing the project requires US$2.3 billion in loans from various foreign government-owned banks, in addition to funding by the Panamanian government and the Panama Canal Authority. Since it's estimated that the value of tolls will increase significantly over the next 20 years, the hope is that the expected flow of post-Panamax vessels through the canal will eventually pick up the tab.

arrangements, you could also take an organized tour of Isla Barro Colorado, one of the world's most famous tropical research stations, or visit an Emberá or Wounaan village on the shores of the Río Chagres. If you want to spend the night in the area, it's worth staying at either the Canopy Tower or the Gamboa Rainforest Resort.

All of the attractions in the Canal Zone are located along the highway that runs from Panama City to Gamboa, the small town where the Río Chagres enters Lago Gatún. They can be reached by taking the Gamboa bus, which departs frequently from Albrook bus terminal (US$0.85).

Summit Botanical Gardens & Zoo

Located 10km past the Miraflores Locks, Summit Botanical Gardens & Zoo (☑ 232-4854; adult/child US$1/free; ⊙ 9am-5pm) was established in 1923 to introduce tropical plants from around the world. Around 15,000 plant species line marked trails and paths. The small zoo onsite was originally setup to help GIs identify animals while serving in tropical rainforests. In recent years, upkeep of the park has declined. Under the jurisdiction of the Panama City municipality, Summit depends on city funding and organization, thus improvements are often slow to implement.

Parque Nacional Soberanía

A few kilometers past Summit Botanical Gardens, across the border into Colón Province, the 22,104-hectare Parque Nacional Soberanía (admission US$5) is one of the most accessible tropical rainforest areas in Panama. It extends much of the way across the isthmus, from Limón on Lago Gatún to just north of Paraíso, and boasts hiking trails that brim with a remarkable variety of wildlife.

Leaflets and information about the park, including a brochure for self-guided walks along the nature trail, are available from park headquarters (Autoridad Nacional del Ambiente; ☑ 276-6370) near Gamboa.

🏃 Activities

Hiking & Bird-Watching

If you plan on hiking, you should note that the trail heads are quite far from the Autoridad Nacional del Ambiente (ANAM) station. If arriving by taxi, have the driver wait for you to pay the fee and then take you to the trailhead. Hiking trails in the park include a

section of the old Sendero Las Cruces (Las Cruces Trail), used by the Spanish to transport gold by mule train between Panama City and Nombre de Dios, and the 17km Pipeline Rd, providing access to Río Agua Salud, where you can walk upriver for a swim under a waterfall. A shorter, very easy trail is the Sendero El Charco (the Puddle Trail), signposted from Carretera Omar Torrijos, 3km past the Summit Botanical Gardens & Zoo.

Pipeline Rd is considered to be one of the world's premier bird-watching sites. Not surprisingly, it's intensely popular with bird-watchers, especially early in the morning. Over 500 different species of birds have been spotted on the trail and it's fairly likely you will spot everything from toucans to trogons.

A healthy cluster of golden-collared manakins is usually found at the end of the first 100m of the road, on the left-hand side. Other typical sounds on the first 2km of the road come from white-bellied antbirds, black-bellied wrens, collared aracaris, keel-billed toucans and buff-throated woodcreepers. Also keep an eye out for rarities such as the tiny hawk, the hook-billed kite, the great jacamar and the black-tailed trogon.

In order to fully appreciate the wildlife on Pipeline Rd, it's wise to hire a guide – it would be a shame to give it short shrift.

Emberá & Wounaan Communities

The Río Chagres, which flows through the park and supplies most of the water for the Panama Canal, is home to several Emberá and Wounaan communities. Although the Darién is the ancestral home of these two indigenous groups, a wave of migration to the shores of the Río Chagres commenced in the 1950s. However, following the establishment of the national park in the 1980s, the government stopped the practice of slash-and-burn agriculture, which has severely affected their livelihood. Today, several villages are turning to tourism for survival.

Before visiting these communities, it's important to realize that over the past 50 years, both the Emberá and the Wounaan have had a turbulent history of land grabs, legal battles and political misrepresentation. Both groups have been forced to modernize, though the Emberá and the Wounaan still maintain their incredibly rich cultural heritage. If you arrive expecting to see villagers living traditional lifestyles in harmony with the land, then you will be disappointed. However, the Emberá and the Wounaan still have a lot to show to visitors, especially their traditional dances, music, handicrafts and the surrounding national park.

The neighboring Emberá community of Ella Puru (☑6537-7223) and Wounaan community of San Antonio (☑6637-9503) regularly receive tourists and with prior notice you can arrange a pickup from the docks in Gamboa. Tour prices depend on the activities you arrange. There is no shortage of possible excursions, ranging from guided rainforest walks to watching traditional dances.

Visitors also praise Embera Village Tours (☑6758-7600; www.embervillagetours.com), the agency of Anne Gordon de Barrigón, a former animal trainer who married into this warm Emberá community. The tour is well done and provides loads of cultural insight.

Fishing

Fishing is permitted on the Río Chagres and Lago Gatún. If you're interested in arranging a private tour, contact Panama Canal Fishing.

Panama Rainforest
Discovery Center PARK
(☑6588-0697; www.pipelineroad.org; adult/child US$20/4; ⊙6am-4pm) Geared towards ecotourism and environmental education, Panama Rainforest Discovery Center is an excellent facility for bird-watchers and nature lovers. Since you are probably coming to watch wildlife, it's worth making an effort to roll out of bed early. You will be kindly rewarded for the effort. In fact, those arriving after 10am pay US$10 less in admission, a sure sign that the value is less. During premium hours, only 25 visitors are admitted to minimize the impact on wildlife. With advance reservations, groups can set up special night tours.

A 32m-high observation tower is great for spotting blue cotinga and toucans. The visitors center provides information and has 13 species of hummingbirds feeding nearby. Guides can point out wildlife. Currently, a 1.2km circuit of forest trails offers options that range from easy to difficult. By the lake you can view aquatic birds like wattled jacanas, least grebes, herons and snail kites. Other animals around include monkeys, crocodiles, coatis and butterflies.

You can also contact the center to participate in bird migration counts. It's run by the Fundación Avifauna Eugene Eisenmann (☑264-6266; www.avifauna.org.pa), a nonprofit group with the mission to protect Panama's bird fauna and rainforest habitat. Within the center, scientific research includes studies of migratory birds, green macaws and

raptors as well as investigations into carbon capture.

No buses access the park. It is best to negotiate with a taxi, rent a car or go with an organized tour. The center is located 1.6km from the entrance to the Pipeline Rd. You must pass the town of Gamboa, at the end of Gaillard Rd, and follow the signs.

🛏 Sleeping

★ Canopy Tower Ecolodge &
Nature Observatory LODGE $$$
(☑264-5720; www.canopytower.com; s/d/ste incl meals & guided walk US$159/229/259; ℗) Located in Parque Nacional Soberanía, this former US Air Force radar station now serves a very different function, namely ecotourism. Open only to guests of the recommended onsite lodging, the Canopy Tower is an ecologically minded three-story, cylindrical lodge and observatory that offers guests the chance to immerse themselves in the sights and sounds of the rainforest. From the third and rooftop levels, you have a 360-degree view over the national park and you can even see ships passing through the canal a mere 2km away. The bird-watching in the surrounding area is top-notch and there's no shortage of other tropical wildlife, including howler monkeys, sloths and a slew of frogs and lizards.

In addition to the viewing platforms, there is also a small ground-floor museum, a tropical biology library, a cozy sitting area and a handful of attractive guest rooms ranging from quaint singles to luxurious four-person suites. Each room is awash in tropical hues, natural hardwoods, firm beds and a few hammocks to help you pass the time easier. Rates include three meals and guided nature walks in Parque Nacional Soberanía. Even if you're not spending the night, a day visit will allow you to visit the viewing platforms and partake in a few guided walks through the park.

To reach the Canopy Tower, pass the entrance to Summit Botanical Gardens & Zoo on your way to Gamboa, and take the second road to the right – the turnoff is marked with a Canopy Tower sign. Follow the road for 1.6km until you reach the top of Semaphore Hill and the entrance to the hotel.

Monumento Natural Isla Barro Colorado

This lush island in the middle of Lago Gatún is the most intensively studied area in the

Neotropics. Formed by the damming of the Río Chagres and the creation of the lake, in 1923 Isla Barro Colorado (BCI) became one of the first biological reserves in the New World. Home to 1316 recorded plant species, 381 bird species and 120 mammal species, the island also contains a 59km network of marked and protected trails. It is managed by the Smithsonian Tropical Research Institute (STRI), which administers a world-renowned research facility here.

Although the 15-sq-km island was once restricted only to scientists, a limited number of tourists are now allowed to enter as part of a guided tour. The trip includes an STRI boat ride down an attractive part of the canal, from Gamboa across the lake to the island. Reservations are essential – book as far in advance as possible. Reservations can be made through the Panama City visitors services office of **STRI** (☑ 212-8000; www.stri.org; Av Roosevelt, Tupper Bldg, Ancón district; adult/student US$70/40; ◉ 8:30am-4:30pm Mon-Fri).

To visit, a 45-minute boat ride leaves Gamboa pier at 7:15am on weekdays and at 8am on weekends. There are no public visits on certain holidays. Hikes are demanding and last two to three hours. The entire trip lasts four to six hours, depending on the size of the group and on the weather. A buffet lunch (with vegetarian options) is included. For more visitor information, you can download the free PDF on the STRI website.

Gamboa

A pleasant community of broad, curving streets, old wooden canal houses and leafy walks, Gamboa is an ideal base for wildlife-watchers who want some quiet too. The small town is the base of many foreign scientists working for STRI. Unfortunately, if you want groceries or great options for eating out, you will have to backtrack toward the city.

To arrive, take a taxi (US$30 to US$40) from Panama City or the Gamboa-bound bus (US$0.65) from the Albrook Bus Terminal.

🛏 Sleeping

Ivan's Bed & Breakfast   B&B $$
(☑ 6981-4583, 314-9436; www.gamboaecotours. com; Av Jadwin 111; r per person US$50; ❄🖂) Decked with memorabilia, this comfortable canal house tends to draw bird-watchers and hikers keen on quick access to Pipeline Rd. Prices are the same for private or shared bathrooms. The 3rd-floor rooms with shared bathrooms are fresher than those at floor level. A 2nd-floor living area is cozy and tasteful, while the covered terrace is ideal for an afternoon beer.

Guests can rent bicycles or a golf cart (each US$10 daily) to get around the area. Reserve ahead for large-portioned dinners, which include salad and dessert. English-speaking Ivan and his wife can arrange bird-watching and fishing tours, as well as airport transfers.

★ Canopy B&B   B&B $$$
(☑ 833-5929, reservations 264-5720; www.canopy tower.com; Av Jadwin 114; s/d incl breakfast from US$88/132; ❄🖂) In an old canal house, this lovely B&B has a clean design of classic features mixed with bold patterns. Heated towel racks and hair dryers add a nice touch. In the morning, pancakes, eggs and wheat toast are served at a huge breakfast table. You can also cruise the pleasant, shady neighborhood on a rental bike (US$5 per hour).

Upstairs rooms cost slightly more but are significant upgrades. Dinner (US$23) is an optional extra.

Gamboa Rainforest Resort   RESORT $$$
(☑ 314-9000; www.gamboaresort.com; d from US$170; P❄@🖂🖂) Near the junction of the Panama Canal and the Río Chagres, 9km past the turnoff for Canopy Tower on the road to Colón, is the US$30-million Gamboa Rainforest Resort. Although it's just a resort located in a rainforest as opposed to an environmentally friendly ecolodge, it's hard to deny its grandeur. All 110 luxurious guest rooms offer sweeping vistas of the jungle-flanked Río Chagres.

There's echoes of Disneyland, with an on-site golf course, spa, gym, marina, swimming pool and bar-restaurant. There's even an aerial tram that brings you up into the canopy, as well as a healthy offering of guided nature walks and bird-watching trips (which cost extra). The website offers special package deals, which often include activities, meals and transfers.

PACIFIC ISLANDS

Wedged between two oceans, Panamá is an island-hoppers' dream – spend some time on the Pacific side of things, especially if you're a fan of fiery sunsets and scenic coastlines.

Isla Taboga

POP 1000

A tropical island with only one road and no traffic, Isla Taboga is a pleasant escape from the rush of Panama City, only 20km offshore. With the addition of an annual festival and boutique lodgings in the works, it's becoming more of a destination. Named the 'Island of Flowers,' it is covered with sweet-smelling blossoms much of the year. First settled by the Spanish in 1515, the quaint village is also home to the second-oldest church in the Western Hemisphere. While there are better beaches elsewhere, these are a salve for the most hardened urbanite.

History

Taboga is part of a chain of islands that was inhabited by indigenous peoples who resided in thatched huts and lived off the bounty of the sea. In 1515 Spanish soldiers announced their arrival by killing or enslaving the islanders and establishing a small colony. It then became a favorite haunt for English pirates.

On August 22, 1686, the ship of English buccaneer Captain Townley was offshore from Taboga when it was attacked by three Spanish ships. During the ensuing battle, Townley destroyed one of the ships and took two vessels captive as well as a fourth ship that had arrived as reinforcement. Townley sent a messenger to the president of Panama demanding supplies, the release of five pirates being held prisoner and ransom for the Spanish captives. When the president refused, a standoff ensued, with Townley sending him a canoe with the heads of 20 Spaniards. With that, the pirate's demands were soon met.

For years, peace eluded the little island in a strategic location. During the 1880s, when the French attempted to build the canal, Taboga became the site of an enormous sanatorium for workers who had contracted malaria or yellow fever.

The US Navy used the broad hill facing the town for artillery practice during WWII and even installed a number of anti-aircraft guns and machine-gun bunkers atop the island. Though abandoned in 1960, these ruins can still be visited today.

◉ Sights

Fine beaches lie in either direction from the ferry dock. Many visitors head right to the island's most popular beach, arcing between Taboga and tiny Isla El Morro.

Walk left from the pier to the village. After a fork, a high road leads to a modest church with a simple square. Founded in 1550, it's the second-oldest church in the Western Hemisphere; inside is a handsome altar and lovely artwork. Further down the road, a beautiful public garden bares the statue of the island's patroness, Nuestra Señora del Carmen.

🏃 Activities

Snorkeling

On weekends, fishermen at the pier take visitors around the island to good snorkeling spots and caves on the western side, which are rumored to hold pirate treasure. During the week you can snorkel around Isla El Morro, which doesn't have coral, but attracts some large fish.

Diving

Pacific-style diving has rocky formations, schools of fish and a wide variety of marine life. On a good dive you can see jack, snapper, jewfish, eels, rays, lobsters and octopuses. With a little luck, you may also come across old bottles, spent WWII-era shells and artifacts from pirate days (look but don't take). Dive outfitters in Panama City occasionally make the trip.

Bird-Watching

Taboga and nearby Urabá are home to one of the world's largest breeding colonies of brown pelicans. The colony has up to 100,000 pelicans, about half of the world population of this species. Refugio de Vida Silvestre Islas Taboga y Urabá was established to protect their habitat, and covers about a third of Taboga as well as the entire island of Urabá, just off Taboga's southeast coast. May is the height of nesting season, but pelicans are seen from January to June.

Whale-Watching

Keep an eye out while on the ferry. From August to October migrating humpback and sei whales can be seen leaping from the water near Taboga in spectacular displays.

🎊 Festivals

Fiesta del Mar   FESTIVAL
(www.fiestadelmarpanama.com; admission $6) Only in its second year, this festival highlights local culture, with live Panamanian Calypso music, dancing, a pageant and food events. Held at the end of January, it draws 4000 guests to this tiny island.

PIRATES IN THE BAY

From the late 17th century, Panama Bay was the scene of pirate exploits unsurpassed anywhere in the New World. It served as both hideout and attack springboard. After Captain Henry Morgan's successful 1671 sacking of Panama City, other buccaneers flooded in to pillage and plunder along the Pacific coast.

In May, 1685, the largest number of fighters ever assembled under a buccaneer flag in the Pacific played cat-and-mouse with a Spanish armada of 18 ships. English captain Edward Blake's French and English pirate fleet had plenty of muskets but was deficient in cannons, so avoided long-range fighting.

When the two great forces crossed paths on May 28, Blake, who was itching for a close encounter, ordered two of his principal ships to attack. Fearing the cannons, both men refused to obey. The forces exchanged fire, but with odds stacked against Blake he ordered the slower ships to flee while his and another fast vessel delayed the conquistadors.

The pirates managed some risky evasive maneuvers between rocky islets and anchored that night, expecting the Spanish armada to engage them the next day. Instead, the Spanish fleet fled to Panama. Soon dissent arose among the buccaneers and the short-lived, French-English pirate confederacy dissolved.

Today, almost the only evidence of pirates in the Archipiélago de Las Perlas are distant descendants of the Spaniards and their slaves. Forests once felled to build ships have grown back. Storms, termites and wood worms have destroyed the old Spanish structures, though a church and a stone dam on Isla Saboga testify to the Spaniards' presence.

Exploiting this buccaneer reputation, the popular US TV show *Survivor* set its reality TV series here in autumn 2003.

Nuestra Señora del Carmen　　FESTIVAL
(⊘ July 16) Island patroness Nuestra Señora del Carmen is honored with a seafaring procession. Seemingly everyone partakes in games, fire-breathing or dancing.

🍴 Sleeping & Eating

The island is a day trip from Panama City, though there is a handful of lodgings. Prices are high here for what you get. Stands on the beach sell food, but check the hygiene standards before committing.

Vereda Tropical Hotel　　HOTEL **$$**
(☑ 250-2154; www.hotelveredatropical.com; d with fan/air-con incl breakfast US$72/83; ❋ 🛜) Atop a hill with commanding views, this boutique hotel charms with tropical tones, mosaic tiles and rod-iron railings. The dining patio (mains US$9-16) has gaping views and Julio Iglesias serenading from the speakers. Service may be a little slow. It's about 100m up a winding path off the main road.

Cerrito Tropical　　B&B **$$**
(☑ 390-8999; www.cerritotropicalpanama.com; d/apt incl breakfast from US$88/110; ❋ 🛜) This smart Canadian and Dutch–owned B&B occupies a quiet nook atop a steep road. Rooms are stylish, some are more spacious and not all feature TVs. Meals ranging from burgers to seafood are available on a large shady deck

until 8pm. Extras include BBQs and picnic lunches. To get here, go right uphill at the end of Calle Francisco Pizarro.

It can also arrange tours such as fishing, hiking and whale-watching, and daytime packages with lunch and showers for nonguests.

Zoraida's Cool　　GUESTHOUSE **$$**
(☑ 6566-9250, 6471-1123; s/d/tr US$35/45/50) Overlooking the bay, this turquoise house is run by Rafael, the widow of Zoraida. Rooms are small and mattresses plastic-wrapped, but it's the cheapest around. The clincher is a hammock deck ideal for a snooze with Pacific views. Turn left as you exit the dock and walk for a few minutes until you see a sign leading you up the hill.

Donde Pope Si Hay　　PANAMANIAN **$**
(mains US$4-7; ⊘8am-8pm) A simple eatery serving fresh fish, cold green coconut water and *patacones* (plantains), there is nothing mysterious about Pope beyond its name.

❶ Information

Ferries from the Causeway in Panama City land at a pier near the north end of the island. As you exit the pier, the main beach is to your right. To your left, you'll see a narrow street that is the island's main road. From this point, the street meanders

5.2km before ending at the old US military installation atop the island's highest hill, Cerro El Vigia.

There are no cash machines on the island, so bring money. For more information, visit the excellent English-language site, www.taboga.panamanow.com.

ⓘ Getting There & Away

The scenic 45-minute boat trip out to Isla Taboga is part of the island's attraction. Ferries depart from Isla Naos on the Causeway in Panama City. The easiest way to reach the dock is by taxi (US$6). Note that the police check ferry passengers for drugs upon arrival.

Barcos Calypso (☑ 314-1730; round-trip US$12) Ferries depart from Panama City to Isla Taboga at 8:30am and 3pm Monday and Friday; 8:30am on Tuesday, Wednesday and Thursday; and 8am, 10:30am and 4pm on weekends. Returns from Isla Taboga are Monday to Thursday at 4pm; Friday at 9:30am and 4:30pm; and Saturday and Sunday at 9am, 3pm and 5pm.

National Tours (☑ 6615-1392, 6617-0450; round-trip US$14) This small fast ferry reaches Isla Taboga in under 30 minutes. Daily departures from Panama City's Balboa Yacht Club are at 8:30am and 3pm. It returns from Isla Taboga 9am and 4pm daily. There is no indoor seating, so it isn't ideal for bad weather. Phone service is poor, so buy tickets onsite.

Archipiélago de Las Perlas

Named for the large pearls found in its waters, the Pearl islands comprise 90 named islands and more than 100 unnamed islets, each surrounded by travel-magazine-worthy, white-sand beaches and turquoise waters. Home to the palatial mansions of the rich and powerful, Isla Contadora is the best known. In January 1979, after the Shah Mohammed Reza Pahlavi was ousted from Iran, he packed up his large fortune to Isla Contadora. It's one of 90 named islands in the Archipiélago de Las Perlas, any one of which is fit for a king – or a shah. Recent real estate developments, which would add luxury homes and resorts to areas with poor longtime settlements, are increasingly under fire.

History

Pearls brought the archipelago to the Old World's attention. Vasco Núñez de Balboa, within days of discovering the Pacific Ocean, learned of nearby islands rich with pearls from a local guide. Balboa was anxious to visit, but he was told that a hostile chief ruled them and cautiously decided to postpone. Nonetheless, Balboa named the archipelago

'Islas de Las Perlas,' and declared it and all its undiscovered riches Spanish property. The year was 1513, and Balboa vowed to return one day to kill the chief and claim his pearls for the king of Spain.

Before he could fulfill his vow, Spanish governor Pedro Arias de Ávila dispatched his cousin Gaspar de Morales to the islands for the pearls. Morales captured 20 chieftains and gave them to his dogs. The purportedly hostile chief, a man named Dites, saw the futility of resisting so instead presented Morales with a basket of large and lustrous pearls. With an appetite not sated, the Spanish took just two years to exterminate the indigenous population.

In 1517, the same year that Morales raided Las Perlas, Pedrarias (as the governor was often called) falsely charged Balboa with treason, and had him and four of his closest friends beheaded.

In the years that followed the Spaniards harvested the islands' oyster beds. Having slain the entire native population, they imported slaves from Africa to pearl dive. Their descendants live on the islands today.

ⓘ Information

Tourists mostly visit four islands: Isla Contadora, the most accessible, developed and visited island; Isla San José, the site of an exclusive resort; and neighboring Islas Casaya and Casayeta, frequented by pearl shoppers. Uninhabited isles offer ample opportunity for independent exploration, especially if you have a sense of adventure and the help of a local guide.

There are no ATMs, so bring sufficient cash.

Isla Contadora

POP 350

Isla Contadora (Counting House Island) was once the accounting center for pearls before they were shipped to Spain. While multimillionaires once made their island their refuge, a government crackdown on tax evasion is embittering the once-sweet deal. Many empty mansions are now rented to vacationers.

With frequent air and sea connections to Panama City, Isla Contadora is the only island in the archipelago with a developed tourist infrastructure. A prestigious destination, it caters to its wealthy residents and moneyed tourists from the mainland. In the low season it's more accessible for all. Beaches are spectacular, the snorkeling is world class, and the island is a great jumping-off point for independent exploration of the archipelago.

LA PEREGRINA

Archipiélago de Las Perlas has produced some of the world's finest pearls. However, none are as celebrated or well documented as the La Peregrina (the Pilgrim Pearl). Enormous and pear-shaped, this white pearl weighs 203.84 grains or 31 carats. Four hundred years ago, it earned the slave who discovered it his freedom.

In the mid-16th century the pearl was given to King Phillip II of Spain, who later presented it as a wedding gift to his wife, Queen Mary I of England. Later the British Marquis of Abercorn acquired it from the son of French emperor Napoleon III.

In 1969 actor Richard Burton purchased it for US$37,000 for his wife, Elizabeth Taylor. La Peregrina was briefly lost when Taylor's dog scampered away with the pearl in its mouth. In 2011 the pearl was auctioned as part of her estate, fetching $11 million dollars.

◉ Sights & Activities

Beaches

The island's 12 gold-sand beaches are virtually abandoned except during major holidays. Five are particularly lovely: Playa Larga, Playa de las Suecas, Playa Cacique, Playa Ejecutiva and Playa Galeón. Although spread around the island, all can be visited in as little as 20 minutes in a rented ATV (all-terrain vehicle).

Playa Larga (Long Beach) occupies a long stretch of coast. It's probably best not to swim here because of the water quality. Around the corner to the south is Playa de las Suecas (Swedish Women's Beach), where you can legally sunbathe in the buff. Continuing west 400m, you'll find Playa Cacique, a fairly large and unvisited beach ideal for a little peace and quiet. On the northern side of the island, Playa Ejecutiva (Executive Beach) is another intimate escape – the large house on the bluff to the east is where the shah of Iran once lived. Playa Galeón (Galleon Beach), to the northeast, is another good spot for snorkeling when the surf is small.

Snorkeling & Diving

The snorkeling and diving around Contadora is fantastic. In five nearby coral fields you can see schools of angelfish, damselfish, moray eels, parrot fish, puffer fish, butterfly fish, white-tip reef sharks and much more. Even off Playa Larga, the most popular of Isla Contadora's beaches, you can often spot sea turtles and manta rays.

The coral fields are found offshore from the eastern end of Playa de las Suecas, Punta Verde, near the southern end of Playa Larga, both ends of Playa Galeón and the western end of Playa Ejecutiva. There is also a lot of marine life among the rocks in front and east of Playa Roca.

Coral Dreams   DIVING
(☑ 6536-1776; www.coral-dreams.com) This small PADI-certified outfit with experienced instructors is located in front of the Contadora Airport. Snorkeling tours go to Isla Mogo (Survivor Island) for three hours (US$40); 50-minute dives cost US$75. They also do whale-watching (July to October) trips with a *hydrofono* to hear them and rent snorkel equipment.

Sailing & Boating

One of the best ways to appreciate the beauty and isolation of the Archipiélago de Las Perlas is to explore them on a chartered sailboat.

If you want to go island-hopping, you can contract a fishing-boat captain (US$35 per hour). Bring cash because they definitely do not take credit.

Las Perlas Sailing   BOATING
(☑ 6413-7128; www.lasperlassailing.es.tl) Offers day charters on a 38ft catamaran with snorkel equipment, lunch and drinks (US$100 per adult), in addition to other excursions. Those with previous sailing experience can rent one- and two-person sailboats as well as a range of motorboats. Sportfishing excursions are a high-end affair.

ATVs & Golf Carts

They're the only way to get around the island aside from walking. Rent them at the Hotel Punta Galeón Resort & Spa and some other hotels for US$30 per hour.

Whale-Watching

Migrating humpback whales can be seen from July to October. Fishermen take tourists out (and you might see whales while on another excursion), but it's worth going with a naturalist guide.

Isla Contadora

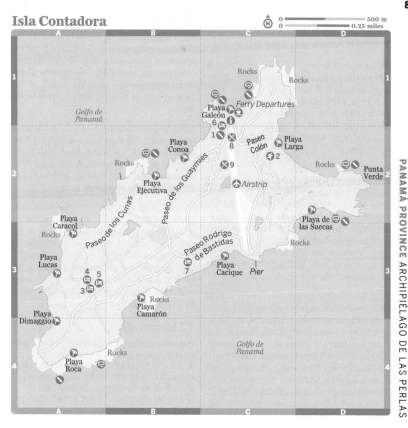

0 ————— 500 m
0 ————— 0.25 miles

Isla Contadora

Activities, Courses & Tours
1 Coral Dreams C2
2 Las Perlas Sailing C2

Sleeping
3 Casa del Sol A3
4 Contadora Island Inn A3
Gerald's Place .... (see 8)
5 Perla Real A3
6 Point C1
7 Villa Romántica B3

Eating
8 Gerald's Place C2
9 La Fonda de Clarita C2

Whale Watching Panama   TOUR
(☎ 6662-1946; www.whalewatchingpanama.com; ⊙ Jul-Oct) To see humpback whales and dolphin pods in the Pearl Islands, these day trips and multiday trips are led by expert biologist guides. Some trips have a spiritual focus (ie animal communication or shamanic whale-watching with yoga). The company adheres to international guidelines for whale-watching.

🛌 Sleeping

Many accommodations will meet you at the airport and provide transportation (via golf cart) to the resort or hotel.

★ Perla Real   B&B **$$**
(☎ 6513-9064, 250-4095; www.perlareal.com; d/ste/villa incl breakfast US$95/125/185; ❄ ⚡) Looking more Santa Fé than tropical, this comfortable inn is one of the best options on the island. Spacious rooms have French doors and prim decor with painted ceramic sinks, stenciled walls and soft cotton bedding. Ideal for long stays, suites come with an equipped kitchen and living space. The quiet residential area is a 10-minute walk from the beaches.

Friendly and well-managed, the B&B also loans kayaks and snorkel gear, and golf carts cost US$45 for 24 hours – a deal in these parts.

★ **Gerald's Place**   HOTEL **$$**

(☑250-4159; www.island-contadora.com; d incl breakfast US$84) With a good location near the ferry landing, Gerald's is central and comfortable, with consistently good service. Rooms may lack views, but are modern and well equipped, with flat-screen TVs and air-conditioning.

Contadora Island Inn   B&B **$$**

(☑6699-4614; www.contadoraislandinn.com; d incl breakfast US$95-130; 圈�) In a pleasant, large home with wooden decks, this B&B is relaxing and personalized. Modern rooms are ample and lovely, with tile floors, brocade bedspreads and French doors that fling open to catch the breeze; some have balconies and all have hot-water showers. The management also rents private homes.

Villa Romántica   INN **$$**

(☑250-4067; www.contadora-villa-romantica.com; d garden/sea view incl breakfast US$96/114, ste US$156; 圈�) Overlooking lovely Playa Cacique, this small inn caters to romantic escapes, though the vibe is more 'Vegas Weekend' than 'Hawaiian Honeymoon.' Shell walls, gold mirrors and Roman columns with your waterbed? Check. The restaurant (mains US$7.50 to US$20) serves sandwiches, pastas and seafood. Welcome cocktail included. It's closed through October.

Casa del Sol   INN **$$**

(☑250-4212, 6518-8284; www.panama-isla-contadora.com; s/d incl breakfast US$77/88; 圈�) Located in a residential neighborhood, this pleasant inn features small rooms where your continental breakfast is served. The grounds are lovely but there is no living-room space, making it a little cramped if you are spending time in. Also rents houses and has good ATV rental prices.

Point   HOTEL **$$$**

(☑836-5434; www.cunadevida.com; d US$174; 圈@圈) On a dramatic cliff above Playa Galeón, this is the island's only 'resort.' Now under new management and pending renovation, the 48 rooms are still small for the price tag. A wooden boardwalk leads to the swimming pool, a spa and bar and restaurants. Food quality may depend on how recently the supply ship has visited.

✖ Eating

Isla Contadora's poor reputation for dining is due to sporadic food shipments from the mainland that results in poor variety. Even fresh fish can also be hard to come by. Three small supermarkets serve the island. At the time of writing, new restaurants were in the works.

La Fonda de Clarita   PANAMANIAN **$**

(mains US$5; ☉6:45am-2pm & 6-8:30pm) This outdoor eatery has plain, good food that's popular with the locals. Fish and chips is on the menu, but lunch specials such as chicken with rice and lentils are bountiful.

Gerald's Place   INTERNATIONAL **$$**

(mains US$8-20; ☉7:30am-10am, noon-3pm & 6-11pm; �) This thatched restaurant attached to the hotel of the same name has the best food on the island. It's certainly where you would go for a little ambience, though it's still casual. Options include good pizzas and seafood with vegetable sides, all cooked by a friendly German.

ℹ Information

Welcome Center (☑6544-8962; ☉8am-7pm) Privately run, this is the only place for general info. It also books boat tours (fee US$10), rents kayaks and golf carts (both US$25 per hour), and sells the only espresso on the island.
ULAPS Health Clinic (☑250-4209; ☉24hr) A short walk from the airstrip. If closed, visit the house at the back for emergencies.

ℹ Getting There & Away

Air Panama (☑316-9000; www.airpanama.com) Direct flights from Panama City to Isla Contadora (round-trip US$140, 20 minutes). Has two daily departures on weekdays and multiple departures on weekends.
Sea Las Perlas (☑391-1424; www.sealasperlas.com; one-way adult/child US$45/35) Catamaran ferry service (one hour 40 minutes) leaves from Balboa Yacht Club on the Panama City Causeway for Isla Contadora daily at 8am, returning at 3pm. There's an 11am departure on Sunday.

ℹ Getting Around

Because the island is only about a square kilometer in size, there are no taxis. It's easy to walk everywhere, but it's hilly. Most tourist facilities are on the northern side of the island, within walking distance of the airstrip. Hotels shuttle guests to and from the airport via golf cart, and there is no shortage of ATVs for rent.

Isla San José

Home to the most exclusive resort in the Pearl islands, Isla San José has a sinister history as a US chemical-weapons testing ground. During a 2001 inspection, the entire island was placed under temporary quarantine following the recovery of unexploded ordnance, which led to a tiff between Panama and the US over who should pick up the cleaning bill.

Most of the 45.3-sq-km island is covered in a bank of rainforest networked by all-weather roads installed by the US military decades ago. Beyond the roads, the only development on the island is the cliffside resort.

If you wanted to really get away, **Hacienda del Mar** (☑ 269-6634, in Panama City 269-6613; www.haciendadelmar.net; cabin from US$375; ❄) has 37 tan-sand beaches, nine year-round rivers and seven accessible waterfalls all to itself. Each stand-alone luxury cabin overflows with amenities, and has views to a picture-perfect sweep of beach. Plunge into the laundry list of tours or just soak up your exclusive slice of paradise.

Prices fall to roughly half in low season. Flights between Panama City and Isla San José (US$135 round-trip) are arranged through Hacienda del Mar. Leave a few days between your visit and international flights, as there can be weather delays.

OFF THE BEATEN TRACK

ISLA SABOGA

Isla Saboga has been populated for centuries (its church is the oldest in Panama), though the 400-resident population, once all pearl divers, has struggled with poverty. **Turismo Comunitario Saboga** (☑ 391-3048; islandecotour@gmail.com), a new community tourism initiative, is hoping to buoy this old Afro-Pacific culture with guided visits by locals that include hiking jungle paths, snorkeling and swimming. Foundation Almanaque Azul pioneered the project. Boatman Pedro does transfers (US$40 round-trip for six passengers) from Isla Contadora. Guests can stay at **Casa de Fermina** (US$25 per room), a four-room cement dwelling in the middle of the hilltop village. Installations are basic but it can be a very interesting experience – and sharp contrast – to the fantasy island next door.

Islas Casaya & Casayeta

Oysters are still harvested on the archipelago, and their pearls are just as legendary as they were when Balboa first arrived. Although pearls are sometimes offered for sale on other islands, the best places to shop for them are Isla Casaya and neighboring Isla Casayeta, about 12km to the south of Contadora.

When you're looking at pearls, you should know that pearl sellers tend to keep their goods in oil, so that they'll have a lovely shine when presented – always dry the pearl that intrigues you before you buy. Prices are generally very reasonable, and there's always room for bargaining.

Accommodations on either Isla Contadora or San José can arrange transportation to the pearl shops on Islas Casaya and Casayeta.

PACIFIC COAST

Every weekend, thousands of stressed-out Panama City residents hop into their cars or board buses and head west on the Interamericana – their destination: the beach.

La Chorrera

POP 60,000

One of the first major towns you hit along the Interamericana is La Chorrera, famous throughout Panama for its *chicheme* (nonalcoholic drink made from milk, mashed sweet corn, cinnamon and vanilla). **La Feria de La Chorrera**, held in late January or early February, includes parades, a rodeo, the odd cockfight or two, and drum dances, which have their origin in African music brought by slaves. Join what looks like a Friday bank line at **El Chichemito** (cnr Calles L Oeste & 26 Norte) to sample the homemade *chicheme* (US$0.25). It goes nicely with a *boyo chorrenano* (tamale filled with marinated chicken and spice).

East- and west-bound buses stop at the gas station on the Interamericana. Buses for Panama City (US$1.25, one hour) leave every 15 minutes – take the express to avoid frequent stops.

Capira

Quesos Chela (Interamericana; ☺ 10am-5pm Mon-Sat) is located 57km from Panama City in the nondescript townstron of Capira. This famous cheese shop is an institution that few Panamanian drivers can pass without stopping. It's a plain shop that usually has piping-hot fresh cheese (string, mozzarella, farmers, ricotta) and homemade meat empanadas for sale. The cheese shop is right next door to a gas station and a supermarket on the right-hand side of the road if you're heading west.

Parque Nacional y Reserva Biológica Altos de Campana

This obscure and relatively unknown national park is a favorite for bird-watchers. Common sightings include the scale-crested pygmy-tyrant, orange-bellied trogon and chestnut-capped brush-finch; rare avians including the slaty antwren, the white-tipped sicklebill and the purplish-backed quail-dove are occasionally spotted here.

This park requires at least several hours to be appreciated because it's best viewed on foot. Starting at the road's end, beyond the microwave tower, trails will take you into some lovely forest, which is on the much greener Atlantic slope. The difference between the deforested Pacific and the lush Atlantic slopes is nowhere more evident.

The easy-to-miss turnoff for this national park is 25km southwest of La Chorrera, on the western side of the Interamericana. It's at the top of a steep and windy section of the Interamericana known locally as the Loma Campana. From the turnoff, a rocky road winds 4.6km to an **ANAM ranger station** (admission US$5; campsite per night US$5) at the entrance to the park, which is located on Cerro Campana; pay fees here. Camping is allowed; there is water but no facilities.

No buses go up the road leading to the park. You pretty much need to have your own vehicle, rely on the services of a guide company or do some rather serious hiking to get in. However, getting to the turnoff for the park is easy. Virtually any bus using that section of the Interamericana will drop you there – there's a bus stop beside the turnoff. Getting picked up isn't a problem either as there are many buses that pass by the turnoff during daylight hours.

SURFING IN PANAMÁ PROVINCE

The beaches to the southwest of the capital are a popular destination for Panamanian surfers, especially since they're easy to access and offer relatively consistent surf year-round. The following list will help you get started, though don't be afraid to ask local surfers to let you in on their hidden spots.

Playa Malibú Near Gorgona. Sand-bottom right and left break. Best during medium to low tide. Consistent, good tubes and long rides when there is a strong swell.

Playa Serena In Coronado, past the security gate. Right point break with good tubes. Long rides when there is a strong swell.

Frente de Teta Rock-sand-bottom break at the mouth of the Río Teta. Long lefts at low tide, and rights and lefts at medium to high tide.

Punta Teta Point break over rocks to the south of the Río Teta mouth. Lefts and rights with good tubes, especially at medium tide going up.

Rinconcito Rock-bottom point south of Punta Teta with a long, right break on a good swell. Named after California's famous Rincón break.

Frente Palmar South of San Carlos. Beach break, partial rock bottom that is popular with beginners.

Punta El Palmar South of San Carlos. Rock-bottom point break. Right peeling waves at medium to high tide when there is a good swell.

Hawaiisito South of San Carlos. Rock-bottom point break. Lefts at full high tide. Closes out if there is a strong swell.

Frente Río Mar Somewhat rocky beach break in front of Río Mar. Rights and lefts at medium to high tide.

Punta Río Mar South of the Río Mar, near jutting rocks. Walk and paddle at low tide. Rights best. Breaks only at low tide.

Punta Chame

POP 390

Just before the Interamericana reaches the coastline, there is a turnoff immediately east of Bejuco, which leads to the tiny sliver of a peninsula known as Punta Chame. The road out to the sea winds past rolling hills before opening up to flat land that consists mainly of shrimp farms and mangroves. The brackish water makes farming near impossible, though the environment here is unique to this region, and well worth the diversion.

Punta Chame, a one-road town on a long, 300m-wide peninsula, is getting more vacation homes and weekenders since the road in was paved. To the north of the peninsula, a scenic but muddy bay is popular with windsurfers and kitesurfers from December to April, during trade wind season. Outside of those months wakeboarding is popular. Beaches at Playa Chame on the east coast of the peninsula have lovely tan sand and a wilderness backdrop. The area is notorious for stingrays, so swim with caution and shuffle your feet while walking out.

Guests adore Hostal Casa Amarilla (www.hostalcasaamarilla.com; d from US$77, tr with shared bathroom from US$44; ✳️ 🛜 ✉️), a French-run B&B also serving exquisite French and Mediterranean cuisine (not to mention homemade pastries) in an open-air restaurant (three-course dinner US$13). Rooms vary and include cute yellow cabins and rustic bamboo lodgings with mosquito nets over the beds.

Panama's first extreme sports resort, Nitro City (📞 202-6875, 223-1747; www.nitrocitypanama.com; d/ste incl breakfast from US$259/360; adult/child day-pass US$30/15; P 🛜 ✉️) is pretty much what you would expect in a beach haven bankrolled by energy drinks. Stylish lodgings have sleek decor, stone sinks and bamboo ceilings; pro suites boast their own outdoor hot tub. But the real draw is a circus of adrenaline offerings, from a skate park to mountain and motorbike courses, wakeboarding and kitesurfing (lessons available). Tamer offerings include volleyball and soccer areas as well as a stunning pool replete with island. There's also game and video rooms. Hyperactive teens do well here, and young Panama City weekenders don't seem to mind the US$18 burgers with live rasta-rock backbeat. Still, the management is attentive and there's really nothing else of its kind around. On weekdays, lodging prices fall by nearly half.

To get to Punta Chame from the Interamericana, catch a bus at the stop at the Punta Chame turnoff at Bejuco – a bus to the point (US$1.75) leaves hourly from 6:30am to 5:30pm daily.

Pacific Coast Beaches

Starting just south of the town of Chame and continuing along the Pacific coast for the next 40km are dozens of beautiful beaches that are popular weekend retreats for Panama City residents. About half of these beaches are in Panamá Province, while the remainder are in Coclé Province.

Most beaches can be reached by local bus or taxi at the turnoffs from the Interamericana.

Gorgona

Six kilometers southwest of the turnoff for Punta Chame is the turnoff for Gorgona, a small ocean-side community that fronts a curving beach of mostly black sand. Gorgona is best accessed by car. Bring your sandals – it gets very hot.

For a leisurely bite, try La Ruina (📞 240-5126; www.laruinatavern.com; mains US$5-12; ⏱️ noon-midnight Thu-Sun), which serves stem glasses of *ceviche* (seafood marinated in lemon or lime juice, garlic and seasonings) and authentic chicken Bocatoreño-style, curried with coconut rice. You can sit outside at the leatherette booths and bide the wait chatting with the owner or tapping along to the country tunes. It's run by a friendly US army retiree and his Panamanian wife. Check for live rock weekend nights.

Playa Coronado

Four kilometers southwest of the turnoff for Gorgona is the turnoff for Playa Coronado, an affluent beachside community that is a haven for water sport lovers. A newly built mall and hospital confirms its growing status. The salt-and-pepper beach here is one of the most developed strips of sand along the coast, extremely popular with Panama City denizens on the up and up. For a chiller approach, check out the bird-watching trail near the village gate.

If you're looking to live it up in unchecked luxury, then look no further than the Coronado Golf & Beach Resort (📞 264-3164; www.coronadoresort.com; d from US$149; P ✳️ @ ✉️), the granddaddy of Pacific coast resorts.

Pacific Coast Beaches

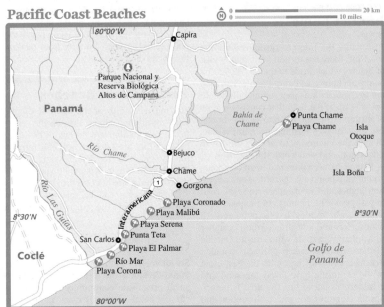

With 78 amenity-laden rooms, a top-notch beachside golf course, swimming pools, tennis courts, equestrian center, casino, day spa, gym, marina and a whole slew of bars and restaurants, you may not be able to find the time to actually visit the beach. Kids get their own miniclub where they can play Wii. Even if you're not staying here, the town's nightlife revolves around the hotel, so dress smart and stop by the attached nightclub.

The recommended **El Litoral B&B** (☑240-1474; www.litoralpanama.com; d incl breakfast US$95; ❄@🖘🌊) is a cute yellow house with smart air-conditioned rooms. The kicker is a sumptuous patio breakfast with choices like cappuccino, crepes, waffles and juice. The lovely French-speaking owner offers yoga and can arrange Spanish classes or kitesurfing. It's in front of Coronado Golf & Beach Resort.

A good bet for lunch and dinner, chef-run **El Rincon del Chef** (☑345-2072; mains $7-16; ⊙1-9pm Tue-Sun, 9am-9pm Fri-Sat) serves grilled meats, pastas and Panamanian classics. It's located 300m from the Interamericana on the right.

Playa El Palmar

Ten kilometers west of the Playa Coronado is the turnoff for this lovely white-sand beach, which is located by the village of San Carlos.

Although much less developed than Coronado, El Palmar is still popular with week-ending families from the capital, but the atmosphere is more low-key.

The most stylish digs is **Manglar Lodge** (☑345-4014, 240-8970; d US$110; ❄🖘), professionally run by surfer Ivan. Outdoor showers help you rinse off the sand, there are pleasant manicured grounds and ample rooms with contemporary styles. It's at the end of the road at the mouth of the river.

The wave-front **Palmar Surf Camp** (☑240-8004; campsite per person US$10, d/q/ste US$70/90/130; P❄🖘) aims at surfers or those who want to learn the ropes. Motel-style rooms feature cool murals, cable TV and free coffee. Check on midweek discounts. Surf lessons are US$35 for three hours; you can also rent kayaks. It's a US$2 taxi from the Interamericana.

Another option for lessons, **Panama Surf School** (☑6673-0820; www.panamasurfschool.com; Calle 4ta Sur s/n) is run by a well-known local surfer. Some English is spoken and lessons run US$40 for two hours, including board. There may be dorm rooms available next door.

At the turnoff for El Palmar, **Carlitos** (Interamericana; pizzas US$4-7) cooks Argentine-style empanadas and thin-crust pizzas.

Río Mar

Just five minutes up the road from Playa El Palmar, Río Mar is a small rocky inlet where a few new highrises cast a shadow. A right turn on the road in, **Río Mar Surf Camp** (☑ 345-4010; www.riomarsurf.com; d/q US$50/70; ❋ 🕑 ≋) offers bargain-rate rooms and surf lessons. Rooms are pleasant and sit on immaculate green grounds with a pea-sized pool. There is no kitchen but visiting surfers get refrigerator and grill access for feeding purposes. Lessons are US$20 per hour and boards rent for US$15 to US$35 per day. Call ahead to reserve (weekends are busier), since it seems the management tucks out for the waves now and then, leaving a grumpy caretaker.

NORTHEAST PANAMÁ PROVINCE

Heading toward the Darién and the Comarca de Kuna Yala, there are some excellent attractions still within an easy day trip from Panama City. Lago Bayano has boating, bird-watching and caving, while Narganá and its surrounding area has great rainforest trails.

Área Silvestre de Narganá

Just before you reach the town of El Llano on the road to the Darién, you'll see the turnoff for Cartí, a small town inside the **Área Silvestre de Narganá** (admission US$6) wildlife reserve. This reserve was created by the Kuna, primarily to try to keep squatters from settling on their land. However, it consists of 960 sq km of species-rich primary forest, a perfect choice for conservation.

The road into the reserve is pretty rough, and you'll need a 4WD with a strong engine and plenty of clearance. However, it's worth the trip in, especially if you're a bird-watcher – this is the best place in Panama to spot the speckled antshrike, the black-headed ant thrush and the black-crowned antpitta.

🛏 Sleeping

⭐ **Burbayar Lodge**   LODGE **$$$**
(☑ 6400-8972; www.burbayar.com; per person incl 3 meals & tours first night US$190, then US$155; Ⓟ) 🍴 Among Panama's best jungle retreats, this ecologically minded, low-impact lodge is located in an enchanted hillside setting. The love child of a Spanish traveler who came to Panama and stayed, it's affectionately crafted from reused wood and recycled materials, with terraced lookouts and a quirky open-air chapel. Lodging is in simple cabins with mountain views and river stone showers.

All guests get a guide to explore options like visiting Emberá communities, hiking or bird-watching. Best of all, the staff are contagiously enthusiastic. On the Mesoamerican Biological Corridor, the lodge sits surrounded by primary and secondary forest with waterfalls, caverns and trails. One of the last great frog reserves, the area boasts more than 30 species. Rare birds include the speckled antshrike, and species easy to spot include toucans, as well as howler monkeys, Geoffrey's tamarin, white-faced tamarin monkeys and sloths. Also around but harder to spot are jaguars, pumas, ocelots, margays and tapirs.

Burbayar works with local schools and local communities. The lodge recycles all trash, uses solar power and filters water. A tiny generator provides some electricity, but gas lanterns and candles lend a rustic appeal. Booking in advance is essential. If you don't have your own car, note that the price includes round-trip transportation from Panama City (leaving at 8am and returning the following afternoon at 5pm). It's on the road to Cartí at the 17km mark, roughly 96km from Panama City and 24km from Cartí.

Lago Bayano

Created when the Río Bayano was dammed in 1976, the artificial **Lago Bayano** nonetheless is a great nature excursion. The lake takes its name from Bayano, the man who led the largest slave revolt of 16th-century Panama. The area, with little development and lots of waterbirds, is home to Emberá, Wounaan and Kuna communities.

On the south side of the lake, visiting the **Bayano Caves** is an excellent day trip. Cavers wade up Río Tigre through a sculpted Paleolithic cave that's 850m long, full of bats and amphibians. At times it's necessary to wade or swim, depending on water levels. Exploring the cave requires round-trip boat transportation, a guide, headlamps and helmets.

Guided tours are available through Panama City tour agencies or Kuna guide **Igua Jiménez** (☑ 6700-3512; iguat28@yahoo.com); tours usually include a visit to a nearby indigenous community as well. It's located 1½ hours east of Panama City via the Interamericana.

Coclé Province

POP 233,700 / AREA 6075 SQ KM / ELEV 1626M

Best Places to Eat

➡ Kacos (p104)

➡ Pipa's (p102)

➡ Ederra (p104)

➡ Xoko (p101)

➡ La Casa de Lourdes (p100)

Best Places to Stay

➡ Posada Cerro La Vieja (p107)

➡ Togo B&B (p102)

➡ Golden Frog Inn (p98)

➡ Los Mandarinos (p99)

➡ Park Eden (p99)

Why Go?

Coclé – land of sugar, salt and presidents. More sugar has been refined in this province, more salt has been produced here, and more Panamanian presidents have been born in Coclé than in any other province. These are facts in which the people of Coclé take great pride, but the province isn't just about political legacies and table condiments.

Coclé boasts a medley of landscapes from abandoned coastlines to towering cloud forests, with vast agricultural and pastoral land in between. Edging along the Pacific Ocean, the province is home to beaches attracting weekend warriors from Panama City. Edging along the highlands, the gorgeously set mountain town of El Valle is a popular retreat from the big city. The bustling regional capital of Penonomé proves the best place to pick up an authentic panama hat.

When to Go

➡ **Dec–Apr** High season on the Pacific coast means a party scene. Visits to the sugar refinery can be made from mid-January. A wild Carnaval takes place at the tail end of this season in Penonomé.

➡ **Jul–Oct** Rainy season means muddy trails but highland waterfalls with the full faucet flowing; it's also the only time to see Panama's national flower, the ghost orchid, in bloom.

➡ **Oct–Dec** Bring on the noise. Anton's rowdy festival Toro Guapo in October is followed by weeks of Fiestas Patrias (national holidays) in November and celebrations of Penonomé's patron saint in early December.

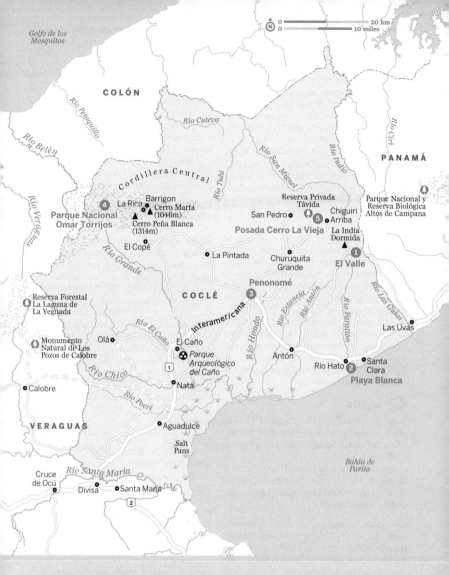

Coclé Province Highlights

① Hike to waterfalls, dine in colonial opulence and cruise the handicrafts market in the lovely highland retreat of **El Valle** (p94)

② Feast seaside on a whole fresh fish with *patacones* before cruising the endless sands around beach town **Playa Blanca** (p101)

③ Shop for an authentic panama hat or get caught up in the mayhem of a festival in the regional capital of **Penonomé** (p102)

④ Hike through dense rainforest and camp in utter solitude in the little-known **Parque Nacional Omar Torrijos** (p107)

⑤ Enjoy a wild panorama of misty peaks and spa pampering at **Posada Cerro La Vieja** (p107)

El Valle

POP 5700

Officially known as El Valle de Antón, this picturesque town is nestled in the crater of a giant extinct volcano, and ringed by verdant forests and jagged peaks. Like Boquete, El Valle is a popular weekend getaway for urbanites in need of a little fresh air and scenery. With an extensive network of trails, it's a superb place for walking, hiking or horseback riding. Nearby forests offer excellent bird-watching, and the valleys of El Valle are home to an impressive set of waterfalls as well as some rare golden frogs.

History

Three million years ago, this volcano erupted with such force that it blew off its top, creating a crater 5km across – one of the largest in the Americas. In the eons that followed, the crater gradually filled with rainwater to create a large lake. However, through erosion or collapse, a breach opened at the present site of Chorro de Las Mozas and the entire lake drained. The resulting flood created an extensive network of waterways, which attracted indigenous populations to the area. Their early petroglyphs can still be seen throughout the valley.

◉ Sights

Some of the biggest attractions of El Valle are the handful of waterfalls that cascade down the surrounding hillsides into the valley floor.

Follow Av Central through town until it branches. The branch to the right – Calle del Macho – leads to the canopy tour, a waterfall and some petroglyphs.

Chorro de las Mozas   WATERFALL

(Young Women's Falls) The most accessible of the waterfalls around El Valle is the Chorro de las Mozas, which is located about 1km outside the southwest corner of town. This is the original site where the prehistoric lake breached to form these scenic cascades. Though the access is not well marked, these winding cascades with deep pools are gorgeous. It's popular with locals enjoying El Valle's year-round, near-perfect spring weather.

Chorro El Macho   WATERFALL

(Manly Falls; admission US$3.60; ⊙dawn-dusk) The most famous waterfall in the El Valle area is the 85m-high Chorro El Macho, which is located a few kilometers north of town near the entrance to the canopy tour. As its somewhat humorous name implies, this towering waterfall is more dramatic than its dainty counterpart, and makes for some excellent photographs. Here, below the falls, you'll find a large swimming pool made of rocks, surrounded by rainforest and fed by river water. There is also a series of short hiking trails that wind into the surrounding forest.

For an unforgettable aerial view of El Macho, El Valle's famed canopy tour is a truly hair-raising experience.

La Piedra Pintada   ROCK PAINTINGS

(Colored Stone; admission US$1.50) Located in the northwestern corner of the valley, La Piedra Pintada is a huge boulder adorned with pre-Columbian carvings. Locals often fill in the grooves of the petroglyphs with chalk to facilitate their viewing, but their meaning isn't clearer. That doesn't prevent children from giving their interpretation of the petroglyphs for US$2 (in Spanish only).

The trail to the rock is well worn and easy to do without a guide. But due to thefts from vehicles left near the trail entrance, it's best to come by bus even if you've got your own wheels. The site can be reached by a yellow school bus with 'Pintada' above the windshield. It passes along Av Central every 30 minutes, from 6am to 7pm (US$0.25 one way).

El Níspero   ZOO

(☑983-6142; adult/child US$3/2; ⊙7am-5pm) About 1km north of Av Central is a zoo named El Níspero. If you're sensitive to caged animals, you should probably skip this one. With that said, El Níspero is one of the best places for seeing Panama's *ranas doradas* (golden frogs). These endangered amphibians are unbelievably striking in color, and extremely photogenic.

They are also one of Panama's most important cultural symbols, and have long been revered by the indigenous peoples of the country. Unfortunately, they are extremely sensitive to human intrusion and climate change so, as their numbers continue to deplete, it's increasingly unlikely that you'll see them in the wild.

El Valle Amphibian
Conservation Center   WILDLIFE RESERVE

(EVACC; www.fightforthefrogs.com/valle.html) More a conservation center than a zoo, the excellent El Valle Amphibian Conservation Center was created in conjunction with the Houston Zoo to save amphibians from a deadly virus currently threatening them around the world. Run by a dedicated team of conservationists, the center exhibits native Panamanian species and, in particular, the golden frog.

The research area is private and devoted to quarantine, treatment and captive breeding efforts. It is located in the grounds of El Níspero.

Pozos Termales   HOT SPRINGS
(Thermal Baths; Calle los Pozos; admission US$2.25; ☉8am-5pm) Pozos Termales is the perfect place to soak the afternoon away. This renovated complex features a series of pools with varying temperatures and supposed curative properties. Post-bath, there is a bucket for applying healing mud to your skin. The next step is to take the requisite photo or two, and then head to the showers.

It's a 10-minute walk from town, located on the west side in a remote, forested area (follow the signs).

Museo de El Valle   MUSEUM
(Av Central; admission US$0.75; ☉10am-2pm Sat & Sun) This museum contains exhibits of petroglyphs and ceramics left by the indigenous peoples who lived in the area hundreds of years ago. There is also some religious art (the museum is owned by the church next door), mostly statues of Christ and the Virgin, as well as some historical

and geological information on El Valle's volcano.

It's on the eastern side of El Valle's conspicuous church.

Square-Trunked Trees   OUTDOORS
(Calle Club Campestre; suggested donation US$2) El Valle's peculiar *arboles cuadrados* (square-trunked trees) can be found directly behind the Hotel Campestre. After a short 10-minute hike through the forest, you'll come across a thicket of trees that aren't exactly round, but they're not exactly square, either. Much local pride is invested in the concept of these geometric formations.

Aprovaca Orquídeas   GARDEN
(☏983-6472; admission US$2; ☉9am-4pm) For the best selection of *orquídeas* (orchids) in the area, visit this pleasant garden. Some 32 volunteers work to maintain the lovely flowers inside the greenhouse and the grounds, and they welcome visitors to show off the 96 varieties of orchids cultivated – it's well worth a visit. Look for the 'Orquídeas' sign on the way into town.

🏃 Activities

Hiking

Ringed by 1000m-tall mountains, and surrounded by humid cloud forest, El Valle is a hiker's paradise. From the town center an extensive network of trails radiates out into the valley and up into the hills, and there

GOLDEN FROG REFUGE

A symbol of good fortune since pre-Columbian times, the golden frog is also an icon of Panama's incredible wildlife. Then one day these already rare frogs started to disappear. It turned out that kitrid, a deadly microscopic fungus, was the culprit. The problem was not just local. The fungus has reached epidemic levels on five continents, decimating the population of not only frogs but also toads and salamanders.

The fungus enters the animals by infecting their skin cells. Since kitrid kills over 90% of the creatures that it comes into contact with, it would seem that there's little to be done. But scientists have found that, while it cannot be prevented in the wild, kitrid is effectively treated in captivity.

The disease has brought these creatures dangerously close to extinction. With collaboration from the Houston Zoo, the El Valle Amphibian Conservation Center set about collecting all the frogs they could find to protect those that weren't already infected and heal those that were. It was the biggest amphibian rescue mission in anyone's memory.

At first the frogs were homeless, since a research center was yet to be constructed. Luckily, Hotel Campestre in El Valle volunteered to house them in the meantime (imagine the room-service bills). The hotel is now under new management and the amphibians have their own home, where scientists and volunteers work around the clock taking care of them and researching their condition.

EVACC features educational exhibits and houses 40 species.

El Valle

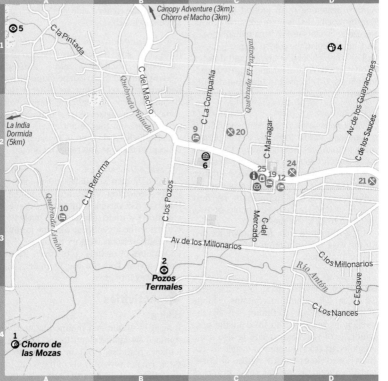

El Valle

Top Sights
1	Chorro de las Mozas	A4
2	Pozos Termales	B3

Sights
3	Aprovaca Orquídeas	E3
4	El Níspero	D1
	El Valle Amphibian Conservation Center	(see 4)
5	La Piedra Pintada	A1
6	Museo de El Valle	C2
	Square-Trunked Trees	(see 14)

Activities, Courses & Tours
7	Alquiler de Caballos	F2
8	Panama Explorer Club	F2

Sleeping
9	Anton Valley Hotel	C2
10	Cabañas Potosí	A3
11	Crater Valley Resort & Adventure Spa	F3
12	Don Pepe	C2

13	Golden Frog Inn	F1
14	Hotel Campestre	F1
15	Hotel y Restaurante Los Capitanes	E2
16	La Casa de Juan	E3
	La Casa de Lourdes	(see 22)
17	Los Mandarinos	E1
18	Park Eden	E4
19	Residencial El Valle	C2
	Santa Librada	(see 24)

Eating
	Bruschetta	(see 9)
20	Buon Appetito	C2
21	El Valle Gourmet & Coffee Shop	D2
	Hotel y Restaurante Los Capitanes	(see 15)
22	La Casa de Lourdes	E1
23	Pinocchio's	F2
24	Restaurante Santa Librada	D2

Shopping
25	Mercado de Artensanía	C2

independently, trails are not always clearly marked, and it is recommended that you seek out local advice before hitting the trails.

Canopy Tours

For the uninitiated, a canopy tour consists of a series of platforms anchored into the forest canopy that are connected by zip lines. Originally used by biologists to study the rainforest canopy, today they function primarily as adrenaline fixes.

Canopy Adventure ADVENTURE SPORTS
(in El Valle 983-6547, in Panama City 612-9176; canopy ride US$54; 8am-4pm) Canopy Adventure uses cable zip lines to take harnessed riders whizzing through the rainforest dozens of meters above the jungle floor. You'll ride from one platform to another (there are four in all), at times gliding over Chorro El Macho.

Bird-Watching

The forests around El Valle offer numerous opportunities for bird-watching, especially if you're looking for hummingbirds – commonly spotted species include the green hermit, the violet-headed hummingbird and the white-tailed emerald.

Rates for a bilingual naturalist guide are around US$60 per person per day.

Horseback Riding

Alquiler de Caballos HORSEBACK RIDING
(646-5813; Calle El Hato; horse rental per hr US$12) The stable here has over 30 horses, which make for some fine transportation to explore the nearby mountains. Guides speak Spanish only. Call ahead for free transport from your hotel.

Tours

Panama Explorer Club ADVENTURE TOUR
(983-6939; www.crater-valley.com) Based at Crater Valley Resort, the Panama Explorer Club is an adventure tourism outfit that offers a wide range of activities. Available tours billed per person include hiking La India Dormida (US$20, three to four hours), tree climbing (US$25, two hours), class III river rafting (US$88) and mountain-biking tours (from US$12.50 per hour). It's kid-friendly, with a ropes course too.

Mario Urriola ADVENTURE TOUR
(6569-2676; serpentariomaravillastropicales@hotmail.com) Mario is a reputable, locally based naturalist guide specializing in birding and wildlife-watching.

are possibilities for anything from short day hikes to overnight excursions.

Serious trekkers should consider excursions to the tops of Cerro Cara Coral, Cerro Gaital and Cerro Pajita to the north, Cerro Guacamayo to the south, and Cerro Tagua to the east.

It's also possible to make an ascent to the top of La India Dormida, where there are well-defined, safe trails. In local myth, the 'Sleeping Indian' was a local maiden who fell in love with a conquistador. After her father refused to allow their marriage she took her own life. She was buried in the hills, which eventually took the shape of the mountain rising over the valley. Legend has it that she is awaiting the day when her forbidden love can be pursued.

For the most part, the valley floor has been cleared for agricultural and pastoral land, though the peaks remain covered in dense forest. Although it is possible to hike

THE HOLY GHOST ORCHID

While hiking though the forests around El Valle, be sure to look for Panama's national flower, a terrestrial orchid known as the *flor del espiritu santo*, the 'holy ghost orchid.' This stunner, named by Spanish missionaries during the colonial era, is perfectly shaped like a red-spotted dove emerging from ivory petals.

The flower is most commonly found along the forest floor beside a trail, but it also grows on the branches of large trees. The orchid blooms from July to October, and has an unforgettable aroma. Do not pick them as the species is threatened by over-harvesting.

🛏 Sleeping

Although reservations are generally not necessary, be advised that El Valle can get busy on weekends and on national holidays as urban dwellers flee the capital and head for the hills.

Due to the chilly climate, all of the rooms in El Valle have hot-water showers.

Santa Librada GUESTHOUSE $

(☑ 6591-9135; Av Central; d US$20-35) Behind the popular restaurant, a passageway leads to three basic but clean doubles, a much-needed value option for couples.

La Casa de Juan GUESTHOUSE $

(☑ 6807-1651, 6453-9775; www.lacasadejuanpanama.blogspot.com; Calle Cocorron No 4; camping per tent US$10, dm/s/d US$10/15/20; 🛜) This bare-bones Sanford and Son setup brims with the clutter of ATV, outdoor weight-lifting equipment and wagon wheels, but it is the sole hostel-style option that's passable. Though decrepit, the house is clean and Señor Juan is a social host also offering guided walks.

★ Golden Frog Inn INN $$

(☑ 983-6117; www.goldenfroginn.com; ste incl breakfast US$70-140; 🅿 ❄ 🛜 🏊) Attentive and relaxing, this deluxe American-owned lodge is the perfect place to laze after a long day of play. Start with the swimming pool and migrate to the open-air living spaces and library. The expansive grounds include orchids and a cinnamon tree; adjoining trails mean you can hike right out the door. Massages are organized onsite.

Rooms come equipped with kitchens stocked with fresh fruit and coffee. From Calle Central, turn right on Calle El Hato and follow the signs to the inn.

Residencial El Valle HOTEL $$

(☑ 983-6536; www.hotelresidencialelvalle.com; Av Central; d/tr/q US$55/66/83; 🅿 🛜) Visitors become loyalists, given the high level of service offered at this motel-style lodging. This long-standing hotel offers clean no-fuss rooms and has a nice roof deck and bike rentals. Attached is a popular restaurant.

Don Pepe HOTEL $$

(☑ 983-6425; www.hoteldonpepe.com.pa; Av Central; s/d/tr US$39/50/65; 🅿 🛜) The renovated Don Pepe offers bright rooms (those on the 3rd floor are best) with tiled bathrooms, firm mattresses and craftsy touches. A sprawling roof deck with hammocks is great for a siesta or stargazing. There's also wi-fi and an onsite internet cafe.

Hotel Campestre HOTEL $$

(☑ 983-6146; www.hotelcampestre.com; Calle Club Campestre; s/d incl breakfast US$71/83; 🅿 ❄ 🛜) Dating from the 1920s, El Valle's oldest hotel features forested walking paths. Remodeled rooms include sleigh beds and stone baths, yet door handles are incongruently flimsy. Staff is a little slow, though the new management is planning day trips to Playa Blanca, which will allow visitors to enjoy both beach and mountain settings.

When the kitrid fungus threatened to wipe out all local amphibians, the hotel temporarily housed the golden frogs that scientists were able to save. Be assured that the frogs' stay in Room 29 is long over, and no one orders crickets by room service any more.

Hotel y Restaurante Los Capitanes HOTEL $$

(☑ 983-6080; www.los-capitanes.com; Calle El Ciclo; s/d/tr from US$44/66/77; 🅿 🛜) Owned and managed by a former captain in the German merchant marine, this spick-and-span destination runs like a well-oiled ship. With excellent valley views, octagonal rooms have firm beds, leatherwork tables and spacious hot-water bathrooms. Amenities include a good restaurant and a kiddie pool for the little ones.

Anton Valley Hotel HOTEL $$

(☑ 983-6097; www.antonvalleyhotel.com; Av Central; d/ste US$83/91; 🅿 ❄ 🛜 🏊) Popular with package tours, this small hotel packs in 16 renovated rooms with high-quality linens and orthopedic mattresses, plus original details such as bamboo beds and stonework. Some are really on the small side and service can be slack, considering the price. Don't get too excited about the pool, it's the size of a peanut.

Cabañas Potosí
CABIN **$$**

(☑ 983-6181; Calle La Reforma; campsite US$15, d/tr US$49/59, 4-person cabin US$49; P) Good for a peaceful sleep, Cabañas Potosí is situated about 1.5km west of the town center. The parklike grounds offer lovely views of the craggy ridges ringing the valley. Old-school wooden cabins with stone columns and Adirondack chairs have two beds apiece. Guests have kitchen privileges. Campers have level ground and a rushing stream nearby.

To get there, follow Av Central to a left-hand branch called Calle La Reforma. It reaches the Cabañas Potosí after about 800m.

Park Eden
B&B **$$$**

(☑ 938-6167; www.parkeden.com; Calle El Nance; d/ste incl breakfast US$121/149, 2/4-person cabin incl breakfast US$143/165, 5-person house US$264; P ✱) A beautiful country retreat run by an American-trained designer and his Ecuadorian wife, this gorgeous home offers three tastefully appointed rooms, plus a separate two-story house, a cottage and a little room behind the cottage. Regardless of which you choose, the friendly couple and their gardens are simply a delight. Breakfast includes the option for waffles, *carimañolas* (yucca roll with chopped meat and boiled eggs), eggs and bacon, fruit and juices. Bikes are available for rent.

La Casa de Lourdes
BOUTIQUE HOTEL **$$$**

(☑ 983-6450; www.lacasadelourdes.info; d from US$193; ✱ 🛜) A classic country villa insulated by fields that make it quiet and secluded, this is the real deal. Though service can be uneven, La Casa is a unique small-scale offering. Four rooms have modern styles, including playful animal prints and oversized photos. Bathrooms feature bathtubs. Best booked in advance; it's located past the grounds of Los Mandarinos.

Los Mandarinos
LUXURY HOTEL **$$$**

(☑ 983-6645; www.losmandarinos.com; d incl breakfast from US$173, ste US$277; P ✱ @ 🛜 ✹) In El Valle's lush countryside, these Tuscan villas target your desire to rejuvenate in a sumptuous setting. Winding walkways link imposing stone and Spanish tile lodgings, though they look slightly better at a distance. Modern rooms are decked in finery, some with king-sized beds, oversized tiles and stone baths.

The fountain of youth concept follows through with a ritzy 'anti-aging' spa (though strangely not with the Irish pub). Guests are split between those making the health pilgrimage and well-to-do families on vacation.

Crater Valley Resort & Adventure Spa
RESORT **$$$**

(☑ 983-6942; www.crater-valley.com; d incl breakfast from US$128; P ✱ 🛜 ✹) With offerings like rock climbing, guided rainforest hikes, a swimming pool and spa, Crater Valley caters to all, from the active to the inert. Surrounded by beautifully tended grounds, guest rooms are all different and executed with varying degrees of care – some are clearly dated. All feature hammock patios.

Prices fluctuate depending on the time of year, the day of the week and the size of the room, so it's best to book ahead.

✖ Eating

Restaurante Santa Librada
PANAMANIAN **$**

(Av Central; mains US$3-5) Cheap and cheerful, Santa Librada does hearty portions of Panamanian staples such as *lomo de arroz* (beef with rice) and *bistec picado* (spicy shredded beef), as well as sandwiches and breakfast. Try the locally famous *sancocho de gallina* (a stewlike chicken soup).

Hotel y Restaurante Los Capitanes
INTERNATIONAL **$**

(Calle El Ciclo; mains US$5-15; ⊙ 7:30am-8pm Mon-Fri, to 9pm Sat & Sun) Serving pasta, seafood and tasty German staples such as sauerkraut and *imbiss* (meatloaf), this open-air restaurant has a relaxed and quiet setting. Don't miss the freshly baked cakes and fruit shakes. The long list of imported beers includes dark and dreamy *Warsteiners*.

Pinocchio's
PIZZERIA **$**

(☑ 983-6975; Calle El Hato; pizzas US$4-10; ⊙ 11am-9pm Thu-Sun) This much-loved pizzeria does pizza pies with a range of toppings. You can also get rotisserie-cooked chicken or meaty burgers. Save room for the tasty lemon pie.

Buon Appetito
PIZZERIA **$**

(☑ 6401-6301; mains US$6-9; ⊙ 6-9pm Thu, noon-9pm Fri & Sat, noon-8pm Sun) Run by a couple from Milan, this is the real deal, locals say, serving pastas, lasagna, focaccia and pizza, Italian-style. Watch for the daily dessert special. It's run out of the family home. There's no real street address; it's on the 'calle de la Panadería Cano.'

El Valle Gourmet & Coffee Shop   CAFE $
(Av Central; sandwiches US$6; ⊗9am-4pm Tue-Thu, 8am-9pm Sat, 8am-6pm Sun) With gourmet sandwiches and smoothies, this is also a good stop to stock up on picnic items before heading for the trails. You can also find goat cheese, cured meats and olives here.

La Casa de Lourdes   INTERNATIONAL $$
(☑983-6450; mains US$10-19; ⊗noon-3pm & 7-10pm) Associated with a celebrated Panamanian chef, Lourdes has an outgrown reputation that can fall short when you realize that half the diners are eating burgers. Still, it's hard to beat its sheer elegance, set around a garden patio in a lovely colonial building. The rotating menu includes mesclun salad with roast mango, cashew-encrusted sole, and lemon tarts with almond crust.

From Calle Central, go right on Calle El Ciclo (likely there is no sign here); follow signs to Casa de Lourdes (near Los Mandarinos).

Bruschetta   CAFE $$
(Av Central; mains US$7-13; ⊗11am-10pm Wed-Mon) Bruschetta features generous versions of its namesake as well as salads, tacos and sandwiches. Unusual treats include the carrot-orange juice. While it is one of the more ambient cafes around, the place could be cleaner. It's located at the Anton Valley Hotel.

🛍 Shopping

Mercado de Artensanía   MARKET
(Av Central; ⊗8am-6pm) El Valle is home to one of Panama's largest handicrafts market. Mostly Ngöbe-Buglé, but also some Emberá and Wounaan, bring a variety of handicrafts to sell to tourists (most of whom are Panamanians from the capital). If you're self-catering, the market also stocks a good selection of fresh produce from around the country.

Although the market runs every day, stop by on Sunday for the full-on affair. One of the most popular items up for sale in the markets are *bateas*, which are large trays carved from a local hardwood and used by the Ngöbe-Buglé for tossing rice and corn. You can also find figurines, colorful baskets made from palms, gourds painted in brilliant colors, clay flowerpots, panama hats, and birdcages made of sticks.

ℹ Information

ATP (☑983-6474; Av Central; ⊗9:30am-5:30pm) This small information booth at the center of town next to the handicrafts market can be very helpful, with information on bicycle rentals and guides.

Banco Nacional de Panama (Av Central) Has an ATM.

Centro de Salud de El Valle (☑983-6112; Av Central; ⊗24hr) For your health needs, turn to this clinic near the western end of Av Central.

Post office (Calle del Mercado; ⊗8am-4pm) Behind the handicrafts market.

ℹ Getting There & Away

To leave El Valle you can hop aboard a bus traveling along Av Central; on average, they depart every 30 minutes. The final destinations are painted on bus windshields. If your next destination isn't posted, catch a bus going in the same direction and transfer.

To reach El Valle from the Interamericana, disembark from any bus at Las Uvas (marked by both a sign for El Valle and a pedestrian overpass), about 5km west of San Carlos. Minibuses pick up passengers at this turnoff and travel to El Valle (US$1.50, one hour, every 30 minutes). It takes 2½ hours to get here from Panama City.

ℹ Getting Around

Despite El Valle's small size, taxis ply Av Central all day long. You can go anywhere in town for US$2 or US$3, or US$10 per hour. Many hotels offer bike rentals (around US$2 per hour), which are a great way to get around.

Santa Clara

With sparkling white sand and towering coconut palms, this is a great destination if you want to lounge about for days without having to worry about someone stealing your stretch of sand.

Santa Clara itself was once little more than a sparsely populated fishing village edging between patches of dry tropical rainforest and the vast blue expanse of the Pacific. Upscale beach villas now dot the landscape. However, there's plenty of local flavor here to soak up in between beach sessions, making a nice change from some of the country's more popular destinations.

THE BEST FESTIVALS OF COCLÉ

If you're looking for the best parties in the province, Antón celebrates its **patron saint festival** from January 13 to 16 and folkloric festival **Toro Guapo** from October 13 to 15. On these dates, the whole of Coclé crowds into this ranching center for music, parades and animated festivities.

🛏 Sleeping & Eating

If you go down the first turnoff for Santa Clara from the Interamericana for about 1km, you'll see signs for Balneario Santa Clara and Las Veraneras.

Restaurante y Balneario Santa Clara   CAMPGROUND $

(campsite per person US$5; P) This popular campsite is a steal – for only a few bucks per night you can get a private *rancho* (cabin) on the beach as well as access to clean toilet and shower facilities. It's US$2 to use the facilities for day visits. Even if you're not camping here, this is one of the few restaurants (meals US$5 to US$14) in the area, and the catch of the day – whatever it is – tastes fantastic when served in front of a Pacific sunset.

Restaurante y Cabañas Las Veraneras   CABIN $$

(☑ 993-3313; www.aventuraspanama.com/las veraneras; 5-person cabin from US$76; P ❄ 🏊) These *cabañas* on a slope set back from the beach come in different sizes and designs. The loveliest are the split-level thatched cabins built on stilts, which overlook the crashing waves. Amenities include hot water, cable TV and a swimming pool. The small thatched restaurant-bar (mains US$5 to US$14) fronts the beach. It's the perfect setting for fresh *ceviche* (seafood marinated in lemon or lime juice, garlic and seasonings) topped off with a sundowner, but service is achingly slow.

XS Memories   MOTEL $$

(☑ 993-3096; www.xsmemories.com; campsite per person US$4, motor-home hookup from US$20, d from US$40; P ❄ 🛜 🏊) You won't find many RV resort/sports bars in Panama but this friendly North American–owned outfit definitely has the market cornered. Three spacious guest rooms feature air-con, platform beds, hot water and tile floors. There are also over 20 hookups for motor homes providing water, sewers and electricity.

Campers can pitch their tents and all can partake of an inviting swimming pool smack in front of the sports bar. The cluttered bar is a kind of homegrown TGI Fridays, serving good juicy cheeseburgers, grilled steaks and pork chops to the drone of football. Follow the billboard to get here – it's just north of the turnoff for Playa Santa Clara, 100m from the Interamericana.

Xoko   SPANISH $$

(Interamericana s/n; US$3.50-14; ⊗ 11am-9pm) Ignore the unfortunate architecture, which is more pool hall than elegant eatery. Xoko is a worthy roadside stop with a pleasing selection of tapas such as clams in white wine sauce, delicious *papas bravas* (fried potatos with a spicy sauce) and tuna tatami. Bigger appetites might prefer a steak, served for a change with nicely grilled vegetables.

ℹ Getting There & Away

To get to Santa Clara, just take any bus that passes through on the Interamericana and tell the bus driver to drop you in town. When it's time to leave town, just stand at any of the bus stops and hail a bus going in the direction you want to go.

From Santa Clara, onward buses leave every 30 minutes west to Antón (US$0.75, 30 minutes) or Penonomé (US$1.25, one hour). Northbound buses heading as far as David (US$12, 5½ hours) and points along the way run hourly. Heading east, buses to San Carlos (US$1.50, 30 minutes), Chame (US$1.75, 45 minutes) and Panama City (US$3.50, 1¾ hours) run every 20 minutes.

ℹ Getting Around

Except for late at night, there are always taxis parked beside the turnoff on the Interamericana for Santa Clara (the town, not the beach). You can take one for US$2 to get to any Santa Clara destination. The beach is 1.8km from the Interamericana.

Farallón (Playa Blanca)

A picture-perfect stretch of powder-white sand, the village of Farallón, most commonly known as Playa Blanca, sits about 3km west of the Santa Clara turnoff. A decade ago, Farallón was a fishing village with the ruins of the Panamanian military base that was destroyed during the US invasion to oust Noriega. However, resort fever has recast Playa Blanca as one of the hottest beach destinations in Panama.

In addition, a highly controversial international airport is under construction in nearby Río Hato. Supporters deem it another necessary step in making Panama a tourist destination, with easier access for those headed straight to the beach. Detractors worry that it will speed coastal development at an even faster pace. Needless to say, locals are divided about whether or not Farallón's sudden spate of development is exactly what the town needs, though it's unlikely that the boom will stop anytime soon.

Visitors are urged to go beyond the resorts – lots of the original village charm is still here, though it is apparent that apartments, condos, gated communities and shopping malls have created an alternate reality. It's no small wonder that Farallón survived as long as it did, especially considering that Playa Blanca is one of the most beautiful beaches along the Pacific coast.

If you're just visiting for the day, and you don't have the cash to blow on a night of hedonistic luxury, Royal Decameron Beach Resort & Casino offers day passes that give you full access to the facilities. Of course, beaches are public land in Panama, so as long as you don't get into trouble, no one is going to stop you lying out in front of either hotel and working on your tan.

🛏 Sleeping & Eating

Togo B&B
B&B $$$

(☑ 6613-5233; www.togopanama.com; d incl breakfast from US$138, extra person US$25; P ❋ 🛜) A lovely little getaway, Togo B&B occupies a renovated beach home with recycled materials used to create a sleek and stylish design. Rooms are ample and airy, with cool tile bathrooms, gorgeous original artwork and private terraces. The prime spot on the property is a lush garden laced with hammocks. Breakfasts offer generous portions of fresh fruit, eggs and *tortilla frita*.

Guests can borrow a bike or rent kayaks. A private passageway crosses the street to the beach. Apartments and a pool are in the works. It's adults only and gay friendly.

Royal Decameron Beach Resort & Casino
RESORT $$$

(☑ 993-2255; www.decameron.com; d 2-night all-inclusive from US$528; P ❋ @ 🛜) Panama's answer to Vegas, Royal Decameron Beach Resort & Casino is a whopper, with 600 rooms and enough pools, bars, clubs and restaurants to count on both hands. Strolling a gated compound affixed with a bracelet ID may not be your idea of travel. But if you like buffet food and Latin nightlife, replete with clubs and casinos, you'll be *en tu salsa*, as they say. Families find plenty to do, including a nightly kids' show.

If you're planning on staying at the Decameron, check out the discounted all-inclusive packages that are sometimes available if you book in advance. Transportation to and from Panama City is included.

JW Marriott Golf & Beach Resort
RESORT $$$

(☑ 908-3333; www.thebristol.com/buenaventura; 340 Calle 3ra Buenaventura; d from US$316; P ❋ @ 🛜) Like heaven but even more exclusive, JW Marriott Golf & Beach Resort has 126 luxury rooms and eight villas located around trails, open space and artificial lagoons. Any whim is yours for the asking, from strawberries and champagne in your room to beach butler service and couples' massages. Private condos and townhouses sit within the complex, which has tennis courts, a world-class spa and a Jack Nicklaus golf course.

Five distinct restaurants plot to keep you onsite, with menus designed by an award-winning Panamanian chef. As with the Decameron, go online to save yourself a few bucks before arriving.

Pipa's
SEAFOOD $$

(mains US$9-20; ⏰ 10am-7pm) For lunch, check out Pipa's, a thatched beachfront restaurant serving seafood with gourmet touches (think Thai mussels or fresh lobster). One of the delights of dining here is enjoying a cold beer or tropical cocktail while you look out on the waves, feet buried in the sand.

The service is friendly and those taking advantage of the beach can shower and rent thatched beach shelters (US$20) to escape the sun. More infrastructure is in the works.

Penonomé
POP 20,000

The provincial capital of Coclé Province is a bustling crossroads city with a rich history. Founded in 1581, Penonomé blossomed so quickly that it served as the temporary capital of the isthmus in 1671 after the destruction of the first Panama City (now known as Panamá Viejo) and until Nueva Panamá

Penonomé

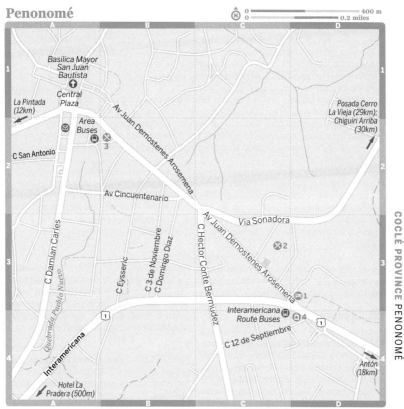

(now known as Casco Viejo) was founded a few years later.

Today, the lifeline of the city is the Interamericana, which bisects Penonomé and ensures a steady stream of goods flowing in and out. If you're heading west, it's likely that you will pass through here at some point, though it's worth hopping off the bus for the city's two principal attractions, namely its annual festivals and its traditional panama hats. Penonomé also serves as good jumping-off point for the nearby artisan town of La Pintada.

✪ Festivals & Events

Carnaval   RELIGIOUS

Held during the four days preceding Ash Wednesday, Carnaval is a huge happening in Penonomé. In addition to traditional festivities, which include dancing, masks and costumes and a queen's coronation, floats here are literally floated down a tributary

of the Río Zaratí. The plaza and every street for three blocks around it are packed with people.

Patron Saint Festival   FESTIVAL

A big crowd pleaser, this festival is generally held on December 8 and 9 (or the following Saturday if both these dates fall on weekdays). Following a special mass, Catholics carry a statue of the saint through the

PANAMA HATS

A panama hat, or simply a panama, is a traditional brimmed hat made from palm (*Carludovica palmata*). Although originally from Ecuador, the hat became fashionable during the construction of the canal, when thousands were imported for use by the workers. After American president Theodore Roosevelt donned a panama during his historic visit to the canal, their iconic status was sealed.

Unlike their Ecuadorian counterparts, which are woven from crown to brim in one piece, this kind is made by a braiding process, using a half-inch braid of palm fiber. The finished braid is wound around a wooden form and sewn together at the edges, producing a round-crowned, black-striped hat. It's a common sight in the rural parts of Panama, and it's not uncommon for political contenders to don hats to appear as 'one of the people.'

Penonomé is known throughout Panama as the place to buy the hats that bear the country's name. The highest-quality Penonomé hats are so tightly put together that they can hold water – prices range from US$15 up to US$150. Hat vendors stand outside stores and restaurants near the gas station by the entrance to town. You can also try **Mercado de Artesanías Coclé** (⊙8am-4pm) at the eastern end of town and Mercado de Artesanías La Pintada in the nearby town of La Pintada.

streets. Yet the mass and procession seem incidental to the celebration taking place outside the church for two days.

🛏 Sleeping & Eating

Hotel La Pradera　　　　　　HOTEL **$**
(☑997-0106; hotelpradera@cwpanama.net; Interamericana; d/tw US$44/55; P❋🛜) This newish yellow colonial feels ritzy for Penonomé, and it is undoubtedly the best value of the budget options. Smart earth-tone rooms include built-in cabinets, cable TV, a lounge chair and desk.

Hotel Dos Continentes　　　　HOTEL **$**
(☑997-9326; Interamericana; d/tr US$30/43; P❋🛜) Near the the Interamericana fork, this sprawling hotel is secure and spacious. Rooms are worn but serviceable, with ironed sheets. Ask for a room in the back for considerably less street noise. The immaculate onsite restaurant is popular for cheap and cheerful *típico* (US$5); natives swear its fried chicken is the best in Panama.

Ederra　　　　　　　　　SPANISH **$**
(Cañas y Tapas; mains US$3-10; ⊙4pm-12:30am) One of those great provincial hangouts that you're happy to stumble upon, Basque-owned Ederra has a warm spirit. Tapas such as ham croquettes or chorizo served with wine are a highlight. The paella Costa Brava also comes recommended. Decor features local art and a bamboo bar. It's in a small shopping plaza a few blocks behind the Hotel Dos Continentes.

Mercado Público　　　　　MARKET **$**
(Av Juan Demostenes Arosemena s/n; mains US$2; ⊙breakfast Sat & Sun) The city market serves hearty breakfasts on weekends, with *hojaldras* (fried dough), *bistec encebollado* (steak with onions and spices) and eggs.

Kacos　　　　　　INTERNATIONAL **$$**
(☑6873-3296; www.icacosadventure.com; Via El Coco s/n; mains US$7-20; ⊙noon-10pm Mon-Sat) More than a country restaurant, Kacos also has fishing, activities, a playground and a small adventure park. It's ideal for families. The breezy, open-air restaurant serves standards such as good club sandwiches and more local fare including *pernil* (thinly sliced pork) with *patacones* (fried green plantains cut in thin pieces) or tilapia farmed onsite. Service is attentive and friendly. It's 4km from the Interamericana.

ⓘ Information

For banking, try **BBVA** (Interamericana) or **Banco Nacional de Panamá** (Av Juan Demostenes Arosemena) and **HSBC** (Av Juan Demostenes Arosemena), both along the city's main street. All have ATMs.

The **post office** (Av Juan Demostenes Arosemena) is in the Palacio Municipal half a block off the central plaza. There's a **mercado público** (Public Market; ⊙4:30am-3:30pm) that's fun to browse near the central plaza. There is no tourist office in town.

The city's principal **hospital** (Interamericana) is at the eastern end of town.

ℹ Getting There & Away

Interamericana route buses stopping in Penonomé via the Interamericana use a small parking lot opposite the Hotel Dos Continentes as a passenger pickup and drop-off point. Buses pass through in either direction every 15 minutes. From Penonomé there are frequent buses to Panama City (US$5.25, 2½ hours, every 20 minutes) and David (US$10, 4½ hours, every 35 minutes).

Area buses, such as those to Churuquita Grande (US$0.85, 45 minutes, every 30 minutes), Aguadulce (US$2, 30 minutes, every 20 minutes), La Pintada (US$1, every 30 minutes), San Pedro, Chiguiri Arriba (US$2.20, 80 minutes, seven per day) and El Copé (US$2, one hour), use a terminal two blocks southeast of the central plaza.

ℹ Getting Around

Due to its size and importance, Penonomé has no shortage of taxis. The best place to hail one is by the Esso gas station, near the entrance to town. You can also find one near the central plaza. The fare for any destination in town is not usually more than US$3, and often it's less.

La Pintada

This small foothill town, just 12km northwest of downtown Penonomé, boasts an artisans' market and a cigar factory. If you're staying in Penonomé for the night or simply passing through the area, it's worth stopping at La Pintada to pick up some attractive handicrafts and a few fresh-rolled cigars direct from the source.

La Pintada's famous Mercado de Artesanías La Pintada (Pintado Artisans' Market; ☑ 983-0313; ☺ 9am-4pm) specializes in Penonomé-style panama hats. The material used in panamas occasionally varies from one town to the next, though here hats are made of *bellota* (palm fiber) and *pita,* a fiber related to cactus. There are several *bellota* and *pita* plants growing in front of the market, so you can see what they look like. Other items of particular interest are dolls wearing handmade folkloric costumes, *seco* (the local firewater) bottle covers made from hat palm, and handmade brooms.

The market is easy to find. As you drive through La Pintada on the main road from Penonomé, you'll come to a very large soccer field on the left side of the road. The market is on the far side of this field.

The second obligatory stop in La Pintada is Cigars Joyas de Panama (☑ tours 6622-1151; www.joyasdepanamacigars.com). The factory's owner, Miriam Padilla, began growing tobacco in La Pintada with three

COCLÉ PROVINCE LA PINTADA

OFF THE BEATEN TRACK

PANAMA'S OLDEST CHURCH

Founded on May 20, 1522, Natá is the oldest surviving town in Panama. The conquistadors came here to claim prodigious quantities of gold. Today, little remains of its rich history aside from a few colonial houses and the lovely, well-preserved Iglesia de Natá, one of the oldest churches in the Americas. This is Panama's oldest continental church; there's a predecessor on Isla Saboga.

Upon the founding of Natá, 60 soldiers took up residence and enslaved the local indigenous population. Indigenous artisans made the church's remarkable carvings. A close look at at the Altar of the Virgin shows the culture's influence in the sculpted fruit, leaves and feathered serpents on its two columns. Artists positioned carved angels at its base to signify their power.

Ecuadorian artist José Samaniego created the *Holy Trinity* painting to the right of the altar in 1758. For many years it was kept censored from public view, since its Trinity shows three Christlike individuals, a considerable breach of Church canon.

During a 1995 restoration, three skeletons were discovered under the floor beneath the Trinity painting. Their identities remain a mystery. Four belfry bells date from the 20th century. The originals, made of solid gold, were stolen years ago. The columns are made of *níspero,* a hardwood found in Bocas del Toro Province. The entire ceiling has been replaced with pine and cedar.

Natá can be reached by all the buses that use this stretch of the Interamericana; they pass in either direction every 15 minutes or so. Natá is 30 minutes from Penonomé and 15 minutes from Aguadulce.

SUGAR IN THE RAW

The origins of the sugar industry are in the European colonization of the Americas, particularly in the Caribbean. Although it was possible for Europeans to import sugar from the colonies in Asia, the advent of slavery in the New World meant that sugarcane could be grown for a fraction of the cost. This in turn led to lower prices for the European consumer, which took precedence over the lives of the slaves forced to work in the fields.

During the 18th century, European diets started to change dramatically as sugar increased in popularity. Coffee, tea and cocoa were consumed with greater frequency, and processed foods such as candies and jams became commonplace. The demand fueled the slave trade, though the actual process of refining sugar became increasingly mechanized.

In industrialized countries, sugar is one of the most heavily subsidized agricultural products. Sugar prices in the US, EU and Japan are on average three times the international market cost as governments maintain elevated price floors by subsidizing domestic production and imposing high tariffs on imports. As a result, sugar-exporting countries are excluded from these markets, and thus receive lower prices than they would under a system of free trade. For countries like Panama, sugar production is mainly a domestic industry as it's not profitable to export sugar to countries that levy a high tariff on imports.

Harvesting sugarcane manually is exhausting work as the stalks can grow to a height of 4m, and they are fibrous and difficult to cut down. A new tendency to harvest sugarcane using self-propelled machines has made it difficult for rural Panamanian farmers to find employment.

The next time you're driving through cane country, look for signs advertising *jugo de caña* as there's nothing quite like a glass of fresh sugarcane juice.

Cubans in 1982, though they went their separate ways in 1987 when the Cubans emigrated to Honduras to open a cigar factory. Left to her own devices, Miriam sent choice samples of her tobacco to tourists and other people she'd met in Panama over the years, seeking investors for a factory. Today, Miriam and her son, Braulio Zurita, are La Pintada's largest employers, employing 80 workers who make a total of 22,000 cigars a day. The employees work at rows of desks in a long, concrete-sided, aluminum-roofed, one-story building the size of a large home, which is the pride of the neighborhood.

The cigars are made in an assembly process that begins at one end of the building with leaf separation from stem, and ends at the other end of the building with the packaging of the final product. From here, the cigars are shipped primarily to the USA, France and Spain. Here, you can buy a box of Joyas de Panama's highest-quality cigars for half the price you would find them outside the country. The cigars also come flavored with a hint of vanilla, rum or amaretto.

Miriam and Braulio speak English, and cigars are clearly much more than a business to them.

To get to the factory from the artisans' market, just drive southeast from the market, straight toward Penonomé (ignore the Pana American Cigar Co, which is en route to Joyas de Panama). You'll come to Cafe Coclé, on your right; take the well-maintained dirt road just beyond it (the road that initially parallels the paved road, not the next right). Follow this road for about 1km until you see a simple thatched-roof restaurant on the right side of the road immediately followed by the open-sided cigar factory with a corrugated metal roof.

Reserva Privada Távida

The Reserva Privada Távida is a private mountain reserve that's part of the Mesoamerican corridor. Once used for livestock, the area is now undergoing reforestation and offers ample trails for hiking or horseback riding, including one spectacular waterfall.

🛏 Sleeping & Eating

★ **Posada Cerro La Vieja** LODGE $$
(📞 983-8900; www.posadalavieja.com; s/d incl breakfast US$83/98, 2-person cabin at waterfall US$198; 🅿 ❄ 🛜 ♨) This incredible mountain lodge sits atop a summit with sweeping views. Surrounded by gardens, green valleys and shrouded peaks, it resembles the famous karst formations outside Guilin, China. The property sits inside Reserva Privada Távida. A favorite of Panama's politicos, the lodge has housed former presidents and the owner has no shortage of stories to tell.

Guests have their pick of rooms in the main lodge, nearby cabins or two exclusive cabins set by a stunning waterfall. The spacious cabins are coolly modern, with large windows, colonial-inspired furnishings and private terraces. The thatched waterfall cabins, some 10 minutes away by 4WD, luxuriate in privacy. With views and walks right out the door, the site has an alfresco dining area and hammock terrace where you'll want to laze the hours away. There is a delicious swimming hole under Cascada de Távida, so bring your suit. These cabins have fully equipped kitchens in addition to cable TV and hot-water showers, which you will find in the main cabins too.

At the restaurant you will find quality dining, with a selection of Chilean wines and produce fresh from local organic gardens. A holistic spa offers everything from manicures and facials to mud baths with mountain views and herbal oil massages. You can get here via the paved road to Chiguiri Arriba, 29km to the northeast of Penonomé.

🏃 Activities

Guided hiking tours (from US$20 per person) from Posada Cerro La Vieja range from easy nature walks to arduous treks, taking in river, waterfall and forest scenes. Area wildlife includes three-toed sloths, night monkeys, deer and armadillos. Four species of toucan and many species of hummingbird also live here, and can occasionally be seen from the comfort of the creek-fed swimming pool.

ℹ Getting There & Away

To get here from central Penonomé, take the well-marked turnoff for Churuquita Grande, several hundred meters northwest of the Hotel Dos Continentes. Proceed past Churuquita Grande and follow the signs to Chiguiri Arriba and the Posada Cerro La Vieja.

Alternately, go to Penonomé's area bus terminal and take a 'Chiguiri Arriba' bus (US$2.20, 80 minutes) or *chiva* (pickup truck with bench seating in the back). Buses depart at 6am, 10am, 11am and 12:30pm, 2pm, 4:30pm and 6pm.

Parque Nacional Omar Torrijos (El Copé) & La Rica

This park is truly one of Panama's hidden gems, though difficult access and relative obscurity have kept the tourist crowds away. It encompasses some of the most beautiful forests in Panama, with montane forest on the Pacific side of the continental divide and humid tropical forest on the Caribbean side.

El Copé is also home to the full complement of Panama's wildlife, including such rare bird species as the golden-olive woodpecker, red-fronted parrotlet, immaculate antbird and white-throated shrike-tanager, as well as all four species of felines, Baird's tapirs and peccaries.

One of the wonderful surprises to greet visitors to El Copé is the excellent condition of the park's trail system, renovated by US Peace Corps volunteers, Autoridad Nacional del Ambiente (ANAM) rangers and members of Panama Verde (a Panamanian student ecological group). Another surprise: this park offers the easiest and surest point from which to see both the Pacific and Atlantic Oceans (from the lookout above the cabin).

🏃 Activities

Hiking

Next to the ranger station you'll find two side-by-side trails – the leftmost trail follows the ridgeline and summits a nearby mountain in about an hour. Here you'll be rewarded with panoramic views of both oceans and the surrounding canopy.

If you take the rightmost trail, you'll be following the Caribbean slope of the continental divide, though be advised that this trail does not end, and should under no circumstances be attempted without a guide. However, if you can arrange a guide through the ranger station, this is a fantastic trail that passes several rivers, winds up and down several mountain peaks and penetrates deep into the heart of the forest.

COOL ROADSIDE ATTRACTIONS

Hot and flat, Aguadulce is surrounded by fields and fields of sugarcane. Yet several cool attractions make it a worthy stop on the Interamericana.

From mid-January to mid-March, **Ingenio de Azúcar Santa Rosa** (Santa Rosa Sugar Refinery; ☎ 987-8101/2; www.azunal.com; ⊙ 7am-4pm Mon-Fri, 7-11:30am Sat), located 15km west of Aguadulce, processes over 6500 tons of raw sugarcane daily, all by hand. The process involves 4000 workers in round-the-clock production. It's a fascinating time to visit the refinery (with 24-hour's notice). Ask for Gonzalo Peréz for tours in English. From Aguadulce, the turnoff for the mill is on the right-hand side of the Interamericana and marked by a sign (there's a gas station opposite).

Located 9km from Aguadulce, **Tidal Flats** serve as a crucial habitat for marsh and shore birds. The area draws local and international bird-watchers to view roseate spoonbills and wood storks. Access by taxi.

On Aguadulce's central plaza, **Museo de la Sal y Azúcar** (Museum of Salt & Sugar; ☎ 997-4280; Plaza 19 de Octubre; adult/child US$1/0.25; ⊙ 9am-5pm Tue-Sat, 2-5pm Sun) documents the history of these industries and their role in Panamanian life.

Aguadulce can be visited by bus from Penonomé (US$2, 30 minutes, every 20 minutes) and Panama City (US$6, three hours, every 20 minutes). Taxis can take you around town.

Behind the ranger station you'll find the entrance to a short interpretative trail that points out local species of trees and plants. This trail is only about 500m in length, but it's a great introduction to the flora of the region.

Another hiking option is to spend a night with the Navas family (see below).

Be advised that there are poisonous snakes in the park including the infamous fer-de-lance – as a precaution, inform others of your intentions, always hike in boots and stick to the trails.

🛏 Sleeping & Eating

About 200m up the road from the ranger station is a small **ANAM cabin** (campsite US$5, r per person US$5) with four beds and a kitchen with simple cooking facilities and basic toilet and cold-water shower. It also has a loft and living room, allowing a total of 10 to sleep comfortably if you have your own gear. Either way, you'll need a sleeping bag – it cools off at night in the mountains so bring some warm clothing as well. If you've brought your own tent, there is a groomed spot alongside the cabin where you can pitch for the night.

Another excellent way of visiting the park is taking advantage of the services of the friendly Navas family. They rent rooms in their **house** (Casa Navas; ☎ 983-9130; Barrigon; per person incl 3 meals & guide US$35) in Barrigon or *cabaña* **Albergue Navas** (☎ 983-9130;

La Rica; per person incl 3 meals & guide US$35) in La Rica, a beautiful community inside the park. Accommodations at both places are rustic, but very well maintained and inexpensive, with all meals included. The family – Santo and Anna Navas and their sons – work as guides, as they have done in the past for scientists and bird-watchers. They help to maintain the park and its trails and their knowledge and love of the area is quite apparent.

Barrigon can be reached by car or public transportation from El Copé. From Barrigon it's a two- to three-hour hike or a horseback ride to La Rica, where you'll find a cool and pleasant community with a beautiful river and swimming holes, with access to secluded, orchid-covered waterfalls, virgin rain- and cloud forest, and excellent bird-watching.

From La Rica, you can take day hikes to the summits of Cerros Marta and Peña Blanca, visit the impressive waterfalls of Chorros de Tife and even hike to the ruins of the plane that crashed, killing president Omar Torrijos.

La Rica is remote (no phone, electricity or road), and the hiking is strenuous, but it is a nature-lover's dream and comes highly recommended. All the arrangements can be made through Santo and Anna Navas (Spanish only). Call ahead, or ask around for the Navas family when you reach Barrigon.

ⓘ Information

There is a **ranger station** (admission US$5; ⊙ 6am-8pm) just inside the entrance of the park where visitors can pay for accommodations, camping permits and admission fees.

ⓘ Getting There & Away

The turnoff for this national park is on the Interamericana, 18km west of Penonomé. From the turnoff it's another 32.8km to the park's entrance. The road, paved for the first 26km, winds through rolling countryside dotted with farms and small cattle ranches. The paved road ends at the small town of El Copé. The remaining 6.8km of the drive to the park is on a dirt road that's so bad that a 4WD vehicle with a very strong motor and excellent tires is needed. There is no public transportation to the park. If you don't have a car, catch a bus from Panama City (US$6.50, three hours) or Penonomé (US$2, one hour) to El Copé and transfer from there in a minibus to Barrigon (US$0.30, 15 minutes), the closest village to the park. From there it's a one-hour hike into the park.

If you're driving, take the turnoff as marked from the Interamericana and proceed 26km. You will then see a sign directing you to the park (to the right) and another to the park's Sede Administrativa (administrative office). There's no reason to go to the administrative office, so stay to the right and continue until you reach the park's entrance.

Parque Arqueológico del Caño

Parque Arqueológico del Caño (adult/child US$1/0.50; ⊙ 9am-noon & 12:30pm-4pm Tue-Sat, 9am-1pm Sun) is perhaps the best place in Panama to get a sense of the nation's indigenous traditions. A small museum contains pottery, arrowheads and carved stones from a culture that lived in El Caño about 1500 years ago. Other attractions include dozens of stone columns and an excavation pit, which contains a burial site where five skeletons remain intact.

The turnoff for the town of El Caño is about 8km north of Natá on the Interamericana. The park is another 3km down an occasionally mud-slicked road. El Caño is not served by bus, but you can take a taxi here from Natá.

COCLÉ PROVINCE PARQUE ARQUEOLÓGICO DEL CAÑO

Península de Azuero

POP 199,500 / ELEV SEA LEVEL TO 3478M / AREA 6147 SQ KM

Best Artisan Workshops

➡ Ocú (p118)

➡ La Enea (p123)

➡ Parita (p117)

➡ La Arena (p116)

➡ San José (p118)

Best Places to Stay

➡ Casa de Campo (p127)

➡ Eco Venao (p131)

➡ Hotel Cambutal (p132)

➡ Posada Los Destiladeros (p129)

➡ La Casa del Puerto (p122)

Why Go?

Esteemed as the country's heart and soul, Península de Azuero is a farming and ranching hub in addition to the strongest bastion of Spanish culture left in Panama. These days the buzz is 'Tuscany of the Tropics,' with rolling hills alongside a long and lovely coastline. Surf is up.

Here, the passage of time is a countdown to the next festival, be it Corpus Christi, La Mejorana or Carnaval. Costumes range from swirling devils to curtsying *reinas*, teenage queens turned dolls in the lace finery of *polleras* (national dress of Panamanian women). It's a party to beat the band. Joining the throngs on sticky rum-soaked streets for these celebrations is a first-rate introduction to the real Panama.

Over time, the peninsula has seen stark transformations – from verdant rainforest to cattle country, indigenous land to Spanish stronghold and, finally, from sleepy backwater to surf central and Panama's next travel hot spot.

When to Go

➡ **Jul–Sep** Traditional Azuero is ground zero for Panama's best festivals and these months feature some major celebrations all over the peninsula, featuring oxcart parades, *seco* (alcoholic drink made from sugarcane) and live bands.

➡ **Late Aug–Nov** Thousands of endangered olive ridley sea turtles come ashore to nest on the broad beach of Isla de Cañas; visitors come to watch the nighttime hatchings with guides.

➡ **Dec–Mar** Dry season is the best time to surf Pacific swells, and options from wilderness beaches to surf villages abound. Also hit Carnaval in Las Tablas – the country's best – in February or March.

Chitré

POP 41,600

One of Panama's oldest settlements, the hot city of Chitré is hardly geared toward travelers, but it's an agreeable stop on the way to the peninsula. Though it has mostly cement structures, a handful of ornate red-tiled row homes hark back to the early days of Spanish settlement. Colonial records indicate that there was a village here as early as 1558. The capital of Herrera Province, it's the largest city on the Península de Azuero, and the cultural and historic capital of the region.

For most travelers, Chitré serves as a springboard for nearby attractions like the ceramic shops in La Arena, the Humboldt Ecological Station at Playa El Aguillito, historic Parita, the *seco* (alcoholic drink made from sugarcane) factory at Pesé and the wildlife refuge at Cenegón del Mangle. Some of the country's best festivals are just a quick bus ride away, but Chitré does host a few wild parties of its own.

Sights

The town's cathedral and the adjacent central square, Parque Union, are one block south of Calle Manuel Maria Correa between Av Obaldía and Av Herrera. There are numerous hotels and restaurants within a short walk of the square.

Museo de Herrera   MUSEUM

(996-0077; Paseo Enrique Geenzier; adult/child US$1/0.25; 8am-4pm Mon-Sat) This anthropology and natural history museum contains many well-preserved pieces of pottery dating from 5000 BC until the Spanish conquest, some of which were found at the excavation sites outside Parita. There are also replicas of *huacas* (golden objects placed with indigenous peoples at the time of burial) found on the peninsula, as well as photos and maps of archaeological sites.

On the museum's 2nd floor you'll find photos of Azuero residents, authentic folkloric costumes and religious artifacts (including the original bell of Chitré's cathedral, which was cast in 1767). Signs are in Spanish only.

Catedral San Juan Bautista   CATHEDRAL

The 18th-century cathedral was substantially remodeled in 1988. Unlike many cathedrals that impress through ostentation, this one is striking for its elegant simplicity and fine balance of gold and wood. Today, the ceiling is polished mahogany, and figures of saints, teak crosses and vivid stained glass windows adorn the walls.

Festivals & Events

Carnaval   RELIGIOUS

Chitré's Carnaval festivities, held each year on the four days before Ash Wednesday, feature parades, folkloric dancing, water fights and lots of drinking.

Fiesta de San Juan Bautista   RELIGIOUS

Chitré's patron saint festival, the Fiesta de San Juan Bautista, held on June 24, starts with a religious service followed by bullfights (the animals are teased but not harmed), cockfights and other popular activities.

Founding of the District
of Chitré 1848   HISTORY

Festivities on October 19 celebrate the 1848 founding of Chitré with parades, historical costumes and much merriment.

Sleeping

If you plan to attend any of the festivals in or around Chitré, you need a reservation – rates go up on these dates too. For Carnaval, rooms often book up months in advance, though you can always visit on a day trip.

Hotel Santa Rita   HOTEL $

(996-4610; cnr Calle Manuel Maria Correa & Av Herrera; d with/without air-con US$29/23;) One of the city's first hotels, Santa Rita is economical but basic. High-ceiling rooms feel musty around the edges, though bathrooms smell scoured with bleach. Perks include some private balconies, very friendly attention and cable TV.

Hotel Rex   HOTEL $$

(996-4310; Calle Melitón Martín s/n; d/tr US$55/72;) With a prime location on Parque Union and good dining downstairs, Rex is a solid midrange choice. Clean tile rooms have brick walls, cable TV, fresh towels and water thermoses.

Hotel Versalles   HOTEL $$

(996-4422; www.hotelversalles.com; Paseo Enrique Geenzier; d/ste US$50/85;) Spacious rooms feature comfortable beds and tile floors, and the onsite restaurant and bar is good for an evening meal and a nightcap. The high price tag is mostly justified with the swimming pool, ideal for those hot Azuero days. There's also onsite car rental.

Península de Azuero Highlights

1 Ride the waves and stay in cool lodgings at **Playa Venao** (p131), a surf destination still evading the mainstream

2 Enjoy the down-home ambiance of **Pedasí** (p125), with lovely boutique lodgings, family-run eateries and long bike rides to the beach

3 Spot sea turtles arriving by the thousands during their annual nesting at **Isla de Cañas** (p132)

4 Squeeze through the multitudes dancing in the soaked streets at Carnaval in **Las Tablas** (p123)

5 Visit a mask-maker's studio and stroll the colonial center of historic **Parita** (p117)

6 Go bird-watching at **Playa El Aguillito** (p115), a tidal mudflat that attracts rare migratory seabirds

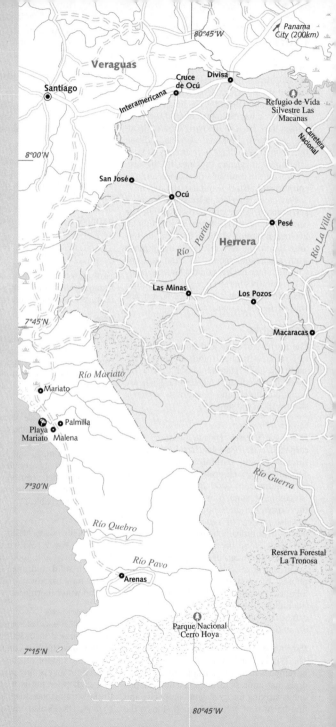

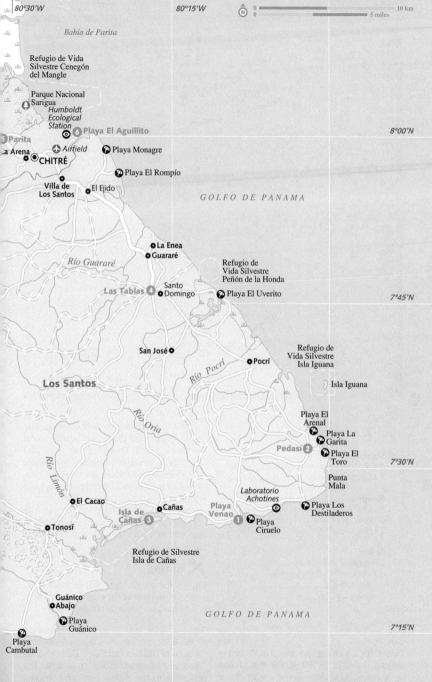

80°30'W 80°15'W

N 0 ———————————— 10 km
0 ———————————— 5 miles

Bahía de Parita

Refugio de Vida
Silvestre Cenegón
del Mangle

Parque Nacional
Sarigua
*Humboldt
Ecological
Station*

5 Parita 8°00'N

6 Playa El Aguillito

La Arena

CHITRÉ Airfield **Playa Monagre**

Villa de
Los Santos El Ejido **Playa El Rompío**

GOLFO DE PANAMA

La Enea
Guararé

Refugio de
Vida Silvestre
Peñón de la Honda

Río Guararé

Las Tablas 4 Santo
Domingo **Playa El Uverito** 7°45'N

Refugio de
Vida Silvestre
Isla Iguana

San José

Pocrí

Río Pocrí

Isla Iguana

Río Oria

Playa El
Arenal

**Playa La
Garita**

Pedasí 2 **Playa El
Toro** 7°30'N

Los Santos

Punta
Mala

Río Limón

*Laboratorio
Achotines*

El Cacao

Isla de
Cañas 3 Cañas

**Playa
Venao 1** **Playa
Ciruelo** **Playa Los
Destiladeros**

Tonosí

Refugio de Silvestre
Isla de Cañas

Guánico
Abajo

GOLFO DE PANAMA 7°15'N

**Playa
Guánico**

**Playa
Cambutal**

80°30'W 80°15'W 80°00'W

Chitré

N 0 ___ 400 m
   0 ___ 0.2 miles

Chitré

◉ Sights

1 Catedral San Juan Bautista	C2
2 Museo de Herrera	C1

🛏 Sleeping

3 Hotel Rex	C2
4 Hotel Santa Rita	C1
5 Hotel Versalles	A1

🍽 Eating

6 Restaurante El Meson	C2
7 Restaurante y Refresquería Aire Libre	C2
8 Salsa y Carbon	C2

Los Guayacanes   HOTEL **$$$**
(☑996-8969; www.losguayacanes.com; Vía Circunvalación; d/ste US$138/160; 🅿✳@🛜🏊) Billed as a resort, Los Guayacanes' cookie-cutter constructions leave dreamers wanting. The ample space could prove particularly useful for families. Built around an artificial lake just outside town, it features a swimming pool, disco, tennis courts, spa and gym, connected by walkways. Rooms are tasteful and bright.

There's complimentary credit for the next-door casino and a good onsite restaurant serving club sandwiches and standard fare.

🍴 Eating

Chitré's fishers get their fish to market the same day, so most of the seafood served here is fresh and surprisingly cheap.

★ Salsa y Carbon   PARRILLA **$**
(☑996-6022; cnr Calle Julio Botello & Francisco Corro; mains US$7; ⊙7am-10pm) This open-air Colombian thatched BBQ house grills the best steak in the region. Meat and chicken

are exceptionally tender, served with salad and arepas (savory corn cake). It's nothing extravagant but consistently good.

Restaurante y Refresquería
Aire Libre   PANAMANIAN $
(Av Obaldía; mains US$3-5; ☺6:30am-10pm) Get your greasy-spoon fix at this open-air plaza cafe. It serves two kinds of fried chicken and seafood like *camarones al ajillo* (shrimp with garlic), served with crisp, thick-cut fries.

Restaurante El Meson   PANAMANIAN $
(☎996-4310; Calle Melitón Martín s/n; mains US$4-12; ☺7:15am-10pm; 🐾) This plaza restaurant with long hours has a long list of offerings, from sandwiches to steak and seafood. The chicken tacos will fully satisfy small appetites. Full breakfasts include fried yucca or *tortillas de maíz* with eggs and coffee. The ambiance is glass tables and tall wooden chairs.

❶ Information

The city website is www.chitrenet.net/chitre.html.

ATP Office (La Arena) Offers tourist information.

Banco Nacional de Panamá (Paseo Enrique Geenzier; ☺9am-1pm Mon-Thu & Sat, to 3pm Fri) Has an ATM.

HSBC (Av Herrera; ☺9am-1pm Mon-Fri) Has an ATM. Located just north of the cathedral.

❶ Getting There & Away

AIR
At the time of writing there was no regular flight service to Chitré from Panama City. Look for possible changes, as there is an airport just outside of town.

BUS
Chitré is a center for regional bus transportation. Buses arrive and depart from **Terminal de Transportes de Herrera** (☎996-6426), 1km south of downtown, near Vía Circunvalación. The terminal has a 24-hour restaurant and a car rental agency. To get there, **Radio Taxi** (☎996-4442) charges US$2. The 'Terminal' bus (US$0.30) leaves from the intersection of Calle Aminta Burgos de Amado and Av Herrera.

Tuasa (☎996-2661) and **Transportes Inazun** (☎996-4177) buses depart from Chitré's Terminal de Transportes de Herrera for Panama City (one way US$9.05, four hours, every hour from 6am to 11pm). Other buses departing from Chitré operate from sunrise to sunset.

To get to David or Panama City from Chitré, take a bus to Divisa and then catch a *directo* (direct bus) to either city (US$7 or US$8). Buses leave from the Delta station at the intersection of the Interamericana and the Carretera Nacional. You likely won't have to wait more than 30 minutes.

BIRD-WATCHING AT PLAYA EL AGUILLITO

Seven kilometers from Chitré, Playa El Aguillito is a mudflat created by silt deposited by the Río Parita and the Río La Villa. At low tide, it stretches more than 2km from the high-water mark to the surf, supplying a bounty of plankton and small shrimp to thousands of migrating birds.

Regulars include roseate spoonbills, sandpipers, warblers, black-necked stilts, white-winged doves, black-bellied plovers, yellow-crowned amazons, yellowlegs and ospreys. The beach is also home to common ground-doves, found only in this one spot in Panama. At high tide, birds congregate around salt ponds to the immediate east of Playa El Aguillito. The artificial beach is a failed attempt to create a sunbathing beach by destroying a mangrove forest back in the 1960s.

Chitré native and 'friend of the birds' Francisco Delgado heads Humboldt Ecological Station. Since 1983, the group has monitored more than 15,000 birds with the assistance of international scientists. Their work shows that annual visits to the same feeding grounds is an important survival mechanism for long-distance migratory birds. This is particularly true for species like the western sandpiper, which can fly for days on end without stopping to eat. The station displays a map of migratory routes of bird species. Guests can speak with volunteers if they have time, or Francisco himself, who speaks English and Spanish.

Playa El Aguillito is reached from Chitré via Av Herrera just past the airport. A bus leaves the Chitré station for the beach every 20 minutes or so during daylight hours. The one-way fare is US$0.50. A taxi ride from town costs US$4 one way.

To reach Chitré from the Interamericana, ask your bus driver to stop in Divisa, at the Delta gas station, where you can catch any Chitré-bound bus.

ℹ Getting Around

When the highway reaches Chitré, it becomes Paseo Enrique Geenzier, changing its name again a dozen blocks further east to Calle Manuel Maria Correa. The Carretera Nacional re-emerges at the southern end of town.

If you need to travel by vehicle, a taxi is the best way to go. They're cheap – most fares in town are between US$1.50 and US$2.

Around Chitré

Some of the most interesting sights in the Península de Azuero are just a short bus ride away from downtown Chitré.

La Arena

The tiny village of La Arena produces some of the highest-quality pottery in the country, and is one of the best places to watch sculptors working their trade. The pottery mimics the pre-Columbian designs of the Ngöbe-Buglé people who once lived nearby. Buy direct here to help support artisans. This famous ceramics center sits about 5km west of downtown Chitré, bisected by the Carretera Nacional.

The best of the town's several pottery factories is Ceramica Calderón (near Calle del Río Parita & Carretera Nacional), where you can buy traditional painted ceramics at wholesale prices. These pieces are made on the premises in a workshop directly behind the roadside showroom. All pottery is made by hand with the help of a foot-powered potter's wheel. The principal artisan is Angel Calderón, who's been making ceramics professionally for almost 50 years. If you visit Angel's shop, be sure to take a look at the impressive ovens out back.

Although there are no places to stay in La Arena, downtown Chitré is just 5km away and US$0.30 by bus. A taxi ride from Parque Union to La Arena shouldn't cost you more than US$2.

Atop a hill in La Arena, El Mirador (Lookout; mains US$5-9; ⊙4pm-midnight) is a popular spot where tourists from around Panama congregate to take in the views of the city and the surrounding plains. The food is standard at best, though the twinkling lights of Chitré make for an atmospheric night out. To find El Mirador from downtown Chitré, head west on Paseo Enrique Geenzier for about 2.5km and turn left onto the road that begins just past the large 'Chino Bar' sign. At the fork, turn right and continue for another 400m until you reach the top of the hill.

Parque Nacional Sarigua

Ten kilometers north of downtown Chitré, this national park (admission US$5; ⊙8am-4pm) is arguably the most important pre-Columbian site in Panama. The Sarigua site has been dated back 11,000 years based on shell mounds and pottery fragments,

BUSES FROM CHITRÉ

DESTINATION	COST (US$)	DURATION (MIN)	FREQUENCY
Divisa	1.25	30	every 15min
La Arena	0.30	15	every 15min
Las Minas	3	45	every 30min
Las Tablas	1.50	45	every 20min
Macaracas	2.50	60	hourly
Ocú	2.50	60	hourly
Parita	0.70	20	every 45min
Pedasí	3.25	60	hourly
Pesé	1.10	20	every 30min
Playa El Aguillito	0.50	12	every 20min
Playas Monagre & El Rompío	1.25	30	every 20min
Santiago	3	75	every 30min
Villa de Los Santos	0.35	5	every 10min

although much of it has yet to be excavated. The main hurdle preventing wide-scale excavation is the fact that the entire national park is a 'tropical desert.'

Created in 1984, it consists of 80 sq km of wasteland that was once dry tropical rainforest and coastal mangrove patches. Unfortunately, Sarigua is mostly the end product of slash-and-burn agriculture. People moved into the area, cut down all the trees, set fire to the debris, planted crops for a few harvests and then left. Because the forest that had held the thin topsoil in place was removed, the heavy rain that falls here every year carried the topsoil into creeks and then into rivers and out into the sea.

What you see in Parque Nacional Sarigua today is the nutrient-deficient rock that was once underneath the topsoil. The park even formerly served as the waste-disposal site for Chitré, Parita and other cities in Azuero.

A visit to Sarigua is a sober reminder of the earth's fragility, and the rapid speed with which humans can alter the environment. From the *mirador* (lookout) behind the ranger station, you can gaze out at the dry, cracked earth and swirling dust storms that used to be a living, breathing ecosystem. If you have your own transportation, you can also drive a few kilometers into the park, though much of Sarigua is off-limits to the public. The coastal edges of the park are also home to privately owned commercial shrimp farms, which stand as a testament to the rapid destruction of Panama's wetland habitats.

To get here from the Carretera Nacional, take the Puerto Limón turnoff, a couple of kilometers northwest of Parita. After 1km you'll notice the foul smell of a nearby pig farm. After another 1km you'll come to the park turnoff. Follow the signs for 2km, until you come to a structure on the left – this is the ANAM station.

Buses do not go to the park. A round-trip taxi ride to the ANAM station from Chitré costs about US$20.

Parita

POP 2500

Just 6km northwest of downtown Chitré, the colonial town of Parita is one of those hidden gems that travelers love to stumble across. Founded in 1558 and named after the departed Ngöbe-Buglé chief, Parita is full of 18th-century colonial structures. Buildings have thick walls and solid beams, red-tiled roofs and sweeping arcades. Despite its historic core, Parita is known to few outside the Península de Azuero, so it's unlikely that you will see any tourists here, Panamanian or otherwise.

Parita follows a grid pattern. As you come to intersections near the town's center (which is about 500m from the Carretera Nacional) and glance both ways, you'll see buildings that look much the same as they have for centuries.

The church in Parita is the only one in Panama that has its steeple located directly over its entrance rather than over a corner of the structure. This is very unusual as bell towers are always extremely heavy, and therefore are generally built on pillars that rest upon a massive foundation. In fact, it is a major curiosity to the residents of Parita that the steeple hasn't collapsed upon the entryway. Although the church was completed in 1723, you'll never see a Parita resident loitering near the entrance.

Beside the church is a grassy square in which cattle-roping demonstrations are held from August 3 to 7, during the town's patron-saint festivities.

Two doors down from the southeastern corner of Parita's church, a workshop specializes in the restoration of altars – it is the only such restoration center in the country. The artisans working here, Macario José Rodriguez and José Sergio Lopez, have been restoring the altars of Panama's colonial churches since the 1970s. Both men speak some English and they are very friendly – chances are they'll let you take a look around.

One of the country's top mask-makers is Dario López ([☎]974-2933). To visit his home workshop, return to the Carretera Nacional and find the service station near the turnoff. Darido's house is about 100m northwest of the gas station, on the opposite side. Visitors can identify his home by the masks hanging beside his front door. Darido has been making colorful masks for folkloric dancers since the 1960s. While he continues to make masks and satin costumes worn by dirty-devil dancers, these days most are exported to the USA and to Europe. In the shop they typically cost between US$20 and US$80, with some small masks under US$10.

There are no lodgings in Parita, but downtown Chitré is just 10km away. A taxi ride from Parque Union to Parita shouldn't cost you more than US$5, and there are several buses an hour that won't cost you more than US$1.

PENÍNSULA DE AZUERO AROUND CHITRÉ

THE FIESTAS DE AZUERO

Famous throughout Panama, the traditional festivals of Azuero were created around customs from early Spanish settlers. This is a side of Panama that few foreigners are ever given the opportunity to see. While you may lose a day from a *seco* hangover, taking part in the wilder side of the peninsula is hard to forget. Some of the best-known festivals:

Festival de San Sebastián January 20 in Ocú

Carnaval The four days before Ash Wednesday in Chitré, Parita, Las Tablas and Villa de los Santos

Semana Santa March/April in Pesé and Villa de los Santos

Feria de Azuero Late April/early May in Villa de Los Santos

Fiesta de Corpus Christi Forty days after Easter in Villa de los Santos

Fiesta de San Juan Bautista June 24 in Chitré

Patronales de San Pablo & San Pedro June 29 in Pedasí and La Arena

Fiestas Patronales de Santa Librada July 20 in Las Tablas

Fiesta de la Pollera July 22 in Las Tablas

Festival del Manito Ocueño, Fiesta Popular, Matrimonio Campesino, El Duelo del Tamarindo & El Penitente de la Otra Vida August (dates vary) in Ocú

Feria de la Mejorana, Festival de la Virgen de las Mercedes September 23 to 27 in Guararé

Founding of the District of Chitré October 19 in Chitré

La Grita de la Villa November 10 in Villa de los Santos

Refugio de Vida Silvestre Cenegón del Mangle

This 775-hectare refuge near Parita protects a mangrove forest at the mouth of the Río Santa María, an important wildlife area and nesting ground for wading birds. The most commonly sighted species here are great egrets, cattle egrets and tri-colored herons – in fact, many of the herons that now inhabit the Palacio de las Garzas (Palace of the Herons), the official residence of the Panamanian president, came from this reserve.

The refuge is accessed by a 500m-loop trail that follows a boardwalk through the mangrove forest. Along the way, keep your eyes fixed on the waters below as the abundance of wading birds also attracts hungry caimans and crocodiles. The herons are here year-round, though opportunistic reptiles tend to congregate during the June-to-September mating season. Watch your step – you really don't want to fall in!

The primary attraction of the refuge is the birds, though locals claim that Los Pozos (the pools) have health-giving properties.

The refuge is not reachable by bus; instead, it's a 45-minute drive north of Chitré via the Carretera Nacional, easily accessible as a day trip. Take the signposted turnoff to Los Pozos. After 1km the road forks at a church in the village of Paris; take the right branch and it becomes a dirt road. Proceed 4km on this road, after which you'll come to a sign with an arrow indicating you're 2km from the wells and the entrance to the refuge.

Interior Azuero

Interior towns near Chitré offer a glimpse of rural life, with worthwhile traditional festivals, artisan workshops and liquor production from the endless sea of sugarcane plantation.

Home to the country's largest *seco* factory, Pesé, 19km southwest of Chitré, has seasonal tours of Seco Herrerano (974-9621; 9am-5pm Mon-Sat, mid-Jan–mid-Mar) FREE, started in 1936. During harvest guests can visit the distillery and taste free samples of this liquor produced from sugarcane. The town is also famous for its annual Good Friday re-enactment of the crucifixion.

About 20km west of Pesé, sleepy Ocú produces Panama's finest panama-style hats. The genuine article is so tightly braided it is waterproof. Visitors are welcome at the workshops of Ezequela Maure or Elena Montilla (☑974-1365). To find their houses, drive or walk about 1km on Av Central from the town plaza until you reach a fork in the road. A dirt road splits to the left, while the main paved road sweeps right; if you pass the Jorón El Tijera restaurant, in the fork of the road, you've gone too far. Ezequela's house is on the left side of the street, about four houses south of the fork. Elena's house is two doors down.

Ocu's festivals also have wide notoriety, including Festival del Manito Ocueño, held during the third week in August, and the late-January Festival de San Sebastián, Ocu's patron saint. Both feature folklore programs and an agricultural fair.

Just outside Ocú, the small village of San José is home to the internationally renown women's co-op Artesanía Ocueña (☑974-1059; www.artesaniasocu.com; Avenida Central s/n). The group sells intricate *montunos* (traditional folklore outfits), *polleras* (traditional dresses from the Península de Azuero)

and handmade items such as tablecloths and place mats with exquisite embroidery. To visit the workshop, take the turnoff (the sign says 'Los Llanos') on the left side of the road as you head north of Ocú toward the Interamericana. The turnoff is about 1km from the central plaza. From there it's a 15-minute drive along a dirt road until you reach the community. If it's closed, ask around for Ana Marin or Guillermina Montilla. You can also catch an 'Ocú–Los Llanos' *chiva* (rural bus; US$0.65) in front of the main plaza in Ocú.

From Chitré, frequent buses visit Pesé (US$1.10, 20 minutes) and Ocú (US$2.50, one hour).

Villa de Los Santos

POP 5900

A quintessential Azuero town, Villa de Los Santos is where Panama's first move toward independence from Spain began on November 10, 1821. Residents now honor their freedom-fighting ancestors by hosting truly wild parties. The Los Santos calendar does not skimp on celebrations; on the contrary, its busy itinerary of local and national holidays makes it one entertaining destination.

INSIDE AZUERO'S INTRIGUING PAST

Spanish settlements were so effective in wiping out the indigenous populations of Azuero that little is known about these communities. During the 1940s a major tomb excavation just 10km outside Parita yielded some of the finest pre-Columbian artifacts ever discovered in Panama.

Discoveries included painted pots in the form of bird effigies and exquisitely carved batons shaped like stylized alligators, made from manatee ribs. Perhaps the most amazing find was an urn with the remains of a man wearing a necklace made of more than 800 human teeth.

In the colonial era, the now-parched Azuero was covered by dry tropical rainforest and thick mangroves. Early communities subsisted on hunting and fishing, with small-scale agriculture which included rice, beans and manioc. Several tribes shared the peninsula, though the region was controlled by a powerful Ngöbe-Buglé chief named Parita.

For decades Parita and his fierce warriors held off Spanish settlement. Yet when Gaspar de Espinosa raided in the early 16th century, Parita was found lying dead, surrounded by his slaughtered wives, attendants and 161kg of gold ornaments. They were presumably killed by another tribe on the peninsula. Also found were 20 native captives lashed to house posts by cords around their necks – about to be buried alive with the great chieftain.

Following this episode, the Spanish rapidly colonized the Península de Azuero and exterminated its residents. A few Ngöbe-Buglé communities safely fled to the rainforested mountains in present-day Chiriquí Province. These same communities were so fearful of intervention that they placed deadly traps along trails until only a few decades ago.

Aside from its festivals, Los Santos boasts colonial structures dating back to the early days of the Spanish settlers. It is also home to a noteworthy museum dedicated to Panamanian independence as well as one of the country's most magnificent churches.

◉ Sights

Museo de la Nacionalidad   MUSEUM
(Calle José Vallarino; adult/child US$1/0.25; ◷9am-4:30pm Tue-Sat, to 1pm Sun) This modest museum, opposite Plaza Simón Bolívar, occupies the former house where Panama's Declaration of Independence was signed in 1821, declared here 18 days before the national declaration. Pre-Columbian ceramics and colonial-era religious art comprise most of the exhibits, and there's also a lovely garden courtyard.

Over the years, this handsome brick-and-tile residence served as a jail, a school and a legislature. It predates the town's church, but no one knows exactly when it was built.

Iglesia de San Atanacio   CHURCH
This church was granted national monument status by the government in 1938 and is truly a national treasure. Alongside Plaza Simón Bolívar, the church opened its doors to the public in 1782 after nearly nine years of construction. It's a fine example of the baroque style, with lots of intricately carved wood depicting cherubs, saints, Jesus and the Virgin.

Almost everything is original, and some objects even predate the structure itself. The 12m arch in front of the altar, for example, bears its date of manufacture (1733) and the names of its two creators.The altar is made of mahogany and rosewood and is covered nearly from base to top in gold leaf. In a glass sepulcher in front of the altar is a life-size wooden statue of Christ that is carried through the streets of Villa de Los Santos on Good Friday, behind a candlelit procession.

Carlos Ivan de Leon   GALLERY
(☑966-9149; Calle Tomas Herrera; ◷noon-1pm & 6-10pm) Master mask maker Carlos Ivan de Leon makes the most elaborate and frightening masks in Panama at his house near Calle Segundo Villareal. He specializes in devil masks for the famous *baile de los diablos sucios* (dance of the dirty devils).

Masks are sold to professional dancers or international collectors. Several are on display at the ATP office. Look for the house with a black front door and a sign featuring his family name (De Leon) nearby. Carlos speaks Spanish only.

✺ Festivals & Events

Other notable festivals include Carnaval, celebrated four days before Ash Wednesday (February/March), and April's Semana Santa.

Fiesta de Corpus Christi   RELIGIOUS
(Body of Christ Festival) Forty days after Easter in Villa de Los Santos. The Fiesta de Corpus Christi is Los Santos' biggest festival.

La Grita de la Villa   HISTORY
(Cry of the Village) The anniversary of the historic *grito* (cry) of independence, also known as La Grita de la Villa, is celebrated in Los Santos on November 10. This patriotic occasion is usually overseen by the president of Panama and is highlighted by a parade, musical and dance performances and a healthy amount of drinking in the streets.

FIESTA DE CORPUS CHRISTI

One of the most riotous events in the country, Fiesta de Corpus Christi has been celebrated ever since Pope Urban IV sanctioned the event in 1264. Yet the local version coolly incorporates animistic traditions passed down from generation to generation in the Península de Azuero.

As a means of converting the indigenous peoples of the region, Spanish missionaries used the festival to highlight the concept of good versus evil. At the core of the festival is a series of dances including the famous *baile de los diablos sucios* (dance of the dirty devils), which emphasizes the Christian belief in the Apocalypse.

Though God, heaven and the angels win out in the end, it doesn't prevent local artisans from creating some truly mind-blowing masks and costumes. Held from Thursday to Sunday, 40 days after Easter, the festival attracts hundreds of performers ranging from singers and dancers to theater troops and magicians.

Check it out in Villa de Los Santos.

Feria de Azuero FAIR
(Azuero Fair) This fair features folkloric dancing, agricultural attractions and various competitions among local singers performing regional songs. Held late April or early May.

🛏 Sleeping & Eating

With the city of Chitré just 4km away, there is a range of other sleeping options that may come in handy when Los Santos is packed to the brim during festivals.

Hotel La Villa HOTEL $
(🖉966-9321; www.hotellavillapanama.com; d US$40-45; P❄☀) A low-key affair, though the swimming pool is a nice touch, especially in the dry and dusty Azuero summer. Rooms of varying sizes and shapes have steamy showers and chilly air-con, and the attached bar-restaurant serves up all of your Panamanian favorites. The colorful design scheme incorporates artisan crafts from Los Santos festivals.

Kevin's Hotel HOTEL $
(🖉966-8276; d US$32-46; P❄🛜) Set back from the Carretera Nacional, this low-key hotel features a wide range of nearly identical-looking, concrete-box–style rooms. The price is right, with private hot-water bathrooms and satellite TV available for just a few extra dollars. The restaurant is a popular truck stop serving hearty dishes including grilled meats and seafood casseroles.

Sol de Luna HOTEL $$
(🖉923-0630; www.soldelunahotel.com; Carretera Nacional; s/d incl breakfast US$57/67; ❄🛜☀) A new addition, this standard hotel on the main road makes good with 22 deluxe motel-style rooms. There's also attentive service and a beautiful pool, solar panels and pool water is recycled for plant watering. It's very family friendly. An onsite restaurant serves fresh juices, burgers and seafood. Plans are in the works for a water park.

❶ Information

ATP Office (🖉966-8013; fax 996-8040; Calle José Vallarino; ⊙9am-4pm Mon-Fri) Provides information on any upcoming celebrations in the area.
Banco Nacional de Panamá (cnr Av 10 de Noviembre & Calle Tomas Herrera)
Police Station (Av 10 de Noviembre)

❶ Getting There & Around

Chitré–Las Tablas buses stop on the Carretera Nacional, and Chitré–Villa de Los Santos buses stop on Calle José Vallarino half a block from the Carretera Nacional. Fares to these destinations or anywhere in the province are usually between US$0.50 and US$3.

Buses to Panama City depart from Calle José Vallarino at Av 10 de Noviembre, and also from Calle Segundo Villarreal, 1½ blocks northeast of Plaza Simón Bolívar.

Taxis are a quick way to get around Villa de Los Santos and between Villa de Los Santos and Chitré. The fare won't exceed US$3 if you stay within these cities. Taxis can usually be found near the bus stop on the Carretera Nacional and northwest of Plaza Simón Bolívar.

Playas Monagre & El Rompío

Ten kilometers northeast of Villa de Los Santos are Playas Monagre and El Rompío, which serve as popular beach day trips for local families. El Rompío is less frequented than Monagre and thus has less litter, but both have a lot of driftwood on them and the sand is dark and hot on sunny days. The presence of strong rip currents means that swimming is not a great idea, though there's still plenty of fun in the sun to be had.

A bus leaves the Chitré station for Playas Monagre and El Rompío (US$1.50, around 20km, hourly) from sunrise to sunset. This bus passes through Villa de Los Santos on the way to the beaches and can be hailed from the Carretera Nacional in town. Look for a bus with 'Monagre' on its windshield. The fare from Villa de Los Santos to either beach is US$0.75. A taxi ride from Chitré to either beach costs about US$8; a taxi from Villa de Los Santos costs half that.

Road to Las Tablas

The Carretera Nacional from Villa de Los Santos to Las Tablas runs mostly past small farms and cattle ranches, with almost no remaining forest in sight – indeed, the province is the most heavily deforested in the country. However, the drive is still scenic in its own right, especially since it passes a few much-loved Azuero institutions.

About 3km southeast of Los Santos along the Carretera Nacional is **Kiosco El Ciruelo** (⊙6am-10pm Fri-Sun), a rustic truck stop where everything is cooked on a wood-fire grill. Among the offerings is a traditional specialty of Los Santos Province: tamales made with corn, pork and various spices, and wrapped in plantain leaves.

From Kiosco El Ciruelo, travel another 6km until you see a bright-blue public phone on the eastern side of the road. Just beyond the phone is a small hut beside a large pile of coconut husks. Located here is Casa de la Pipa (House of Coconut Juice), which sells fresh, ice-cold coconut water.

As you travel the two-lane Carretera Nacional toward Las Tablas, you'll occasionally see stands with sausages dangling in front of them. Pork sausages made on the Península de Azuero are nationally famous for their high quality, and a few links of this delicious meat shouldn't cost you more than a dollar or so.

If you're traveling the highway around Carnaval time, you'll also see dozens of smashed-up cars on the roadside, sobering remnants of Carnaval placed to encourage safe driving. Still, it's best to avoid any unnecessary highway travel during Carnaval.

Guararé

POP 3800

Tiny Guararé, located on the Carretera Nacional between Villa de Los Santos and Las Tablas, is just another sleepy Azuero town until the last week in September, when the town explodes to life with Feria de la Mejorana, Panama's largest folkloric festival.

Founded by Manuel Zárate in 1950 to stimulate interest and participation in traditional practices, the Feria de la Mejorana has become the best place to see Panama's folklore in all its manifestations. Dance groups from all over the country – and even some from other Latin American countries – attend this annual event, which includes a colorful procession in which decorated floats parade through the streets in oxcarts.

Folkloric dances that were once part of other celebrations in other places are today sometimes seen only at this event. For example, this is the only festival in which a dance known as La Pajarita (Paper Bird) is performed. In contrast to the various exuberant devil dances, a calm, religious quality pervades La Pajarita. Given the great success of La Mejorana, Guararé is looking to hold folkloric events on a monthly basis; check with local tourism offices for updates.

A good warm-up for the festivities is a visit to Museo Manuel F Zárate (☑994-5644; Calle 21 de Enero; adult/child US$0.75/0.25; ⊙9am-4pm Tue-Sat). Zárate was a folklorist devoted to conserving the traditions and folklore of the Azuero region. The museum, in Zárate's former home, contains *polleras*, masks, *diablito* (little devil) costumes and other exhibits. It's two blocks behind the church and about six short blocks from the main road (turn off at the gas station).

For interesting excursions, look no further than Guararé Folk Tours (☑6686-2632, 6772-2863; guararefolktours@gmail.com), offering horseback riding (US$20 per hour), a *pollera* tour (US$20 for three visitors), and mangrove and seasonal waterfall visits. Developed in tandem with Peace Corps efforts, these tours employ local guides and showcase local cultural and natural heritage.

A local training ground for young festival artists, Academy of Customs & Traditions Gabriel Villarreal (☑994-4581, cell 6949-6885; pfalconett@hotmail.com; Edificio Melo; ⊙3-7pm Mon-Fri, Sat am) offers classes in mejorana, dancing, accordion, violin, and *cantaderas* (folk songs). Visitors are always welcome to watch. Contact coordinator Pastor Falconett. The Melo Building is white with a blue *pollera* design, located near Guararé center.

Just off the Chitré–Las Tablas highway, Residencial La Mejorana (☑994-5794; d US$33; 🅿🌀🛈) is a fairly large, fairly clean and fairly nondescript hotel decent enough to crash in for the night. If there's a festival in town, you could only be so lucky as to get a room here. Prices vary according to the size of the room, though all are equipped with air-con and private hot-water bathrooms, and have that certain air of sterility to them.

An excellent rural option, La Casa del Puerto (☑994-4982, cell 6772-2863; www.panamacasadelpuerto.com; 2-/3-/4-person apt US$45/60/100) is located 10km out on the oceanfront. Run by a retired Peace Corps alumna, it feels more like staying at the home of a faraway friend. Perks include hot water, attentive service and tips, and a beach out the back door. Host Bonnie can arrange local excursions and pick up guests in Guararé or Chitré, with advance notice.

Guararé is beside the Carretera Nacional, 20km south of Villa de Los Santos. You can hop on any bus that travels the highway in the direction of Guararé; you'll be dropped off at the town. Call ahead for a local taxi (☑994-5410); they can be hard to hail during the festival.

La Enea

This small village northeast of Guararé produces the finest *polleras* in Panama. Once the daily attire of Spain's lower classes in the 17th and 18th centuries, the *pollera* is today the national costume, distinguished by its stirring beauty and elegance. It is almost entirely handmade, from the attractive embroidery on the blouse and skirt to the delicate filigree ornaments tucked around the gold combs in the hair. The traditional assortment of jewelry worn with a *pollera* can cost upwards of US$20,000.

By convention, the *pollera* consists of two basic pieces: a blouse that rests upon the shoulder tops and a long skirt divided into two fully gathered tiers. Each dress requires no less than 10m of fine white linen or cotton cloth. Elaborate needlework in a single color brings contrast to the white background.

Located halfway between Guararé and La Enea, Señora Dilsa Vergara de Saavedra (☑994-5221, cell 6529-0445.) is a *pollera* maker and judge known to many queens and for many contests. She's known for giving interesting presentations and offers a nice selection of items to show.

If you're interested in purchasing a *pollera,* be advised that every dress is made to order.

To reach La Enea, take a taxi (US$3) from Guararé.

Las Tablas

POP 10,400

Las Tablas is ground zero for the street dancing, booze-soaked celebrations and all-out mayhem associated with the festivals of the Península de Azuero. Home to the country's most famous Carnaval, Las Tablas is the best place in Panama to let go of your inhibitions, sample some *seco* and seriously cut loose.

As the capital city of Los Santos Province, Las Tablas has a fine church and a small museum devoted to former Las Tablas statesman and three-time president Belisario Porras. The city is also famous for its combined patron saint–*pollera* festival, a colorful mix of religious ceremony and beauty contest.

JUNTA DE EMBARRE

The Spanish cultural heritage of Azuero lives on in various forms, including some bizarre and antiquated traditions. One is *junta de embarre,* which literally translates to 'meeting of mud covering.' Following a local wedding, villagers will gather to build a crude mud hut for the newlywed couple. This practice symbolizes the joining together of two households as well as the beginning of a new family. Although this custom is dying out in larger towns and cities, the tradition continues to thrive in some of the more traditional areas of in the peninsula.

⊙ Sights

Almost everything of interest to travelers is within five blocks of the plaza.

Museo Belisario Porras   MUSEUM
(Av Belisario Porras; adult/child US$0.50/0.25; ⊙9am-12:30pm & 1:30am-4pm Tue-Sat, 9am-noon Sun) Opposite the Central Plaza is the mudwalled former home of three-time president Belisario Porras, during whose administration the Panama Canal opened. The museum contains many artifacts from Porras' life and serves as a monument to the achievements of this widely revered man.

Porras was president for all but two years during the period from 1912 to 1924. He is credited with establishing Panama's network of public hospitals, creating a national registry for land titles and constructing scores of bridges and aqueducts.

As an aside, Porras' male descendants wear their whiskers in his unusual style – a thick, prideful mustache resembling the horns of a Texas longhorn steer.

Iglesia Santa Librada   CHURCH
(Av Belisario Porras) This baroque-style church near the central plaza opened its doors on March 9, 1789, but sustained major damage during a 1950 fire. The walls and the base of the pulpit are original, as are the painted faces on the ornate 23-karat gold-leaf altar. Cedar wood was used in the construction of the altar, renovated in 2001.

🎎 Festivals & Events

★ **Carnaval**   FESTIVAL
The best Carnaval in Panama, it is held during the four days that precede Ash

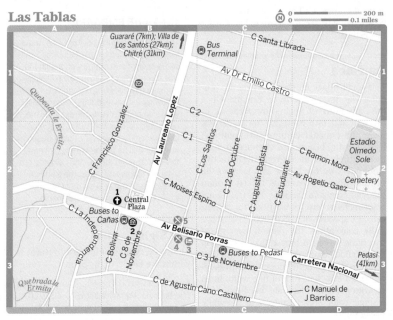

Las Tablas

Sights
1 Iglesia Santa Librada.............................B2
2 Museo Belisario Porras.......................B3

Sleeping
3 Hotel Piamonte B3

Eating
4 Boquitas Caseras.................................B3
5 Los Portales...B3

Wednesday. At dusk, floats and musicians are paraded on parallel streets. Crowds pack the sidewalks and fireworks light up the night. The queens appear on Saturday night and their coronation is held on Sunday. Monday is masquerade day and on Tuesday townswomen don *polleras*.

By tradition, the town is divided into two groups, *calle arriba* (high street) and *calle abajo* (low street); both compete intensely in every aspect of the fiesta. Each calle has its own queen, floats and songs. Each day begins with members parading in street clothes and singing songs that poke fun at the rival group. Jokesters toss tinted water, blue dye and shaving cream at the opposing

side. No one is spared – so dress expecting to get filthy.

**Fiestas Patronales de Santa
Librada** RELIGIOUS
On July 20 church services are accompanied by street celebrations that recall a medieval fair, with gambling, dancing, singing, and excessive eating and drinking – it's a strange juxtaposition of the sacred and the profane.

Fiesta de la Pollera FESTIVAL
Features a parade of beautiful young women who model the national costume as they pass through the streets on July 22, all while being judged on their grace and on the artisanship, design and authenticity of their costumes.

🛏 Sleeping & Eating

Hotel Piamonte HOTEL **$**
(✆923-1603; hotelpiamonte@hotmail.com; Av Belisario Porras; d US$33, annex s/d US$22/29; P✼☎) Clean and kept with frilly bedspreads, Piamonte is a friendly place to lay your head. Ask for a room with window. There's a downstairs restaurant and the annex across the street has bargain rooms without air-con or hot water.

Hotel La Luna INN $$
(☎6525-9410; www.hotel-laluna.com; Playa Uverito; d/tr/q US$60/75/80; ❉ 🛜 ⚟) Located 11.5km out of town on the beach, this modern house is an upscale option for those who want to celebrate the local festivities in style. Run by the charming Lucas from Milan, this two-story minimalist house has glass-front rooms, modern art and a kidney-shaped pool. Rooms have hot water and cable TV.

You can organize fishing tours, horseback riding and other activities onsite. A taxi from the center of town costs US$8.

Boquitas Caseras CAFE $
(Av Belisario Porras; mains US$2) This snack shop is a perfect hunger fix if you have a few minutes between buses: think marinated meatballs, potato salad and empanadas in a clean little cafe.

Los Portales PANAMANIAN $
(Av Belisario Porras; mains US$3-8) Housed in a handsome colonial building, this atmospheric yet low-key spot serves grilled meats and tasty seafood including *corvina ceviche* (marinated sea bass in lemon or lime juice, garlic and seasonings). Before hitting the road, stop by in the morning for a tasty farm-style breakfast to start your day the right way.

🛈 Information

Banco Nacional de Panamá (Av Laureano Lopez) Near Calle 2.
BBVA (Av Belisario Porras) Bank with ATM.
Post office (Calle 2)

🛈 Getting There & Away

The Carretera Nacional becomes Av Laureano Lopez at the northern edge of town and re-emerges as the road to Santo Domingo on the southeastern side of town. From Las Tablas' **bus terminal** (cnr Avs Laureano Lopez & Dr Emilio Castro) buses run hourly to Santo Domingo (US$0.35, 10 minutes), Cañas (US$3, 1½ hours), Chitré (US$1.50, 30 minutes), Tonosí (US$3, 1½ hours) and Pedasí (US$2.40, one hour).

There are 10 daily departures to Panama City (US$10, 4½ hours), with additional buses during festivals.

Pedasí

POP 1700

Unpretentious and picturesque, Pedasí's streets are lined with tiled colonials where inhabitants greet evening as they have for generations – rocking on the porch. For years, this sleepy retreat bloomed only at festival times. But outsiders are discovering the big appeal of small-town life and wilderness beaches.

Pedasí has become the focus of an intensive push to develop the southwestern coastline, with comparisons ranging from Tuscany to California. The hometown of former president Mireya Moscoso, Pedasí has a new airport (not yet in service) and promises of coming immigration and customs offices that could certainly make life easier for resident expats. But once the condos come, will the appeal still hold?

Pedasí serves as the gateway to the Azuero coastline, and is a convenient base for exploring Refugios de Vida Silvestre Isla Iguana and Isla de Cañas.

🕥 Sights & Activities

The Carretera Nacional passes down the western part of Pedasí, while the beaches start just a few kilometers to the east. None of the streets in Pedasí are marked with street signs.

Snorkeling and diving around the nearby islands surrounded by large coral reefs are major attractions. Sportfishers can land wahoo, tuna, mahimahi, amberjack and Pacific mackerel. For guided trips (around US$200 for two passengers), ask at Pedasí Sports Club or Casita Margarita.

Pedasí Sports Club DIVING
(☎995-2894; www.pedasisportsclub.biz; Calle Central s/n) The PADI-certified Pedasí Sports Club offers two-tank dives (US$95 and up) to Isla Frailes and Isla Iguana. Snorkelers (US$65) can join dive trips to Iguana. It also offers a river kayak tour (US$65), sportfishing (US$180), turtle-watching (US$65) and horseback riding (US$65). Staff speak English and Spanish.

🎊 Festivals & Events

Pedasí holds patron-saint festivals on June 29 and November 25, or the nearest Saturday to them. Although these events are nowhere near as chaotic as some of the more famous festivals in Azuero, they are nevertheless fun affairs, with long parades and lots of merriment. On July 16 a small celebration for fishers is held at Playa Arenal, a beach 3km northwest of town.

AZUERO EARTH PROJECT

The most highly deforested area of Panama, the Azuero has seen generations of cattle ranching degrade what was once tropical dry forest. Gone are the scarlet macaws and spider monkeys. Yet habitat destruction and advancing soil erosion isn't only detrimental to wildlife, it also affects ranchers. Enter Azuero Earth Project (p128), a nonprofit working to right these wrongs with the help of both volunteers and an elite team of experts collaborating from various fields.

Creating local economic benefits is key to sustainability. Current studies show that locals can win with a greener approach – but it will take time. Ranchers who set aside 10% of their land can double their income by growing hardwoods. The trick is convincing subsistence farmers to wait years for a pay-off when they are used to living day to day.

Currently, the center works closely with the community promoting organiculture, recycling and education about conservation, working with local elementary schools. Community outreach works with land owners and developers, government agencies and NGOs to work toward sustainable solutions.

🛏 Sleeping

Residencial Moscoso   HOTEL $
(☑995-2203; residencialmocoso@gmail.com; Av Central s/n; s/d US$25/30; 🅿❄) These clean but worn dark-tile rooms are bare-bones utilitarian. Don't mind the bare metal spigot that delivers your cold shower. Service is indifferent and internet isn't available.

Dim's Hostal   GUESTHOUSE $$
(☑995-2303; mirely@iname.com; Av Central s/n; s/d incl breakfast US$33/49; 🅿❄@🛜) Dim's has a family atmosphere and a coveted backyard patio, complete with breakfast tables, hammocks and a mango tree. Rooms and beds vary in quality (with some sagging mattresses) but the owners are delightful and service-oriented. A highlight is the huge breakfast spread served on the patio, where your friendly host cooks up eggs and *tortillas de maiz* made to order.

Peak Hostel   HOSTEL $$
(☑995-2776, 6258-1875; peakhostel@gmail.com; dm US$10, s/d/tr US$45/55/65; ❄) Pedasí's first hostel has a prime location on the plaza with a nice backyard garden. The attractive concrete-slab rooms with murals could use some fixing (look for leaks), though some are fine. Showers feature hot water. On the other hand, dorms are musty and overstocked with bunks.

La Rosa de los Vientos   B&B $$
(☑6530-4939, 6778-0627; www.bedandbreakfast pedasi.com; Camino a Playa del Toro; d/tr/q incl breakfast US$60/80/90; 🅿🛜) With the feel of a rural hacienda, this lovely red-tile Spanish colonial has three smart rooms with Guatemalan weavings and antique tiles abutting an acid-stained concrete deck. Owners Isabelle and Robert speak English, French and Spanish and provide warm hospitality. It's designed to be ecofriendly, so there is no aircon, but fans do the trick.

There's bicycles for borrowing and the couple plans to add horses soon. It's 2km from Pedasí on the road to Playa del Toro (taxis cost US$2.50). The beach is easily accessed on foot.

Pedasito Hotel   BOUTIQUE HOTEL $$
(☑995-2121; Calle Agustín Mocoso No 2; s/d with pool incl breakfast US$83/106; ❄🛜❄) Billed as boutique, this small hotel has a fresh, modern look. Ample rooms feature polished concrete floors, king-sized beds and stenciled walls. Those with pool access (mind you, it's pea-sized) have private terraces accessed by sliding glass doors. The onsite restaurant has patio seating and worthwhile international fare and seafood. There's an onsite surf shop and massages are available.

Hostal Doña María   HOTEL $$
(☑995-2916; www.hostaldonamaria.com; Av Central s/n; s/d/tr incl breakfast US$40/55/70; 🅿❄@) Ideal for couples, this caring family-run lodging has good tiled rooms with firm beds in plush quilted covers. The upstairs patio has soft sofas that peer out onto the street and a stack of magazines to peruse. Showers feature hot water and there's an open-air kitchen for guest use. Upgrades to cable TV or a queen-sized bed are extra (US$5).

An annex features extra rooms in back, with some disabled access.

Casita Margarita
B&B $$

(☏995-2898; www.pedasihotel.com; Av Central s/n; d incl breakfast US$109; 🅿️❄️@🛜) Stylish and sweet, the Casita is a reliable choice. Rooms are furnished with king-sized beds, flat-screen TVs, folk art and cool oversized tiles. Local information is quite good but don't expect great walk-in service. Unlike most spots, they accept credit cards and offer an honor bar. Kids under 10 stay free.

Pedasí Sports Club
HOTEL $$

(☏995-2894; www.pedasisportsclub.biz; Av Central s/n; s/d/tr incl breakfast US$55/66/77; 🅿️❄️@ 🛜❄️) Usually booked first for diving packages, these 10 newish motel-style rooms may lack character but they are impeccably clean and cool, with air-conditioning, wi-fi, satellite TV and hot-water showers. There's a pea-sized pool perfect for dips and equipment checks.

★ Casa de Campo
B&B $$

(☏6780-5280; www.casacampopedasi.com; Av Central s/n; d incl breakfast US$94; ❄️🛜❄️) Hospitable and simply lovely, this chic renovated colonial B&B says getaway. The mainstreet location is deceptive: out back there's a pool and lush landscaped grounds. Longtime locals, hosts Obedin and Koby are truly gracious and helpful. Guests share a family table for big breakfasts of Panamanian *tortillas de maíz* and eggs or fruit and cereal with fresh bread.

For a soothing day trip, ask about their private cliffside retreat.

✖️ Eating

Pasta e Vino
ITALIAN $

(☏6695-2689; mains US$5; ⊘6:30-10pm Tue-Sun) The essence of simplicity, this Italian-run restaurant has two chalkboard offerings nightly: pastas, a wine list and salad. Food is simple but authentic, like the pesto with black olives and fresh cheese. It's all about service: you are actually in Danilo and Elena's living room. The yellow house is three blocks past the plaza on the road to Playa El Toro.

★ Fonda Mama Fefa
PANAMANIAN $

(Calle Los Estudiantes s/n; set meal US$2.25; ⊘5am-2pm Mon-Sat) Matriarch of creole cooking, Mama Fefa usually runs out of lunch by noon (though you can linger longer). Cheap and cheerful, these huge *platos típicos* include meat or fish, rice, salad and a drink. Devotees share the space at a few outdoor tables. Take the side street abutting Dim's Hostel for a block and a half, it's on the right.

Maudy's Café
CAFE $

(Av Central s/n; mains US$3-6; ⊘8am-5pm Mon-Sat, closed Sep-Oct; 🛜🖊️) A Dutch-Panamanian venture into the deep end of blended drinks. Pineapple-mint or banana beet with carrot and OJ are refreshing zingers in one serious juice bar. You can also get fruit salad, baguette sandwiches or fruit sorbet at open-air tables flanked by resident parrots and with kids' toys underfoot.

Bakery
CAFE $

(☏995-2878; www.thebakerypedasi.com; Av Central s/n; mains US$4-7; ⊘7am-10pm) Known for exquisite breakfasts with homemade wheat or sourdough breads and organic coffee, this Israeli-run bakery does a brisk business. There's also bread-bowl soup and sandwiches with vegetarian options. The shady porch overlooks the main street.

Dulcería Yely
BAKERY $

(☏995-2205; cakes US$0.35-2; ⊘7am-9pm) This lovely cake shop on a side street near the Residencial Moscoso is an institution of delectable sweets. The sandwiches are tasty too (and cheap! burgers are US$2). While you're here, grab a *chicheme* (a concoction of milk, sweet corn, cinnamon and vanilla) and browse the photos of politicians and celebrities courting Yely.

Smiley's
AMERICAN $

(☏995-2863; Av Central s/n; mains US$4-12; ⊘12pm-9:30pm) Catering to expats, this friendly bar-restaurant serves up grilled fish and deli sandwiches such as minced BBQ pork with coleslaw. There's also good nightlife, with live music on Tuesday and Friday, sports matches on the tube, and an extensive drink menu to match. Locals get excited about the ribs night.

Villa Libera
PIZZERIA $

(☏6791-2387; mains US$6-9; ⊘6-10pm) Run by an energetic young Italian couple, this simple pizzeria with candlelit tables serves thin wood-fired pizzas in addition to seafood or steaks cooked on volcanic stones. A popular hangout for locals, it's located on a branch off the road to Playa Toro.

Mamallena's
CAFE $

(Calle Agustín Mocoso s/n; mains US$6; ⊘6:30am-3:30pm Tue-Sat) This Aussie-run surfer cafe has an assortment of tasty bites on a tiny patio facing the plaza. Expats dig the Vietnamese spring rolls. There's also Caesar salad and a flat but filling spaghetti bolognese. For dessert there's cupcakes and rum balls.

Tiesto PIZZERIA $
(Calle Ramón Ramos s/n; mains US$1-5; ⊙2-10pm Wed-Mon) With brick-oven pizzas topped with local cheese and tasty US$2 chicken tacos, this plaza-front Panamanian cafe proves a magnet for locals and backpackers alike. Sweets include oatmeal cookies and pineapple cake.

Gregory DINER $
(Calle Agustín Mocoso s/n; mains US$5-10; ⊙noon-10pm Tue-Sun) Cute and Canadian-owned, this pocket-sized diner serves burgers on fresh rolls, hot wings and milkshakes with a slick red and black backdrop. If you want bacon on your burger or heat in your wings, it's your spot.

Isla Iguana SEAFOOD $
(Av Central s/n; mains US$4-9; ⊙11am-10pm Thu-Tue) For filling seafood with a Chinese accent, try this roadside restaurant that somehow manages the feel of a friendly truck stop. One shrimp chow mien could feed three people. Located just before the gas station.

Centro Comercial Pedasí SUPERMARKET $
(Av Central s/n; ⊙7am-9pm) The principal supermarket sits in front of Dim's.

ℹ Information

ANAM (⊙8am-4pm Mon-Fri) The ANAM office in the south of town has extremely poor service (and no phone), but in theory it provides information about Isla Iguana and Isla de Cañas.

ATP (☑995-2339; ⊙9:30am-5:30pm) Helpful but slow, the ATP office lies one block past the main road in the north of town. It has a list of boat contacts for Isla de Cañas.

Azuero Earth Project (www.azueroearthproject.org; ⊙8am-5pm Mon-Fri) This volunteer-friendly NGO focuses on behind-the-scenes work in conservation and community education. Visitors can check out the research center library, with naturalist guides and maps for sale. Talks are given the first Saturday of the month and an outdoor information board features a community events calendar. It's on a side street behind the gas station by the town entrance.

Banco Nacional de Panama (Av Central s/n) Has an ATM (one of two in town on Av Central) near the entrance to town.

ℹ Getting There & Away

Buses from Las Tablas leave every 45 minutes between 6am and 4pm (US$3, one hour) from next to the Centro Comercial. Buses to Playa Venado (US$2, 30 minutes) leave at 7am, noon and 2pm. Buses to Cañas (US$2, 45 minutes) leave at 7am.

The coastline is easily accessed by private vehicle or **taxi** (☑995-2275); the taxi stand sits on Av Central. Standard one-way fares include Playa El Toro US$3.50, Playa La Garita US$5, Playa Estiladero US$7, Playa Venado US$24 and Cambutal US$60 to US$80. Cambutal runs expensive due to the often dismal condition of the road.

Around Pedasí

Refugio de Vida Silvestre Isla Iguana

The 55-hectare **Refugio de Vida Silvestre Isla Iguana** (admission US$10) is centered on a deserted island ringed by coral fields, though unfortunately many of the reeds died in the 1982–83 El Niño (a change in weather patterns that shifts ocean currents and starves marine life along the eastern Pacific coast). However, the surviving coral is pretty spectacular and the water is shallow enough for snorkeling. As with most reefs in the Pacific, the fish here are enormous.

Humpback whales also inhabit the waters around Isla Iguana from June to November. These large sea mammals, 15m to 20m long, mate and bear their young here and then teach them to dive. The humpbacks are the famous 'singing whales' – occasionally you can hear their underwater sounds when diving here.

Although the island is supposed to be maintained by ANAM, Panama's environmental agency, the main beach is often strewn with litter, which can be hard to control as it comes in with the tide. Also, the US Navy used the island for target practice during WWII and unexploded ordnance is occasionally discovered here. Needless to say, it's unwise to stray off the beaten paths.

Isla Iguana is reachable by boat from Playa El Arenal, a beach 3km northwest of the Accel station in Pedasí. At the beach, boaters can take parties to the island for around US$60. ATP in Pedasí can also help you arrange for a boat. Hold payment until the return trip and be clear on when you want to be picked up.

THE TUNA COAST

The Azuero coastline is often referred to as the 'tuna coast'. Home to a large population of yellow-fin (ahi) tuna, the area serves as a benchmark indicator for the health of global tuna stocks.

Among the most sought-after fish in the world, yellow-fin tuna has spawned a billion-dollar industry. Found in subtropical and tropical waters, tuna reach lengths of over 2m and can weigh upwards of 200kg. Although typically processed and canned, tuna is increasingly flash frozen and sold in fillets for sushi. Left raw, tuna is blood red in color, with a smooth texture and a rich buttery taste.

Thirty kilometers southwest of Pedasí, **Laboratorio Achotines** (Tuna Laboratory; ☑ 995-8166; www.iattc.org; tours US$1) tracks the movement and behavior of these fish, tagging them to study migration patterns. The tuna lab is also the only place in the world with tuna spawning in captivity daily. But instead of making sashimi lunches for staff, they use the process to study tuna eggs and larvae. Affiliated with the Inter-American Tropical Tuna Commission, a global regulatory consortium on tuna fishing, the lab routinely sets quotas for catches along the Pacific coast of the Americas.

Visitors can tour Laboratorio Achotines by appointment and watch an interesting educational video. Another highlight is to show up for the feeding of prize-sized tunas.

Azuero Coastline

Gorgeous and a little remote, the rolling green coast of Azuero has seen a recent boom in lodgings. Many do not take children – easy to understand if you note the number of cliffs and swimming pools – so check ahead if you have little ones.

Playas El Toro & La Garita

The two closest beaches to Pedasí serve as a popular day trip for residents of Pedasí, especially since the ocean here is usually safe for swimming. However, the waves can pick up if there's a strong surge coming in.

At Playa El Toro you can actually drive onto the beach if you have a vehicle, but Playa La Garita is flanked by a rocky slope, and a hike of about 100m through light scrub and dirt (which turns to mud if there's been any recent rain) is required to reach the beach. Despite their close proximity to Pedasí, both beaches are quite isolated and private. Neither offers much snorkeling – the water is simply too murky. An open-air restaurant serves seafood and beer.

You can hire a taxi in Pedasí to reach these beaches (US$5 one way); if you're driving from central Pedasí, turn east off the Carretera Nacional onto the paved street beside the Residencial Moscoso and drive about 250m to the Cantina Hermanos Cedeño bar. Then take the road just past the bar for 1km until the road forks. Follow the signs for 2km to the beaches.

Playa Los Destiladeros

🛏 Sleeping

⭐ **Posada Los Destiladeros** CABIN $$
(☑ 6673-9262, 995-2771; www.panamabambu.net; d incl breakfast from US$60, beachfront cabin from US$125, tr ste US$200; [P][❄][@][≋]) A sweet and seductive clutch of cabins with dizzy views of the pounding surf. Accommodations range from modern rooms to Africa-inspired thatched huts with vaulted ceilings. There are no TVs. The French chef-diver owner Philippe Atanasiades has crafted each to showcase his own taste and travels. Hand-hewn wicker canopy beds sit alongside Polynesian carvings and modern baths, and it works.

The restaurant is a popular destination for nonguests. Reserve ahead for a candle-lit three-course dinner featuring the catch of the day and ultrafresh vegetables. There is also a good wine list. To get here, drive through Pedasí and take the left hand turnoff in El Límon.

Villa Camilla RESORT $$$
(☑ 995-9595, 994-3100; www.villacamillapanama.com; d US$225-450, 4-person ocean loft US$250; [P][❄][@][≋]) A modern fortress, Villa Camila is a gorgeous adobe compound with sleek lines and chic accents. Privacy is primary – the villa has hosted the likes of Michael Jordan and Shakira. Don't expect TVs; the concept is unplugged. Rooms are ample, low-lit and cool, and a long footpath of river stones leads though manicured grounds to the beach.

SURFING LOS SANTOS

Though untapped by the international crowd, Los Santos Province is the source of some serious surf. Panamanians mostly hit the coastline near Pedasí, though there is no shortage of wicked spots (just a shortage of transportation to them).

Playa Lagarto At Pedasí. Beach bottom. Breaks at all tides. Good rights, lefts. Closes out when surf too big.

Playa El Toro Near Pedasí. Rock-bottom point break with lefts, rights. Gets big with a strong swell. Best surfed at medium tide.

Playa Los Destiladeros Near Pedasí. Right point over rock bottom, left point over rock bottom, beach break with pebble bottom. Best at medium tide.

Ciruelo Before Venado. Rock-bottom point break, rarely surfed. Can get really good left tubes when there is a strong swell and no wind.

Playa Venao South of Venado. Sand-bottom beach break popular with local surfers. This spot catches just about any swell. Best surfed at medium to high tide.

Playa Madroño A 30-minute walk from Venado. Surf can get really good, with hollow tubes at low tide. Need to arrive early in the day before the wind picks up.

Playa Guánico A 45-minute walk south of Venado. Two rock-bottom point breaks with rights and lefts. One beach break with rights and lefts.

Playa Raya One hour past Venado. Waves 4m to 5m on big swells with serious tubes. Many big sharks here as well.

Playa Cambutal Beyond Tonosí. Beach breaks with rights and lefts. Catches just about every swell. Best at medium to high tide.

Playa Negra West of Playa Cambutal, around the first point. Point break over rocks, best during medium to high tide.

411 West of Punta Negra. Locally famous point break with a long right over a rock ledge. Best during medium to high tide.

Dinosaurios Next to 411. Rock-bottom break with rights, lefts at medium to high tide. Can get very big with strong swells.

Horcones Beach Break West of Dinosaurios. Sand-bottom beach break with rights, lefts. Good most tides.

Dos Rocas Near Horcones. Rock-bottom point break beside two jutting boulders. Can get good rights at medium tide.

Corto Circuito At road's end toward Cerro Hoya. Rock-bottom point break with powerful peak. Breaks over a rock ledge and throws a huge tube, then peels for about 100m with a great wall.

Chef-made meals are available for extra. Yet the best part may be lolling about the delicious infinity pool set amid tall palms. The serenity here should not be underestimated – consider how in love you are before booking this lovely bubble of solitude.

La Playita

Popular among Panamanian day-trippers, the nice beach at La Playita (adult/child US$3/1) has shower and bathroom services attached to the resort. An onsite restaurant serves typical Panamanian fare (mains US$8). Weekends may be crowded.

More rustic retreat than resort, the shady and somewhat outdated cabins at Resort La Playita (☎ 996-2225; www.playitaresort.com; d/q cabin US$88/120; P ✳ ☎) sit surrounded by an informal zoo of clipped-wing guacamayas and ñandus. For most, the sight of these animals is less than encouraging. Playita has some recently upgraded rooms with air-con and hydromassage showers, but the best is No 5, with its atmospheric collection of memorabilia and cozy throws with a private balcony.

Resort La Playita is about 13km southwest of Pedasí, down a rugged dirt road. Arriving from Pedasí, the bus passes the entrance at 7am, and returns at around 3:30pm.

Playa Ciruelo

A pretty half-moon bay, Playa Ciruelo has lodgings and a fishing-village atmosphere.

Fishing tours are easy to book, but keep in mind that you will want a covered boat for shade with a decent motor. Recommended Agusto López (☑6671-9421) – aka 'Pimply' – meets both standards and is known as one of the best local guides for fishing tours.

The Cañas–Las Tablas bus passes at around 7:30am bound for Las Tablas and heads towards Cañas at 4pm. A taxi from Pedasí costs US$14.

🛏 Sleeping & Eating

Hostal Casa Estrella INN $$
(☑6571-3090; www.casadeestrella.com; d US$55-66; P❋🛜) An excellent value, the American-owned Hostal Casa Estrella has four pristine blue rooms with driftwood beds and sea views. Showers have hot water. The house is inviting and immaculate, with hammocks on a shady deck and a comfortable family living area. Enrique, the friendly host, runs fishing trips and the spot is also popular with surfers.

Sereia do Mar INN $$
(☑838-5962, 6523-8758; www.sereiadomar.net; d/tr incl breakfast US$88/98; P❋🛜) The mellow Sereia do Mar has four fresh rooms with adobe-style molding and walk-out porches with breathtaking sea views. Rooms come equipped with TV, refrigerator and hot-water showers. Guests are fairly on their own here, though it's a relaxing spot and even offers discounts for weeklong stays. Meals are available upon request.

Hostal del Mar CABIN $$
(☑6634-1245; www.hostaldelmarpedasi.com; d US$65) With just four tiny cabins dripping with passion fruit vines, these simple rooms with hammock decks are mostly aimed at surfers (with the Punta Marfil break out front). Lanterns are loaned if you want to descend the steep path to the beach at night; it becomes submerged in high tides.

Pritti Pizza PIZZERIA $
(pizzas US$6.50-9; ☉8am-9pm) In a thatched *rancho* on the main road, this spartan restaurant makes a worthy pitstop if your stomach's grumbling. Thin-crust pizzas are fired in a brick oven. Chill out to reggae while you wait.

Playa Venao

A long, protected beach, Playa Venao recently transformed from a wild beach to an outright destination. Surfers lay the first claim to its waters – waves are consistent and break in both directions.

Area accommodations can set up surf lessons. Ask around for recommended instructor Trico Rangel (tricosurfschool@gmail.com; class US$25-30); he speaks a bit of English, does board repairs and is locally based.

The Playa Venao turnoff is 33km by road southwest of Pedasí, or 2km past the Resort La Playita turnoff. The Cañas–Pedasí bus (US$2) passes between 7:30am and 8am in the evening. Confirm exact times with your hotel. You can also take a taxi from Pedasí (US$24).

🛏 Sleeping & Eating

⭐Eco Venao LODGE $
(☑832-0530; www.venao.com; campsite per person US$5.50, dm/d without bathroom US$11/28, 2-person cabin US$44, 6-person house US$275; P❋🛜) On the jungle side of the main access road, American-owned Eco Venao offers cool mountain ambiance. Perfect for surfers and adventurers, its excellent low-to-high-end options offer something for everyone. The lush 57-hectare property means mini-adventures are close at hand, from howler monkey visits and a playground to a short waterfall hike.

Dorm rooms are without reservation and rustic (though comfy) with mosquito nets and fans. Privates range from traditional thatched huts with composting toilets to colonial-style guesthouses with colorful weaves and wood accents. The newest addition, a six-person Cali-style minimalist house high on the hill, provides a gorgeous retreat. Low season means huge discounts.

Guests can rent horses (US$10), surfboards (US$15 per day) or kayaks (US$25 to US$35 per day) and do yoga. 'Eco' means that trash separation and recycling are practiced, as well as reforestation and a small footprint, with minimal roads and footpaths that lead to the beach.

La Choza

HOSTEL $

(www.playavenaohostel.com; campsite per person US$7, dm US$15, d with/without air-con US$55/40; ❄ 🛜) A skip to the waves, this new option is perfect for shoestringers. Somewhat cramped dorms have polished cement floors, fans and comfortable beds with white linens. Hot showers are delivered via a bare spigot. Some private rooms feature bunks and all rooms have shared bathrooms. There's kitchen use and a nearby mini-market for supplies. Reserve via sister operation El Sitio Hotel.

El Sitio Hotel

HOTEL $$$

(⌨832-1010; www.elsitiohotel.com; d US$109-193; ❄🛜⌨) New on the scene, El Sitio's best feature is its location right on Venao beach. With ample, classic rooms, it's hard to recognize that it's actually built from shipping containers. Service is attentive and professional. Activities include jungle tours and seasonal whale-watching (from US$35 per person in groups). There's also massage, a good restaurant and a surf shop.

Villa Marina

HOTEL $$$

(⌨397-1058; www.villamarinapanama.com; d incl breakfast US$198; P❄⌨) Sharing Playa Venao but with an earlier access (just past La Playita), Villa Marina is a stunner. Set amid tranquil gardens, this regal resort exudes charm, from the spurting fountain to the wide shady porch. Guest rooms are bright with ocean breezes, while the larger master bedroom has French doors opening to the beach.

Guests can spend their days lounging around on hammocks, horseback riding on the beach, snorkeling and surfing in the sea or on boating and fishing excursions.

Boboré

INTERNATIONAL $

(⌨6634-4550; at Eco Venao; mains US$4-10; ⊙8am-9:30pm) Located at Eco Venao but open to the public, this relaxed thatched restaurant serves beachgoers with an appetite. While surfers usually down the daily special (US$4), there are also Spanish- and Asian-influenced dishes cooked up by Chef Aldo. The burgers are huge. There is occasionally live music.

El Sitio Restaurant

INTERNATIONAL $$

(⌨832-1010; mains US$9-18; ⊙7:30am-10pm) Your best bet for sunset dining or drinks on Playa Venao. Open-air El Sitio offers homemade shrimp ravioli and polenta and sesame-crust tuna that can be spot on. Yet its reputation has been spotty thanks to turnover in the cooking staff. A dedicated pastry chef prepares nice tropical crème brûlée and coconut macaroons.

Playas Cambutal & Guánico

Playas Cambutal and Guánico, 16km and 22km away from Tonosí respectively, are two excellent surfing beaches along the southern coast of the Península de Azuero. Both are reachable by dirt road from Tonosí, but access is difficult. First take the Cañas bus from Las Tablas at 7am or 2pm (US$4, 1¼ hours). From Cañas, a bus goes to Tonosí (US$1.50, 30 minutes) and from Tonosí to Playa Cambutal (US$1.50, 20 minutes).

New community conservation organization **Tortuagro** (⌨6264-1936; Cambutal) patrols the beach with volunteers during turtle season; it is also in the process of setting up tours. Get in touch with Yaqueline Vásquez for more information (Spanish only).

At Playa Cambutal, the recommended beachfront **Hotel Cambutal** (⌨832-0948; www.hotelplayacambutal.net; d incl breakfast US$149; ❄🛜⌨) offers the most comfortable lodgings in the area with an ecofriendly approach. It also has a good restaurant, and can arrange fishing boats, nature walks (US$35), turtle sighting (US$10), horseback riding (US$15, two hours) and kayaking.

If you have your own transportation, give some thought to camping on the beaches between July and early September as you'll likely see some nesting sea turtles. Since there aren't any stores near the beaches, be sure to take provisions.

Isla de Cañas

From July through early November, thousands of olive ridley sea turtles come ashore at night to lay eggs on the broad beach of **Isla de Cañas** (admission US$10). This is one of five places that these endangered turtles nest in such numbers – the others are two beaches on the Pacific side of Costa Rica, and two beaches in Orissa, India, on the Bay of Bengal.

The turtles arrive late at night, so there's no point in hiring a guide during daylight hours. Instead, agree on a meeting place and an hour when the guide can take you. When that time arrives, the guide will walk you across the island to the beach and, if you're lucky, you'll arrive at the same time as the expectant mothers. Keep in mind that sea turtles are easily frightened, particularly by bright lights such as flashlights and cameras. Instead of hoping to resist the temptation to use these items, just leave them behind – your eyes will adjust to the moonlight and you can take plenty of mental pictures.

Tour operator Frederik Lacoste (☑ 6980-0110; www.islacañasmarina.com) offers recommended turtle and general ecotours of the reserve by boat, paddle board or sea kayak, the latter two being fun alternatives for exploring the waterways. You can also arrange turtle tours through the Pedasí branch of ATP.

There's a small restaurant on the beach as well as some nameless cabañas (per person US$20) if you wish to stay on the island. Bring a mosquito net and lots of insect repellent, long pants, a windbreaker or bug jacket and mosquito coils if you have them.

To access the island, a bus runs from Pedasí to Cañas (US$2, 45 minutes) at 7am and noon. From here, take a Tonosí-bound bus, which stops in Puerto de Cañas (US$1.50, 30 minutes). If this sounds like too much work, coordinate a guided trip with your hotel in Pedasí or at Pedasí Sports Club (p125).

If you are driving, the turnoff for Isla de Cañas is easy to miss. It's beside a bus stop on the south side of the Carretera Nacional, 6.5km west of the turnoff for the town of Cañas; next to the bus stop there's a brown-and-yellow sign that reads 'Bienvenidos Isla de Cañas via Puerto 2.5km.' The bus stop is served by Toyota Coaster buses that travel between Las Tablas and Tonosí hourly from 7am to 4pm.

From the turnoff, a 5km drive or hike on a dirt road takes you to the edge of a mangrove forest. There's usually a boater there who will shuttle you to and from the island.

If there's no boater to greet you, find the truck wheel hanging from a tree at the mangrove's edge and hit it hard five times with the rusty wrench atop it. If the sun's out and the tide's up – if there's water in the mangrove – a boater will fetch you.

Once you reach the island, you will be approached by a guide. As a rule every foreign visitor must be accompanied by an island guide. Paying local guides provides a worthy local alternative to inhabitants selling turtle eggs on the black market. As it is, about half of the eggs that are laid on the beach are dug up and sold illegally in Panama City – the other half are placed in hatcheries to ensure survival.

Macaracas

POP 1900

Forty kilometers southwest of Chitré, the tiny town of Macaracas is the site of an annual festival folklórico (⊙ January 5 to 10), highlighted by dramatic theater performances including the popular story of *The Three Wise Men*.

The nearby Río La Villa, a secluded river just outside of town, is ideal for swimming and very popular on weekends. To get there, take a right off the main road at the San Juan gas station. Continue for 750m until you pass over a metal bridge, then turn right into the gravel lot.

Above the pharmacy on the main road, Pensión Lorena (☑ 995-4181; d US$25; P ✳) has spartan rooms with cold-water showers; it'll do in a pinch. The attached restaurant also serves up hot meals, but don't expect anything more than Panamanian staples.

Buses run between Macaracas and Chitré (US$2.50, one hour, hourly), and Macaracas and Tonosí (US$3, one hour, hourly) from 7am to 4pm.

Veraguas Province

POP 227,00 / ELEV SEA LEVEL TO 3478M / AREA 10,050 SQ KM

Best Places to Eat

➡ Anachoreo (p140)

➡ Chano's Point (p145)

➡ La Panaderia (p145)

➡ Los Pibes (p145)

➡ La Buena Vida (p145)

Best Places to Stay

➡ Hostal La Qhia (p140)

➡ Hibiscus Garden (p142)

➡ La Buena Vida (p143)

➡ Time Out (p144)

➡ Oasis Surf Camp (p144)

Why Go?

Nearly 500 years ago, the Spanish were lured here by the region's natural beauty, with robust rivers, stunning peaks and the promises of vast gold reserves. Though the gold ran out and colonies failed, the essence of Columbus' first impression remains.

The Galápagos of Central America, the wildlife-rich Unesco World Heritage Site of Isla Coiba draws divers, birdwatchers and paradise seekers. Surf village Santa Catalina has become a destination in its own right. Hikes to waterfalls and swimming holes around the highland village of Santa Fé offer an off-the-beaten-path retreat.

The isolated Caribbean coast of Veraguas will soon be accessible by the Carretera de Caribe, a now half-constructed cross-peninsula road bound to change the future of the region and places on the way, like Santa Fé. In short, this deforested region of ranchers and subsistence farmers is redefining itself. Tourism may help recast its fragile fortunes.

When to Go

➡ **Feb–Mar** The best months to hit the world-class surf breaks in Santa Catalina and along the Veraguas coast.

➡ **Dec–Feb** Three species of turtle nest on the beaches of Malena in Western Azuero Península; community volunteers guide these very off-the-beaten-path trips.

➡ **Dec–Apr** Dry season means the the best weather for the beach, but the May–Nov rainy season means waterfalls near highland Santa Fé are big – though trails may be muddy. In October many services are closed.

Veraguas Province Highlights

1 Explore the astounding natural beauty of **Parque Nacional Coiba** (p145), above or below the water line

2 Surf some seriously sick waves at **Playa Santa Catalina** (p141), Panama's legendary surf spot

3 Retreat to the highland village of **Santa Fé** (p137), famous for its waterfalls, steep hills and lush forests

4 Visit the **Iglesia San Francisco de Veraguas** (p136), one of the best examples of baroque religious art and architecture in the Americas

5 Get inspired off the beaten path with a retreat to the crowd-free **Isla Gobernadora** (p147)

6 Adventure to the **Western Azuero Península** (p148), with remote coastal appeal and community turtle tours

History

The fourth and final voyage of Columbus brought him here in search of a water passage that would, by his calculation, pass south of Asia into the Indian Ocean. The year was 1502, and the great explorer spent most of it commanding his little worm-eaten fleet up and down the Caribbean coast from Venezuela to Nicaragua. Unable to find a strait, but seeing gold-laden natives in the region, the admiral cast anchor between Veraguas and Colón Provinces.

In February 1503 Columbus gave orders to establish a hillside colony beside the mouth of Río Belén. The Quibian, the area's native inhabitants, massacred an exploratory party that had gone up river. When Spanish corpses came floating down the river, Columbus loaded the ships and set sail for Hispaniola (the island of modern-day Dominican Republic and Haiti).

In his journal Columbus wrote: 'I departed, in the name of the Holy Trinity, on Easter night, with the ships rotten, worn out, and eaten with holes.' He died three years later believing he'd seen Asia, unaware that he'd found instead the second-largest landmass on earth.

Over the next 30 years, the Spanish attempted several other expeditions, which all ended in similar disaster. The conquistadors returned to the area two decades later and eventually overcame the Quibian. After finding gold, they established mines, and in 1560 founded the town of Concepción (which has since disappeared), 10km west of the Río Belén. African slaves were brought in to extract gold and run the smelter in Concepción. With mines completely spent by 1590, many miners fled or took to farming throughout Pacific Veraguas and the Península de Azuero.

Santiago

POP 44,500

About 250km from Panama City, the sprawling town of Santiago is a bustling hub of rural commercial activity. Halfway between the capital and the Costa Rican border, and just north of the Península de Azuero, Santiago is a crossroads town where you can easily get a hot meal and a clean bed. For the casual tourist there's little reason to stop, though it's a good place to break up a long drive and recharge for the night.

Most of the town's commerce and services, including stores, banks, gas stations, internet cafes, restaurants and hotels, are along the Interamericana and Av Central, which splits off from the highway.

For regional tourism information, stop by the ATP tourist office (☑998-3929; Av Central). ANAM (☑998-4387, 998-0615; Interamericana) has information on area parks, including Parque Nacional Coiba, and supplies fishing permits.

Approximately 25km south of Santiago is the port of Puerto Mutis, which is the most popular disembarkation point for boats heading to Isla de Coiba.

Note that Santiago is also a convenient base for visiting the Iglesia San Francisco de Veraguas (San Francisco of Veraguas Church).

There are ATMs at the bus terminal and across the street from it. If you are headed to Santa Catalina, Isla de Coiba or Santa Fé, these are the closest cash machines you'll find.

Backpackers will appreciate the cheap living at the homestay-like Hostal Veraguas (☑958-9021, 6669-6126; www.hostalveraguas.com; Barriada San Martín; dm/d US$10/20, outside dm US$6; @ ⛷), popular with Peace Corps volunteers. Host Lidia goes out of her way for guests, who can even gather herbs for tea in the garden. It's located five blocks behind the University of Panamá chapel.

Also along the Interamericana, Hotel Plaza Gran David (☑998-3433; d US$33; P ✳ @ ⛷ ⛳) is well regarded locally, mainly because of its swimming pool. Rooms are decked in stucco and tile; some of them are drive-up. They also feature TV and hot water.

If you're looking to stock up, there's a supermarket in front of the bus terminal.

From the bus terminal (☑998-4006), buses depart for David (US$9, three hours) hourly from 9am to 2am, and for Panama City (US$9.50, four hours) hourly from 3:15am to 9:15pm.

Buses to destinations in Veraguas depart from Santiago's bus terminal on Calle 10, near Av E. For Santa Fé, buses depart half-hourly from 5am to 7:30pm (US$2.90, 1½ hours). You can also hail these on the turnoff from the Interamericana, north of Calle 24. To reach the surf destination of Santa Catalina, you must first take a bus to Soná and transfer. Buses to Soná depart half-hourly from 7am to 6pm (US$2.10, one hour). From Soná to Santa Catalina (US$4.65, 1½ hours) there are four departures daily. Buses charge extra for surfboards.

If you don't have your own wheels, taxis are easy to hail and they go anywhere in town for US$2 or less. You can also hire Radio Taxi (☑958-8075) to the Iglesia San Francisco de Veraguas (US$8 one way) or the towns of Soná (US$30), Santa Catalina (US$70) or Santa Fé (US$30).

San Francisco

In the small town of San Francisco, 16km north of the Interamericana on the road from Santiago to Santa Fé, the historic San Francisco of Veraguas Church is one of the best and oldest examples of baroque art and architecture in the Americas.

The centerpiece is the highly ornate altar of ash and bitter cedar. Although most colonial altars in the Americas were brought over from Europe, this one was carved by local indigenous people and finished around 1727.

In addition to images of the crucifixion, Virgin and saints, there are finely carved and well-preserved images of the artisans and prominent indigenous people. Their faces are cleverly inserted into the religious scenes – some atop the bodies of cherubs. One large carving also includes items that had special meaning for the natives – an eagle piercing its own heart with its beak, three large dice, a Spanish sword, a lantern and a human skull.

The original bell tower survived until 1942, when it suddenly collapsed without warning. It had also served the Spanish as a lookout tower to monitor the movements of local people and slaves.

To reach the church, head 16km north on the San Francisco turnoff from the Interamericana, until you reach the police substation near a stop sign. Veer right, proceed 400m, and then turn right again at the Supermercado Juan XXIII de San Francisco. Another 100m on, you'll see the church on the left.

A bus leaves the Santiago terminal for San Francisco (US$1, 30 minutes, every 30 minutes from 7am to 6pm). An alternative is to hire a taxi in Santiago (US$16 round trip).

Near the church, El Chorro del Spiritu Santo (Holy Spirit Waterfall) has a fine swimming hole. Follow the road as it winds around the church, and then take the road just behind the church. After a few hundred

WORTH A TRIP

CERAMICA LA PEÑA

A ceramic workshop and artisan market (☉9am-4:30pm Mon-Fri), La Peña sells wood carvings and baskets made by the Emberá and Wounaan peoples of the Darién, woven purses and soapstone figurines made by local Ngöbe-Buglé people, and masks from the town of Parita. There's also a good selection of pots and sculptures available for purchase, some made onsite. It's on the Interamericana, 8km west of Santiago.

meters, take the first right; after another several hundred meters the road will bring you to the small cascades.

San Francisco has no lodgings, though it's convenient to Santiago or Santa Fé.

Santa Fé

POP 3000

This tiny mountain town lies in the shadow of the Continental Divide about 52km north of Santiago. At an altitude of 500m, Santa Fé is cooler than the lowlands, and much of the surrounding forests remain as they did when the Spaniards founded the town in 1557.

Like Boquete, Santa Fé has fresh clean air and bucolic surroundings, yet it sees fewer foreign visitors, though the real-estate frenzy is starting to creep here too. With lush mountainsides, waterfalls and mountain streams right outside the town, Santa Fé is an ideal destination for hikers, birdwatchers and those simply wanting to soak up the beauty of the highlands.

⊙ Sights

With hilly contours, the town layout is confusing to visitors but pleasant to walk nonetheless. The road from Santiago splits off from the Interamericana and winds through lovely valleys, branching out in three directions at the southern edge of town. The middle 'branch' forks yet again after a few more blocks.

A number of lovely waterfalls, empty mountain streams and accessible swimming spots are all within walking distance from town.

Santa Fé

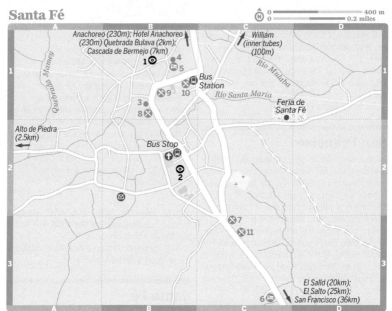

Santa Fé

⊙ Sights

1	Café El Tute Coffee Plant	B1
2	Mercado	B2

Activities, Courses & Tours

3	Cooperativa Santa Fé	B1
4	Fundación Hector Gallego	B1

Sleeping

5	Hostal La Qhia	B1
6	Hotel Santa Fé	C3

Eating

7	Blue Iguana	C3
8	La Matera	B1
9	Restaurante de la Cooperativa	B1
10	Restaurante de la Terminal	B1
11	Super Santa Fe	C3

Quebrada Bulava   RIVER

There's a lovely swimming hole at the Quebrada Bulava, a 20-minute walk from town. Head along the right branch of the fork at the cemetery, take the second right, and you'll soon reach several spots that make for a nice dip. Continuing on, you'll reach a bridge – cross it and take the second turnoff on the right.

Here a local named William rents inner tubes (US$7) and life jackets, which allow you to float idly down the river; it eventually merges with Río Santa Maria. He can also arrange a taxi return.

Cascada de Bermejo   WATERFALL

An excellent half-day road and trail walk (four hours round trip) leads to this tall waterfall with a delightful swimming hole in the dry season. Follow past William's inner-tube rentals; after taking the Bulava bridge take your first left to a steep uphill. Here the road becomes dirt; continue until the waterfall, following yellow arrow signs into the trail.

You can return looping onto the main road (going right leaving the trail and left at every intersection). In rainy season you should inquire with locals about conditions before going.

El Salto   WATERFALL

Further afield, the impressive waterfall known as El Salto lies about two hours south of Santa Fé along a bad 4WD road, only accessible during the dry season. On foot, it is a full eight-hour excursion with time for bathing.

There are also three waterfalls in Alto de Piedra. Since access can be difficult and affected by recent weather conditions; it is necessary to hire a local guide to visit these areas. Aventuras Cesamo is available for hikes and bird-watching.

Cerro Tute   MOUNTAIN

With excellent open views of the valley, Cerro Tute is home to the area's famed bird life and features a cliff blasted with up currents that seemingly prevent anyone from falling off. An extensive trail network winds through primary and secondary rainforest. It's a few kilometers south of town, on the western side of the Santiago–Santa Fé road. Best with a guide.

Alto de Piedra   OUTDOORS

The vast, mountainous area of Alto de Piedra contains thousands of hectares of pristine wilderness, extending from the northern edge of Santa Fé to the Caribbean Sea. Part of the northern portion of the province that remained roadless so long, a dirt road now penetrates the area. It's wise to access this sector with an area guide.

As hikes go this now-improved road is a little dull, but it is worth doing as a loop circuit. It's reachable by a signposted gravel road that leaves the western side of town.

Mercado   MARKET

Just past the entrance to town, this open-air market sells fruits and vegetables, woven handmade bags, a wide range of hats, leather goods and many other interesting items. It's a fun place to browse.

🏃 Activities

The expansive views, rugged hills and mountains around Santa Fé are perfect for exploring on horseback.

Best explored with a guide, Cerro Tute and Alto de Piedra offer some fine bird-watching. Many specialties of eastern Chiriquí and Veraguas Provinces can be found here, including the rufous-winged woodpecker and the crimson-collared tanager. Both areas require a 4WD vehicle, a horse or strong legs.

Aventuras Cesamo   HORSEBACK RIDING

(📱954-0807, 6972-0571; www.aventurascesamo.blogspot.com) Reputable local guide Cesar Miranda takes visitors on horseback rides using his own horses. He also guides Alto de Piedra and area walks to waterfalls.

Chong & María   AGROTOURISM

(📱6525-4832; half-day tour per person US$5) To see an organic family farm up close, visit with Chong & María, hospitable *campesino* (farmer) hosts happy to bring you in and show you around their very small-scale operation. Though they only speak Spanish, this lovely couple finds a way to communicate with non-Spanish-speaking visitors that makes the trip still very worthwhile.

You can also check out their orchids and sample María's homemade cooking over lunch (US$3). It's excellent for families too, who can take advantage of the country quiet and a nearby swimming hole. Make sure you book ahead.

CAFÉ EL TUTE COFFEE PLANT

Santa Fé's famous Café El Tute Coffee Plant is the flagship institution in a four-decade-old cooperative. Started by Father Héctor Gallego, who was working in Veraguas in the late 1960s, the original aims of the cooperative were to wrest power from local coffee barons and to put the profit from the crop back in the hands of the farmers.

According to the co-op's history, the initial idea came when the priest decided to purchase a 50kg sack of salt from the lowlands rather than from the company store in town. By showing the local farmers that he could circumvent the rich and powerful ruling families, he rallied the necessary support to start the co-op. Although government forces wary of his teachings eventually murdered the priest, the co-op continues to thrive today.

Café El Tute, the locally grown coffee, is only sold for domestic consumption, though every step of the growing, harvesting and roasting process is 100% organic. Stop by for a tour (1st person US$15, each additional person US$5) in Spanish. The same organization also runs the Restaurante de la Cooperativa, where you can pick up some Café El Tute to try yourself.

You can book your visit to Café El Tute a day ahead with Lilia at Fundación Hector Gallego (📱954-0737; ⊙8am-8pm Mon-Sat, to 5pm Sun), a few doors up from Hostal La Qhia. In addition to coffee, the cooperative also grows cinnamon, orchids and oranges.

Inocencio & Pedra Virola TOUR

(☑6738-9906; per person US$30) If you are interested in visiting a Ngöbe-Buglé community, Inocencio and Pedra Virola offer tours of Río Piedra. They do not speak English but their daughter may be able to help translate. Part of the fee goes to providing students with school supplies and improving the local clinic. The tour includes a guide, transportation and lunch.

✽✥ Festivals & Events

Feria de Agricultura FAIR

(Agricultural Fair) If you're in the area, don't miss this lively event hosted by the producers of northern Veraguas in early February. The agricultural fair features traditional dancing, horse races, a multitude of food stands and an occasional boxing match or rodeo competition. It's held at the Feria de Santa Fé, in the eastern part of town.

Exposición de Orquídeas FLOWERS

(Orchid Show) Collectors from all over Panama display their finest orchids at the Féria de Santa Fé during the popular orchid exposition each August; the ATP tourist office (p136) in Santiago can provide you with the precise date.

📛 Sleeping

Keep your eyes peeled as more hotels and B&Bs are in the works around Santa Fé.

★Hostal La Qhia GUESTHOUSE $

(☑6592-5589, 954-0903; www.panamamoun tainhouse.com; dm US$11, d & tr with shared/private bathroom US$33/39; ℗) Surrounded by lush gardens and hammocks, this original bamboo-and-stone chalet makes a great base camp for mountain adventures around Santa Fé. Clean, snug rooms feature crisp bedding and excellent breakfasts (extra). Upstairs rooms are complete charmers but the bamboo construction means conversations carry. Dorms and rooms with private bathrooms occupy a small cement addition with an outdoor kitchen.

At the time of writing, the guesthouse was for sale. Check the website for the latest update before just showing up. For now, it's a good source of local information and responsible tours. Wi-fi may be added.

Hotel Santa Fé HOTEL $

(☑954-0941; www.hotelsantafe.com; s/d/tr/q US$22/28/33/39, deluxe tr US$42-47; ℗❀🖂) This quiet, motel-style lodging features tidy cement rooms with cable TV and hot showers. They are centered around a grassy courtyard and shady porch. The restaurant serves Panamanian food but isn't always open. The owner, Miriam, can impart local knowledge and put visitors in touch with guides. The main drawback here is that town is a hard walk uphill.

Hotel Anachoreo HOTEL $$

(☑6053-4310; www.anachoreo.com; s/d/tr/q incl breakfast US$33/44/56/68) In a brand new hillside home with panoramas of the countryside, this Dutch-Cambodian enterprise is a small hotel with ample high-ceiling rooms, some still under construction. Kids under six stay free. Fragrant flower, herb and vegetable gardens flank the property on all sides. The mulitlingual owner gives good local tours with a jeep and offers directions for hiking trails.

🍴 Eating

★Anachoreo ASIAN $

(☑6911-4848; mains US$7-10; ⊙5-9pm Wed-Sun) Run out of Hotel Anachoreo, this intimate (read: one table) restaurant ranks among the finest eating this side of Panama City. The Cambodian owner-chef is a wonderful cook and delightful presence. Don't miss Fish Amok: wrapped in banana leaves and steamed in ginger and fresh lemongrass. Wow. Enormous organic salads come from produce grown in the backyard. Reserve ahead!

La Matera PIZZERIA, CAFE $

(☑6053-4310; Calle Principal; pizza US$9; ⊙5-8:30pm Thu-Fri, 11am-8:30am Sat & Sun; 🖂) With modern design, this hip Argentine eatery offers exquisite thin-crust pizzas, empanadas and wine. Table games keep you busy at the wooden tree-trunk tables. It's all very cozy and inspired, a great hangout (finally) in Santa Fé. It also sells artisan goods.

Blue Iguana AMERICAN $

(☑6079-4253, 6011-4080; Av Central; mains from US$4; ⊙closed Tue & Wed) Pulled pork sandwiches, pizza and burgers. Run by North Americans for North Americans, the menu here is gringo deluxe and it's duly popular with the expat crowd. The patio with mountain views is popular for drinks. It's located just after the supermarket at the entrance to town.

Restaurante de la Terminal CAFETERIA $

(Bus Terminal; mains US$3; ⊙11am-7:30pm) You wouldn't expect much from bus terminal food, but this no-nonsense cafeteria offers some of the best *comida típica* (regional specialties) around and it's friendly and clean.

Super Santa Fe SUPERMARKET $
(Av Central; ☺7:30am-8pm) The town's most complete grocery store is on the right-hand side as you come into town.

❶ Information

In town, none of the streets have names, and even directions given by locals can be confusing. It's best to confirm that you're on track before you walk right out of town. Note that Santa Fé has no ATM and no gas station. Plan to stock up on cash or fuel in Santiago.

❶ Getting There & Away

Buses from Santa Fé to Santiago (US$2.90, 1½ hours) depart every 30 minutes from 5am to 6pm. Note that if you are trying to reach the surf town of Santa Catalina in one day, you must leave Santa Fé by 9am to make all the bus connections in time.

Las Palmas

There's nothing of special interest in sleepy Las Palmas, a town 10km south of the Interamericana and 32km northwest of the town of Soná. But if you love waterfalls and have your own wheels, you'll want to know about the nearby cataract and its enticing swimming hole. The scene is set amid light forest, and you'll likely have the place to yourself.

To get to the falls from the Interamericana, take the Las Palmas turnoff and drive 10km. Bypass the first road into town, but turn left at the second road just before the town's cemetery. Follow this dirt road for 200m and then take the fork to the right. This last 1km to the falls, along a much rougher road, requires a 4WD vehicle. If you're not driving one, it's best to play it safe and walk the last 1km to the falls. Be sure to lock up and take your valuables with you.

Santa Catalina

The secret about one of Central America's top surf spots is out. With a number of beach breaks, the right and left breaks of Santa Carolina are comparable to Oahu's Sunset Beach on a good day. The fishing village has a laid-back feel, with one good outdoor pizzeria that forms the nexus of the dining and nightlife scene.

Since the recent paving of the access road, foreign investment has been shoring up.

Rumors run the gamut from the construction of a mega-resort and airstrip to the establishment of a protected area and a marine park. In the meantime, enjoy it while it's still remote, undeveloped and home to some seriously wicked surf.

Though cell-phone service was recently added, there are still no banks and very few places take credit cards. Make sure you arrive with cash. For general information and surf forecasts, check out www.santacatalina beach.com.

🏃 Activities

Many of the local fishers know a variety of superb snorkeling and spear-fishing spots as well as some remote surf breaks. Their lifelong knowledge and love of the area is apparent, and although you will need some basic Spanish to contract them, it's a good way to support the community. Look for guides on the beach or simply ask around. You can also find locals who will lead horseback-riding tours through the nearby forests.

Javier Elizondo TOUR
(☑6544-1806; www.birdcoiba.com; full day per person US$110-250) Responsible local guide Javier offers visits to Parque Nacional Coiba, both all-inclusive day trips and overnights. Prices decrease with the number of participants so it's worth getting a group together with other travelers. Options include birding, snorkeling, a visit to the former penal colony or hiking. A native English speaker with good local knowledge.

Surfing

The best waves are generally from December to April, though there's surf here year-round. Unlike the Caribbean, the Pacific offers fairly consistent sets, though a good swell will really give a boost to the surfing here. Be advised that many of the breaks in the area are over rocks, and can easily snap your board if you don't know what you're doing. Most of the accommodations in town rent boards and offer surfing lessons.

Santa Catalina Surf Shop SURFING
(☑6963-0831; www.santacatalinasurfshop.com; ☺8am-3pm & by appt) Run by a friendy Southern California couple, this surf shop specializes in getting good gear to those loath to travel with extra baggage. Rents buys and sells quality boards and accessories. Across from La Buena Vida.

Surf and Shake SURFING
(www.surfandshake.com; ⊙9am-6pm) On the road to the beach just 150m in from the main street, Surf and Shake rents boards and sells leashes, boards and surf wear. Run by a duo of German surfers, it's also a good spot for surf info in English and German. If it's after hours you can try knocking.

Fishing
The area is famous for big fish, including yellow-fin tuna, wahoo, snapper, Spanish mackerel, jacks and rooster fish. Though there's no major sportfishing operator in town, many local fishers rent their boat and services for the day. Prices depend on the number of people in your party and your destination since gasoline is very expensive. Cabañas Rolo arranges half-day trips (US$30 per person, minimum two) to Isla Cébaco with a knowledgeable local captain.

If you'd prefer to go after reef fish including snapper and grouper, there are some hidden spots along the coast that are perfect for spear fishing. Plenty of rocky ledges serve as hideouts for lobster, though be sure to only harvest adults – lobster are in danger of being overfished throughout Panama. Scuba Coiba can set you up with the gear you need, and the local fishers can help you get your feet wet.

If you are sportfishing in Parque Nacional Coiba, you must obtain a fishing permit (US$60) from any mainland ANAM office (the nearest is Santiago).

Diving & Snorkeling
Diving and snorkeling are a great way to see some of the spectacular marine life around Isla de Coiba. There is an incredible variety of fauna and even whale sharks have been sighted here. Two-tank dives start at US$115 per person, though diving in the park costs more since the distance is much greater. Snorkelers can join dive trips to Coiba

LEARNING TO SURF

If you are learning to surf, the best place to go is **Estero Beach**. It's your best bet since you can stand in the water and surf both high and low tide. It's probably not time to consider the point – that's best left for advanced surfers.

German native Teresa Biegmann runs a surf shop in Santa Catalina

(US$60), but the cost does not include the park fee or lunch. Scuba Coiba also offers multiday trips to Isla de Coiba (three nights US$550), which include entry into the national park, lodging at the ANAM station on Coiba, and meals; there's a two-person minimum for these trips. Visitors usually check all shops to see which has a trip visiting their preferred destination.

★**Panama Dive Center** DIVING
(☑6665-7879; www.panamadivecenter.com; ⊙7am-7pm) Friendly and professional, this PADI-certified dive center is a good local resource for information. It offers snorkeling (US$60), all-day two-tank dives (US$130) and courses. Equipment is pretty new. It also gives interesting options for longer dive trips, camping on Isla Jicarón and freediving. It's on the main road in town, walking toward the beach.

Coiba Dive Center DIVING
(☑6780-1141; www.coibadivecenter.com) A reputable PADI-certified dive shop located on the main road, with snorkel gear available for rent.

Scuba Coiba DIVING
(☑6980-7122; www.scubacoiba.com) Run by an experienced Austrian dive master, offering dives, courses and multiday trips to Isla de Coiba (three nights US$630), which include entry into the national park, lodging at the ANAM station on Coiba and meals. Less experienced divers have given it mixed reviews for guide attentiveness. It's on the main road into town near Cabañas Rolo.

🛏 Sleeping

Santa Catalina has frequent water shortages, so mind your usage. A flashlight is handy for power outages. Also, the internet is slow and spotty.

In & Around Town

★**Hibiscus Garden** LODGE $
(☑6615-6097; www.hibiscusgarden.com; Playa La Gartero; dm/s/d without bathroom US$10/18/30, s/d with bathroom from US$25/40; P❄@☎) On Playa La Gartero (10km before Santa Catalina), these relaxed German-run lodgings fuse modern with rustic, with stylish installations and minimal fuss. There are playful mosaics throughout. Rooms have recycled driftwood beds and private hammock terraces. An open-air dorm catches the breeze

SURFING IN VERAGUAS PROVINCE

Although it's not as popular among the international surfing community as Bocas del Toro, Veraguas is home to the country's best surf. Serious surfers should head straight to Playa Santa Catalina, which has some of the biggest breaks in the whole of Central America, though there are plenty of other less crowded spots to get your surf on.

Playa Santa Catalina As good as it gets. Sharp rock bottom, right and left break. Main wave is the right. Incredible tubes, long rides with lots of power. Surfed mostly medium to high tide.

Estero Beach Break A 15-minute walk from Santa Catalina. A long beach break, has lefts and rights over sand bottom. Popular with beginners at low tide.

Punta Brava Just west of Estero. Point breaks at low tide over sharp rock bottom. Has lefts and rights, but the lefts are the best. Very powerful. Has a great tube section. Booties needed.

Punta Roca A 30-minute walk from Santa Catalina. Left point break surfed at low tide over a rock-bottom ledge, with short rides but big hollow tubes.

Isla Cébaco Island near Santa Catalina. Four breaks, with rights and lefts. Area known for sharks.

Playa Mariato Faces Isla Cébaco. Soft rock-bottom break with lefts, rights.

and views. Unlike the beaches of Santa Catalina, this gulf beach is calm, secluded and very swimmable.

For some, the distance from town is a drawback, though a shuttle (round trip US$5) is offered. You won't get bored: horseback riding (three hours, US$20), wakeboarding, surf lessons and fishing trips are offered. Children under 14 stay free. The restaurant (mains US$6.50 to US$15) serves wonderful salads, sandwiches on homemade German bread and a daily special, or you can use the community kitchen.

Boarder's Haven HOSTEL $
(☑ 6572-0664; dm US$25; ✳) For shoestringers, this tiny guesthouse is ideal: just seven single beds in three rooms with real mattresses, shared bathrooms and a petite kitchen that's fully equipped. It sits on the main road with a worn table and stack of magazines outside. Monthly rates are available.

Hostal Oasis HOSTEL $
(☑ 6671-7049; www.santacatalinapanamahostals.com; dm/d US$12/22; ☎) A cute new hostel on the main road into town. The two-story wood house has a wrap-around porch and murals. Oasis features boy and girl dorms and budget rooms. Cement stall showers have hot water. Guests get small lockers and free coffee. It offers a free beach shuttle at 9:30am daily, and is affiliated with the Oasis surf camp.

La Buena Vida CABIN $$
(☑ 6572-0664; www.labuenavida.biz; cabins from US$66; P ✳ ☎) These cool roadside cabins with restaurant will whisk you away from it all. Rainforest cabins charm with their sea-themed mosaics and colorful tiles crafted by the American couple that has welded, tiled and painted the place into eclectic perfection. 'Gecko' is the most deluxe, while the 'butterfly' cabin offers the delicious option of showering outdoors.

Cabins include a fridge, screened windows and air-conditioning, with one larger group cabin with kitchen that's a steal. Yoga and professional massages are available onsite. The owners have ironed out every little detail here, from local tips and recommendations to quality lunchboxes for tours. La Buena Vida composts, recycles and sells local artisan goods. It's on the main street in Santa Catalina.

Santa Catalina Inn HOTEL $$
(☑ 6872-3117; www.santacatalinainn.com; d US$55; ✳) While the roadside location won't grab you, these good, clean doubles are nonetheless a decent value and the air-con provides needed respite from the heat. A thatched restaurant serves meals. Hot water and private room balconies are a perk. It's across from Surf and Shake, about 200m from the bus stop.

VERAGUAS PROVINCE SANTA CATALINA

Blue Zone
HOSTEL $

(☑6458-5305; www.bluezonepanama.com; campsite per tent US$5, dm/s/d US$10/18/20; [P][@]) This attractive adobe hostel has a cluster of dark cement rooms arranged around circular spaces. There's also a campsite and long-term rates are offered. There are hot showers, free coffee and homemade goodies too.

Cabañas Rolo
CABIN $$

(☑6494-3916; www.rolocabins.net; dm US$11, d/tr without bathroom US$20/30, with bathroom US$55/65; [P]) One of Santa Catalina's few locally owned hotels, these rustic cabins are a favorite of baby-faced surfers from around the world. Each has one to three good beds, a fan and a shared cold-water bathroom that sees much traffic. Two newer cabins feature ample, more upscale rooms with air-conditioning and bathrooms with hot-water showers.

Truck-stop–quality coffee comes free in the morning and guests get use of an open-air kitchen. The owner, Rolo Ortega, speaks Spanish and English, offers surf lessons (US$25, 1½ hours), rents surfboards and kayaks (US$10 to US$15 per day) and can arrange surf trips to Isla Cébaco (from US$200 per group).

Sol y Mar
CABIN $$

(☑6920-2631, 596-1521; www.solymarpanama.com; 2-/3-/4-person cabin US$73/85/96; [P][※][≋]) Surrounded by green vegetation, these hilltop cabins have hammock porches, electric hot-water showers, satellite TV and air-con. Guests rave about the special attention that owner Luis showers upon them. Yet for those without wheels, it's a bit of a commute. Steep stairs lead to cabins, with sea views at the highest. It's about 1km before town.

Wahoo Rock
HOTEL $$

(☑6673-5790; d/tr US$55/75; [※]) Above a minimarket, this new two-story wooden house features good rooms set around a wrap-around porch. Boasting zany design (think pink and brown accents and polished concrete baths), rooms also include cable TV and air-con. The thatched restaurant out back has decent meals when other eateries are closed. On the main road.

🏖 Beach

To access the following lodgings, take a left-hand turnoff after arriving in town – it's the only other major road in town. All lodgings here are on right-hand side roads except for Oasis Surf Camp, which is at the end of the road (cross when the tide is right).

Surfer's Paradise
HOSTEL $

(☑6709-1037; surfcatalina@hotmail.com; campsite per person US$8, dm US$13, s/d/tr US$36/48/55; [P][※]) You could watch the tubes roll in all day at this hilltop camp with a box seat to the waves. While the location is prime, the rooms are just long, adequate cement boxes with fans and single beds. There is also a thatched restaurant with views. Guests can take surf classes and rent boards. Air-con is extra.

Oasis Surf Camp
CABIN $

(☑6588-7077; www.oasissurfcamp.com; camping per person US$10, d with fan/air-con US$40/50, ste US$150; [P][※][🛜]) This Italian-run surf camp has long been a staple of Santa Catalina and its beachfront setting is one of the best. Bright multicolor cabins overlooking the black-sand beach have adequate facilities including hot showers and ample hammocks. The new star suite is a two-bedroom wooden house with a kitchen and great balcony views.

Breakfast and authentic Italian meals with fish, bruschetta and salads are served at the open-air restaurant. You can also rent a variety of surfboards (US$10 to US$15). It's 2km from Santa Catalina's main road, on Playa Estero near the mouth of the river. Closed October.

Time Out
CABIN $$

(☑6617-1692; www.cabanastimeout.com; d US$119; [※][≋]) Geared at upscale surf bums, North American–run Time Out boasts Santa Catalina's nicest rooms on the water, in front of the coveted point break. New cabins are tasteful and well equipped, with LCD TV, air-con and hot water. In addition to the onsite resto-bar (and room service) there's a hammock hut with views and a sparkling freshwater pool.

Hotel Santa Catalina
HOTEL $$

(Kenny's; ☑6871-4847; www.hotelsantacatalina panama.com; d/tr/q US$70/75/80; [※][@][🛜]) With manicured grounds strewn with hammocks and Spanish-tile roofs, this newer hotel is a strong midrange option. Tile rooms somewhat crowded with beds feature electric hot-water showers and individual lockers for gear. A big draw is the surft break out front. Guests get free use of kayaks, bicycles and foam boards and there's onsite dining.

Surfside Inn HOTEL **$$**

(www.surfsidepanama.com; dm US$15, d US$44-55; ✳☎) Killer views of the surf break are the first thing that grabs you. Room prices vary depending on the view and amenities like hot water. There's free coffee and a guest kitchen. We hope to see better days for this spot, as it's under new management, but we found it disheveled and a bit broken down (mind the stairs!).

✗ Eating

There are several places in town and on the beach where you can buy excellent fresh fish to prepare yourself. There are also a number of small shops that sell basic groceries.

Los Pibes ARGENTINE **$**

(mains US$5-12; ⊘6:30-10pm Thu-Tue) This good-vibe Argentine eatery is an original – from its menus of nachos, steak and small Argentine-style empanadas to its margs and mojitos drenched in crushed ice. The kitchen will even cook the fish you catch. Surfers can gorge on mammoth burgers topped with bacon or eggs, or choose healthy salads with basil and gouda. It's 1km from town.

La Buena Vida AMERICAN **$**

(www.labuenavida.biz; mains from US$5; ⊘6am-2pm) If you're hitting the water early, this will be the first spot open for a bite. Great bets are the breakfast burritos or the Greek scrambles with feta, olives, tomatoes and eggs in this funky tiled cafe perched above the main street. There are also fresh fruit drinks and a lunchtime selection of salads, tacos and sandwiches on homemade bread.

Pizzeria Jamming PIZZERIA **$**

(pizzas US$5-8; ⊘from 6:30pm) Something of a Santa Catalina institution, this open-air *rancho* offers delicious thin-crust pizzas baked in a stone oven. Nightlife tends to concentrate here – perhaps it's the cheap beer, though there's also good wine and picnic tables conducive to sharing. It gets crowded, so arrive early in the night. You will find Jamming on the road to the beach-facing hotels.

La Panaderia BAKERY **$**

(The Bakery; ☎6549-7464; ⊘6:30am-4pm) Across from La Buena Vida, this tiny bakery run by a French and Spanish couple is a local institution. Come before 9:30am, as bread sells out, and breakfasts (think omelets and pancakes) are slow to get served. There's also great coffee, lunchboxes to go, cakes and delectable muffins.

Chano's Point SEAFOOD **$$**

(☎6736-1652; mains US$10-17) Venezuelan-run, this thatched restaurant offers lovely seafood meals and frozen fruit drinks. Start with fresh local clams or salad with tart passion-fruit dressing. The fish in coconut curry served Hawaiian-style with fresh pineapple borders on the divine. And bring your patience because the wait for food is long. It's off a right-hand turn on the way out to Estero Beach.

Pingüinos ITALIAN **$$**

(mains US$8-12) This thatched Italian-owned restaurant on the public beach is the best spot for a sunset beer. Pasta dishes are a tad pricey given their somewhat reckless preparation. We recommended the whole fried fish with *patacones* (slices of fried green plaintain). At breakfast there's US$3 pancakes.

① Getting There & Away

To reach Santa Catalina from Panama City, first take a bus to Santiago, then another to Soná where buses leave to Santa Catalina (US$4.65, 1½ hours) at 5am, 11am, 2pm or 4:30pm. The driver may be able to take you to a listed hotel for an additional fee. If you miss the bus, hire a taxi from Soná to Santa Catalina from US$60. Direct Soná/Panama City buses run every two hours.

From Santa Catalina, three buses serve Soná daily, leaving at 7am, 8:20am and 1:15pm. In Santa Catalina, the bus stops at the intersection with the beach road. If you're staying outside of the center, most lodgings are a 1km walk on mostly flat but unshaded terrain. Note that there are never taxis in town, unless of course someone is arriving from Soná.

To get to the ocean-side surf hotels from the bus terminal, take the dirt road on the left side of the road into Santa Catalina just before the road ends. Each hotel has its own sign marking the turnoff.

Parque Nacional Coiba

With the exception of the Galápagos and Isla de Coco, few destinations off the Pacific coast of the Americas are as exotic (and difficult to access) as this national park centered on the 503-sq-km Isla de Coiba. Although just 20km offshore in the Golfo de Chiriquí, Coiba is a veritable lost world of pristine ecosystems and unique fauna.

Parque Nacional Coiba

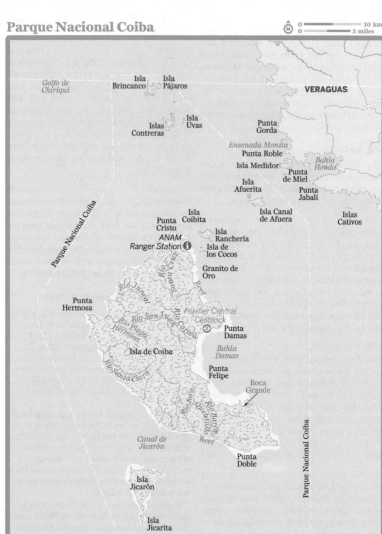

Golfo de Chiriquí

Isla Brincanco

Isla Pájaros

VERAGUAS

Islas Contreras

Isla Uvas

Punta Gorda

Ensenada Monita

Punta Roble

Isla Medidor

Bahía Honda

Punta de Miel

Isla Afuerita

Punta Jabalí

Islas Cativos

Parque Nacional Coiba

Isla Coibita

Punta Cristo

Isla Canal de Afuera

ANAM Ranger Station ℹ

Isla Ranchería

Isla de los Cocos

Granito de Oro

Reef

Punta Hermosa

Río Cacique

Río Juncal

Río San Juan

Río Catival

Former Central Cellblock

Punta Damas

Río Playa Hermosa

Isla de Coiba

Bahía Damas

Punta Felipe

Río Santa Clara

Boca Grande

Canal de Jicarón

Río Negro

Río Barco Quebrado

Reef

Punta Doble

Isla Jicarón

Parque Nacional Coiba

Isla Jicarita

PACIFIC OCEAN

Left alone for the past century due to its status as a notorious penal colony (p149), Coiba offers intrepid travelers the chance to hike through primary rainforest, snorkel and dive in a marine park with increasingly rare wildlife. However, as it has virtually no tourist infrastructure in place, you're going to have to work hard (and empty the pockets) to get here.

ART ISLAND: ISLA GOBERNADORA

If you ever wanted to watch the moon rise from your thatched hut, Art Lodge (☎6636-5180; www.artlodgepanama.com; all-inclusive per person per day US$95-115) satisfies the urge, and comfortably so. Both original and inspiring, this island retreat is run by two very hospitable French artists. The setting is Isla Gobernadora, home to a quiet fishing village, forested trails and a few white-sand beaches. And the idea is that it stays that way.

To create income for island women, Valerie and Yves have put together community art cooperatives that use found objects to make gorgeous belts, handbags and decorations crafted with quality and design sense. Guests can tour the village and workshops, talk with locals, snorkel, practice yoga and beachcomb. While the hillside lodge has a stony beach (a few good ones are within walking distance), there is a stream perfect for dips and a lovely lounge area with art, games and futons. Meals incorporate fresh local seafood, fruit and vegetables. Open-air *ranchos* have double beds with mosquito nets and showers half-walled by foliage. While alfresco living may not be for all, it is certainly paradise for some.

For those on a tight budget who want to enjoy Isla Gobernadora, contact the Art Lodge for help arranging a homestay with locals in basic accommodations.

Due to its remoteness, the Art Lodge requires a three-day stay. A visit includes transportation to and from the mainland (either Santa Catalina or Puerto Mutis), all meals, a daily excursion and a welcome cocktail. A taxi from Santiago to Puerto Mutis costs US$18.

🏃 Activities

Wildlife-Watching

Over 147 bird species have been identified here. While bird-watchers covet sighting the Coiba spinetail, a little brown-and-white bird found only on Coiba, most are awed by the scarlet macaws, which are limited in Panama to Parque Nacional Coiba. The birds nest at Barco Quebrado on the southern tip of Isla Coiba, but are frequently sighted in flight, with an easy to recognize call.

Due to penal colony restrictions, Coiba has not had a proper wildlife survey, though it's believed to be home to about 40 different species of mammal. Two rare mammals are endemic to the island, namely the Coiba agouti and the Couti howler. While these are difficult to spot, it's common to watch the howlers and white-faced capuchins playing on the beach.

Seventeen species of crocodile, turtle and lizard, as well as 15 species of snake – including the very dangerous fer-de-lance, coral snakes and boa constrictors – are found here. Enormous crocodiles might inhibit your swim plans. Although snakes tend to be extremely shy, you should always walk slowly and carefully through the jungles and wear thick leather boots.

In prison times, cattle were brought to the island to supply meat for prisoners. Now there are some 2500 of these untamed animals loose on the island. The cows are being removed but meanwhile cause soil damage, which creates a mudflow that damages coral reefs.

The waters surrounding Coiba have a notorious reputation for big sharks – a considerable deterrent for penal colony escapees and heaven for avid divers. Black-tip and white-tip reef sharks are the most sighted, though hammerheads school in large numbers here as well. Lucky divers may see the occasional whale shark. Unlucky divers may see the occasional tiger shark, though the danger is overestimated.

The marine life in the park is simply astounding. The warm Indo-Pacific current through the Gulf of Chiriquí creates a unique underwater ecosystem atypical of this region, attracting large populations of pelagics and enormous schools of fish. Over 23 species of dolphin and whale have been identified, and humpback whales and spotted and bottle-nosed dolphins are frequently seen. Killer whales, sperm whales and Cuvier's beaked whales are also present, but in much fewer numbers.

The waters around Coiba are also home to large numbers of manta rays, as well as the occasional sea turtle (leatherback, olive ridley and the increasingly rare green). In addtion to seriously large fish, you're almost guaranteed to spot schools of snapper and jacks as well as large grouper and barracuda.

WESTERN AZUERO

Most visitors access the Azuero via Chitré, but a few hours south of Santiago the west coast of the peninsula offers some amazing off-the-beaten-path attractions. Between December and February you can find three species of turtle hatching on the beaches of Malena. Community volunteers work toward their preservation. To volunteer, contact **Malena Beach Conservation Association** (Asociación Conservacionista de Playa Malena; www.playamalena.org; tours from US$10 per person, lodging per person incl breakfast US$10). Basic Spanish is necessary. The organization also offers lodging and economical horseback riding (US$10 per hour), boat tours and nature walks.

Providing luxury camping (mid-December through mid-May), meals and smart rooms, **Hotel Heliconia** (Tanager Tourism; ☑ 6676-0220; www.hotelheliconiapanama.com; tented rancho s/d US$18/30, s/d incl breakfast US$50/75; ❄) is in nearby Palmilla. The excellent retreat was thoughtfully crafted by Dutch biologists who also offer recommended area tours. They also work with the local community in sustainable tourism projects and in the reforestation of their own property. From Santiago, coaster buses leave hourly for Mariato, then go on to Palmilla (US$4, 1½ hours). Get off in Palmilla.

Hiking

Other trails include **Sendero de los Pozos**, which leads to thermal baths built in an old tile installation; it's a 30-minute walk from the station. The **Sendero de Santa Cruz** takes two hours. Since there are no markers, it's best to do these longer trails with a guide.

Sendero del Observatorio　　　HIKING
(Observatory Trail) Starting at the ANAM ranger station, this 500m-long trail terminates at a secluded bird-watching platform. The trail starts behind the cabins, with a second part that starts behind the kitchen. After a few hundred meters you will reach the top of a hill with views out to neighboring Isla Coibita.

Sendero de Los Monos　　　HIKING
(Monkey Trail) Near the Granito de Oro islet, this trail is only accessible by boat. It's only a few kilometers long, though it accesses several beaches and is home to several species of monkey. You're most likely to spot howlers and capuchins in the dry season when the foliage isn't as dense.

Scuba Diving, Snorkeling & Swimming

The cove near the ANAM ranger station is home to a tiny island that you can snorkel around during high tide. If you choose to do this, be warned that the current on the island's far side is sometimes very strong. If you're a poor swimmer, do not venture outside the cove.

Two other popular spots for swimming and snorkeling are the islet of Granito de Oro and the mangrove forest close to Punta Hermosa in the west. Both the mangroves and Granito de Oro can be reached only by boat.

The majority of visitors to Coiba arrange their diving through tour operators or dive centers based in Santa Catalina.

Coiba Dive Expeditions　　　DIVING
(☑ 6689-6112, 232-0216; www.coibadiveexpeditions.com; 7-day all-inclusive US$2100) Recommended by reputable guides, this conservation-oriented dive tour is run on a 16-guest, 115ft dive boat where guests sleep. Offers seven-to-12-day dive expeditions to Coiba, with nature tours, penal colony visit and kayaking included.

Sportfishing

The seas around Coiba are home to some seriously large fish, and lucky anglers can hook everything from marlin and sailfish to roosters and tarpon. To fish, you must obtain a sportfishing permit (US$60) for the park, through your outfitter or **ANAM** (Autoridad Nacional de Ambiente; ☑ 998-0615; www.anam.gob.pa).

One option is to use the local boats around Santa Catalina. Professional outfitters run about US$2500 per person for all-inclusive three-night/four-day packages, some with private charter flights, group minimums of four passengers.

Coiba Adventure　　　FISHING
(☑ captain 6623-9868, in USA 800-800-0907; www.coibadventure.com) This recommended sportfishing operation is run by Tom Yust, widely regarded as Panama's top sportfishing

captain. Tours can be customised, and take the hassle out of navigating local logistics. Rates vary depending on the time of year, boat used and size of the party, and include transportation from Panama City, meals, accommodations and fishing charters.

Pesca Panama   FISHING

(☑ in USA 800-946-3474; www.pescapanama.com) The Arkansas-based outfitter Pesca Panama runs trips to Coiba for fly-fishing and sport-fishing aboard a barge. The weeklong trip includes meals, six days of fishing and five nights on board.

☞ Tours

Even if you're normally a fiercely independent traveler, Coiba is one destination where it's probably worth joining up with an organized tour. Although you may be able to save a few dollars organizing your own transport to Coiba, you'll have an easier time getting ANAM to grant you access to the island's interior if you go with an operator. Being part of a chartered expedition also means that you can explore more of the marine park, which is more convenient and ultimately may be cheaper than arranging activities on your own.

Ancon Expeditions   ECOTOUR

(☑ 269-9415; www.anconexpeditions.com) Ancon has had a major role in the conservation of Coiba, and its tours emphasize the unique ecology and environment. Trips are guided by an experienced naturalist guide. Itineraries can cater to visitor interests, and prices depend on group size, length of stay and activities.

Arturis   TOUR

(Asociación Rural de Turismo Sostenible de la Zona de Amortiguamiento del Parque Nacional Coiba; ☑ 6529-5802, 933-0325; http://arturiscoiba.blog spot.com; 2 days & 1 night per person US$100) Arturis is a network of local service providers offering transportation, camping and guides to Coiba for one-day and multiday trips. Spanish only is spoken. Boats leave from Puerto Mutis or Santa Catalina; students get discount rates. For information, contact Faustino Sánchez.

Fluid Adventures   KAYAKING

(☑ 6560-6558; www.fluidadventurespanama.com; 3 days & 2 nights per person US$469) Run by a young Canadian, this Santa Catalina–based outfitter offers kayaking trips around Isla de Coiba. Day trips (US$105) reach Coiba by

---

GREAT ESCAPES: ISLA DE COIBA

Virtually absent of human development, Isla de Coiba is an ecological gem. With an approximate area of 503 sq km, it is the largest of a group of islands lying around 20km off the Pacific coast of Veraguas. After hosting pre-Columbian cultures as well as a colonial-era pearl industry, Coiba was sectioned off as a penal colony in 1912. Its impenetrable jungles and vast expanses of shark-infested waters in every direction served the purpose well.

While it was an unsavory period of history, the island's status as a penal colony was instrumental in preventing the widespread rainforest destruction that has swept through Panama. With the exception of agricultural and pastoral land surrounding the prison, virtually the entire island features primary rainforest teeming with wildlife, including several endemic species that have never been studied in depth. Coiba's underwater world is equally spectacular, boasting one of the largest coral reefs on the Pacific coast of the Americas.

In 1991 the Panamanian government established Parque Nacional Coiba, allowing for the continued operation of the penal colony, which deterred mainland squatters from arriving. In 2004 a second law doubled the size of the park to include several outlying islands and their surrounding waters. In 2005 Unesco declared it a World Heritage Site.

However, despite national and international legislation protecting both terrestrial and marine ecosystems of Coiba, it remains very vulnerable. According to Fundación Mar Viva, there is not enough funding to patrol and protect the park from illegal fishing and other incursions. Developers see it as prime real estate. On several occasions the government has tried to lighten existing park legislation to allow for foreign investment.

Coiba has survived hardcore criminals and the challenges of Pacific-coast drug trafficking, overfishing and the disappearance of species. Recent changes in regulation earmark all park fees for its upkeep, another reason to visit this incredible place.

motorboat for a head start. Departure dates are few. Camping, guides, all meals and transportation are included and equipment is top-notch.

Tanager Tourism ADVENTURE TOUR
(☑6676-0220, 6667-6447; www.tanagertourism. com; 3-day all-inclusive per person US$500) Run by a keen Dutch couple, these guided tours use local fishing boats and include meals, snacks and drinks. Not included are the park entrance fee and the cost of the dorm at the ranger station. Since trips are tailored, it's best to book several weeks in advance to give time for adequate preparation. Tours start and end in Malena, on the Azuero coast. Requires two-guest minimum.

🛏 Sleeping & Eating

Ranger Station Cabins CABIN $
(☑999-8169; campsite/dm per person US$10/20) The only accommodation on the island is the ANAM ranger station, which offers six spartan cabins that share common cold showers and toilets. Owing to the isolation of Coiba, you shouldn't expect too much. You can also use a tent or a jungle hammock. Insect repellent is a must!

The entire station has a certain deserted island charm, given it is a deserted island. Electricity is produced by a diesel generator that runs from dusk to dawn. Depending on the available gas supply, use of air-conditioning may be restricted, though no one will stop you from turning it on if you bring your own fuel in from the mainland. Of course, if you've made it this far, you probably have some man-vs-wild experience and can take a warm tropical night.

If traveling as part of a tour, you will not have to worry about meals as everything will be arranged for you. Independent travelers must purchase supplies in advance on the mainland as there is no food available on the island. Guests can cook at the ranger station, where kitchen and dining renovations are in the works.

ℹ Information

Visitors to the island (even day-trippers) register upon arrival at the ANAM ranger station. It is very difficult to arrive on the island as an independent traveler, since you must confirm that there is space for lodging, though the phone lines are not always working (and when they are, there's no guarantee anyone will be around).

The majority of the island is a restricted area, though there is a large distance between the ANAM station and the now defunct main prison complex (open to tours).

Coiba is home to the second-largest eastern Pacific coral reef and some of the finest diving and snorkeling to be found along the Pacific coast from Colombia to Mexico. The entire island is covered with a heavy virgin forest, except for the prison camps and along the lower courses of the larger streams where there are swampy woodlands. Rocky headlands project along the coast, and there are sandy beaches broken by mangroves at river mouths.

In addition to Coiba (503 sq km), islands within the park include Isla Jicarón (20 sq km), Isla Brincanco (330 hectares), Isla Uvas (257 hectares), Isla Coibita (242 hectares), Isla Canal de Afuera (240 hectares), Isla Jicarita (125 hectares), Isla Pájaros (45 hectares) and Isla Afuerita (27 hectares).

On the northern end of the island, the **ANAM Ranger Station** (☑999-8169, in Santiago 998-4387; park fee US$20) consists of several basic cabins, a camping pitch, showers and toilets. It is located beside an attractive beach alongside a scenic cover. One former prisoner did not want to leave the island and still works at the ANAM station and often interacts with Spanish-speaking visitors.

ℹ Getting There & Away

The most common departure point for boats heading to Isla de Coiba is Puerto Mutis, a small port about 25km southwest of Santiago, though more and more boats go from Santa Catalina. Typically, this trip takes about two to three hours, though it varies depending on the size and speed of both the boat and the waves. Boats also depart for Coiba from the port of Pedregal near David and Santa Catalina, though these two destinations are less convenient. There is also an airstrip on Coiba Island, though this is reserved for private charter flights.

If you're on Coiba as part of an organized tour, your operator will take care of all the necessary transportation arrangements. However, if you're planning on trying to reach the island independently, the best place to hire a boat and a guide is Puerto Mutis. Prices are negotiable and ultimately dependent on the price of fuel, the size of your party and your intended length of stay (eg whether or not your driver has to return to the mainland). Make sure your boat has life jackets, plenty of fuel, adequate horsepower and a functioning radio.

Please keep in mind that the open sea can get extremely rough, and many fishers have been lost at sea over the years. Before making the journey you need to have absolute confidence in the seaworthiness of both your vessel and its captain.

Parque Nacional Cerro Hoya

On the southwestern side of the Península de Azuero, this 326-sq-km park protects the headwaters of the Ríos Tonosí, Portobelo and Pavo, as well as 30 endemic plant species, and rare fauna including the elusive carato parakeet. The national park also contains some of the last remaining rainforest on a huge peninsula that is one of the most agriculturally devastated regions of Panama. Although the park was created in 1984, much of the forest had been chopped down prior to that, and unfortunately, it will be a long time before the park really looks like a park.

There are no accommodations for visitors in or near the park, and the trails into it are ill defined. In short, until the park is more accessible and facilities are developed for tourists, visits to the park are reserved for intrepid types truly looking to get away from it all. Getting there may require 4WD transportation or a boat and horseback-riding combination. Visitors should call the ANAM office (☎ 994-7313) in Las Tablas for current access information.

For a guided bird-watching tour, try Tanager Tourism (☎ 6667-6447, 6676-0220; www.tanagertourism.com; 2-person tour US$75); price includes transportation and food.

It's also possible to reach the park by a road that winds along the western edge of the Península de Azuero. However, even with a 4WD vehicle (dry season only), visitors are only able to get as far as Restigue, a hamlet south of Arenas, at the edge of the park.

Chiriquí Province

POP 416,900 / ELEV SEA LEVEL TO 3478M / AREA 8653 SQ KM

Best Places to Eat

➡ Rock (p172)

➡ Il Forno (p175)

➡ Daily's Diner (p174)

➡ Cuatro (p157)

➡ Big Daddy's Grill (p171)

Best Places to Stay

➡ Lost & Found Lodge (p160)

➡ Los Quetzales Cabins (p176)

➡ Coffee Estate Inn (p170)

➡ Bocas del Mar (p159)

Why Go?

Chiriquí claims to have it all: Panama's tallest mountains, longest rivers and most fertile valleys are here. The province is also home to spectacular highland rainforests and the country's most productive agricultural and cattle-ranching regions.

Bordering Costa Rica to the west, Chiriquí is often the first province in Panama encountered by overland travelers and serves as a subtle introduction to Panama's immense beauty.

On the coast, the pristine Golfo de Chiriquí boasts powdery white-sand beaches and a rich diversity of marine life. Although the mist-covered mountains near Boquete have been colonized by waves of North American and European retirees, the town is a good base for adventures such as white-water rafting and hiking the flanks of Panama's highest point, Volcán Barú (3478m). Boquete is also the center of Panama's coffee industry, which means that a potent cup of shade-grown arabica is never more than a cafe away.

When to Go

➡ **Apr–May** The best time to spot the resplendent quetzal nesting in highland destinations such as Parque Nacional Volcán Barú and Parque Internacional La Amistad. Boquete's Orchid Fair lights up April.

➡ **Dec–Apr** High season on the Pacific coast has little precipitation, making it the best time to hit highland trails that get muddy and damaged during the rainy season.

➡ **Jan–Mar** Boquete's Feria de las Flores y del Café draws crowds to the fairgrounds in January. Early February brings Fiesta de Concepción, and David's huge Feria de San José takes place over 10 days in early March.

History

When the Spaniards first visited Chiriquí in the early 15th century, they were astonished by what they found. Instead of discovering one or two main population groups, they encountered a large number of tribes living in relative isolation. Often separated by only a few kilometers, each group maintained a distinct language, culture and religion.

Spanish missionaries arrived and began their conversions. In the early 17th century a group led by Padre Cristóbal Cacho Santillana rounded up 626 indigenous people from across the region. Hoping that his work would be easier if he could identify similarities in the languages, Santillana started to record a vocabulary of the most common words, and he was successful in identifying six distinct languages.

Sadly, measles brought by the colonists swept through the towns and killed half of the study population. The survivors, having had enough of the Spaniards, their linguistic studies and their religion, took to the hills. Unfortunately, their fate was already sealed – of the Cotho, Borisque, Dorasque, Utelae, Bugabae, Zune, Dolega, Zariba, Dure and others, only the Ngöbe-Buglé survived. Today, the Ngöbe-Buglé are the most populous of Panama's seven indigenous groups, though their numbers are but a fraction of what they once were.

During the 17th century and into the 18th century Chiriquí Province was the subject of pirate attacks, much like the rest of Panama. It was just outside Remedios in 1680 that English buccaneer Richard Sawkins, attempting to lead an assault against the well-defended city, was fatally wounded. Six years later, English privateers from Honduras sacked the towns of Alanje and San Lorenzo. Even the Miskito tribes from up north behaved like pirates after invading the region in 1732, and plundering and burning the city of David.

In the 19th century, farmers from North America and Europe viewed the climate and slopes of the Chiriquí highlands as prime for coffee, timber and other crops. Their descendants still work the fields today. Though the wave of immigration hasn't subsided, recent arrivals are mainly foreign retirees and real-estate speculators, which has led many *chiricanos* to question who it is that actually owns the land they love so much.

LOWLANDS

Chiriquí has much more to offer than its famous highland rainforests – the lowlands are home to Panama's second-largest city, David, as well as large stretches of striking Pacific coastline.

David

POP 104,500

Although it feels more like a country town, David is Panama's second-largest city and the capital of Chiriquí Province. Think more major agro industry than cultural hub; you will be disappointed if you have museums, clubs and fine dining on your mind. Yet, with a powerful wave of foreign capital flowing into Chiriquí, David is rapidly gaining wealth and importance. With tens of thousands of North American and European retirees expected to settle in the region in years to come, it's poised to boom.

For travelers, David is a pit stop on the way to surrounding destinations. Half way between San José, Costa Rica and Panama City, the city is an important transportation hub. If the road has you weary, slip into the slow pace, grab a *jugo de caña* (sugarcane juice) in downtown's Parque de Cervantes, the heart of the city, or day trip to the beach or highlands.

✷✷ Festivals & Events

Feria de San José de David   FAIR
This big international fair is held for 10 days each March; contact the ATP tourist office for exact dates, as they vary from year to year.

Fiesta de Concepción   RELIGIOUS
A half-hour drive west of David, Concepción celebrates its patron saint's day on February 2, or the following Saturday if it lands on a weekday.

🛏 Sleeping

Bambú   HOSTEL $
(☎730-2961; www.bambuhostel.com; Calle de la Virgencita, San Mateo Abajo; dm US$10-12, d with/ without bathroom US$30/25; P✳❄🖥) This chill little house is run by a friendly Cantonese-speaking NYC musician. There's a regular dorm and Darien-style dorm (a thatched hut on stilts) out back with mosquito nets. Includes electric hot-water showers in so-so bathrooms. There's cable TV and air-con in doubles. The star feature is the sprawling

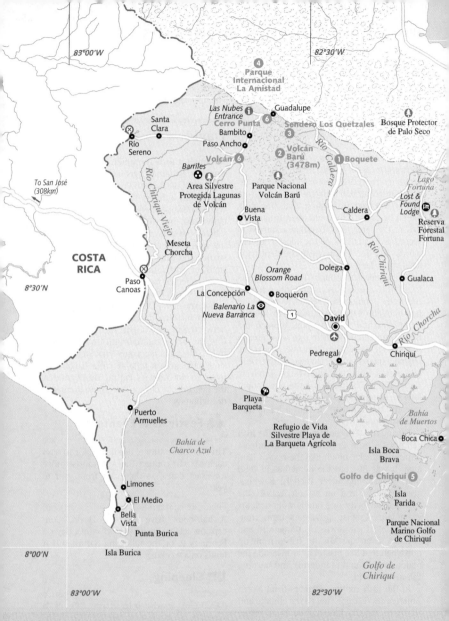

Chiriquí Province Highlights

① Fuel up for highland adventures with local mountain-grown coffee in **Boquete** (p163), the town of eternal spring

② Ascend burly **Volcán Barú** (p172) for views of both the Pacific and Atlantic coastlines – if the weather is clear!

③ Hike through cloud forests along the **Sendero Los Quetzales** (p173) in search of the elusive quetzal

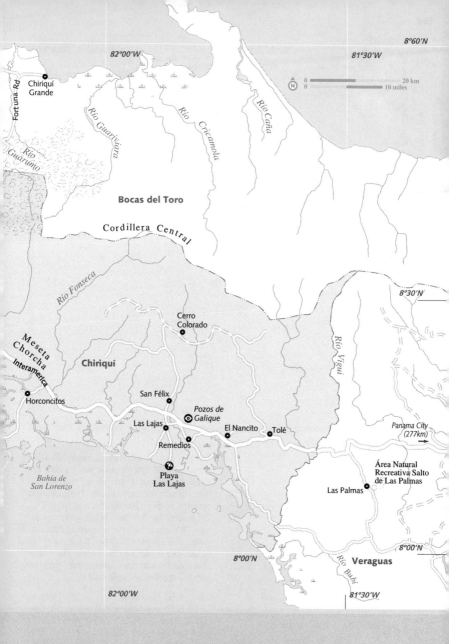

4 Wonder why you're the only one around in the pristine and bio-rich **Parque Internacional La Amistad** (p177)

5 Island-hop and explore the clear blue seas of the national marine park **Golfo de Chiriquí** (p159), the 'other side' of Chiriquí

6 Wake up surrounded by wilderness while staying in the cool jungle lodges around **Volcán** (p174) and **Cerro Punta** (p176)

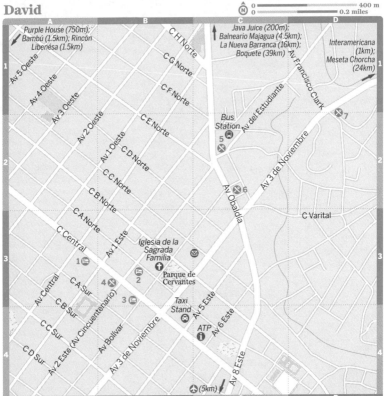

David

Sleeping
1	Gran Hotel Nacional	A3
2	Hotel Castilla	B3
3	Hotel Puerta del Sol	B3

Eating
4	Casa Vegetariana	B3
5	Cuatro	C2
6	Mercado	C2
7	Super Barú	D2

garden with a swimming pool, bar (open until 11pm) and the requisite hammocks.

Purple House　　　　　　　　　HOSTEL **$**
(☏774-4059; www.purplehousehostel.com; cnr Calle C Sur & Av 6 Oeste; dm US$8, d with/without bathroom US$27/25; 🅿❋@🛜) Warm and welcoming Peace Corp veteran Andrea pioneered David's first hostel and has served as able den mother ever since. Guests have

use of a communal kitchen, cable TV, DVD rentals and a splash patio for cooling off. Tiled bunk rooms are clean, purple and tidy, though without air-con. Doubles offer optional add-ons like air-con and cable TV.

Located in the San Mateo commercial area, it's close to lots of restaurants and shops. It's sometimes closed for some or all of October – call or email first. The house also recycles and has a community partnership selling Ngöbe-Buglé crafts.

Gran Hotel Nacional　　　　　　HOTEL **$$**
(☏775-2222; www.hotelnacionalpanama.com; Calle Central; d/ste US$94/110; 🅿❋@🛜🏊) David's most upscale hotel offers modern yet fairly sterile rooms more suited to domestic business-people than discerning tourists. But the hotel isn't short on amenities, and the onsite bar-restaurant, pizzeria, casino and secure parking sweeten the deal. New rooms are visibly smarter. The large swimming pool is welcome in the reputed hottest city in Panama.

Hotel Castilla
HOTEL **$$**

(☑774-5260; www.hotelcastillapanama.com; Calle A Norte; s/d/ste US$61/72/77; ℗❄@) Professional and super-clean, this hotel offers cheerful rooms with matching beds and desk sets in deco style. Each is equipped with creature comforts such as a hot-water shower, phone and cable TV.

Hotel Puerta del Sol
HOTEL **$$**

(☑774-8422; www.hotelpuertadelsol.com.pa; Av 3era Este, apartado 329; d/tw US$76/86; ℗❄@🕏) A secure midrange choice, this hotel offers tasteful tiled rooms with wood furnishings. Rooms are on the small side, but the setting is pleasant with amenities that include hot-water showers and cable TV.

✗ Eating

If you're looking for cheap produce, look out for the bustling mercado (cnr Avs Bolívar & Obaldía). An enormous new market is under construction, between Calle I Sur and Av 1era Este.

Java Juice
CAFE **$**

(Interamericana; mains US$2.50-6; ☑) Iced coffees, fruit smoothies, salads and grilled burgers are the fare at this casual cafe in San Mateo, located in front of the grocery store. Good vegetarian selection.

Casa Vegetariana
CAFETERIA **$**

(Av 2 Este; meal US$2; ☺7am-4pm; ☑) This cheerful Chinese-style mini-cafeteria packs in the crowds for inexpensive plates of sautéed greens, eggplant, fried rice and beans served on no-nonsense metal plates. For lunch, go early – everything will run out!

Super Barú
SUPERMARKET **$**

(cnr Avs Francisco Clark & 3 de Noviembre) Self-caterers can head to the Super Barú, a large US-style supermarket.

★Cuatro
PANAMANIAN **$$**

(☑730-5638; cnr Avs Obaldía & del Estudiante; mains US$12-16; ☺noon-3pm & 6:30-10:30pm Mon-Sat) Only one spot does great local food in David with sophistication and even happy surprises. Classic Panamanian basics like cassava, tamales and new corn get gourmet treatment. Start with hot corn blinis with red onion marmalade. Honey-glazed pork ribs are tender and fish come in exquisite sauces. The chef, Luis Mendizábal, honed his craft in top European and Panama City restaurants.

Rincón Libenésa
MIDDLE EASTERN **$$**

(☑774-2700; Calle F Sur, Interamericana; mains US$4-12) Located three blocks past the McDonald's off the Interamericana, this authentic Lebanese restaurant provides welcome relief from a steady diet of rice and beans. Homemade hummus, tabbouleh and baba ghanoush will make you stop and wonder if you're in the Middle East – 15 seconds later, the sounds of blaring reggaetón will remind you where you are.

🍷 Drinking & Nightlife

Chiricanos are not big on bars and clubs, but they go wild when it's festival time. A certain amount of nightlife centers around the casinos and you will always find livelier crowds around the 15th and 30th of the month – the local pay days.

WORTH A TRIP

DAVID DAY TRIPS

Spice up your travels with these excursions:

➡ Take a soak in the Los Pozos de Caldera (p165) hot springs. Take a bus to the town of Caldera, hike along the dirt road for one hour and enjoy the spring.

➡ Learn to appreciate rum before you down a tumbler or two. Contact Señor Garcia (☑772-7073) FREE to arrange a private tour of the Carta Vieja rum factory on the outskirts of town.

➡ Swim with *chiricanos* at Balneario Majagua or Balneario La Nueva Barranca (p162). Hop on a Boquete- or Concepción-bound bus and jump off at either of these popular local swimming spots.

➡ Beat the David heat at the beach. Grab some friends and take a taxi to the lovely dark-sand Playa Barqueta (p158).

ⓘ Information

ANAM (Autoridad Nacional de Ambiente; ☎775-7840; fax 774-6671; ⊙8am-4pm Mon-Fri) Provides tourist information and advice, and gives permits to camp in the national parks. It's 4.5km south of David's center.

ATP (☎775-2839; Calle Central btwn Calles 5ta & 6ta; ⊙8:30am-4:30pm Mon-Fri) Provides information on Chiriquí Province.

Chiriquí Hospital (☎777-8814; cnr Calle Central & Av 3 Oeste) One of the best hospitals in the country.

HSBC (Av Central) With branches on Calle C´ Norte near the park and on Av Obaldía north of the bus station.

Post Office (Calle C Norte; ⊙7am-6pm Mon-Fri, to 4:30pm Sat)

ⓘ Getting There & Away

AIR

David's airport, the Aeropuerto Enrique Malek, is about 5km from town. There are no buses to the airport; take a taxi (US$5) or a shared taxi (US$2).

Air Panama (☎721-0841; www.flyairpanama. com) Has multiple flights daily from Panama City (US$117, 45 minutes).

BUS

The Interamericana does not go through the town, but skirts around its northern and western sides. The David **bus terminal** (Av del Estudiante) is about 600m northeast of the central plaza. Most buses begin service around 7am.

For Guadalupe, passengers can get on a Cerro Punta bus, which continues on; passengers for Volcán also take the Cerro Punta bus, but get off earlier. For Las Lajas, visitors will have to continue to the beach via taxi.

Tracopa (☎775-0585; www.tracopacr.com) Direct buses between David and San José, Costa Rica (US$21, eight hours), daily at 8:30am and noon from the David bus terminal.

ⓘ Getting Around

David has a complex network of local buses, though the easiest way to get around is by taxi; fares within the city are generally under US$2. If you're planning on renting a car, all of the major car-rental companies have booths at the airport.

You can hire a taxi to Pedregal (US$3.50), Boquete (US$25) and Playa Barqueta (US$30).

Playa Barqueta

This long and lovely dark-sand beach southwest of David is a popular weekend escape, although it remains quiet during the week. As inviting as the ocean seems, its riptides are very strong, and there are some steep underwater drops as you wade in. However, La Barqueta is a great place to break out the surfboard. Besides, wading in up to your ankles sure beats sweating through your socks on the David streets.

From September to November it's turtle-hatching season on this beach. Since turtles don't run by the calendar year, it's hard to predict the event, but local lodgings are likely to be in tune with the latest news. For information about volunteering, contact Purple House (p156).

BUSES FROM DAVID

DESTINATION	COST (US$)	DURATION	FREQUENCY
Boquete	1.75	1hr	every 20min until 9:30pm
Caldera	2.40	45min	hourly until 7:30pm
Cerro Punta	3.50	2¼hr	every 20min until 8pm
Changuinola	9.70	4½hr	half-hourly until 6:30pm
Guadalupe	3.50	2½hr	every 20min until 8pm
Horconcitos	2	45min	11am & 5pm
Las Lajas	5	1½hr	4 daily
Panama City	15-18	7-8hr	every 45min, 6:45am-8pm
Paso Canoas	2.10	1½hr	every 10min until 9:30pm
Puerto Armuelles	3	2½hr	every 15min until 9pm
Santiago	9	3hr	hourly until 9pm
Río Sereno	5.10	2½hr	every 30min until 5pm
Volcán	3	1½hr	every 20min until 8pm

GETTING TO COSTA RICA

The most heavily trafficked Panama–Costa Rica border crossing is at Paso Canoas (open 24 hours), 53km west of David on the Interamericana. Allow at least one to two hours to get through the formalities on both sides. Buses from David depart frequently for the border (US$2.75, 1½ hours, every 30 minutes) from 4:30am to 9:30pm. On the Costa Rican side of the border, you can catch regular buses to San José or other parts of the country.

The least trafficked crossing into Costa Rica is the border post at Río Sereno (9am to 5pm Monday to Saturday, to 3pm Sunday), located 47km west of Volcán. Buses to the border depart from David and travel via La Concepción, Volcán and Santa Clara (US$6.50, three hours, every 30 minutes). On the Costa Rican side of the border, you can take a 15-minute bus or taxi ride to San Vito, where you can catch buses to regional destinations.

From David, there are also taxis to Paso Canoas (US$40 to US$50) or Río Sereno (US$70). Note that you can be asked for an onward ticket if you are entering Costa Rica. If you do not possess one, it is acceptable to buy a return bus ticket back to Panama. Also note that Costa Rica is one hour behind Panama – opening and closing times here are given in Panama time.

Capping the eastern end of the beach is Las Olas Resort (☎772-3000; www.beachresortpanama.com; d/ste US$98/116; P❋@🛜❄). It has a number of terraced rooms and suites decorated with natural colors and featuring sweeping ocean views. Facilities include several bars and restaurants, a spa, gym, yoga, equestrian center and marina. Rates are cheaper in low season (April to November), and all-inclusive deals are available online.

There is no public transportation connecting Playa Barqueta to David, though it's easy to access by private vehicle or taxi (US$30, one hour). If you can fill the cab, you should be able to negotiate a reasonable price, especially if you arrange for a ride back to David.

Golfo de Chiriquí

The undisputed gem of the Chiriquí lowlands is the Golfo de Chiriquí, home to the Parque Nacional Marino Golfo de Chiriquí, a national marine park with an area of 147 sq km protecting 25 islands, 19 coral reefs and abundant wildlife. The marine park also protects the 30-sq-km Isla Boca Brava, a lovely little island with hiking trails and beautiful outer beaches. It's home to monkeys, nesting sea turtles and 280 recorded bird species. This area is accessed via the mainland village of Boca Chica.

Visitors can surf, kayak the calm interior waters, snorkel or wildlife-watch underneath the rainforest canopy, yet the biggest draw to the area is high-stakes sportfishing. A new luxury development on

Isla Palenque means further development is on its way.

🛏 Sleeping & Eating

Hotel Boca Brava   HOTEL $$
(☎851-0017; www.hotelbocabrava.com; Isla Boca Brava; hammock/dm US$8/11, d without bathroom US$39, d/ste US$50/94; ❋) On Isla Boca Brava, this hotel with rustic to deluxe offerings is ideal for mingling with other travelers. Budget travelers might pick the hammock room over the too-warm dorm. Doubles are snug, with the best deal being the 'hostel' option with shared bathroom. The hotel can arrange excursions such as snorkeling, whale-watching or just lounging on an uninhabited island.

Only some rooms have air-con. The attached Restaurante Bar Boca Brava (meals from US$7) occupies a cool space on an overhanging deck with expansive water views. It's the perfect setting for a sunset Brava Colada cocktail. Reasonably priced meals range from fresh fish to burgers.

★ Bocas del Mar   RESORT $$$
(☎6395-8757; www.bocasdelmar.com; Boca Chica; ste/superior incl breakfast US$185/215; ❋🛜❄) New on the scene, this elegant Belgian-owned resort has 11 ultra-mod bungalows in citrus tones. Amenities range from a two-tier infinity pool and spa to suites with private hot tubs. A full menu of excursions ranges from horseback rides to kayaking, fishing, funboards and snorkeling. Kids will not get bored here. Service is good. Recommended for families.

WORTH A TRIP

LOST & FOUND LODGE

On the way to Bocas province in the Talamanca mountain range, this original cloud forest lodge offers a utopian take on jungle living. Only accessed on foot, Lost & Found Lodge (☑ 6432-8182; www.lostandfoundlodge.com; dm/d/tr without bathroom US$14/33/48) is a backpacker community perched on a steep hill facing a gaping mountain panorama.

The Canadian owners have plotted every detail, from foosball tournaments to a tricked-out treasure hunt that takes visitors mucking through rivers and labyrinths, competing for a coveted bottle of cheap wine. Bunks are stacked high, but you can also choose a private room that's basic but clean. Shared bathrooms are stall-style and well maintained. Rates decrease with each night of your stay.

The open-air kitchen is stocked with basic provisions (pasta, eggs, sauces and vegetables) for sale, though you can also order meals. There's also a minipub set up far from sleepers.

Activities are varied and well priced. A highlight is the Lost World Tour which takes hikers to an impressive waterfall and visits an indigenous community. You can also visit a local coffee producer or hike the trails.

While Rocky the resident kinkajou is here because he cannot be released into the wild, other animals come for the buffet of bananas occasionally left out for them – not the best wildlife practice, but one you might see throughout the country and should discourage.

Given the isolation, it's necessary to call or email for reservations 24 hours in advance. From David, the lodge provides a shuttle (US$30), or you can take the bus (US$3.50). After one hour, the bus reaches a sign for the lodge near Km 42. From here, hike 15 minutes. You can also take a bus from the Bocas side, starting in Changuinola or Almirante (around US$8).

Discounts are given for longer stays. The lodge also provides good shuttle tours between Bocas and Boquete, making active stops at places of interest.

Follow the signs from Horconcitos, and take the left-hand turn before Boca Chica (also on the mainland).

Boutique Hotel Cala Mia BOUTIQUE HOTEL $$$
(☑ 851-0059; www.boutiquehotelcalamia.com; Isla Boca Brava; ste incl breakfast US$240; ☀) ◢
Lauded Cala Mia offers luxuriant oceanfront tranquility. Though there are better beaches around, a massage spa occupies its own islet. Thatched bungalows have ample living spaces and handcrafted local furniture. The resort is solar powered, provides organic locavore-style meals around a big community table, and donates 5% of room rates to local indigenous groups.

Kayaks and snorkeling are included; other activities use the resort's own boats and guides. It's on the virtually uninhabited Isla Boca Brava. You can get a water taxi from the Boca Chica dock to Boutique Hotel Cala Mia for US$35.

ⓘ Getting There & Away

To reach Boca Chica, first take a David bus (US$2) to the Horconcitos turnoff, located 39km east. You can also take any passing bus (those heading from David to Panama City), as long as you ask the driver to drop you at the Horconcitos turnoff.

From the turnoff, a bus (US$3, 50 minutes) leaves four times daily for Boca Chica. For the hours of service, call **Jimi** (☑ 6857-2094). You can also take a taxi (US$20). At the Boca Chica dock, hire a water taxi (per person US$3) to take you 200m to the Boca Brava island dock at Restaurante Bar Boca Brava. A water taxi from the Boca Chica dock to Boutique Hotel Cala Mia costs US$35.

If you drive your own vehicle, you can safely leave it near the village dock.

Playa Las Lajas

With one of the longest beaches of Central America, the 20km palm-fringed Playa Las Lajas seems to stretch forever. The town sits 51km east of David and 13km south of the Interamericana. It gathers serious crowds on the weekends and has started on the road to mainstream commercial development. Over the New Year holiday it becomes a crazy, drunken scene. During the week it often lies empty so you can savor the glorious expanse all by yourself.

Ngöbe-Buglé people sell handicrafts in a wooden-walled structure 500m west of the turnoff – most of the residents of San Félix, 3km north of here, are Ngöbe-Buglé.

🛏 Sleeping & Eating

Changes are happening fast. Consult www.laslajasbeach.com for information on lodgings and food.

La Spiaza HOSTEL $
(📞6620-6431; www.laspiazapanama.com; dm US$8, d US$20-30; 🛜) With open-air *ranchos* and attractive earthy constructions, the Italian-run La Spiaza is the best bargain lodging/pizzeria at the beach. It sits across the road from the beach in a shadeless compound.

Casa Laguna B&B B&B $$
(📞6896-0882; www.casalagunapanama.com; d with/without bathroom incl breakfast US$100/70; ❄🛜❄) Run by a young Italian couple, this small B&B is a popular option for couples. Rooms are ample and cool. There are also open-air *ranchos* around the property for relaxing and it's a three-minute walk to the beach. Immense breakfasts include yogurt, fruit and pancakes, and other meals are available upon request. The pool is small and above ground.

Finca Buena Vista B&B $$
(📞6814-8693; www.finca-buenavista-laslajas.com; Calle 12 de Octubre s/n; d incl breakfast US$80; ❄) On the outskirts of Las Lajas, this German-run B&B has sweeping views and warm hospitality. Spacious rooms feature private patios, small fridges and hot water. Those with lofts are ideal for families. Hosts are happy to arrange fishing, mangrove boat trips to spy on crocs, and trips to the local indigenous community.

Las Lajas Beach Resort RESORT $$$
(📞832-5463; www.laslajasbeachresort.com; d/ste US$99/138; ❄🛜❄) A lovely destination. Rooms are impeccable, ample and cheery, with beds decked in embroidered *molas* (colorful hand-stitched appliqué textiles made by Kuna indigenous people) and plenty of amenities. There's also plenty to do. Guests can float in the infinity pool, rent body boards (US$6), ride horses (US$25) or visit a Ngöbe community (US$40 per person) in small numbers.

The breezy open-air restaurant serves American-style breakfasts and big cheeseburgers, and offers a rotating dinner menu (US$8 to US$14).

🛈 Getting There & Away

To reach Las Lajas, take any bus from David (US$2.70, 90 minutes) that travels by the Las Lajas turnoff on the Interamericana. At the turnoff, take a taxi (US$6) to where the road reaches the sea. Turn right and proceed 1.5km until you arrive at the cabins. Ask your lodging for taxi contacts in advance.

The Road to Veraguas Province

Heading out to Veraguas Province there are a number of interesting attractions to check out along the way, particularly if you have your own wheels.

Twenty-four kilometers east of David, on the northern side of the Interamericana, the enormous **Meseta Chorcha** (Chorcha Plateau) beguiles photographers. From the west, you'll see a white streak running down its glistening granite face – it's actually an extremely tall but inaccessible waterfall.

Nearly opposite the turnoff for Playa Las Lajas is **Cerro Colorado**, one of the world's largest copper mines, with approximately 1.4 million tons. It's not open for tours.

Soak your travel-worn bones at **Pozos de Galique** (Springs of Galique), three no-frills hot springs. Bring cold drinks and try to visit early morning before the day heats up and crowds descend. The easy-to-miss

---

OFF THE BEATEN TRACK

RURAL GULF ADVENTURES

Not long ago, selling shark fins was the only viable income for rural residents of the Chiriquí coast. Now, with the help of Fundación Mar Viva, local cooperative **Aventuras Rurales del Golfo** (ARUG, Rural Gulf Adventures; www.arugpanama.com) will be taking visitors to see sharks, along with other amazing underwater wildlife.

Its success will depend on independent travelers attracted to a home-spun tour. Options include taking a one-hour boat ride from Pedregal to Islas Paridas for snorkeling. Aventuras Rurales del Golfo also offers sustainable travel around the town of Malena, on the coast of Península de Azuero, where there are mangroves, trails and turtles. Visitors can camp or stay in family lodgings. To learn more, check out the website.

PUNTA BURICA

This lush peninsula jutting into the Pacific is a lovely spot for absorbing the beauty of both the rainforest and the coastline.

A very remote and rustic getaway, Mono Feliz (☑ 6595-0388; monofeliz@gmail.com; per person campsite/cabin US$8/25; 3 meals US$25; P ✿) offers cabins with mosquito nets, a freshwater pool frequented by monkeys and an outdoor kitchen for guest use. Guests can cook for themselves or pay US$25 extra for home-cooked meals. With your own gear you can camp onsite, with access to pool and bathrooms. Activities include nature walks (an excursion to Isla Burica at low tide is a highlight), fishing, surfing, bird-watching and horseback riding. English is spoken.

To arrive, start with an early bus from David to Puerto Armuelles (US$3, 2½ hours). From the Puerto Armuelles *mercado municipal* take a truck to Bella Vista. From here it's a one-hour downhill walk. Mono Feliz is directly in front of Isla Burica. For private transportation from Puerto Armuelles, contact Spanish-speaking Yanilka (☑ 6595-0388; per person one way US$10) or from the marina Eric (☑ 6652 9930; one way US$35) does boat shuttles, weather permitting.

With a 4WD, there is dry season (mid-December to mid-April) access. From Puerto Armuelles keep heading south along the coast toward Costa Rica. Go through the Petro terminal and then veer directly onto the beach (attempt only at low tide). Continue up to a dirt road marked with a 'Mono Feliz' sign, about 30 minutes on.

turnoff for the road to the springs (which requires a 4WD vehicle to access) is 4km east of the turnoff for Playa Las Lajas. The 3.8km-long turnoff leading to the springs is 30m west of a small bridge with 'Galique' written on it.

About 5km west of the town of Tolé is a turnoff for El Nancito, a small community known for its rock carvings. Locals say that the carved boulders were made more than 1000 years ago, though no one really knows for sure.

From the Interamericana, turn north onto the road to El Nancito (for walkers, it's 3km uphill). When you reach the 'Cantina Oriente' sign, turn west and drive 75m until you come across some rather large boulders. If taking public transportation, jump off any eastbound bus at El Nancito, and then hike the 3km to the boulders. Be aware you'll have difficulty catching a return bus after sunset.

The Road to Boquete

Interesting attractions line the way to Boquete. If you have your own wheels, you can really explore the area, though most places can be accessed via public transportation.

Popular swimming spots take the edge off the heat. On the road to Concepción, Balneario La Nueva Barranca is a little gem on the river with a bar-restaurant and clean facilities. Balneario La Cascada (admission US$1), 8.4km north of David, has two waterfall-side swimming pools and a small bar. Take the bus on 'Calle F Sur' in David to get there. Both spots can get very crowded on weekends, though the atmosphere is always 'family fun in the sun.'

About halfway between David and Boquete, the small town of Dolega boasts Book Mark (☑ 776-1688; ☺ 9am-5pm Tue-Sun), a fine secondhand book shop with English-language titles and obscure works. Any Boquete-bound bus can drop you off. Here, you can also turn off west on the Orange Blossom Road, a scenic new paved connection that comes out just south of Volcán.

The area's most famous attraction, Los Pozos de Caldera (p165) are natural hot springs renowned for health-giving properties. The springs are located on private land near the town of Caldera, 14km east of Boquete.

To get to the springs, take a bus or drive to the town of Caldera (the turnoff to Caldera is 13km south of Boquete). From where the bus drops you off, continue to the end of town; here you'll see a sign indicating the turnoff to the springs. You'll turn right along this rugged dirt road, accessible by 4WD only. If you're walking it's about one hour from here. Continue along the road until you reach a suspension bridge. Cross it, and take the first left leading up the hill. After 100m, you'll see a gate that marks the entrance to the property.

If you're driving, don't leave anything in the car as there have been reports of break-ins here. If you get overheated in the springs, the pleasant Río Caldera is just a stone's throw away, and is a pleasant spot to cool off. Hourly buses run from both David and Boquete (both US$2, 45 minutes) to the town of Caldera.

HIGHLANDS

The highland rainforests are the heart of Chiriquí Province – from the rugged mountains of Parque Internacional La Amistad to the misty hills of Boquete, this is the only spot in Panama where you might need a sweater. While Panamanians relish the chill, you'll appreciate locals' laid-back hospitality and the astounding natural beauty throughout the region.

Boquete

POP 6000

The Napa Valley of coffee, the mountain town of Boquete is known throughout Panama for its cool, fresh climate and pristine natural setting. Flowers, coffee, vegetables and citrus fruits flourish in Boquete's rich soil, and the friendliness of the locals seems to rub off on everyone who passes through.

Boquete would have remained a small town, but gained a deluge of expats after the AARP (American Association for Retired Persons) named it a top retirement spot. With gated communities dotting the hillsides the face of Boquete is slowly being transformed.

Boquete is one of the country's top destinations for outdoor lovers. It's a hub to hike, climb, raft, visit coffee farms, soak in hot springs, study Spanish or go on a canopy tour. And, of course, there's nothing quite like starting your day with a glass of freshly squeezed OJ, or perking up with a cup of locally grown coffee.

⊙ Sights

With its flower-lined streets and forested hillsides, Boquete is ideal for taking picturesque strolls. Visit Parque de las Madres, with flowers, a fountain and a children's playground. At the attractive fairgrounds and riverside there's an old railway and an exhibition wagon left over from the days when a train linked Boquete with the coastal town of Puerto Armuelles.

Mi Jardín es Su Jardín   GARDENS

(⊙daylight) FREE Mi Jardín es Su Jardín is a magnificent garden surrounding a luxurious private estate. The residence is off-limits to the public, but you are free to stroll about the gardens unhindered.

El Explorador   GARDENS

(☏775-2643; Calle Jaramillo Alto; adult/child US$5/2; ⊙10am-6pm daily mid-Dec–mid-Apr, Sat & Sun only mid-Apr–mid-Dec) This private garden is located in a hilly area about 45 minutes' walk from the town center. The

---

SURFING IN CHIRIQUÍ PROVINCE

More difficult to access, surfing in Chiriquí is less popular than in other provinces, though there is great surf to be had. To go beyond these suggestions, hire a local guide or tour operator.

Isla Silva de Afuera Remote island with a right and left break. The right: a big peak breaking over a shallow rock ledge at medium tide. Occasionally throws a big tube with steep drops and no wall. The left: breaks over a rock reef at medium tide. This spot catches almost every swell.

Isla Silva de Adentro Remote island with a right-hand break over a reef that can get really big with strong swell.

Morro Negrito Near Morro Negrito town. About five breaks, variety of lefts and rights with occasional tubes.

Playa Las Lajas East of David. Beach-bottom break with rights and lefts but infrequent waves.

Playa Barqueta (p158) Near David. Beach-bottom break with rights and lefts. Breaks at all tides, but medium to high tide is best.

Punta Burica On the Costa Rican border. Four left points that break along the point for long, tubing rides. Catches any swell. Better than Pavones in Costa Rica and less crowded.

Boquete

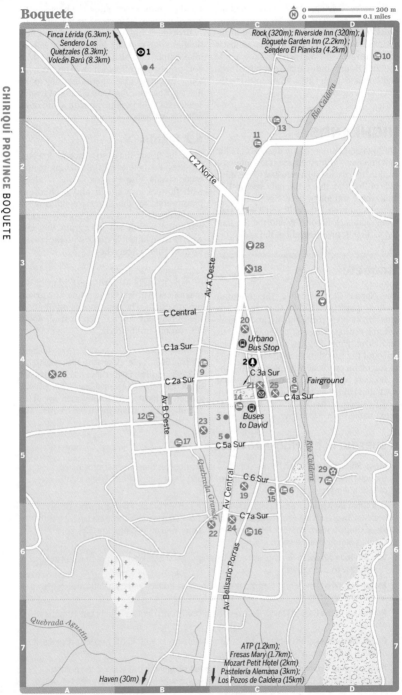

Boquete

gardens are designed to look like something out of *Alice in Wonderland,* with no shortage of quirky eye-catching displays, including fanciful suspension bridges, koi ponds and playful sculptures.

Los Pozos de Caldera   HOT SPRINGS
(admission US$1; ☉ dawn-dusk) An undeveloped hot spring said to have health-giving properties. Arrange a tour (US$25) which includes a visit to a petroglyph site or take a taxi (US$40 round-trip) with the caveat that you will have to walk the last part of a very rough dirt road for one hour each way. A Boquete bus goes to Caldera (US$2, 45 minutes) every two hours.

🏃 Activities

Adventure-hub Boquete has the lion's share of outfitters in the region, so it's not a stretch to book coastal trips like seakayaking or sportfishing here. Hostels and various agencies rent bicycles and scooters, a good way to explore the charms of the surrounding hillsides.

Hiking

With its breathtaking vistas of mist-covered hills and nearby forests, Boquete is one of the most idyllic regions for hiking and walking. Several good paved roads lead out of town into the surrounding hills, passing coffee farms, fields, gardens and virgin forest.

Although saunterers will be content with picturesque strolls along the river, the more ambitious can climb Volcán Barú (p173). There are several entrances to the park, but the trail with easiest access to the summit starts near Boquete.

You can access the Sendero Los Quetzales (p173) from Boquete, though the trail is uphill from here – you'll have an easier time if you start hiking from Cerro Punta. On the other hand, if you're not interested in a thru-hike but just a taste, Boquete provides a more central departure point. In the past, landslides have affected the trail. Ask locals about conditions before heading out. Using a guide is highly recommended.

Sendero El Pianista   HIKING
(Pianist Trail) This pleasant day hike winds through dairy land and into humid cloud forest. You need to wade across a small river after 200m, but then it's a steady, leisurely incline for 2km before you start to climb a steeper, narrow path. The path winds deep into the forest, though you can turn back at any time.

To access the trailhead, take the first right fork out of Boquete (heading north) and cross over two bridges. Immediately before the third bridge, about 4km out of town, a track leads off to the left between a couple of buildings. Don't go alone and exercise caution as robberies have been reported here.

THE NGÖBE-BUGLÉ

The Ngöbe-Buglé are composed of two separate ethnolinguistic categories, the Ngöbe and the Buglé, though the distinction is minor, and both are commonly referred to in conjunction with one another. As Panama's largest indigenous population, the Ngöbe-Buglé number close to 200,000. Like the Kuna, they retain their own autonomous region with its own system of governance and economy while maintaining their language, representation in the Panamanian legislature and full voting rights.

The Ngöbe-Buglé are largely confined to the Chiriquí highlands, and predominantly survive on subsistence agriculture, much like their pre-colonial ancestors. Their social structure is based on a system of small villages comprising *chozas* (thatched huts) with dirt floors. In the villages, men practice slash-and-burn agriculture in order to produce staple crops such as plantains, bananas, corn, cassava and rice. During the coffee-harvest season, many of the younger men work as laborers in the fields around Boquete, which generates a significant amount of income for the village.

In the villages, women are primarily responsible for raising the children, though many work as skilled artisans, especially since their crafts can fetch a high price. The two most common items produced by Ngöbe-Buglé women are the *chacara* (a woven bag of plant fibers that is meant to mimic the landscapes of the rainforest) and the *naguas* (a traditional dress of hand-sown appliqué, worn by both women and girls). Throughout Chiriquí Province, you can find both items for sale in traditional markets and shops.

Like other indigenous groups in Panama, the Ngöbe-Buglé are struggling to maintain their cultural identity, especially as foreign pressures continue to descend on the *comarca* (autonomous region). However, although the Ngöbe-Buglé are not as politically organized as the Kuna, they are far greater in number, and they control large tracts of undeveloped land. As a result, they have been more successful than other groups such as the Emberá and Wounaan in maintaining their cultural identity and resisting the drive to modernize.

Rafting

Those who seek a bit of adventure shouldn't miss the excellent white-water rafting within a two-hour drive of Boquete. Ríos Chiriquí and Chiriquí Viejo both flow from the fertile hills of Volcán Barú, and are flanked by forest for much of their lengths. At some places, waterfalls can be seen at the edges of the rivers, and both pass through narrow canyons with awesome sheer-rock walls.

The Río Chiriquí is most often run from May to December, while the Chiriquí Viejo is run the rest of the year; the rides tend to last four and five hours, respectively. Depending on the skill level of your party, you can tackle thrilling Class III and Class IV rapids or some seriously scary Class V rapids.

Not all rafting companies offer the same level of service and safety. When booking a trip, inquire if the outfitter uses a safety kayak for descents and if guides are certified in Wilderness First Responder. These should be minimum requirements for a safe trip.

Boquete Outdoor Adventures   ADVENTURE SPORTS
(☑ 720-2284; www.boqueteoutdooradventures. com; Av Central, Plaza Los Establos) This recommended, reliable outfitter offers quality rafting trips (US$90) and tailored vacations ideal for families. Its sportfishing adventures on the Golfo de Chiriquí are value-priced (US$600 to US$800 for four passengers). Guides are bilingual and the company uses local service providers.

Canopy Tours

Boquete Tree Trek   ADVENTURE TOUR
(☑ 6450-2599, 720-1635; www.aventurist.com; Av Central, Plaza Los Establos; canopy tour US$65; ☺ 7:30am-1pm & 2-4:30pm) Travelers love this three-hour canopy tour with 12 zip lines, a rappel and a Tarzan-swing in secondary forest. The lines pick up some serious speed, so you might want to consider going a little heavy on the handbrake. The company sells other tours and also offers lovely accommodations in rural cabins with transportation from the center.

Bird-Watching

Coffee Adventures   BIRD-WATCHING
(☑6634-4698, 720-3852; www.coffeeadventures.
net; 2-person half-day tour US$55) Dutch natu-
ralist guides Terry and Hans are locally renowned as great birding and nature guides.
They also offer hiking in the cloud forest,
including Sendero los Quetzales, visits to
indigenous communities and informative
coffee tours. They also have cabin accommodations on a small coffee farm.

Finca Lérida   BIRD-WATCHING
(☑720-1111; www.fincalerida.com; US$75) Finca
Lérida, located about 6km northwest of
town, is a stunning coffee farm owned by
one of Boquete's founding families. It's considered one of the premier bird-watching
spots in Panama, with hundreds of species. A
half-day bird-watching trip includes a knowl-
edgable guide, lunch and transportation.

The extensive grounds and forested trails
here are prime habitat for the quetzal, a
Central American symbol and the national
bird of Guatemala. Nearly extinct there, it
has found refuge in Chiriquí Province. The
quetzals are most likely to be seen January
through to August.

Coffee Tours

A trip to Boquete just isn't complete without
learning the secrets of a perfectly blended
cup of joe.

Cafe de la Luna   TOUR
(☑6677-7748; per person US$15-30) If you are
looking to learn about small-scale organic
coffee production, check out this extended
tour that includes roasting and tasting. In
addition to guiding the tour, American coffee afficionado Richard Lipner is the brains
behind the beans. The tour takes 1½ to 2½
hours and cost depends on the number of
participants.

Finca Lérida   TOUR
(☑730-1230; www.fincalerida.com; 2½hr tour
US$35) A tour of the family-run estate Finca
Lérida is quite thorough, showing both the
business side of a small farm and the process of production from coffee cherry to cup.
Part of the tour focuses on the farm's transition to organic and sustainable practices,
with composting and reduced water consumption.

Café Ruíz   TOUR
(☑720-1392; www.caferuiz.com; 3hr tour US$30;
⊙9am Mon-Sat) Located on the main road
about 600m north of the town center, Café
Ruíz is Panama's most famous coffee-grow-
er, and now produces the award-winning
Gesha coffee. The tour includes transportation to a nearby coffee farm, a presentation
on the history of coffee in Boquete, a tour
of a roasting facility and a tasting session.
Reservations are required.

CHIRIQUÍ PROVINCE BOQUETE

HIGHER GROUNDS

During the 19th century, farmers from North America and Europe discovered that the
cool climate and rich volcanic soil of Chiriquí were perfectly suited for the cultivation
of coffee. Since dried beans are relatively nonperishable and thus easy to ship, coffee
quickly surpassed other cash crops, and became an important source of revenue for the
area. Although lesser known than the Costa Rican competition, Panamanian coffee is
highly praised for its high caffeine content and acidic, multidimensional flavor.

In the early 1990s the collapse in the world quota cartel system dealt the industry a
severe blow. Growers could no longer rely on a stable price for their harvest. In turn, a
few growers switched tactics, planting quality low-yield varieties aimed at the gourmet
market instead of the usual high-yield crops.

Selectivity paid off. The biggest coup was the emergence of the Gesha (also called
'Geisha') variety on the world scene. After winning first place in multiple international
cupping competitions, Gesha became a rock-star bean. Originally from Ethiopia (the
birthplace of coffee), Gesha is coveted for its light body with citrus and honey notes and
jasmine-like aroma. It has been auctioned for up to US$375 per kilo.

In late 2012 Starbucks got into the spirit and started selling Gesha at US$7 per cup. You
can also find it for sale online, but because it is grown in small quantities it is often sold
out. While Boquete's Finca Esmeralda was the first to make good on Gesha, it's now found at
Café Ruíz (Calle 2 Norte), Finca Lerida and a growing number of local estates.

Kotowa Coffee Estate TOUR

(☎720-3852) This gourmet grower offers the most comprehensive coffee-estate tour in the area. Guests learn about the estate's history (beginning with a Canadian's arrival in 1918), get a full tour of the production facilities and processing mill, and have a tasting session. Call ahead for current prices; reservations are requested with 24 hours' notice.

Truck Tours

Boquete Mountain Safari DRIVING TOUR

(☎6627-8829; www.boquetesafari.com; Av Central; half-day 4WD US$35) Boquete Mountain Safari offers scenic back-country tours in open jeeps. Highlights of the cloud-forest safari include stops around Boquete to check out coffee estates, basalt formations and waterfalls – or you can beeline for the Caldera hot springs. This outfit also rents scooters.

🎓 Courses

Habla Ya Language Center LANGUAGE COURSE

(☎720-1294; www.hablayapanama.com; Av Central, Plaza Los Establos; ⊙8am-6pm Mon-Fri, 9am-noon Sat) Habla Ya Language Center offers both group and private lessons. A week of group lessons starts at US$175. The language school is also well connected to local businesses, so students can take advantage of discounts on everything from accommodations to tours and participate in volunteer projects.

Spanish by the River LANGUAGE COURSE

(☎720-3456; www.spanishatlocations.com) The sister school to the popular Spanish school in Bocas del Toro is located 5km south of Boquete near the turnoff to Palmira. Standard/intensive lessons cost US$185/275 for a one-week course. Discounts come with comprehensive packages and longer stays. Offers homestays (nightly US$15), simple dorms (US$10) or private rooms (US$18).

🎉 Festivals & Events

Feria de las Flores y del Café FAIR

(Flower & Coffee Fair; ⊙ January) The town's annual fair, the Feria de las Flores y del Café is held for 10 days each January. While there's coffee in the name, it's strangely missing from exhibits, though you will find plenty of rum and children's carnival rides.

Feria de Las Orquídeas FLOWERS

(Orchid Fair; April) Showing over 150 varieties, the orchid fair is held every April. It's not all flowers; sundown brings rock concerts and dancing. Contact ATP (p172) for exact dates.

🛏 Sleeping

Because of the cool climate, all of the places to stay in Boquete have hot-water showers, but don't waste too much time looking for the air-conditioner – you're not going to need it.

🛏 In town

Refugio del Río HOSTEL $

(☎720-2088; www.refugiodelrio.com; Av B Oeste; dm US$11, d without bathroom US$33/28, cabin US$35; P@🛜) With the comfy feel of a large, well-kept home, this budget stop features a huge guest kitchen and good location. Sprawling rooms are pleasant and well furnished, though could be tidier. The dormitory features a row of single beds with snug covers but saggy mattresses. Reserve ahead for the cool tree house cabin overlooking the babbling river out back.

Mamallena HOSTEL $

(☎730-8342; www.mamallenaboquete.com; Av Central; dm US$11, d/tr without US$25/33, d/tr/q US$28/37/47; P🛜) On the plaza, this ex-boarding house is backpacker central, complete with kitchen, coin-op laundry and free pancake breakfasts. For its huge capacity it seems rather cozy. Four-bed dorms boast orthopedic mattresses. Smokers retreat to the sheltered patio area with grill. Service-oriented, the hostel runs tours and shuttles (to Bocas and Volcán) through an onsite agency and offers local information.

Hostal Boquete HOTEL $

(☎720-2573; Calle 4a Sur; d US$33-40; P@🛜) Overlooking the Río Caldera, Hostal Boquete provides a budget option for couples. Rooms with cable TV are cramped and just OK, but guests have kitchen use and river access.

Hostal Nomba HOSTEL $

(☎720-2864, 6497-5672; www.nombapanama.com; Av A Oeste; dm/d without bathroom US$10/24; P🛜) This pared-down chill-out hostel is fairly sterile but good for tight budgets (there's a slight discount for smaller rooms). An onsite bar, darts and foosball keep it lively. The in-house outfitter offers regular excursions and bike rentals.

Pensión Marilós GUESTHOUSE $

(☎720-1380; marilos66@hotmail.com; cnr Av A Este & Calle 6 Sur; s/d without bathroom US$10/14, s/d US$15/20; P🛜) With the feel of a well-worn family home, Marilos offers a bit of peace and quiet at bargain rates. Rooms

THE RESPLENDENT QUETZAL

The Central American lore of the resplendent quetzal originated during the era of the Maya and the Aztecs, who worshipped a deity known as Quetzalcoatl (Plumed Serpent). This mythical figure was often depicted as wearing a crown of male quetzal tail feathers, and was believed to be responsible for bestowing corn upon humans.

A popular legend regarding the scarlet-red breast of the quetzal originated during the colonial period. In 1524 in the highlands of Guatemala, the Spanish conquistador Pedro de Alvarado defeated Tecun Uman, the last ruler of the Quiché people. As Uman lay dying, his spiritual guide, the quetzal, stained its breast with Uman's blood and then died of sadness. From that day on, all male quetzals bore a scarlet breast, and their song hasn't been heard since.

Even today, quetzals are regarded in Central America as a symbol of freedom and it's commonly believed that they cannot survive if held in captivity. In Panama, the quetzal is something of a legend, as bird-watchers from far and wide continue to brave the elements for the chance to see the most famous bird in Central America.

The best time to spot a quetzal is between April and May. At this time they nest in the highlands and wait for their young to hatch. They're not out courting or foraging. You can look for their nests in rotted trunks carved out by their beaks.

---

are warmly decorated with assorted knick-knacks and doo-dads reminiscent of the guest bedroom at grandma's house. There's even a mild-mannered dog to pet and the owner Frank can help you make the most of your time in Boquete.

Pensión Topas   GUESTHOUSE $
(☑720-1005; www.coffeeadventures.net/topas. html; Av Belisario Porras; s/d US$25/35; P🅿🛜🍽) Built around a small organic garden and pool, this German-run lodging features Tintin murals and tidy rooms. A shady outdoor patio provides ample shared space and perks include a slackline, foosball and volleyball. Hosts can get unexpectedly boisterous, leading guests to give it mixed reviews.

★Isla Verde   CABIN $$
(☑720-2533; islaverde@cwpanama.net; Av B Oeste; d apt US$150, cabins from US$90; P🅿@🛜) Set riverside in a beautiful, lush garden with Buddha statues, these delicious two-story alpine cabins feature luxurious mattresses, vaulted ceilings, complete kitchens and roomy bathrooms. It's probably the best in-town retreat, with prompt service and even professional massages available. Cabins cost US$20 extra for each additional person (US$10 for kids). Look for the highly anticipated onsite restaurant set to open as we go to press.

La Casa de La Abuela   HOTEL $$
(☑730-9484; www.lacasadeabuela.com; Av Central s/n; s/d incl breakfast US$80/112; 🛜) This new brick hotel is a smart addition to Boquete. Eighteen earth-tone rooms, some with balconies, have tile floors, flat-screen TVs, hot showers and modern installations. There is nice outdoor patio seating though the roadside location can be noisy at times.

El Oasis   HOTEL $$
(☑720-1586; www.oasisboquete.com; Calle de la Feria; d incl breakfast US$72; P🅿@🛜) Although it's in walking distance of town, El Oasis is across the river from Boquete proper and a good deal quieter. Rooms are immaculate but pricey for what you get (plastic furniture). The garden restaurant serves good soups.

Mozart Petit Hotel   CABIN $$
(☑720-3764; www.petithotelmozart.com; Calle Volcancito Principal; d US$39-85, q US$53-110; P🅿🛜) A chill rural retreat, this artist's inn features a cool countryside setting and occasional art classes. Cabins have rustic furnishings, terraced patios and sweeping views to the Pacific on a clear day. English and German are spoken. It's best for those with their own wheels, since it's about 5km from the town center, near the ATP office.

★Haven   BOUTIQUE HOTEL $$$
(☑730-9345; www.boquetespa.com; Av A Oeste; d/deluxe US$165/195; ❄🛜🍽) New to Boquete, this slightly removed, sleek design hotel and spa provides a chic retreat. British-owned, it has only eight rooms with cool space-saving designs. Water features, river stones and palms throughout the property set the scene for relaxation. A full spa with dry sauna, steam room, indoor pool, yoga facilities and Jacuzzi seals the deal. Professional and service-oriented.

It's 2km from the town center, watch for signs for the left-hand turn as you approach town.

Riverside Inn
INN **$$$**

(☑ 720-1076; www.riversideinnboquete.com; Calle Jaramillo Alto; d incl breakfast US$180; P @ 🛜) A casual stunner, this exclusive four-room inn has a relaxed and intimate setting and an excellent restaurant (The Rock). Living areas feature original artwork and a grand stone fireplace. Rooms are expansive and modern with vaulted ceilings, soft cotton bedding and Jacuzzi baths. Though the setting is lovely, the flat riverside location lacks the mountain panoramas of other inns.

Hotel Ladera
HOTEL **$$$**

(☑ 730-9000; www.hotel-ladera.com; camino a Palo Alto; s/d incl breakfast US$98/119; P ❄ 🛜) A good value, this upscale roadside hotel features an appealing ultramodern style and attentive staff at the front desk. Rooms feature an outdoor terrace or balcony and two queen-sized beds with wicker headboards. There's onsite dining as well as room service. The hotel often hosts events and art shows.

Hotel Panamonte Inn & Spa
INN **$$$**

(☑ 720-1327; www.panamonte.com; d/ste incl breakfast US$133/425; P ❄ @ 🛜) This historic 1915 inn wins you over with sprawling flower gardens, serene spaces and handsome rooms. You can relax here, knowing that John Wayne, Ingrid Bergman and Richard Nixon did so too. Choose between the original rooms, blooming with character down to the details, or new, larger terrace rooms outfitted as modern deluxe. All come with North American–style breakfast.

Service is impeccable and the restaurant is among Panama's best. The day spa is the perfect complement to a mountain getaway. It's located on a quiet road at the northern end of town.

Downtown Hotel
HOTEL **$$$**

(☑ 720-2455; boqueteguesthouses@gmail.com; Av A Este; d/tr US$139/159; P 🛜) Design-oriented, this hotel features 10 modern suites with living room and kitchenette. It's all spic and span but feels lacking in the personality department. Details like Egyptian cotton bedding, down duvets, flat-screen TVs and safe boxes work to justify the price tag. Rooms look out on a small grass courtyard with an iron gazebo.

🛏 Surrounding Hillsides

Boquete Garden Inn
INN **$$**

(☑ 720-2376; www.boquetegardeninn.com; d incl breakfast US$99-119; P @ 🛜) Perched on the edge of the Río Palo Alto, this garden inn is run by a welcoming British-Canadian couple. The grounds overflow with blossoming tropical flowerbeds. Lounging around the riverside patio bar with other guests proves a fine cap on the day. Rooms with some canopy beds are lovely and modern, and service stands out.

Villa Marita Lodge
LODGE **$$**

(☑ 720-2165; www.villamarita.com; d/ste US$72/149, cabin US$94; P @ 🛜) On the edge of a plateau overlooking a vast expanse of coffee farms, these cute cabins offer striking views of Volcán Barú – when it isn't cloudy. There is onsite dining and wi-fi in public areas. Though clean and bright, it seems a little overpriced.

★ Coffee Estate Inn
B&B **$$$**

(☑ 720-2211; www.coffeeestateinn.com; Calle Jaramillo Alto; 2-person cabin incl breakfast US$198; P @ 🛜) 🌿 In the lap of coffee-estate luxury, these lovely orange-grove bungalows are surrounded by a 1.5km network of private trails that wind through gardens and forest. It is all about escape here, though guests also rave about the attentive service of hosts Jane and Barry. Cabins are spacious and smart, with complete kitchens, heated floors and private terraces with valley views.

The estate is also home to a working coffee farm, the source of your morning brew, and oranges, as well as a delicious coffee liqueur. Guests get a complimentary coffee tour (three-night minimum) and the recommended option of custom romantic dinners. The inn has an extensive library, recycles, promotes energy conservation and offers reusable containers for restaurant take-out.

Finca Lérida
LODGE **$$$**

(☑ 720-1111; www.fincalerida.com; Calle 2 Norte; d/ste incl breakfast US$165/275; P @ 🛜) Famous for its legendary bird-watching, Finca Lérida is a working coffee farm that happens to be an avian hot spot that's one of the best places in the country to see quetzals. You can also tour the coffee farm. Standard rooms are tastefully decorated with countryside motifs, each with deck and outdoor seating to watch the hummingbirds. Suites feature Jacuzzis.

Guests and day-trippers can dine at the onsite restaurant, which features excellent salads made with local produce and house-made yogurt-dill dressing, in addition to well-prepared Panamanian favorites, sandwiches and homemade rhubarb pie.

Hotel Los Establos　　　BOUTIQUE HOTEL **$$$**
(☑720-2685; www.losestablos.net; d/ste incl breakfast US$215/330; P @) Former stables, these lavish quarters surrounded by manicured grounds and a coffee farm bear no trace of their past. Decor is elegant but a little fussy, heavy on brocade, carved mirrors and gold highlights. Guest bedrooms and suites have elegant furnishings and private terraces with views. Guests start their stay with complimentary wine or coffee. There's also a spa.

✖️ Eating

Boquete has numerous well-priced restaurants to choose from, and the produce and coffee here is among the best in Panama. Fresh produce is sold at the mercado municipal, on the northeastern corner of the plaza.

★ Big Daddy's Grill　　　SEAFOOD **$**
(☑6683-3354; Av Central s/n; mains US$5-10; ⊙noon-9pm Tue-Sat, to 8pm Sun) The next best thing to dining in Baja, this friendly eatery serves the most enormous and satisfying fish tacos. Floridians Larry (the big daddy) and Elizabeth use the fresh fish they catch off the Chiriquí coastline. There are also lovely salads, margaritas rimmed with chili salt and (if you must) corn dogs. The backyard patio offers privacy and better ambiance.

Sugar & Spice　　　BAKERY, DELI **$**
(Av Central & Calle 7a Sur; sandwiches US$4; ⊙8am-6pm Thu-Sat & Mon-Tue, to 4pm Sun) Throngs gather at this artisan bakery, a modest storefront with a couple patio tables for American-style sandwiches, organic salads and oh-so-good brownies. You can also take away fresh breads including wholegrain and ciabatta.

Café de Encuentro　　　CAFE **$**
(Calle 6 Sur; mains US$3-7; ⊙7am-noon) In a converted carport and garden, this family-run eatery is a find. All guests are *mi amor* to the affectionate Olga, who cooks breakfast like nobody's business. The menu ranges from Panamanian fare to pancakes and bacon. Expect to wait, but given the scarcity of US-style morning fare, you will want to.

Restaurante Nelvis　　　CAFETERIA **$**
(Av A Oeste; meals US$3.50; ⊙10am-4pm Mon-Sat) Packing in the locals at lunchtime, this favorite serves up no-nonsense lunches with attentiveness. Rice, lentils and a selection of chicken or beef dishes are staples.

Pastelería Alemana　　　BAKERY **$**
(pastries US$3; ⊙8am-noon) On the main road 2km south of town, this spot serves up decadent pies and authentic German breads alongside strong cups of coffee.

El Sabrosón　　　CAFETERIA **$**
(Av Central; mains US$2-5) This much-loved local institution cooks up cheap and filling Panamanian cuisine served cafeteria-style. Although Boquete is rapidly being colonized by gringo-friendly boutique eateries, this is one local institution that stays true to its roots.

Fresas Mary　　　DESSERTS **$**
(Calle Volcancito Principal; snacks US$3) With strawberry milkshakes to make you shiver with pleasure, this cute roadside stand makes a worthy stop.

Supermercado Romero　　　SUPERMARKET **$**
(Av A Este; ⊙24hr) One block east of the plaza, this has the best selection of groceries.

★ Il Pianista　　　ITALIAN **$$**
(Palo Alto sector; mains US$5-15) One of the pleasures of Boquete is driving the loopy hillside roads where you will find Il Pianista. Husband cooks and wife serves at this creekside Sicilian restaurant with riverstone walls and just a few tables. A bottle of wine and pizza or calzones make the perfect leisurely lunch but don't come in a rush. Service is as slow as magma.

Local buses loop by here or follow signs for Boquete Garden Inn; it's just above it.

Art Café La Crêpe　　　FRENCH **$$**
(Av Central; mains US$6-13; ⊙11am-3pm & 5-9pm Tue-Sun) Fresh and festive, this American-run French cafe serves faithful incarnations of its namesake in a kindergarten-inspired ambiance of primary colors. Francophiles will embrace menu options that include pâté, rilletes and tenderloin with blue cheese. For lunch there is a daily special with dessert and appetizer. There's also brunch on weekends.

Mike's Global Grill　　　INTERNATIONAL **$$**
(☑730-9360; Av Central Oeste; mains US$6-12; ⊙11am-10pm Wed-Mon) This homesick restaurant is the lovechild of a couple who met at the South Pole. To further the wanderlust

theme, dishes range from Asian fusion to American chili, falafel and brick-oven pizzas. The ambiance is friendly-chill, with a long bar and sofas and stacks of magazines. At night it's a popular watering hole for expats, with occasional live music.

Panamonte Inn INTERNATIONAL **$$**
(☑720-1327; mains US$13; ☺7am-10pm) This sophisticated restaurant has a longstanding reputation. Chef Charlie Collins takes a modern approach, exquisitely preparing everything from grilled filets to mushroom-stuffed ravioli. Local staples such as trout are transformed to buttery softness. While the powder-blue dining room rings romantic, you may prefer a tiny table near the crackling hearth in the bar-lounge. Ideal for cocktails or wine.

Wine Bar/Pomodoro ITALIAN **$$**
(Camino a Valle Escondido; mains US$8-17; ☑) The sister bar-restaurant to the popular Panama City outlet, this classic Italian spot serves fresh pastas and pizzas alongside a laundry list of great wines. There's a nice riverside patio and a trampoline and playground to keep kids busy. Adults won't mind passing the time at the pool table either.

Rock INTERNATIONAL **$$$**
(☑720-2516; www.foodforsenses.com; Calle Jaramillo Alto; 4-course lunch US$20; ☺11:30am-9:30pm Wed-Mon) This is cosmopolitan dining at its best, at least in the highlands. Attached to the Riverside Inn, the Rock takes itself very seriously. The pork ribs with papaya sugarcane sauce come widely recommended. There's also lovely pasta and seafood.

The restaurant can be a lively spot for a drink, with an extensive wine list and full bar and live jazz on Monday and Wednesday. Two-for-one cocktails are served from 6pm to 7pm.

🍷 Drinking & Entertainment

With much to do all day, Boquete leaves little for the evenings, unless it's festival time. Come darkness you can hear a pin drop, so don't expect a wild night out on the town. Bars close at midnight on weekdays and 2am on weekends.

Zanzibar BAR
(Av Central) A low-key jazz bar with the cure for what ails ya, Zanzibar is the place to mingle with travelers and locals. Your best chance of hearing live music is on weekends,

though most nights of the week you'll find a friendly face sitting at the bar. Happy hour runs from 5pm to 7pm.

La Cabaña CLUB
(Calle de la Feria; cover US$2; ☺7pm-2am Fri & Sat) Boquete's only disco is riverside, with DJs, reggaetón, a young crowd and a steady current of rum and cola to keep it flowing.

Boquete Community Playhouse THEATER
(☑6533-0967; www.bcpboquete.com; Calle de la Feria) Hosts local theater and special events. Check with your hotel or the tourist office about current offerings.

ℹ Information

ATP (☑720-4060; ☺8am-5:30pm) About 1.5km south of Boquete, this office sits atop a bluff overlooking town. Here you can grab a Kotowa coffee, pick up maps and obtain information on area attractions. A 2nd-floor exhibit details the history of the region (Spanish only).
Banco Nacional de Panama (Av Central) Has ATM.
Centro Medico San Juan Bautista (☑720-1881; Calle 2 Norte) For medical care.
Global Bank (Av Central) Bank with ATM.
Post office (☺7am-6pm Mon-Fri, to 5pm Sat) Handy to mail some coffee home.

ℹ Getting There & Around

Buses to Boquete depart from David's main bus terminal (US$1.75, one hour, every 30 minutes) from 6am to 9:30pm. Buses to David depart from the south side of Boquete's plaza every 30 minutes from 5am to 6:30pm.

Boquete's small size lends itself to easy exploration. The *urbano* (local) buses winding through the hills cost US$0.50. They depart on the main road one block north of the plaza. Taxis charge US$2 to US$3 for most places around town.

For scooter or bike rentals (about US$3 per hour), check out local hostels. Cars can be rented at **Thrifty** (☑721-2477; Av Central, Plaza Los Establos; ☺8am-5pm Mon-Sat), which is a great option to explore more of the local area.

Parque Nacional Volcán Barú

This 143-sq-km national park (admission US$5) is home to Volcán Barú, Panama's only volcano and the dominant geographical feature of Chiriquí. Volcán Barú is no longer considered active; in fact, there is no record of its most recent eruption. Yet the volcano has not one but seven craters.

Its 3478m summit is the highest point in Panama, and on a clear day it affords views of both the Pacific and Caribbean coasts.

The national park is also home to the Sendero Los Quetzales, one of the most scenic treks in the entire country. As its name implies, the trail is one of the best places in Central America to spot the rare resplendent quetzal, especially during the dry season (November to April). However, even if the Maya bird of paradise fails to show, the park is home to more than 250 bird species as well as pumas, tapirs and the *conejo pintado* (a spotted raccoon-like animal).

After a series of severe landslides, the Quetzals trail has suffered extensive damage. While it is still walkable, there are sections that are very indistinct and under heavy debris. We recommend that you hike the trail with a guide; ANAM plans to soon make this a requirement. In recent times many travelers have gotten lost on this stretch and resources for rescue are practically nonexistent.

�֯ Activities

Volcán Barú   HIKING
(Barú Volcano) With summit views of both oceans, climbing the volcano is a goal of many visitors. It might not be worth it in poor weather, as the going is strenuous and rough. In addition, there is little to see in cloud cover. You can enter the park on the eastern and western sides of the volcano. The eastern access, known as 'El Salto,' includes a drive through beautiful forest.

From Boquete, the eastern summit access is the easiest, but it involves a strenuous uphill hike along a 14km road that goes from the park entrance – about 8km northwest of the center of Boquete – to the summit. The road is paved to the ranger station and 2km beyond. If you drive or taxi as far up as possible and then walk the rest of the way, it takes about five or six hours to reach the summit from the park gate; walking from town would take another two or three hours each way.

On this route, it's best to camp on the mountain at least one night; and you should be prepared for the cold. Camping will also allow you to be at the top during the morning, when the views are best.

The other park entrance is just outside the town of Volcán, on the road to Cerro Punta. This rugged road into the park (requiring a 4WD vehicle) goes only a short way off the main road to the foot of the volcano. The view of the summit and the nearby peaks from this entrance are impressive, and there's a lovely loop trail that winds through secondary and virgin forest. Access from this side is steep and technical.

★ **Sendero Los Quetzales**   HIKING
(Quetzals Trail) Sendero Los Quetzales near Cerro Punta is one of Panama's most beautiful trails. The 8km route takes between four and seven hours. It runs between Cerro Punta and Boquete, crisscrossing Río Caldera. You can hike from either direction, but it is easiest from west to east: the town of Cerro Punta is almost 1000m higher than Boquete, so hiking east offers more downhill.

While the trail is easily visible in most parts, down bridges can be a serious affair. At the time of writing, a suspension bridge was being installed over the Río Caldera.

The trail itself takes four to five hours walking west to east, though getting to and from the trailhead adds another couple of hours of walking on either side. A 4WD taxi can take you to the trailhead on the Cerro Punta side for about US$25 per person; taxi drivers know the area as Respingo. Road conditions may be very poor from landslides. The trail is 5km uphill from the main road and 2km from the last paved road. When you exit the trail, it's another 8km along the road to Boquete, though you may be able to catch a taxi along the road. In total, the hike is about 23km, so plan accordingly if you intend to walk the entire trail.

After arriving in Boquete, stay overnight or take a bus to David and then Cerro Punta; note that the last Cerro Punta bus leaves David at 6pm. You can also leave your luggage at one of the hotels in David to save yourself the hassle of backtracking. Take only the bare essentials with you on the walk (and a little cash for a good meal and/or lodging in Boquete).

🛏 Sleeping

**Parque Nacional Volcán
Barú Camping**   CAMPGROUND **$**
(campsite US$5) Camping is available in the park and on the trail to the summit from the Boquete side, along the Sendero Los Quetzales or at the ranger station at the entrance to the Sendero Los Quetzales on the Cerro Punta side.

ℹ Information

Admission to the park is paid at either of the trailheads leading to the summit or at the ranger station on the Cerro Punto side of the Sendero Los Quetzales.

The best time to visit is during the dry season, especially early in the morning when wildlife is most active.

Be advised that overnight temperatures can drop below freezing, and it may be windy and cold during the day, particularly in the morning – dress accordingly.

❶ Getting There & Away

The trailhead leading to the summit of Volcán Barú is best accessed from the town of Boquete while the Sendero Los Quetzales is best approached from Cerro Punta.

Volcán

POP 8200

Volcán is the first town of major size that you pass along the route to La Amistad, though the town is dwarfed by its namesake. Clinging to the flanks of the towering Volcán Barú, the town of Volcán has a pleasant feel and serves as a good base for excursions and eating, though the lodgings pickings are slim. However, if you're feeling nostalgic for the days when Boquete was just another mountain town in Chiriquí, this may be the perfect stop for you.

The road that links Concepción and Volcán forks in the center of town: one arrow points left toward Río Sereno, on the Costa Rican border (47km); the other points right toward Cerro Punta (16km), the entrance to the Sendero Los Quetzales.

◎ Sights & Activities

⭐ **Arte Cruz Volcán –**
Artesanía en Madera GALLERY
(☏6622-1502; ⊙8am-noon & 1-5:30pm) On the western side of the Concepción–Volcán road, 3km south of Volcán, you'll see Arte Cruz Volcán – Artesanía en Madera, where artist José de la Cruz González makes and sells exquisite wooden signs, sculptures and furniture as well as impressive etchings on crystal and glass.

José trained in fine arts in Italy and Honduras, and his work has been commissioned by buyers worldwide. Visitors are treated to José's entertaining demonstrations.

Barriles RUINS
FREE These pre-Columbian ruins (located on private land) are about a five-minute drive from the center of town. The settlement, inhabited in the period during

300–900 AD, was believed to have up to 1000 residents. Some artifacts are display onsite though not all were found here.

Área Silvestre Protegida
Lagunas de Volcán PARK
FREE Four-and-a-half kilometers from Volcán, this protected area encompasses the highest lake system (1240m) in Panama. The two picturesque lakes swell in the rainy season, with lush, virgin forest at their edges and Volcán Barú in the background. To get to the lakes from the Concepción–Volcán road, turn west onto Calle El Valle (near central Volcán) and follow the signs.

Surrounding woodlands are excellent sites for bird-watching – of special interest are the masked duck, the northern jacana, the rose-throated becard, the pale-billed woodpecker and mixed flocks of tanagers, flycatchers and antbirds. No buses go to the lakes, but you can hire a taxi in Volcán to bring you here. If you take your own vehicle, be advised that there have been reports of thefts from vehicles.

Highland Adventures ADVENTURE TOUR
(☏6685-1682; hlaaizpurua@hotmail.com; Av Central) With some English, Gonzalo Aizpurua is a good source of information, though rarely in the office since he's usually in the field. Guided activities include rainforest mountain-biking, birding or hiking Parque Internacional La Amistad (US$90 for two people) and guided climbs to the top of Volcán Barú (US$130 for two people, 12 hours). His stand is 1.5km after the police station.

🛏 Sleeping & Eating

Mount Totumas Cloud Forest CABIN $$
(www.mounttotumas.com; s/d US$50/80, cabin US$140; @🛜) ✈ This 160-hectare ecoresort borders Parque Internacional La Amistad, 20km from Volcán. Far and away from creatures without wings or paws, the cloudforest setting is a biologist's dream. There are spacious rooms, hammock decks with views, and well-equipped kitchens. Off the grid, hot water and electricity comes via a micro-hydroplant. Guests can sign up for guided hikes or horseback riding.

Contact via the website. Transportation is available from Volcán (US$40 one way), otherwise guests need a high-clearance 4WD.

Daily's Diner AMERICAN $
(mains US$2.50; ⊙7:30am-8:30pm) On the way into Volcán, this converted gas station is a

tour de force of home cooking. The glass-front diner is run by the tiny and formidable Daily. We recommend the American-style breakfasts and other gringo treats, such as wholegrain cookies and cinnamon rolls. The menu is incredibly diverse, ranging from outstanding burgers to Thai curries.

Portions are on the small side but prices are very reasonable. It's best on a weekday, since the resident expats hold court on the weekends.

★ Il Forno   ITALIAN $$
(☑ 6827-0621; mains US$10-18; ☉ noon-9pm Thu-Sun; ☕) In the center of Volcán, chef-run Il Forno serves up satisfying and authentic Italian fare, ranging from thin-crust pizzas to beef carpaccio, homemade pasta and churrasco beef plates. Il Forno also makes its own ricotta cheese. The atmosphere is rustic but inviting.

Cerro Brujo Gourmet   INTERNATIONAL $$$
(☑ reservations only 6669-9196; sector Brisas del Norte; mains US$12-18; ☉ noon-3pm & 6-10pm) Another excellent food destination, this is a vibrant and relaxed colonial country house with no menu – just two daily options. Patti Miranda's mouthwatering creations include garden salad, squash-blossom soup, baked chicken with blue cheese and dill, or grilled steak, with banana flambé for dessert.

Grab a taxi there or take the signed turnoff on the main road about 1km in on a dirt road.

❶ Getting There & Away
Buses from Volcán to David depart from the Shell station on Av Central every 15 minutes from 5am to 7:30pm (US$3, 1½ hours). There are also pickup truck taxis available by the Río Sereno–Guadalupe fork in the road.

Santa Clara

About 30km from Volcán, on the highway to Río Sereno, is the tiny village of Santa Clara, which is little more than a grocery store and a gas station. It's also home to Finca Hartmann (☑ 6450-1853; www.fincahartmann.com; 2-/4-person cabin US$80/140; ℗), a working shade-grown coffee farm situated in highland rainforest with a rich variety of wildlife.

Ardent conservationists, the Hartmanns have hosted a number of Smithsonian-affiliated scientists over the years. The family rents out basic but handsomely constructed cabins in fantastic surroundings. Though there's no electricity, cabins have clean potable spring water, flush toilets and even hot showers.

The bird-watching is simply superb, with more than 280 unique species. The hiking trails pass through a variety of habitats between 1300m and 2000m. Sr Hartmann is an excellent host with a wealth of information – ask to see his 'museum' (a lifetime's collection of Panamanian insects and pre-Columbian artifacts). The farm charges admission (US$15) for bird-watching or coffee tours. The coffee harvest season runs roughly from October to January.

The entrance to Finca Hartmann is located a few hundred meters past the gas station, on the left-hand side – look for the small sign.

Paso Ancho

Along the road to the Parque Internacional La Amistad, a great place to stop for a few nights is Las Plumas (☑ 771-5541; www.las-plumas.com; Paso Ancho; 4-person guesthouse US$66-143; ℗), a friendly Dutch-owned spot on the edge of Paso Ancho village. Las Plumas occupies a tranquil setting on 2.3 hectares of land, and consists of several roomy guesthouses that can accommodate four people in two bedrooms. Each guesthouse is beautifully furnished with solid wooden furniture, leather couches, tiled bathrooms and orthopedic mattresses – there's even satellite TV, though the man attraction is the beauty of the surrounding forest. There is a minimum stay of three nights, with discounted weekly and monthly rates.

Bambito

There's no shortage of tiny mountain towns along this route, though Bambito is worth a quick look, even if only to visit Truchas de Bambito (fishing US$5), a rainbow trout farm where thousands of fish are raised in outdoor ponds. The chilly spring-water-fed ponds produce some healthy (and very meaty) trout, which are also for sale. The fishing fee includes a pole.

Just over 3km past Bambito in the hamlet of Nueva Suiza, Hostal Cielito Sur B&B (☑ 771-2038; www.cielitosur.com; d incl breakfast from US$105; ℗) is a sweet highland retreat. Owned by a friendly Panamanian-American couple, it offers four spacious guest rooms with hot-water bathtubs, hairdryers, living rooms with fireplaces and private riverside patios. Breakfast is local, with fresh farm eggs and coffee from the surrounding property. Lounge spaces abound, from the *bohío* (rustic hut) strung up with hammocks to a shared Jacuzzi bathhouse. You can also arrange canoeing, bird-watching and Quetzal Trail transfers here.

Before leaving Bambito, look for a small store 1.5km north of the Hotel Bambito named Alina, which sells fruit jam, candy and milkshakes using the region's famous wild strawberries. It's a charming spot that any local can point out to you – be sure to stock up if you're on your way to an expedition in Parque Internacional La Amistad.

Cerro Punta

At an altitude of 1800m, this tranquil highland town is reminiscent of an alpine village. Indeed, you'd be forgiven for thinking you were in Switzerland – as you near Cerro Punta, everything starts to look European, with meticulously tended agricultural plots and European-style houses with steep-pitched tin roofs. Not surprisingly, a Swiss colony was founded here many decades ago, and you can still hear Swiss-German spoken in the area.

Visitors come to Cerro Punta primarily during the dry season (January to April) in order to access the two nearby parks: Volcán Barú and La Amistad. However, the town itself makes a lovely stop, especially since the area is known for its succulent strawberries – be sure to pick some up at a roadside stand.

Located on the main road, friendly Hotel Cerro Punta (771-2020; http://hotelcerropunta.zxq.net; s/d/tr US$24/30/36; P ☎) offers a row of mint-green concrete rooms that are a bit tired and beat up. If you're on your way to either national park, enjoy the private hot-water bathroom – it's the last one you'll see for a while.

A bus runs from David to Cerro Punta (US$3.50, 2¼ hours, every 20 minutes) en route to Guadalupe, stopping at Volcán and Bambito along the way. If you're coming from Costa Rica, you could catch this bus at the turnoff from the Interamericana at Concepción. If you're in Volcán, you can catch one at the parking lot opposite the Shell station.

If you're driving, the main road continues through Cerro Punta and ends at Guadalupe, 3km further. Another road takes off to the west, heading for the Las Nubes entrance to Parque Internacional La Amistad, 6.8km away – the turnoff is marked by a large wooden sign.

Guadalupe

Three kilometers past Cerro Punta, Guadalupe is the end of the road, though it's a glorious area where you can walk among meticulously tended farms and gardens. This little community is full of flowers, and the agricultural plots curling up the steep hillsides are out of a picture book. With that said, respect the signs that read: 'Esteemed Visitor: we are making all Guadalupe a garden – please don't pick the flowers.'

About 600m beyond the Los Quetzales Lodge & Spa, at the turnoff to the Cabañas Los Quetzales Cabins, lies the Finca Dracula Orchid Sanctuary (771-2070; www.fincadracula.com; admission US$10; ☺8-11:30am & 1-4pm Tue-Sun), one of Latin America's finest orchid collections. There are over 2000 species on display here, and the extremely knowledgeable staff take great pride in showing off this impressive sanctuary to interested guests.

Every 20 minutes a bus runs from David to Guadalupe (US$3.50, 2¼ hours) via Volcán, Bambito and Cerro Punta. If you're driving, Guadalupe is the end of the road.

🛏 Sleeping

⭐ Los Quetzales Cabins   CABIN $$
(771-2182; www.losquetzales.com; dm US$20, 4-person cabin US$140-160; ☎) Affiliated with the lodging in the village, these spectacular rustic retreats are tucked into the rainforest. The forested setting with darting hummingbirds, lookout balconies and trout ponds is among the finest in Panama. Some cabins have electricity, and all feature propane lanterns and fireplaces with wood, though hot showers are provided.

You can hike straight from the cabins and make arrangements for a cook or for groceries to be delivered. They are located 2km from the main lodge up a 4WD road (transportation is provided).

Los Quetzales Lodge & Spa   LODGE $$
(771-2182; www.losquetzales.com; camping per tent US$15, dm/d US$18/85, r in lodge incl breakfast from US$85; ☎) Located in town, this cozy lodging is a favorite for bird-watchers and hikers. Rooms feature vaulted ceilings, wood furnishings and private hot-water bathrooms, though most guests tend to congregate around the bar-restaurant and cozy fireplace lounge. Families can ask about their new farmhouse rentals with activities in Bajo Grande, 3km away.

Couples might want to splurge on one of the five cedar-walled suites with a romantic hewn-stone fireplace, private bathtub and rainforest-facing balcony. Also on the premises are three riverside hot tubs and an equestrian center. All guests also have access to a full-service spa and a private network of trails adjoining Parque Nacional Volcán Barú. The park is less than an hour's walk from the hotel, which can also provide transportation.

Parque Internacional La Amistad (Las Nubes)

The 4070-sq-km Parque Internacional La Amistad (admission US$5, campsite US$5; ⊘ 8am-4pm) was established jointly in 1988 by Panama and Costa Rica. In 1990 La Amistad was declared a Unesco World Heritage Site, and later became part of the greater Meso American Biological corridor. In Panama, the park covers portions of Chiriquí and Bocas del Toro (p201) Provinces, contains seven of the 12 classified life zones and serves as a refuge for a great number of endangered flora and fauna.

🏃 Activities

Although most of the park is high up in the Talamanca Mountains and inaccessible, there is no shortage of hiking and camping opportunities available for intrepid travelers. Unlike the Wekso entrance in Bocas del Toro Province, the Las Nubes sector is home to an established trail network, and is more accessible to independent hikers. However, the Naso population has a more established presence in Wekso, so it's better to approach the park from Bocas if you're interested in spending some time with this indigenous group.

Hiking

Sendero La Cascada   HIKING
(Waterfall Trail) Starting at the Las Nubes ranger station, this 3.4km round-trip hike takes in three *miradores* (lookouts) as well as a 45m-high waterfall with a lovely bathing pool.

Sendero El Retoño   HIKING
(Rebirth Trail) From the Las Nubes ranger station this trail loops 2.1km through secondary forest, crosses a number of rustic bridges and winds through bamboo groves.

Lost World Tours   ADVENTURE TOUR
(☑ 6920-3036; www.boquetetobocas.com; 2/3 passengers US$450/350 per person) The Amistad Trek is run by the Lost & Found Lodge and led by a former Peace Corps volunteer. This strenuous three-day hike starts in Cerro Punta and traverses to Bocas del Toro Province, with accommodations in indigenous villages.

Watching-Wildlife

Most of Parque Internacional La Amistad is inaccessible terrain high up in the Talamanca. It's worth making the trek, as the park is home to a recorded 90 mammal species and all six cat species. There's more than 400 bird species including resplendent quetzals and harpy eagles.

🛏 Sleeping & Eating

Las Nubes Ranger Station   HUT $
(☑ ANAM 775-3163; dm US$15) The basic ranger station at Las Nubes has a visitors' dormitory with bunk beds. Due to its popularity among international school groups, reservations are advisable. Guests have kitchen access; stock up on provisions in Cerro Punta. Bring your own bedding, and a mosquito net is a good idea.

To reserve, call ANAM in David or the Co-op Restaurant at the park entrance.

Co-op Restaurant   PANAMANIAN $
(☑ 771-2566; dishes US$2-5; ⊘ 8am-4pm) Near the entrance to the park, this wonderful restaurant is run by a local women's co-op. There's outdoor seating on a deck with hummingbirds buzzing about. Fresh-cooked meals include soup, rice and beans or grilled cheese. In addition to bottled water, there's hot tea for chilly days, as well as homemade strawberry jam.

It's also a good place to inquire about local guides who can lead excursions into primary rainforest.

ℹ Information

Admission to the park (US$5) is paid at Las Nubes, near Cerro Punta. Camping permits (US$3 per person) are payable at the ranger station.

If you plan to spend much time at Las Nubes, be sure to bring a jacket. This side of the park, at 2280m above sea level, has a cool climate – temperatures are usually around 24°C (75°F) in the daytime and drop to about 3°C (38°F) at night.

ℹ Getting There & Away

The Las Nubes entrance is about 7km from Cerro Punta; a sign on the main road in Cerro Punta marks the turnoff. The road starts out good and paved, but by the time you reach the park it's a rutted track suitable only for 4WD vehicles. From Cerro Punta, you can take a taxi (US$6 for two people).

Bocas del Toro Province

POP 125,500 / ELEV SEA LEVEL TO 3300M / AREA 8,745 SQ KM

Best Places to Eat

➡ Raw (p188)

➡ Up In the Hill (p199)

➡ Guari Guari (p189)

➡ Om Café (p189)

Best Places to Stay

➡ La Loma Jungle Lodge (p198)

➡ Casa Cayuko (p198)

➡ Gran Kahuna Hostel (p193)

Why Go?

With Caribbean islands dotting a shock of blue waters, Bocas is all that's tropical. Panama's principal tourist draw, the archipelago consists of six densely forested islands, scores of uninhabited islets and Parque Nacional Marino Isla Bastimentos, Panama's oldest marine park.

The longtime roost of Chiquita Banana, the mainland boasts the binational gem of Parque Internacional La Amistad, shared with Costa Rica. It's also home to diverse wildlife including the elusive jaguar, traditional Ngöbe-Buglé settlements, and the Naso, one of few remaining American tribes with a traditional monarchy.

Most visitors come for a hefty dose of sun and surf. Few are disappointed with the Bocas cocktail of water fun and thatched luxury. Those bent on a Caribbean getaway should get here soon, as unspoiled beauty rarely stays that way.

When to Go

➡ **Dec–Mar & Jun–Aug** The biggest swells for surfers to ride; green turtles can be found nesting on Isla Bastimentos in July and August.

➡ **Feb–Apr & Aug–Oct** Dry conditions and calm seas mean the best visibility for snorkeling and diving with better access to ocean caves. From February, turtle nestings are monitored for six months in Humedal de San-San Pond Sak.

➡ **Mid-Nov** Bocas breaks into mayhem for its anniversary celebration, along with myriad celebrations of Días Patrias. A booming month for national tourism.

History

Christopher Columbus visited Bocas del Toro in 1502, during his fourth and final New World voyage. Taken by its beauty, he affixed his name to many sites.

During the 17th century, the archipelago became a haven for pirates repairing and building ships, felling the forests and feeding upon nesting sea turtles. Despite rumors of buried treasure, none of their loot has been found (or reported).

After French Huguenots settled the coast in the 17th and 18th centuries, a Spanish militia was sent to Bocas to dislodge them. Their diseases and destruction virtually wiped out the indigenous populations.

In the early 19th century wealthy aristocrat settlers arrived in Bocas with many black slaves from the USA and Colombian islands. When slavery was abolished in 1850, the blacks became fishers and subsistence farmers. Towards the end of the 19th century Jamaican blacks joined them to work in the burgeoning banana industry.

In 1899, however, United Fruit Company overtook a small American-owned banana company. As United Fruit established vast plantations across the entire peninsula it also constructed elaborate networks of roads, bridges and canals. Entire towns and cities popped up to house workers.

Now Chiquita Brands International, the company grows and exports three-quarters of a million tons of bananas annually. The largest workforce in the province, they are also the most diverse nationwide, with West Indian, Latino, Chinese and indigenous workers.

ARCHIPIÉLAGO DE BOCAS DEL TORO

For most travelers, the archipelago *is* Bocas – Caribbean clichés aside, there's no shortage of postcard beaches, emerald waters and swaying palms.

Isla Colón

The archipelago's largest and most developed island is home to the provincial capital of Bocas del Toro. Starting in the mid-1990s, foreign investors flooded the island, creating new hotels, restaurants and condos while infrastructure for water, trash and sewage lagged far behind. Today, the island, which runs on diesel, struggles to find a balance between satiating development and serving community needs.

Note that the town, the archipelago and the province all share the name Bocas del Toro or simply Bocas. Isla Colón and Bocas del Toro town are also referred to as Bocas Isla.

🏃 Activities

Cycling

Whether you're heading to Boca del Drago on the paved road, or taking the dirt path to Playa Bluff, a bicycle can seriously increase your mobility. Note that the cycle to Boca del Drago from Boca town is taxing, especially when the sun is beaming. If you're unsure of your fitness level, it's advised that you head to Punta Bluff instead, even though the road can flood after heavy rains. Bikes are available from some hostels and from Ixa's Bike World (p183) in Boca town.

Bird-Watching

While the bird-watching on the islands isn't as good as that on the mainland, it can still be rewarding. Particularly rare birds, or at least those poorly known to Panama, have been recorded on the islands in recent years, and include the semiplumbeous hawk, white-tailed kite, zone-tailed hawk, uniform crake, olive-throated parakeet, red-fronted parrotlet, lesser nighthawk, green-breasted mango, chestnut-colored woodpecker, snowy cotinga, brown-capped tyrannulet, yellow-bellied elaenia, stubtailed spadebill, purple martin, tree swallow and black-cowled oriole.

Fishing

The best budget option for aspiring anglers is to go surf casting with the local water-taxi drivers. The hand lines are a bit tricky at first, though you'll get the hang of it. It's best to go early in the morning when the fish are biting.

Hiking

If you're looking to seriously get off the beaten path, there is a network of undeveloped hiking trails that fan out across the island. One of the more popular hikes starts at the end of the coastal road in Mimbi Timbi and carries on along the coast to Boca del Drago. You will need about six hours of daylight to complete the hike and you must carry in all your fresh water. The trail winds past caves, caverns and plenty of vine-entangled

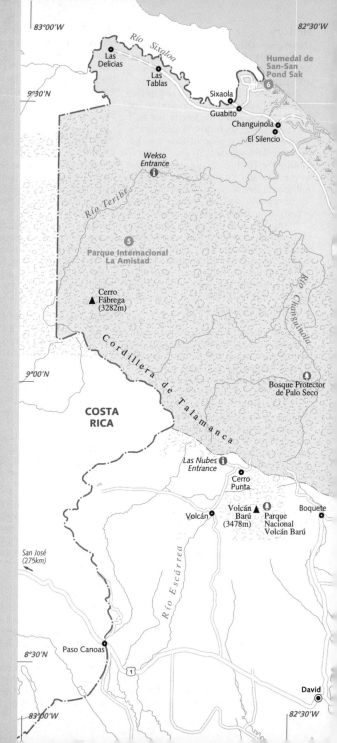

Bocas del Toro Province Highlights

1 While the days away sipping coconuts and snorkeling at laid-back resorts in the **Archipiélago de Bocas del Toro** (p179)

2 Swim through a bat cave or soak up the rays on the pristine beaches of chill **Isla Bastimentos** (p195)

3 Take the party from boat bars to cocktail lounges in lively **Bocas town** (p183)

4 Surf some of the sickest breaks you'll find in the **Caribbean** (p197) – just watch those shallow reefs!

5 Explore **Parque Internacional La Amistad** (p201), where the Naso (Teribe) live under one of the world's last tribal monarchies

6 Spot manatees and river otters while boating through the oft-overlooked wetlands of **Humedal de San-San Pond Sak** (p201)

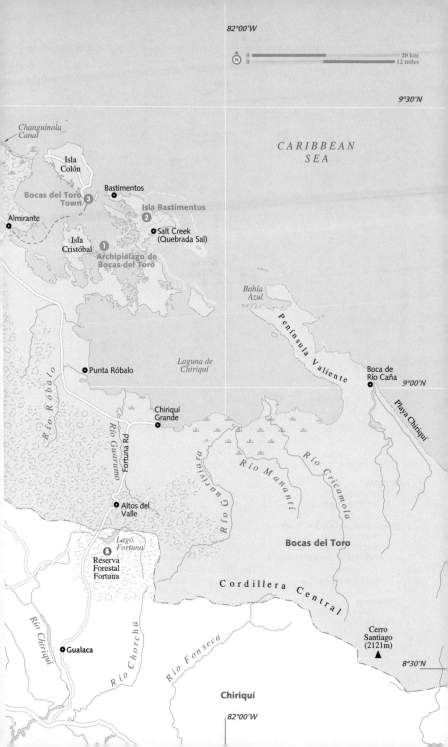

Archipiélago de Bocas del Toro

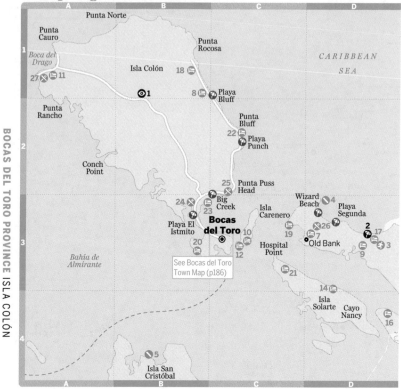

Archipiélago de Bocas del Toro

◉ **Sights**
1 La Gruta..B1
2 Red Frog Beach.................................... D3

➕ **Activities, Courses & Tours**
3 Bastimentos Sky.................................. D3
4 Dark Wood Reef................................... D3
Institute for Tropical Ecology &
Conservation............................. (see 11)
5 Punta Juan Buoy................................. B4

🛏 **Sleeping**
6 Al Natural Resort...................................F4
Aqua Lounge............................... (see 12)
7 Beverly's Hill.. D3
8 Bluff Beach Retreat............................ B1
9 Bocas Bound Hostel............................ D3
10 Buccaneer Resort................................. C3
11 Cabañas Estefany.................................A1
12 Casa Acuario... C3
13 Casa Cayuko...F4
El Faro del Colibri........................ (see 12)

14 Garden of Eden......................................D3
Gran Kahuna Hostel...................... (see 12)
15 La Loma Jungle Lodge............................E4
16 Los Secretos...D4
17 Palmar Tent Lodge...............................D3
18 Playa Bluff Lodge................................. B1
19 Point..C3
20 Punta Caracol Aqua Lodge...................B3
21 Solarte del Caribe Inn..........................C3
22 Tesoro Escondido...................................C2
Tierra Verde.................................... (see 12)
23 Villa Paraiso..B3

🍴 **Eating**
Bibi's..(see 10)
24 Guari Guari..B3
La Gruta (Bahía Honda)................ (see 1)
25 Paki Point..C2
Pickled Parrot................................(see 10)
26 Up In the Hill...D3
27 Yarisnori Restaurant............................ A1

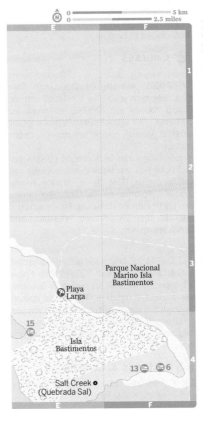

Bocas serves as a convenient base for exploring the archipelago, as *taxis marinos* (water taxis) ply the waters and can whisk you away to remote beaches and snorkeling sites for a few dollars. However, as most travelers learn after spending their first few days idly wandering the streets, the allure of Bocas is simply slowing down and soaking up the Caribbean vibes.

◎ Sights

Bocas town is laid out in a grid pattern, with most of the hotels and restaurants on Calle 3.

Bocas Butterfly Farm GARDENS
(☑757-9008; adult/child US$5/2; ☺9am-3pm Mon-Sat, 9am-noon Sun) A great morning trip from Bocas town is the adorable Bocas Butterfly Farm, which houses species from every corner of Panama. There is no road access: hire a water taxi for US$1 one way.

🕴 Activities

Ixa's Bike World BICYCLE RENTAL
(Av H; ☺8am-6pm) Repairs and rents a wide selection of bicycles.

Boat Tours

The most popular tours in the area are all-day snorkeling trips, which are perfect for non-divers wanting a taste of the area's rich marine life. A typical tour costs US$20 per person and goes to Dolphin Bay, Cayo Crawl, Red Frog Beach (US$2 entry) and Hospital Point.

A trip to the distant Cayos Zapatillas costs US$25 (plus an additional US$10 for admission to the marine park) and includes lunch, beach time and a jungle hike on Cayo Zapatilla Sur.

Many 'tours' are really little more than boat transportation to a pretty spot. If you have your own snorkel gear (or if you rent it), you can also charter motor boats. Agree on a price before you go.

Transparente Tours TOUR
(☑6583-0351, 757-9915; transparentetours@ hotmail.com; Calle 3, Bocas del Toro; ☺9:30am-5:30pm) This recommended tour operator provides guides, gear, drinks and radios on excursions.

Diving & Snorkeling

With nearly 40 rivers unloading silt into the seas around Bocas del Toro, the archipelago's waters are notorious for their poor visibility. If it has rained a lot in recent days, visibility may be limited to only 3m.

jungle. A bicycle will help speed things up a bit, though you'll be carrying it part of the way, especially if it's been raining recently.

Kayaking

Although you will need to be wary of boat traffic and the occasional swell, a great way to travel between islands is by sea kayak. Some of the dive shops rent kayaks.

Bocas del Toro

Colorful and utterly Caribbean, this town of clapboard houses was built by the United Fruit Company in the early 20th century. Today, Bocas is a relaxed community of West Indians, Latinos and resident gringos, with a friendly atmosphere that easily rubs off on visitors. In fact, travelers to this island town have a reputation for canceling future plans – it's an easy place to get stuck and an even easier place to linger.

Although experienced divers accustomed to crystal-clear Caribbean diving may be disappointed with Bocas, the islands still have much to offer. The emerald-green waters of the archipelago are home to the usual assortment of tropical species and with a little luck you might see barracuda, stingrays, dolphins and nurse sharks. Better sites include **Dark Wood Reef**, northwest of Bastimentos; **Hospital Point**, a 50ft wall off Cayo Nancy; and the base of the buoy near **Punta Juan** north of Isla Cristóbal.

Costs run around US$60 for a two-tank dive and US$70 for a full-day tour.

Starfleet Eco Adventures   DIVING
(☑757-9630; www.starfleetscuba.com; Calle 1) PADI open-water and advanced-diver courses are available. Starfleet offers instruction in English and enjoys a strong reputation among locals and travelers.

La Buga   DIVING
(☑757-9534; www.labugapanama.com; Calle 3; ☺8am-8pm) New on the scene, La Buga has nonetheless become a well-regarded dive shop. Trips are made twice daily. Highlights include night dives and visiting the caves off Bastimentos (US$70). It also does surf rentals and lessons, stand-up paddles (US$20 per day) and kayak rentals (US$5). While you explore options, grab a bite at its cute cafe.

Bocas Water Sports   DIVING
(☑757-9541; www.bocaswatersports.com; Calle 3) A longtime PADI dive center operating in Bocas.

Dutch Pirate   DIVING, SNORKELING
(☑6567-1812; www.thedutchpirate.com; Av H) Diving trips in many languages are offered by the Dutch Pirate. There is a booking office in Old Bank, though it's best to phone ahead to reserve.

Sailing

Catamaran Sailing Adventures   SAILING
(☑757-7048; www.bocassailing.com; Av Sur; snorkel tour US$45; ☺8:30am-11am & 4-8pm) With affordable overnight adventures and options for snorkeling, fishing and dolphin watching, Catamaran Sailing Adventures has popular tours on a 42ft catamaran that are kid-friendly too.

Yoga

Bocas Yoga   YOGA
(www.bocasyoga.com; Calle 4; US$5) Geared at both locals and travelers, this Hatha yoga studio run by the effervescent Laura makes a good break from the party scene. Offers daily classes in English.

🐟 Courses

Spanish by the Sea   LANGUAGE COURSE
(☑757-9518; www.spanishbythesea.com; Calle 4) A language school in a relaxed setting. Group lessons are US$185 per week for 20 hours. The school also offers a popular survival Spanish course to jump-start your travels.

Homestays can be arranged (US$18 per night), or you can bunk down in clean and comfy dorms (US$10) or private rooms (US$25). Spanish by the Sea also organizes parties, dance classes and open lectures. English, Spanish, French, German and Dutch are spoken.

Habla Ya   LANGUAGE COURSE
(☑730-8344, 757-7352; www.hablayapanama.com; Av G & Calle 9 Sur; ☺8am-5:30pm) This Spanish school, also with an outlet in Boquete, has a great reputation. It offers a special 'Spanish for travelers' course. There are air-conditioned classrooms and special rates on lodging in the school's own dorms and private rooms, and tours.

✯ Festivals & Events

Bocas celebrates all of Panama's holidays and a few enjoyable local ones besides.

May Day   DANCE
While the rest of Panama is celebrating Labor Day, local girls perform the Palo de Mayo (Maypole dance). Celebrated May 1.

Día de la Virgen del Carmen   RELIGIOUS
Bocatoreños make a pilgrimage to La Gruta, the cave in the middle of the Isla Colón, for a mass in honor of the Virgen del Carmen on the third Sunday in July.

Feria del Mar   FESTIVAL
The 'Fair of the Sea' is held on Playa El Istmito, a few kilometers north of Bocas, from September 28 to October 2.

Fundación de la Provincia de Bocas del Toro   HISTORY
Celebrating the foundation of the province in 1904, this is a day of parades and other events; it's a big affair, attracting people from all over the province, including the Panamanian president. November 16.

🛏 Sleeping

The town of Bocas is a major tourist draw, though many don't realize there is no town beach. Water shortage can be a problem, so it's recommended that you take short showers. Reservations are a good idea between December and April and during national holidays and local festivals. Discounts may be considerable in low season.

Touts on the street who call themselves guides might try to get you to change your lodging plans if you're walking around with luggage. They likely are working on commission and their tales (that your hostel is out of business, dirty, etc) shouldn't be trusted.

★ Hostel Heike   HOSTEL $
(☎757-9708; www.hostelheike.com; Calle 3; dm with/without air-con US$12/10, r per person US$11; ❄@🛜) Awash with colorful murals and natural woods, Heike is the perfect spot for chilling Caribbean-style. Expertly managed by a friendly Panamanian, it gets rave reviews. Free basic Spanish classes are given daily at 2pm; there's also free water and hot drinks. A sprawling roof deck with hammocks is the perfect spot for a cold beer and a good book.

Private rooms have bunks, not double beds.

Hostal Hansi   GUESTHOUSE $
(☎757-9085; http://hostalhansi.bocas.com; cnr Av D & Calle 2; s without bathroom US$13, s/d/tr US$15/25/30; @🛜) The idea here is family friendly and the German-owned guesthouse prides itself on having a quiet interior and hot showers. Rooms have fans and are generally spotless and comfortable. Doubles sport their own balcony. Guests can cook in an ample kitchen, where guests get fridge space precisely organized by room number – surely a UN-worthy model of hosteling.

Casa Verde   HOSTEL $
(☎6633-8050; www.casaverdebocas.com; Av Sur; dm US$14, d US$33-44; ❄@🛜) A popular new crashpad with waterfront location, Casa Verde is all about chilling out (witness the sunbathers tubing off the dock). The vibe is friendly and attentive, rooms are OK for the price, and a deckside cafe serves well-priced soups, salads and smoothies. Bathrooms have hot water and there's free coffee. It's affiliated with the Palmar Tent Lodge (p198).

Hotel Las Olas   HOTEL $
(☎757-9930; www.hotelolas.com; Calle 6; s/d/tr/q incl breakfast US$42/48/68/88; ❄@🛜) Shining like a yellow beacon from the southern tip of Bocas town, this three-story hotel has clean polished-wood rooms with electric hot-water showers. Some readers have complained about discord among the staff, but in general it's a difficult value to beat. Also offers tours and bicycle rentals.

Mondo Taitú   HOSTEL $
(☎tel 757-9425; www.mondotaitu.com; Av G; dm/d without bathroom US$10/24, dm with air-con US$12; ❄@🛜) Though it looks as if a strong wind could collapse it, this is Bocas' backpacker hub. Built on good vibes, this hostel makes good with a chill social atmosphere, freebies and good nightlife right at home at the bar. It's probably not the choice for those who mind grunge. There's a communal kitchen, lounge area, laundry facilities, free bikes and surfboards.

Hotel Dos Palmas   HOTEL $
(☎757-9906; residencialdospalmas@yahoo.com; Av Sur; d/tr US$28/35; ❄) Proudly '100% Bocatoreño,' Dos Palmas offers basic wooden rooms with old-fashioned furnishings. Run by a friendly matriarch, it's no cookie-cutter lodging, though some might find it a little musty. It sits above the water and boasts exceptional views of the bay.

International Hostel   HOSTEL $
(☎757-7374; hostelinternational@gmail.com; Calle 3; dm US$10-12) With a loud paint job, this Israeli-run hostel has the standard offerings, including kitchen use. There are some fans in rooms, and rooms with open-lattice walls (good for a breeze but less so if you worry about skeeters). Coffee is complimentary.

Hotel Casa Max   HOTEL $
(☎757-9120; casa1max@hotmail.com; Av G; s/d US$30/35, s/d with air-con US$40/45) This sprawling turquoise Caribbean house has a handful of brightly painted wooden rooms, some with bathrooms that are dated and worn. The service isn't much to speak of. Dreamy balconies overlook the town and ocean, there's an onsite cafe with international cuisine (seperately run), and the location is good.

Hotel del Parque   HOTEL $
(☎757-9008; www.hdelparque.webs.com; Calle 2; s/d/tr US$37/45/50; ❄🛜) A classic Caribbean

Bocas del Toro Town

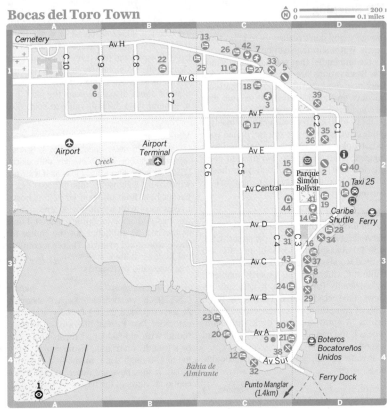

house fronting the plaza, this tranquil place has B&B style within budget reach. Ample rooms have big windows, cool cement floors, hot showers and firm beds in crisp linens. The terraces provide views of the plaza and hammocks for cat naps. The guest kitchen could use some scrubbing. The amiable owner also runs the Butterfly Farm.

Casa Amarilla   HOTEL **$**
(☏757-9938; www.casaamarilla.org; Calle 5; d/tr US$40/45; ❋@🔊) In a cute yellow house, these four motel-style rooms come decked out with amenities. Each has a laptop with internet connections, flat-screen TV, mini-fridge and hot water. If you need anything, the American owners are usually around.

Lula's   B&B **$$**
(☏757-9057; www.lulabb.com; Av Norte; d/tr/q incl breakfast US$55/77/88; ❋@🔊) A place of

rocking chairs and porches, this lovely B&B is a welcome addition to the Bocas scene. Rooms are immaculate, with hot-water showers and a snug design. The hosts, originally from Atlanta, give first-rate service, in addition to big southern breakfasts. There's also an onsite surf school (US$54 for a half-day).

Cocomo   B&B **$$**
(☏757-9259; www.cocomoonthesea.com; cnr Av Norte & Calle 6A; s/d/tr incl breakfast US$60/80/90; ❋🔊) A sweet clapboard house with a tropical garden and waterfront hammock deck, Cocomo wants for nothing. A local pioneer, this American-run B&B knows service. If the weather's bad, this is a snug spot to hole up in. Rooms have hot water. All-you-can-eat breakfast includes pastries, fruit, yogurt and omelets. There's kayak rentals (US$10) and you can swim right off the dock.

Bocas del Toro Town

◎ Sights
1 Bocas Butterfly Farm A4

✪ Activities, Courses & Tours
2 Bocas Water Sports D2
3 Bocas Yoga C1
4 Catamaran Sailing Adventures D3
5 Dutch Pirate C1
6 Habla Ya A1
7 Ixa's Bike World C1
8 La Buga.. D3
9 Spanish by the Sea............................... C4
  Starfleet Eco Adventures.............. (see 8)
  Transparente Tours .... (see 4)

🛏 Sleeping
10 Bocas Paradise D2
11 Casa Amarilla.. C1
12 Casa Verde.. C4
13 Cocomo.. C1
14 Hostal Hansi... D3
15 Hostel Heike... C2
16 Hotel Bocas del Toro............................ D3
17 Hotel Cala Luna C2
18 Hotel Casa Max...................................... C1
19 Hotel del Parque D2
20 Hotel Dos Palmas C4
21 Hotel Gran Bahía C4
22 Hotel La Veranda B1
23 Hotel Las Olas.. C4
24 International Hostel C3
25 Lula's... C1
26 Lula's Hostel C1
27 Mondo Taitú C1
28 Tropical Suites D3

✕ Eating
  Alberto's Pizzeria .... (see 17)
29 Buena Vista Bar & Grill D3
30 Carlos' Steak House.............................. C4
31 El Chitré C3
32 El Ultimo Refugio................................... C4
33 La Casbah C1
34 Lilli's Cafe.. D3
35 Om Café D2
36 Panadería & Dulceria Alemana D2
37 Raw D3
38 Super Gourmet....................................... C4
39 Tom's D1

🍷 Drinking & Nightlife
40 Barco Hundido D2
41 El Toro Loco.. D2
  Mondo Taitú Bar.......................... (see 27)
42 Riptide C1
43 Wine Bar.. C3

🛍 Shopping
44 Tropix Surfshop..................................... C2

Lula's Hostel HOSTEL **$$**
(☏757-9057; http://luabb.com/hostel-lulas; Av H; dm/d without bath US$20/60; ❋🛜) It's not every day that your hostel has its own swim-off dock. This super-cute mint-green cottage is a great addition to the local hostel scene, with big solid bunks and recent renovations. There's no onsite host; after leaving a deposit for keys, guests are on their own. Kayaks (US$10 per half-day) available for rent.

Hotel Cala Luna HOTEL **$$**
(☏757-9066; www.calalunabocas.com; Calle 5; s/d/tr US$55/65/80; ❋@) Atop the legendary Alberto's Pizzeria, the Italian-owned Cala Luna was built with fine attention to detail. The hotel features cathedral windows, tasteful wood details and crisp, functional rooms. As an added bonus, guests can watch planes coming in for a landing 30m above their heads from a pair of lookouts on the roof.

Hotel La Veranda INN **$$**
(☏757-9211; http://laverandapanama.tripod.com; Av H; d without bathroom US$29, d/tr US$56/66; ❋🛜) This residence-turned-inn was built in 1910 and has been maintained with pride, down to its gleaming hardwood floors and pretty antique windows and doors. None of the six guest rooms are alike, except that all contain early-20th-century antique furnishings. The veranda is perfect for a morning cup of coffee or an afternoon sundowner.

Bocas Paradise INN **$$**
(☏757-9546; www.bocasparadisehotel.com; Calle 1; d/ste from US$66/110; ❋🛜) On the waterfront, these upmarket rooms have brocade beds, carved hardwood furniture and little balconies with wooden loungers. Installations are shiny new and the bathrooms are quite spacious. Perks include kitchenettes and minibars. The onsite restaurant is a huge hit with expats – think comfort food and apps.

Hotel Gran Bahía HOTEL **$$**
(☏757-9626; www.ghbahia.com; Calle 3; s/d incl breakfast from US$73/80; ❋🛜) This historic Bocas landmark was built in 1905 by the United Fruit Company to serve as its local headquarters. Though it isn't a standout, some careful restorations have revived its original splendor. Second-floor rooms are considerably more attractive than the ground-floor counterparts, with wicker

furniture, safe boxes and original oak floors. Service is professional if a little aloof.

★ **Hotel Bocas del Toro**   INN $$$
(☏757-9018; www.hotelbocasdeltoro.com; Calle 2; d incl breakfast from US$129; ❈@🖤) A fine getaway, this three-story waterfront house is decked in comforts, with spacious hardwood rooms that feature firm beds with luxuriant linens, warm decor and seafront balconies. Perks include great service, travel-agency assistance and kayak rentals. There's also a deckside restaurant-bar and spa treatments are available. American-run, the hotel is a member of APTSO, Panama's sustainable tourism alliance.

Punta Caracol Aqua Lodge   CABIN $$$
(☏612-1088; www.puntacaracol.com; s/d incl 2 meals US$374/430) A poster child for Caribbean luxury, Punta Caracol has a handful of exquisite cabins perched on a boardwalk over warm waters. Two-story thatched cabins feature king-sized canopy beds, big skylight windows and soft lighting. There are solar panels and local renewable materials used in construction, but everything eco stops there, since the resort is built on a reef.

Accessed only by boat, it's the ultimate in tranquility. Nonguests can dine at the deckside restaurant (mains US$10 to US$25), with fresh seafood, tasty oversized cocktails and tropical style.

Tropical Suites   HOTEL $$$
(☏757-9880; www.bocastropical.com; Calle 1; ste incl breakfast from US$226; ❈@🖤) Boasting the island's only elevator, this hotel bleeds modern comforts such as Jacuzzi tubs, flatscreen TVs, hairdryers and a room safe. But if you're looking for personality you might want to go elsewhere. The ample rooms easily fit three and kitchens have range-tops and refrigerators. A nice perk is the Caribbean breakfast offered at Lilli's Cafe next door.

✖ Eating

Although Bocas town is a small place, there's no shortage of great restaurants serving up an impressive offering of international cuisine. A number of food carts ply their wares around town – local favorites include the 'Chicken Lady' and 'Batidos & Plantas Medicinales,' but ask for bottled water in your *batido* (fruit shake). Supermarkets are found on Calle 3.

DON'T MISS

OREBA CHOCOLATE TOUR

Lauded as a Bocas highlight, this guided tour takes you on an organic chocolate farm run by the indigenous Ngöbe community to wide acclaim. Swiss experts have classified it as some of the highest grade cacao in the world. Tour the farm, see tree sloths, sample chocolate and enjoy a traditional lunch. The trip (four-person minimum) is guided in Spanish and English.

Though it's on the mainland near Almirante, most visitors book the Oreba Chocolate Tour (☏6649-1457; quintero2380@gmail.com; per person US$25) ✐ through Lula's (p186) or through Super Gourmet. The cost does not include the boat trip from Bocas (US$7 round trip).

★ **Raw**   SUSHI $
(☏6938-8473; Calle 2; mains US$8-10) Just a little plank restaurant on the water, but the offerings are spot on. Carafes of sake accompany fresh tofu spring rolls and amazing tacos with tuna tartar and pickled onions. The salads are wonderful and service is attentive. At night candles are lit and the full bar specializing in original martinis starts humming.

Super Gourmet   SUPERMARKET $
(Calle 3; ⊙9am-7pm Mon-Sat) This boutique grocer stocks special treats including rotisserie chicken, Mexican food, wine and frozen bagels. It also has a section of sustainable local gifts, which include handmade soaps and outstanding local Bocas chocolate.

Panadería & Dulceria Alemana   BAKERY $
(Calle 2; snacks US$1-5; ⊙7am-8pm Mon-Sat, 8am-4pm Sun) Frothy cappuccinos and moist slabs of carrot cake are the order of the day at this German bakery, where you can also find fresh wholegrain bread and great sandwiches.

Lilli's Cafe   CAFE $
(Calle 1; plates US$5-8) Whether you feast on eggs Benedict with crab or an oversized burger, be sure to try the homemade 'Killin' Me Man' pepper sauce. After all, nothing says the Caribbean like an ocean view and fire on the palate.

Tom's
PANAMANIAN **$**

(☑6776-9280; Av H; mains US$6-10; ⊘10am-5pm Mon-Sat) Locals of every stripe agree that Tom's is the spot for a tasty lunch (fixed menu US$6) that doesn't break the bank. Head upstairs in a concrete market building and you'll find it on a shaded 2nd-floor terrace overlooking the water. Seafood or chicken is usually paired with rice or fries. They also deliver.

El Chitré
PANAMANIAN **$**

(Calle 3; plates US$2-4) Patronized by locals and travelers alike, this no-frills cafeteria is the best spot in town for cheap but tasty grub.

Alberto's Pizzeria
PIZZERIA **$**

(Calle 5; pizzas US$10; ⊘noon-10pm Mon-Sat) These fresh pizzas with toppings such as artichokes, kalamata olives and gorgonzola satisfy big appetites. Sardinian-run, Alberto's is a favorite local haunt where you can even play ping-pong while anticipating your dinner.

Om Café
INDIAN **$$**

(cnr Av E & Calle 2; mains US$6.50-15; ⊘8am-noon & 6-10pm Fri-Tue) Guaranteed to make your brow sweat, this welcoming Indian cafe cooks up classic curries and vindaloo with crisp hot naan. Service may be slow, so order up one of the original cocktails to keep you company (we like the Tipsy Turban – a dizzy mix of passion fruit, rum and sugar).

Look for a new Thai restaurant from the same owner on Calle 3.

La Casbah
MEDITERRANEAN **$$**

(☑6477-4227; Av H; mains US$8-15; ⊘6-10pm Tue-Sat) Popular with locals and travelers alike, this Mediterranean restaurant serves up gazpacho, goat-cheese salad and well-prepared meats and seafood. The fish of the day comes in cucumber and coconut sauce, and there's a nice baked veggie plate for non-meat-eaters. Reserve ahead.

Buena Vista Bar & Grill
AMERICAN **$$**

(Calle 1; mains US$7-13) The best burgers on the island, nachos and brownie sundaes with local chocolate... you can see why this seaside cafe hauls in hungry expats. Run by a welcoming Panamanian-American couple, it is a good bet for a decent bite and may be the only spot around where service can be swift. Dinner ups the ante with a surf-and-turf menu.

El Ultimo Refugio
SEAFOOD **$$**

(☑640-1878; Av Sur; mains US$8-13; ⊘11:30am-10pm) This rustic, mellow American-run place on the edge of the sea specializes in seafood dishes. Service is friendly and the tranquil location makes it a great spot for a quiet, romantic dinner out.

Guari Guari
MEDITERRANEAN **$$$**

(☑6627-1825; 6-course meal US$23; ⊘6-10pm Thu-Sun) When dinner should be an event (ie without a blaring TV), this plain restaurant doesn't disappoint. Run by a Spanish cook and her German partner, it's highly personal. Reservations are a must. Service is unhurried as diners sample four appetizers, a main course and dessert. The fixed menu changes but highlights include skewered shrimp, pork tenderloin and greens.

It's 2km from the center of town, near the gas station.

Carlos' Steak House
GRILL **$$$**

(☑6518 9627; Calle 3; mains US$17-30) At these prices, you would expect more than a hand-stenciled cardboard sign out front. Still, the locally adored Carlos is the man to seek if you've finally tired of fresh fish. It's pretty casual, with both the grill and a handful of tables alfresco watching the world pass by on Calle 3. Steaks cooked to perfection with Argentine chimichurri sauce.

🍸 Drinking & Nightlife

Wine Bar
WINE BAR

(Calle 3; ⊘5-11pm Mon-Sat) Upstairs in a worn wooden building, this ambient lounge has crushed velvet sofas, low lit chandeliers and friendly wait service. It's probably the best watering hole in town for intimate conversations, with tasty bites to curb your hunger.

Mondo Taitú Bar
BAR

(Av G) You're guaranteed a good time at the Mondo Taitú Bar. On Tuesday and Friday the party-loving owners entertain their guests with a variety of themed events, though the creative cocktail list and hookahs make Mondo a good choice any night. If you're feeling brave, order a tequila suicide – a snort of salt, a squeeze of lime in the eye and a shot of bad tequila (at least it's free!).

El Toro Loco
SPORTS BAR

(Av Central; ⊘noon-midnight) Expat-owned, El Toro Loco is the closest thing you'll find to Hooters. With a two-drink minimum, you can hear live rock and eat hot dogs and cheese fries with a draft pint.

Barco Hundido
BAR

(Calle 1) Most nights in Bocas end at the Barco Hundido, an open-air bar that's affectionately known as the 'Wreck Deck' – the name comes from the sunken banana boat that rests in the clear Caribbean waters in the front. A short boardwalk extends from the bar to an island seating area perfect for stargazing.

Riptide
BAR

(Av H; ⊙9am-midnight) If you haven't the budget to booze it up with your buddies on a private yacht, this weathered boat-bar may be the next best thing. A gringo magnet, it's a good spot to gather around a horseshoe-shaped bar and shoot the breeze. There are daily food specials – some swear by the fried chicken, but general reviews are very mixed.

🛍 Shopping

You'll find a large selection of *molas* (colorful hand-stitched appliqué textiles made by Kuna indigenous people) and a range of other handicrafts for sale by Kunas at stands near the park.

Tropix Surfshop
OUTDOOR EQUIPMENT

(☑757-9727; Calle 3; ⊙9am-7pm) Sells custom-made surfboards and a few used boards, as well as a large selection of bikinis and other island apparel.

ℹ Information

EMERGENCY

Police (☑104)

DANGERS & ANNOYANCES

The surf can be dangerous and there are frequently strong riptides – use caution when going out into the waves.

Unlike in most other places in Panama, tap water is not safe to drink in Bocas del Toro archipelago. Bocas town has a water-treatment plant, but locals say the tap water isn't to be trusted. The water is certainly fine for brushing your teeth, but you're probably best off siding with caution and purchasing bottled water for drinking or, preferably, purifying yours.

The archipelago of Bocas del Toro is a conservative place and local law prevents men (and obviously women) from walking down the streets shirtless. Even if you are on your way to the beach, wear a shirt or you will be sent back to your hotel if spotted by police.

INTERNET RESOURCES

Bocas Breeze (www.thebocasbreeze.com) The island's monthly bilingual publication lists events and covers some current issues.

Bocas.com (www.bocas.com) The official tourism website.

National Geographic (www.gobluecentralamerica.org) A National Geographic–produced geotourism map guide to Bocas del Toro.

MEDICAL SERVICES

Hospital (☑757-9201; Av G; ⊙24hr) The island's only hospital has a 24-hour emergency room.

MONEY

Banco Nacional de Panamá (cnr Calle 4 & Av E; ⊙8am-2pm Mon-Fri, to noon Sat) Exchanges traveler's checks and has a 24-hour ATM.

POST

Post office (Calle 3, Governmental Bldg) For all your letter-writing, postcard and general posting needs, the post office is in the large government building overlooking Parque Simón Bolívar.

TELEPHONE

Cable & Wireless (Calle 1) Phone cabins.

TOURIST INFORMATION

ANAM (Autoridad Nacional de Ambiente; ☑757-9442; Calle 1) Not really set up as a tourist information office, but staff can answer questions about the national park or other protected areas. If you want to camp out in any of the protected areas, you must first get a permit from this or any other ANAM office.

ATP Tourist Office (Autoridad de Turismo Panama; ☑757-9642; ⊙8:30am-3:30pm Mon-Fri) In Centro de Facilidades Turísticas e Interpretación (Cefati) on the eastern waterfront. A color map in English and Spanish is available.

Bocas Sustainable Tourism Alliance (☑6956-9520; www.discoverbocasdeltoro.com) This English-speaking website offers good

---

SUSTAINABLE BOCAS

Bocas is not ready for massive tourism, though it presents itself otherwise. What can you do to make your visit sustainable? Stop using small plastic water bottles; support sustainable tourism with a visit to the Ngöbe-run restaurant in Bahía Honda; make sure your boat in Dolphin Bay keeps a respectable distance from the dolphins; and use the co-op of local boaters (Boteros Unidos), who show more consciousness in their boating practices.

Daniel Suman, coastal planner

reference information for travelers. Arranges tours and visits to a Ngöbe crafts workshop on Isla San Cristóbal. The organization does not have a walk-in office.

❶ Getting There & Away

AIR

Since Aeroperlas went out of business, the number of flights to Bocas have halved. Book ahead as early as possible.

Air Panama (📞 757-9841; www.flyairpanama. com) Flies to Panama City (US$116, one hour) once or twice daily. Office at the airport.

Nature Air (📞 in USA 800-235-9272; www. natureair.com) Flies from San José, Costa Rica (US$135, 1½ hours), in the early morning several times per week.

BOAT

If you don't fly into Bocas you'll have to take a water taxi (US$4) from Almirante on the mainland. On the waterfront, Taxi 25 makes the half-hour trip between 6am and 6:30pm, every 30 minutes.

Caribe Shuttle (📞 757-7048; www.caribeshut tle.com) To reach Puerto Viejo, Costa Rica, this combination boat-bus trip (US$32) runs twice daily. There's also an option to go on to Cahuita (US$38) or San Jose (US$70). They provide a hotel pickup but you must reserve one day in advance.

❶ Getting Around

BUS

A cross-island bus goes to Bocas del Drago from Bocas plaza (US$2.40, one hour), with six departures between 5:30am and 8:30pm. As it's used as a school bus, afternoon trips tend to experience delays. The latest schedule is in the *Bocas Breeze*.

WATER TAXIS

To reach nearby islands, you can hire boaters operating motorized boats and canoes along the waterfront. As a general rule, you should always sort out the rate beforehand, and clarify whether it is for one way or a round trip. Always pay on the return leg – this guarantees a pickup – though most boaters will want some money up front to buy petrol. Though rates vary, you will get a better deal if you speak Spanish, are with a group and arrange for a pickup.

Boteros Bocatoreños Unidos (📞 6022-9554; Calle 3; ⊙ 6:30am-6:30pm) Locals claim this service consistently offers fair prices; destinations include Isla Carnero and Bastimentos. Staff are trained in safe boating and sustainable tourism practices. Boats go to Almirante (US$4, 20 minutes) every half-hour.

Boca del Drago

Located on the western side of Isla Colón, this sleepy beach earned fame for its huge numbers of starfish, a 10-minute walk around the bend. The recent addition of commercial stands and increased boat-taxi traffic are taking their toll on the beach, which has seen a lot of erosion. Still, the calm and relaxed atmosphere at Boca del Drago will draw beach bums. The swimming and snorkeling here are good, especially when the sea is calm and the water is clear. Though it's not as stunning as the wilderness beaches on Isla Bastimentos, the lack of surge means that this is the safest spot for swimming in the archipelago.

The beach is also home to a branch of the Institute for Tropical Ecology & Conservation (ITEC; www.itec-edu.org), a nonprofit education, research and conservation organization. The field station here offers field ecology courses to undergraduate and graduate students, provides facilities for tropical researchers, operates marine conservation programs and engages in community development. For more information on research, employment and volunteer opportunities at the station, contact ITEC via the website.

Though it's a far cry from luxury, Cabañas Estefany (📞 6956-4525; gilbertosan chez-25@hotmail.com; dm US$12, d with kitchen US$35, 6-person cabin US$75; @) is one of the few beach lodgings on Isla Colón. Its wooden *cabañas* are bare-bones, some without fans and all with cold showers. Secure a room with a fan as it can get quite buggy. The cabins are often booked by researchers from the nearby ITEC, so it's recommended that you call ahead.

Overlooking the water, the open-air Yarisnori Restaurant (mains US$7-25; ⊙ 8am-6pm Mon-Sat) is a local favorite, due in large part to the warm hospitality of Señora Juani. Grab an outdoor table on the sand and feast on the catch of the day, served with beans and coconut rice. Breakfast is good too. Yarinori is adding lodging soon.

To get here from Bocas, take a local bus, water taxi (US$15 to US$20 round trip) or taxi (US$15 one way).

La Gruta

If sun, sand and surf aren't your persuasion, then consider a trip to La Gruta (The Cave; admission US$2; ⊙ dawn-dusk), where you can wade through waist-high water while trying not to disturb the thousands of sleeping bats overhead. Admission is paid to the Comunidad Bahía Honda. The entrance to the cave, which is marked by a statue of the Virgin Mary, is 8km from Bocas town along the road to Boca del Drago. A round-trip taxi should cost about US$20 (depending on fuel costs and length of stay), or you can take the bus.

Playa Bluff & Around

A string of beaches on the eastern side of Isla Colón can be reached by an unpaved road that skirts up the coast from Bocas town. With bad roads, this has traditionally been the terrain of surfers but, as more lodgings pop up, travelers are discovering this more secluded option. Playa Bluff stretches for 5km all the way to Punta Rocosa. October to March are sure months to enjoy the beach without worrying about hatching turtles.

Sights

Playa El Istmito BEACH
(Playa La Cabaña) Playa El Istmito, also called Playa La Cabaña, is the closest beach to Bocas town, though it's on Bahía Sand Fly and the *chitras* (sand flies) that live here have an itchy bite. This is not the most attractive beach; unless you're walking, it's worth heading further north.

Playa Punch BEACH
Further up the coast from Playa El Istmito is Playa Punch, which is dangerous for swimming but good for surfing.

Playa Bluff BEACH
This secluded wilderness beach is pounded by intense waves. Though you wouldn't want to get into the water here without a board, the soft yellow sand and palm-fringed shores are pristine. It serves as a nesting area for sea turtles from May to September.

It's 8km from Bocas town, next to the road after you round Punta Bluff.

Activities

★Anaboca TOUR
(La Asociación Natural Bocas Carey; ☑ 6529-7153, 6843-7244; www.anaboca.org; per person hiking/turtle tours US$10/15) ✐ This nonprofit run by the local community addresses marine turtle conservation. In season (May to September), certified guides offer nighttime tours to view turtle hatching on Playa Bluff. You can also arrange overnight community

stays (food and lodging US$45), a good idea if you are there to watch hatching in the wee hours.

Sleeping & Eating

Playa Bluff Lodge LODGE $$
(☑ 6798-8507; www.playablufflodge.com; d incl breakfast US$110; ⊛) This highly recommended lodge is run by a welcoming Dutch family. Rooms are modern and attractive, nestled into a rainforest location with lily ponds and huge trees with the occasional sloth. A boon for families, its casual onsite bar-restaurant (open to nonguests) features a billiard table and kids' area. There's also a pool, an exotic frog diorama and jungle treks (US$45).

The location is literally the end of the road, 8km from Bocas, across from the beach. Transfers are included with a three-night stay.

★Tesoro Escondido CABIN $$
(☑ 6782-0512; www.tesoroescondido.info; d/tr from US$35/50, 2-/3-/4-person cabins US$65/80/95) ✐ Exuding a very homespun charm, this seafront lodge with thatched cottages works its magic. But it's not for everyone – the overgrown rainforest means there might be unwelcome visitors. Mosaic tables and recycled-bottle construction lend a bohemian air, but its most remarkable feature is the Swiss cooking. Can you say best chocolate ever tasted? Guests dine on fixed menus (US$10 to US$14) with fab desserts.

Snorkel gear is free to borrow. It's located on the right just before Playa Bluff.

★Bluff Beach Retreat INN $$$
(☑ 6677-8867; www.bluffbeachretreat.com; Playa Bluff; 2-person cabins US$250/325; 9-person house US$795; ☎⊛) ✐ This lush property facing Playa Bluff makes the perfect honeymoon getaway. One large home with a lap pool and two smaller cabins feature open floor plans, lovely hardwood details and slatted windows that keep out the sun and prevent the need for air-conditioning. Guests get the use of bicycles; it's also the site of yoga retreats with the Canadian owner.

There's a three-night minimum stay here. Owners are professional and accommodating. There's also the option to ride horses on their nearby fruit farm. It's 5km from Bocas.

Villa Paraiso INN $$$
(☑ 6494-3042; www.villaparaiso.info; ste US$165-180; ⓟ❀☎⊛) With a waterfront location 2km from Bocas, this family-orientated

California-style home offers comfortable suites. The construction is contemporary classic, with rooms surrounding a saltwater pool. Lodgings feature kitchenettes and a BBQ grill as well as kayak and bicycle loans. It's 3km from Bocas.

Paki Point CAFE $$
(mains US$6-12; ⊙10am-6pm) This outdoor deck restaurant with graffiti art and water views serves jalapeño burgers and seafood with cold beers and margaritas. For cyclists making the arduous trip to Playa Bluff, it's a godsend. You can also rent surf boards (US$15 per day).

ℹ Getting There & Away

There's no public transportation to the beaches, but a 4WD taxi will take you to any of them and pick you up at an appointed time for a negotiable price – expect to pay taxis US$10 to US$12 one way for two to four people to Playa Bluff. Prices fluctuate since the road is sometimes in ruinous condition.

Many people cycle this route. With a steady effort, it's about an hour one way from Bocas town, but be warned that the sun is unrelenting and it isn't a flat route. Take plenty of water and sunscreen.

Isla Carenero

A few hundred meters from Isla Colón is the oft-forgotten Isla Carenero. The island takes its name from 'careening,' which in nautical talk means to lean a ship on one side for cleaning or repair. In October 1502 Columbus' ships were careened and cleaned on this cay while the admiral recovered from a bellyache.

In recent times many hotels have been added, and nature isn't as wild as on islands further out. Yet Carenero remains a nice alternative if you're seeking peace and quiet. It's also a good place to day trip for a leisurely lunch.

🏃 Activities

Escuela de Mar SURFING
(☑757-9137, 6785-7984; http://bocasbuccaneerresort.com/surfing-school; ⊙8am-6pm) For quality surf classes (US$45 for three hours) or kayaks rentals ($10 for three hours), stand-up paddles (US$30 per day) and boards (US$15 per day), check out this surf school at Bibi's run by Argentine Luis. Call ahead if you can.

EXPLORE MORE: BOCAS DEL TORO

Tired of crowds? Find adventure by hiring a boat to try out these excursions:

Cayo Crawl Get lost in these mangrove-dotted channels near Isla Bastimentos.

Cayos Zapatillas Set out for these pristine white-sand beaches and virgin forests.

Dolphin Bay Spot dolphins frolicking at this densely populated breeding ground.

Swan Cay Spot red-billed tropic birds and white-crowned pigeons in this cay near Isla de Los Pájaros.

🛏 Sleeping & Eating

⭐**Gran Kahuna Hostel** HOSTEL $
(☑757-9551; www.grankahunabocas.com; dm/d US$12/45; ❋@🛜) Wildly popular in its new waterfront location, this surfer inn is adorable, with yellow cement cabins, bright rooms and even a picket fence. It offers a huge flat-screen, house guitars, a kitchen and onsite bar. The cleanliness is impressive, not so the service – you might have to drag the desk person away from what they're doing to check in.

Aqua Lounge HOSTEL $
(☑757-9042; www.bocasaqualounge.info; dm/d/tr incl breakfast US$11/25/36; 🛜🏊) Rough and rustic, this backpacker palace is a matchstick construction on the dock facing Bocas. Guests love it or leave it, but it says Spring Break in so many ways. The onsite bar (open late) is hugely popular, then there's the aquatic trampoline...

Casa Acuario INN $$
(☑757-9565; www.casaacuario.com; d US$88-102; ❋🛜) Visually dreamy, this tropical inn sits above crystal-blue waters teeming with tropical fish. Rooms are impeccably outfitted with smart fixtures and rustic, crafty touches. The big draw is the private decks with open-air dining.

El Faro del Colibri CABIN $$
(☑6791-0840, 757-7315; www.farodelcolibri.com; d incl breakfast from US$98; ❋🛜) A new addition, these canary yellow cabins line a wooden dock. With individual swim-up decks and

wood floors, they are lovely and considerably private. The buffet breakfast includes eggs, bread, fruit, yogurt and coffee. The aimiable Italian owner, Adrian, mans the lighthouse office.

Buccaneer Resort
CABIN $$
(☑ 6847-9306, 757-9042; www.bocasbuccaneer resort.com; d/tr/ste cabin US$77/88/99; ✳ 🎨) Located on a lovely strip of sand, this low-key resort is more of a humble clutch of romantic cabins. Elevated units have polished hardwood floors and walls, a thatched roof, a screened porch and a modern tiled bathroom with some composting toilets. Wi-fi only works in the office. Guests get breakfast vouchers for Bibi's.

Tierra Verde
HOTEL $$
(☑ 757-9042; www.hoteltierraverde.com; s/d/tr incl breakfast US$65/75/85; ✳ @ 🎨) Run by brothers, this attractive three-story hotel sits back from the beach in shady palms. Designed in a contemporary island style, seven spacious rooms feature wood details and windows that allow in ample light. There's hot water and the option of airport pickups (US$10).

Pickled Parrot
INTERNATIONAL $
(☑ 757-9093; mains US$5.50-10; ⊙ 11am-9pm) Locals claim this seaside deck restaurant serves the best food on the island. Burgers with blue cheese, stuffed chilies, firecracker shrimp and *ceviche* (seafood marinated in lemon or lime juice, garlic and seasonings) are lovingly prepared by a cantankerous chef. And there are drinks.

Bibi's
SEAFOOD $$
(mains US$6-15; ⊙ 8am-10pm) In front of the Buccaneer, this thatched, over-the-water restaurant and outfitter makes fresh salads, tasty soups and lightly fried fish. The service couldn't be friendlier and the sea views will keep you lingering.

❶ Getting There & Away
Isla Carenero is a quick and easy US$1 boat ride from the waterfront in Bocas town. Water taxis dock at the small marina on the tip of the island. From here, there is a path that leads to Isla Carenero's fledgling town and continues across the island.

Isla Solarte & Around
Isla Solarte (Cayo Nancy) is distinguished by Hospital Point, named after the United Fruit Company hospital built here in 1900 to isolate victims of yellow fever and malaria. At the time, it was not yet known that these diseases were transmitted by mosquitoes. Although the hospital complex eventually included 16 buildings, it was abandoned after two decades of operation following the blight that killed all of United Fruit's banana trees.

Today, most visitors to Solarte are day-trippers on boat tours, who dock just off Hospital Point to snorkel the 20m underwater wall. Though much of the island is private, an attractive option for anyone looking for a little tropical seclusion is Solarte del Caribe Inn (☑ 6554-4428; www.solarteinn.com; d US$88; 🎨), with the air of a country inn, complete with a spacious open-sided dining room and cozy guest rooms with lovely hardwood floors and private bathrooms with flushing compost toilets. Unlike some remote lodgings, Solarte is close enough to Bocas to make impromptu trips without much production.

Fenced in by mangroves on an islet connected to Solarte, Garden of Eden (☑ 6967-0187; www.gardenofedenbocaspanama.com; d incl breakfast US$187; ✳) is a lovely, secluded resort that won't mind if you bare all. Three snug bungalows have sweet sea views and private balconies. There is no air-conditioning, but you can count on a decent breeze and fans, as well as hot-water showers. Guests (adults only) get free rein to paddle the kayaks, self-serve drinks or lounge at the pool or the tiny white-sand beach. Guests get one free water taxi to Bocas per day, otherwise the cost to get out here (US$25 round trip) is steep.

Isla Solarte is a quick and easy boat ride from the waterfront in Bocas town, but lodgings on the far end are considerably more expensive to reach. If you want to snorkel at Hospital Point, you can either organize a private tour or negotiate a price with a water taxi.

Isla San Cristóbal
Half an hour away from Bocas town is another world – the Ngöbe community on Isla San Cristóbal. These subsistence farmers and fishers have a strong sense of Ngöbe identity, though they live mostly in difficult circumstances.

On a day trip, you can see how the Ngöbe prepare and dye fibers to make *chacara* bags, tour medicinal gardens and enjoy a traditional meal cooked over the wood fire. For a visitor, it's an opportunity to see life as it's lived without much gloss. Visitor fees (day

SURVIVING A RIPTIDE

Rip currents are formed when excess water brought to shore by waves returns to the sea in a rapidly moving depression in the ocean floor. They are composed of three parts: the feeder current, the neck and the head.

The feeder current consists of rapidly moving water that parallels the shore but isn't always visible from the beach. When this water reaches a channel, it switches direction and flows out to sea, forming the neck of the rip. This is the fastest-moving part of the riptide, moving with a speed of up to 10km/h. Finally, the head of the riptide current occurs past the breakers where the current quickly dissipates.

If caught in a riptide, immediately call for help. Conserve your energy and do not fight the current – this is the principal cause of drownings as it's almost impossible to swim directly back to shore. Instead, try one of two methods. The first is to tread water and let yourself be swept out past the breakers; once you're in the head of the rip, you can swim out of the channel and ride the waves back to shore. Or you can swim parallel or diagonal to shore until you're out of the channel.

Rip currents usually occur on beaches with strong surf, but temporary rips can occur anywhere, especially when there is an offshore storm or during low tide. Indicators include a brownish color to the surface of the water caused by swept-up sand and debris. Also, look for surface flattening, which occurs when the water enters a depression in the ocean floor and rushes back out to sea. If you're ever in doubt, it's best to inquire locally about swimming conditions.

tours US$20 per person with lunch) benefit the local community. The Peace Corps has helped develop Isla San Cristóbal Hostel (☑6832-9118; www.keteka.com/destinations/latin-america/panama/isla-san-cristobal; tours, meals and 2-night lodging US$75), a community-run ecolodge with basic mosquito-net draped beds, rainwater catchment showers and composting toilets. Boat taxis (US$60 round trip) charge by boat, not per person. For arrangements, you can also contact Bocas Sustainable Tourism Alliance (p190).

Also on the island, Dolphin Bay is famous for sightings of dolphin pods. If you're a fan, consider staying at Dolphin Bay Hideaway (☑6772-9917, 6417-7351; www.dolphinbayhideaway.com; d incl 2 meals US$120-160; ☎) 🖉, a charming and highly recommended inn run by Transylvanian Erika and her husband, who is from the island. Located on the mangrove, it's a lovely two-story home with a big wooden deck, docks with hammocks and a lily pond. Rooms are romantic and well appointed, with canopy beds and pitchers of water, but you are also entitled to 'all the coconuts you can drink.' They also offer tours around the area.

Isla Bastimentos

POP 1500

Although it's a mere 10-minute boat ride from the town of Bocas del Toro, Isla Bastimentos is a different world. The northern coast of the island is home to palm-fringed wilderness beaches that serve as nesting grounds for sea turtles, while most of the southern coast consists of mangrove islands and coral reefs that fall within the boundaries of the Parque Nacional Marino Isla Bastimentos.

The main settlement on Bastimentos is the historic West Indian town of Old Bank, which has its origins in the banana industry. The island is also home to the Ngöbe-Buglé village of Quebrada Sal (Salt Creek).

Long the stronghold of Afro-Caribbean culture in Bocas, Bastimentos is changing in nature, in not small part due to Red Frog Beach Rainforest Resort & Marina, a luxury development project that went bust, but not before generating real-estate buzz around the previously pristine Red Frog Beach.

Día de Bastimentos (Bastimentos Day; November 23) is celebrated with a huge parade and drumming demonstrations on the island.

⊙ Sights

◉ Old Bank

Located on the western tip of the island, Old Bank (Bastimentos Town) is a small enclave of 1500 residents of West Indian descent. Until the 1990s most of the adults in Old Bank traveled daily to Changuinola to work in banana fields, though today residents have taken to fishing, farming small plots or just hanging out.

Although Old Bank is very poor and devoid of any real sights, it has a much more pronounced Caribbean vibe than Bocas town and it's a relaxing place to stroll around and soak up the atmosphere. It's also the best place in Bocas del Toro to hear Gali-Gali, a fascinating Spanish-English Creole that's native to the island.

There are no roads, just a wide concrete footpath lined on both sides with colorfully painted wooden houses.

⊙ Around the Island

Bastimentos has some amazing beaches, though be careful swimming as the surf can really pick up on the north coast of the island.

Wizard Beach BEACH
(Playa Primera) The most beautiful beach on Bastimentos Island is awash in powdery yellow sand and backed by thick vine-strewn jungle. Although Wizard Beach is connected to Old Bank via a wilderness path, the mere 30-minute walk can turn into an all-day trek through the muck if it's been raining heavily.

In good weather, you can continue walking along the coast to Playa Segunda (Second Beach) and Red Frog Beach.

Red Frog Beach BEACH
(admission US$3) A stunner, Red Frog Beach is home to the *rana rojo* (strawberry poison-dart frog). The recent wave of development here is likely to affect this sensitive species – up to 300 visitors arrive daily in the high season. From Bocas, water taxis go to a small marina on the south side of the island, from where it's an easy, signposted 20-minute walk.

Playa Larga BEACH
(Long Beach) Playa Larga and much of the eastern side of the island fall under the protection of Parque Nacional Marino Isla Bastimentos. Sea turtles nest here from April to August. To get here, follow the path past Red Frog Beach.

⊙ Salt Creek

This remote Ngöbe-Buglé village, also known as Quebrada Sal, is on the southeastern side of the island. Reached via a long canal cut through the mangrove forest, this Ngöbe-Buglé village has 60-odd houses, an elementary school, a handicrafts store, a general store and a soccer field. The community largely depends on fishing and subsistence farming, travels mostly by canoe, and resides in wooden, thatched-roof huts without electricity or running water.

The Quebrada Sal is slowly modernizing and villagers are friendly and open to visitors, especially if you can speak Spanish. If you have the time, it's worth hiring a local guide to walk with you along the roughly one-hour cross-island trail to Playa Larga (US$12 per person). A recommended guide is Señora Kony Gonzales. Water taxis can also drop you off at the entrance. You will need to pay the US$2 entry fee and sign the visitors logbook.

⊙ Parque Nacional Marino Isla Bastimentos

Established in 1988, Panama's first marine park (admission US$10) protects various areas of the Bocas del Toro archipelago, including parts of Isla Bastimentos and the Cayos Zapatillas. The marine park is an important reserve for countless species of Caribbean wildlife.

You can get current park information from the ATP or ANAM offices in Bocas del Toro. The dive operators and boaters in Bocas are also good sources of information about the park and its attractions. To camp in the park, first obtain a permit from ANAM.

★**Nivida Bat Cave** CAVE
(Bahía Honda) One of Bastimentos' most fascinating natural wonders, Nivida is a massive cavern complete with swarms of nectar bats and a subterranean lake suitable for swimming. Half the fun of the place is getting there via motorboat through a channel of lush vegetation. To reach Nivida, go only with a reliable guide (around US$25 per person) such as Oscar from Roots (p199).

Laguna de Bastimentos LAKE
Getting to this jungle lake surrounded by dense vegetation is a challenging hike. This swath of rainforest is the terra firma section of the Parque Nacional Marino Isla Bastimentos. Go only with a reliable guide.

🏃 Activities

Bastimentos Sky ZIP LINE
(☑ 6507-4646, 757-8001; www.redfrogbeach.com/bocas-del-toro-zipline.html; per person US$55)

Seven zip lines, a swinging bridge and vertical rappel are a few of the highlights of this new attraction, brought to you by the Red Frog Beach development and a well-known Costa Rican zip-line designer. The tour lasts two hours and reaches heights of 45m.

Uwe   SNORKELING
(2 6741-1535; 3hr tour US$15) A standout guide for snorkel tours (there must be a reason he's called the 'fish whisperer'). Uwe speaks several languages and takes groups to lesser-known destinations including wonderful mangrove areas covered in sponges. Group minimum is four guests.

Oscar   ADVENTURE TOUR
(2 6515-9276) Oscar is a reliable local guide who can take visitors to the bat caves, hiking to Laguna Bastimentos and to other island attractions.

Señora Kony Gonzales   TOUR
(2 6092-7259; Salt Creek) English-speaking guide to Salt Creek. Leads community tours (US$2), visits to a bat cave (US$12) and Playa Larga (US$12). Monkeys and sloths might be viewed as well.

🛌 Sleeping

Though the majority of the action is on Isla Colón, the mostly rustic digs in Old Bank offer an alternatively laid-back, Caribbean atmosphere. Those not in Old Bank are mostly resorts, some quite high-end, that most often include transfers from Bocas in their rates. Some do not allow children, so check first if with the family.

SURFING IN BOCAS

With beginner beach swells, ripping reef breaks and some seriously suicidal barrels, Bocas del Toro is emerging as an international surf destination. The following is a rundown of the major surfing spots in the archipelago.

If you don't have your own board, you can rent from Tropix Surfshop (p190) or Mondo Taitú (p185) in Bocas town. If you're heading out to Isla Bastimentos, arrange your board in advance as there are no surf shops there.

Isla Colón

Beginner surfers looking for a bit of reef experience should check out **Playa Punch**, which offers a good mix of lefts and rights. Although it can get heavy when big, Punch generally offers some of the kindest waves around.

Just past Punch en route to Playa Bluff is a popular reef break known as **Dumpers**. This left break can get up to 3m and should only by ridden by experienced surfers as wiping out on the reef here is a dangerous affair. There is also an inner break known as **Inner Dumps**, which also breaks left but is more forgiving than its outer brother.

Be careful walking out on the reefs as they are sharp and full of urchins – don't go barefoot. If you wipe out and get cut up, be sure to properly disinfect your wounds. Although saltwater heals, seawater doesn't, especially in the Caribbean where the warm water temperature means the ocean is full of live bacteria.

The island's most notorious surf spot is **Playa Bluff**, which throws out powerful barreling waves that break in shallow water along the beach, and have a reputation for snapping boards (and occasionally bones). The waves close quickly, but the tubes here are truly awesome, especially when the swells are strong.

Isla Bastimentos

If you're looking for a solid beach break, both **Wizard Beach** and **Red Frog Beach** offer fairly constant sets of lefts and rights perfect for beginners and intermediates. When the swells are in, however, Wizard occasionally throws out some huge barrels, though they tend to close up pretty quickly.

Isla Carenero

The truly experienced may want to tackle **Silverbacks**, an enormous barreling right that breaks over a reef and can reach heights of over 5m. On a good day, Silverbacks is a world-class break that wouldn't look out of place on Hawaii's North Shore. Silverbacks breaks off the coast, so you're going to need to hire a water taxi (around US$5) to get out there.

🛏 Old Bank

Hostel Bastimentos · HOSTEL $

(🖉757-9053; Old Bank; dm US$6, d US$12-18, d with air-con US$30; @🛜) On a hill off the main path, this sprawling yellow clapboard has a bright selection of 28 rooms and hammock decks. Spaces are creaky but serviceable and the host, Dixon, couldn't be nicer. Backpacker-ready, it includes two kitchens and a common room with a bar, TV and dartboard.

Pension Tío Tom · GUESTHOUSE $

(🖉tel/fax 757-9831; tiotomscabin@gmail.com; Old Bank; d US$22-27, 2-person bungalow US$34; 🛜) This plank-and-thatch building has been offering cheap, clean and unfussy rooms for years. A highlight is the waterfront deck strewn with hammocks. There are family-style rooms and all come with private bathrooms. The German owners also offer hearty meals (dinner US$7), organize tours and rent kayaks.

Beverly's Hill · CABIN $$

(🖉757-9923; www.beverlyshill.blogspot.com; Old Bank; s/d without bathroom US$14/20, d US$40-50; 🛜) 📎 These jungle cabins occupy a lush green garden replete with red frogs. Immaculate thatched rooms feature fans and firm mattresses. Hammocks abound and some rooms offer hot-water showers. The onsite composting and water filtration system makes this one of the most environmentally friendly hotels on the island.

🛏 Around the Island

Bocas Bound Hostel · HOSTEL $

(🖉757-8012; www.bocasbound.com; dm US$13, d with/without bathroom US$50/30; ❄🛜) From the public dock it's a five-minute walk to this popular new cement hostel, part of the original plans for a high-end resort. Large concrete structures have long dorms in narrow rooms and an open-air kitchen, all tidy and clean. There's a separate restaurant (mains US$6 to US$17) and general store. While short on charm, it's functional.

It's 15 minutes further on foot to Red Frog Beach.

Point · HOTEL $

(🖉6561-9462, 757-9704; sloopj4@yahoo.com; Old Bank; d US$30; @) At the northern tip of Bastimentos, these standard rooms boast excellent views of the point break (bring your own board). Service may be indifferent, but there are creature comforts including hot-water showers, a fridge and a coffee maker.

Palmar Tent Lodge · LUXURY CAMPGROUND $$

(🖉6880-8640; www.palmartentlodge.com; dm tent US$15, d/tr tent from US$50/60) On the edge of the jungle and famous Red Frog Beach, Palmar introduces glamping to Bocas, with accomodations in solar-powered circular tents, some with private outdoor showers. The thatched lounge offers open-air meals and socializing. A laid-back attitude is required as there's no locked area for your stuff and scorpions do live here. Most guests love it anyway.

Transfers from Isla Colon are US$10 round trip, plus the $3 beach entry fee.

Los Secretos · HOTEL $$

(🖉6631-2337; http://lossecretosbocas.com; d incl breakfast US$75; ❄🛜🏊) A newer option, this pink Caribbean-style home sits high on a forested hill. It's a hike up many stairs from the dock, but you'll find five rooms with balconies and modern hotel comforts (though air-con is extra), including a swimming pool. Popular with passersby, a pizzeria (closed Monday) sits down in the shade by the mangroves. The owners hail from Florida.

Water taxis cost US$15 one way.

★ Casa Cayuko · RESORT $$$

(www.casacayuko.com; s/d incl 3 meals from US$235/295; ☺closed Nov) 📎 Owned by a teacher and a former Outward Bound instructor, this hushed retreat is a launch pad for tropical adventure. Kayak and snorkel gear are included to explore the nearby reefs, mangroves and rivers. Guided excursions run extra but include choice, unique offerings. Guests choose from rooms with fans and hardwood details in a post-and-beam lodge or private jungle cabins.

The resort runs on solar power and cached rainwater. Located on the white-sand beach of Punta Vieja, it's 45 minutes by boat to Bocas. There's no phone. It's closed through November.

★ La Loma Jungle Lodge · ECOLODGE $$$

(🖉592-5162; www.thejunglelodge.com; r per person all inclusive US$133) 📎 Integrated into the forest and the community, this chocolate farm offers tasteful, sustainable lodging to rave reviews. The location is hidden in mangroves, accessed by boat. A steep hill leads past a rushing creek to sedate, ultra-private bungalows with hand-carved beds. Each has a propane-fuelled, rainwater-fed bathroom, a mosquito net and solar-powered energy system.

Meals include fresh-baked bread and organic vegetables grown on the premises – you can even pick your own. La Loma donates a percentage of profits to the Bahía Honda Ngöbe community.

Tranquilo Bay RESORT $$$
(☑ 380-0721; www.tranquilobay.com; 3 nights all-inclusive per person US$1115; ❄ @ �) ✔ Notably family-friendly, this American-run lodge creates a fantastic environment for play and relaxation. The grounds feature six comfortable cabins with orthopedic beds, fine linens and locally crafted hardwood furnishings and art. Guests dine at the main lodge with a wrap-around porch and ocean views. Tailored excursions run by biologist guides include wildlife-watching, or you could just beach it.

The lodge composts, captures rainwater, uses a minimum of plastics and educates staff on water usage. Created around 52 hectares of conservation land, Tranquilo Bay also works with local scientists and conservation agencies and does not print marketing material. Transportation is US$155 per person, round trip. It's near the island's remote southeast tip.

★ **Al Natural Resort** RESORT $$$
(☑ 757-9004; www.alnaturalresort.com; d incl 3 meals from US$260) This desert-island hideaway lends a bohemian twist to all-inclusive. Based on traditional Ngöbe-Buglé architecture, the round wood-and-palm bungalows have an open design that delivers sea views. Being exposed to the elements is not everyone's cup of organic, young-leaf tea, especially if the rain and wind pick up. Still, the hosts are uncommonly gracious and the meals (wine included) are well prepared.

It's ideal for surfers and divers. The resort also loans kayaks to paddle out to snorkel spots. Rates dip US$80 after the first night. It's closed mid-May through mid-July.

✖ Eating

★ **Up In the Hill** CAFE $
(www.upinthehill.com; chocolate from US$2) Organic chocolate and gourmet coffee are reason enough to hike to this charming outpost on Bastimentos. To get there, head right from the Old Banks docks onto the main road and follow the signs. It's a 15-minute walk.

Roots CARIBBEAN $
(Old Bank; mains US$4-15; ⊙ 11:30am-9pm Wed-Mon) A deck bar with boat docking, this Bocas institution is famous for local meats and seafood, perfectly accented with fresh coconut milk. Co-owner Oscar Powell has also done much for the community of Isla Bastimentos and he's a personable fellow with a sharp sense of humor.

❶ Information

DANGERS & ANNOYANCES
Readers have reported a number of muggings on the trail between Old Town and Red Frog Beach (an alternate trail). Never go on any trail after dark and always travel with a friend. Never bring valuables, just a towel and water.

GETTING THERE & AWAY
To get to Isla Bastimentos from Bocas del Toro, just walk down to the waterfront and ask a boater to take you over. The ride will cost about US$4 to get to Old Bank or the public dock for Red Frog Beach (the beach lies 20 minutes further on by footpath).

MAINLAND

The mainland jungles of Bocas del Toro Province teem with wildlife and are pocketed with remote indigenous villages – the contrast with the archipelago couldn't be greater.

Almirante

A clutch of stilted homes on the water, this unkempt village has seen better days. Water taxis to Bocas del Toro depart here. Seeing disoriented travelers arrive, local taxis will try to charge US$5 for the trip between the bus terminal and the dock, but in reality the walk only takes five minutes, and should cost US$1 per person. Taxi 25 has a water shuttle to Bocas del Toro (US$4, 30 minutes). An air-conditioned bus to Changuinola (US$1.50) leaves every 15 minutes between 6am and 8pm. Taxis to Changuinola (from US$20) can be bargained, particularly if you start your walk from the dock to the bus terminal.

South of Almirante, **La Escapada** (☑ 6618-6106; www.laescapada.net; coastal road Km 48.5; d US$70-85; Ⓟ ❄) is a quiet coastal lodge with comfortable rooms and decks over the water. The welcoming owners, retirees from Florida, can also offer fishing and boating.

Changuinola

POP 32,600

Headquarters of the Chiriquí Land Company, the very same people that bring you Chiquita bananas, Changuinola is a hot and rather dusty town surrounded by a sea of banana plantations. Although there is little reason to spend any more time in the town than you have to, overland travelers linking to Costa Rica will have to pass through here. Changuinola also serves as the access point for the Humedal de San-San Pond Sak, the Parque Internacional La Amistad and Las Delicias.

◎ Sights

Canal OUTDOORS

In 1903 a 15km canal connecting the Río Changuinola and Bahía de Almirante was dug parallel to the Caribbean shoreline to facilitate the barging of bananas from the fields to ships. The 30m-wide channel allowed transfer of the fruit without interference from the open sea. Abandoned years ago, it is now a decent spot to view wildlife.

🛏 Sleeping & Eating

Hotel Hawaii HOTEL $

(📋 758-6025; Av 17 de Abril; s/d/tr US$24/26/33; ❋◉🐨) Basic but good, Hawaii has ample plain rooms with clean bathrooms equipped with spigot showers. Beds are clad in white sheets.

Hotel Semiramis HOTEL $

(📋 758-6006; Av 17 de Abril; d/tr US$30/35; ❋🐨) With 24-hour service (presumably friendly to truckers or trysts), this shiny tiled hotel does the trick for a night. It has hot water, proper rooms and even a car-rental service.

Resto Cotty's PANAMANIAN $

(Av 17 de Abril; meals US$2.50; ⊘24hr) On the main road, this clean cafeteria-style restaurant prepares Panamanian fare. A plate of curried chicken and rice is gratifying and quick.

ℹ Information

Av 17 de Abril (also called Av Central) runs north to south and serves as the town's main artery. The same street also has a Banco Nacional de Panamá and an immigration office.

The **ANAM office** (Autoridad Nacional del Ambiente; 📋767-9485, 758-6603; ⊘8am-4pm Mon-Fri), near the center of town, should be able to provide information on national parks in the province, though service is lax.

The post office is located near the airport.

ℹ Getting There & Away

AIR

From Panama City, **Air Panama** (📋316-9000; www.flyairpanama.com) flies to Changuinola (US$116 one way) several times per week. If your destination is Bocas del Toro, it's best to fly direct to the island.

Travelers can take a taxi (US$3) to/from the airport in Changuinola from the center of town.

BUS

Buses depart near the city center, close to a number of restaurants, bars, markets and hotels. Buses for Costa Rica depart next to the Shell gas station. Other buses leave from **Terminal Urrica** (📋758-8115) with departures between 6am and 7pm.

TAXI

You can take a taxi from Changuinola to the Costa Rican border at Guabito (US$3 per person, 15 minutes).

BUSES FROM CHANGUINOLA

DESTINATION	COST (US$)	DURATION	FREQUENCY
Almirante (with boat connections to Isla Colón)	1.50	45min	every 30min
Altos del Valle (Bosque Protector de Palo Seco)	8	2hr	every 30min
David	10	4¾hr	every 45min
El Silencio (Parque Internacional La Amistad)	0.80	30min	every 20min
Guabito-Sixaola	1	30min	every 30min
Las Tablas (Las Delicias)	2	1¾hr	hourly
Panama City	29	12hr	daily 7am
San José (Costa Rica)	12	6hr	daily 10am

Humedal de San-San Pond Sak

These relatively undiscovered wetlands (admission US$5) are located a mere 5km north of central Changuinola, yet they harbor an incredible variety of tropical fauna. In addition to sloths, river otters, white-faced monkeys, caimans, iguanas, sea turtles and poison-dart frogs, the fresh waters of San-San are also one of the few known Central American habitats for the manatee. It is well worth a visit to check out the manatee viewing center, which has somehow gone under the radar of the general public.

This protected area is administered by Aamvecona (p203), a conservation organization consisting mainly of volunteers that works in close conjunction with ANAM. Onsite, a free visitors center at the beach at the mouth of the Río San-San has displays on wildlife. Prices for day tours vary. A manatee tour costs US$15 per person, but the boat costs an additional US$60 (for up to 10 passengers) for a day tour. If you can, form a group to keep costs down. There's basic lodging (US$20 per person) and lunch (US$5).

To arrange a trip, stop by the Changuinola ANAM office (Autoridad Nacional de Ambiente; ☑758-6603) or contact Aamvecona directly and speak with Kherson Ruiz.

Although it's possible to visit the wetlands in a day trip from Changuinola, the best way to appreciate the area is to stay overnight. Located inside the park on a stunning wilderness beach is a rustic house on stilts, which has three simple rooms, cold-water showers, a flush toilet (fed by rainwater) and a cooking area. However, the biggest perk about staying here is that guests are allowed to accompany the rangers at night to observe the turtle nesting sites.

Bring your own food and drink, as well as a sleeping bag or blanket – bedding is not provided. You will also want to bring a mosquito net and bug spray as the sand fleas and mosquitoes show no mercy.

Parque Internacional La Amistad (Wekso)

The 4070-sq-km Parque Internacional La Amistad was established jointly in 1988 by Panama and Costa Rica – hence its name, La Amistad (Friendship). In 1990 La Amistad was declared a Unesco World Heritage Site and later became part of the greater Mesoamerican Biological corridor. In Panama, the park covers portions of Chiriquí (p177) and Bocas del Toro Provinces, contains seven of the 12 classified life zones, and serves as a refuge for a great number of endangered flora and fauna.

La Amistad is also home to members of three indigenous groups: the Naso (Teribe), Bribrí and Ngöbe-Buglé. Although these groups are still clinging to their traditional ways of life, their numbers are dwindling fast, especially as outside influences continue to invade their culture. However, in an effort to preserve their identity while simultaneously providing a means of income, the Naso have created an ecological center at Wekso, the former site of the infamous US-run Pana-Jungla survival school. Today, this ecotourism project is thriving as more and more travelers discover the beauty of both the rugged wilderness of La Amistad and the ancestral culture of the Naso.

History

According to the colonial records of the Spanish empire, the Naso were present in mainland Bocas del Toro when the first explorers arrived in the region in the 16th century. The Spaniards referred to the Naso as the Teribe, or the Tjër Di (Grandmother Water) in Naso, which is the guiding spirit

> ### DON'T MISS
>
> ## ADVENTURE IN NASO COUNTRY
>
> On the border of Parque Internacional La Amistad and the proposed Naso reservation, a unique jungle lodging and sustainable tour operator is a recommended step off the gringo trail. At Soposo Rainforest Adventures (☑ 6631-2222; www.soposo.com; per person day tour US$90, 2-day all inclusive package per person US$140), guests stay in stilted thatched huts, eat traditional foods and immerse themselves in Naso culture.
>
> The project, spearheaded by an ex-Peace Corps volunteer and her Naso husband, has been lauded by travelers. It was created to offer the Naso people an alternative income, bolster cultural self-esteem and protect natural resources in the face of a massive hydroelectric project which is changing the nature of the area. A highlight is a three-day trip up the Teribe river to the village of the Naso monarch. There are also trips to San-San Pond Sak to see the manatees and search for hatching turtles.
>
> From Changuinola, it's a 30-minute taxi ride to the village of El Silencio, from where there's river access to the lodging.

that forms the backbone of their religious beliefs. The Spaniards gradually squeezed the Naso off their lands, and drove the population to exile in the highlands near the Costa Rican border.

Although the establishment of the modern Panamanian state has enabled the Naso to return to their ancestral home, their survival is threatened by the lack of their own *comarca* (autonomous region). This scenario contrasts greatly with other Panamanian indigenous population groups such as the Kuna, the Emberá, the Wounaan and the neighboring Ngöbe-Buglé. The plight of the Naso is further amplified by the fact that the tremendous ecotourism potential in Parque Internacional La Amistad is at odds with a massive hydroelectric project planned in the region. Although proposals for establishing a *comarca* are on the table, in true Panamanian form progress is being held up by bureaucracy.

It is estimated that there are only a few thousand Naso remaining in Panama, the majority of whom live in Bocas del Toro Province and survive as subsistence farmers. Although they remained virtually autonomous for generations, the Naso have recently started losing their cultural self-sufficiency due to missionary activity, Latino encroachment and youth migration. Today, most Naso are bilingual (Naso and Spanish), wear Western-style clothing and practice some form of Christianity. However, strong elements of ancestral Naso culture remain, especially considering that they are one of the few remaining indigenous groups in the Americas to retain their traditional monarchy.

⊙ Sights

Before the US invasion of Panama in 1989, Wekso was named Pana-Jungla, and served as a US-run survival school that trained Panamanian and international troops in jungle warfare. Although it was disbanded in 1990 following the ousting of General Noriega, the ruins of the old structures remain scattered around the Wekso grounds. Highlights include the barracks, mess hall, chapel, armory and the serpentarium.

🏃 Activities

Although most of Parque Internacional La Amistad is inaccessible, the park is home to a recorded 90 mammal species (including six cat species) and more than 400 bird species (including resplendent quetzals and harpy eagles).

Visitors can hire local guides for US$20 to US$30, depending on the length of the hike. A 3.5km loop trail at Wekso cuts through secondary and virgin rainforest, with good opportunities for wildlife-watching. You can also take a dip in the river (the current is too fast for crocodiles), though be careful of the current. A network of trails link various Naso communities together, though it's best to tackle these with a guide.

From Wekso, it's a five-hour hike into the Parque Internacional La Amistad. The Caribbean side of La Amistad is much less developed than the Pacific side. You will need to hire the services of local boaters and guides, and you must be completely self-sufficient. The terrain is extremely rugged, without hiking trails, and the river rages during the rainy season. If you're prepared for a serious trek, you're almost certain to have an adventure.

🛏 Sleeping & Eating

Permits to camp in the park are payable at the ranger station.

Guest Lodge   CABIN **$**
(☑ 6574-9874; http://odesen.bocas.com; lodging per person US$20, 3 meals US$14) The heart of Wekso is the Naso-run guest lodge which benefits the tribe. Rooms are basic and there is a secure water supply, flush toilets and an outdoor shower. It's staffed by community members who prepare meals, lead guided jungle tours and can explain about Naso culture and history.

Readers reported an armed robbery here in 2011. According to a local resident, the presence of many part-time workers and no real security measures leaves Wekso more open to security issues. On the other hand, in 15 years of operating, there has been only one reported incident.

❶ Information

Wekso is administered by **Odesen** (Organization for the Sustainable Development of Naso Ecotourism; ☑ 6569-3869; http://odesen.bocas. com), a community-based development organization that promotes ecotourism in the park as well as the cultural preservation of the Naso. Its direct contact is Raul Quintero.

Keep in mind that the guides at Wekso, all of whom are local residents, speak only Spanish and Naso. Although you don't have to be fluent in Spanish to arrive here, a basic understanding of the language is recommended.

Note that the Las Nubes entrance to the park is only accessible from Chiriquí Province. Admission to the park is paid at the Wekso entrance near Changuinola.

❶ Getting There & Away

To reach Wekso, you first have to catch a bus from Changuinola to the hamlet of El Silencio (US$0.80, 40 minutes, every 20 minutes), and then take a 45-minute boat ride up the Río Teribe. In El Silencio, you can hire a five-person boat for around US$60 to US$75. If you tell the ANAM office in Changuinola that you want to go to Wekso, they can radio ahead and make sure there is someone at the river's edge.

Once on the river you'll pass hills blanketed with rainforest and intermittent waterfalls. The backdrop is the glorious Talamanca range and the jungle comes all the way down to the river. After about 45 minutes on the river, a sign on the right bank announces your arrival at Wekso.

Las Delicias

Set in rainforest hills, the small indigenous community of Las Delicias lies along the Sixaola River, 20km from the Costa Rican border crossing at Guabito. The community has shifted its income source from harvesting and logging to preservation and ecotourism.

WORTH A TRIP

TURTLE PATROL IN SAN-SAN POND SAK

There are only eight sea-turtle species in the world and half of those can be found nesting in the Archipiélago de Bocas del Toro, primarily on the long beaches on the northern side of Isla Bastimentos. The loggerheads appear from April to September, the leatherbacks in May and June, the hawksbills in July and the greens in July and August.

Sea turtles leave the water only to lay their eggs. Two months after the eggs are laid, the hatchlings break loose from their shells, leave their sandy nests and enter the sea – if they are not stolen or first eaten by raccoons, birds or dogs. Many hatchlings, which are guided to the sea by moonlight, die because people using flashlights unintentionally steer the tiny turtles into the rainforest, where they may be preyed upon, get lost or die from starvation.

Human predators and the encroachment of development may be their greatest obstacle. Throughout Panama, many communities still eat turtles and their eggs, greatly contributing to turtles' dwindling populations.

The community-based organization **Aamvecona** (Association of Friends & Neighbors of the Coast & its Environment; ☑ 6494-5001; www.aamvecona.org), based in the Humedal de San-San Pond Sak, is working toward turtle preservation, with projects active between February and July. This location is known as the most important nesting ground for leatherback turtles in the entire southeastern Caribbean. Aamvecona accepts volunteers on turtle nesting and hatching projects. It also offers nature tours and has inaugurated a small cabin for visitors.

Visiting is one way you can make a positive contribution. Attractions include waterfalls, abundant wildlife and impressive viewpoints over the Sixaola River Valley and the Talamanca Mountains.

On a day trip, you can boat the Sixaola and Yorkin Rivers, hike through rainforest or go horseback riding. Lunch prepared by villagers is usually fresh fish. Prices are quite reasonable, at around US$20 to US$30 per person. There are also rustic cabins (per person US$20) available, though hardy travelers can string up a hammock or pitch a tent at one of the *ranchos*. Remember that it's relatively undeveloped (there's no electricity), so bring your own supplies, especially a water purifier, flashlight, mosquito net and bug repellent.

Make arrangements to visit Las Delicias through the Changuinola ANAM office or by phoning the community tourism management at Las Delicias (✆6600-4042) directly. To reach the community, take a bus from Changuinola to Las Tablas (US$2, 1½ hours, hourly), followed by a taxi to Las Delicias (US$10). You can also negotiate a price with one of the 4WD taxis in Changuinola.

Bosque Protector de Palo Seco

Set high in the Talamanca range, the 1600-sq-km Bosque Protector de Palo Seco (BPPS; admission US$5) is a lush cloud forest, home to monkeys, sloths, armadillos and butterflies. Bird-watching is superb – keep an eye out for rarities such as the bat falcon, the wedge-billed woodcreeper and the golden-winged warbler. Unique to this area are ashy-throated bush-tanagers. It's 29km south of Chiriquí Grande on the road to David (also called 'Fortuna Rd').

Pay the park admission fee and obtain information about current hiking conditions at the ANAM station at the entrance. ANAM maintains three trails in the park, each

SAVING THE PENÍNSULA VALIENTE

Located some 40km southwest of Bocas del Toro town, the hilly Península Valiente extends 30km into the Caribbean Sea. With dramatic cliffs and pristine beaches, this entire peninsula is part of the self-governing Ngöbe-Buglé Comarca. Until now, this roadless area has remained largely inaccessible.

In 2011, the mayor of one of the towns in the Comarca was implicated in the illegal sale of 189 hectares of Comarca land adjacent to Playa Chiriquí to Costa Rican investors developing a tourist venture known as Desarrollo Turístico Cañaveral.

At the center of the controversy is Playa Chiriquí, a stunning 25km beach. Between two Ngöbe communities, it was one of the most important hawksbill sea turtle nesting sites in the Caribbean until the 1950s. While local hunting almost wiped out these populations, hawksbills and leatherbacks are making a comeback thanks to the efforts of the Caribbean Conservation Corporation and Ngöbe community.

Playa Chiriquí and the adjacent wetland ecosystems have also been declared a Wetland of International Importance under the Ramsar Convention on Wetlands – Damani-Guariviara Wetland. This wetland is one of only two areas in Panama inhabited by the endangered West Indian manatee.

Over the years, outlandish proposals have ranged from the government creating an 80-hotel resort complex known as 'New Cancun' to earlier plans to put Damani beach in the hands of US developers. Opposition of most Ngöbe peoples to all these proposals from outsiders has been crucial in stopping the projects.

Large-scale tourist development would have irreversible effects on this fragile coastal ecosystem, home to critically endangered species. Ngöbe peoples' land tenure, access to resources, community cohesion and traditional culture would also certainly be endangered.

Environmental groups and Ngöbe communities are beginning to organize small-scale ecological tourism alternatives. But the hot debate about big development is unlikely to ebb in the coming years.

Daniel Suman is a professor of environmental and coastal law at the University of Miami.

INDIOS CONEJOS

According to the Naso, *indios conejos* (rabbit Indians) are fierce warriors living deep in the jungle. Completely nocturnal, they possess superhuman attributes and are deadly with a bow and arrow. By some accounts they are pale white with striped backs and dwarfish in size. If you meet an elder Naso, ask about them. Elders are fond of telling stories of battles with these mythical warriors that took place during their youth. According to them, these wily foes can easily be killed if ambushed while sleeping during the day. Historians suggest that the lore could stem from real battles that took place with the Miskito tribe.

about 45 minutes in duration, allowing visitors the chance to get a taste of the region's natural wonders.

ANAM has two-story sleeping facilities with a **dorm** (per person US$5); bring your own food and bedding. Guests have access to the kitchen as well as bathrooms. To ensure they have room for you, contact the Changuinola ANAM office.

A clutch of cabins in the forest, **Celestine** (☑6474-7827; hapenagosg@hotmail.com; adult/child US$30/15; ℗) is owned by a local doctor and his wife Elvia. With solar-powered electricity and hot water, lodging includes three meals as well as guided walks led by a Ngöbe-Buglé villager. Guests can hike one hour to a Ngöbe village. There is also an excellent river for bathing, as well as waterfalls and a variety of cool frogs and birds. Access is slightly more difficult after an area landslide.

These sights lie less than 17km from Lago Fortuna, a picturesque reservoir and power plant surrounded by some of the finest forest in Panama, which is strictly protected as the reservoir watershed.

To arrive from David, take any bus heading toward Changuinola. Ask to stop just before Altos del Valle and disembark at Km 68.5, which is right by the ANAM station. Don't go at night because these spots are set back from the road and easy to miss. From Bosque Protector de Palo Seco, buses pass every 30 minutes heading north to Changuinola (US$5, two hours) or south to David (US$5, 2½ hours).

Colón Province

POP 242,000 / ELEV SEA LEVEL TO 979M / AREA 4890 SQ KM

Best Surf Spots

➡ Isla Grande (p216)

➡ Isla Mamei (p216)

➡ Playa Grande (p216)

➡ Turtles Beach (p216)

➡ V-Land Beach (p216)

Best Places to Stay

➡ Casa de La Bruja (p217)

➡ Hostel Puerto Lindo (p219)

➡ Sister Moon Eco Lodge (p220)

➡ Casa Rayo Verde (p217)

➡ Sierra Llorona Panama Lodge (p210)

Why Go?

With an edgy reputation more true crime than travel, Colón rarely makes travel wish lists. But there is more to this Caribbean province than its downtrodden capital. Think pristine beaches and lowland rainforests, colonial splendors and modern engineering marvels. Portobelo, with its growing music and art scene, shows the best of vibrant Congo culture. The luxury train between Panama City and Colón remains one of the greatest rail journeys in the Americas.

The region's incredible history dates back to the earliest European explorers. Black roots also run deep; Colón is the birthplace of today's ultra-popular *punta* music (better known abroad as reggaetón).

During the colonial era these coastal cities ranked among the world's richest; their gold and silver stores enticed pirates from English privateer Sir Francis Drake to Admiral Edward Vernon. Today, the fallen fortresses and cannons embedded in the coral reefs recall the fallen Spanish empire.

When to Go

➡ **Dec–Apr** Dry season is a great time for snorkeling or diving for Caribbean treasure, as visibility is at its best. It's high season for lodging and beaches fill up.

➡ **Oct** Pilgrims set out walking from all over Panama weeks ahead to attend the Black Christ Festival, an enormous event with masses and street celebrations in Portobelo.

➡ **May–Jul** A relatively good time to visit, with some rain showers and off-season prices.

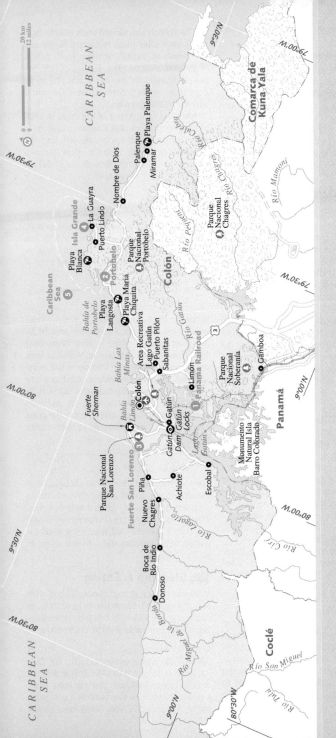

Colón Province Highlights

1 Ride through lush vistas in a 1st-class luxury car heading from Panama City to Colón along the historical **Panama Railroad** (p211)

2 Explore hallowed colonial ruins or find festival frenzy in **Portobelo** (p213), once the Caribbean's greatest port

3 Live out your *Pirates of the Caribbean* fantasy at **Fuerte San Lorenzo** (p212), a historic Spanish fort that once stood guard over the Caribbean

4 Soak up the natural beauty and laid-back vibe of **Isla Grande** (p219), a picture-perfect gem of a Caribbean island

5 Find sharks, cargo ships and military planes while scuba diving the **Caribbean sea** (p216) around Portobelo

Colón

POP 134,000

With its colonial grandeur crumbling and its neighborhoods marginalized, Colón is the city that Panama forgot, in spite of vigorous development meant to court Caribbean cruise ships. Prior to 1869 the railroad connecting Panama City and Colón was the only rapid transit across the continental Western Hemisphere. A last whiff of prosperity was seen during the construction of the Panama Canal.

On the city's edge, the Zona Libre (Free Zone) was created in 1948. Today, this sprawling 482-hectare complex is the largest free-trade zone in the Americas. With more than 1600 companies and dozens of banks, it links overseas producers with the Latin American market. From close up, it's an island of materialism floating in a sea of unemployment and poverty. Very little of the US$10 billion in annual commerce seems to benefit locals.

Recent improvements in city safety are attributed to tighter gang control and an arms-for-food program that got many guns off the streets. The improved Ruta 3 between Panama City and Colón is now a four-lane highway, resulting in much quicker travel times.

History

In 1850 the city of Colón (originally called Aspinwall for a Panama railroad founder) was established as the Caribbean terminus of the Panama Railroad. It became a boom town attracting east-coast Americans who favored this 'shortcut' to California at the height of gold-rush fever. Even with boating the Atlantic and Pacific oceans and crossing the isthmus, it was considered a faster and less dangerous journey than crossing the US heartland and facing hostile indigenous groups.

Following the completion of the US transcontinental railroad in 1869, Colón faded into obscurity less than 20 years after its founding.

At the peak of Colón's economic depression in 1881 the French arrived to build an inter-oceanic canal, but the city was burnt to the ground four years later by a Colombian hoping to spark a revolution. In the years to follow, the city blossomed, entirely rebuilt in French colonial architectural style. Rivaling Panama City in beauty and wealth, life in the Canal Zone was pleasurable and highly profitable.

The French abandoned their efforts eight years later after huge monetary losses and the death of 22,000 workers from yellow fever and malaria. The US seized the opportunity, reinventing the vibrant provincial capital as workers from around the world arrived by the shipload.

After the completion of the canal in 1914, unemployment caused Colón's economy to disintegrate and the city spiraled into the depths of depravity. Today, most of the colonial city is still intact, though the buildings are on the verge of collapse.

◎ Sights

The Zona Libre occupies the southeastern corner of the city while the cruise-ship port, Colón 2000, is located just north of it. If you turn left on Calle 13, you'll pass the passenger train terminal, 200m before the port of Cristóbal.

◎ Zona Libre

Second only to Hong Kong's, Colón's free-trade zone is a huge fortresslike area of giant international stores selling items duty free. However, most stores only deal in bulk merchandise; they aren't set up to sell to individual tourists. Individual purchases are sent to Tocumen International Airport in Panama City, where they may be retrieved upon a visitor's departure. To enter the Zona Libre, present your passport at the security office.

◎ Colón 2000

Only a decade old, this sterile shopping and entertainment sector geared toward cruise-ship travelers sits on the east side of Colón. Though lacking in any Panamanian flavor, it is safe to peruse and features a good selection of restaurants and souvenir shops as well as a casino.

🛏 Sleeping & Eating

Visitors to Colón should choose a hotel with security in mind. Many hotels have 24-hour security guards. Most hotels have dining options, which are also good at Colón 2000.

Meryland Hotel HOTEL $$
(☎441-7055; www.hotelmeryland.com; cnr Calle 7 & Av Santa Isabel; s/d US$44/55; P❄@🛜) A massive stone building, this business hotel fronts an attractive city park in a comparatively safe part of Colón. Small tiled rooms

with gold tones and wrought-iron furniture have air-con, cable TV and hot-water bathrooms, though you're paying for security not luxury. The restaurant saves you the trouble of having to leave the hotel at night.

Radisson HOTEL $$
(☑446-2000; www.radisson.com; Colón 2000; d/ste US$119/169; P ❄ @ 🛜 🏊) Really you could be anywhere, but this luxury chain hotel has the friendliest staff and the best digs in Colón. Rooms are comfortable and sufficiently stylish, with minibar and flat-screen TVs, and you can always let off steam with some laps in the pool. Big off-season discounts are available.

Arrecifes SEAFOOD $
(☑info 441 9308; Calle 3 at Paseo Gorgas; mains US$10-12; ☺noon-8pm Mon-Sat) Local business owners lunch at this nondescript port building cooking up great Caribbean seafood in the gated port area. Expect no frills and no water views, just generous portions of *criollo*-style seafood, stewed in onions, peppers and tomatoes, and whole fried snappers.

ⓘ Information

The safest place to withdraw money is the BNP ATM in the Colón 2000 cruise-ship port.

DANGERS & ANNOYANCES

Apart from the cruise port on the eastern side of the city and the bustling Zona Libre (free trade zone), Colón has a dangerous reputation. Violent crime rates have lowered, but visitors should exercise caution when walking around, even during the day. Paseo de Washington, the renovated waterfront area, and Av Bolívar are safe to peruse by day. Always travel by taxi at night.

ⓘ Getting There & Away

Plans are in the works to add an overnight ferry to Cartagena, Colombia, which would be Panama's only direct boat service to Colombia outside the Darién.

BUS

From Panama City, a regular bus service to Colón (US$3.50, one to 1½ hours, every 30 minutes) departs from the Albrook Bus Terminal.

Colón's *terminal de buses* (bus terminal) is at the intersection of Calle Terminal and Av Bolívar. It serves towns throughout Colón Province, including Escobal (US$1.25, 35 minutes), La Guayra (US$3, two hours; from here you can catch the boat to Isla Grande), Nombre de Dios (US$3.80, 2½ hours) and Portobelo (US$1.60, 1½ hours). These all depart hourly.

If you are headed east of Colón from Panama City, these buses can be boarded at Sabanitas, the turnoff for Portobelo, thus avoiding a trip into Colón. Be aware that buses may have standing room only, particularly on weekends.

TRAIN

Panama Railway Company (PCRC; ☑317-6070; www.panarail.com; Carretera Gaillard; one way adult/child US$25/$15) This glass-domed luxury passenger train takes a lovely ride from Panama City to Colón daily, leaving at 7:15am and returning at 5:15pm. The train follows the canal, at times surrounded by nothing but thick vine-strewn jungle. If you want to relive the heyday of luxury train travel for an hour or two, this is definitely the way to do it.

Note that the Panama City terminus is actually located in the town of Corazal, a 15-minute cab ride from the capital.

ⓘ Getting Around

While in Colón, it's not a good idea to walk around unknown neighborhoods. Fortunately, taxis congregate at the bus terminal, train station and the Zone Libre, and fares across the city are usually under US$2.

A round-trip taxi for two costs around US$60 to Fuerte San Lorenzo and US$30 to Gatun Locks.

Around Colón

◎ Sights

Canal Expansion Observation Center LOOKOUT
(Centro de Observación de la Ampliación del Canal; ☑276-8325; www.micanaldepanama.com; adult/child US$15/10; ☺8:30am-3:30pm) Still a work-in-progress, this new and pricey observation center offers an exclusive view of the Panama Canal expansion, slated to be completed in 2015. Visits take slightly over an hour. Covered decks view Lago Gatún and the locks; there is also a theater with videos in English, exhibits, a cafe and gift shop. A short rainforest trail has sloths and monkeys.

The turnoff for the new observation center is just past the railroad tracks, to the left; for the locks, continue straight at the turnoff. The center is accessible to travelers with disabilities.

Gatún Locks CANAL
(adult/child US$5/free; ☺8am-4pm) The Gatún Locks, just 10km south of Colón city, raise southbound ships 29.5m from Caribbean waters to the level of Lago Gatún. From

there the ships travel 37km to the Pedro Miguel Locks, which lower southbound ships 9.3m to Lago Miraflores, a small body of water that separates the two sets of Pacific locks. The ships are then lowered to sea level at the Miraflores Locks.

Not only are the Gatún Locks the largest of the three current sets, but their size is simply mind-boggling. In *The Path Between the Seas*, David McCullough notes that, if stood on its end, a single lock would have been the tallest structure on earth at the time it was built, taller by several meters than even the Eiffel Tower. Each chamber could have accommodated the *Titanic* with room to spare.

Workers poured a record-setting 1,820,000 cu meters of concrete to construct the Gatún Locks. The concrete was brought from a giant mixing plant to the construction site by railroad cars that ran on a circular track. Huge buckets maneuvered by cranes carried the wet concrete from the railroad cars and poured it into enormous steel forms. Locomotives moved the forms into place. This protracted process continued virtually uninterrupted until the Gatún Locks were completed after four years.

A viewing stand opposite the control tower offers a prime view of the locks in action. The two-hour process is the most interesting stage of the canal transit and the English brochure clearly describes what you're watching.

Buses to the Gatún Locks leave the Colón bus terminal hourly (US$1.25, 20 minutes). If you arrive by taxi you can stop here before heading on to Gatún Dam – another 2km away. A taxi ride from Colón to the locks and dam and back should cost US$60 per party, but agree on a price before leaving.

Gatún Dam   OUTDOORS

The Gatún Dam, which was constructed in 1908 to shore up the Río Chagres and to create Lago Gatún, was the world's largest earthen dam at the time. Before Lake Mead was formed by the 1936 completion of the Hoover Dam on the Nevada–Arizona (USA) border, Lago Gatún was the world's largest artificial body of water.

In fact, when Lago Gatún was created it submerged 262 sq km of jungle, entire villages (which were relocated) and large sections of the Panama Railroad. Today, power generated by the dam drives all the electrical equipment involved in the operation of the Panama Canal, including the locomotives that tow ships through the locks.

Although the sight of the dam is impressive enough, if the spillway is open you can watch millions of gallons of water rushing out. Before going, ask the guard at the entrance to the Gatún Locks if the spillway is open.

If you arrive at the Gatún Locks by bus, then it's a leisurely 30-minute walk to the dam. To get there, cross over the bridge spanning the Gatún Locks, turn left and follow the road for approximately 2km.

South of Colón

Prized for its lush setting and remoteness, Sierra Llorona Panama Lodge (☑6574-0083; www.sierrallorona.com; d US$55-88; ⓟ☒) is a 200-hectare rainforest reserve with 213 species of tropical bird. With extensive gardens and excellent trails with observation platforms, it is easy to cover the grounds. Trail difficulty ranges from easy-peasy to backbreaking. The lodge caters best to fans of the atmospheric natural setting (no casinos here!).

Rooms offer rustic styling without air-conditioners or TVs, though mountain breezes keep it cool and there's no need for TV with the rainforest on your doorstep.

After you have explored the reserve, you can organize private tours to some of the country's top bird-watching hot spots, such as nearby Parque Nacional Soberanía and Parque Nacional San Lorenzo. A day pass (US$20) allows visitors to hike the trails with a local guide and enjoy a three-course lunch with good vegetarian options.

Although it's possible drive yourself in a 4WD, you should probably arrange for a pickup with the company recommended on the website, since the road into Sierra Llorona can be hairy, particularly during rainy season. Those driving from Panama City can follow the Transisthmian Hwy toward Colón, and take the Santa Rita Arriba turnoff, just a few kilometers before the Sabanitas turnoff. Once on this road, follow signs for the lodge, which is approximately 4.5km from the Transisthmian Hwy.

Parque Nacional San Lorenzo

Centered on the ruins of the crumbling Spanish colonial fortress of Fuerte San Lorenzo, the 9.6-sq-km park (www.sanlorenzo.org.pa) also includes the former US military

RIDE THE PANAMA RAILROAD

One of the best ways to fully appreciate the extent of the canal is to travel from Panama City to Colón along the historic Panama Railroad (☑ info 317-6070; www.panarail.com; one way adult/child US$25/US$15; ⊙ departs from Panama City 7:15am, Colón 5:15pm daily). The rails fell into disrepair during the Noriega regime, but in 1998 the Panama government partnered with Kansas City Southern, an American-based railway holding company, to create the Panama Canal Railway Company (PCRC). The joint venture sought to re-establish the Atlantic–Pacific rail link and create a profitable alternative to the Panama Canal trade route. In 2001 PCRC also introduced a passenger service with a fully operational vintage train.

If you're looking to relive the golden age of railway travel, the vintage train features exotic wood paneling and blinds, carpeted interiors, glass-domed cars and open-air viewing decks. The hour-long ride parallels the canal, sometimes traversing thick rainforest.

While you're sipping a hot cup of coffee and admiring Panama's scenic interior, consider for a moment this cool train trivia:

➡ Peaking at US$295 a share, the Panama Railroad was the highest-priced stock on the New York Stock Exchange (NYSE) in the mid-1800s.

➡ With a total construction bill of US$8 million, it was, at the time, the most expensive railroad per kilometer ever built.

➡ Despite being only 76km long, the Panama Railroad required 304 bridges and culverts.

➡ During the first 12 years of its operations, the Panama Railroad carried over US$750 million in gold and silver, and collected 0.25% on each shipment.

➡ In 1913 the railroad hauled 2,916,657 passengers and transported 2,026,852 tons of freight across the isthmus, which was the heaviest per-kilometer traffic of any railroad in the world.

➡ An estimated 12,000 laborers died during its construction, mainly from malaria and yellow fever.

➡ Disposing of the dead was such a problem that the Panama Railroad administration started pickling the bodies in barrels and selling them to medical schools, the proceeds of which were used to build a hospital in the Panama Canal Zone.

base of Fuerte Sherman, as well as 12 different kinds of ecosystem including mangroves, marshlands, semideciduous forests and humid rainforests. Since the departure of the US military in 1999, native fauna has slowly recolonized the area, though the future of the San Lorenzo protected area remains uncertain.

As part of the Mesoamerican Biological Corridor, San Lorenzo protects and fosters species' migration between the continents, a fact touted by conservation biologists and ecotour operators alike. However, locals mostly see the area as unoccupied land, and everyone from poachers and loggers to slash-and-burn farmers is encroaching on the reserve.

Fortunately, conservation and tourism may win out in the end, due in part to the massive quantities of unexploded ordnance (UXOs) left in the area by the US military.

For decades the jungles surrounding Fuerte Sherman were used for target practice and survival training, though America's hasty exit from Panama in 1999 didn't leave much time for cleaning up shop.

Today, most travelers set their sights on the ruins of Fuerte San Lorenzo, but there are plenty of opportunities here for jungle exploration. The secondary forests of the protected area are rich in bird life and there's no shortage of mountainous trails and waterfall-fed ponds to discover.

History

Following the destruction of Nombre de Dios by Sir Francis Drake in 1573, the Spanish moved to fortify the Caribbean coast. Of principal concern was the Río Chagres, which flowed inland to the town of Venta de Cruces (near the modern town of Gamboa), and then linked up with the trade route leading to the city of Panamá. In 1595, by order of Phillip II of Spain, Fuerte San Lorenzo was built into the side of a steep cliff near the river mouth. Fuerte San Lorenzo, Portobelo and Panamá, the 'three keys' of the Americas, became known as the strategic hearts of the Spanish trade empire.

Once established, Fuerte San Lorenzo was under constant pirate attack. In 1596, only one year after its completion, Drake seized San Lorenzo. Although later recovered and rebuilt with greater fortifications, San Lorenzo was again assaulted, this time by Sir Henry Morgan in 1671. Captain Morgan (of the spiced-rum fame) succeeded in overpowering its guns and sailing up the Río Chagres. A few months later Morgan burnt Panamá to the ground, pilfered its riches and sailed back to England with galleons laden with Spanish treasure.

In 1680 a new fortification was built on the highest part of the cliff, but this was no match for British Admiral Vernon, who destroyed San Lorenzo yet again in 1740. In 1761 the Spanish once more rebuilt San Lorenzo, though the decision to abandon the overland trade route in favor of sailing around the Cape Horn meant that the fort didn't suffer further attacks. As a result, Fuerte San Lorenzo was abandoned by Spain in 1821 when Panama became independent. The fort was subsequently used as a Colombian prison, a post office for inbound English mail and a campsite for gold miners en route to California.

In order to defend the Panama Canal Zone, the US military built Fuerte Sherman in 1911 with the purpose of defending the Atlantic side of the canal. Although post-WWII changes in war technology meant that the fortifications were rendered obsolete, the area surrounding the fort became an important jungle warfare training center. In 1963 these operations came under the responsibility of the US-army-run 'School of the Americas' in nearby Fuerte Gullick, but five years later the 'Jungle Operations Training Center' became an independent entity. Fuerte Sherman subsequently became the main jungle operations school for the US army and was used as a training center for Vietnam-bound Special Forces.

On June 30, 1999, under the Torrijos-Carter treaties, Fuerte Sherman, nearby Fuertes Davis and Gullick, and the Parque Nacional San Lorenzo were handed back to the Panamanian Government.

COLÓN PROVINCE PARQUE NACIONAL SAN LORENZO

◉ Sights

Fuerte San Lorenzo and the Parque Nacional San Lorenzo are located west of the city of Colón and northwest of Lago Gatún. The ruins of San Lorenzo are located 9km southeast of Fuerte Sherman on the Caribbean coastal highway and lie along the northwestern boundary of the protected area. Although there is no official entrance to the reserve, there is a visitors center in the village of Achiote, located along the northeastern edge of the reserve between the villages of Piña and Escobal.

Fuerte San Lorenzo   FORT
(www.sanlorenzo.org.pa; ⊘ 8am-4pm) FREE Declared a Unesco World Heritage Site in 1980, Fuerte San Lorenzo is perched at the mouth of the Río Chagres on a promontory west of the canal. Despite its violent history, much of San Lorenzo is well preserved, including the moat, the cannons and the arched rooms. The fort also commands a wide view of the river and bay far below, which was one of the reasons the Spanish chose to fortify the site.

Like its contemporary fortresses at Portobelo, San Lorenzo was constructed of blocks of cut coral and armed to the teeth with row upon row of cannons. If you inspect the cannons closely, you'll notice that some of them are actually British-made, which bespeaks the time in the 17th century when Sir Francis Drake and his pirate brethren occupied the fort.

There's no bus service to the fort; taxis go from Colón (around US$60 round trip for two). If driving, go to the Gatún Locks, continue past the stoplight near the northern entrance to the locks and follow the signs to the dam, 2km away. Drive over the dam and follow the 'Fuerte San Lorenzo' signs. These lead to the entrance of Fuerte Sherman where you'll be asked to show identification. Once you've done this, you will be allowed to proceed the remaining 9km to Fuerte San Lorenzo.

The park is renowned for bird-watching, but hikers will be more than satisfied with guided romps through its dense secondary forest. You can also take some lovely walks to waterfalls and natural ponds, visit organic shade-grown coffee farms and hike to splendid lookouts with views of the protected area and the Río Chagres.

Centro El Tucán OUTDOORS

(☎226-6602, 6628-9000; ⊙8am-4pm Mon-Fri)
The protected area at San Lorenzo is best
explored with a guide, easily arranged at the
Centro El Tucán, a community learning and
visitors center that lies on the edge of the
reserve. Guides generally charge US$60 per
group for a two-hour hike, though longer
and more difficult treks can also be arranged. El Tucán also has an excellent documentation center on the flora and fauna,
human ecology and history.

The visitors center is located in the village of Achiote, 13km north of Escobal, on
the edge of the reserve. Since there is no
public transportation to the town and there
are few taxis in the area, Achiote is best accessed by private vehicle.

🛏 Sleeping

The helpful staff at the Centro El Tucán can
arrange homestays in Achiote. There are
also opportunities for unofficial camping in
the reserve, though you will need to be self-
sufficient.

You can also bed down for a night or
two in the former den of dictators, namely
Building 400 of the notorious School of the
Americas.

❶ Getting There & Away

As there is no public transportation to either
Fuerte San Lorenzo or Parque Nacional San Loren-
zo, this area is best explored by private vehicle. It
is, however, possible to take a taxi to Fuerte San
Lorenzo from Colón (around US$60 round trip).
Taxis are uncommon closer to the reserve.

Portobelo

POP 4000

This Caribbean fishing village is so laid-back
and languorous, it is incredible to ponder
that it was once the greatest Spanish port in
Central America. Mules once carried Peruvian gold and Oriental treasures to Panama
City via the fortresses at Portobelo. Though
English privateers destroyed them several
times throughout their history, many of
these atmospheric colonial fortresses still
stand. Throughout the village, homes are
situated among these atmospheric ruins.

Today, Portobelo's residents scratch out a
living fishing, tending crops or raising livestock. Though economically depressed, Portobelo is experiencing something of a cultural
revival, with interest surging in Congo art
and dancing. The town bursts to life every
October 21 for the Festival de Cristo Negro

COLÓN PROVINCE PORTOBELO

SWEET DREAMS IN THE DEN OF DICTATORS

The borders of the San Lorenzo protected area are home to Fuerte Espinar, which was
known as Fuerte Gullick prior to the US handover. Within this compound is the infamous
Building 400, which was the former home of the School of the Americas.

Established in 1949, the School of the Americas trained more than 34,000 Latin
American soldiers before moving to Fuerte Benning, Georgia, in 1984. The school was
created to keep communism out of Latin America, which quickly translated into teach-
ing Latin American soldiers how to thwart armed communist insurgencies.

The school graduated some of the worst human-rights violators of our time, including former Argentine dictator Leopoldo Galtieri, who 'disappeared' thousands during
Argentina's Dirty War of the 1970s, and El Salvador's Roberto D'Aubuisson, who led
death squads that killed Archbishop Oscar Romero and thousands of other Salvadorans
during the 1980s.

In a bizarre twist, Building 400 is now a giant resort, Meliá Panamá Canal (☎470-
1100; www.solmelia.com; s/d US$115/125; P ✴ @ 🛜 ☼). Not too surprisingly, all evidence
that the hotel has ever been anything but an upscale fun center is missing.

The US$30-million hotel features guest rooms that are comfortable but somewhat
dated, a cluster of outdoor and indoor pools complete with swim-up bars, and a formal
restaurant overlooking Lago Gatún. Service can be slow. A wide range of tours operated
by Aventuras 2000 include an onsite canopy zip line and fishing, as well as canal, Emberá village and Fuerte San Lorenzo visits.

In the past, overnight guests at Building 400 arrived via convoy or Blackhawk chop-
per. Today, it's recommended that you arrive via private vehicle; take the Quatro Altos
turnoff on the Transisthmian Hwy and follow signs for the hotel.

Portobelo

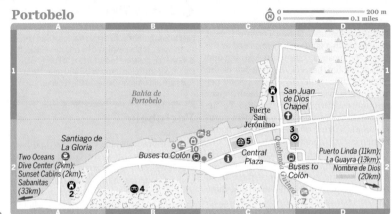

Portobelo

(Black Christ Festival), one of the country's most vibrant and spiritual celebrations.

Portobelo also attracts dedicated scuba divers, with no less than 16 major dive sites in the adjacent waters. Though the visibility can't compare to more traditional Caribbean diving destinations, the variety of underwater attractions include a 110ft cargo ship and a C-45 twin-engine plane.

History

Colombus named 'Puerto Bello,' the Beautiful Port, in 1502, when he stopped here on his fourth New World voyage. Over time, the name shortened to 'Portobelo.'

Portobelo consisted of no more than 10 houses when the celebrated Italian engineer Juan Bautista Antonelli arrived in 1586 on a mission to examine the defensibility of the Caribbean. After noting how well Portobelo's bay lent itself to defensive works, King Félipe II ordered that Nombre de Dios be abandoned and Portobelo colonized. However, it wasn't until after Nombre de Dios was completely destroyed by Sir Francis Drake in 1596 that the transfer took place.

The city of San Felipe de Portobelo was founded in 1597 and its 200-year history was riddled with numerous invasions at the hands of English privateers and the Royal Navy. Portobelo was first attacked in 1602 by English pirate William Parker, but it was the infamous Sir Henry Morgan who sacked the city in 1671.

However, not all of the invasions were the product of superior tactics or numbers. In 1679 the crews of two English ships and one French vessel united in an attack on Portobelo. They landed 200 men at such a distance from the town that it took them three nights of marching to reach it. As they neared Portobelo, they were seen by a farmer, who ran ahead to sound the alarm, but the pirates followed so closely behind that the town had no time to prepare. Unaware of how small the buccaneer force was, all the inhabitants fled.

The pirates spent two days and nights in Portobelo, collecting plunder in constant apprehension that the Spaniards would return in great numbers and attack them. However, the buccaneers got back to their ships unmolested, then distributed 160 pieces of eight to each man. At the time, one piece of eight would pay for a night's stay at the best inn in Seville.

Attacks on Portobelo continued unabated until the city was destroyed in 1739 by an attack led by Admiral Edward Vernon. Portobelo was rebuilt in 1751, but it never attained its former prominence and in time became a virtual ruin. Later, much of the outermost fortress was dismantled to build the Panama Canal and many of the larger stones were used in the construction of the Gatún Locks. There are, however, still considerable parts of the town and fortresses left, and today Portobelo is protected as a national park and a Unesco World Heritage Site.

⊙ Sights

Fuerte San Fernando   FORT
`FREE` In 1601 Fuerte San Félipe and Fuerte San Diego were built near the mouth of the bay, but were subsequently destroyed by Admiral Vernon in 1739. Fuerte San Fernando was later built over the ruins. American engineers dismantled much of the fort later, using its walls to create the breakwater protecting the northern end of the Panama Canal.

Boats can be hired from the water's edge (US$4 per person round trip) to bring you across the bay to the fort.

Fuerte Santiago   FORT
`FREE` Approaching from the west, the first fort is Fuerte Santiago. Built after Vernon's attack, some walls were 3m thick, made entirely of cut coral. Known to the Spaniards as 'reef rock,' coral was a popular building material since it's easily shaped, tough as granite yet light as pumice. Ruins include officers' quarters, artillery sheds, a sentry box, barracks and watchtowers.

After a recent mudslide, some coral walls had to be replaced with cement reinforcements.

Fuerte San Jerónimo   FORT
`FREE` Fuerte San Jerónimo, closer to Portobelo center, was the largest fortress ever built to protect the bay. Eighteen cannon embrasures face the mouth of the bay, some exactly where the Spanish troops left them in 1821, the year Panama declared independence. Beyond the impressive gateway of San Jerónimo are the remains of the officers' quarters, barracks and a guardroom.

If you're short on time, San Jerónimo is more complete and makes for a better visit than Fuerte Santiago.

Mirador Perú   LOOKOUT
On a hill overlooking Santiago and much of the bay is a small but well-preserved watchtower called Mirador Perú, which was built at the same time as Fuerte Santiago. There are steps carved into the hillside to reach the lookout, and the views of the coastline from here are expansive.

Real Aduana de Portobelo   HISTORIC BUILDING
(admission US$1; ⊙8am-4pm) The handsome, two-story Royal Customs House of Portobelo was originally built in 1630 to serve as the *contaduría* (counting house) for the king's gold. Treasure brought across the isthmus was recorded and stored here until it could be placed on galleons and sailed to Spain. According to early records, no less than 233 soldiers were garrisoned in this building alone.

The customs house consists of two main rooms, which are now used as permanent exhibition halls. One room displays dozens of purple velvet robes, which are placed on the statue of the Black Christ every October when thousands of devotees descend on Portobelo to worship the icon. Among the donors are boxer Roberto Durán and salsa star Ismael Rivera. The other room contains replicas of Spanish-colonial rifles, sketches of Portobelo's forts, 20th-century black-and-white photos of the town and a few dozen rusty cannonballs.

The building's 2nd floor features an intriguing collection of photos and drawings of the Spanish-colonial fortresses that exist throughout Latin America. Also, don't overlook the bronze cannon at the entrance – it was recovered from a sunken galleon and bears a Spanish coat of arms as well as the date of manufacture (1617).

PORTOBELO'S TOP FIVE ESCAPES

➡ Take a water taxi to Puerto Francés for private swims and jungle hikes.

➡ Snorkel around Spanish cannons encrusted in the coral landscape.

➡ Kayak on the tranquil Río Claro.

➡ Watch a sunset from El Fuerte de San Fernando.

➡ Join a Congo dance workshop and sweat to cool African rhythms.

🏃 Activities

Diving & Snorkeling

It's not Belize or the Bay Islands, but if you're an avid scuba diver you'll have a good time here. In addition to the famous sunken cargo ship and military plane, the waters around Portobelo are also home to soft coral-laden walls, offshore reefs and rock gardens, some also apt for snorkeling. Dive centers have snorkel gear and information.

The good news is that you'll probably see several pelagic animals including nurse sharks, black-tip reef sharks and eagle rays. The bad news is that you probably won't see them very well, especially if it has been raining. Generally speaking, you can expect about 10m of underwater visibility, but don't be surprised if it gets as low as 3m. Fortunately, scuba diving along this stretch of the Caribbean is fairly cheap and a bad day of diving is always better than a good day of work.

Dive operators in Portobelo are located along Sabanitas–Portobelo road, about 2km west of town. If you're planning to dive, it's best to phone ahead or make a reservation via the internet. A two-tank dive will cost around US$90 per person.

Two Oceans Dive Center   DIVING
(☑ 6678-8018, in Panama City 399-4781; www.2oceansdivers.com) A PADI dive center mostly active on weekends and in high season, located at Coco Plum Lodge. Excursions are made from a comfortable catamaran.

Scubaportobelo   DIVING
(☑ 261-3841; www.scubapanama.com) Outfitter Scubaportobelo offers all-inclusive scuba packages. It's located on the road into town, on the left.

Swimming

If you're looking for a day of fun in the sun, nearby Playa Blanca is a great day trip from Portobelo. Closer, you'll find the small cove beach La Huerta and Puerto Francés, which has a covered hammock hut and bathroom (arrange ahead of time for a key; local boat drivers know the caretakers).

🎓 Courses

Agrupaciones de Congo   DANCE
(☑ 6693-5690; Calle Principal, Casa Artesanal; per hr US$20) This established local group preserves the longstanding tradition of Congo dancing. Aristela Blandon gives tailored dance classes and provides a fascinating background on the slave history behind this unique tradition in Spanish. Participants can also purchase a CD of original music.

🎉 Festivals & Events

On the last Sunday of each month there is an Afro Mass with a town fair displaying local food and traditional crafts. Holy Week is also an interesting time to be here.

Festival de Diablos y Congos   FESTIVAL
The most intriguing local tradition is Festival de Diablos y Congos, a festival of rebellion and ridicule that mocks the colonial

---

SURFING IN COLÓN PROVINCE

One of Panama's least surfed provinces will make you a believer with its great unknown breaks.

Playa Maria Chiquita In front of Maria Chiquita. Beach break with lefts and rights, but limited to big swell.

Isla Grande In front of La Guayra, it's best reached by water taxi. Reef bottom break with three peaks, rights and lefts.

Isla Mamei Next to Isla Grande, it's reached by boat or paddling from Isla Grande. Left-hand point break over shallow reef.

Playa Palenque/Cuango In front of Cuango village. Beach break with rights and lefts. Surfers seldom seen here.

Playa Grande Mainland East of Isla Grande. Beach break with some reef. Waves break left and right.

Turtles Paddling distance from Playa Grande. Waves are great; unreal tubes, if it is glassy with a big swell.

V-Land Near Devils Beach in Sherman. Unbelievable right-point reef break with great tubes when there's big swell and it's glassy.

CELEBRATING REBELLION

To see authentic Portobelo, see the Festival de Diablos y Congos where we celebrate our *cimarrón* ancestors, slaves who survived by rebellion. We dance, and instead of wearing our Sunday best, we wear clashing rags. We speak in reverse, as *cimarrones* did, to keep the Spaniards guessing. Survival is all about liberty, it's a beautiful thing to see.

Portobelo resident Aristela Blandon is a community mediator and dance teacher.

Spaniards. During the festivity, blacks assume the role of escaped slaves and take 'captives.' It is held two weeks after Carnaval, sometimes coinciding with March 20, Portobelo's patron saint day.

The tradition of Los Congos (named for its participants) dates from the slave-trading days when blacks escaped into the jungle and formed communities of exiles. In satire, a prisoner is taken and a huge ransom demanded, though the prisoner is freed upon paying a token ransom (US$1 will suffice). The Congos perform before audiences dressed in outlandish outfits that include tattered clothes, hats that resemble crowns and wooden swords.

Beware that a wild group may descend upon an innocent pedestrian and demand thousands of dollars. If you ever find yourself an innocent 'victim' of this tradition, try not to freak out – they'll settle for a few coins.

Festival de Cristo Negro   RELIGIOUS
(Black Christ Festival) Every October 21, pilgrims from all over Panama arrive in Portobelo to partake in this festival which honors a miracle-giving 1.5m-high statue of the Black Christ housed in the Iglesia de San Félipe. After the sun sets the statue is paraded down the streets, while pilgrims bedecked in purple robes and thorned crowns dance and drink until the wee hours.

🛏 Sleeping & Eating

Particularly during festivals, local families may rent out spare rooms starting at US$15 – ask at ATP.

Captain Jack's   HOSTEL **$**
(☑ 448-2009; www.captainjackvoyages.com; dm US$13; @ ☎) Run by a sailboat captain from New Jersey, this bare-bones hostel (think plastic-covered mattresses and funky showers) is nonetheless a hub of merrymaking. Perhaps its best feature is the upper deck restaurant-bar serving great grub (US$7 to US$26) from 11am to 10pm. Unfortunately, we are not sure if the Vietnamese cook (responsible for the pho and spring rolls) is staying on.

★ **Casa de la Bruja**   GUESTHOUSE **$$**
(☑ 6764-0725, 226-2035; sandraeleta@gmail.com; d US$50, 4-person loft US$80, 2-bedroom house US$175; P ✶) Quite out of the ordinary, this chill photographer's home is adapted for guests. Side by side there are two ample houses; just lovely, with a grassy seafront perfect for lounging. The bright, open interiors showcase photography and local Congo art.

It is fine to cook here or you can pay extra for prepared meals. Guests can organize onsite excursions to snorkel and sightsee or take a Caribbean cooking workshop (US$15 per person) from Doña Cecelia, a whiz of Afro-Caribbean cooking whose specialties include *fufu* (fish soup) and *tortillas changa* (grilled with maize and coconut).

Coco Plum Eco Lodge   HOTEL **$$**
(☑ 448-2102; www.cocoplum-panama.com; s/d/tr US$45/55/65; P ✶) An attractive motel-style lodging, the friendly Coco Plum has been around for years. On the waterfront, the feel of the place is ocean kitsch, replete with nets, shells and pastels, but the effect is cozy. The attached bar-restaurant (mains US$6 to US$15) is popular with travelers – check out the octopus in coconut milk or seafood stew.

It's on the road into town on the left. Two Oceans Dive Center is attached and there's a salon with games and TV.

Casa Rayo Verde   GUESTHOUSE **$$**
(☑ 202-0111; info.rayoverde@gmail.com; d US$60; ✶ ☎) A recent addition, this attractive four-room home is recommended by guests. The property faces the water and has quaint rooms with mini-fridges and private bathrooms. Guests can enjoy the shared terrace and the guesthouse helps fund art, music and carpentry initiatives in the local community.

Run by the resort across the bay, the group plans to add another lodging, Casa de Cultura Congo, that will be more high end.

THE LEGEND OF THE BLACK CHRIST

Festival de Cristo Negro (p217) honors the statue of the same name, which has many miracles attributed to it. Normally housed in the Iglesia de San Félipe, the Black Christ statue's exact origins are a matter of speculation. All definitive church records were lost in the fire that followed Henry Morgan's sacking of Panamá in 1671. However, there's no shortage of fanciful stories surrounding the origins of the statue.

One story has it that a ship bound for Cartagena, Colombia, tried to leave Portobelo five times, but on each occasion a storm blew the ship back to the town's edge, nearly sinking it. The crew lightened their vessel by tossing a heavy box overboard. On their sixth attempt to sail out, the weather calmed and they were able to go on their way. Several days later, local fishers found the discarded box floating off Portobelo and discovered the Black Christ inside.

A second story claims that the box was instead found floating at sea during a cholera epidemic. After being retrieved by local fishermen, the statue was placed inside the Iglesia de San Félipe. Almost immediately, as the story goes, the epidemic passed and the infected were instantaneously cured.

Sunset Cabins CABIN $$
(☑ 448-2147; www.panamaportobelocabins.com; d/cabin US$53/75; P ✳) Nondivers are welcome at this comfortable seafront lodging run by Scubapanama. A bright structure has motel-style doubles with balconies, electric showers and air-con. The cute cabins are charming but pocket-sized – best for a couple or a family with small children. For all-inclusive scuba packages, see the website.

Shopping

Taller Portobelo ARTS & CRAFTS
(☑ 6777-5022; ⊘ 9am-noon & 2-5pm) Fascinating for art and culture buffs, Taller Portobelo is an artist-run workshop of Congo art. Feel free to ask the attendant about the historical and cultural significance of the work on display; the art is also for sale. It's located behind Casa de Brujas. If the shop is closed, ask around for Gustavo.

Information

Just off the main road through town, **ATP** (☑ 6485-7028, 448-2200; ⊘ 9:30am-5:30pm Tue-Fri & Sun) has good information. Ask Mirsa Jimenez for information about dance classes, volunteering with the school or working on community projects; only Spanish is spoken. Across the street from the tourist office is an **internet cafe** (per hr US$1.50; ⊘ 8:30am-4pm Mon-Fri).

Portobelo consists of about 15 square blocks beside a paved two-lane road that intersects with the Panama City–Colón road at the town of Sabanitas, 33km to the west. East of Portobelo, the road forks after 9km. The right branch of the road extends 14km further east to Nombre de Dios; the left branch extends 11km to the hamlet of La Guayra, where you can hire boats to Isla Grande.

Getting There & Away

Buses to Portobelo (US$1.60, 1½ hours, every 30 minutes) depart from Colón's Terminal de Buses from 6:30am to 6pm.

From Panama City you can avoid Colón. Take the Colón bus and get off at El Rey supermarket in Sabanitas, 10km before Colón. Next, catch the bus coming from Colón to Portobelo when it passes through Sabanitas (US$1.25, 1¼ hours). Since it's often full, take as little luggage as possible.

Getting Around

Taxis exist but can be scarce. On the Sabanitas–Portobelo road you can flag down any bus headed in your direction. After dark there is no public transportation.

Water taxis leave from Fuerte Santiago. Co-op **Santiago de La Gloria** (☑ 448-2266) charges a two-person minimum to Playa La Huerta (US$30), Playa Blanca (US$45) and the beach at Puerto Francés (US$35); all fees are for a round trip.

Around Portobelo

Playa Blanca

A 20-minute boat ride from Portobelo will bring you to this lovely white-sand beach, which fronts a tranquil cove and is surrounded by dense wilderness. Since it is impossible to access the beach by car or bus, you'd be forgiven for thinking that Playa

Blanca is an uninhabited island floating in the Caribbean.

Playa Blanca has some of the least disturbed reefs between Colón and the Archipiélago de San Blás and its sheltered waters have better visibility than those of nearby Portobelo. There's a colorful reef in the center of the cove that's a mere shell's toss away from the beach, as well as a second reef that sits in deeper waters about 100m offshore.

Any boat in Portobelo can bring you to Playa Blanca (two to three passengers US$45 round trip), though it's possible to arrange for a pickup if you make a reservation in advance.

Puerto Lindo

Located 6km before El Guayra, this snoozy village with a protected bay increasingly favored by sailboats voyaging to the San Blás or Cartagena, Colombia. Excursions to the nearby Isla Mamey visit a beautiful beach and surrounding mangroves.

To get to Puerto Lindo, take any bus bound for El Guayra.

🛏 Sleeping

Hostel Puerto Lindo   HOSTEL $

(📞 6436-7601; hostelpuertolindo@gmail.com; dm US$7, s/d US$10/16, d with air-con US$20) With a waterfront location, this new Panamanian-run hostel is proving a hit with backpackers who enjoy affordable rates and a good vibe. Outings can be made to nearby islands for snorkeling or paddling by kayak. The hostel can also recommend sailboats to Colombia.

Hostel Wunderbar   HOSTEL $

(📞 6626-8455, 448-2426; www.hostelwunderbar. com; dm US$11-15, d US$25-30) This place is run by a German-Austrian couple who traded their sailboat for a hostel. The setting is relaxed, with mosaic tiles adorning the shady outdoor kitchen. Guests choose between the cement privates and cheaper thatched dwellings, but everyone shares an outdoor shower and bamboo toilet stalls.

There are also bicycle rentals, horseback riding day trips (US$35) and canoe trips to the mangroves. Internet may be available for extra.

Isla Grande

POP 900

Palm trees and white-sand beaches form the backdrop to this lovely little island, just

---

ICING GLASS

If you're missing your daily dose of spirulina, look no further. Regional specialty *icing glass* has yet to make the menu at Starbucks, but its sweet and potent taste is strangely addictive. This icy blend of condensed milk and seaweed is sold at roadside stands, sometimes even out of recycled rum bottles. Now *that's* organic.

15km offshore from Portobelo. A popular getaway for Panama City folk fleeing the urban grind, Isla Grande is an ideal setting for snorkeling, scuba diving or simply soaking up the island's relaxed vibe. A few hundred people of African descent live on Grande, most of whom eke out a living from fishing and coconuts – you'll get a taste of both when you sample the fine island cuisine.

Owing to its location on Panama's northern Caribbean coast, Isla Grande gets an awful lot of rain year-round. Terms like 'rainy' and 'dry' seasons don't apply here, though torrential showers are usually intense and short-lived.

🏊 Activities

This 5km-long, 1.5km-wide island has two trails, one that loops the shoreline and another slippery cross-island trail. The lovely beaches on the northern side of the island can be reached by boat (water taxis dock in front of Cabañas Super Jackson) or on foot.

Some fine snorkeling and dive sites are within a 10-minute boat ride of the island. If you are interested in diving, contact one of the Portobelo-based operators. Diving is limited to between April and December, when seas are calmer.

For around US$50 one of the boaters in front of Cabañas Super Jackson will take you on a half-day adventure. The possibilities are quite appealing – the mangroves east of Isla Grande are fun to explore, or you could go snorkeling off the coast of the nearby islets.

🎉 Festivals & Events

Isla Grande Carnaval   FESTIVAL

(🕑 Feb-Mar) Isla Grande celebrates Carnaval in rare form. Women wear traditional *polleras* (tnational dress) while men wear ragged pants tied at the waist with old sea rope, and everyone dances the conga. There are also satirical songs about current events and a lot of joking in the Caribbean calypso tradition.

Festival de San Juan Bautista   FESTIVAL

Isla Grande celebrates Festival of San Juan Bautista with swimming and canoe races on June 24.

La Virgen del Carmen   RELIGIOUS

The Virgen del Carmen is honored with a land and sea procession, baptisms and masses on July 16.

🛏 Sleeping & Eating

Cabañas Super Jackson   CABIN $

(☎448-2311; d/tr/q US$30/40/50; ❄) Closest to the main pier, this Isla Grande landmark offers a handful of budget rooms with the character and ambiance of a hospital waiting room. There are more comfortable spots on the island, but these are convenient and relatively cheap.

Sister Moon Eco Lodge   LODGE $$

(☎6948-1990; www.hotelsistermoon.com; dm US$25, s/d/tr/q US$40/69/89/109; ❄ ⛴) The best bang for your buck on the island, this lovely clutch of hillside cabins is surrounded by swaying palms and crashing waves. The fabulous views are best appreciated from a porch hammock. Its 'ecolodge' billing just means no hot water or air-conditioning. The hotel bar-restaurant is built right over the water and features the island's famous coconut-infused seafood.

Day passes are US$20. It's a 10-minute walk east of Cabañas Super Jackson.

Bananas Village Resort   RESORT $$$

(☎263-9510; www.bananasresort.com; d incl breakfast from US$153, oceanfront ste from US$203; P ❄ @ ⛴) Located on the northern side of the island and only accessible by boat or trail, Grande's most upscale accommodation consists of two-story A-frame jungle cottages fronted by the sea. Cheerful rooms have white-wicker furniture and French doors – those upstairs are slightly larger with private balconies.

Guests can kayak, play volleyball and use snorkeling gear without extra charges. Weekend prices climb steeply. Day-trippers pay US$35 for use of the facilities, a welcome cocktail and lunch.

❶ Getting There & Away

Isla Grande is a 10-minute boat ride from La Guayra, a tiny coastal hamlet that is connected to Colón via frequent buses. Boats arriving at Isla Grande dock in front of the Cabañas Super Jackson, which serves as the island's unofficial landmark.

Buses to La Guayra leave from the Colón bus terminal (US$3, 1½ hours). These buses can be also be boarded at Sabanitas, the turnoff for Portobelo, La Guayra, and Nombre de Dios. Buses return from La Guayra at 8am, 9am and 1pm.

Resorts can bring guests and day-trippers from Panama City; Bananas resort charges US$60 per person for a round-trip shuttle, which leaves at noon and returns at 4pm.

In La Guayra, there are always skippers hanging about near the water's edge, waiting to take people to the island. The 10-minute boat ride costs US$3 to US$5 per person; secure parking US$3.50 per day.

Comarca de Kuna Yala

POP 33,100 / ELEV SEA LEVEL TO 748M / AREA 2360 SQ KM

Best Off-the-Beaten-Path Spots

➡ Cayos Holandeses (p232)

➡ East Lemons (p230)

➡ Cayos Los Grullos (p232)

➡ Beyond Achutupu (p234)

Best Places to Stay

➡ Dolphin Lodge (p234)

➡ Cabañas Kuanidup (p231)

➡ Cabañas Tigre (p233)

➡ Sapibenega (p234)

➡ Yandup Lodge (p233)

Why Go?

Imagine a turquoise tropical archipelago with an island for every day of the year. With white sand and waving palms, these Caribbean islands cheat no one's version of paradise. The Comarca is home to the Kuna, the first group in Latin America to gain indigenous autonomy. Though they have had contact with Europeans since Columbus sailed these waters in 1502, clan identity is paramount, and many Kuna make tenacious efforts to preserve a traditional way of life.

In 2009 the road to Cartí was completed, making the region far more accessible than it has ever been. Still off the beaten track, this narrow, 226km-long strip on the Caribbean coast stretches from the Golfo de San Blás to the Colombian border.

Community islands are acre-sized cays packed with bamboo huts, livestock and people. Visitors often prefer the more remote outer islands with few inhabitants. Most areas require landing fees.

When to Go

➡ **Dec–Apr** During trade-wind season there's little rain. It can get hot in the thatched huts, but conditions are ideal for sailing with winds from the north and northeast.

➡ **Oct** Isla Tigre celebrates traditional dance at the Nogagope, which brings communities together for a week of dancing as well as canoe races and an art fair.

➡ **May–Aug** Good visibility for snorkeling, though rainstorms are around and so are annoying *chitras* (sand flies). Thunderstorms mean it's not a preferable time to sail.

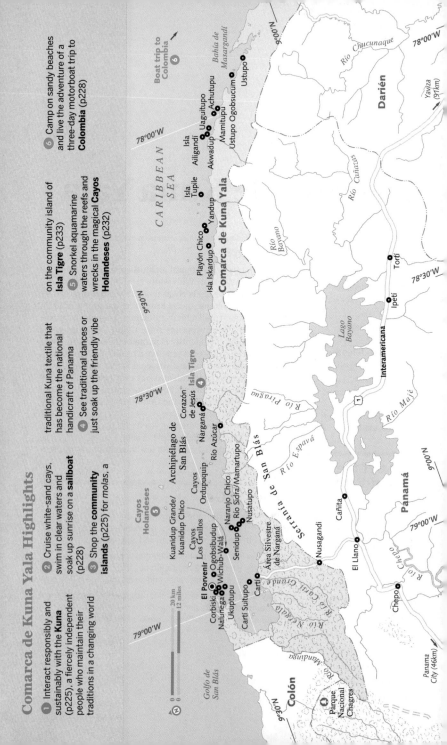

Comarca de Kuna Yala Highlights

① Interact responsibly and sustainably with the **Kuna** people (p225), a fiercely independent people who maintain their traditions in a changing world

② Cruise white-sand cays, swim in clear waters and soak up sunrise on a **sailboat** (p228)

③ Shop the **community islands** (p225) for *molas*, a traditional Kuna textile that has become the national handicraft of Panama

④ See traditional dances or just soak up the friendly vibe on the community island of **Isla Tigre** (p233)

⑤ Snorkel aquamarine waters through the reefs and wrecks in the magical **Cayos Holandeses** (p232)

⑥ Camp on sandy beaches and live the adventure of a three-day motorboat trip to **Colombia** (p228)

The Kuna

History

Although the Kuna have lived in eastern Panama for at least two centuries, scholars fiercely debate their origins. Language similarities with people who once lived several hundred kilometers to the west would indicate that the Kuna migrated eastward. However, oral tradition has it that the Kuna migrated to San Blás from Colombia after the 16th century, following a series of devastating encounters with other tribes armed with poison-dart blowguns.

Regardless of the Kuna's origins, scholars agree that life on the islands is relatively new for them. Historians at the end of the 18th century wrote that the only people who used the San Blás islands at that time were pirates, Spaniards and the odd explorer. However, the Kuna flourished on the archipelago due to the abundance of seafood. They supplemented this with food crops, including rice, yams, yucca, bananas and pineapples, grown on the nearby mainland.

Today, there are an estimated 70,000 Kuna; 32,000 live on the district's islands, 8000 live on tribal land along the coast and 30,000 live outside the district. So communal are the island-dwelling Kuna that they inhabit only 49 of the nearly 400 cays; the rest are mostly left to coconut trees, sea turtles and iguanas.

Culture

The traditional Kuna belief structure is based around three principal concepts: god, nature and the cosmos.

According to Kuna religion, the world was created by God, Paba Tummat, and the Great Mother, Nan Tummat, who continue to keep watch over everyone's daily actions. Although Kuna shamans often look into the future and make minor divinations, everything in life is believed to be preordained by God and the Great Mother. In fact, the Kuna make great efforts in their daily lives to ensure that their actions follow the will of Paba and Nan Tummat, even though they do not know their fate.

The Kuna identify strongly with nature, and their rich oral traditions are full of songs, hymns and prayers that recount the beauty and majesty of the wind, the land and the sea. To the Kuna, people and nature are considered parts of the same entity and thus the rules of nature follow human life from birth to death. The Kuna love and admire nature, and believe that true happiness is only experienced within its presence.

Kuna cosmology is based on the doctrine that the knowledge of a concept allows the knower to manipulate the power of the concept. As a result, Kuna myths and legends have both a literal and a symbolic meaning. For example, the story of the Iberokun, who descended to the earth in order to teach the Kuna how to have chiefs, is often associated with most of the moral and ethical teachings of the Kuna.

Lifestyle

Not surprisingly, the cornerstone of the Kuna political organization is the Iberokun or community gathering house. Here, men gather nightly for heated discussions about local events, to make decisions about important problems and to listen to the advice of chiefs. Generally, each island has at least three chiefs and their authority is officially recognized by the Panamanian government. Every year there are two general assemblies for representatives from all of the islands in the Comarca where major issues affecting the Kuna are discussed.

Historically, the Kuna were matrilocal, meaning that when a man marries, he moves into the household of his wife's parents and comes under the control of his father-in-law. Today, this pattern is yielding to neolocality, in that newlyweds will establish residence away from both parents. As recent as a generation ago, Kuna households had an average size of seven to 12 people, but today households often comprise as few as five people.

The distinctive dress of the Kuna is immediately recognizable no matter where you are in Panama. Most Kuna women continue to dress as their ancestors did. Their faces may be adorned with a black line painted from the forehead to the tip of the nose, with a gold ring worn through the septum. Colorful fabric is wrapped around the waist as a skirt, topped by a short-sleeved blouse covered in brilliantly colored *molas*. The women wrap their legs, from ankle to knee, in long strands of tiny beads, forming colorful geometric patterns. A printed headscarf and many necklaces, rings and bracelets complete the wardrobe. In sharp contrast to the elaborate women's wear, Kuna men have adopted Western dress, such as shorts and sleeveless shirts.

In recent years Kuna culture has come under increasing threat of Westernization, particularly as young Kuna are drawn away from the islands and toward Panama City in search of employment and increased opportunities. However, Kuna culture has survived countless generations of foreign encroachment, and communities are just as committed to preserving their identity today as they were when the Spanish first arrived.

Economy

Until the late 1990s, the district's principal currency was the coconut. (In recent years the sale of *molas* has outpaced coconuts as the Kuna's number one revenue source.) The Kuna are coconut barons: a good year's harvest reaches more than 30 million. Coconuts are bartered to Colombians, whose old wooden schooners can hold 50,000 to 80,000 coconuts. In return, the Colombians provide clothing, coffee, vinegar, rice, sunglasses, canned milk, batteries, soups and other goods.

In Colombia the coconuts are exported or used in the production of candy, gelatin capsules, cookies, shampoos and other products. Colombia has many processing plants for coconuts, but Panama, oddly, has none.

Shrewd businesspeople, the Kuna regulate the price of coconuts on a yearly basis to prevent buyers from bargaining down individual sellers. Every year, Kuna chiefs agree on one price for coconuts. A Kuna found selling coconuts below or above price is severely punished by the community. By stabilizing the sale of coconuts and enforcing trade restrictions, the chiefs prevent price wars among the Kuna.

In another protectionist move, Kuna law prohibits outsiders from owning property in the district. A conscious move to ensure limitations on tourism in the region, the law also prevents foreigners from speculating on real estate and driving up living costs. Today, lodgings are 100% owned and managed by local Kuna families and are fairly uniform in offerings and quality.

🛏 Sleeping & Eating

Carefully selecting your accommodations on the islands is key, since their remoteness makes it difficult to change your mind. Camping on an uninhabited island isn't wise because you run the risk of encountering drug traffickers in the night. The Kuna do not allow the Panamanian coast guard or US antidrug vessels to operate in the archipelago, so the uninhabited islands are occasionally used by Colombian drug traffickers running cocaine up the coast.

There are only a handful of lodgings on the islands and none on the mainland. Most of these are basic but comfortable. Most densely populated islands in the district have a store selling basic items, as well as pay phones for domestic and international calls. The phones are public, but there's usually a Kuna standing nearby charging a telephone tax of US$1 per call or more. Cell phones may work in some areas.

Since there are almost no restaurants, each lodging provides meals for guests. They are usually seafood based, with lobster for extra. Quality varies, as some local fishing stocks have been depleted, but there is always a healthy supply of fresh coconuts.

🤿 Activities

Most lodgings offer complete packages, where a fixed price gets you a room, three meals a day and boat rides to neighboring islands for swimming, snorkeling and lounging on the beach. If you seek community life, you can also arrange visits to more populated islands. Before swimming off the shores of a heavily populated island, however, take a look at the number of outhouses built over the ocean – they may change your mind.

Snorkeling is good in places, but many coral reefs are badly damaged. You can often rent snorkeling equipment from your hotel. Serious snorkelers should bring their own gear. Jaunts to hike the mainland jungles are arranged with a guide. Most travelers are content with simply soaking up the Caribbean sun and perfecting their hammock-swaying.

🎊 Festivals & Events

Kuna Revolution of 1925   HISTORIC
One of the biggest holidays in Kuna Yala is the commemoration of the anniversary of the Kuna Revolution of 1925 on February 25. It marks the day when the Kuna rebelled against the Panamanian police occupying the islands, and expelled them from the Comarca. On Isla Tigre this event is remembered through an emotional reenactment of the rebellion.

Nogagope   DANCE
The Nogagope celebrates a traditional dance and takes place from October 10 to 12 on Isla Tigre. The event is marked by communities from outlying islands converging on the island and dancing for three days straight.

KUNA LIVING 101

Lodging considerations in the Comarca are vastly different from those on the mainland. Here, a spot in a thatched hut with sand floor can cost anywhere between US$30 to US$130 per night. So what's the difference?

Often it has more to do with access, ambience and organization than anything. Densely populated community islands are more likely to have budget options, but they will not live up to your image of a remote tropical paradise. Resort islands generally have a higher price tag, but may not offer many opportunities to interact with locals. When planning, consider why you're going and the following:

Space Does the island have shade? Privacy? Are there pleasant areas to swim or do you have to take a boat to swim and snorkel sites?

Access Is the island too remote, requiring expensive transfers to do anything?

Hospitality Ask other travelers about their experience.

Water Is it potable? Consider bringing a filter.

Bathrooms Are there modern installations or does the toilet sit at the end of a dock?

Safety Do excursion boats have life vests and good motors?

Lodgings generally include three meals (but not drinks), one outing per day (snorkeling or a community visit, for example) and transportation to or from the airport or Cartí, but do confirm ahead. Fees to visit Kuna islands and drinking water may be separate. It is always wise to bring snacks, insect repellent, a first-aid kit and a flashlight. Rates are generally lower from April to November.

When booking, remember that internet is not prevalent and any cell-phone number is only good until that phone accidentally falls into the ocean. But approach your hosts with good humor and patience, and they will probably reciprocate in spades.

The event is proceeded by a huge *feria* (festival) from October 13 to 16 that includes more dancing as well as art expositions and various games and canoe races.

🛍 Shopping

Molas are the most famous of Panamanian traditional handicrafts. Made of brightly colored squares of cotton fabric sewn together, the finished product reveals landscape scenes, birds, sea turtles, fish and beasts – often surrounded by a mazelike, geometric pattern. Traditional geometric designs are usually valued more than modern ones. Craftsmanship varies considerably. The simplest are peddled for upwards of $10; elaborate designs are works of art valued at several hundred dollars. You can find *molas* on the islands (or, rather, the *mola*-sellers will find you).

Mola work originated from the transfer of designs used for body painting to the cloth, particularly on blouses. When the Panamanian government tried to modernize the Kuna by prohibiting traditional dress, the *mola* emerged as a symbol of independence. Even when Kuna schools were administered by Panamanian officials, girls wore special *molas* in school colors as a sign of silent protest.

Today, there is a wonderful sense of pride among Kuna women regarding *molas*. In addition to being an integral part of the Kuna culture, *molas* are wholly unique to the Comarca.

Molas are classified by differences in the technical process:

Abiniguat One color; refers to a single layer of color sewn onto a base layer.

Obagalet Two colors; refers to two layers sewn onto a base layer.

Mor-Maralet A few colors; refers to two or more layers sewn onto a base layer.

Morgonikat Many colors; refers to two or more layers sewn onto a base layer with additional filler layers, embroidery and/ or appliqué.

ℹ Information

Flights are limited, so book as far in advance as possible. You should also reserve your hotels in advance, especially since package deals are the norm in the Comarca. There's no cash machine, so visit an ATM *before* reaching the islands.

From May through November temperatures are generally lower. When there's no breeze and the mercury rises, the humidity sets in and life on the

San Blás islands can cease to be paradise. During January and February the trade winds kick in.

In the Comarca it helps to have a good command of Spanish as few Kuna outside the tourist centers speak English. In fact, many older Kuna do not speak Spanish. In more remote areas your guide or boatman may have to do the talking for you. A few words of Kuna will win you friends and favors wherever you go.

The Kuna are very particular about what foreigners do on their islands. As a result, tourists must register and pay a visitation fee, between US$3 and US$12 per person, on nearly every island. The price varies and you're expected to pay regardless of whether you stay for a week or only half an hour. On smaller, privately owned islands, you must seek out the owner, obtain permission to stay and pay a fee of around US$5 per person.

Visitors are expected to pay to take photographs of the Kuna people (around US$1 per subject or photo). If you want to take someone's photo, ask his or her permission first. You may not be required to pay for a photograph taken of an artisan from whom you buy crafts, but it depends on the person. Some islands may charge you US$50 just for possessing a video camera.

❶ Getting There & Away

Previously, the only practical means of visiting the Comarca de Kuna Yala was to fly there, or to depart from a nearby port on a private sailboat. In 2009 a 4WD road was finished, linking the coast of Cartí to the Interamericana. Hired jeeps make the trip. At the northwest end of the province, El Porvenir is the gateway to the San Blás islands, and one of the most popular destinations for visitors. From here, boat transportation can be arranged to other islands, several of which have basic hotels. If you're planning on staying at any of the far-flung islands, you can also fly into one of several remote landing strips scattered throughout the Comarca.

A GUIDE TO THE KUNA LANGUAGE

Feeling a little tongue-tied? The following glossary will help you break the ice with the Kuna. Note: the second entry in all listings is Spanish, the third is Kuna.

Getting Started

Yes.	Sí.	Elle.
No.	No.	Suli.
Thanks.	Gracias.	Dot nuet.
Please.	Por favor.	Uis anga saet.
OK.	Esta bien.	Nued gudii o.
Good.	Bueno.	Nabir, nuedi.
Welcome.	Bienvenidos.	Nuegambi uese be noniki.

Greetings

Hello.	Hola.	Na.
How are you?	¿Como esta usted?	Bede nued guddi?
Fine, thank you. And you?	Bien, gracias. ¿Y usted?	An nuedi. Bedina?
Fine.	Bien.	Nuedi.
What is your name?	¿Cual es su nombre?	Igi be nuga?
My name is...	Mi nombre es...	An nuga...
Nice to meet you.	Encantado.	An yeel itoe.
Where are you from?	¿De dónde es usted?	Be bia lidi?
I am from...	Soy de...	An... ginedi.

Feelings

I'm hungry.	Tengo hambre.	An ukur itoe.
I'm thirsty.	Tengo sed.	An gobie.
I'm cold.	Tengo frío.	An dambe itoe.
I'm warm.	Tengo calor.	An uerba itoe.
I'm sleepy.	Estoy cansado.	An nue gapie.
I'm happy.	Estoy contento.	An yee ito dii.

AIR

Book as far in advance as possible as demand far exceeds supply. Note that planes may stop at several islands in the archipelago, loading and unloading passengers or cargo before continuing on.

Flights depart from Albrook airport in Panama City and take 30 minutes to an hour. A one-way ticket to each destination ranges from US$40 to US$80; prices vary according to season and availability.

Air Panama (⏰ 316-9000; www.airpanama. com) Daily flights to Achutupu, Cartí, Corazón de Jesús, Playón Chico and Río Sidra.

CAR

The El Llano–Cartí road is the only road that leads into the district. It connects the town of El Llano, on the Carretera Interamericana 70km east of Panama City, to the San Blás coastal hamlet of Cartí. The road begins near El Llano at the turnoff for Nusagandi.

It's best to take a shared 4WD with a powerful engine, a winch and good tires. Ask your Panama City hostel to arrange transportation. Both Kuna Yala Expeditions (p229) and driver **Germain Perez** (⏰ 6734-3454; http://cartihomestaykunayala.blogspot.com; per person US$25) offer transfers for US$50 round-trip, per person.

BOAT

Sailboats travel to Colombia via the archipelago, but most board in Colón Province. Lodgings in Panama City have more information about these privately run trips.

San Blas Adventures (The Darien Gapster; www. sanblasadventures.com; all-inclusive per person US$350) More of a tour than just transport, this popular new four-day service takes backpackers between Cartí and La Miel (the Colombian border), visiting Kuna communities, camping on beaches and snorkeling along the way. Fiberglass boats have outboard engines.

Useful Expressions

Let's go.	Vamos.	Anmar nae.
How much does this cost?	¿Cuánto cuesta?	Qui mani?
I want to buy it.	Quiero comprarlo.	An bag-bie.
Do you speak English?	¿Habla inglés?	Be sumake merki galla?
Come here.	Venga aquí.	Uesik dage.
Look at that.	Miralo.	Dake.
Speak slowly, please.	Hable despacio por favor.	Uis binna sunmake.
I don't understand.	No entiendo.	Aku ittoe.
I'm sorry.	Lo siento.	An oakue.
foreigner	extranjero	uaga

On the Plate

rice	arroz	oros
bread	pan	madu
fish	pescado	ua
lobster	langosta	dulup
coconut	coco	koibir
coffee	café	cabi

Saying Goodbye

Good bye.	Adiós.	Degi malo.
Good luck.	Buena suerte.	Nuedgine, nuegan bi.
I'll see you tomorrow.	Hasta manãna.	An banedse be dakoe.
I had a good time.	Me divertí.	An yer ittosa.

COMARCA DE KUNA YALA THE KUNA

A good alternative to the sailboat crossing (avoiding cramped overnight quarters) and rough seas. See the website for useful planning details.

ℹ Getting Around

Few of the islands in the archipelago are more than 10km from the district's mainland. All of the heavily inhabited islands are very close to the coast to permit access to agricultural areas and vital natural resources, such as water, firewood and construction materials. Also on the mainland are the giant trees from which the Kuna make their chief mode of transportation – the *cayuco* (a dugout canoe made from a burned and hollowed-out trunk). There are nine towns on the mainland, all within 100m of the sea, though there are no restaurants or hotels in these towns.

AIR

Inter-island flights are occasionally available, though it's a good idea to inquire directly at regional airstrips since schedules fluctuate wildly.

BOAT

Boatmen await the arrival of planes to shuttle people to their island destination (US$2 to US$80). If you want to travel by boat between island groups or explore some of the far-flung islets, you can either hire local guides at the docks or have your hotel make the arrangements.

Inquire about your ride in advance if you don't like small seacraft (some go quite slowly).

It is becoming more common to see pleasure yachts and sailboats in the region, though it is not without controversy. Upset at the perceived competition, the Kuna Congress is thinking of outlawing these 'floating hotels.' Yet individual Kunas who live in remote areas are often supportive, since the boats support locals by buying their produce and *molas*.

Cartí, El Porvenir & Around

Cartí

POP 400

Cartí is the collective name for a group of islands and a small strip of coast that is a 45-minute boat trip south of El Porvenir. If you've arrived in the Comarca by 4WD, the coastal hamlet of Cartí will be your first port of call. There is also a small airstrip (currently closed) just outside town.

Most places here are all in Cartí Suitupo or 'Crab Island,' a mere 100m from the mainland and one of the most densely populated islands in the Comarca: crowded as Manhattan

---

SAILING THE KUNA YALA TO COLOMBIA

If you're a backpacker or don't mind living like one in the name of adventure, consider this. Small sailboats can take passengers to Colombia via the scenic Archipiélago de San Blás for the same price as a flight. But the trip may not be for everyone.

Potential guests should know that these boats are not official charters. Passengers help out in exchange for cheap passage. But in exchange you usually get a few days of sun and sand in the San Blás, often with a snorkeling trip or two. The rough open-sea passage to Cartagena accounts for half the duration of the trip. Before you book, find out the following:

➡ Are accommodations a cabin or floor space?

➡ What is the size of boat and the number of passengers?

➡ Is the boat equipped with adequate life boats and life vests for all passengers?

➡ Does it have an adequate safety equipment and a functioning radio?

➡ Does the captain have a charter license?

➡ What are the meals like? (Some boats serve beans and rice three times a day.)

We have heard happy reports, but travelers have also complained about boats skimping on meals, overcrowding or traveling despite bad weather in order to fit in more trips. Bring snacks and ask ahead whether the boat needs fresh groceries (hard to stock when boats spend extended periods in the islands). Don't skimp on research – check a boat or captain's existing references with hostels and other travelers before committing. If you are only traveling for the novelty of sailing, consider a trip that sticks to the Kuna Yala.

The best place to inquire about scheduled departures is at any of the youth hostels in Panama City. A typical five-day sailing trip including food and activities (but not island fees) costs around US$500. Another alternative is the motorboat trip offered by San Blas Adventures (p227), which stops to camp on beaches.

at rush hour and terribly polluted. Although there are plenty of other real estate options in the area, islanders have it easy here, especially since Cartí Suitupo is a popular port of call for cruise ships. Be warned that if there's a cruise ship docked here, your cultural experience will take on a whole new definition.

The small **museum** (☑6085-9592; admission US$3; ☉8am-4pm) offers a better cultural and historical understanding of the Kuna. A guided tour with Delfino Davies (he speaks some English) will elucidate everything from Kuna coming-of-age rituals to funerary rites. For general tours, contact Kuna guide **Hernan Martinez** (☑6517-7417), who speaks English.

Cartí Suitupo also serves as a base for exploring nearby **Isla Aguja** (Needle Island), a picture-perfect retreat with lazy palms, golden sands and gentle surf.

🛏 Sleeping

Cartí Homestay   HOSTEL **$**
(☑6517-9850, 6734-3454; www.cartihomestayku nayala.blogspot.com; r per person all inclusive US$35; @) Catering to backpackers, Cartí Homestay is the best place around to meet young Kunas and strike up a conversation, though the inflatable Jägermeister bottle in the corner is a good indicator of the kind of cultural interactions you might expect. Internet (via stick modem) is US$1 per hour. The hosts can also coordinate speedboats to Puerto Obaldia for Colombia-bound travelers.

Dormitory Cartí Sugdup   HOSTEL **$**
(☑6755-5066; r per person US$8) Nothing is cheaper than this 2nd-story flophouse facing a dock on Cartí Suitupo, with a leaky roof and passable shared facilities. Food is available downstairs.

El Porvenir

POP 2000

Situated at the northwestern end of the Comarca, El Porvenir was long considered the gateway to the Archipiélago de San Blás. At the time of writing, flights were suspended, but this may change in the future. In addition to a landing strip and a dock, the town boasts a police station and two (sometimes working) public phones.

☉ Sights

Porvenir Museum   MUSEUM
(admission US$2) This small museum features models of a Kuna burial site, a cooking area and community congress along with photos and artifacts. It is worth employing a guide to explain the items. To visit, find someone on the island to unlock it.

🛏 Sleeping

El Porvenir Hotel   HOTEL
(☑6692-3542; r per person all inclusive US$45) Although there's little reason to spend the night here, if flights resume, El Porvenir Hotel has worn but serviceable motel-style rooms with electricity. The sprawling lawn is attractive, but you are neither mired in the cultural aspects of a community island or enjoying the isolation of a resort island.

Corbiski

Corbiski (aka Pelican Island) is a populated community island with plenty of opportunities to interact with locals in a friendly atmosphere. While it's a convenient place to set off on snorkeling trips, Corbiski does not have great swimming or snorkeling off the island itself.

English-speaking local entrepreneur Elías Perez at **Kuna Yala Expeditions** (☑6708-5254) offers day tours in covered *pangas* (small motorboat) with fast, two-stroke motors. Excursions include kayaking mangroves (US$50 per person), a visit to the mainland cemetery and hike (US$5 per person) and snorkeling Cayo Holandeses (US$50 per person, four passengers minimum). Though service is good, the boating can be a bit fast. Bottled water is included. They also offer camping (US$55 per person) with tent and boat transfer included.

Hotel Corbiski (☑6708-5254; www.corbiski. com; r without bathroom per person all inclusive US$65) offers bamboo-walled lodging with laminated floors and neat, spacious rooms. Clean shared bathrooms occupy cement stalls. Lodgings include purified water and transportation to and from Cartí or El Porvenir. The owner, Elias Pérez, is the school principal; travelers interested in volunteering at the school are encouraged to contact him.

Nalunega

POP 500

With a name that translates to mean 'Red Snapper Island,' it's no wonder that Nalunega's inhabitants spend most of their days fishing the surrounding seas. However, tourism has played an important role on this community

RESPONSIBLE TRAVEL IN KUNA YALA

When visiting the Comarca de Kuna Yala, consider how your visit may affect the community. Tourism revenue can play a vital role in the development of the region, particularly if you are buying locally produced crafts or contracting the services of a Kuna guide. However, Western interests have already caused an irreversible amount of damage to the region. Go aware of your surroundings, and sensitive towards your impact.

One look at the paradisiacal setting, the rainbow flag and the distinctive Kuna dress and you might feel transported into the pages of *National Geographic*. Don't snap that shutter just yet. If the Kuna appear unfriendly, consider their predicament. When cruise ships visit, the number of people on an already congested island can triple. Nonetheless, nearly two-thirds of the populace (the tourists) turns paparazzi on the other third (the Kuna). It's an unsavory scene repeated again and again.

Trash is a problem on the islands, and there is no effective plan for its removal. For the Kunas, the cost of removal to the mainland is too high, and there is no designated site or 'culture' of waste management, since all refuse was relatively innocuous until outside influence prevailed. You may see litter and burning piles of plastics. With no current solution to the issue, do what you can to pack out your own garbage, if necessary, and try to consume fresh products with minimal packaging – ie choose coconut water over cola.

The way you dress (or fail to) is another issue. Kuna men never go shirtless and Kuna women dress conservatively, with their cleavage, bellies and most of their legs covered. Arriving in Kuna villages in bikinis or shirtless is interpreted as a sign of disrespect. In general, it is not worth risking offending local sensibilities.

To rein in the situation, the Kuna charge fees for photographs taken of them as well as visitation fees for each island. Forget the way things work back home. Remember this is their territory and their rules apply. If you can't afford the photo fee, just tuck away your camera and strike up a conversation instead.

island for decades, mainly because Nalunega is home to the Comarca's oldest hotel.

Unfortunately, the 1972 Hotel San Blás (6705-3820; r without bathroom per person all inclusive US$50) has been temporarily closed but plans to reopen. Installations are pretty basic. While this isn't a destination hotel, it is handy if you arrive too late for a boat transfer further afield.

Wichub-Walá

POP 100

Just a five-minute boat ride from El Porvenir, the community island of Wichub-Walá is often touted by travelers as a good place to meet and interact with the Kuna. People here are friendly but not as overtly commercial as islanders living closer to the road at Cartí.

Reached via a sandy labyrinth through thatched dwellings and alleyway soccer matches, Kuna Niskua Lodge (225-5200; r per person all inclusive US$80) is a two-story thatch and bamboo structure. Though undergoing some renovation, it's utterly basic, with electricity only at night, cold water and no door locks. The host may be scarce, so guests need to be independent. Yet the

charm of surrounding street life is infectious. Transfer from Cartí is included.

East Lemons

A lovely island chain popular with yachts (there's a mooring close to a good scuba site), visitors are likely to spend time here if traveling by sailboat.

Visitors here may be approached by a motorized dugout canoe with traveling master *mola* maker Venancio Restrepo (6500-7302). He carries buckets of beautiful *molas* (US$20 to US$70) made by himself or others.

Isla Banedup

Sailboats moor alongside this tiny private isle, where you can stop by for seafood meals (US$10) at Banedup (6962-4668; www.diagditours.com; cabin per person all inclusive US$120). This family-run island with freshwater sinkhole recently added three cabins. The price tag is on the high end, possibly because you get the hospitality of Hilario, a gregarious young entrepreneur and super-host who studies tourism in the capital. Tours include snorkeling Isla Perra and Isla Pelicano.

Río Sidra & Nearby Islands

Río Sidra

Located 15km east of Cartí Suitupo, Río Sidra serves as a secondary gateway to the Archipiélago de San Blás. Like El Porvenir, Río Sidra's small dock isn't too far from the airport and it's quick and easy to hop on a boat elsewhere. That 'elsewhere' is usually Kuanidup Grande, Naranjo Chico or the far-flung Cayos Los Grullos, Holandeses and Ordupuquip.

Río Sidra is extremely congested and the effects of Westernization are more prevalent here than on other islands (50 Cent isn't exactly traditional Kuna music). If you do need to spend the night, there are a few rooms for rent in the community of Mamartupo, though don't expect anything too comfortable.

Local historian and master *mola*-maker Lisa Harris (☑6753-2085) offers a recommended walking tour (US$20 per person, minimum four people) on the mainland to a waterfall, with a focus on birds, medicinal plants and Kuna legends. Her *molas* receive wide acclaim; some are quite affordable. Any local can point you to her house, but try to make contact in advance.

Kuanidup Grande

Just 30 minutes by motorized *cayuco* from Río Sidra, the tiny islet of Kuanidup Grande is only large in comparison to its nearby kid brother, Kuandip Chico. In fact, the only residents of Kuanidup Grande, aside from the guests lucky enough to be staying here, are some lazy iguanas and a few flocks of birds. Simply put, Kuanidup Grande is breathtaking – with manicured grounds, pristine beaches of powdery white sand, swaying coconut palms and little else.

At Cabañas Kuanidup (☑6742-7656, 6635-6737; www.kuanidup.com; r per person all inclusive US$90) you will find a clutch of solar-powered bamboo-and-thatch cabins with sandy floors and private bathrooms. Outings include a waterfall hike, and a visit to the prized Cayos Holandeses or a nearby nudist island. The clincher is a stunning beach. There's billiards and volleyball, but most guests pass the time by simply swinging in the hammocks and meditating to the sounds of the lapping waves.

Some huts have tarps under the thatch, which kills a bit of the ambience. But it's well managed, with secure boats, a septic system and purified drinking water included. Regional transportation is included.

Isla Senidup

A tiny islet divided by chain-link fence, this is a popular destination for backpackers.

🛏 Sleeping

Cabañas Franklin　　　　　　CABIN $
(Tuba Senika; ☑6902-2863; dm US$26, cabin per person US$30) Franklin is a bit of a personality among Kunas, a blue-eyed older gent conversant in English and with signs in Hebrew in his thatched office. His lodging is consistently popular, with cabins scattered under palms, cement and tiled stall bathrooms and sand that is regularly raked.

Guests play volleyball in the water, but also can partake of snorkeling excursions (US$6). Transfers are extra (US$20 round-trip).

Cabañas Senidup　　　　　　CABIN $
(☑6945-4301, 6513-0091; cabanas_senidub@hotmail.com; dm US$26, cabin per person all inclusive US$31) This place is less popular than the competition, though the lodgings are comparable. Dorms seem a little crowded, however. Usually there is one host on site who speaks English. Guests also have access to beach games and volleyball and free use of snorkel gear. Of course, lobster is extra.

Transfers to Cartí run US$20 round-trip.

Naranjo Chico

Three kilometers northwest of Río Sidra is the island of Naranjo Chico, Little Orange or Narascandub Pipi, depending on who you ask. Naranjo Chico is a mix between a community and resort island – it is populated, but it's also possible to find solitude.

🛏 Sleeping

Robinson's Cabins　　　　　　CABIN $
(☑6721-9885; r per person all inclusive US$30) For shoestringers who want nothing more than some thatch over their head and sand beneath their toes, this is it. The charismatic Robinson is good for wacky conversation – he studied in the US and has plenty to say. There is little to do here, but dining outdoors around the picnic table provides the perfect opportunity to mix with fellow travelers.

In low season, rates are discounted but transfers to Cartí (US$15) are charged separately. If Robinson is full, his cousin

Ina's place next door offers identical rates and lodgings. Having moved from a previous location known as Robinson's Island, the location can be confusing for boat drivers.

Cabañas Narascandub Pipi CABIN $$
(☑6501-6033, 256-6239; r per person all inclusive US$65) These decent cabins offer quiet with a lovely swimming beach. Robinson's Cabins occupies the other side of the island

The Cays

The undisputed gems of the Archipiélago de San Blás are the Cayos Los Grullos, Holandeses and Ordupuquip, a triangle of three virtually uninhabited island chains that are separated by calm blue-green waters and surrounded by shallow reefs. At the lower left corner of the triangle are the Cayos Los Grullos, which are a mere 10km northwest of Río Sidra. Heading clockwise, the tip of the triangle is formed by the Cayos Holandeses (Dutchmen Keys), while the Cayos Ordupuquip are located in the southeastern corner. Despite the lack of tourist facilities in the cays, yachties love to anchor near these islands, though it takes skill behind the wheel to keep your boat afloat here.

Approximately 100m north of Cayos Holandeses is a spot known as Wreck Reef, which earned its name by snaring all kinds of vessels over the years. The reef's notoriety stems from the fact that it's fairly far offshore from the closest island, though the water south of the reef is barely 1m deep – the ocean floor north of the reef plunges 100m in half that distance. From a captain's perspective, this means that the ocean floor rises 100m to a dangerously shallow depth in half that distance.

Over the years, many experienced sailors have met their end here, though these days it's mostly smugglers that meet their doom. In 1995 a smuggler's boat filled with TV sets slammed into the reef at night. Although the smugglers had hoped to skip out on import taxes by sailing from Colón's Zona Libre to Cartagena, Colombia, they instead helped the local Kuna communities catch up with their favorite Venezuelan soap operas without paying a cent.

Unless you're on an organized tour – or you have your own yacht – you're going to need to hire a boat and a guide to come out here. Depending on the distance between your hotel and your destination, you can expect to pay between US$50 and US$100 round trip to reach the cays. Be aware that the seas can get very rough out here, so make sure you have confidence in the seaworthiness of your captain and his vessel. You're also going to want to make sure there are enough life jackets on board for everyone – and don't forget your snorkeling gear! Needless to say, the snorkeling in the Cayos Holandeses is astounding, though you'll see plenty of tropical fish and colorful reefs anywhere in the cays.

Corazón de Jesús & Nearby Islands

Corazón de Jesús & Narganá

The densely populated islands of Corazón de Jesús and Narganá, which are linked by an arcing wooden footbridge, are of little interest to travelers, especially since they're the most Westernized Kuna communities in the Comarca. Here Kuna families inhabit concrete cinderblock houses, wear Western clothing and hold all-island baseball tournaments. People are friendly and the visit makes an interesting contrast to some of the more traditional islands.

For travelers arriving by plane from Panama City, the coastal airstrip in Corazón de Jesús serves as a gateway to nearby Isla Tigre, one of the most traditional islands in Comarca, just 7km east of Narganá.

At the southwestern end of the bridge is the island of Narganá. It's home to the district's only courthouse and jail, so there are a lot of policemen on the island. If any ask for your passport, politely present it – jotting down tourists' names in little books gives them something to do.

Banco Nacional de Panamá (Narganá; ☺8am-3pm Mon-Fri, 9am-noon Sat) changes large bills and cashes Amex traveler's checks for a nominal fee. There is no ATM.

In 'downtown' Nargana, **Hospedaje Noris** (☑6099-7706, 6039-6842; s/d with fan US$10/20, with air-con US$15/30; ❄) will do if you find yourself stuck waiting for a flight. Otherwise, the two-story concrete hotel is rather musty. Consider the air-con the best few extra bucks you ever spent. Ask for the owner Paco at the public dock.

Isla Waidup

This tiny private isle is a stone's throw from Narganá.

CHOCOSANOS

Historically, most of the boats claimed by Wreck Reef were the victims of *chocosanos* – 'storms that come from the east' in Kuna. *Chocosanos* are ghastly tempests that whip up monstrous waves that can overrun entire islands. Such waves have swept many Kuna and their homes out to sea, though there are early warning signs, such as a purple-black easterly sky and a lack of breeze and birdsong.

When a *chocosano* is approaching, Kuna elders traditionally combat the storm by blowing into conch shells. The sound alerts their benevolent god, Paba Tummat, who tries to intervene and disperse the *chocosano*.

At the southern end of Wreck Reef, a freighter lies with its hull fully exposed and its deck flat against the ocean floor – a hulking vessel that was once flipped like a pancake by a mighty *chocosano*.

Waidup Lodge   CABIN **$$**
(☑ 6103-0436, 6044-2691, 225-7619; per person all inclusive US$75) Three simple cabins on stilts work their charm with good mattresses, woven fiber walls and waterfront balconies. Recently built, it features modern bathrooms in the rooms (but water is unheated). Still, it's more private than other spots. A small bar-restaurant is at your service and the water is swimmable. Tours go to nearby Isla Tigre.

Isla Tigre

Just a short boat ride from Corazón de Jesús and Narganá, Isla Tigre ranks among the most traditional islands in the Comarca – though the whole island is lit with solar energy. With wide walkways separating homes, the island is tidy and uncrowded, which makes it easy to interact with local Kuna. However, an island guide must accompany visitors. Isla Tigre is also home to some of the biggest festivals and events in the Comarca. Traditional dances are performed free of charge but visitors should offer a tip.

A water taxi from Corazón de Jesús should run US$30 for two passengers.

Cabañas Tigre   CABIN **$**
(☑ 6099-2738; r per person US$10, child US$5; meals from US$4) The best feature here is the chill reception – guests have their own ample space but also get to see a fair amount of typical village life, with locals who are more open and relaxed toward travelers than elsewhere. They also recycle. Pleasant beachside *cabañas* have cement floors, colorful hammocks and shared facilities.

The ocean here is crystal clear and fairly placid, perfect for kayaking (from December to June) or snorkeling. Tigre has three new bamboo-and-thatch cabins under construction, which will raise rates since they feature private bathrooms. Snorkel gear (US$2) and meals are extra (US$4 to US$25), the highest prices are for lobster.

Playón Chico & Nearby Islands

Playón Chico

With regular air connections to Panama City, Playón Chico serves as a popular gateway to San Blás, especially since it's located near the archipelago's most expensive hotel on Isla Iskardup. If you're looking for more modestly priced accommodations, Playón Chico also serves as a convenient jumping-off point for nearby Yandup.

While much of the island is still covered by traditional dwellings, the main drag in Playón Chico is home to everything from missionaries and concrete churches to video shops and liquor stores. Although Playón Chico isn't set up to receive tourists, a quick stroll from the airstrip to the docks reveals the conflicting pressures shaping modern Kuna life.

Yandup

Just five minutes by boat from Playon Chico, the tiny islet of Yandup is home to the recommended **Yandup Lodge** (☑ 261-7229; www.yandupisland.com; s/d cabin all inclusive US$160/230), run by a very attentive Spanish-Kuna family. Accommodations are simple but comprise lovely octagonal thatched-roof cabins with private bathrooms. Light comes from solar panels and water from the mainland. The island's grassy grounds, palm shade and powder-fine beach might be reason enough to just stay put.

Guests can be catered to with vegetarian meals and tailored excursions, which include cultural visits as well as the usual snorkeling and hiking.

Isla Iskardup

This picturesque private island features minimal infrastructure. Gorgeous *molas* and traditional handicrafts bring the clutch of thatched waterfront cabins at Sapibenega (Kuna Lodge; ☑ 215-3724, 215-1406; www.sapibenega.com; s/d/tr all inclusive US$185/260/315) to life. Yet, lovely as it is, it is not so different from other options half the price. They also feature plank floors and bamboo walls. Solar-powered electricity and composting flush toilets provide creature comforts. The breezy bar-restaurant serves scrumptious seafood spreads and cocktails made to order.

Guests should fly into Playón Chico, from where it's a 10-minute motor canoe ride to the island.

Achutupu & Nearby Islands

Achutupu

With regular air connections to Panama City, Achutupu (like Playón Chico to the west) serves as a popular gateway to San Blás, especially since it's located near the archipelago's second most expensive hotel (on Uaguitupo).

Although the densely populated island of Achutupu isn't set up to receive overnight visitors, it's a popular day trip for visitors from Uaguitupo who are interested in seeing Kuna village life. Of particular interest is the community gathering house at the center of the island, which often hosts important meetings, rituals and celebrations.

Uaguitupo

Although it's a mere 100m from Achutupu, the grassy isle of Uaguitupo is a private and pristine island aimed at high-rolling travelers. Visitors can fly into the nearby airport of Mamitupu.

Much more relaxed and traditional than its upmarket brethren, Dolphin Lodge (Uaguinega Lodge; ☑ 6090-8990, 396-4805; www.dolphinlodgesanblas.com; s/d/tr all inclusive US$155/250/300; @) receives rave reviews

and many repeat visitors. Taking up virtually all of Uaguitupo, it features a clutch of handsome thatched cabins with wooden floors and wicker furniture. Rooms feature cold-water showers, 24-hour solar electricity and environmentally-friendly flush toilets.

A great spot to kick back, the breezy restaurant faces the breakers. The English-speaking staff is extremely attentive to guests, especially if you're looking to hire a boat to explore the surrounding area.

Akwadup

Pretty and petite, this palm-frond isle is well removed from the usual tourist route, but the breezy mint-green octagonal cabins over the waterfront at Akwadup Lodge (☑ 396-4805; www.sanblaslodge.com; s/d/tr all inclusive US$185/320/390; @) might make you think you're in the Bocas. The private decks beckon you to laze away the sunset with beer in hand – although romance might be your agenda if you've come all the way to the middle of palm-frond nowhere. These so-secluded lodgings represent the top-end of offerings in the archipelago: fine Kuna hospitality and fussy details (by local standards) include vaulted thatched ceilings, fully functioning private bathrooms, screened doors and 24-hour electricity.

Dining is fresh and simple, featuring local ingredients like lobster, fish, yucca and coconut. Excursions – including cultural visits, snorkeling and fishing – are handily nearby.

Beyond Achutupu

Those sailing to Colombia should be advised that tourist infrastructure is virtually nonexistent west of Achutupu and Uaguitupo. Scenery is striking, and although several islands allow foreigners, the southern stretches of the Comarca are mostly off-limits.

Be advised that the ocean can be treacherous here, particularly further away from the islands in open water. Here, 3m swells are the norm, worse if there's a storm. If you've been frightened by the sea in other parts of the archipelago, you can expect to be terrified here. Again, if you plan to travel these waters and have any doubts about your boatman, consider hiring another one before attempting this trip.

Darién Province

POP 47,000 / ELEV SEA LEVEL TO 3478M / AREA 8653 SQ KM

Best Off-the Beaten Path Spots

➡ Parque Nacional Darién (p245)

➡ Sambú (p244)

➡ Pacific Coast (p245)

➡ Río Sambú (p244)

Best Places to Stay

➡ Filo de Tallo (p240)

➡ Sambu House (p245)

➡ Punta Patiño Lodge (p243)

➡ Tropic Star Lodge (p245)

Why Go?

One of world's richest biomes is the 5760-sq-km Parque Nacional Darién, where the primeval meets the present with scenery nearly unaltered from one million years ago. Even today in the Darién, the Emberá and Wounaan people maintain many of their traditional practices and retain generations-old knowledge of the rainforest. In a stroke of irony, the Darién has remained so pristine because of its volatile reputation.

But while the southern Darién is home to Panama's most spectacular rainforests, the north is home to scenes of habitat destruction. Safety is a real concern here, yet the region's issues are complex and require careful consideration. It is not for everyone, but with careful planning and the right destinations, the Darién offers spectacular opportunities for intrepid travelers yearning for something truly wild.

When to Go

➡ Travelers to the Darien should always check on current security issues before going.

➡ **Dec–April** Less precipitation makes dry season the best time to hit trails that will turn muddy and unstable during rainy season. Travel connections are also more reliable.

➡ **May, Oct–Nov** With rivers running high and heavy rainfall, these months are generally the most difficult time to visit the region.

➡ **Year-round** Multiday sailboat charters and backpacker boat shuttles between San Blas and Colombia touch down in Puerto Obaldia for border crossing.

Darién Province Highlights

① Search for capybara while exploring the lush jungle reserve of **Reserva Natural Punta Patiño** (p243) on the edge of Golfo de San Miguel

② Hike along the spectacular jungle trails surrounding **Rancho Frío** (p246), a ranger station on the edge of Parque Nacional Darién

③ Look for harpy eagles and interact with the Emberá around **Mogué** (p243), a traditional village by the Río Mogué

④ Enjoy excursions into indigenous communities and the dreamy savannah-like setting of ecolodge **Filo de Tallo** (p240)

⑤ Go for a world record at the **Tropic Star Lodge** (p245), a remote fishing lodge that's the site of some of the world's largest catches

History

Living within the boundaries of the Darién, the group commonly known as the Chocóes emigrated from Colombia's Chocó region long ago. Anthropologists use two linguistic groups – the Emberá and the Wounaan – though, with the exception of language, the groups' cultural features are virtually identical. Both groups prefer to be thought of as two separate peoples.

Before the introduction of guns, the Emberá and Wounaan were experts with the *boroquera* (blowgun), using envenomed darts with lethal toxins from poisonous frogs and bullet ants. Many scholars believe that they forced the Kuna out of the Darién and into the Caribbean coastal area they now inhabit.

The Emberá and Wounaan are known for their incredibly fine dugout canoes. Known as *piraguas,* their shallow bottoms are ideal for dry season when rivers run low. The Panama Canal Authority has long employed Emberá and Wounaan craftsmen to make the *piraguas* which are used by officials to reach upper parts of the canal's watershed. Until the late 1990s, the US Air Force solicited the Emberá and Wounaan for help with jungle living. Many of them trained US astronauts and air-force pilots at Fuerte Sherman, near Colón, in tropical wilderness survival.

Today, the majority of the 8000 Emberá and Wounaan in Panama live deep in the rainforests of the Darién, particularly along the Ríos Sambú, Jaqué, Chico, Tuquesa, Membrillo, Tuira, Yapé and Tucutí.

Culture

The Emberá and Wounaan survive on subsistence agriculture supplemented by limited fishing and poultry raising. Historically, both groups were more reliant on slash-and-burn agriculture and hunting, which are practices now restricted in the national park. Increased commercial rice and maize plantations offer work for seasonal migrant laborers.

The Emberá and Wounaan are also exceptional woodcarvers and basket weavers. Boas, frogs and birds are traditionally carved from dark cocobolo hardwood; now tiny animal figurines are also made from tagua nuts. The women produce some of the finest baskets in Latin America. Woven from palm fibers, each requires months of intensive labor. These products fetch a high market price, and provide a much-needed secondary income for most communities.

Emberá and Wounaan homes are extremely well-suited to the rainforest. Built on stilts 3m to 4m off the ground, flooring uses thin, strong, strips of plentiful palm bark. The vaulted design protects occupants and food from ground pests and swollen rivers. Beneath, medicinal plants and edible vegetables and roots are grown. Many homes are thatched and open-sided for breezes, with mud ovens.

Western clothing is replacing traditional attire, except for older individuals. Women, who traditionally wore only a skirt, increasingly don bras and shirts. Many wear traditional jewelry, especially wide silver bracelets and elaborate silver-coin necklaces. They also stain their bodies with purplish black designs made with juice from the jagua fruit. The dye is believed to have health-giving properties and wards off insects.

Like the Kuna, the Emberá and Wounaan have a strong measure of political autonomy, though under threat of increasing external pressures. These include encroachment by Latino settlers and habitat destruction by loggers, accelerated in recent years due to the paving of the Interamericana. Missionaries, particularly evangelicals, have almost entirely eliminated the core religious values of both groups. Youth flee to the cities for employment prospects, which has prompted fears that both cultures are dwindling fast.

☞ Tours

The Darién is the only major part of Panama where a guide is necessary. If you speak Spanish, you can hire guides locally for about US$20 to US$30 per day. However, transportation costs can be very expensive. If you go with a tour operator, they will take care of all arrangements without a language barrier, teach you about the incredible local ecology, cook for you and humor you when you have blisters. Another option is to go with an independent guide.

★ **Jungle Treks** ADVENTURE TOUR
(☑ 6438-3130; www.jungletreks.com) Run by a veteran naturalist guide, this recommended outfitter specializes in expedition-style travel for groups of six or more. Destinations include Río Sambú and the Pacific coast. Custom trips are possible, with a three-day minimum. English-speaking.

Ancon Expeditions GUIDED TOUR
(☑ 269-9415; www.anconexpeditions.com) The sole operator in the Darién for many years, Ancon

is highly recommended for the quality and professionalism of their tours. Trips run from four days to two weeks. Destinations include Ancon's private lodge in Punta Patiño on the Pacific coast, the Río Sambú area and remote indigenous communities. Special programs for bird-watchers and hikers are excellent.

Panama Exotic Adventures   TOUR
(☐ in Panama City 223-9283; www.panamaexotic adventures.com) With an ecolodge in Metetí and longtime experience in the region, this French-run outfit offers three- to eight-day trips with hands-on visits to indigenous communities, kayaking and outings. Ask about tailor-made trips.

ℹ️ Information

Printed information on the Darién becomes rapidly outdated. Always seek up-to-date information, usually best from a guide who leads frequent trips to the area.

Local Autoridad Nacional del Ambiente (ANAM; National Environment Authority) offices in towns such as Yaviza or La Palma can provide some information on the park and potentially help you find guides (usually rangers with days off). Travelers must also check in with the police in these towns before heading out into the jungle.

Panama City's Instituto Geográfico Nacional usually sells topographical maps for some regions of the Darién.

DANGERS & ANNOYANCES

The greatest hazard in the Darién is the difficult environment. Trails, when they exist at all, are often poorly defined and are never marked. The many large rivers that form the backbone of the Darién transportation network create their own hazards. Any help at all, much less medical help, is very far away. If you get lost, you are done for. To minimize these risks, it's recommended that you explore the Darién either as part of an organized tour or with the help of a qualified guide.

Dengue and malaria are serious risks. Consult your doctor before you go about necessary medication, and cover up as much as possible, especially at dawn and dusk. Areas of the Parque Nacional Darién are prime territory for the deadly fer-de-lance snake. Odds of getting a snake bite are low, but be careful and always wear boots on treks. Although they don't carry Lyme disease, ticks are widespread. Bring tweezers and a few books of matches to ensure you're able to remove the entire tick if it's burrowed well into your skin.

The US State Department warns travelers against visiting remote areas of the Darién off the Interamericana. This blanket advisory includes the entirety of Parque Nacional Darién, although certain destinations may be OK to visit.

Particularly treacherous, however, are the areas between Boca de Cupe and Colombia, the traditional path through the Darién Gap. With minimal police presence, you're on your own when trouble arises. Avoid Balsal, El Naranjal, Púcuro, Limón, Paya and Palo de las Letras. The areas north and east of these towns are also considered dangerous, including the mountains Altos de Limón, the Río Tuquesa and the trail from Puerto Obaldía.

Although the no-go zones in the Darién are well removed from the traditional tourist destinations, their dangers cannot be underestimated. Narco-traffickers who utilize these jungle routes don't appreciate encountering travelers trekking through the woods. Parts of the Darién Gap are areas of activity for former Colombian guerrillas or runaways. Missionaries and travelers alike have been kidnapped and killed in the southern area of the Darién.

Despite these warnings, parts of the Darién can be visited safely.

ℹ️ Getting There & Away

The Interamericana terminates 266km from Panama City in the frontier town of Yaviza – the vast wilderness region of the Darién lies beyond. The highway starts again 150km further on in Colombia. This break between Central and South America is known as the Darién Gap – literally the end of the road.

There are eight buses daily from Panama City to Yaviza between 3:30am and 7am (US$16, 4.5 hours). Be sure to tell the bus driver your destination.

With irregular frequency, **Air Panama** (☐ 316-9000; www.flyairpanama.com) has flights to Jaqué, El Real Sambú and Puerto Obaldia. There is also a ferry from Panama City to La Palma.

ℹ️ Getting Around

In the vast jungles of the Darién Province, rivers are often the only means of travel, with piraguas providing the transport. In La Palma you can hire a motorized boat for US$175 to US$200 per day, which can take you to the Río Mogué or the Río Sambú. From either of these rivers you'll have to negotiate with indigenous villagers (in Mogué or La Chunga) to take you further upriver in piraguas. A boat can be hired from Puerto Quimba to La Palma.

THE ROAD TO YAVIZA

The Interamericana runs from Panamá Province along the spine of the Darién Province, with Yaviza the end of the road (for now). Police checkpoints are frequent on this road, so have your passport ready and be prepared

SURVIVING THE DARIÉN

Parque Nacional Darién is the most ecologically diverse land-based national park in all Central America, yet it is also one of the least-visited parks. Chalk it up to reputation – with its high stakes and poisonous snakes, the Darién isn't for all. Yet as a destination it is fascinating and fulfilling – provided you are prepared and take the necessary precautions.

Security
In years past the Darién has proved the perfect hideout for armed groups coming to rest from military action in Colombia. Today, as Colombia stabilizes, this infiltration is less of an issue, but the jungle is still an ideal hideout for rogue factors. The Panamanian police take defending the area very seriously and it's unwise to go against their recommendations.

When planning your trip, first consider your destination. Established routes are recommended both for your safety and for legal reasons. The police have been known to detain those on unauthorized routes, suspecting their activity – even if they are with a guide.

Safety
Even if you have crossed Central America by bus alone, solo travel here is not recommended. First off, trails are unmarked and it is terribly easy to get lost. No one is likely to come to your aid. But you might also find poisonous snakes and scorpions – who could end your trip (or your time on earth) unexpectedly.

Preparations
Though remote, the Darién is not cheap. Travelers should make a careful trip budget. Most people that are loath to take tours do so here. Decide whether going with an independent guide and paying all the fuel and food costs separately will really work out to your advantage – since the cost of fuel can be astronomical. Those who contract a local guide should speak Spanish, otherwise the whole endeavor is prone to frustrating misunderstandings. If problems arise, speaking Spanish will help you find the solution.

Keep your baggage to a minimum on any jungle trek. You will need insect repellent, sun block, a hat and rain gear. Food can only be found in the few towns and it is not available at the ranger stations. Bring some drinking water and a means of purifying water.

Plan your trip to coincide with the dry season (mid-December to mid-April); otherwise, you'll be slogging your way through thick mud being attacked by moth-sized mosquitoes.

Engines break, flights are delayed, in short: travel delays are about as common as raindrops in the Darién. Go with extra food and cash, a flashlight, matches, good personal equipment and flexibility in your schedule.

Guides
Paying more usually means getting more. A naturalist guide will have a different skill set than a *guía local* (local guide). Consider your needs and criteria when making a selection. The following are essential:

➡ Experience in the area, and extensive local contacts and problem-solving skills

➡ A planned itinerary with realistic travel times and contracted transportation

➡ Good equipment (tents etc) if you do not have your own. and any necessary permits

The following are desired:

➡ Skill at spotting animals

➡ Knowledge of local history, animals and plants

➡ Knowledge of English (or another language)

➡ First-aid kit and skills

➡ Handheld radio and/or cell phone for areas with coverage

Fellow travelers can be excellent guide references, but it is important to meet your guide – particularly if you will be traveling solo. If contracting your guide in the Darién, converse with locals, find someone you trust and ask them for references.

Find out ahead of time if gas, transportation, food and fees are included. Don't assume that a local guide is experienced – some have sold trips despite never having set foot in the national park. ANAM (📞299-4495) is a good point of reference.

DEFORESTATION IN THE DARIÉN

As little as 50 years ago, more than 70% of Panama was covered by forest. Deforestation is the country's gravest environmental problem. Today, trees continue to be felled at a rapid pace, with the Darién serving as the ecological ground zero.

Logging trucks and river barges move the trunks to mills. Floated lumber is sprayed with a chemical that prevents rot but also wreaks havoc on the local environment, particularly on the health of agricultural plots and fish stocks.

At stake are not only local animal populations, but also migratory animals seeking seasonal food supplies. Rainforest destruction also threatens the traditional cultures of the Emberá and the Wounaan. Deforestation results in regional water shortages during the dry season, as well as number of other environmental problems ranging from pollution to erosion.

For much of the rural population, hunting and logging have been a way of life for generations. Many communities feel that their economic welfare is dependent on these practices. In 2011, ANAM (Panama's national environmental agency) asked the UN-backed convention governing trade in illegal species (CITES) to help regulate trade in its rare hardwoods because of rampant illegal logging.

Fighting the problem isn't easy. Panama's national parks are sparsely staffed, though their territory is colossal. In the Parque Nacional Darién, only 20 rangers protect 5760 sq km, an area more expansive than some countries.

For more information on the environmental situation in Panama, visit the home page of ANCON (☑314-0060; www.ancon.org).

to discuss your travel plans. Occasionally, a soldier will lecture you about the dangers near the border – that's because it's their job to go there if something happens.

Forty-five kilometers east of Lago Bayano, is the town (or towns) of Ipetí: Ipetí Emberá, Ipetí Kuna and Ipetí Colono. Each is occupied by a different cultural group (Kuna, Emberá and Latino). Activities here include walks along the Río Ipetí to a series of natural swimming pools fed by small waterfalls. You can also hire one of the villagers to take you here by dugout canoe, a unique opportunity to watch wildlife at an unhurried pace.

Ask around for homestays. A small handicrafts store sells Emberá woven baskets and you can receive a traditional jagua body painting for a few dollars. This henna-like plant extract leaves a temporary tattoo for up to two weeks.

A recommended English-speaking Kuna naturalist guide, Igua (☑6700-3512) leads boat tours to nearby Lago Bayano and can lead hikes into the rainforest, though it helps to have a decent command of Spanish.

Twelve kilometers past Ipetí is the village of Tortí, a useful stop with a restaurant, police station and health clinic. Hospedaje Tortí (☑6743-3697; d with/without bathroom US$18/14; P❄) has squat cinderblock rooms, each with a decent mattress and clean towels for cold-water showers. Rooms

with bathrooms have air-con. Roadside restaurant Avicar (dishes US$3-5) serves traditional country-style Panamanian dishes and you're likely to share a table with some pretty interesting characters.

Metetí

Located 1km southeast of the police checkpoint, Metetí buzzes with passing traffic, but few stay. The town's primary function is to get travelers to La Palma via a scenic boat ride. Yet lodging options are preferable to those in Yaviza. For last-minute purchases there is a good-sized grocery store.

Bleach-scented Hotel Felicidad (☑299-6544; d US$23; ❄) is one of the more decent hotels, with clean cement rooms. Nearby Restaurante Johana (mains US$3.50) serves meat dishes with rice and plantain, and fresh juice but no beer.

Ecolodge Filo de Tallo (☑in Panama 223-9283, 6673-5381; www.panamadarien.com; 4-day package per person from US$1050) sits perched upon a grassy knoll on the outskirts of Metetí. Once a shooting range for the Noriega camp, the transformation of this space to ethno-adventure tourism couldn't be stranger. Run by Panama Exotic Adventures, the lodge is primitive but handsome, with three well-spaced thatched huts with bamboo walls. Firm beds are draped in mosquito netting and attached bathrooms are set with pastel river stones and handcarved basins. The open-air living and dining area sports a stunning panorama of the region. French-run, the lodge provides good international and Panamanian cuisine served with wine. Activities include kayaking and visiting a Wounaan village. While the lodge occupies a deforested sector just on the tip of the Darién, it is one of the best lodgings in the region and provides a good dose of indigenous culture. It is also certified as carbon-neutral by Forest Finance. Packages include all meals and activities and transportation to/from Panama City.

For the boat to La Palma, take the turnoff for Puerto Quimba, a port on the Río Iglesias. The paved road between Metetí and Puerto Quimba is about 20km long. A passenger pickup shuttles between Metetí and Puerto Quimba every 30 minutes from 6am until 9pm (US$3), or take a taxi (US$10).

From Puerto Quimba, unscheduled boats to La Palma leave several times a day between 7:30am to 6:30pm (US$5); they depart from La Palma roughly between 5:30am and 5pm. A one-way charter (US$40) may also be an option.

Traveling to La Palma by boat from Puerto Quimba is an excellent alternative to flying straight in from Panama City. The scenery along this 30-minute river trip is virgin jungle and dense mangrove forests – and you're bound to meet interesting characters on board.

Yaviza

Part bazaar and part bizarre, this concrete village is the end of the road. Here the Interamericana grinds to a halt and beyond lies the famous Darién Gap. Rough edged and misshapen, it's hardly a destination unless you had cockfighting in mind. For travelers, it is an essential stop to check in for entry to Parque Nacional Darién.

The ANAM (☏ 299-4495) office of Parque Nacional Darién can offer updated information on trails and safety; register here and pay your park fee (foreigners US$15). Note that you must have prior permission from SENAFRONT (Servicio Nacional de Fronteras; ☏ in Panama City 527-1000; www.senafront.gob. pa) in Panama City in order to go any further. The office also can suggest local guides (US$10 to US$20 per day). If you do not need a local guide, your best bet is to register with SENAFRONT and ANAM in Panama City and take the boat to La Palma from Puerto Quimba.

The best sleeping option is Ya Darien (☏ 294-4334; d US$25; ✳) where tidy rooms have cold-water showers and the help is as slow as molasses. Hotel 3Americas (☏ 299-4439; r from US$25) has worn, plain rooms and the distraction of a cockfighting pit.

GETTING TO COLOMBIA

The Interamericana stops at the town of Yaviza and reappears 150km further on, far beyond the Colombian border. Overland crossings through the Darién Gap on foot are not recommended.

The Caribbean crossing between Puerto Obaldía, Panama, and Capurganá, Colombia, has become a better option than in the past. Air Panama flies to Puerto Obaldía. From here, there are no buses. You must boat or walk to the Colombian village of Sapzurro. On foot, this takes about 2½ hours, but the track is indistinct in places, and sporadic regional insecurity makes boating the better option. Just on the border, the Panamanian village of La Miel is building a hostel and features a gorgeous beach (20 minutes on foot to Sapzurro).

From Sapzurro, ferries go to Capurganá; alternatively, it's a two-hour walk. As the security situation constantly changes, it's best to get an update with solid information about the route beforehand.

Sailing or boating to Colombia is by far the safest option after flying.

San Blas Adventure (Darien Gapster; ☏ 6696-1554, 6731-2530; www.thedariengapster.com; 4-day trip US$350) More of a tour than just transport, this popular service takes backpackers from Colombia to Panama, up through the Darién and San Blas Islands, camping and snorkeling on the way. On the Panamanian side, the trip starts in Portobelo or Cartí and ends in Sapzurro, Colombia. Travel is on a covered boat with outboard motors. There are regular set departures and the website features useful details for planning.

There are eight buses daily between Panama City and Yaviza (US$16, 4½ hours).

To arrange a private boat to El Real (US$70 for three passengers), contact Chicho Bristan (🖳6539-2007, 299-6566) of El Real to pick you up in Yaviza.

INTERIOR DARIÉN

Rivers and ocean are the inroads to the heart of the Darién, where the cultures of Emberá and Wounaan meet African-Darienita culture. Cruising the waterways and hiking trails are the only ways to explore the slow-paced interior.

La Palma

POP 1400

The provincial capital of Darién Province, La Palma is a one-street town located where the wide Río Tuira meets the Golfo de San Miguel. Pastel stilt houses lord over the muddy waterfront, a scene abuzz with commerce, bars and evangelist messages.

Most travelers pass through La Palma for one of two reasons: they're here to catch a plane to somewhere else, or they're here to take a boat ride to somewhere else. The two most popular boating destinations are the Ancon nature reserve and lodge at Reserva Natural Punta Patiño and the Emberá villages that line the banks of the Río Sambú.

Every facility of possible interest to the traveler is located on the main street, which is within 300m of the airstrip. La Palma is home to the only bank in the Darién Province, Banco Nacional de Panamá. There is also a hospital, a port and a police station (if you intend to go anywhere near the Colombian border and you speak Spanish, you should talk to the police here first), as well as three hotels, three bars and several food stands.

The waterfront Hospedaje Pablo & Benita (🖳299-6490; Calle Central Abajo; s/d US$10/12) has thin walls and mattresses but good sea views. The friendly owners can help arrange visits to the Emberá community of Mogué. The comparatively upscale Hotel Biaquira Bagara (🖳299-6224; d with/without bathroom US$25/17; 🖳) is simple and sweet, with hardwood decks, wicker furniture and firm beds. There is a basic market below: if you're boating upriver, stock up on groceries here.

There's no shortage of cheap and somewhat cheerful eateries in town. La Unción (🖳299-6372; mains US$2-5) offers decent *comida criollo* – typical food like stewed chicken, rice and fried plantains, served along with fiery sermons on the satellite TV.

At the time of writing, Air Panama (🖳316-9000; www.flyairpanama.com/tickets)

THE LAST ROADLESS PLACE

Since the first Interamericana Congress met in Buenos Aires in 1925, the nations of the Americas have been dedicated to the completion of a great hemispheric road system. Today, only 150km of unfinished business prevents that system from being realized – the Darién Gap. This defiant stretch of wilderness, which separates the continents of North and South America, is the sole barrier in the way of an otherwise unbroken 30,600km highway winding from Circle in Alaska, to Puerto Montt, Chile.

Constructing this missing link would increase trade and travel options. Colombia's civil war got in the way for years, during that time the Darién Gap was both buffer zone and safe haven for rogue factors. Today, narco-trafficking in the region has become the greater issue. But there is still a lobby for a unified Pan-American Hwy (Interamericana).

Detractors, many Panamanians, cite the cost of excavating rugged terrain, the threat of foot-and-mouth disease spreading to North America and the still-delicate issue of security. In 2012, SENAFRONT (the National Border Service) reported seizing 5 tons of drugs.

Road building also provides a quick conduit for resource extraction. A road through the Darién Gap would likely spur the deforestation of one of the world's finest remaining tropical rainforests, precipitating a devastating habitat loss for its unique flora and fauna. A cultural shift in remote communities would inevitably follow.

Currently, Panama's mostly paved Interamericana Hwy travels deforested cattle country to end at the sweaty, ramshackle town of Yaviza in Darién Province. The road frequently deteriorates due to weather and heavy use by trucks. About 266km separate Yaviza from Panama City.

was not flying here, but there is an airstrip; check if flights have resumed.

To hire a boat and a guide, look in the vicinity of the dock for a responsible captain with a seaworthy motorboat (US$120 to US$300 per day, gas included).

Reserva Natural Punta Patiño

On the southern shore of the Golfo de San Miguel, 25km from La Palma, is this private 263-sq-km wildlife preserve owned by AN-CON and managed by the organization's for-profit arm, Ancon Expeditions. The only way to reach the preserve is by boat or plane. Landing on the tiny strip of ocean-side grass that's called a runway in these parts is definitely part of the experience.

The species-rich primary and secondary forest is one of the best places to spot harpy eagles. There are many other birds and a good chance of seeing everything from three-toed sloths and howler monkeys to crocodiles.

In the waterways around the reserve, you'll almost certainly see brown pelicans, magnificent frigate birds and laughing gulls. Also look for terns (royal, sandwich and gull-billed), American oystercatchers and waders on the beach near the lodge. Cetaceans like bottlenose dolphins and humpback whales frequent the waters.

In the mangroves, you'll have a good chance of spotting Amazon kingfishers, white ibises, and great and little blue herons as well as waders including willet, whimbrels and spotted sandpipers. A specialty of the area is the black oropendola, which occurs more than normal near Mogué. Late afternoon and early morning are good times to look for crab-eating raccoons venturing to the water's edge.

A swampy flat supports communities of capybaras, the world's largest rodents. Commonly spotted mammals include gray foxes around the lodge (especially at night) and tayras in patches of nearby dry forest.

One of the best parts of visiting Patiño is staying at ANCON's Punta Patiño Lodge (📝 in Panama City 269-9415; www.anconexpedi tions.com; per person 3-night package incl guide, meals & lodging US$750). Its wooden cabins have air-con, comfortable mattresses and private cold-water showers – you won't miss hot water in these climes. Staff are extremely attentive and meals are fresh and well prepared. The lodge itself is perched atop a ridge with arresting gulf panoramas. Activities include guided nature hikes, night tours and boating the mangroves. Or just relax on a wilderness beach.

Ancon Expeditions' Coastal Darien Explorer tour includes the round-trip airfare between Panama City and Punta Patiño, lodging, food and activities. This can also be combined with a trip up the Río Mogué to the Emberá village of Mogué and a guided hike to a harpy-eagle's nest. Punta Patiño is also a destination on Ancon's highly recommended two-week Darién Explorer Trek.

Independent travelers can hire boats in La Palma to reach Punta Patiño. Notify Ancon Expeditions in advance to reserve a cabin.

Mogué

Although there are countless indigenous villages in the Darién, the majority of tourists ultimately end up spending a night or two in Mogué, an Emberá village located on the banks of the Río Mogué, roughly between Punta Patiño and La Palma. Villagers here are keen to show off their culture and lifestyles, and extremely adept at finding harpy-eagle nests in the surrounding jungle.

Despite the fact that Mogué is set up for tourism, it is still very much a traditional village. Mogué sees fewer visitors than Emberá villages in Panamá Province and Kuna villages in the Comarca. Everything done for the benefit of tourists certainly has a price tag, but the atmosphere in the village is extremely relaxed and there is no pressure to buy crafts, give gifts or spend money.

While in Mogué visitors can watch a performance of traditional dance, purchase crafts including woven baskets and taguanut carvings or get a jagua-juice 'tattoo,' in the same manner that the Emberá paint themselves. Like henna, the tattoo stains the skin for up to two weeks, so it's wise to consider where you'll be heading after the Darién before you get painted. Although just a faint tattoo will appear immediately on your skin, the next morning when you wake up, you'll be about as blue as a Smurf.

Aside from interacting with the Emberá villagers, the majority of whom speak Spanish, the highlight of Mogué is taking a guided two-hour walk to a nearby harpy-eagle nest. Although there are no guarantees that you'll spot the bird, the local 'harpy-eagle whistler' will do his best to call it back to its nest. The hike itself winds through lush secondary

THE MOTHER OF ALL EAGLES

The harpy eagle, Central America's most striking raptor, is considered by many to be the most powerful bird of prey in the world. Unfortunately, opportunities to see the bird in the wild are limited as they are rare throughout most of their range and hard to spot in the canopy. Fortunately, you're in the Darién, and the area surrounding Reserva Natural Punta Patiño is home to a healthy nesting population. Although your chances of spotting one is still low, it's better here than anywhere else in Central America.

Harpy eagles are enormous birds with a wingspan of 2m and a height of 1.5m – they are immediately recognizable. Adults tend to have white breasts with a broad black chest band and faint leg barring as well as grey upper parts. They also have piercing yellow eyes that can be seen from the forest floor, as well as powerful yellow talons and a hooked bill.

Harpies rarely soar above the treetops, instead they hunt by attacking prey through the canopy. Monkeys are plucked from the foliage, unwary birds are taken from tree limbs and snakes are swept off the forest floor. However, the majority of the harpy's diet consists of sloths, which are extremely vulnerable basking in the morning sun. A harpy will sit nearby – sometimes for days – until it is hungry, and then snatch the sloth at its leisure.

Anyone who has had the privilege to watch a harpy eagle hunt will tell you that it is simply awesome. A harpy can hunt a large male howler, crush the monkey's skull with her talons and carry it back to the nest unhindered. With massive claws as big as a grizzly bear's, and legs as thick as a man's wrist, the harpy is nature's Terminator.

With females weighing up to 9kg, such a large predator obviously has high energy requirements. As a result, harpies hunt all but the largest forest mammals. As an apex predator (like the jaguar), the harpy eagle probably never occurred in high densities, though deforestation has removed much of its prey base and its habitat. Furthermore, its habit of perching for long spells, even when people approach, makes it vulnerable to poachers.

forest brimming with tropical birds. Bring a camera as harpy eagles are not easily startled by human presence, and thus easily photographed if you have a telephoto lens.

Visitors may sleep in a tent underneath the communal gathering hall, or string up a jungle hammock (bring your own). A private outhouse and cold shower are unlocked when tour groups arrive. Meals include hearty portions of rice, beans, meat and plantains – tasty and unbelievably filling. Although the village sounds are part of the whole experience, light sleepers may want to bring earplugs.

Several outfitters and guides offer overnight excursions to Mogué.

Río Sambú

The mouth of the wide, brown Río Sambú is 1½ hours by boat south of Punta Patiño. Boats pass through spectacular jungle, gliding past traditional Emberá and Wounaan villages. Fortitude is a must. You will have to deal with hours on board under a broiling tropical sun with leaking gasoline cans onboard. Minor hardships include a lack of showers and toilets, and the abundance of creepy crawlies and biting insects. But a trip up the Río Sambú offers true adventure.

It is essential to bring gasoline from La Palma to fuel the canoe that you'll hire upriver. At night, you can make camp with a tent or a jungle hammock or even sleep on the floor of an Emberá or Wounaan family home. If you can speak Spanish, finding a host family for the night isn't difficult, and even getting a hot meal is easy. Rates will start at around US$10 per person for shelter and US$5 for a meal.

If you speak Spanish, boats and guides can be hired in La Palma, but once you reach the Río Sambú, you'll need to hire another guide and a separate, smaller *piragua* to navigate the narrow, shallow sections upriver. In rainy season, the river is navigable by *piragua* all the way to Pavarandó, the most inland of the eight indigenous communities on the Sambú.

Sambú

Riverside Sambú is an interesting stop, populated by Emberá and Cimarron people (whose ancestors escaped the slave trade by living in the jungle). Urban by Darién standards, it has an airstrip, hospital and pay phone. Given the ease of flying in here, it makes a good launch point to visit riverside Emberá and Wounaan communities and absorb the slow jungle pace.

From Sambú visitors can plan enjoyable trips to Puerto Indio (with permission from the Emberá and Wounaan) and visit petroglyphs or mangrove forests. Bocaca Verano is a lagoon with crocodiles and prolific birdlife. Local guide Lupicinio, found in front of Sambú house, guides hiking excursions (US$15 per person) to see harpy eagles and tours to Bocaca Verano in dry season.

For boat tours, Juan Murillo takes visitors fishing (four passengers US$120) in the Golfo de San Miguel in his 75-HP boat. Since there are no phones, ask around for either guide.

The only jungle B&B around, Sambu House (☏ 6687-4177, 268-6905; www.sambuhaus edarienpanama.com; s/d incl meals US$75/125) is a North American–owned attractive yellow clapboard run by friendly Mabel. Cozy but simple, this might be the only place to get pancake breakfasts in the Darién. You can also arrange cultural tours here.

The Emberá community runs Werara Puru (☏ 299-6090; per person US$12), a *cho-za* (hut) built to lodge tourists, located a 10-minute walk from town. When we visited the space was under renovation. Near the airstrip, Mi Lindo Sueño (☏ public phone 333-2512; r with shared bathroom US$10) has plain concrete rooms.

You can get cheap and tasty meals at Co-midas Benedicta (meals US$2.50), where Anthony Bourdain dined when in Sambú. If it's a party you want, check out Mis Cabañas del Nuevo Milenio (☺ Sat & Sun), a woodsy juke-joint with music blasting half the village away. You can get a beer here, though it may not be cold.

For flights, Air Panama (☏ 316-9000; www. flyairpanama.com) flies twice weekly, currently Wednesday and Saturday, from Panama City (US$150 round-trip, one hour). Always confirm your return ticket in advance. If the airline can't fill a flight, it may be delayed. This also goes for flights out of Sambú.

The *panga* (small motorboat) to Puerto Quimba (US$20) goes three times a week, with one stop in La Palma. Trips are not scheduled far in advance, ask around and try to confirm a date for a return trip.

PARQUE NACIONAL DARIÉN

Parque Nacional Darién is the most ecologically diverse land-based national park in all of Central America. Although it's often overshadowed by the security situation in the province, there is no doubt that it is the crown jewel of Panama's national parks, mostly sought after by specialists like biologists and botanists.

El Real

POP 1200

Riverside El Real dates from the conquistador days when it was merely a fort beside Río Tuira. The settlement prevented pirates from sailing upriver to plunder Santa María,

DARIÉN PROVINCE EL REAL

TROPIC STAR LODGE

Overlooking Bahía Piña on the Pacific Coast, near the southern tip of the Darién, the legendary Tropic Star Lodge (☏ in USA 800-682-3424; www.tropicstar.com; 3-day/4-night per person nonfishing/fishing package from US$2280/3550; ✱@✉) boasts the most International Game Fish Association (IGFA) world records. No expense has been spared in this remote luxury lodge. With everything done just right, there's a sense of camaraderie among guests, many of whom are professional sportfishers, millionaires and celebrities.

Stand-alone cabins have modern conveniences and satellite TV. Immaculate grounds with dramatic ocean views invite guests to lounge in manicured gardens, wade in the palm-shaded pool and dine on the catch of the day in the sophisticated bar-restaurant. There's even a 'palace' built onsite by a Texas oil tycoon as his home away from home in 1961.

Of course, all of this shouldn't distract you from why you're really here – to fish. The lodge's fleet of 31ft Bertrams, the Ferraris of sportfishing boats, are outfitted with top-notch gear and manned by some of the best captains in the world.

Packages include the use of a boat with a captain and mate, all meals, and fishing tackle and leaders. Rates vary according to the number of people on the boat. Cost increases in winter (December to March).

Tropic Star arranges charter flights (extra) to and from Panama City.

ⓘ RESPONSIBLE TRAVEL IN THE DARIÉN

Travelers should carefully consider the impact they might have upon visiting Emberá and Wounaan communities in the Darién. Unlike Kuna Yala, the Darién sees few foreign visitors. Yet as hosts, these groups are very hospitable.

Make an effort to respect the sensibilities of your hosts. Although some women still go topless, these are still fairly conservative societies. Most villagers are happy to pose for a photo, but you should always ask first. Photos of communities sent back in thanks (via a guide) are treasured. After all, these societies have scant access to cameras.

Instead of giving out candy or coins to village children, consider buying dictionaries, Spanish-language books and much needed supplies to donate to local schools.

Tourism has a long way to go to develop in the region, which is one reason why a visit to an Emberá or Wounaan village is so refreshing. As visitors, we need to keep in mind that we will all need to work together to promote cultural preservation.

---

where gold from the Cana mines was stored. Today, El Real is one of the largest towns in the Darién, though it's still very much a backwater settlement.

El Real is the last sizable settlement before the national park. Those heading up to Rancho Frío must either hire a local guide or be part of a tour – ANAM will not let you proceed unescorted. Before your arrival, you must register with **SENAFRONT** (Servicio Nacional de Fronteras; ✆ in Panama City 527-1000; www.senafront.gob.pa) and ANAM Panama City, where you can pay the entry fee (foreigners US$15).

Options are slim here and it's best to make food purchases prior to the hike. If you arrive in town too late to start the trek to Rancho Frío, you can spend the night at a rustic *pensión*. At **Fonda Doña Lola** (meals US$3) you can have a heaped plate of rice and chicken. Veteran boatman **Chicho Bristan** (✆ 6539-2007, 299-6566) offers charter trips between Yaviza and El Real (US$70 for three passengers). Though the park cannot be accessed by vehicle, Chicho can arrange a 4WD vehicle (US$30) to take you partway, leaving you in Pirre 1, a 1½-hour hike to Rancho Frío.

Another way to Rancho Frío is to charter a boat (US$80 plus gasoline) up the Río Pirre to Piji Baisal. From Piji Baisal, it's a one-hour hike to the station. A guide is indispensable as there are no signs to mark the way.

Rancho Frío

Thirteen kilometers south of El Real, as the lemon-spectacled tanager flies, is the Rancho Frío sector of Parque Nacional Darién. It's home to **Pirre Station**, or Pirre 2, not be confused with the station at the top of Mount Pirre near Cana. Rare bird species represented here include the crimson-bellied woodpecker, the white-fronted nunbird and the striped woodhaunter. To steal a line from the famous naturalist guide Hernán Araúz, Rancho Frío is 'Panama's foremost theater of life.'

The real strength of this sector is the excellent trail network. A two-day trail goes to Mt Pirre ridge and a one-hour trail winds through thick jungle to a series of cascades. Neither should be attempted without a guide as they are unmarked, and if you get lost out here you're finished.

Visitors must get prior permission from SENAFRONT in Panama City and pay **ANAM** (✆ 299-4495) US$15. At Pirre Station, there are **barracks** (per person US$15) with a front room with fold-out cots for visitors, a small outdoor dining area beside a very basic kitchen, a *palapa* (open-sided shelter) with a few chairs and a number of flush toilets and cold-water showers. There is also a shady **campsite** (per person US$6) where you can either pitch a tent or string up a jungle hammock. Electricity is run off batteries and use must be kept to a minimum.

Visitors must bring their own food and purified water. Cooking fuel is scarce, so let the rangers do the cooking (US$10 to US$15 a day is most appreciated). Be sure to try the *zapote* growing at the station – this fruit has a fleshy orange meat with the appearance, taste and texture of mango and it's highly addictive.

Pirre Station can only be reached by hiking or by a combination of hiking and boating or 4WD transportation. The four-hour hiking route takes the 'road' connecting El Real and Rancho Frío, yet this barely discernible path is pretty much impossible without a guide – though you can find one in Pirre 1 for US$15.

Understand
Panama

Panama Today

The waistline of the Americas, Panama has always been a crucial connection. The appearance of this land bridge three million years ago created a biological boom. Species moved, adapted and flourished through this one narrow isthmus. Like one great cocktail party, the event had no bedtime. Back then, it was plants, amphibians, primates, flowers and insects. Today's Panama has become a mix of ambitions, economic forces and peoples: among them Chinese immigrants, Latinos, North Americans and indigenous groups.

Best in Film

Hands of Stone (release 2013) The anticipated biopic of boxing legend Roberto Durán, with Robert Di Niro.
Quantum of Solace (2008) Agent 007 is out for revenge, with scenes in Casco Viejo.
The Tailor of Panama (2001) A reluctant spy lets loose.

Best in Print

Getting to Know the General (Graham Greene; 1984) A portrait of General Omar Torrijos by his longtime friend.
Empire of Blue Water (Stephen Talty; 2008) An intriguing pirate history and NY Times bestseller.
Panama (Carlos Ledson Miller; 2007) Explores the turmoil of the Noriega years with snapshots of history.
Confessions of an Economic Hitman (John Perkins; 2005) Explores the shadowy world of overseas business.

Best Dining Websites

www.buenprovechopanama.com
www.panamarestaurantreviews.com
www.panamarestaurantweek.com

The Expanding Canal

The fastest growing economy in Latin America for the last two years, Panama owes much of its prosperity to the Panama Canal. The 80km belt of locks links the Atlantic to the Pacific, and east with west. In the last century, the canal has cast the isthmus as the western hub of global commerce. Each year, more than four million containers travel it, their hulls filled with everything from bananas and grains to oil, lumber and shiny new cars. You may have never visited Panama, but it is quite likely that both the fruit in your juice and the accessories in your pocket once did.

One of the world's largest transportation projects, the Panama Canal's US$5 billion dollar expansion is expected to double the current capacity and triple the traffic in the canal by digging deeper to accommodate bigger vessels and by adding a third lane. It already hauls in US$2 billion yearly.

A financial boon for Panama, the expanded Panama Canal is expected to be completed on the heels of the canal's 100-year anniversary – slightly behind schedule. The canal is also expected to shift trade patterns, upsetting the prosperity of North American west coast ports.

Detractors fear that the project – along with the tab for a new US$1.2 billion dollar Panama City subway system, a proposed beltway in Panama Bay, a new international airport and other projects – will shackle the country with serious debt. Or is the infrastructure upgrade a savvy investment? With the supersizing of merchant ships worldwide, the gamble bodes necessary if Panama is to remain a key shipping hub.

Sitting on Green Riches

Although the canal has defined Panama for the last century, it's what lies just beyond this engineering marvel that could define the next 100 years. A third of the country is set aside as protected areas and national parks, and the culture and customs of Panama's indigenous populations remain largely intact. Yet visitor numbers are nowhere near those of neighboring Costa Rica. Many outsiders assume that Panama is all about its capital and commerce. But while Panama races toward rapid-fire development, the resources it has always had and oft neglected have started to attract attention.

Panama's intrigue, which dates from the voyages of Columbus and its plundering by pirates, may be its one treasure that remains intact. One of the most biodiverse places in the world, Panama is a refuge for an incredible array of species. Its first-rate nature destinations range from lush, untapped rainforests to solitary beaches and uninhabited isles. Everyone is asking: is it packaged and tourist ready? Not exactly. Yet many travelers will find that's precisely its charm.

Dividing the Pie

Always a creature of potential, Panama lives with a sharp contrast between its urban and rural counterparts. Panama City is all sparkling skyscrapers, cement mixers and scaffolds, yet an hour outside of the capital indigenous Emberá paddle dugout canoes. The modern and ancient strangely coexist, but each year there is friction at their boundaries.

While poverty has reduced by 10% in the last decade, Panama still has the second worst income distribution in Latin America. Many provincial residents have relocated to Panama City in search of opportunities. City dwellers blame the most recent growth spurt for increasing traffic, pollution and crime. Ironically, many residents welcomed the 2009 world economic crisis in relief – that mega-developments and real-estate speculation would go away. It worked, for a while. Today, whispers of opportunity have investors trickling back.

There is hope that the country's investments in infrastructure will pay off. But many Panamanians are weary of increasing political cronyism. More and more, disgruntled citizens are protesting the privatization of public resources and taking it to the streets. When the government attempted to privatize Colón's profitable free trade zone in October, 2012, protests erupted, leaving three protesters dead in clashes with police. The rest of the country joined Colón in solidarity marches and protests. When chaos hit a fever pitch with riots and looting in the capital, the controversial plans were scrapped. For Panama, it's time to put more focus on community interests.

POPULATION: **3.5 MILLION**

AREA: **75,420 KM2**

GDP: **55.8 BILLION**

GDP GROWTH: **8.5%**

INFLATION: **6.1%**

UNEMPLOYMENT: **4.4%**

if Panama were 100 people

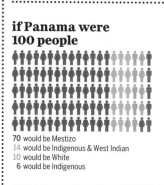

70 would be Mestizo
14 would be Indigenous & West Indian
10 would be White
6 would be Indigenous

belief systems
(% of population)

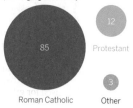

85 Roman Catholic
12 Protestant
3 Other

population per sq km

PANAMA   COSTA RICA   USA

≈ 30 people

History

The crossroads of the Americas, the narrow isthmus of Panama has always played a central and even strategic role in the history of the Western Hemisphere, from hosting the biological exchange of species to periodic encounters – and clashes – between many cultures. Once an overland trade route that linked the great civilizations of ancient Peru and Mexico, in the post-Colombian conquest it became the overland route for the siphoning off of Inca treasures. With two oceans so near, transit is a longtime theme. As the Panama Railroad once brought prospectors to the California gold rush, today the Panama Canal has become the roaring engine of global commerce.

Lost Panama

Panama: Four Hundred Years of Dreams and Cruelty, by David A Howarth, chronicles the history of the isthmus from Balboa's 1513 exploration through 1964, with scintillating tales of conquistadors and buccaneers.

The coastlines and rainforests of Panama have been inhabited by humans for at least 10,000 years, and it's estimated that several dozen indigenous groups including the Kuna, the Ngöbe-Buglé, the Emberá, the Wounaan and the Naso were living on the isthmus prior to the Spanish arrival. However, the historical tragedy of Panama is that despite its rich cultural history, there are virtually no physical remains of these great living civilizations.

Unlike the massive pyramid complexes found throughout Latin America, the ancient towns and cities of Panama vanished in the jungles, never to be seen by the eyes of the modern world. However, tales of lost cities still survive in the oral histories of Panama's indigenous communities, and there is hope among Panamanian archaeologists that a great discovery lies in waiting. Considering that much of Panama consists of inaccessible mountains and rainforests, perhaps these dreams aren't so fanciful.

What is known about pre-Columbian Panama is that early inhabitants were part of an extensive trading zone that extended as far south as Peru and as far north as Mexico. Archaeologists have uncovered exquisite gold ornaments and unusual life-size stone statues of human figures as well as distinctive types of pottery and *metates* (stone platforms that were used for grinding corn).

TIMELINE	11,000 BC	2500 BC	100 BC
	The first humans occupy what is now Panama, and their populations quickly flourish thanks to the rich resources found along both the Pacific and Atlantic coastlines.	Panama is home to some of the first pottery-making villages in the Americas including the Monagrillo culture, which existed between 2500 to 1700 BC.	Panama becomes part of an extensive trade network of gold and other goods that involves many disparate civilizations and extends from Mesoamerica to the Andes.

Panama's first peoples also lived beside both oceans, and fished in mangrove swamps, estuaries and coral reefs. Given the tremendous impact that fishing has had on the lives of isthmians, it seems only fitting that the country's name is derived from an indigenous word meaning 'abundance of fish.'

New World Order

In 1501 the discovery of Panama by Spanish explorer Rodrigo de Bastidas marked the beginning of the age of conquest and colonization in the isthmus. However, it was his first mate, Vasco Núñez de Balboa, who was to be immortalized in the history books, following his discovery of the Pacific Ocean 12 years later.

On his fourth and final voyage to the New World in 1502, Christopher Columbus went ashore in present-day Costa Rica and returned from the encounter claiming to have seen 'more gold in two days than in four years in Spain.' Although his attempts to establish a colony at the mouth of the Río Belén failed due to fierce local resistance, Columbus petitioned the Spanish Crown to have himself appointed as governor of Veraguas, the stretch of shoreline from Honduras to Panama.

Following Columbus' death in 1506, King Ferdinand appointed Diego de Nicuesa to settle the newly claimed land. In 1510 Nicuesa followed Columbus's lead, and once again tried to establish a Spanish colony at Río Belén. However, local resistance was once again enough to beat back Spanish occupation, and Nicuesa was forced to flee the area. Leading a small fleet with 280 starving men aboard, the weary explorer looked upon a protected bay 23km east of present-day Portobelo and exclaimed: '¡Paremos aquí, en nombre de Dios!' ('Let us stop here, in the name of God!'). Thus was named the town of Nombre de Dios, one of the first Spanish settlements in the continental New World.

The Sack of Panamá: Sir Henry Morgan's Adventures on the Spanish Main, by Peter Earle, details the Welsh pirate's looting of Panamá in 1671.

Much to the disappointment of Columbus' conquistador heirs, gold was not abundant Panama. Add tropical diseases, inhospitable terrain and less than welcoming natives to the mix, and it's easy to see why Nombre de Dios failed several times during its early years as a Spanish colony. However, a bright moment in Spanish exploration came in 1513 when Balboa heard rumors about a large sea and a wealthy, gold-producing civilization across the mountains of the isthmus – almost certainly referring to the Inca empire of Peru. Driven by equal parts ambition and greed, Balboa scaled the Continental Divide, and on September 26, 1513, he became the first European to set eyes upon the Pacific Ocean. Keeping up with the European fashion of the day, Balboa immediately proceeded to claim the ocean and all the lands it touched for the king of Spain.

AD 1501	1506	1513	1519
Spaniard Rodrigo de Bastidas becomes the first European to see Panama; Christopher Columbus came one year later and explored Bocas, coastal Veraguas and Portobelo.	Christopher Colombus dies and Diego Nicuesa is appointed to settle the territory known as Veraguas.	Searching for a city of gold, Vasco Nuñez de Balboa leads a grueling overland expedition and is the first European explorer to see the Pacific Ocean.	Pedrarias founds the city of Panamá, which becomes a major transit point for gold plundered from Peru, packed overland to the Pacific coast and transferred by galleon to Spain.

ISTHMUS

The Empire Expands

In 1519 a cruel and vindictive Spaniard named Pedro Arias de Ávila (or Pedrarias, as many of his contemporaries called him) founded the city of Panamá on the Pacific side, near where Panama City stands today. The governor is best remembered for such acts as ordering the beheading of Balboa in 1517 on a trumped-up charge of treason, as well as ordering murderous attacks against the indigenous population, whom he roasted alive or fed to dogs when the opportunity permitted.

Despite his less than admirable humanitarian record, Pedrarias established Panamá as an important Spanish settlement, a commercial center and a base for further explorations, including the conquest of Peru. From Panamá, vast riches, including Peruvian gold and Oriental spices, were transported across the isthmus by foot to the town of Venta de Cruces, and then by boat to Nombre de Dios via the Río Chagres. Vestiges of this famous trade route, which was known as the Sendero Las Cruces (Las Cruces Trail), can still be found today throughout Panama.

As the Spanish profited from the wealth of plundered civilizations, the world began to notice the prospering colony, especially the English privateers lurking in coastal waters. In 1572 Sir Francis Drake destroyed Nombre de Dios, and set sail for England with a galleon laden with Spanish gold. It was also during this expedition that Drake climbed a high tree in the mountains, thus becoming the first Englishman to ever set eyes on the Pacific Ocean.

Hoping to stave off further ransacking and pillaging, the Spanish built large stone fortresses at Portobelo and Fuerte San Lorenzo. However, these fortifications weren't enough to stop the Welsh buccaneer Sir Henry Morgan from overpowering Fuerte San Lorenzo and sailing up the Río Chagres in 1671. After crossing the length of the isthmus, Captain Morgan destroyed the city of Panamá, made off with its entire treasure and arrived back on the Caribbean coast with 200 mules loaded with loot.

After Panamá burnt to the ground, the Spanish rebuilt the city a few years later on a cape several kilometers west of its original site. The ruins of the old settlement, now known as Panamá Viejo, as well as the colonial city of Casco Viejo, are both located within the city limits of present-day Panama City.

Of course, British privateering didn't cease with the destruction of Panamá. In 1739 the final nail in the coffin was hammered in when Admiral Edward Vernon destroyed the fortress of Portobelo. Humiliated by their defeat and robbed of one of their greatest defenses, the Spanish abandoned the Panamanian crossing in favor of sailing the long way around Cape Horn to the western coast of South America.

The famous crossing of the isthmus included 1000 indigenous slaves and 190 Spaniards, including Francisco Pizarro, who would later conquer Peru.

1671	1698	1739	1821
Henry Morgan overpowers Fuerte San Lorenzo, sails up the Chagres and sacks the city of Panamá. After a crushing defeat, a new walled city is built in present-day Casco Viejo.	A Scottish trading colony established in the Darién fails and plunges Scotland into economic depression. The financial losses heavily influence the union of Scotland with England in 1707.	Following numerous pirate attacks, Spain finally abandons the short but perilous trans-isthmian trade route in favor of sailing all the way around Cape Horn in South America.	Liberator Simón Bolívar leads the northern swath of South America to independence from Spain, and Panama joins the newly formed union of Gran Colombia.

SALVAGING SUNKEN GALLEONS

During the period of colonization between the 16th and 18th centuries, Spanish galleons left home carrying goods to the colonies and returned loaded with gold and silver mined in Colombia, Peru and Mexico. Many of these ships sank in the Caribbean Sea, overcome by pirates or hurricanes. During these years, literally thousands of ships – not only Spanish but also English, French, Dutch, pirate and African slave ships – foundered in the green-blue waters of the Caribbean.

The frequency of shipwrecks spurred the Spaniards to organize operations to recover sunken cargo. By the 17th century, Spain maintained salvage flotillas in the ports of Portobelo, Havana and Veracruz. These fleets awaited news of shipwrecks and then proceeded immediately to the wreck sites, where the Spaniards used Caribbean and Bahamian divers, and later African slaves, to scour sunken vessels and the seafloor around them. On many occasions great storms wiped out entire fleets, resulting in a tremendous loss of lives and cargo.

The Empire Ends

Spain's costly Peninsular War with France from 1808 to 1814 – and the political turmoil, unrest and power vacuums that the conflict caused – led Spain to lose all its colonial possessions in the first third of the 19th century.

Panama gained independence from Spanish rule in 1821, and immediately joined Gran Colombia, a confederation of Colombia, Bolivia, Ecuador, Peru and Venezuela, a united Latin American nation that had long been the dream of Simón Bolívar. However, internal disputes lead to the formal abolishment of Gran Colombia in 1831, though fledgling Panama retained its status as a province of Colombia.

Birth of a Nation

Panama's future forever changed from the moment that the world's major powers learned the isthmus of Panama was the narrowest point between the Atlantic and Pacific Oceans. In 1846 Colombia signed a treaty permitting the US to construct a railway across the isthmus, though it also granted them free transit and the right to protect the railway with military force. At the height of the California gold rush in 1849, tens of thousands of people traveled from the east coast of the US to the west coast via Panama in order to avoid hostile Native Americans living in the central states. Colombia and Panama grew wealthy from the railway, and the first talks of an inter-oceanic canal across Central America began to surface.

Heat, starvation and botfly infestations were just some of the challenges faced in the US Army's disastrous 1854 Darién expedition, chronicled by Todd Balf in *The Darkest Jungle*.

1855	1856	1878
An estimated 12,000 laborers die building the Panama Railroad, particularly from malaria and yellow fever. Despite being only 76km long, the Panama Railroad requires 304 bridges and culverts.	The Watermelon War of 1856 becomes the first US intervention. Large-scale race riots result from white US soldiers mistreating locals. Marines eventually put down the conflict.	The French are granted the right to build a canal though Panama. After malaria and yellow fever claim over 22,000 lives, the French declare bankruptcy and abandon the project altogether.

THREE LIONS/GETTY IMAGES ©

➡ Panama Railroad (p211)

The idea of a canal across the isthmus was first raised in 1524 when King Charles V of Spain ordered that a survey be undertaken to determine the feasibility of constructing such a waterway. In 1878, however, it was the French who received a contract from Colombia to build a canal. Still basking in the warm glory of the recently constructed Suez Canal in Egypt, French builder Ferdinand-Marie de Lesseps brought his crew to Panama in 1881. However, Lesseps severely underestimated the task at hand, and over 22,000 workers died from yellow fever and malaria in less than a decade. By 1889, insurmountable construction problems and financial mismanagement had driven the company bankrupt.

Spanish readers and history buffs should pick up *El Caballo de Oro*, by Juan David Morgan, a novel about the building of the Panama Railroad in the quest for California gold.

The US saw the French failure as a lucrative business opportunity that was ripe for the taking. Although they had previously been scouting locations for a canal in Nicaragua, the US pressured the French to sell them their concessions. In 1903 Lesseps' chief engineer, Philippe Bunau-Varilla, agreed to the sale, though the Colombian government promptly refused.

In what would be the first of a series of American interventions in Panama, Bunau-Varilla approached the US government to back Panama if it declared its independence from Colombia. On November 3, 1903, a revolutionary junta declared Panama independent, and the US government immediately recognized the sovereignty of the country. Although Colombia sent troops by sea to try to regain control of the province, US battleships prevented them from reaching land. Colombia did not recognize Panama as a legitimately separate nation until 1921, when the US paid Colombia US$25 million in 'compensation.'

Growing Pains

Following independence, Bunau-Varilla was appointed Panamanian ambassador to the US, though his first act of office paved the way for future American interventions in the region. Hoping to profit from the sale of the canal concessions to the US, Bunau-Varilla arrived in Washington, DC, before Panama could assemble a delegation. On November 18, Bunau-Varilla and US Secretary of State John Hay signed the Hay-Bunau-Varilla Treaty, which gave the US far more than had been offered in the original treaty. In addition to owning concessions to the canal, the US was also granted 'sovereign rights in perpetuity over the Canal Zone,' an area extending 8km on either side of the canal, and a broad right of intervention in Panamanian affairs.

The Panama Railroad (www.panamarailroad.org) website contains photographs, historical information and fascinating travelogues, including one written by Mark Twain in 1868.

Despite opposition from the tardy Panamanian delegation as well as lingering questions about its legality, the treaty was ratified, ushering in an era of friction between the US and Panama. Construction began again on the canal in 1904, and despite disease, landslides and harsh weather,

1887	1902	1912	1914
French impressionist painter Paul Gauguin moves to Isla Taboga after working with a French crew on the first Panama Canal attempt.	US President Theodore Roosevelt convinces the US Congress to take control of the abandoned French project. At the time, Colombia was in the midst of the Thousand Days War.	Isla de Coiba becomes a penal colony whose brutality becomes infamous. It's closed in 2004 and now operates as a national park renown for its biodiversity.	The Panama Canal is finally completed after a decade of monumental effort, thanks to the work of 75,000 laborers, many thousands of whom perish during the construction.

the world's greatest engineering marvel was completed in only a decade. The first ship sailed through the canal on August 15, 1914.

In the years following the completion of the canal, the US military repeatedly intervened in the country's political affairs. In response to growing Panamanian disenchantment with frequent US interventions, the Hay-Bunau-Varilla Treaty was replaced in 1936 by the Hull-Alfaro Treaty. The US relinquished its rights to use its troops outside the Canal Zone and to seize land for canal purposes, and the annual sum paid to Panama for use of the Canal Zone was raised. However, increased sovereignty was not enough to stem the growing wave of Panamanian opposition to US occupation. Anti-US sentiments reached a boiling point in 1964 during a student protest that left 27 Panamanians dead and 500 injured. Today, the event is commemorated as Día de Los Mártires (National Martyrs' Day).

As US influence waned, the Panamanian army grew more powerful. In 1968, the Guardia Nacional deposed the elected president and took control of the government. Soon after, the constitution was suspended, the national assembly was dissolved and the press was censored, while the Guardia's General Omar Torrijos emerged as the new leader. Torrijos' record is spotty. Though he plunged the country into debt as a result of a massive public works program, Torrijos was successful in pressuring US President Jimmy Carter into ceding control of the canal to Panama. The Torrijos-Carter Treaty guaranteed full Panamanian control of the canal as of December 31, 1999, as well as a complete withdrawal of US military forces.

Old Panama and Castilla Del Oro, by CLG Anderson, is a narrative history of the Spanish discovery, conquest and settlement of Panama as well as the early efforts to build a canal.

The Rise & Fall of Noriega

Still feeling triumphant from the recently signed treaty, Panama was unprepared for the sudden death of Torrijos in a plane crash in 1981. Two years later, Colonel Manuel Antonio Noriega seized the Guardia Nacional, promoted himself to general and made himself the de facto ruler of Panama. Noriega, a former head of Panama's secret police, a former CIA operative and a graduate of the School of the Americas, quickly began to consolidate his power. He enlarged the Guardia Nacional, significantly expanded its authority and renamed it the Panama Defense Forces. He also created a paramilitary 'Dignity Battalion' in every city, town and village, its members armed and ready to inform on any of their neighbors if they showed less than complete loyalty to the Noriega regime.

Things went from bad to worse in early 1987 when Noriega became the center of an international scandal. He was publicly accused of involvement in drug trafficking with Colombian drug cartels, murdering his opponents and rigging elections. Many Panamanians demanded

Mountains were moved and 25,000 perished in the process. Panama Fever, by Matthew Parker, makes real the magnitude of building the Panama Canal, documenting the imperial vision, and the back-breaking work of the laborers from the West Indies.

HISTORY THE RISE & FALL OF NORIEGA

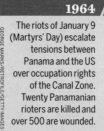

1964	1968
The riots of January 9 (Martyrs' Day) escalate tensions between Panama and the US over occupation rights of the Canal Zone. Twenty Panamanian rioters are killed and over 500 are wounded.	The Panamanian army overthrows president-elect Arnulfo Arias after just 11 days in office. Seizing the power gap, General Omar Torrijos becomes Panama's leader.

GEORGE MARKS/RETROFILE/GETTY IMAGES ©

➡ Panama Canal (p73)

Noriega's dismissal, protesting with general strikes and street demonstrations that resulted in violent clashes with the Panama Defense Forces. In February 1988 Panamanian President Eric Arturo Delvalle attempted to dismiss Noriega, though the stalwart general held on to the reins of power, deposing Delvalle and forcing him to flee Panama. Noriega subsequently appointed a substitute president who was more sympathetic to his cause.

Noriega's regime became an international embarrassment. In March 1988 the US imposed economic sanctions against Panama, ending a preferential trade agreement, freezing Panamanian assets in US banks and refusing to pay canal fees. A few days after the sanctions were imposed, an unsuccessful military coup prompted Noriega to step up violent repression of his critics. After Noriega's candidate failed to win the presidential election in May 1989, the general declared the election null and void. Meanwhile, Guillermo Endara, the winning candidate, and his two vice-presidential running mates were badly beaten by some of Noriega's paramilitary Dignity Battalions, and the entire bloody scene was captured by a TV crew and broadcast internationally. A second failed coup in October 1989 was followed by even more repressive measures.

On December 15, 1989, Noriega's legislature declared him president and his first official act of office was to declare war on the US. The following day, an unarmed US marine dressed in civilian clothes was killed by Panamanian soldiers while exiting a restaurant in Panama City.

US reaction was swift and unrelenting. In the first hour of December 20, 1989, Panama City was attacked by aircraft, tanks and 26,000 US troops in 'Operation Just Cause,' though the US media preferred to label it 'Operation Just "cuz."' Although the intention of the invasion was to bring Noriega to justice and create a democracy, it left more than 2000 civilians dead, tens of thousands homeless and destroyed entire tracts of Panama City.

On Christmas Day, the fifth day of the invasion, Noriega claimed asylum in the Vatican embassy. US forces surrounded the embassy and pressured the Vatican to release him, as entering the embassy would be considered an act of war against the tiny country. However, the US memorably used that psychological tactic beloved of disgruntled teenagers, namely bombarding the embassy with blaring rock music (Van Halen and Metallica were among the selections). The embassy was also surrounded by mobs of angry Panamanians calling for the ousting of Noriega.

After 10 days of psychological warfare, the chief of the Vatican embassy persuaded Noriega to give himself up by threatening to cancel his asylum. Noriega surrendered to US forces on January 3, and was flown

The US Army's School of the Americas, previously based in Panama, trained some of the worst human-rights abusers in Latin America – including Manuel Noriega. For information on the school's history visit www.soaw.org.

1977	1980	1983	1988
The Torrijos-Carter Treaty is signed, allowing for the complete transfer of the canal and the 14 US army bases from the US to Panama by 1999.	Panamanian boxer Roberto Durán beats Sugar Ray Leonard for the world welterweight championship.	Following General Torrijos' death in a plane crash in 1981, former CIA operative Manuel Noriega rises to power and ushers in an era of repression.	US President Ronald Reagan invokes the International Emergency Economic Powers Act, freezing Panamanian government assets in US banks and prohibiting payments by American businesses to the Noriega regime.

immediately to Miami where he was convicted of conspiracy to manufacture and distribute cocaine. After his US prison sentence ended in 2007, he was extradited to Paris in April, 2010. A re-trial found Noriega guilty and sentenced him to seven years in prison, but he was conditionally released in order to serve 20 years in Panama, starting in December, 2011, where he is incarcerated today.

Modern Woes

After Noriega's forced removal, Guillermo Endara, the legitimate winner of the 1989 election, was sworn in as president, and Panama attempted to put itself back together. The country's image and economy were in shambles, and its capital had suffered damage not only from the invasion itself, but from widespread looting that followed. Corruption scandals and internal fighting were rampant during the Endara administration. There was 19% unemployment and a deep disconnect with the country's significant poor population, as his administration was peopled by wealthy businessmen. By the time he was voted out of office in 1994, he was suffering from single-digit approval ratings.

In the 1994 elections, the fairest in recent Panamanian history, Ernesto Pérez Balladares came into office. Under his direction, the Panamanian government implemented a program of privatization that focused on infrastructure improvements, health care and education. Although Pérez Balladares allocated unprecedented levels of funding, he was viewed as corrupt. In the spring of 1999, voters rejected his attempt to change constitutional limits barring a president from serving two consecutive terms.

In 1999 Mireya Moscoso, the widow of popular former president Arnulfo Arias, Panama's first female leader and head of the conservative Arnulfista Party (PA), took office. Moscoso's ambitious plans for reform were not realized. As Panama celebrated its centenary in 2003, unemployment rose to 18%. Moscoso was accused of wasteful spending – as parts of the country went without food, she paid US$10 million to bring the Miss Universe pageant to Panama. She was also accused of looking the other way during Colombian military incursions into the Darién. She left office in 2004 after failing to fulfill even a single campaign promise.

She was followed by Martín Torrijos, a member of the Revolutionary Democratic Party (PRD) and the son of former leader Omar Torrijos. Although there has been much debate regarding the successes and failures of his administration, he did implement a number of fiscal reforms including an overhaul of the nation's social security. Furthermore, his proposal to expand the Panama Canal was overwhelmingly approved in a national referendum on October 22, 2006.

Learn how one company's tropical meddling 'set the template for capiltalism' in *Bananas: How the United Fruit Company Shaped the World*, by Peter Chapman.

1989	1994	1999	2006
The US invades Panama, and extradites Noriega to Miami where he is later convicted on charges of conspiracy and drug trafficking. He is incarcerated until September, 2007.	Ernesto Pérez Balladares is sworn in as president after an internationally monitored election campaign. Balladares emphasizes his party's populist Torrijos roots rather than its former association with Noriega.	Mireya Moscoso is elected Panama's first female president. The US ends nearly a century of occupation by closing all of its military bases and turning over control of the canal.	Seventy-eight per cent of Panamanian voters cast a 'yes' ballot in support of an expanded canal which could double its present capacity; expansion is underway.

Current Panama

On May 3, 2009, Panama bucked the Latin American leftist trend by electing conservative supermarket magnate Ricardo Martinelli president. Part of the conservative party Democratic Change (CD), Martinelli was a pro-business choice who has proved even more ambitious in political and development plans than the public had first expected.

The future of Panama remains uncertain. After the world economic crisis, high inflation kept international investors at bay. But signs of returning prosperity may herald a comeback of the gold-rush aplomb that had Panama with the highest growth rate in the Americas before the election of Martinelli. As his government winds down and Panama looks toward 2014 elections, the future is anyone's guess.

The Path Between the Seas, by acclaimed historian David McCullough, makes vivid the elephantine undertaking of creating the Panama Canal.

2010

After Noriega finishes his US prison sentence, France indicts him on charges of money laundering, but before he can serve his seven-year term, he is extradited by Panama to serve a 20-year sentence there.

2011

Following a period of economic growth, Panama signed a US–Panama Trade Promotion Agreement into law in October 2011.

ALFREDO MAIQUEZ/GETTY IMAGES ©

➡ Panama Canal expansion project (p77)

The Panamanian Way of Life

At the crossroads of the Americas, the narrow isthmus of Panama bridges not only two continents, but two vastly different paradigms of Panamanian culture and society. Roughly an hour from the gleaming skyscrapers of Panama City you can find an indigenous family paddling a dugout canoe. Sharp contradictions simply coexist in Panama. But when they clash it raises the question: what exactly is the Panamanian national character?

The National Psyche

Panamanian identity is in many ways elusive. Perhaps it's only natural given the many years that Panama has been the object of another country's meddling. From the US-backed independence of 1903 to the strong-armed removal of Noriega in 1989 – with half-a-dozen other interventions in between – the USA left behind a strong legacy in the country.

Nearly every Panamanian has a relative or at least an acquaintance living in the USA, and parts of the country seem swept up in mall-fever, with architectural inspiration straight out of North America. Panamanians (or at least the ones that can afford to) deck themselves out in US clothes, buy US-made cars and take their fashion tips straight from Madison Avenue.

Others are quite reticent to embrace the culture from the north. Indigenous groups like the Emberá and Kuna struggle to keep their traditions alive as more and more of their youth are lured into the Western lifestyles of the city. On the Península de Azuero, where there is a rich Spanish cultural heritage of traditional festivals, dress and customs, local villagers raise the same concerns about the future of their youth.

Given the clash between old and new, it's surprising the country isn't suffering from a serious case of cognitive dissonance. However, the exceptionally tolerant Panamanian character weathers many contradictions – the old and the new, the grave disparity between rich and poor, and the stunning natural environment and its rapid destruction.

Much of the famous Panamanian tolerance begins in the family, which is the cornerstone of Panamanian society, and plays a role in nearly every aspect of a person's life. Whether among Kuna sisters or Panama City's elite, everyone looks after each other. Favors are graciously accepted, promptly returned and never forgotten.

This mutual concern extends from the family into the community, and at times the whole country can seem like one giant extended community. In the political arena, the same names appear time and again as nepotism is the norm rather than the exception. Unfortunately, this goes hand-in-hand with Panama's most persistent problem: corruption.

Formal marriage is rare outside of the middle and upper classes. Some estimate that 60% of children are born to short-term unions.

Panamanians view their leaders' fiscal and moral transgressions with disgust, and are far from being in the dark about issues. Yet they accept things with patience and an almost fatalistic attitude. Outsiders sometimes view this as a kind of passivity, but it's all just another aspect of the complicated Panamanian psyche.

Lifestyle

In spite of the skyscrapers and gleaming restaurants lining the wealthier districts of Panama City, a third of the country's population lives in poverty. Furthermore, almost 750,000 Panamanians live in extreme conditions, struggling just to satisfy their basic dietary needs and living on less than a dollar a day. Those hardest hit by poverty tend to be in the least populated provinces: Darién, Bocas del Toro, Veraguas, Los Santos and Colón. There is also a substantial number of poor people living in the slums of Panama City, where an estimated 20% of the urban population lives. Countrywide, 9% of the population lives in *barriados* (squatter settlements).

In the Emberá and Wounaan villages of the Darién, traditional living patterns persist much as they have for hundreds of years. The communities are typically made up of 30 to 40 *bohíos* (thatched-roof, stilted, open-sided dwellings), and they survive on subsistence agriculture, hunting, fishing and pastoralism. However, life can be extremely difficult in these frontier villages – the life expectancy is about 10 years below the national average and the majority of the Emberá and Wounaan communities lack access to clean water and basic sanitation.

For the *campesinos* (farmers), life is also hard. A subsistence farmer in the interior might earn as little as US$10 per day, far below the national average of US$12,770 per capita. The dwelling might consist of a simple cinder block building, with a roof and four walls and perhaps a porch. Families have few possessions and every member assists with working the land or contributing to the household.

The middle and upper classes largely reside in Panama City environs, enjoying a level of comfort similar to their economic brethren in Europe and the USA. They live in large homes or apartments, have a maid, a car or two, and, for the lucky few, a second home on the beach or in the mountains. Cell phones are de rigueur. Vacations are often enjoyed outside of the country in Europe or the USA. Most middle-class adults can speak some English and their children usually attend English-speaking schools.

Celebrations, weddings and family gatherings are a social outlet for rich and poor alike, and those with relatives in positions of power – nominal or otherwise – don't hesitate to turn to them for support.

Population

The majority of Panamanians (70%) are mestizo, which is generally a mix of indigenous and Spanish descent. In truth, many non-black immigrants are also thrown into this category, including a sizable Chinese population – some people estimate that as much as 10% of the population is of Chinese ancestry. There are also a number of other sizable groups: about 14% of Panamanians are of African descent, 10% of Spanish descent, 5% of mixed African and Spanish descent, and 6% are indigenous. Generally, black Panamanians are mostly descendants of English-speaking West Indians, such as Jamaicans and Trinidadians, who were originally brought to Panama as laborers.

Indigenous Groups

Of the several dozen native tribes that inhabited Panama when the Spanish arrived, only seven now remain. While indigenous culture is much

RESPONSIBLE TRAVEL

Traveling sensitively in Panama means being mindful of the environment around you. Try to patronize locally owned businesses and small business owners, and spend your money where it will go directly to the people working for it.

Don't support businesses that keep exotic pets. It's an offense to keep a parrot, toucan or macaw in a cage. In some restaurants you may see endangered species on the menu; avoid *tortuga* (sea turtle), *huevos de tortuga* (turtle eggs), *cazón* (shark), *conejo pintado* (paca), *ñeque* (agouti) and *enado* (deer).

more vibrant and present than in neighboring countries, an inordinately high percentage of the indigenous population lives in poverty. In the *comarcas* (autonomous regions), illiteracy runs between 10 and 30 percent. Access to health care and education are serious issues.

Smaller indigenous populations include the Bokotá, who inhabit Bocas del Toro Province, and the Bribrí, found both in Costa Rica and in Panama along the Talamanca reserve. Both of these groups maintain their own language and culture, but their numbers and political influence are less than the larger groups.

Ngöbe-Buglé

Panama's largest indigenous group is the Ngöbe-Buglé (pronounced No-bay Boo-glAY), who number around 156,000 and occupy a *comarca* that spans the Chiriquí, Veraguas and Bocas del Toro Provinces. Similar to the Kuna, the Ngöbe-Buglé enjoy a high degree of political autonomy and have been successful in managing their lands and protecting their cultural identity. Unlike the Emberá and the Wounaan, the highland Ngöbe-Buglé have largely resisted outside cultural interventions, primarily because their communities are scattered among huge tracts of undeveloped land. In recent years, their youth have been increasingly heading to the cities for work, and missionaries have made numerous inroads in their attempt to convert the indigenous population to Christianity. Religion aside, the Ngöbe-Buglé continue to live much as they have throughout history by relying almost exclusively on subsistence agriculture.

The Kuna

Perhaps the most well-known group in the West, due to their distinctive dress, are the Kuna, who inhabit the Archipiélago de San Blás and run their native lands as a *comarca*. Regarded as having one of the largest degrees of sovereignty in Latin America, the Kuna are fiercely protective of their independence and routinely introduce new legislation to protect their lands from foreign cultural invasion. In recent years, this has resulted in barring foreigners from owning property in the *comarca*, imposing restrictions on tourism in San Blás and introducing standard fees for visitation, photography and video throughout the region. This tenacity has proved successful, as one of the highlights of visiting San Blás is witnessing first-hand the vibrancy of the Kuna's unique culture.

In 2011, the Panamanian government recognized the Kuna's wish to change their official spelling from Kuna to Guna, also changing Kuna Yala to Guna Yala, owing that the hard 'k' sound does not exist in their language. With Kuna still in widespread use, it has been used throughout this text for consistency, though documents are beginning to reflect this change.

MOLAS

To learn about the culture, history and sewing of world-famous Kuna *molas*, visit www.quiltethnic.com.

Emberá & Wounaan

The Emberá and Wounaan inhabit the jungle of the eastern Panamá Province and the Darién, and although both groups distinguish themselves from one another, the difference is more linguistic than cultural. Historically, both groups have eked out a living on the edges of the jungles through hunting, fishing, subsistence farming and rearing livestock, though rapidly increasing deforestation has reduced the extent of their traditional lands. Today, the majority of Emberá and Wounaan inhabit the fringes of the Darién and live beyond the range of destruction brought forth by loggers, farmers and ranchers. However, an increasing number of communities are turning to tourism for survival, particularly in the Canal Zone where traditional lifestyles are no longer feasible. There are also Emberá refugees from Colombia, who fled heavy fighting in the Chaco region by the thousands in early 2004.

A People Who Would Not Kneel: Panama, the United States and the San Blás Kuna, by James Howe, describes the struggles the Kuna underwent in order to gain the independence they enjoy today.

The Naso

The Naso (Teribe) inhabit mainland Bocas del Toro and are largely confined to the Panamanian side of the binational Parque Internacional La Amistad. Unlike other indigenous population groups, the Naso do not have an independent *comarca* of their own, which has resulted in the rapid destruction of their cultural sovereignty in recent years. Another strike against them is the tremendous tourism potential of the international park, which has prevented the Panamanian government from coming to their aid. Today, traditional villages are rapidly disappearing throughout the region and only a few thousand Naso remain. However, in an effort to ensure their cultural survival, a few villages have banded together to create an ecological center near the Wekso entrance to the park, which aims to draw more visitors to the region and employ more Naso as tourist guides.

Sports

Owing to the legacy of US occupation, baseball is the preferred pastime in Panama. This is indeed a rarity in Latin America where *football* (soccer) is normally the national craze. Panama has sent more players to the US big league teams than any other Central American country.

Although there are no professional teams in Panama, the amateur leagues host games in stadiums throughout the country. Panamanians have their preferred teams but are usually more interested in their favorite players in the US major leagues.

Mariano Rivera, the record-setting Panamanian pitcher for the New York Yankees, is a national hero, and New Yorkers and Yankees fans alike can easily strike up a conversation with most Panamanians. Carlos Lee from Aguadulce is an outfielder for the Miami Marlins. Carlos Ruiz from Chiriquí is a catcher for the Philadelphia Phillies. Batting champ Rod Carew, another Panamanian star, was inducted into the Hall of Fame in 1991. Roberto Kelly, who played for the Yankees for many years, is also fondly remembered.

Boxing is another popular spectator sport and a source of pride for Panamanians (and Latin Americans) ever since Roberto Durán, a Panama City native and boxing legend, won the world championship lightweight title in 1972. He went on to become the world champion in the welterweight (1980), light middleweight (1983) and super middleweight (1989) categories. There are four Panamanians in the International Boxing Hall of Fame: Roberto Durán, Eusebio Pedroza, Ismael Laguna and Panama Al Brown. Currently, Panama also has three reigning world boxing champions.

Panama's first Olympic gold came in 2008 when Irving Saladino won the long jump in Beijing.

Multiculturalism

Panama has a rich mix of cultures with immigrants from around the globe as well as a diverse indigenous population. Shortly after the Spanish arrived, slaves were brought from Africa to work in Panama's mines and perform grunt labor in the colony. Slaves that escaped set up communities in the Darién jungle, where their *cimarrones* (descendents) still live today. Subsequent waves of immigration coincided with the construction of both the Panama Railroad in 1850 and the Panama Canal – the French effort in the late 1800s and the American completion in the early 1900s. During these times, thousands of workers were brought to Panama from the West Indies, particularly Jamaica and Trinidad.

Workers also came from the East Indies and from China to labor – and many to die – on these massive projects. The majority of the Chinese settled in Panama City, and today you can see two Chinatowns (one is near Casco Viejo, the other in El Dorado). In fact, there are two daily Chinese newspapers and even a private school for the Chinese. The term for Chinese Panamanians is 'Once' (pronounced '*awn*-say').

Mixed-race offspring – and mixed marriages – are increasingly common today. Among the East Indian community, Hindus complain that their culture is disappearing: where once it was common for young men to return to India to find a bride, this is no longer the case. This intermixing of races happens across the nation, although indigenous groups and whites – representing each end of the economic scale – are least likely to marry outside of their group.

Although Panama is a much more racially tolerant society than many other Latin American countries, there is distrust among groups, particularly between indigenous groups and mestizos. This stems largely from mestizo land grabs – by loggers, ranchers and settlers – that have pushed indigenous communities off their lands. Indigenous communities also view the government as corrupt and largely indifferent to their plight – to some extent, they are in fact correct.

Class distinctions also persist. While politicians from the president on down take pride in mingling with the public and maintaining some semblance of a classless society, the *rabiblancos* (whites) control the majority of the wealth and nearly all of the power. Within that group are several dozen wealthy families who are above the law – people able to escape arrest by mentioning the names of others who could complicate life for a lowly police officer.

Class divisions and racism exist in Panama. Members of a certain class marry only members of that same class. And at the almighty Union Club (*the* social club of Panama City), memberships are rarely given to people with dark skin.

Racism is abhorrent no matter where it's found, but racism in Panama is mild compared to the brand found in many other countries. Panama has no counterpart to the Ku Klux Klan and there are no skinheads committing hate crimes. For all its inequities, Panama is closer to the ideal in this respect than most developed nations.

Media

Panama has a number of daily newspapers – ranging from sensationalist rags to astute independents. However, in Panama City, the most popular form of mass media is television. Mainstream broadcast views tend to represent business and the oligarchy, which is for the most part what urban viewers want to hear.

Outside the capital, however, radio is the most important medium. There are approximately 90 radio stations on the dial, though most Panamanians have two or three favorites – morning talk shows are particularly popular and represent a wide range of viewpoints.

The Martinelli government has taken media criticism hard, even pursuing imprisonment and fines for journalists, for 'offending the honor' of a public figure. This is a legacy of Noriega, who used such laws to suppress the voices of critics. International human-rights and press-advocacy organizations have decried Panama as supporting one of the most repressive regimes in the Americas because of the various 'gag laws' that bureaucrats can use to stifle opposition.

In the current media environment, underfunding is another issue. There's a lamentable lack of investigative reporting and broad-spectrum coverage on controversial issues. Still, many young Panamanians in particular have turned to the web to inform and be informed. For an alternative view on national issues, some interesting sites include www. kaosenlared.net (see the Latin American coverage, in Spanish), the environmental website www.ciampanama.org and www.thepanamanews. com (in English).

Religion

Religion in Panama can best be observed by walking the streets of the capital. Among the scores of Catholic churches, you'll find breezy Anglican churches filled with worshippers from the West Indies, synagogues, mosques, a shiny Greek Orthodox church, an impressive Hindu temple and a surreal Baha'i House of Worship (the headquarters for Latin America).

Freedom of religion is constitutionally guaranteed in Panama, although the preeminence of Roman Catholicism is also officially recognized, with 85% of the country filling its ranks. In fact, children in school have the option to study theology, though it is not compulsory. Protestant denominations account for 12%, while there are also small numbers of Muslims and Baha'i and approximately 3000 Jews (many of them recent immigrants from Israel), 24,000 Buddhists and 9000 Hindus also live in Panama.

Additionally, the various indigenous tribes of Panama have their own belief systems, although these are fading quickly due to the influence of Christian missionaries. As in other parts of Latin America, the evangelical movement is spreading like wildfire.

Although Catholics are the majority, only about 20% of them attend church regularly. The religious orders aren't particularly strong in Panama either – only about 25% of Catholic clergy are Panamanian while the rest are foreign missionaries.

Women in Panama

Women enjoy more opportunities in Panama than they do in most other Latin American countries. Panama even had a woman president, Mireya Moscoso, whose term ended in 2004. At the forefront of the country's political arena is the PNF (Feminist National Party), which was founded in 1923 and is one of the oldest feminist parties in Latin America. Historically, the PNF has been strongly critical of the male-dominated government and has secured numerous social reforms for women and children. In 1941 the PNF helped women secure the right to vote, while in 1981 they helped ratify the law that eliminated all forms of discrimination against women. The Family Code, adopted in 1995, upholds the equal rights of women and abolished discriminatory clauses in the code of 1917.

In spite of these advances, women still face many obstacles in Panamanian society. Machismo and gross stereotypes are more prevalent in rural areas than in urban ones, but even in the cities women have to face lower wages and sexual harassment, and are nearly twice as likely to be unemployed. Although women make up nearly half of the workforce, they remain underrepresented in positions of power and in public service, with 17% representation in parliament.

Overall, women are having fewer children and are having them later in life. Many postpone motherhood to enter the workplace – a pattern that exists in Europe and the USA. Panama also has a growing number of single mothers, particularly at the lower income bracket. This problem is compounded by the facts that women have no right to an abortion (it's illegal in Panama) and that the teenage pregnancy rate is high. According to a 2000 UN survey, 22% of women were married, widowed or divorced before the age of 20. At the same time, they are expected to work and help support the household. As the legal age for marriage for girls is 14 (boys 16), teenage marriage is still prevalent.

In indigenous communities, women face many hardships, including poor access to health care and a low level of prenatal care. Prevailing stereotypes also mean that girls are less likely to attend school – among indigenous populations, more than half of women are illiterate compared to one-third of men. Women also enter motherhood at much younger ages and bear more children than their mestizo counterparts.

Music

While Panamanians have an inordinate degree of affection for '80s rock, there is far more diversity happening in this small country. It helps to have a population of many cultures. From West Indies calypso music to jazz, salsa, reggaetón and rock 'n' roll, music is always drifting out of taxis and flat windows and into your experience.

For the lowdown on the Panamanian music scene as well as a guide to its most famous and greatest, take a look at the Music of Panama section of www.panama1.com.

Salsa

With blaring brass horns, the swish of skirts and pulsing rhythms, salsa music is like the very air one breathes in the Latin Caribbean. And Panama is home to the biggest icon of them all.

Renowned salsa singer Rubén Blades is a prominent international figure. Raised in Panama City, Blades has had several international hits, appeared in a few motion pictures and once even ran for president – he finished third.

Salsa has traditionally been the most popular music in Panama, but live salsa has become harder to come by, given the current popularity of reggaetón (known here as *plena*).

El Salsero: Rubén Blades

Salsa singer, songwriter, lawyer, actor and politician Rubén Blades was born on July 16, 1948, and raised in a middle-class neighborhood in Panama City. As a songwriter, Blades is revered for bringing lyrical sophistication to salsa and creating intelligent dance music. His 1978 hit 'Pedro Navaja' still remains the biggest-selling single in salsa history. Today his music continues to be incredibly popular in Panama, throughout Latin America and the West. After a failed attempt at the Panamanian presidency in 1994, Blades later served as the Minister of Tourism under President Martín Torrijos.

A case study in Panamanian versatility, Blades also personifies the love-hate relationship between Panama and the US. Blades inherited musical talent from his mother, a Cuban immigrant who played the piano and sang on the radio, and his father, a police detective who played the bongos. Inspired by doo-wop singing, Blades began singing North American music in his early teens. However, the political upheaval in Panama during the mid-1960s made Blades increasingly patriotic. For a brief period he refused to sing in any language other than Spanish.

Blades has not shied away from politically charged lyrics. In 1980 he became embroiled in controversy over his song 'Tiburon,' which used the shark metaphor to describe American political and military intervention in the Caribbean. It was eventually banned on Miami radio. In the '80s Blades experimented with a fusion of Latin, rock, reggae and Caribbean music while simultaneously completing a masters degree in international law at Harvard University and breaking into Hollywood.

The same year he formed Los Seis de Solar, Blades got his first acting role in the film *The Last Fight* (1983). Portraying a singer-turned-boxer, Blades' character seeks to win the championship against a fighter who was portrayed by the real-life world champion boxer Salvador Sánchez.

In the years to follow, Blades appeared in a string of movies including *The Milagro Beanfield War* (1988), *The Two Jakes* (1990), *Mo' Better Blues* (1990), *The Devil's Own* (1997) and *Cradle Will Rock* (1999). However, his most memorable performances were in Paul Simon's Broadway musical *The Capeman* (1997) and in the cult movie *Once Upon a Time in Mexico* (2003).

After a mediocre stint in national politics as the Minister of Tourism, Blades has returned to the music scene, rapping with Puerto Rican sensation Calle 13 in 'La Perla,' just to keep it real.

Jazz

Jazz was brought to Panama from the US and found a welcoming home. It can be heard in many clubs in Panama. The jazz composer Danilo Pérez is widely acclaimed by American and European jazz critics. He has recorded with many jazz greats from around the world and now serves on the faculty of the Berklee College of Music in Boston, USA.

Reggaetón & Beyond

These days reggaetón permeates all social levels in Panama. Like rap, reggaetón spread from the urban poor to conquer all social strata, though at its heart it's a youth trend. Key artists include Danger Man, who died in gang violence, the romantic ballads of Eddie Lover, alt-cool Los Rakas and the artist known as Flex, who has also been very popular in Mexico. From Colón, Kafu Banton is a popular reggae star.

Rock 'n' roll, in both English and Spanish, is played on most Panamanian FM radio stations, and some decent bands play it in Panama City clubs. For classic rock, Los Rabanes is considered Panama's most well-known sound.

Panamanian Folk

Attend any Azuero festival and you will see Panamanian *típico* (folkloric music) alive and thriving. In *típico* the accordion is dominant. It's well represented by Dorindo Cárdenas, the late Victorio Vergara (whose band lives on as Nenito Vargas y los Plumas Negras) and the popular brother-sister pair of Sammy and Sandra Sandoval.

Arts

Panamanian art reflects its stunning ethnic mix, with indigenous, African and Latin influences informing a diversity that ranges from delicate carvings of wood and tagua nut to flamboyant costumes and extraordinary lace dresses. Perhaps what is most fantastic is that these treasures are found in the depths of the Darién or the dusty villages of the Península de Azuero, where artisans still pursue traditions that have been long handed down.

For the beat on current cultural events and contemporary Panamanian authors, check out www.escritore spanama.com.

Photographers and painters are also helping to reinvent our understanding of this tropical crossroads. Panama has internationally recognized dancers, actors and photographers. Yet in their own country it is difficult for artists to establish a public presence. Though there is promise in endeavors like the MAC (Museo de Arte Contemporáneo), there is almost no government support for museums or training. But art is far from dead. Graffiti murals, small-scale expositions and cooperatives work hard to close the gap.

The Written Word

Often inward-looking, Panamanian literature has not carved much of a presence in international circles.

Several of the country's best novelists wrote around the mid-century. *El Ahogado* (The Drowned Man), a 1937 novel by Tristán Solarte (pen name for Guillermo Sánchez Borbón, a well-known poet, novelist and journalist), ingeniously blends elements of the detective, gothic and psychological genres, along with a famous local myth. *El Desván* (In the Garret), a 1954 novel by Ramón H Jurado, explores the emotional limits of the human condition. *Gamboa Road Gang,* by Joaquín Beleño, is the best work of fiction about the political and social events surrounding the Panama Canal.

In 2006, *Come Together, Fall Apart,* a novella and stories about Panama, debuted fiction writer (and half-Panamanian) Cristina Henríquez. She followed up with the 2010 novel *The World in Half.* Both works offer insight into Panamanian identity, from a sometimes displaced point of view.

Current authors to look for include poet and novelist Giovanna Benedetti, historical novelist Gloria Guardia and folk novelist Rosa María Britton.

Panama in Film

Though Panama has served as the backdrop for several Hollywood films (namely *The Tailor of Panama* and *Quantum of Solace*), the country is just beginning to produce its own commercial features. The first released in Panama was 2009's *Chance,* a tropical comedy about class shenanigans told through the adventures of two maids and the upper-class family they work for.

Burwa dii Ebo (The Wind and the Water) was an official Sundance Film Festival selection in 2008. A narrative drama with social undercurrents, the story follows an indigenous Kuna teenager who moves to

Panama City from the Caribbean islands of his homeland. The movie has yet to be commercially distributed but has already won awards in Toronto and Chile.

The 1992 documentary, *The Panama Deception*, recounts the events that led up to the US removal of Noriega, including his previous collaboration with the CIA. Seeing this movie is a must to understand the complications and nuances of US–Panama relations. Also worthwhile, *Curundú* is a 2011 documentary by Ana Endara Mislov which shows the artistic vision of a charming photographer hoodlum trying to chronicle neighborhood life in this tough Panama City slum.

Pending release in 2013, *Hands of Stone* is a much-anticipated biopic about boxer Roberto Durán, starring Gael García Bernal and Robert De Niro. Much of the film was shot in Panama.

Made by Hand

Panama's indigenous groups still produce high-quality woodcarvings, textiles, ceramics, masks and other handicrafts. The Latin folk tradition from the Península de Azuero (*polleras*, masks and leather sandals) is also worth noting.

Panama's handicrafts are varied and often of excellent quality. The Wounaan and Emberá people in the Darién create carvings of jungle wildlife from cocobolo, a handsome tropical hardwood, and tiny figurines from the ivory-colored tagua nut.

However, the Emberá and Wounaan are most renowned for producing beautiful woven baskets of incredibly high quality. There are two types: the utilitarian and the decorative. The utilitarian baskets are made primarily from chunga palm, but can contain bits of other plants, vines, bark and leaves. They are usually woven, using various plaiting techniques, from single plant strips of coarse texture and great strength, and are rarely dyed. These baskets are often used for carrying seeds or harvesting crops.

The decorative baskets are much more refined, usually featuring many different colors and are created from palm materials of the nahuala bush and chunga palm. The dyes are 100% natural, and are extracted from fruits, leaves, roots and bark. Typical motifs are of butterflies, frogs, toucans, trees and parrots. The baskets are similar in quality to the

Inauguración de La Fe (Inauguration of La Fe), by Consuelo Tomás, is a collection of tales depicting the idiosyncrasies of the popular neighborhoods of Panama City.

HOW TO BUY A MOLA

Molas are as ubiquitous as soccer shirts in Panama. A traditional Kuna handicraft, a *mola* is made of brightly colored squares of cotton fabric laid atop one another. Cuts are made through the layers, forming basic designs. The layers are then sewn together with tiny, evenly spaced stitches to hold the design in place.

Mola means 'blouse' in Kuna, and Kuna women make *molas* in thematically matching but never identical pairs. A pair will comprise the front and back of a blouse. The most traditional colors are black, maroon and orange, while the most traditional designs are abstract and geometric. These days *molas* can feature anything from cartoonish animals to Christmas themes, but the most valued ones are classically designed.

Regardless of the design, the very best *molas* should always have the following characteristics:

➡ Stitches closely match the color of the cloth they are set against.

➡ Stitches are very fine and neatly spaced.

➡ Stitches are pulled evenly and with enough tension to be barely visible.

➡ Curves are cut smoothly and the sewing follows the curves of the cut.

➡ Outline strips are uniform in width, with no frayed edges.

renowned early-20th-century Chemehuevi Indian baskets of California. You can often buy baskets at any of the markets.

The Kuna of the Comarca de Kuna Yala are reknowned worldwide for their *molas* – the blouse panels used by women in their traditional dress and sold as crafts. *Molas* symbolize the identity of the Kuna people to outsiders, and their colorful and elaborate designs often depict sea turtles, birds and fish.

Ocú and Penonomé produce superior panama hats.

Polleras (elaborate traditional outfits of Spanish origin) are handmade in Guararé and in other villages in Las Tablas Province. Also available on the Península de Azuero are handcrafted festival masks from Villa de Los Santos and Parita.

Huacas are golden objects made on the isthmus centuries before the Spanish conquest. They were placed with indigenous leaders at the time of burial, intended to accompany and protect their souls on the voyage to the other world. Most took the form of a warrior, crocodile, jaguar, frog or condor. You can also purchase exact (solid gold) and near-exact (gold-plated) reproductions of these palm-sized objects.

Because of their proximity to mineral-rich Colombia and Brazil, the jewelry stores here often have high-quality gems at excellent prices. Buyers beware: there are many fake gems on the world market, as well as many flawed gems that have been altered to appear more valuable than they really are.

Painting

Trained in France, Roberto Lewis (1874–1949) became the first prominent figure on Panama's art scene. He painted portraits of the nation's leaders and allegorical images to decorate public buildings. Among his most notable works are those in the Palacio de las Garzas in Panama City. In 1913 Lewis became the director of Panama's first art academy, where he and his successor, Humberto Ivaldi (1909–47), educated a generation of artists.

CONGO RENAISSANCE

Started by the descendants of escaped slaves, Congo art tells the story of contemporary Portobelo by retelling their story of self-liberation. The movement started after the US invasion of Panama. Arturo Lindsay, a native Panamanian, artist and professor at Spelman College, says, 'My adopted country had invaded my homeland. Crime and drugs were rampant. There was poverty. The workshop grew out of seeing how I could help.'

Lindsay and photographer Sandra Eleta created Taller Portobelo, an artists' workshop for a community in the throes of hardship. It was art as salvation, and it worked. Lindsay describes Congo as contemporary art with folk elements. Extremely expressive, with color and textures such as beads or broken mirror shards, Congo paintings are often self-portraits. Painted *bastones* (walking sticks) represent those used by slaves to escape to freedom in the mountains and ward off pursuing Spaniards and forest predators.

Congo art has evolved and matured since its initial period, and artists have found the stability that is so hard to come by through commissions and gallery showings. In annual exchanges with visiting US artists, the groups collaborate on earthworks, sustainable architecture and biodegradable installations in addition to painting. Lindsay describes Spelman's Summer Art Colony as a cultural bridge. 'It is not just about work, but creating new friendships and a new network that will bring others into the fold.'

Portobelo is the best place to buy paintings direct but you can also find Congo art in Panama City at Karavan. Look for work by Yaneca Esquina, the movement's best-known artist.

Among the school's students were Juan Manuel Cedeño and Isaac Benítez, as well as the painters who would come to the fore in the 1950s and '60s. This group includes Alfredo Sinclair, Guillermo Trujillo, Eudoro Silvera and others. More recent artists include Olga Sinclair and Brooke Alfaro. Most of these artists are still active, with occasional shows at local galleries.

The largest Panamanian art exposition – the Bienal de Arte – is held every two years at the Museo de Arte Contemporáneo in Panama City.

Photography

Panama has several gifted photographers, including Iraida Icaza, Stuart Warner and Sandra Eleta. Icaza's abstract art is bold and innovative, made with photographic equipment. After living in Tokyo for many years, she now resides in New York.

Warner, who has spent much of his life in Asia, the Middle East, Europe and the USA, captures the human spirit in beautiful landscapes and portraits.

With a recent 40-year retrospective of stunning and thought-provoking work, Sandra Eleta is among the most important photographers in Latin America. Her most lauded work are portraits of the black inhabitants of Panama's Caribbean coast (particularly of Portobelo, where she resides part of the year). She also founded the Panama City gallery Karavan, featuring Kuna and Congo art.

Michel Perrin's *Magnificent Molas: The Art of the Kuna Indian* contains photographs of 300 fabric works of art. Perrin describes the vivid relationship between Kuna art and culture.

ARTS PHOTOGRAPHY

Land & Wildlife

Imagine a country the size of a postage stamp yet so diverse that it boasts 21 times more plant species per square kilometer than Brazil. Panama is gaining fame for its vast tropical forests, hundreds of pristine islands and astounding biodiversity. Though only slightly bigger than Ireland or Austria, Panama is home to an incredible variety of landscapes. In the span of a week, you can hike through highland cloud forests and verdant jungles and take a dip in both the Caribbean Sea and the Pacific Ocean.

The passage of a ship through the Panama Canal requires approximately 52 million gallons of water.

Although Panama is still largely undiscovered, more and more visitors are drawn to its remarkable wildlife. Panama's rainforests are home to countless creatures, from agoutis scurrying across the canopy floor to jaguars prowling the forests. In the sea, shallow coral reef beds support innumerable varieties of tropical fish, while hammerheads and manta rays roam deeper waters. In the air, nearly a thousand avian species make Panama one of the top bird-watching destinations in the world.

Unfortunately, Panama also faces grave environmental threats from the hands of loggers, developers and indifferent or corrupt government agencies, which don't understand that the country's finest gem – its natural beauty – is rapidly disappearing.

The principal threat to Panama's ecology is deforestation, which is picking up momentum throughout the country, most notably in the Darién. In addition, the balance between conservation and development tips in favor of the latter, particularly in tourist hot spots like the Península de Azuero and Bocas del Toro. Unexpected delays in the tourism boom will buy time, hopefully for both sides to re-envision these areas in a way that is both sustainable and profitable.

The Land

Panama is both the narrowest and the southernmost country in Central America. The long S-shaped isthmus borders Costa Rica in the west and Colombia in the east. Its northern Caribbean coastline measures 1160km, compared to a 1690km Pacific coastline in the south, and its total land area is 78,056 sq km.

Panama is just 50km wide at its leanest point, yet it separates two great oceans. The Panama Canal, which is about 80km long, effectively divides the country into eastern and western regions. Panama's two mountain ranges run along its spine in both the east and the west. Volcán Barú is the country's highest point and only volcano.

Like all of the Central American countries, Panama has large, flat coastal lowlands with huge banana plantations. There are about 480 rivers in Panama and 1518 islands near its shores. The two main island groups are the San Blás and Bocas del Toro archipelagos on the Caribbean side, but most of the islands are on the Pacific side. Even the Panama Canal has islands, including Isla Barro Colorado, which has a world-famous tropical rainforest research station.

Wildlife

The country's rich biodiversity owes a great deal to its geological history. Around 65 million years ago, North and South America were joined by a land bridge not unlike what exists today. Around 50 million years ago, the continents split apart and remained separate for millions of years.

During this time, unique evolutionary landscapes were created on both continents. South America experienced an astonishing diversification of many species. The land soon gave rise to many bird families (toucans and hummingbirds included), unique Neotropical rodents (agoutis and capybaras) and groups such as iguanas, poison-dart frogs and basilisks. In North America, which collided repeatedly with Eurasia, animal species that had no relatives in South America (horses, deer, raccoons, squirrels and mice) flourished.

The momentous event that would change natural history for both continents occurred around three million years ago when the land bridge of Panama arose. Species from both continents mingled: northern animals went south and southern animals went north. In the lush forests and wetlands along the isthmus, the great variety of plant species created ideal conditions for nourishing wildlife.

Today, the interchange of species between North and South America is limited to winged migrations, though this annual event can be breathtaking to behold.

A Neotropical Companion, by John Kricher, is an excellent book for learning about ecology, evolutionary theory and biodiversity in the New World tropics.

LAND & WILDLIFE WILDLIFE

Animals

Panama's biodiversity is staggering – the country is home to 218 mammal species, 226 species of reptile, 164 amphibian species and 125 animal species found nowhere else in the world. Panama also boasts 950 avian species, which is the largest number in Central America.

Land & Marine Mammals

Panama's many species of primates include white-faced capuchins, squirrel monkeys, spider monkeys and howler monkeys. Some fascinating varieties, such as the Geoffroy's tamarin, are found nowhere else in Central America. These tiny, gregarious monkeys can live in groups of up to 40 in lowland forest, and many weigh less than 600g. They're identified by their whistles and chirps, mottled black-and-brown fur, white chests and diminutive stature. Spot them in Parque Natural Metropolitano, Monumento Nacional Isla Barro Colorado and in the Darién.

Big cats prowl the jungles of Panama. Although you'd be extremely fortunate to catch even a glimpse of one, their prints are easy to come across. Jaguars, pumas, ocelots, jaguarundis and margays are all found on the isthmus. The jaguar is the largest cat in the Americas, needing large tracts of land in order to survive. Without sufficient space, the big cats gradually exhaust their food supply (which numbers 85 hunted species) and perish. They are excellent swimmers and climbers and at times are spotted resting on sunny riverbanks.

Panama's offshore waters host a fascinating assortment of creatures. Reefs found off both coasts support a plethora of tropical fish, and visitors to the national marine parks might spot humpback whales, reef sharks, bottlenose dolphins, and killer or sperm whales. Underwater, whale sharks, black- and white-tip sharks and occasionally tiger sharks also visit.

One of Panama's biggest coastal draws is the sea turtle. Of the world's seven different species, five can be seen in Panama at various times throughout the year. All sea turtles originally evolved from terrestrial species and the most important stage of their survival happens on land

A Field Guide to the Orchids of Costa Rica and Panama, by Robert Dressler, has 240 photos, and almost as many drawings, of orchids within its 274 pages.

when they come to nest. Although you'll need a bit of luck and a lot of patience, the experience of seeing hatchlings emerge is unparalleled.

Arribadas (arrivals) are rare events that occur when thousands of female sea turtles flood the beach to lay their eggs. This happens occasionally on Isla de Cañas when 40,000 to 50,000 olive ridleys come to nest at a single time. It mostly happens in the wet season (usually September to October) during the first and last quarter of the moon.

Birds

Bird-watchers consider Panama to be one of the world's best bird-watching sites. Quetzals, macaws, amazons, parrots and toucans all have sizable populations here, as do many species of tanager and raptor. Right outside Panama City hundreds of species have been spotted along the famous 17km-long Pipeline Rd in Parque Nacional Soberanía.

One of the most sought-after birds is the harpy eagle (p244), the national bird of Panama. With a 2m wingspan and a weight of up to 12kg, this raptor is the world's most powerful bird of prey and a truly awesome sight. It's recognized by its huge size, broad, black chest band with white underneath, piercing yellow eyes and prominent, regal crests. The harpy's powerful claws can carry off howler monkeys and capuchins, and it also hunts sloths, coatis, anteaters and just about anything that moves. It's best spotted in the Parque Nacional Darién around Reserva Natural Punta Patiño.

The elusive, emerald-green quetzal lives in habitats throughout Central America, but Panama is one of the best places to see it. The male has an elongated wing covert (train) and a scarlet breast and belly, while females have duller plumage. Parque Nacional Volcán Barú is a top spot for sightings, as is Parque Internacional La Amistad. They are best seen in the breeding season from March to June when males grow their spectacular trains and start calling for mates.

Panama's geographical position also makes it a crossroads for migratory birds. Out of the country's 950 bird species, 122 occur only as long-distance migrants (ie they don't breed in Panama). From August to December, North American raptors migrate south into Central America by the millions – at times there are so many birds that they make a black streak across the sky. The canopy tower in Panama's Parque Nacional Soberanía is a particularly good vantage point for watching this migration.

In Bocas del Toro, keep an eye out for kettling hawk migrations – October is the best month to see them in large numbers. The migration of turkey vultures over the islands in early March and again in October is another striking sight. These big, black-bodied, red-necked birds can

SEA TURTLE NESTING

TURTLE	NESTING SEASON	PEAK	HOT SPOTS
leatherback	Mar-Jul (Caribbean)	Apr-May (Caribbean)	Isla Bastimentos
	Oct-Mar (Pacific)	Nov-Jan (Pacific)	Humedal de San-San Pond Sak
loggerhead	May-Sep (Caribbean)	no peak	Isla Bastimentos
	Apr-Sep (Pacific)		Humedal de San-San Pond Sak
green	May-Oct (Caribbean)	Aug-Oct (Caribbean)	Isla Bastimentos
	Jun-Dec (Pacific)	no peak	Humedal de San-San Pond Sak
hawksbill	Apr-Oct (Caribbean)	Jun-Jul (Caribbean)	Isla Bastimentos
	Apr-Nov (Pacific)	Jun-Jul (Pacific)	Humedal de San-San Pond Sak
olive ridley	year-round (Pacific)	Jun-Nov (Pacific)	Isla de Cañas

OBSESSION FOR OCELOTS

Ocelots are nocturnal, elusive and native to Panama. When researchers and wildlife photographers had trouble capturing these cats in Panama's dense rainforest, they turned not to science but to Calvin Klein. Christian Ziegler, a photographer working on assignment for *National Geographic*, remembers, 'After hearing a claim from the San Diego Zoo, I bought Calvin Klein's Obsession when passing through duty-free.' The scent, which contains pheromones that appeal to both humans and animals, was sprayed on a tree.

The result? The ocelots rubbed up against bark doused in the scent. But, according to Ziegler, the attraction (not unlike many a hormonal drive) proved fleeting.

streak the sky and are able to soar for long periods without a single flap as they migrate between southern Canada and Tierra del Fuego.

Endangered Species

According to United Nations data, there are 347 threatened species in Panama. Among the animals appearing on its 'red list' for Panama are the jaguar, the spectacled bear, the Central American tapir, the American crocodile, all five species of sea turtle that nest on Panamanian beaches and dozens of birds, including several eagle species and the military and scarlet macaws.

Laws meant to curb illegal hunting are widely ignored due to the lack of enforcement. For example, keeping a parrot, toucan or macaw in a cage is a fineable offense in Panama. Nonetheless, it's common to see them in cages, even in some public venues.

You can help reduce the threat to Panama's endangered species. If you see caged animals at a hotel, complain to the manager, take your business elsewhere and report the crime to **APPC** (Asociación Panamericana Para la Conservación; ☑317-0298; www.panamericancon.org), a conservation nonprofit organization with experience in wild-animal rescue.

Find out about upcoming seminars and recent publications about tropical ecology and biodiversity topics on the Smithsonian Tropical Research Institute (www.stri.org) website.

Plants

Humid, tropical rainforest is the dominant vegetation in the canal area, along the Caribbean coast and in most of the eastern half of the country – Parque Nacional Darién protects much of Panama's largest tropical rainforest. Other vegetation zones include dry tropical rainforest and grassland on the Pacific coast, cloud forest in the highlands, alpine vegetation on the highest peaks and mangrove forest on both coasts and around many islands. Among the flora, Panama has over 10,000 species of plant including approximately 1200 orchid species, 675 fern species and 1500 species of tree.

National Parks

Today, Panama has around 40 national parks and officially protected areas, and about 33% of the country's total land is set aside for conservation. In many of the national parks and protected areas there are mestizo and indigenous villages. In some scenarios these communities help protect and maintain the park.

To enter a national park, travelers must pay US$5 (US$20 if it's a national marine park) at ANAM (Autoridad Nacional del Ambiente; Panama's national environmental authority; www.anam.gob.pa) headquarters in Panama City, at a regional ANAM office or at an ANAM ranger station inside the park being visited. Permits to camp or stay at an ANAM ranger station can be obtained in these places as well.

In Panama City, the 265-hectare Parque Natural Metropolitano protects vast expanses of tropical semideciduous forest within the city limits.

A short distance from the capital in Panamá Province, Parque Nacional Soberanía is a bird-watcher's paradise where, in a single day, you can see hundreds of species. Lush rainforest also abounds on the nearby biological reserve of Monumento Natural Isla Barro Colorado, where scientists study the area's incredibly rich biodiversity. Also close to Panama City is the historical Fuerte San Lorenzo.

In Coclé Province, Parque Nacional Omar Torrijos is a lovely national park. It remains largely overlooked since access is difficult – access

THE VALUE OF RAINFORESTS

Why should we start getting more serious about saving the rainforest? Even though most of us don't encounter one in our daily lives, rainforests and their future survival affect each and every one of us in more ways than we realize. Here's why.

Carbon Sink Effect

Some of the most common media buzzwords these days are 'climate change' and 'global warming,' and particularly to what extent we are negatively impacting the health and sustainability of the planet. As developing nations modernize, global carbon emissions are on the rise, and evidence of the greenhouse effect can already be felt across the planet.

One of the best defenses humans have against rising carbon dioxide levels is the tropical rainforest. Specifically, tropical rainforests limit the greenhouse effect of global warming by storing carbon and hence reducing the amount of carbon dioxide in the atmosphere. But our best defense against climate change is rapidly being destroyed the world over. In a frightening example of the interconnectedness of human societies, the deforestation of Latin America rainforests is impacting global ecosystems, such as the increasing desertification of the Sahel in Africa.

As a result of changing rainforest dynamics, specifically the decline of densely wooded sub-canopy trees, the ability of tropical rainforests to act as a carbon sink is in jeopardy. This reality, however frightening it may be, affects each and every one of us.

Bioprospecting

One of the most fascinating scientific research projects ever undertaken in Panama could have long-lasting implications for rainforest conservation around the globe.

With cooperation from universities and pharmaceutical companies, Smithsonian Tropical Research Institute scientists are scouring the rainforest for compounds that may one day become new drugs. Bioprospecting has already started producing remarkable results, with findings published in a number of academic journals.

The results place a great deal of importance on the rainforest's biodiversity, especially since further research – and by necessity conservation – potentially equals cures for widespread diseases like cancer and tropical diseases, or assist in developments in areas as disparate as neuroscience and agriculture. Bioprospecting could lead to a huge investment in helping to both unlock the mysteries of the rainforest and consequently preserve them. Ultimately this would make conservation both the end and the means.

Intrinsic Value

Panama's natural vegetation was originally almost all forest, though much of this has been cleared in recent generations to create pastures and agricultural land. Countless flora and fauna species have been wiped out. Beyond the plants and animals that actually inhabit the forests, deforestation also threatens the traditional cultures of the Emberá and Wounaan who have lived in the rainforest for generations. But the effects do not stop there. Migratory animals that pass through the forests annually, such as bats, butterflies and birds, also sustain the impact. A simple argument for saving the rainforest is simply that its intrinsic value is enough to warrant increased conservation efforts.

requires a good 4WD, or at least one hour's walk to reach the entrance. It offers prime bird-watching and the possibility of viewing both the Atlantic and Pacific Oceans.

In Azuero, the Refugio de Vida Silvestre Cenegón del Mangle is a mangrove forest and wildlife refuge that's a prime nesting ground for herons and other birdlife. It also contains a series of pools said to have therapeutic properties.

Although the province of Los Santos has no national parks, there is an attractive wildlife refuge and a protected area frequented by nesting sea turtles. The Refugio de Vida Silvestre Isla Iguana near Pedasí offers snorkeling, and occasional sightings of humpback whales. Nearby, Isla de Cañas is a major nesting site for olive ridley sea turtles.

In Veraguas, Parque Nacional Coiba is one of the largest marine parks in the world. It contains Panama's largest island, the 493-sq-km Isla de Coiba, which is regarded by scientists as a biodiversity hot spot. Also in Veraguas, the 32,577-hectare Parque Nacional Cerro Hoya protects some of the last remaining patches of dry tropical forest on the Península de Azuero. The newest national park is Parque Nacional Santa Fé, around Santa Fé.

In Chiriquí Province, Parque Nacional Marino Golfo de Chiriquí is an impressive 14,740-hectare marine park with 25 islands and numerous coral reefs. The aquatic life here is astounding. In the highlands, Parque Nacional Volcán Barú surrounds Panama's only volcano, a fine destination for hikers and bird-watchers. Volcán Barú (3478m) is Panama's highest peak. Chiriquí also has part of the binational Parque Internacional La Amistad. Although largely unexplored, La Amistad offers several excellent day hikes and local indigenous guides lead overnight excursions.

In the Archipiélago de Bocas del Toro, Parque Nacional Marino Isla Bastimentos protects various areas of the archipelago and is an important nature reserve for many species of Caribbean wildlife. Turtles nest on its beaches and its abundant marine life makes for great snorkeling and diving. On the mainland is the other sector of Panama's share of the binational Parque Internacional La Amistad. Wekso, as this sector of the park is called, is home to several different indigenous groups, pristine rainforest and abundant wildlife. Near the border with Chiriquí Province, the Bosque Protector de Palo Seco contains several hiking trails through lush cloud forest high in the Talamanca range.

Panama's crown jewel is the Parque Nacional Darién, which boasts 576,000 hectares of wildlife-rich rainforest. The heart of this Unesco World Heritage Site is Cana, a former mining valley that is now regarded as one of the best bird-watching spots in the world. Unfortunately, at the time of writing, authorization was closed for visits to this area. The Darién is also home to the Reserva Natural Punta Patiño, a 26,315-hectare wildlife reserve on the southern shore of the Golfo de San Miguel. This private reserve is one of the best places in the country to see the harpy eagle.

The San Lorenzo Project (www.sanlorenzo.org.pa) protects the forests, wetlands and coastal regions surrounding former US military base Fuerte Sherman in Colón Province.

Environmental Issues

According to the Centro de Incidencia Ambiental, 40% of Panama is covered by forest and 33% of its land is set aside for conservation – this is more than any other Central American country. Panama's forests also contain the greatest number of species of all the New World countries north of Colombia.

Unfortunately, it is uncertain as to whether Panamanians will be able to live in harmony with their wilderness areas in the years to come. A little over 50 years ago, 70% of Panama's total land mass was covered by

BIODIVERSITY

forest. Today, deforestation is one of the country's gravest environmental problems. Despite a growing environmental movement, the majority of Panamanians are not behind the issue.

Additionally, Panama's national parks are staffed by few park rangers. Although their areas of coverage are colossal, many rangers aren't given patrol vehicles or radios. In Parque Nacional Darién, for instance, there are usually no more than 20 rangers (generally unarmed and poorly paid) assigned to protect 576,000 hectares – an area larger than some countries. Meanwhile illegal hunting, settling and logging take place inside parks. Unless drastic measures are taken, it may not be long before the country's protected areas are nothing more than national parks on paper.

In recent years, increased foreign investment coupled with the desire to improve tourist infrastructure have started to threaten several of Panama's most pristine ecosystems.

Deforestation

To get an idea of Panama's ecological future, one need only glimpse at what happened (and what's continuing to happen) in the Darién. The region north of Yaviza – the town where the Interamericana presently ends – was covered with virgin forest just over three decades ago. Unfortunately, everything changed when the highway was extended from Chepo to Yaviza.

The loggers initially sought big trees within easy reach, felling all the giants near the highway and trampling young trees with their machinery. Once the giant trees were gone, the loggers cut roads perpendicular to the highway, which led into tall stands of hardwoods. After those stands were removed, more roads were cut and yet more stands were leveled.

Right behind the loggers were thousands of settlers looking to eke out a living by turning the trampled vegetation left by the loggers into cropland. With the mature trees gone, all that was required to create cropland was an ax and a match. After some crackling, sizzling and a lot of smoke, subsistence farmers had fields for planting. Of course, all of this is not only legal, but also actively encouraged by Panamanian law.

However, the story doesn't end here. In a healthy rainforest ecosystem, huge, exposed tree roots prevent heavy rains from washing away the thin layer of nutrient-rich topsoil found in tropical forests. But, if you take out the trees, a big storm over a denuded area will quickly carry the topsoil into rivers and out to sea, leaving only the nutrient-deficient lower soil where the vibrant jungle once stood. In the span of only two to three years, the soil in the Darién couldn't support a decent harvest and little more than grass grew on it. Since cattle eat grass, the ranchers stepped in and bought fields that frustrated farmers could no longer use.

Today, the succession of loggers, farmers and ranchers continues in northern Darién Province, although now the loggers must further explore secondary roads to find trees. The farmers are still a step behind the loggers, unintentional nomads employing the slash-and-burn method so widespread in the developing world. And everywhere the settler-farmers go, ranchers move in behind them. As of 2012, the Panamanian government had paved most of the Interamericana to Yaviza.

Mining

Today, roughly 26% of Panama is mined or under mining concessions, bringing concerns of contaminated water sources, and the destruction of forest and human habitats.

Tropical rainforests cover just 7% of the earth's surface but account for 50% of the world's biodiversity.

TRADING DEBT FOR FOREST

Conservationists are rethinking how to keep valuable resources in countries whose national debt offers a more pressing public concern. The Nature Conservancy (www.nature.org) is among nonprofits purchasing countries' national debt and using later payments toward forest protection programs. Panama has had a total of US$20 million in debt-for-nature swaps in the last decade. The present downturn in this trend has been attributed to the high cost of commercial debt in secondary markets.

A major victory for community interests was the 2012 passing of law 415, which prohibits extraction in indigenous territories and requires their approval for hydro-electric projects. The change came after a shutdown of Ngöbe-Buglé community protests earlier in February, 2012, left two protesters dead.

In spite of objections by prominent environmental groups, the government has approved and expedited large-scale mining projects, most notably a US$6.2 billion dollar project – an investment greater than the present expansion of the Panama Canal – to extract gold and copper.

For more information on mining issues, contact CIAM (p280).

Dams

Dams may become an epidemic in Panama, where proposals have been submitted for almost every river in the country. But none raises as much alarm as the US$50 million hydroelectric dam project underway on Naso tribal territory. The project on the Río Bonyic threatens the settlement and water supply. The reservoir would result in flooding up to the Parque Internacional La Amistad, putting its Unesco World Heritage Site status in danger. Unesco also expressed concern on dam plans on the nearby Río Changuinola. In addition to drawing international opposition, the dam has divided the tribe.

Development

As Panama City grows, sites that have been long earmarked for preservation are coming under threat.

Just outside of Panama City, Panama Bay is a Ramsar wetland site, identified as crucial to the hemisphere as it hosts up to two million shorebirds in their annual migrations. Mangroves in this 85,000-hectare area also play a vital role: as a nursury for fish and shellfish, a natural filter for sewage, and a buffer zone protecting the city from storms. In May, 2012, the government removed Panama Bay's protected status to make way for the development of urban and resort development including hotels and golf courses. Spearheading the campaign for preservation is the Audubon Society (p280).

Also of concern in Panama City are plans to extend the six-lane coastal highway known as Cinta Costera into the sea to wrap around the historic neighborhood of Casco Viejo, a Unesco World Heritage Site. Though it would reduce congested city traffic, it would also threaten the World Heritage status, as well as change the character of this beloved landmark. Neighborhood organizations are up in arms. Unesco opposes any development until studies may be undertaken, though the concrete is already being poured.

Monkey's Bridge: Mysteries of Evolution in Central America, by David Rains Wallace, tells the colorful evolutionary unfolding of fauna and flora on the isthmus, beginning three million years ago and ending in the present.

Isla de Coiba

One of the hottest environmental topics in Panama is the future of Isla de Coiba. This rainforest-covered island and Unesco World Heritage Site is set in one of the largest marine parks on the planet – scientists

ENVIRONMENTAL ORGANIZATIONS

Though there is little public sensitivity to environmental issues in Panama, a number of organizations strive to protect the environment and biodiversity.

Alianza para la Conservación y Desarrollo (ACD; ☎223-9170) is an NGO employing community education and advocacy for conservation, and sustainable alternatives for the indigenous and protected areas of Panama.

ANCON (www.ancon.org) Founded in 1985 by academic and business leaders, ANCON has played a major role in the creation of national parks and on many occasions has spurred ANAM into action.

Audubon Society (☎232-5977; www.audubonpanama.org; Casa No 2006-B, Llanos de Curundu, Panama City) Promoting birds in Panama for more than 35 years, with over 20 bird-watching field trips every year. Find upcoming events online.

Centro de Incidencia Ambiental (CIAM; ☎262-8831; www.ciampanama.org) Promotes environmental advocacy through grass-roots campaigns.

Fundación Albatros Media (☎317-3450; www.albatrosmedia.com; Ciudad del Saber, Panama City) Quality environmental documentaries on Panama.

Fundación Avifauna Eugene Eisenmann (p79) Promotes the preservation of tropical forest to support Panama's astounding diversity of bird life. Created the Panama Rainforest Discovery Center on Pipeline Rd.

Fundación Mar Viva (☎317-4350; www.marviva.net; Ciudad del Saber 168, Panama City) Patrols protected marine areas in Costa Rica and Panama with the goal of ending illegal fishing and replenishing marine life. Also promotes conservation and sustainable use of marine resources.

Nature Conservancy (☎317-0328; www.nature.org; Ciudad del Saber 352 A/B, Panama City) Prominent international conservation agency working extensively in the areas of Bocas del Toro, Península de Azuero, the upper Chagres and the Darién Biosphere Reserve.

Promar (☎757-9367; www.promar.20m.com) Educates about the environmental threats of unsustainable tourism development in the area of Bocas del Toro.

often compare Coiba to the Galápagos Islands. Yet, with annual funding of only US$60,000, it is far from the Galápagos standard. A lack of funding also challenges patrols from combating illegal fishing activity.

In 2004 Panama, Costa Rica, Colombia and Ecuador created a Pacific marine corridor to preserve the area's ecosystems.

Owing to the presence of a penal colony, this island and its surrounding waters remained long untouched, but now that the prison has been phased out, developers and members of the government see glorious tourism possibilities for this ecological gem. There are concerns that big development plans would destroy the fragile ecosystem.

In the past, the unregulated presence of cruise ships has caused disturbing situations, with sometimes as many as 200 tourists visiting the tiny snorkeling island of Granito de Oro – a number that is outrageously unsustainable. Little is being done to preserve the penal colony as a historic site; unfortunately, it is deteriorating rapidly.

Survival Guide

Directory A–Z

Accommodations

Any prices cited here are for accommodations at high-season rates, and they include Panama's 10% tax on hotel rooms.

There is usually no shortage of places to stay in Panama, except during holidays or special events outside Panama City, when advance reservations may be necessary. More popular hostels and small hotels usually require reservations in high season.

Doubles generally have private bathrooms.

B&Bs

Though they're a recent phenomenon in Panama, B&Bs are gaining popularity across the country. Rates are usually midrange. You'll find them at major tourist destinations including Panama City, Boquete and Bocas del Toro. B&Bs offer personalized service, a comfortable room with private bathroom, and breakfast is included.

Camping

Camping facilities are available in many of the national parks; typical fees are US$5 per person per night. Camping isn't available in most towns.

Homestays

Informal homestays are available throughout the country – it's best to inquire about this through local tourist information centers. Travelers who are exploring Kuna Yala and the Darién Province can often find lodging in local villages by asking around. Many villagers are happy to rent out a spare room (or set aside a hammock space) for US$12 to US$40 per night.

Hostels

As Panama becomes more popular with backpackers, hostels are springing up across the country. At the time of writing, none were connected with international youth hostel federations, though facilities are mostly good.

Hotels

Panama has no shortage of places to stay, although getting a hotel room during Carnaval, Semana Santa (Holy Week) and other holiday times can be difficult in some places. Hotel accommodations can also be tight if there is a special event.

Advance reservations are generally possible and are recommended if you're planning on staying at the better accommodations and, in general, in Bocas del Toro town on Isla Colón. Booking online is the most common way of reserving a room.

Before accepting a room ask to see several. The same prices are often charged for rooms of widely differing quality. Even at the US$10-a-night cheapies it's worth looking around. Naturally, hotels want you to rent their most expensive rooms; if you're on a tight budget, make a habit of asking if economical rooms are available. (Some Panamanian hotels have them but don't post their lowest prices.)

SLEEPING PRICE RANGES

The following price ranges refer to a double room with bathroom in high season. Unless otherwise stated tax is included in the price.

$ less than US$48

$$ US$48–$120

$$$ more than US$120

BOOK YOUR STAY ONLINE

For more accommodations reviews by Lonely Planet authors, check out http://hotels.lonelyplanet.com. You'll find independent reviews, as well as recommendations on the best places to stay. Best of all, you can book online.

Lodges

A handful of high-end lodges are scattered about the country. Although these places aren't cheap, they provide an excellent opportunity to be surrounded by nature with access to some spectacular hiking and wildlife-watching nearby.

Resorts

All-inclusive resorts often include meals, activities, private beach access and all the amenities. These can be a good option for travelers with children, as most resorts offer plenty of diversions for kids and adults.

Activities

Panama has scores of ways to spend a sun-drenched afternoon, from hiking through lush rainforest to snorkeling coral reefs. Diving, surfing, bird-watching and fishing are just a few of Panama's star attractions.

Children

Panamanians have a family-oriented culture, and will generally be very accommodating to travelers with children. The same can't be said of many businesses owned by expats, who very clearly state the age requirements of their guests.

High chairs in restaurants are a rarity in Panama, but safety seats in hired cars can be provided upon request. For diapers, creams and other supplies, the best places to stock up are in Panama City and David. Generally speaking, the supermarkets are excellent in Panama, and you can find just about any product you'd find in the US.

Most of Panama is quite safe to travel with children, though places that present greater health risks include Bocas del Toro, where dengue fever is present, and the Darién Province, where malaria and yellow fever, though rare, still exist.

Climate

A number of tours, some low-intensity, can be an enjoyable way for you and your children to see Panama's lush environment. Tour outfits such as Ancon Expeditions offer tailored family outings.

For more ideas about making the most of your family travels, get a hold of Lonely Planet's *Travel With Children*.

Customs Regulations

You may bring up to 10 cartons of cigarettes and five bottles of liquor into Panama tax free. If you try to leave Panama with products made from endangered species – such as jaguar teeth, ocelot skins and turtle shell – you'll face a steep fine and jail time.

Electricity

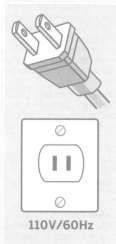

110V/60Hz

110V/60Hz

The power supply in Panama City is 120 volts.

Embassies & Consulates

More than 50 countries have embassies or consulates in Panama City. Their contact details can be found in the Panama white pages, listed under 'Embajada de' followed by the country name in Spanish. Many embassies appear in the yellow pages under 'Embajadas' or 'Consulados.' With the exception of the US and France, most embassies are located in the Marbella district of Panama City.

Ireland, Australia and New Zealand have no representation in Panama.

Canadian Embassy (☎294-2500; www.canadainterna tional.gc.ca/panama; Piso 11, Tower A, Torre de las Americas, Punta Pacifica)

Costa Rican Consulate (☎264-2980; www.embajada costaricaenpanama.com; Av Samuel Lewis, Edificio Omega, 3rd fl, Obarrio; ⊙9am-1pm Mon-Fri)

French Embassy (☎211-6200; www.ambafrance-pa.org; Plaza de Francia, Las Bóvedas, Casco Viejo)

German Embassy (☎263-7733; www.panama.diplo.de; Calle 53 Este, Piso PH, World Trade Center, Marbella)

Netherlands Consulate (☎264-7257; www.embajada-holanda.com/Panama.html; Calle 50, Marbella)

UK Embassy (☎297-6550; www.ukinpanama.fco.gov.uk/ en; Calle 53 Este, MMG Tower, 4th fl, Marbella)

US Embassy (☎207-7000; http://panama.usembassy.gov; Av Demetrio Basillo Lakas 783, Clayton)

Food

In Panama City there is an excellent range of restaurants serving everything from cheap set meals to gourmet cuisine. Outside the capital and major tourist attractions, there is much less variety. Panama's national dish is *sancocho* (chicken-and-vegetable stew). *Ropa vieja* (literally 'old clothes'), a spicy shredded beef combination served over rice, is another common and tasty dish. Rice – grown on dry land – is the staple of Panama. Green salads are hard to come by, but tropical fruit is abundant.

Meat figures prominently in the Panamanian diet. In addition to staples such as *bistec* (steak) and *carne asado* (roast meat), you'll encounter specialties like *carimañola* (a yucca roll filled with chopped meat and then deep fried). The most common snack is the empanada, a turnover filled with ground meat and fried. Another favorite is the tamale, which is cornmeal with a few spices and chicken or pork, wrapped in banana leaves and boiled.

One breakfast staple is *tortillas de maíz*. Unlike those found in Mexico and Guatemala, Panamanian tortillas are much thicker, and are essentially deep-fried cornmeal cakes. They go quite nicely with eggs or roast meat. *Hojaldras* are also served at breakfasts and available at snack bars. Like a doughnut, this deep-fried mass of dough is served hot and covered with sugar.

At *almuerzo* (lunch), many Panamanians opt for *comida corriente*, the meal of the working class. This is an inexpensive set meal of beef, chicken or fish served alongside *arroz* (rice), *frijoles* (black beans), *plátano* (fried plantain), chopped cabbage and an egg or an avocado.

Seafood is abundant. On the Caribbean coast and islands, everyday foods include shrimp, crab, octopus, lobster and fish such as *corvina* (sea bass). Along the Caribbean coast, dishes have a West Indian influence. Seafood is often mixed with coconut milk; coconut rice and coconut bread are also Caribbean treats.

In Panama City you'll often see men pushing carts and selling *raspados* (cones filled with shaved ice topped with fruit syrup and sweetened condensed milk).

Drink

Fresh fruit drinks, sweetened with heaped tablespoons of sugar and mixed with water or milk, are called *chichas*, and are extremely popular. Also be on the lookout for *chicheme* (a nonalcoholic concoction of milk, sweet corn, cinnamon and vanilla).

Coffee is traditionally served very strong and offered with cream or condensed milk. Espresso drinks are available only in major cities and tourist destinations.

The national alcoholic drink is made of *seco*, milk and ice. *Seco*, like rum, is distilled from sugarcane, and popular in the countryside. Popular in the central provinces, *vino de palma* is fermented sap extracted from the trunk of a palm tree.

By far the most popular alcoholic beverage in Panama is *cerveza* (beer), and the most popular local brands are Panamá, Balboa and Atlas.

Gay & Lesbian Travelers

Panamanians are more out than in recent years, though the trend is much more prevalent in the capital than anywhere else. More than in other parts of Central America, you will probably meet openly gay locals, though the culture generally follows an unspoken 'don't ask, don't tell' policy.

Panama City has a few gay and lesbian clubs, advertised only online. Outside the capital gay bars are hard to come by and discrimination is more prevalent. In most instances, gays and lesbians just blend in with the straight crowd at the hipper places and avoid beer halls and other conventional lairs of homophobia.

Panamanian website www.farraurbana.com lists upcoming gay and lesbian events and parties, new club openings and political issues in Panama City. You'll need at least a little Spanish to maneuver through the site.

Health

There are no required vaccines for Panama, but among those recommended are yellow fever, typhoid, rabies and hepatitis A and B. See your doctor well ahead, since most vaccines don't produce immunity until at least two weeks after being given. Request an International Certificate of Vaccination (aka the yellow booklet); it's mandatory for countries that require proof of yellow-fever vaccination.

Tap water is generally drinkable in Panama, except for in Bocas del Toro and the Comarca de Kuna Yala. Visitors who have recently arrived may want to start with bottled water and minimum amounts of tap water.

A superb book called *International Travel and Health*, revised annually and available online at no cost, is published by the **World Health Organization** (www.who.int/ith). Another website of general interest is **MD Travel Health** (www.mdtravelhealth.com), with complete travel-health recommendations for every country, updated daily, also at no cost.

Good medical care is widely available in Panama City and also David, and even sought after with a brisk business of medical tourism, though it's limited elsewhere. Most doctors and hospitals expect cash payment, regardless of whether you have travel health insurance.

Insurance

Prior to your trip, signing up for a travel insurance policy to cover theft, loss and medical problems is a good idea. Be advised, however, that some policies specifically exclude dangerous activities, which can include scuba diving, motorcycling, and even trekking.

You may prefer a policy that pays doctors or hospitals directly, rather than you having to pay on the spot and claim later. If you have to claim later, ensure you keep all documentation.

Check that the policy covers ambulances or an emergency flight home.

Infectious Diseases

DENGUE FEVER

A viral infection, dengue fever (breakbone fever) is transmitted by mosquitoes breeding in standing water. It is especially common in densely populated, urban environments. Flu-like symptoms include fever, muscle aches, joint pains, headaches, nausea and vomiting, often followed by a rash. Most cases resolve in a few days. Take analgesics such as acetaminophen/paracetamol (Tylenol) and drink plenty of fluids. Severe cases may require hospitalization. In recent times, there have been many cases in the province of Bocas del Toro.

HEPATITIS A

The vaccine for hepatitis A is extremely safe and highly effective. The second-most common travel-related infection (after traveler's diarrhea), it's a viral infection of the liver that is usually acquired by ingestion of contaminated water, food or ice. Symptoms include fever, malaise, jaundice, nausea, vomiting and abdominal pain. Most cases resolve without complications, though hepatitis A occasionally causes severe liver damage. There is no treatment.

HEPATITIS B

Hepatitis B is a liver infection usually acquired by sexual contact or by exposure to infected blood, generally through blood transfusions or contaminated needles. The Hepatitis B vaccine is safe and highly effective. A total of three injections is necessary to establish full immunity.

LEISHMANIASIS

Leishmaniasis occurs in rural and forested areas throughout Panama, especially the eastern and south-central regions. The disease causes slow-growing ulcers on the body, but the infection may become generalized, especially in those with HIV. Leishmaniasis is transmitted by sandflies. To protect yourself, follow the same precautions as for mosquitoes, with finer-size mesh on mosquito netting (at least 18 holes to the linear inch).

LEPTOSPIROSIS

Leptospirosis is acquired by exposure to water contaminated by the urine of infected animals. The greatest risk occurs at times of flooding, when sewage overflow may contaminate water sources. Initial symptoms resemble a mild flu and usually subside in a few days, but a minority of cases are complicated by jaundice or meningitis. Minimize your risk by staying out of bodies of fresh water that may be contaminated by animal urine.

MALARIA

Malaria is transmitted by mosquito bites, usually between dusk and dawn. High-spiking fevers may be accompanied by chills, sweats, headache, body aches, weakness, vomiting or diarrhea. Severe cases may lead to seizures, confusion, coma and death.

Malaria pills are recommended for rural areas in the provinces of Bocas del Toro, Darién and Kuna Yala. For Bocas del Toro, chloroquine is taken once weekly in a dosage of 500mg, starting one to two weeks before arrival and continuing through the trip, and for four weeks after departure. In the Darién and Kuna Yala, there are chloroquine-resistant mosquitoes. Your options there are mefloquine, the milder doxycycline, or Malarone.

Protecting yourself against mosquito bites is the best prevention. If you develop a fever after returning home, see a physician, as malaria symptoms may not occur for months.

RABIES

In Panama, rabies is transmitted mainly by vampire bats. If you are bitten by any animal, thoroughly wash the wound and visit a doctor to determine whether or not further treatment is necessary.

TYPHOID

Caused by ingestion of food or water contaminated by *Salmonella typhi*, fever occurs in virtually all cases. Other symptoms may include headache, malaise, muscle aches, dizziness, loss of appetite, nausea and abdominal pain. Either diarrhea or constipation may occur. Possible complications include intestinal perforation or bleeding, confusion, delirium or, rarely, coma.

The vaccine is usually given orally but is also available as an injection. The treatment drug is usually a quinolone antibiotic such asciprofloxacin (Cipro) or levofloxacin (Levaquin).

YELLOW FEVER

A life-threatening viral infection, yellow fever is transmitted by mosquitoes in forested areas. Flu-like symptoms include fever, chills, headache, muscle aches, backache, loss of appetite, nausea and vomiting. Some patients enter a second, toxic phase, which can lead to death.

Vaccination is recommended for travelers visiting Chepo, Darién and the Kuna Yala.

TRAVELER'S DIARRHEA

To prevent traveler's diarrhea avoid untreated tap water, eat fresh fruit or vegetables that are cooked or peeled, and be highly selective when eating food from street vendors.

If you develop diarrhea, drink plenty of fluids, preferably an oral rehydration solution containing lots of salt and sugar. A few loose stools don't require treatment, but if you start having more than four or five stools a day, you should start taking an antibiotic (usually a quinolone drug) and an antidiarrheal

---

MEDICAL CHECKLIST

⇒ Acetaminophen (Tylenol) or aspirin

⇒ Adhesive or paper tape

⇒ Antibacterial ointment (eg Bactroban) for cuts and abrasions

⇒ Antibiotics

⇒ Antidiarrheal drugs (eg loperamide)

⇒ Antihistamines (for hay fever and allergic reactions)

⇒ Anti-inflammatory drugs (eg ibuprofen)

⇒ Bandages, gauze, gauze rolls

⇒ DEET-containing insect repellent for the skin

⇒ Malaria pills – recommended for the Darién

⇒ Oral rehydration salts

⇒ Permethrin-containing insect spray for clothing, tents and bed nets

⇒ Pocket knife

⇒ Scissors, safety pins, tweezers

⇒ Steroid cream or cortisone (for poison ivy and other allergic rashes)

⇒ Sunblock

⇒ Syringes and sterile needles

⇒ Thermometer

agent (such as loperamide). If diarrhea is bloody or persists for more than 72 hours, or is accompanied by fever, shaking chills or severe abdominal pain, seek medical attention.

Internet Access

Most cities and towns in Panama have inexpensive internet cafes. Public wi-fi access is increasingly common in bus terminals, plazas, libraries and restaurants. Hotels and hostels in more tourist-oriented areas are likely to have both internet and wi-fi; the Kuna Yala and Darién regions are exceptions.

Legal Matters

The legal drinking age in Panama is 18, which is strictly enforced in Panama City and generally ignored elsewhere. In Panama you are presumed guilty until found innocent. If you are accused of a serious crime, you will be taken to jail, where you will likely spend several months before your case goes before a judge. Some simple but valuable advice: stay away from people who commit crimes. For example, you can expect to go to jail if the car you are in is stopped and found to contain illegal drugs, even if they aren't yours.

In Panama penalties for possession of even small amounts of illegal drugs are much stricter than in the USA, Europe, Australia and almost everywhere else. Defendants often spend years in prison before they are brought to trial and, if convicted (as is usually the case), can expect sentences of several more years in prison. Most lawyers won't accept drug cases because the outcome is certain: conviction.

If you are jailed, your embassy will offer only limited assistance. This may include a visit from an embassy staff member to make sure your human rights have not been violated, letting your family know where you are and putting you in contact with a lawyer (whom you must pay yourself). Embassy officials will not bail you out.

Remember that you are legally required to carry identification at all times. This should be a photographic ID, preferably a passport. Although this may seem like an inconvenience, police officers reserve the right to request documentation from tourists at all times, and several readers have been forced to spend the night in prison for failure to produce proper ID.

Bear in mind that Panama is a conservative society. Generally speaking, displays of gratuitous flesh are not looked kindly upon, though this is waived once a year when the country hits the Carnaval season.

With that said, it is illegal for men and women to walk around topless, even if you are on your way to the beach. This rule is strictly enforced in Bocas del Toro town on Isla Colón, and you can expect to be stopped on the streets by police officers if you don't cover up.

Maps

International Travel Maps (☑in Canada 604-273-1400; www.itmb.com) publishes an excellent 1:800,000 color map showing the geographical features, cities, towns, national parks, airports and roads of Panama. Maps are available for purchase online.

At **Instituto Geográfico Nacional** (Tommy Guardia; ☑236-2444; near Av Arturo del Valle at Transistmica; ☺8am-4pm Mon-Fri) in Panama City, you can buy topographical maps of selected cities and regions. Various free tourist publications distributed in Panama also have maps, though hiking maps are rarely available at national park ranger stations.

Money

Panama uses the US dollar as its currency. The official name for it is the balboa, but it's exactly the same bill, and in practice people use the terms *dólar* and balboa interchangeably. Panamanian coins are of the same value, size and metal as US coins, though both are frequently used. Coins include one, five, 10, 25 and 50 *centavos* (or *centésimos*) – 100 *centavos* equal one balboa. Most businesses won't break US$50 and US$100 bills, and those that do may require you to present your passport.

ATMs

Throughout Panama ATMs are readily available except in the most isolated places – look for the red *'sistema clave'* sign. Generally speaking, ATMs accept cards on most networks (Plus, Cirrus, MasterCard, Visa, Amex), though a charge is usually levied depending on your issuing bank. The amount that can be withdrawn at one time varies from bank to bank, though it is usually around US$500.

There are several places where it's essential to show up with cash. Among tourist destinations, the following places have no banks, and it's a long way to the nearest ATM: Santa Catalina, Santa Fé, Boca Brava, Isla Contadora, Isla Grande (Archipiélago de Bocas del Toro), Portobelo, Isla de Coiba and the Darién.

Credit Cards

Although they are widely accepted at travel agencies, upscale hotels and many restaurants, credit cards can be problematic almost everywhere else. In short, carry enough cash to get you to the next bank or ATM.

At the time of research, very few businesses on Bocas del Toro accepted credit cards. Find out if your hotel does *before* you go to avoid any unpleasant surprises.

Moneychangers

The only bank that exchanges foreign currency is the Banco Nacional de Panamá counter at Tocumen International Airport. Once you have departed from the airport, the only place that can change foreign currency for dollars is a *casa de cambio* (exchange house), which can be difficult to find outside Panama City.

Taxes

A tax of 10% is added to the price of hotel rooms. When you inquire about a hotel, ask whether the quoted price includes the tax. Note that hotel prices given in this book include the 10% tax.

A 5% sales tax is levied on all nonfood products.

Tipping

The standard tipping rate in Panama is around 10% of the bill, though in small cafes and more casual places, tipping is not necessary. Taxi drivers do not expect tips but tour guides definitely do.

Traveler's Checks

Although they can be cashed at a few banks, traveler's checks are rarely accepted by businesses, and traveler's checks in currencies other than US dollars are not accepted anywhere in Panama. In addition, some banks will only accept American Express traveler's checks. The banks that do accept traveler's checks typically charge an exchange fee equal to 1% of the amount of the check.

Opening Hours

Banks 8:30am to 1pm or 3pm weekdays; some have Saturday hours as well.

Bars Open from around noon to 10pm, later on Friday and Saturday nights (typically 2am).

Government offices 8am to 4pm weekdays; they don't close for lunch.

Grocery stores 8am to around 8pm or 9pm; the El Rey chain stays open 24 hours.

Nightclubs Open around 10pm or 11pm and close at 3am or 4am in Panama City.

Post offices 7am to 6pm weekdays, and to 4:30pm Saturday.

Restaurants Lunch from noon to 3pm and dinner from 6pm to 10pm. Those that offer breakfast open from 7am to 10am. On Sunday many restaurants close. In Panama City and David restaurants open later on Friday and Saturday nights, until about 11pm or midnight.

Shops & pharmacies Around 9am or 10am to 6pm or 7pm, Monday to Saturday.

Travel agencies & tour operators 8am to noon and 1:30pm to 5pm weekdays, and from 8am to noon Saturday.

Photography

Panamanians may be low-key about having their photo taken but it is always best to ask before doing so. General landscape scenes that include locals are usually fine.

In general, indigenous people should not be photographed without their permission. In addition, it may ruin any chance of interaction you have with locals. In the Comarca de Kuna Yala, photographing locals is considered rude. Those who will pose attach a price tag – usually US$1 per photo.

Tropical shadows are extremely strong and come out almost black on photographs. Often a bright but hazy day makes for better photographs than a very sunny one. Photography in open shade or using a flash will help. As a general rule, the best time for shooting is when the sun is low – the first and last two hours of the day. Remember, too, that flash equipment

is forbidden in Panama's churches and museums.

Post

Panama's mail is handled by **Correos de Panama** (www.correos.gob.pa). Airmail to the USA takes five to 10 days; to Europe and Australia it takes 10 days. Panama has neither vending machines for stamps nor drop-off boxes for mail. You may be able to buy stamps and send mail from an upscale hotel to avoid going to the post office and standing in line.

In Panama City packages can only be mailed from the Plaza las Americas post office. Bring all packing materials yourself.

General delivery mail can be addressed to '(name), Entrega General, (town and province), República de Panamá.' Be sure the sender calls the country 'República de Panamá' rather than simply 'Panamá,' or the mail may be sent back.

Public Holidays

Días feriados (national holidays) are taken seriously in Panama, and banks, public offices and many stores close. Public transportation tends to be tight on all holidays and the days immediately preceding or following them – book tickets ahead.

There is no bus service at all on the Thursday afternoon and Friday before Easter, and many businesses are closed for the entire Semana Santa (Holy Week; the week before Easter). From Thursday to Easter Sunday, all bars are closed and alcohol sales are prohibited. Beach hotels are usually booked several weeks in advance for Semana Santa, though a limited choice of rooms is often available.

The week between Christmas and New Year, along with the first week of the year, tend to be unofficial holidays. In addition, various towns have celebrations for their own particular days throughout the year. These other holidays and special events are not official holidays, and businesses remain open.

Most official national holidays are celebrated on Monday to create long weekends. When holidays fall on a Thursday or Friday, they are celebrated on the following Monday; holidays that happen to fall on Tuesday or Wednesday are usually celebrated the prior Monday.

New Year's Day January 1

Martyrs' Day January 9

Good Friday, Easter March/April

Workers' Day May 1

Founding of Old Panama (Panama City only) August 15

Hispanic Day October 12

National Anthem Day November 1

All Souls' Day November 2

Independence Day November 3

First Call for Independence November 10

Independence from Spain November 28

Mothers' Day December 8

Christmas Day December 25

Safe Travel

Crime is a problem in certain parts of Panama City. The city's better districts are safer than in many other capitals: witness the all-night restaurants and activity on the streets at night. On the other hand, it is not safe to walk around at night on the outskirts of Casco Viejo – be careful in the side streets of this district even in the daytime. In general, stay where it's well lit and there are plenty of people around.

Colón has some upscale residential areas, but the city is widely known for street crime. Consult the staff at your hotel on areas to avoid.

Certain areas in the Darién Province bordering Colombia are extremely dangerous. Few travelers have reason to be in these areas. In the past, it has been used as a staging ground by criminals, human traffickers, the Colombian paramilitary and guerrillas. The area that is particularly treacherous goes beyond Boca de Cupe to Colombia, the traditional path through the Darién Gap.

Numerous Colombian boats travel the Caribbean through the Archipiélago de San Blás between the Zona Libre in Colón and Cartagena, Colombia. There have been cases of boats trafficking drugs on northbound voyages. Take this possibility into account if you plan on taking one of these slow cargo boats. On the Pacific there have been incidents as well.

Hiking Safety

Though it's tropical, Panama runs the gamut from hot to cold and hiking is not easy here. You should go adequately prepared. Always ask about the conditions of the trail before heading out – either with local outfitters or rangers. Carry plenty of water, even on short journeys, and always bring food, matches and adequate clothing – jungles *do* get quite a bit colder at night, particularly at higher elevations.

Hikers have been known to get lost in rainforests, even seemingly user-friendly ones such as Parque Nacional Volcán Barú and the Sendero Los Quetzales. Landslides, storms and vegetation growth can make trails difficult to follow. In some cases, even access roads can deteriorate enough for transport to leave you a few miles before your intended drop-off point. This is just the reality of the jungle. Many hikers have gotten lost and there is no official rescue organization to help. If you are heading out without a guide, let your plans be known at your hotel and tell them the number of days you will be gone.

Never walk in unmarked rainforest; if there's no trail going in, you can assume that there won't be one when you decide to turn around and come back out. Always plan your transportation in advance – know where and when the last bus will pass your terminus, or arrange for a taxi pickup with a responsible, recommended transporter.

Police

Police corruption is not as big a problem in Panama as it is in some other Latin American countries. However, it's not unheard of for a Panamanian police officer to stop a motorist for no obvious reason, accuse him or her of violating a law, and levy a fine to be paid on the spot. If there are people around, making a big scene will sometimes fluster the officer into letting you go. Most of the time, however, you become an unwilling participant in a waiting game.

Your best option, unless you want to try to wait out the officer, is to negotiate the fine down. Failure to pay anything can result in your being led to jail with the officer insisting you really did break some law.

Some cities in Panama have tourist police – a division created to deal specifically with travelers. Identifiable by armbands on their uniform, officers in this division may be more helpful.

Swimming Safety

In recent years there have been several deaths in Bocas del Toro Province and on other beaches around the country owing to strong currents. Tourist brochures do not mention the drownings that occur every year in Panamanian waters. Of these, about 80% are caused by rip currents. A rip current is a strong current that pulls the swimmer out to sea. It occurs when two currents that move parallel to the shore meet, causing the opposing waters to choose the path of least resistance, which is a path out to sea. It is most important to remember that rip currents will pull you *out* but not *under*.

If you find yourself caught in a rip current, stay calm and swim parallel to the shore to get out of it – rip currents dissipate quickly. When the current dissipates, swim back in at a 45° angle to the shore to avoid being caught by the current again. Do not try to swim directly back in, as you would be swimming against the rip current and would only exhaust yourself.

If you feel a rip current while you are wading, try to come back in sideways, thus offering less body surface to the current. If you cannot make headway, walk parallel to the beach so that you can get out of the rip current.

Thefts & Muggings

Tourist-oriented crime is uncommon in Panama, but it does happen. Be smart – avoid carrying all your money in one place and avoid entering areas that appear unsafe.

If you go out at night, leave your watch, jewelry and expensive clothing at the hotel. Take only the amount of money you think you'll need, and then a little extra tucked away in a shoe. If you look like you don't have anything of value on you, you're less likely to interest a mugger.

If you are robbed, you should get a police report as soon as possible. This is a requirement for any insurance claims, although it is unlikely that the police will be able to recover the property. If you don't speak Spanish and are having a hard time making a police report, your embassy can often advise and help.

Panama has a long history of business-related crimes, particularly with regard to real estate. If you want to sink money into any kind of Panamanian business, make sure you check it out *thoroughly*. As a general rule: if a deal seems too good to be true, it probably is.

Telephone

Panama's country code is ⏀507. To call Panama from abroad, use the country code before the seven-digit Panamanian telephone number. There are no local area codes in Panama.

Telephone calls to anywhere within Panama can be made from pay phones. Local calls cost US$0.10 for the first three minutes, then US$0.05 per minute. You can buy phone cards at pharmacies, shops and Cable & Wireless offices (the national phone company) in denominations of US$3, US$5, US$10 and US$20. You then plug this into the phone and dial the local number. Some public phones accept both cards and coins, but many accept only cards. Note that calling cell phones (which typically begin with a '6') is much pricier (US$0.25 per minute).

If you are traveling for an extended period, it may be useful to get a SIM card if you have an unlocked cell phone. Otherwise, kiosks in malls sell pay-per-use phones for as cheap as US$20, and many come with minutes loaded. Having a phone can be invaluable for last-minute reservations or directions.

International Calls

Travelers wishing to make international calls can do so with a phone card or via an internet cafe. A phone card has a scratch-off code and can be used from any phone. They come in denominations of US$1, US$3, US$5, US$10 and US$20 and offer English-speaking dial-up instructions. Buy at least US$5 for an international call.

Connecting to an international operator from a residential, business or pay phone is easy. To connect with a local international operator, simply dial 106. For an international operator in the USA, dial 109 (AT&T). To reach a Costa Rican operator, dial 107; for a Colombian operator, dial 116.

The increasing frequency of wi-fi in accommodations also means that if you're traveling with a laptop, you can just connect and call for pennies. Some cafes provide headphones for internet calls.

Time

From the last Sunday in October through to the first Sunday in April, Panama time is in line with New York and Miami. Because Panama does not observe daylight saving time, during the rest of the year (April through October), Panama is one hour behind New York. Panama is five hours behind Greenwich Mean Time (GMT) and one hour ahead of the rest of Central America. If you're coming from Costa Rica, be sure to reset your watch.

Toilets

Panamanian plumbing generally is of high quality, although most places will ask you to place used toilet paper in the trash bins provided instead of flushing it away. That's because narrow piping may cause clogging.

Be advised that in Kuna Yala and in some parts of Bocas del Toro, whatever you flush goes straight out to sea. While you certainly can't stop nature from calling, be sure not to flush anything else down the toilet that doesn't belong in the sea.

Public toilets can be found mainly in bus terminals, airports and restaurants. In Spanish, restrooms are called *baños* and are often marked *caballeros* (gentlemen) and *damas* (ladies). Outside the cities, toilet paper is not always provided, so you may want to consider carrying a personal supply.

Tourist Information

Autoridad de Turismo Panamá (ATP, Panama Tourism Authority; ☏226-7000; www.atp.gob.pa; Vía Israel, Centro Atlapa, San Francisco; ⊗8:30am-4:30pm Mon-Fri), formerly known as IPAT, is the national tourism agency. In addition to this head office, ATP runs offices in Bocas del Toro, Boquete, Colón, David, Paso Canoas, Penonomé, Portobelo, Santiago, Villa de Los Santos, Las Tablas, El Valle and Pedasí. There are smaller information counters at the ruins of Panamá Viejo, in Casco Viejo, and in both the Tocumen International Airport and the Albrook domestic airport.

ATP has a few useful maps and brochures, but often has a problem keeping enough in stock for distribution to tourists. Most offices are staffed with people who speak only Spanish, and the helpfulness of any particular office depends on the person at the counter. Some employees really try to help, but others are just passing the time. As a general rule, you will get more useful information if you have specific questions.

Travelers With Disabilities

Instituto Panameño de Habilitación Especial (IPHE, Panamanian Institute for Special Rehabilitation; ☏261-0500; www.iphe.gob.pa; Camino Real, Betania, Panama City; ⊗7am-4pm) was created by the government to assist people with disabilities in Panama, including foreign tourists. However, the law does not require – and Panamanian businesses do not provide – discounts to foreign tourists with disabilities.

Panama is not wheelchair-friendly; with the exception of wheelchair ramps outside a few upscale hotels, parking spaces for people with disabilities and perhaps a few dozen oversized bathroom stalls, accommodations for people with physical disabilities do not exist in Panama. Even at the best hotels, you won't find railings in showers or beside toilets.

If you have a disability and want to communicate with a person with disabilities who might have been to Panama recently, consider becoming a member of **Travelin' Talk Network** (TTN; ☏in USA 303-232-2979; www.travelintalk. net; membership US$20). This organization offers a worldwide directory of members with various disabilities who communicate among themselves about travel.

Visas & Documents

Onward Tickets

Travelers officially need onward tickets before they are allowed to enter Panama. This requirement is not often checked at Tocumen International Airport, but travelers arriving by land should anticipate a need to show an onward ticket.

If you're heading to Colombia, Venezuela or another South American country from Panama, you may need an onward or round-trip ticket before you will be allowed entry into that country or even allowed to board the plane if you're flying. A quick check with the appropriate embassy – easy to do via the internet – will tell you whether the country that you're heading to has an onward-ticket requirement.

Passports, Tourist Cards & Visas

Every visitor needs a valid passport and an onward ticket to enter Panama, but further requirements vary by nationality and change occasionally. Anyone planning a trip to Panama would be advised to check online to obtain the latest information on entry requirements. Ticketing agents of airlines that fly to Panama and tour operators that send groups there often can provide this information.

A valid passport is required to enter Panama, though additional requirements vary by country. Note that US citizens can no longer enter Panama with just a driver's license and a birth certificate.

Tourist cards are no longer obtained upon arrival, but are included in the price of your air ticket. No matter where you are coming from, you will generally be given a 90-day stamp in your passport when you enter Panama. This means you are allowed to remain in Panama for 90 days without having to obtain further permission from the authorities. After 90 days, visas and tourist cards can be extended at *migración* (immigration) offices.

Travelers entering Panama overland will probably be asked to show an onward ticket and proof of sufficient funds (US$500) or a credit card.

At the time of research, people holding passports from the following countries needed to show only their passports to enter Panama: Argentina, Austria, Belgium, Chile, Colombia, Costa Rica, Czech Republic, Denmark, England, El Salvador, Finland, France, Germany, Greece, Guatemala, Holland, Honduras, Hungary, Ireland, Israel, Italy, Luxembourg, Paraguay, Poland, Portugal, Singapore, South Korea, Spain, Sweden, Switzerland, the UK and Uruguay.

People from the following countries need a passport and a tourist card: Antigua, Australia, Bahamas, Barbados, Belize, Canada, Dominican Republic, Granada, Guyana, Jamaica, Japan, New Zealand, Taiwan, Thailand, Tobago, Trinidad, the USA and Venezuela.

Citizens from countries not on this list will need to obtain a visa, available at Panamanian embassies or consulates. Contact the one nearest you or call Migración y Naturalización in Panama City.

In the event that you lose your passport while in Panama, you'll need proof of when you entered the country to be able to leave. That proof, strangely enough, does not come from an immigration office but from the airline you flew in on. You need to go to the airline's main office in Panama City and request a certification of your entry date (certificación de vuelo). There's no charge, but you'll likely be asked to come back the next day to pick it up. When you leave the country, along with your new passport (obtained from your embassy in Panama City), you'll present your certificación de vuelo to an immigration agent.

Visa Extensions

Visas and tourist cards are both good for 90 days. To extend your stay, you'll have to go to an office of Migración y Naturalización in Panama City, David or Chitré. You must bring your passport and photocopies of the page with your personal information and of the stamp of your most recent entry to Panama. You must also bring two passport-size photos, an onward air or bus ticket and a letter to the director stating your reasons for wishing to extend your visit. You must have proof of funds (US$500) for the remainder of your stay. You will have to fill out a prórroga de turista (tourist extension) and pay US$250. You will then be issued a plastic photo ID card. Go early in the day

as the whole process takes about two hours.

If you have extended your time, you will also need to obtain a permiso de salida (exit permit) to leave the country. For this, bring your passport and a paz y salvo (a certificate stating you don't owe any back taxes) to the immigration office. Paz y salvos are issued at Ministerios de Economia y Finanzas, found in towns with immigration offices, which simply require that you bring in your passport, fill out a form and pay US$1.

These documents can be obtained in Panama City at the Migración y Naturalización and the Ministerio de Economia y Finanzas, Dirección de Ingresos.

Migración y Naturalización (Immigration Office; ☑507-1800; www.migracion. gob.pa; Av Cuba & Calle 28 Este, Calidonia; ◔7:30am-3:30pm Mon-Fri)

Ministerio de Economia y Finanzas, Dirección de Ingresos (☑800-4636; www.dgi. gob.pa; cnr Via España & Calle 52 Este) For a paz y salvo (a certificate stating you don't owe any back taxes).

Women Travelers

Female travelers usually find Panama safe. A minority of Panamanian men may make flirtatious comments, hiss, honk their horn or stare, even if you're accompanied. Don't take it as a challenge. A kind of hormonal babble, this behavior is as much about male bonding as the female passerby. The best response is to follow the lead of Panamanian women: give these men a broad berth, ignore their comments and look away.

While locals might get away with skimpy, stretchy clothing, travelers will naturally attract less attention with a more conservative approach. Shorts mark you as a tourist; it's up to you if you want to wear them. In the interior, dress is more formal, with skirts and nice sandals the norm. It is not legal to go topless, even in beach towns, and even for men.

Women traveling solo will get more attention than those traveling in pairs or groups. Although assault and rape of foreign travelers is rare, avoid placing yourself in risky scenarios. In bars, do not take drinks from strangers. In general, don't walk alone in isolated places, don't hitchhike and always pay particular attention to your surroundings.

If you are taking a long-distance bus, sit next to a woman or a family if you are nervous about come-ons. Be picky about your taxis: though shared taxis (between unknown parties) may be the norm, avoid those with more than one man in them. If the driver tries to pick up another fare, you can offer to pay more to travel alone.

Work

It's difficult for foreigners to find work in Panama. The government doesn't like anyone taking jobs away from Panamanians, and the labor laws reflect this sentiment. Basically, the only foreigners legally employed in Panama work for their own businesses, possess skills not found in Panama, or work for companies that have special agreements with the Panamanian government.

Transportation

GETTING THERE & AWAY

Entering the Country

Passengers entering Panama by air are less scrutinized than those crossing by land. Upon arrival, travelers may have to fill out a tourist card depending on their nationality; the fee is incorporated into the price of the ticket.

The most popular overland crossing is from Costa Rica at Paso Canoas. You may be asked to show an onward ticket – a return bus ticket to Costa Rica will suffice – and a credit card or US$500. Other crossings include the low-key border at Sixaola/Guabito and the seldom-used Río Sereno.

Flights, tours and rail tickets can be booked online at lonelyplanet.com/bookings.

Air

Panama has two international airports. Most international flights arrive to Panama City's **Tocumen International Airport** (www.tocumenpanama. aero), 35km from downtown. Located 5km southeast of the Costa Rican border, David's **Aeropuerto Enrique Malek** (☑721-1072)

frequently handles flights to and from San José.

With frequent flights to the US and throughout Latin America, Panama's national airline **Copa** (www. copaair.com) meets international standards. Low-cost airlines that provide international flights to Panama include **American Airlines** (☑238-4695; www.aa.com), **Avianca** (☑238-4096; www. avianca.com), **Continental Airlines** (☑238-4979; www. continental.com), **Delta Air Lines** (☑238-4793; www. delta.com), **Grupo Taca** (☑238-4116; www.taca.com) and **Iberia** (☑227-3966; www.iberia.com).

Grupo Taca provides services between all the Central American capitals and Panama City. In addition, Copa also serves Costa Rica, Cuba, the Dominican Republic, El Salvador, Guatemala, Haiti, Jamaica and Mexico.

Land

Many travelers arrive in Panama by bus from Costa Rica. It's recommended that you get to the border early in order to ensure that you don't miss onward transportation on the other side. There are no roads into Colombia, and travelers are strongly discouraged from crossing overland due to the instability of the border region.

DEPARTURE TAX

Panama levies a US$40 departure tax for outbound passengers on international flights, which is included in the cost of the ticket.

Border Crossings

There are three border crossings between Costa Rica and Panama. Most travelers cross at Paso Canoas. Note that Panama is always one hour ahead of Costa Rica.

To enter Panama from Costa Rica, you'll need a passport, an onward ticket and proof of solvency – US$500 or a credit card. At the border you'll fill out a US$5 tourist card (some nationalities are exempt, while others need a visa to enter).

PASO CANOAS

On the Interamericana, this chaotic and heavily used border sits between Panama City and San José (Costa Rica). Border hours here change frequently; at last check the border was open 7am to 11pm daily.

Ensure that you have both entry and exit stamps put in your passport. If you don't have an onward ticket and are asked to show one, you can buy a bus ticket from either Panaline or Tica Bus at the border.

Just beyond the immigration window, Banco Nacional de Panamá has an ATM but does not change Costa Rican colones to US dollars. Ask moneychangers on the street for their exchange rate *before* reaching for your cash.

In Panama, taxis and buses are stationed just past the border. It's best to sleep in the nearest Panamanian hub of David. Buses for David (US$2.75, 1½ hours, 5am to 9:45pm) depart every 10 minutes. Buses depart five times daily for Panama City (US$17, eight hours), stopping along the way. Express buses depart twice daily, in the morning and late evening.

The 24-hour taxi stand is near the first bus terminal. Rates to David (US$40 to US$50 per party) vary depending on the number of passengers and the hour.

If you are entering Costa Rica, you may be required to show a ticket out of the country, although this is rarely requested.

SIXAOLA/GUABITO

This crossing (open 8am to 5pm daily) is on the Caribbean coast. Sixaola is the last town on the Costa Rican side; Guabito is its Panamanian counterpart. There are no hotels or banks in Guabito, but stores accept Costa Rican colones or US dollars. Colones are not accepted south of Guabito.

National bus services on either side run until around 7pm. Frequent minibuses travel from Guabito to Changuinola (US$1, 30 minutes), 17km away, during daylight hours. The minibuses leave from the southern side of the elevated entrance road, just past the immigration office. Taxis (US$3 per person) also serve Changuinola.

Changuinola has hotels, several banks, some decent restaurants and an airstrip serving David and Panama City. Travel on to Almirante for transportation to Bocas del Toro.

RÍO SERENO

Tourists are a novelty in this little town at the eastern terminus of the scenic Concepción–Volcán road. Arriving by bus, it's hard to determine where one country ends and the other begins. The Río Sereno crossing is open from 8am to 5pm daily.

The immigration office is near a police communications tower – look for the orange-and-black 'Migracion' sign.

Banco Nacional de Panamá has an ATM, cashes traveler's checks and provides cash advances against major credit cards. Foreign currency cannot be exchanged here.

Along the main road, a bus terminal sits two blocks northeast of the bank. Buses depart to David (US$6.50), hourly, 40km away, via Volcán, with the first bus departing at 5am and the last at 5pm. You can also try a taxi to David (US$70).

Bus

At all three border crossings, you can take a local bus up to the border on either side, cross over, board another local bus and continue on your way. Be aware that the last buses leave the border crossings at Guabito and Río Sereno at 7pm and 5pm, respectively; the last bus leaves Paso Canoas for Panama City at 9:30pm.

Two companies, **Panaline** (☑227-8648; www.viajeros.com/panaline) and **Tica Bus** (☑262-2084; www.ticabus.com), operate daily *directo* (direct) buses between San José (Costa Rica) and Panama City, departing from the Albrook Bus Terminal. Both recommend that you make reservations a few days in advance.

Car & Motorcycle

Driving from the USA or Canada takes about a week or considerably more in order to visit some of the fantastic sights en route. Driving at night is not recommended. Central American roads are narrow, rarely painted with a center stripe, often potholed and subject to hazards such as cattle and pedestrians in rural areas.

If you decide to drive to Panama get insurance in advance, have your papers in order (including a *permiso de salida* – exit permit – from the country of the car's origin) and never leave your car unattended (fortunately, guarded lots are common in Latin America). US license plates are attractive as souvenirs, so you should display these from inside the car.

If you are bringing a car into Panama, you must pay US$5 for a *tarjeta de circulación* (vehicle control certificate) and another US$1 to have the car fumigated. You will also need to show a driver's license, proof of ownership and Panamanian insurance papers, which is best bought upon entering the country at an insurance dealer near *aduana* (customs). Copy the insurance policy and have it officially stamped.

Your passport will be stamped to show that you have paid and followed procedures when you brought the vehicle into the country. A car visa is only valid for one month and can be renewed for up to three months. Overstaying will cost you another US$300 to $500, payable only before expiration.

Sea

It's possible to cross to Colombia by sea, though it can be a rough crossing. Multiday motorboat and sailboat trips depart from Colón Province or the Comarca de Kuna Yala.

DRIVING TO PANAMA FROM NORTH AMERICA

Every year readers tell us about their long-haul road trip across the continent. If you think you're game for a little overland adventure, here is a selection of reader-tested tips for making the most of the big drive:

Think it through Driving yourself through Central America is *not* a cheap option. Advantages include greater comfort and flexibility, but you *will* spend more than you expect on gas, insurance and fees.

Drive defensively Few cars use turn signals, pedestrians cross highways – things are different here. It is not for the faint of heart – be smart, be safe and arrive alive.

Go Japanese Toyotas, Hondas and Nissans are extremely popular in Central America, which makes them substantially easier to service or sell, though you should not expect to recoup your initial expenditure.

Get insurance in the USA or Canada For full coverage, though Panama requires its own insurance.

Learn to service your car Mechanics charge much more in Panama than in other Central American countries.

Be prepared Bring along a good tool kit, an emergency gas canister, plenty of emergency food and water, and industrial-strength duct tape. A spare tire or two is also a good idea, especially if traveling over rough terrain.

Know the law Panamanian law requires that all vehicles be fitted with a catalytic converter.

Nationalize your car It costs approximately 20% to 25% of the vehicle's value in taxation, but it's required if you want to sell. Since any damage reduces value, don't make repairs until afterwards.

Advertise your wares Try online expat forums or take out a classified in *La Prensa* newspaper on Sunday when the majority of car buyers are looking.

GETTING AROUND

Air

Panama currently only has one domestic carrier: **Air Panama** (☎316-9000; www.flyairpanama.com). Domestic flights depart Panama City from Aeropuerto Albrook and arrive in destinations throughout the country.

At the time of writing it was difficult to book tickets online or even get the airline on the phone. It sounds like a hassle, but it will give you a lot of peace of mind to book tickets at the regional airport in person as soon as you know your travel dates. Demand to destinations like Bocas overflows in high season. For most flights it's wise to book as far in advance as possible. Always confirm bookings.

Bicycle

Long-distance cyclists should know that Panama is extremely warm for biking. If that doesn't turn you off, you can cycle through the country easily enough, with lodgings within a day's ride.

Cycling within larger Panamanian cities – particularly Panama City – is ill advised. The roads tend to be narrow, there are no bike lanes, bus drivers and motorists drive aggressively and it rains a lot, reducing motorists' visibility and your tires' ability to grip the road.

The best places for cyclists in Panama City are the coastal routes of Cinta Costera (a dedicated bike trail from downtown to Casco Viejo) and the Causeway. Cyclists also go out to Gamboa via a well-shaded but narrow road. In Panama City, gear, repairs or quality bicycles can be found at **Bicicletas Rali** (Map p56; ☎263-4136; www.rali-carretero.com; Punta Paitilla, Panama City).

Outside the cities, Panama's Interamericana boasts the best quality in Central America, although sections have an extremely narrow shoulder. Roads in many of the provinces (especially in Veraguas and Colón) are in poor shape – plan accordingly and bring lots of spare parts.

Boat

Boats are the chief means of transportation in several areas of Panama, particularly in Darién Province, the Archipiélago de Las Perlas, and the San Blás and Bocas del Toro island chains. And while at least one eccentric soul has swum the entire length of the Panama Canal, most people find that a boat simplifies the transit enormously.

From Panama City there are regular ferries from the Causeway to Isla Taboga and Isla Contadora. Panama City is also the jumping-off point for partial and full Panama Canal transits.

If you're planning an excursion to Isla de Coiba and the national marine park, the best way to reach the island is through an organized boat tour. Local fishers also ply the waters off the coast of Veraguas, though this is a riskier proposition as the seas can get really rough.

The tourist mecca of Bocas del Toro on Isla Colón is accessible from Almirante by frequent water taxis.

Colombian and Kuna merchant boats carry cargo and passengers along the San Blás coast between Colón and Puerto Obaldía, stopping at up to 48 of the islands to load and unload passengers and cargo. However, these boats are often dangerously overloaded. Taking passage on a sailboat, or the new four-day motorboat service to Colombia, is a wiser option.

Since there aren't many roads in the eastern part of Darién Province, boat travel is often the most feasible way to get from one town to another, especially during the rainy season. The boat of choice here is a long canoe, or *piragua*, carved from the trunk of a giant ceiba tree. The shallow hulls of these boats allow them to ride the many rivers that comprise the traditional transport network of eastern Panama. Many such boats – including the ones travelers usually hire – are motorized.

Bus

You can take a bus to just about any community in Panama that is reachable by road. Some of the buses are huge, new Mercedes Benzes equipped with air-con, movie screens and reclining seats. These top-of-the-line buses generally cruise long stretches of highway.

More frequently used – and often seen on the Carretera Interamericana – are Toyota Coaster buses that can seat 28 people. These are affectionately called *chivas,* and are not as comfortable as the Mercedes Benzes, but they aren't bad and they're less expensive. They are an excellent way to visit towns on the Península de Azuero and along the Interamericana.

Panama City is phasing out its converted school buses known as *diablos rojos* (red devils). Replacing them is the Metrobus system. Riders can obtain swipe cards at the Albrook Terminal or main bus stops. Official bus stops are used and the buses are air-conditioned.

Subway

Panama City has been tearing up concrete and pavement all over town in the creation of a new subway system known as Metro.

With its first phase expected to be finished in 2014, the line will link Albrook with Vía Transitsmica, Vía España and Caledonia. Later plans are to extend it to Tocumen International Airport. The terminal, under construction at the time of writing, is across from the Albrook Bus Terminal. Fares will be paid with the same cards used for the Metro bus system.

Car & Motorcycle

Few tourists drive to Panama in their own vehicles, though it is certainly possible to do so. Renting a car is also a possibility. Because of difficult driving conditions, there are speed limits of 80km per hour on all primary roads and 60km per hour or less on secondary roads. Drivers should carry their passports as well as driver's licenses.

If you are involved in an accident, you should not move the vehicles (even if they're blocking traffic) until after the police have arrived and made a report. This is essential for all insurance claims.

If you see oncoming cars with headlights flashing, it often means that there is some kind of road problem or a police speed trap ahead. Slow down immediately. Also be on the lookout for a pile of branches placed on the road near an edge; this often means that a vehicle is broken down just ahead.

Rental

Due to the low cost and ready availability of buses and taxis, it isn't necessary to rent a vehicle in Panama unless you intend to go off the beaten track. There are car-rental agencies in major cities such as Panama City and David. Several agencies also have offices at Tocumen International Airport. To rent a vehicle in Panama, you must be 25 years of age or older and present a passport and driver's license – if you are over 21 and can present a valid credit card, some rental agencies will waive the age requirement.

Prices for rentals in Panama run from US$35 per day for an economy car to US$110 per day for a 4WD vehicle (or a '*cuatro por cuatro*'). When you rent, carefully inspect the car for minor dents and scratches, missing radio antennae, hubcaps and the spare tire. These damages *must* be noted on your rental agreement; otherwise you may be charged for them when you return the car.

There have been many reports of theft from rental cars. You should never leave valuables in an unattended car, and you should remove all luggage from the trunk when you're checking into a hotel overnight – most hotels provide parking areas for cars.

Hitchhiking

Hitchhiking is not as widespread in Panama as elsewhere in Central America; most people travel by bus, and visitors would do best to follow suit. The exception is holiday weekends, when buses are full to overflowing and hitchhiking may be the only way out of a place. If you get a ride, offer to reimburse your driver upon arrival; '¿Cuánto le debo?' (How much do I owe you?) is the standard way of doing this.

Hitchhiking is never entirely safe in any country, but it's not uncommon as you arrive in rural areas.

Local Transportation

Local buses serve the urban and suburban areas, but services can be difficult to figure out and there are few roadside signs indicating destinations. Panamanians are usually friendly, and this includes bus drivers; they'll often be able to tell you where to wait for a particular bus, if you ask in Spanish (few bus drivers speak English). But in general, unless you've come to Panama specifically for its urban-bus experience, leave that for another lifetime and take taxis – they're cheap and will save you a lot of time and hassle.

Taxis

Taxis are cheap and, most of the time, plentiful. Panamanian taxis don't have meters, but there are set fares between sectors of Panama City, though these are not posted. Ask the staff at your accommodation what you should expect to pay to reach

a given destination before heading out. Also, taxis can be difficult to hail late at night and just before and during holidays. At times like these, it's best to call for a radio taxi. Listings for reliable radio taxis can be found in the yellow pages of phone directories throughout Panama, under the heading Taxis.

More expensive 'sedan' taxis operate from particular upscale hotels. These drivers charge at least twice what you'd pay a hailed cab.

Tours

Panama's tourism industry is still young, though the number of tour operators is growing rapidly. While increasingly navigable for the independent traveler, Panama does have special conditions (complex logistics, limited public access and big wilderness) that make contracting a tour operator a good option. Top attractions including the Darién and Coiba are relatively inaccessible without a guide.

Prices vary depending on the services you require and whether you are prepared to join a group. It's increasingly common for hostels to provide their own budget tours for guests.

The following are highly recommended for guided tours of Panama. In general, Panama City and Canal Zone tours may be booked as walk-ins, but book multiday tours well in advance.

Ancon Expeditions (Map p56; 269-9415; www.an conexpeditions.com; Calle 49 A Este, El Dorado Bldg) Created by Panama's top private conservation organization, Ancon offers a superlative level of service and employs the country's best nature guides, many with decades of experience. Regular departures visit the Chiriquí highlands, Bocas del Toro and Isla de Coiba, the Canal Zone and Comarca de Kuna

Yala. The company also operates the Punta Patiño lodge in the Darién. English spoken.

A portion of tour proceeds are used in the ongoing fight to protect Panama's natural heritage.

Ecocircuitos (314-0068; www.ecocircuitos.com; Albrook Plaza, 2nd fl, No 31, Ancón) A great outfitter offering a range of tailored tours throughout the country, including wildlife-watching, adventure tourism and beach destinations. They are also a member of APTSO (Asociación Panameño de Turismo Sostenible), Panama's sustainable tourism alliance. English is spoken.

Yala Tours (6641-6676, 232-0215; www.yalatour spanama.com) This small outfitter specializes in nature travel and indigenous culture. In the canal area, it offers wildlife observation in Lago Gatún by boat or kayak. Day trips include Parque Nacional Soberanía and Emberá village visits. Swiss-run and recommended, with multiple languages spoken. Also has good experience in the Darién for tailored expedition-style trips.

Jungle Treks (6438-3130; www.jungletreks.com) A new company started by a bilingual naturalist guide, Jungle Treks runs a number of unique, recommended expeditions. Destinations include the Darién, the Chiriquí highlands, Veraguas and the Canal watershed. Trips can be custom-made but require six participants and a three-day minimum.

Sendero Panama (393-0747; www.senderopanama. com) A reputable outfitter offering a variety of private tours around Panama, as well as day trips from Panama City. Options include walking, birding, family options and multisport activities. English-speaking and also a member of APTSO.

Scubapanama (☑261-3841; www.scubapanama.com) The country's oldest dive operator, offering a variety of trips throughout the country.

Independent Guides

Skilled independent naturalists and guides are available to visit locations throughout the country.

Ivan Hoyos (☑6678-2657; migratorio@hotmail.com) A naturalist guide with years of experience, specializing in the Darién, Chiriquí highlands and Pipeline Rd. Speaks fluent English and German.

Mario Bernal Greco (☑info 6693-8213) An English- and Spanish-speaking guide from El Valle available for highland tours, birdwatching and visits around Panamá Province.

Roberto Medina (☑6710-4049; robertoisland@hotmail. com) An English-speaking naturalist and bird-watching guide.

Train

The country's only rail line is the historic Panama Railroad, which runs from Panama City to Colón.

In 2001 **Panama Canal Railway Company** (PCRC; ☑317-6070; www.panarail. com; Carretera Gaillard; one-way adult/child US$25/$15) introduced a daily passenger service that included a fully operational vintage train. Aimed at tourists looking to relive the heyday of luxury rail travel, the hour-long ride runs parallel to the canal, and at times traverses thick jungle and rainforest.

Note that the Panama City terminus is located in Corozal, which is a 15-minute cab ride from the capital.

Language

Spanish is the national language of Panama (see also p227 for the basics of the Kuna language, spoken in the Comarca de Kuna Yala). Latin American Spanish pronunciation is easy, as there's a clear and consistent relationship between what you see written and how it's pronounced. Also, most sounds have equivalents in English.

Note that kh is a throaty sound (like the 'ch' in the Scottish *loch*), v and b are like a soft English 'v' (between a 'v' and a 'b'), and r is strongly rolled. There are also some variations in spoken Spanish across Latin America, the most notable being the pronunciation of the letters *ll* and *y*. In our pronunciation guides they are represented with y because they are pronounced as the 'y' in 'yes' in most of Latin America. Note, however, that in some parts of the continent they sound like the 'lli' in 'million'. Read our colored pronunciation guides as if they were English, and you'll be understood. The stressed syllables are indicated with italics in our pronunciation guides.

The polite form is used in this chapter; where both polite and informal options are given, they are indicated by the abbreviations 'pol' and 'inf'. Where necessary, both masculine and feminine forms of words are included, separated by a slash and with the masculine form first, eg *perdido/a* (m/f).

BASICS

Hello.	*Hola.*	o·la
Goodbye.	*Adiós.*	a·dyos

WANT MORE?

For in-depth language information and handy phrases, check out Lonely Planet's *Latin American Spanish Phrasebook*. You'll find it at **shop.lonely planet.com**, or you can buy Lonely Planet's iPhone phrasebooks at the Apple App Store.

How are you?	*¿Qué tal?*	ke tal
Fine, thanks.	*Bien, gracias.*	byen gra·syas
Excuse me.	*Perdón.*	per·*don*
Sorry.	*Lo siento.*	lo syen·to
Please.	*Por favor.*	por fa·*vor*
Thank you.	*Gracias.*	gra·syas
You are welcome.	*De nada.*	de na·da
Yes./No.	*Sí./No.*	see/no

My name is ...
Me llamo ...   me ya·mo ...

What's your name?
¿Cómo se llama Usted?   ko·mo se ya·ma oo·*ste* (pol)
¿Cómo te llamas?   ko·mo te ya·mas (inf)

Do you speak English?
¿Habla inglés?   a·bla een·*gles* (pol)
¿Hablas inglés?   a·blas een·*gles* (inf)

I don't understand.
Yo no entiendo.   yo no en·*tyen*·do

ACCOMMODATIONS

I'd like a single/double room.
Quisiera una   kee·*sye*·ra oo·na
habitación   a·bee·ta·syon
individual/doble.   een·dee·vee·*dwal*/do·ble

How much is it per night/person?
¿Cuánto cuesta por   kwan·to *kwes*·ta por
noche/persona?   no·che/per·so·na

Does it include breakfast?
¿Incluye el desayuno?   een·*kloo*·ye el de·sa·yoo·no

campsite	*terreno de cámping*	te·re·no de kam·peeng
guesthouse	*pensión*	pen·syon
hotel	*hotel*	o·tel
youth hostel	*albergue juvenil*	al·ber·ge khoo·ve·*neel*

Signs

Abierto	Open
Cerrado	Closed
Entrada	Entrance
Hombres/Varones	Men
Mujeres/Damas	Women
Prohibido	Prohibited
Salida	Exit
Servicios/Baños	Toilets

air-con	aire acondicionado	ai·re a·kon·dee·syo·na·do
bathroom	baño	ba·nyo
bed	cama	ka·ma
window	ventana	ven·ta·na

DIRECTIONS

Where's ...?
¿Dónde está ...? don·de es·ta ...

What's the address?
¿Cuál es la dirección? kwal es la dee·rek·syon

Could you please write it down?
¿Puede escribirlo, por favor? pwe·de es·kree·beer·lo por fa·vor

Can you show me (on the map)?
¿Me lo puede indicar (en el mapa)? me lo pwe·de een·dee·kar (en el ma·pa)

at the corner	en la esquina	en la es·kee·na
at the traffic lights	en el semáforo	en el se·ma·fo·ro
behind ...	detrás de ...	de·tras de ...
in front of ...	enfrente de ...	en·fren·te de ...
left	izquierda	ees·kyer·da
next to ...	al lado de ...	al la·do de ...
opposite ...	frente a ...	fren·te a ...
right	derecha	de·re·cha
straight ahead	todo recto	to·do rek·to

EATING & DRINKING

Can I see the menu, please?
¿Puedo ver el menú, por favor? pwe·do ver el me·noo por fa·vor

What would you recommend?
¿Qué recomienda? ke re·ko·myen·da

Do you have vegetarian food?
¿Tienen comida vegetariana? tye·nen ko·mee·da ve·khe·ta·rya·na

I don't eat (red meat).
No como (carne roja). no ko·mo (kar·ne ro·kha)

That was delicious!
¡Estaba buenísimo! es·ta·ba bwe·nee·see·mo

Cheers!
¡Salud! sa·loo

The bill, please.
La cuenta, por favor. la kwen·ta por fa·vor

I'd like a table for ...	Quisiera una mesa para ...	kee·sye·ra oo·na me·sa pa·ra ...
(eight) o'clock	las (ocho)	las (o·cho)
(two) people	(dos) personas	(dos) per·so·nas

Key Words

bottle	botella	bo·te·ya
breakfast	desayuno	de·sa·yoo·no
(too) cold	(muy) frío	(mooy) free·o
dinner	cena	se·na
fork	tenedor	te·ne·dor
glass	vaso	va·so
hot (warm)	caliente	kal·yen·te
knife	cuchillo	koo·chee·yo
lunch	comida	ko·mee·da
plate	plato	pla·to
restaurant	restaurante	res·tow·ran·te
spoon	cuchara	koo·cha·ra
with/without	sin/con	seen/kon

Meat & Fish

beef	carne de vaca	kar·ne de va·ka
chicken	pollo	po·yo
duck	pato	pa·to
lamb	cordero	kor·de·ro
pork	cerdo	ser·do
prawn	langostino	lan·gos·tee·no
salmon	salmón	sal·mon
seafood	mariscos	ma·rees·kos
tuna	atún	a·toon
turkey	pavo	pa·vo
veal	ternera	ter·ne·ra

Fruit & Vegetables

apple	manzana	man·sa·na
apricot	albaricoque	al·ba·ree·ko·ke
banana	plátano	pla·ta·no
beans	judías	khoo·dee·as
cabbage	col	kol

capsicum	*pimiento*	pee·*myen*·to
carrot	*zanahoria*	sa·na·o·rya
cherry	*cereza*	se·*re*·sa
corn	*maíz*	ma·*ees*
cucumber	*pepino*	pe·*pee*·no
grape	*uvas*	*oo*·vas
lemon	*limón*	lee·*mon*
lettuce	*lechuga*	le·*choo*·ga
mushroom	*champiñón*	cham·pee·*nyon*
nuts	*nueces*	*nwe*·ses
onion	*cebolla*	se·*bo*·ya
orange	*naranja*	na·*ran*·kha
peach	*melocotón*	me·lo·ko·*ton*
peas	*guisantes*	gee·*san*·tes

pineapple	*piña*	*pee*·nya
plum	*ciruela*	seer·*we*·la
potato	*patata*	pa·*ta*·ta
spinach	*espinacas*	es·pee·*na*·kas
strawberry	*fresa*	*fre*·sa
tomato	*tomate*	to·*ma*·te
watermelon	*sandía*	san·*dee*·a

Other

bread	*pan*	pan
cheese	*queso*	*ke*·so
egg	*huevo*	*we*·vo
honey	*miel*	myel

LANGUAGE EATING & DRINKING

SPANISH IN PANAMA

Here's a rundown on some of the local expressions and colorful colloquialisms you may hear while traveling in Panama.

salve – street slang for *propina*, or tip

tongo – street slang for 'cop'

hota – street slang for 'police car'

diablo rojo – literally 'red devil'; refers to public buses

¡Bien cuidado! – 'Well taken care of!'; often used by a street person asking for a tip for taking care of your car (in parking lots at restaurants, cinemas, bars)

una pinta/fría – literally, 'one pint' or 'a cold one'; means 'a beer'

Dame una fría. – Give me a cold one (a beer).

guaro – hard liquor

chupata – an all-out drinking party

vuelve loco con vaca – literally 'makes crazy with cow'; refers to drinking *seco* and milk

buena leche – literally 'good milk'; means 'good luck'

salado/a (m/f) – literally 'salty'; refers to someone who is having bad luck

Me estoy comiendo un cable. – literally 'I'm eating a cable'; means 'I'm down on my luck.'

Eso está bien pretty. – refers to something nice

¡Eso está pretty pretty! – refers to something supernice

¡Entonces laopé! – Hey, dude!

¡Juega vivo! – Be alert! (look out for your best interests)

¡Ayala bestia! – Holy cow!

¡Chuleta! – common expression similar to 'Holy cow!'

enantes – just now

Voy por fuera. – I'm leaving right now.

Pa' lante. – Let's go now.

Nos pillamos. – We'll see each other later.

pelao/pelaito – common expression for a child

chombo/a (m/f) – an acceptable reference to a black person of Antillean descent

¡Pifioso! – a show-off, or something that looks cool

Tas buena, mami. – You're looking good, mama.

racataca/meña – both terms refer to women who wear lots of gold jewelry and are perceived as lacking class

mangajo/a (m/f) – someone who is filthy

ladilla – literally 'crab louse'; refers to an annoying person

Eres un comemierda. – said to a pretentious person

rabiblanco/a (m/f) – literally 'white-tipped'; pejorative reference to a member of the socio-economic elite; comes from *paloma rabíblano* (white-tipped dove), a bird that walks with its head held high and its chest thrust out in a seemingly pretentious way

yeye – refers to kids and adults who pretend to be rich (eg by wearing fancy clothes and maybe driving a fancy car) but who in reality are living well beyond their means for as long as they can

vaina – common word used for 'thing,' as in *Pásame esa vaina.* (Pass me that thing.)

nueve letras – literally 'nine letters'; refers to Seco Herrerano, the national drink

jam	mermelada	mer·me·la·da
pepper	pimienta	pee·myen·ta
rice	arroz	a·ros
salad	ensalada	en·sa·la·da
salt	sal	sal
soup	sopa	so·pa
sugar	azúcar	a·soo·kar

Drinks

beer	cerveza	ser·ve·sa
coffee	café	ka·fe
(orange) juice	zumo (de naranja)	soo·mo (de na·ran·kha)
milk	leche	le·che
red wine	vino tinto	vee·no teen·to
tea	té	te
(mineral) water	agua (mineral)	a·gwa (mee·ne·ral)
white wine	vino blanco	vee·no blan·ko

EMERGENCIES

| Help! | ¡Socorro! | so·ko·ro |
| Go away! | ¡Vete! | ve·te |

Call ...!	¡Llame a ...!	ya·me a ...
a doctor	un médico	oon me·dee·ko
the police	la policía	la po·lee·see·a

I'm lost.
Estoy perdido/a.   es·toy per·dee·do/a **(m/f)**

I'm ill.
Estoy enfermo/a.   es·toy en·fer·mo/a **(m/f)**

I'm allergic to (antibiotics).
Soy alérgico/a a   soy a·ler·khee·ko/a a
(los antibióticos).   (los an·tee·byo·tee·kos) **(m/f)**

Where are the toilets?
¿Dónde están los   don·de es·tan los
baños?   ba·nyos

Question Words
How?	¿Cómo?	ko·mo
What?	¿Qué?	ke
When?	¿Cuándo?	kwan·do
Where?	¿Dónde?	don·de
Which?	¿Cuál? (sg)	kwal
	¿Cuáles? (pl)	kwa·les
Who?	¿Quién?	kyen
Why?	¿Por qué?	por ke

SHOPPING & SERVICES

I'd like to buy ...
Quisiera comprar ...   kee·sye·ra kom·prar ...

I'm just looking.
Sólo estoy mirando.   so·lo es·toy mee·ran·do

Can I look at it?
¿Puedo verlo?   pwe·do ver·lo

I don't like it.
No me gusta.   no me goos·ta

How much is it?
¿Cuánto cuesta?   kwan·to kwes·ta

That's too expensive.
Es muy caro.   es mooy ka·ro

Can you lower the price?
¿Podría bajar un   po·dree·a ba·khar oon
poco el precio?   po·ko el pre·syo

There's a mistake in the bill.
Hay un error   ai oon e·ror
en la cuenta.   en la kwen·ta

ATM	cajero automático	ka·khe·ro ow·to·ma·tee·ko
credit card	tarjeta de crédito	tar·khe·ta de kre·dee·to
internet cafe	cibercafé	see·ber·ka·fe
market	mercado	mer·ka·do
post office	correos	ko·re·os
tourist office	oficina de turismo	o·fee·see·na de too·rees·mo

TIME & DATES

What time is it? ¿Qué hora es? ke o·ra es

It's (10) o'clock. Son (las diez). son (las dyes)

It's half past (one). Es (la una) y media. es (la oo·na) ee me·dya

morning	mañana	ma·nya·na
afternoon	tarde	tar·de
evening	noche	no·che
yesterday	ayer	a·yer
today	hoy	oy
tomorrow	mañana	ma·nya·na

Monday	lunes	loo·nes
Tuesday	martes	mar·tes
Wednesday	miércoles	myer·ko·les
Thursday	jueves	khwe·ves
Friday	viernes	vyer·nes
Saturday	sábado	sa·ba·do
Sunday	domingo	do·meen·go

Numbers

1	uno	oo·no
2	dos	dos
3	tres	tres
4	cuatro	kwa·tro
5	cinco	seen·ko
6	seis	seys
7	siete	sye·te
8	ocho	o·cho
9	nueve	nwe·ve
10	diez	dyes
20	veinte	veyn·te
30	treinta	treyn·ta
40	cuarenta	kwa·ren·ta
50	cincuenta	seen·kwen·ta
60	sesenta	se·sen·ta
70	setenta	se·ten·ta
80	ochenta	o·chen·ta
90	noventa	no·ven·ta
100	cien	syen
1000	mil	meel

January	enero	e·ne·ro
February	febrero	fe·bre·ro
March	marzo	mar·so
April	abril	a·breel
May	mayo	ma·yo
June	junio	khoon·yo
July	julio	khool·yo
August	agosto	a·gos·to
September	septiembre	sep·tyem·bre
October	octubre	ok·too·bre
November	noviembre	no·vyem·bre
December	diciembre	dee·syem·bre

TRANSPORTATION

boat	barco	bar·ko
bus	autobús	ow·to·boos
plane	avión	a·vyon
train	tren	tren

... ticket	billete de ...	bee·ye·te de ...
1st-class	primera clase	pree·me·ra kla·se
2nd-class	segunda clase	se·goon·da kla·se
one-way	ida	ee·da
return	ida y vuelta	ee·da ee vwel·ta

first	primero	pree·me·ro
last	último	ool·tee·mo
next	próximo	prok·see·mo

bus stop	parada de autobuses	pa·ra·da de ow·to·boo·ses
cancelled	cancelado	kan·se·la·do
delayed	retrasado	re·tra·sa·do
ticket office	taquilla	ta·kee·ya
timetable	horario	o·ra·ryo
train station	estación de trenes	es·ta·syon de tre·nes

I want to go to ...
Quisiera ir a ...   kee·sye·ra eer a ...

Does it stop at ...?
¿Para en ...?   pa·ra en ...

What stop is this?
¿Cuál es esta parada?   kwal es es·ta pa·ra·da

What time does it arrive/leave?
¿A qué hora llega/sale?   a ke o·ra ye·ga/sa·le

Please tell me when we get to ...
¿Puede avisarme   pwe·de a·vee·sar·me
cuando lleguemos a ...?   kwan·do ye·ge·mos a ...

I want to get off here.
Quiero bajarme aquí.   kye·ro ba·khar·me a·kee

I'd like to hire a ...	Quisiera alquilar ...	kee·sye·ra al·kee·lar ...
bicycle	una bicicleta	oo·na bee·see·kle·ta
car	un coche	oon ko·che
motorcycle	una moto	oo·na mo·to

helmet	casco	kas·ko
mechanic	mecánico	me·ka·nee·ko
petrol/gas	gasolina	ga·so·lee·na
service station	gasolinera	ga·so·lee·ne·ra

Is this the road to ...?
¿Se va a ... por   se va a ... por
esta carretera?   es·ta ka·re·te·ra

(How long) Can I park here?
¿(Cuánto tiempo)   (kwan·to tyem·po)
Puedo aparcar aquí?   pwe·do a·par·kar a·kee

The car has broken down (at ...).
El coche se ha averiado   el ko·che se a a·ve·rya·do
(en ...).   (en ...)

I have a flat tyre.
Tengo un pinchazo.   ten·go oon peen·cha·so

I've run out of petrol.
Me he quedado sin   me e ke·da·do seen
gasolina.   ga·so·lee·na

GLOSSARY

For terms for food, drinks and other culinary vocabulary, see p300. For additional terms and information about the Spanish language, see the Language chapter on p299. This glossary contains some words in Kuna (K) – for more on their language, see boxed text, p227.

ANAM – Autoridad Nacional de Ambiente; Panama's national environmental agency

ANCON – Asociación Nacional para la Conservación de la Naturaleza; National Association for the Conservation of Nature, Panama's leading private environmental organization

árbol – tree

artesanía – handicrafts

bahía – bay

balboa – the basic unit of Panamanian currency

baño(s) – restroom(s)

biblioteca – library

bocas – savory side dishes or appetizers

bohío – see rancho

boleto – ticket; for bus, museum etc

bolitas de carne – a snack of mildly spicy meatballs

boroquera – blowgun once used by the Emberá and Wounaan Indians

bote – motorized canoe

caballero(s) – gentleman (gentlemen)

cabaña – cabin

cacique – Kuna tribal leader

calle – street

campesino/a – rural resident; peasant

carretera – highway

casa de cambio – money-exchange house

cascada – see chorro

catedral – cathedral

cayuco – dugout canoe

centavos – cent(s); 100 centavos equal one US dollar (or one Panamanian balboa)

cerro – hill

certificación de vuelo – certification of entry date into Panama

cerveza – beer

ceviche – marinated raw fish or shellfish

chévere – cool (slang)

chichas – heavily sweetened, fresh fruit drinks

chitra – sand fly

chiva – a rural bus, often a 28-seat Toyota coaster bus

chocosano (K) – storm that comes from the east

chorro – waterfall

cielo – the sky; the heavens

cine – cinema

ciudad – city

cocina – kitchen

cocobolo – a handsome tropical hardwood; used for carving life-sized images of snakes, parrots, toucans and other jungle wildlife

comarca – district

comida corriente – a set meal of rice, beans, plantains and a piece of meat or fish

conejo pintado – raccoon-like animal abundant in Parque Nacional Volcán Barú

cordillera – mountain range

corredor de aduana – customs broker

corvine – a flavorful white fish; Panama's most popular fish dish

cuatro por cuatro – 4WD vehicle

cuidado – caution

Cuna – See Kuna

dama(s) – lady (ladies)

directo – direct bus

día feriado (días feriados) – national holiday(s)

edificio – building

Emberá – indigenous group living in Darién Province

empanada – corn turnover filled with ground meat, chicken, cheese or sweet fruit

feria – festival

fiesta – party

finca – farm

floresta – forest

frontera – border

fuerte – fort

Gali-Gali – the distinct Creole language of Bocas del Toro Province; it combines English, Spanish and Guaymí

galón (galones) – gallon(s); fluid measure of 3.79L

gringo/a – tourist; especially a North American tourist

gruta – cave

guacamayo – macaw

habano – Havana cigar

haras – stable (for horses)

hombre – man

hormiga – ant

hospedaje – guesthouse

huaca(s) – golden object(s); made on the Panamanian isthmus in the pre-Columbian era and buried with Indians

huevo(s) – egg(s)

iglesia – church

Interamericana – the Pan-American Hwy; the nearly continuous highway running from Alaska to Chile (it breaks at the Darién Gap)

invierno – winter

IPAT – Instituto Panameño de Turismo; the national tourism agency

isla – island

kilometraje – mileage

Kuna – the 70,000-strong indigenous tribe living in the Comarca de Kuna Yala

lago – lake

lancha – motorboat

lavamático/lavandería – laundromat

librería – bookstore

llanta – tire

llantería – tire repair shop

lleno – full
lluvia – rain
loro – parrot

manglar – mangrove
mariposa – butterfly
mercado – market
Merki (K) – American
mestizo/a – person of mixed indigenous and Spanish ancestry
metate – flat stone platform; used by Panama's pre-Columbian Indians to grind corn
migración – immigration
Migración y Naturalización – Immigration and Naturalization office
mirador – lookout point
molas (K) – colorful hand-stitched appliqué textiles made by Kuna women
mono – monkey
montaña – mountain
muelle – pier
mujer(es) – woman (women)
museo – museum

Naso – an indigenous group scattered throughout the Bocas del Toro Province; also called the Teribe
Ngöbe Buglé – an indigenous tribe located largely in Chiriquí Province

ola(s) – wave(s)

pájaro – bird
palapa – thatched, palm leaf–roofed shelter with open sides
panadería – bakery
parada (de autobús) – bus stop
Patois – a local dialect on the islands of Boca del Toro; a blend of English, Spanish and Gali-Gali

penca – palm tree leaves
permiso de salida – exit permit
pescador – fisherman
pescar – to fish
pipa – coconut water, served straight from the husk
piragua – canoe carved from a tree trunk
playa – beach
polleras – the intricate, lacy, Spanish-influenced dresses of the Península de Azuero; the national dress of Panama for festive occasions
pozo(s) – spring(s)
preservativo(s) – condom(s)
prohibido – prohibited; forbidden
prórroga de turista – a permit that resembles a driver's license, complete with photo; it allows you to stay in Panama for longer than the 90 days permitted for tourists
propina – tip; gratuity
protector solar – sunscreen lotion
puente – bridge
puerto – port
punta – point
puro – cigar

quebrada – stream

rana – frog
rana dorada – golden frog
rancho – a thatched-roof hut
raspados – shaved ice flavored with fruit juice
regalo – gift; present
río – river

seco – an alcoholic drink made from sugarcane
selva – jungle

Semana Santa – Holy Week; preceding Easter
sendero – trail
serpiente – snake
serranía – mountain range
sol – sun
supermercado – supermarket

tabla – surfboard
tagua – an ivory-colored nut that is carved into tiny figurines
tajadas – ripe plantains sliced lengthwise and fried
taller – workshop
tamales – spiced ground corn with chicken or pork, boiled in banana leaves
tarjeta(s) – plastic phonecard(s)
tarjeta de circulación – vehicle control certificate
tasajo – dried meat cooked with vegetables
taxi marino – water taxi
tigre – jaguar
típico – typical; traditional Panamanian folk music
tortilla de maíz – a thick, fried cornmeal tortilla
tortuga – sea turtle
trucha – trout

urbano – local (as in buses)

valle – valley
verano – summer
viajero – traveler
viento – wind
volcán – volcano

waga (K) – tourist
Wounaan – indigenous group living in Darién Province

Behind the Scenes

SEND US YOUR FEEDBACK

We love to hear from travelers – your comments keep us on our toes and help make our books better. Our well-traveled team reads every word on what you loved or loathed about this book. Although we cannot reply individually to postal submissions, we always guarantee that your feedback goes straight to the appropriate authors, in time for the next edition. Each person who sends us information is thanked in the next edition – the most useful submissions are rewarded with a selection of digital PDF chapters.

Visit **lonelyplanet.com/contact** to submit your updates and suggestions or to ask for help. Our award-winning website also features inspirational travel stories, news and discussions.

Note: We may edit, reproduce and incorporate your comments in Lonely Planet products such as guidebooks, websites and digital products, so let us know if you don't want your comments reproduced or your name acknowledged. For a copy of our privacy policy visit lonelyplanet.com/privacy.

OUR READERS

Many thanks to the travelers who used the last edition and wrote to us with helpful hints, useful advice and interesting anecdotes:

Valerie Anderson, Anna Avilov, Marian van Bakel, Michelle Won Belanger, Kathleen Bennett, Tom de Bock, Étienne Bourassa-Moreau, Deanne Bourne, Jose van Boxmeer, Hope Brady, Dean Bragonier, Arturo Campos, Dan Coplan, Julia Denzel, Han Dercksen, Derek Fenster, Liz Harwood, Kalen Higton, René Hoffmann, Claire Irving, Samta Jain, Lisette Juffermans, Mustafa Karagoz, Steve Latimer, Meta Lehmann, Robert Logan, Yoen de Loor, Heidi Marcon, Casa Mariposa, David McGuire, Annick McIntosh, Bjorn Van Moerkercke, Elizabeth Monterrosa, Ignacio Morejon, Liliane Moussa, Jiri Navratil, Luis Gonzalez Nelson, Janet O'Mara, Arie van Oosterwijk, Corrine Patchett, Irma Peppelenbos, Harrison Pettit, Marlynne Pike, Victoria Pilato, Maria Rivera, Patricia Roberts, Michele Rotman, Margaret Savage, Marian van Sonsbeek, Bas Sterk, Melissa Swenson, Daniel Taber, George Tacik, Izumi Takahashi, Sally Taylor, Darla Thomas, Henny Wels, Johan Wels, Sebas Wesselings, Jonathan White, Mike Wilson, Tibor Wurster, Lauren Ziemski.

AUTHOR THANKS

Carolyn McCarthy

I am very indebted to the many locals, experts and travelers who shared their version of paradise. Ignacio and Judit were Caribbean dream captains. For many reasons, I'm indebted to Ruth Metzel, Rainald, Carla Rankin, Jim Omer, Andrew, Andrea, Obedin and Koby, Alexandra Dennis, Daniel Smetana, Bobby and Katrina, Cherie and Reggie, taxi Karloz, KC, Douglas and Igua. Daniel Suman and Matt Landau provided editorial contributions. Annie, Jennie, Iker, David and Rachel offered respite and support. Thanks guys. *Hasta la proxima!*

ACKNOWLEDGMENTS

Climate map data adapted from Peel MC, Finlayson BL & McMahon TA (2007) 'Updated World Map of the Köppen-Geiger Climate Classification', *Hydrology and Earth System Sciences, 11, 163344.*

Cover photograph: Boy looking out to sea, Kuanidup Grande, Archipiélago de San Blás, Jordan Banks/4Corners.

THIS BOOK

This 6th edition of Lonely Planet's *Panama* guidebook was researched and written by Carolyn McCarthy. The previous edition was also written by Carolyn McCarthy. The 4th edition was written by Matthew D Firestone. This guidebook was commissioned in Lonely Planet's Oakland office, and produced by the following:

Commissioning Editor Catherine Craddock-Carrillo

Coordinating Editors Gabrielle Innes, Ross Taylor

Coordinating Cartographers Csanad Csutoros, Julie Dodkins

Coordinating Layout Designer Lauren Egan

Managing Editor Bruce Evans

Senior Editors Karyn Noble, Martine Power

Managing Cartographers Anita Banh, Diana Von Holdt, Alison Lyall

Managing Layout Designer Chris Girdler

Assisting Editors Janice Bird, Penny Cordner

Cover Research Naomi Parker

Internal Image Research Aude Vauconsant

Language Content Branislava Vladisavljevic

Thanks to Ryan Evans, Larissa Frost, Genesys India, Jouve India, Trent Paton, Raphael Richards, Gerard Walker

BEHIND THE SCENES

Index

NOTES